Praise for *Haldane*

'There is something perennially fascinating about the sensitive polymath. John Campbell has written a magisterial biography of such a figure—an immensely readable account of an extraordinary life. This is, quite simply, a triumph of the art of conveying the texture of human affairs and the events of an era. It is a major and lasting achievement.' — Alexander McCall Smith

'A labour of love. Haldane is rescued from "the condescension of posterity", his achievement in war and peace is finally recognised, and his rightful place in history is secured.' — Gordon Brown

'This captivating, ground-breaking book firmly re-establishes Lord Haldane in the national consciousness as a remarkable statesman of the early twentieth century. Many of his innovations are still flourishing today, and his thoughts on statecraft have much to teach our leaders.' — Sir Anthony Seldon, British political biographer

'An outstanding biography that will have Haldane recognised, at long last, as one of our very greatest twentieth-century statesmen.' — Sir Malcolm Rifkind, former Secretary of State for Defence and Foreign Secretary

'My Grandfather found Haldane to be unfailingly kind and in particular supported him in 1915 when Haldane lost Office. This book brings Haldane marvellously to life, centre stage on the then political map of Britain. It not only remarkably tells Haldane's extraordinary and neglected story, but the exceptional images so cleverly illustrate his life and the turbulent times in which he lived. A must read.' — The Rt Hon Sir Nicholas Soames

'We should thank John Campbell and we should thank Haldane. Haldane saw what our country needed and he quietly and brilliantly introduced those changes and creations, many of which are still with us. We in intelligence, and many others, are much indebted to Haldane. Mr Campbell tells us why.' — Sir Colin McColl KCMG, former chief of MI6

'Most politicians would view themselves as an outstanding success if only one of Haldane's reforms were credited to them. He transformed the British Army, brought into existence many of the great civic universities, and even proposed a Supreme Court 100 years ahead of his time. John Campbell brings Haldane to the front of the political stage, where he belongs, and details well his supreme intellect and political method, which has so much to teach for today's politics.' — The Rt Hon Frank Field DL, former MP

'A welcome and enjoyable biography of a towering yet overlooked figure— Haldane was a transforming war minister, a visionary Lord Chancellor, a passionate supporter of education, and much more. Like the best biographies, this book casts revealing light on the times in which he lived.' — The Rt Hon. The Lord Neuberger of Abbotsbury, former President of the UK Supreme Court

'Few if any of today's public figures can stand comparison with Haldane, architect of so much of what we take for granted in our government and civic society. Campbell's account summons back to life this giant of public administration.' — Professor Sir David Omand GCB, former Director of GCHQ and Home Office Permanent Secretary

'An immensely readable, painstakingly researched biography of a little-known polymath statesman to whom Britain is more indebted than it knows. In this Who's Who of early-twentieth-century politics, Campbell delves deep into Haldane's complex and fascinating personality, in so many ways ahead of his time. He makes his hero our hero.' — Sir Peter Westmacott GCMG LVO, former British Ambassador to Turkey, France and the United States

'A refreshing and compelling new biography of the leading philosopher-statesman of modern Britain. Haldane has had enormous influence, not least in re-organising the British Army to prevent a quick German victory in 1914, as well as in developing British education, the security services and the machinery of modern government.' — Martin Pugh, former Professor of History, Newcastle University, and author of *The Making of Modern British Politics*

'I wish I could have read this as my guidebook before taking on my Prime Ministerial duties, back in 2009. Now I can only hope that current and future leaders will use their chance to do so.' — Gordon Bajnai, former Prime Minister of Hungary

'A meticulously researched life of Haldane which rightly defines him as the ultimate polymath. Haldane's multiple achievements are a lesson to today's politicians: that so much more can be achieved by reaching across party lines when searching for benign change. We have all forgotten how much our military, intelligence services, universities and research communities continue to benefit from Haldane's impact, a century later. This work sets the record straight.' —Sir David Cooksey GBE, Chair of the Francis Crick Institute

'The debt the United Kingdom owes to Haldane is as great as to any other twentieth-century statesman. John Campbell's immensely readable study reminds us of the achievements of this extraordinary public servant. Haldane's instinct to work constructively across the Party divide shows the importance of broad consensus in delivering lasting institutional reform. His search for long-term solutions to our country's needs has never seemed more apposite.' —Robert Gascoyne-Cecil, 7th Marquess of Salisbury, former Leader of the House of Lords

'A remarkably intimate story of an exceptional man who created the British Army of 1914. These carefully considered reforms, resolutely fought for by Haldane in 1907, saved the nation from defeat.' —Major-General Sir Evelyn Webb-Carter

'A truly superb book. Not only is it a remarkable biography of an extraordinary life, it also provides important insights into Haldane's role in laying the foundations of the British university system. It traces how his education in Scotland and Germany moulded his beliefs about the purpose of life and the capacity of universities to inspire minds that contribute to the intellectual advancement and well-being of society. A profoundly humane account of one of Britain's most enlightened and influential, yet insufficiently recognised, reformers of the twentieth century.' —Colin Mayer CBE FBA, Peter Moores Professor of Management Studies, Said Business School, University of Oxford

'The great sadness is that Richard Haldane was Chancellor of St Andrews, Scotland's first university, for only two months before he died in August 1928. In inviting him to fill this key governing role, St Andrews knew it was appointing one of "the most powerful, subtle and encyclopaedic intellects ever devoted to the public service of his country". This great and long overdue book explains why St Andrews was so keen to make him one of its own.' —Sir Ewan Brown CBE FRSE, former senior governor of the University of St Andrews

HALDANE

Haldane

The Forgotten Statesman Who Shaped Modern Britain

JOHN CAMPBELL

in collaboration with

RICHARD MCLAUCHLAN

HURST & COMPANY, LONDON

First published in the United Kingdom in 2020 by
C. Hurst & Co. (Publishers) Ltd.,
41 Great Russell Street, London, WC1B 3PL
© John Campbell, 2020
All rights reserved.

A Cataloguing-in-Publication data record for this book
is available from the British Library.

ISBN: 9781787383111

This book is printed using paper from registered sustainable
and managed sources.

www.hurstpublishers.com

Typesetting by Line Arts Phototypesetters, Pondicherry, India

Imagery: Lexaeon

Permission to quote from the Haldane Papers, Haig Papers, and the Papers
of Dudley Sommer has been granted by the National Library of Scotland; the
Gosse Archive at the Brotherton Library in Leeds by Miss Jennifer Gosse; the
H.H. Asquith Papers at the Bodleian Library Oxford by the Trustees of the
Asquith Bonham Carter Papers; the Margot Asquith Papers at the Bodleian
by Christopher Osborn; and the Milner Papers at the Bodleian by the Warden
and Scholars of New College Oxford. Quotes from the works and writings of
Winston S. Churchill are here reproduced with permission of Curtis Brown,
London on behalf of The Estate of Winston S. Churchill. The Edinburgh Academy
and the Rothschild Archives have granted permission to use material from their
archives. As for private papers, Dick Haldane, Patrick Campbell Fraser, and the
Earl of Oxford and Asquith have all granted permission to reproduce material
from their respective collections. Full acknowledgements can be found at the
back of the book.

Printed and bound in Great Britain by Bell & Bain Ltd, Glasgow

To Shellard,
for your forbearance, love and support
in my pursuit of true statesmanship.

CONTENTS

LIST OF ILLUSTRATIONS

LIST OF ILLUSTRATIONS

TIMELINES OF HALDANE'S LIFE AND TIMES

PERSONAL

1856 (30 July)	Born at 17 Charlotte Square, Edinburgh
1879	Called to the Bar
1886 (Feb.)	Elected MP for Haddingtonshire (renamed East Lothian in 1921)
1890 (Jan.)	QC, 'the youngest Q.C. made for 50 years'
1890	Engagement and breakdown of engagement with Val Munro Ferguson
1905 (Dec.)	Enters Liberal government as Secretary of State for War
1911 (Mar.)	Created Viscount Haldane of Cloan
1911 (Apr.)	Appointed to Judicial Committee of the Privy Council
1912 (Feb.)	Haldane Mission to Berlin
1912 (June)	Appointed Lord Chancellor in Liberal government
1915 (May)	Excluded from coalition government
1924 (Jan.)	Appointed Lord Chancellor in first Labour government; chairman of Committee of Imperial Defence
1924 (Nov.)	Becomes leader of the opposition in the Lords as Labour goes into opposition
1928 (19 Aug.)	Death at Cloan

NATIONAL

Apr. 1880–June 1885	W. E. Gladstone second Liberal Administration
June 1885–Jan. 1886	Marquess of Salisbury first Conservative and Unionist Administration
Feb. 1886–July 1886	W. E. Gladstone third Liberal Administration
July 1886–Aug. 1892	Marquess of Salisbury second Conservative and Unionist Administration

TIMELINES OF HALDANE'S LIFE AND TIMES

Aug. 1892–June 1895	Liberal Administrations, first under Gladstone, then, from March 1894, Earl of Rosebery
June 1895–July 1902	Marquess of Salisbury third Conservative and Unionist Administration
Oct. 1899–May 1902	Second Boer War
July 1902–Dec. 1905	A. J. Balfour Conservative and Unionist Administration
Dec. 1905–Apr. 1908	Sir Henry Campbell-Bannerman Liberal Administration
Apr. 1908–May 1915	H. H. Asquith Liberal Administration
Aug. 1914–Nov. 1918	First World War
May 1915–Dec. 1916	H. H. Asquith Coalition Administration
Dec. 1916–Oct. 1922	Lloyd George Coalition Administration
Oct. 1922–Jan. 1924	Conservative and Unionist Administrations, first under Andrew Bonar Law, then, from May 1923, Stanley Baldwin
Jan. 1924–Nov. 1924	Ramsay MacDonald Administration—first Labour government
Nov. 1924–June 1929	Stanley Baldwin Conservative and Unionist Administration

PREFACE

si monumentum requiris, circumspice
(*If you seek his monument, look around you*)

Epitaph to Sir Christopher Wren on his tomb at St Paul's Cathedral

Sixty years ago, when I was twelve, crammed with my mother and four siblings into an Armstrong Siddeley, my father drove us from our home in Newcastle to Scotland for our summer holidays. Reaching Auchterarder in Perthshire later that morning we saw a valley with some gently rising hills beyond. Twisting along the country lane towards them we caught glimpses of a turreted house high on the hillside. We crossed a narrow stone bridge over a burn and turned into its drive. Sweeping steeply up past great trees and rhododendrons the car scrunched to a halt on a terrace directly beneath the house. A last parental invocation to be polite and ask questions and we tumbled out onto the broad terrace. A glorious 100-mile panorama of the southern Grampians stretched across the horizon below us.

The house was called Cloan. A short white-haired man of sixty, a business partner of my father, and a formidable grande dame with a twinkle in her eye came out of the low front door with their two children to greet us. The tousle-haired boy was my age and wore an open-necked shirt and over-large trousers clamped to his waist with an elastic belt. My hair was well brushed and I recall immediately feeling that I was inappropriately dressed in my new, rather shiny suit. We were ushered into the vast 14-foot-high drawing room. On the ceiling there was a stamp. I was a stamp collector. It was just identifiable as a George V penny red. How did it get there? 'Ah,' our kindly host said, 'that was a party trick of J. M. Barrie, the author of *Peter Pan*.' He went on to explain that, 'back in Lord Haldane's time', forty years ago, Barrie had wagered a fellow guest

xxi

that, without the use of a ladder or pole, he could stick a stamp on the ceiling. Taking one from the writing table, he had apparently licked the back of the stamp, turned over a corner which he stuck to a half-crown, and sent the coin spinning into the air. The half-crown had returned to his outstretched hand; the stamp for forty years had remained on the ceiling.

Dick, the boy with tousled hair, took me to explore the house. We went through various rooms before arriving at the dining room, where lunch was laid. It was quite dark. He turned on the lights. Several portraits lined the walls, but one caught my attention above the fireplace. Lit by its own picture light, it was of a man with a pale serious face, rather dramatically swathed in a dark cloak against an equally dark background. I asked who it was. 'Lord Haldane,' was the reply. 'Who was he?' 'My father's uncle. He lived in this house. He was War Minister; he saved Britain.' Little did I know it, but the whole course of my life changed at that moment.

Dick and I somehow clicked that day and, as the look of my clothes and hair became more sensibly casual, we gradually became the closest of friends. Over our lives we have been involved in many things together. After we had both married, started to have children and become reciprocal godparents, he and his wife Jenny moved permanently to Cloan to run the house and the estate. Since then and for the whole of my adult life it has been an oasis where our families have relaxed together in its pure Highland air.

Until very recently, when Dick moved to a smaller house on the estate, and a cousin acquired Cloan, remarkably little had changed since Haldane's death. His spirit and the possessions he knew and loved lived on in the house. His Lord Chancellor's purse, ministerial dispatch boxes, and set of large military lithographs presented to him by the Kaiser all had their places, together with framed *Punch* cartoons on the back staircase depicting him as a marathon runner, a dove of peace or a bronzed warrior. The ribbons and insignia of his Order of Merit and Knight of the Thistle, and endless silver trowels and commemorative keys used to lay the foundation stones of, or to declare open, a stream of educational and military establishments throughout Britain, shone from their cases in the drawing room. Sitting in Lord Haldane's study, high on the second floor, the view from its windows over the mountains changing with the passing of the seasons, snow-capped on a clear winter's day, sheets of rain moving over the great strath on other wild days, is where I came gradually to understand and, eventually, to love Haldane. This is where he would go to think; and what magnificent thinking he did.

Haldane's presence was palpable at Cloan. What I have since come to realise, with ever-increasing surprise and delight, is that that continuing presence extends well beyond the confines of his Scottish home. Indeed, if you know what you are looking for, it pervades much of our national life today. A walk from my London home, immediately west of Kensington Gardens, to Haldane's home at 28 Queen Anne's Gate in Westminster illustrates the point. Every time I make the journey, I seem to walk in Haldane's footsteps.

We pass, at first, Kensington Palace. There, behind the ornate railings, and topped by a generous ostrich-feathered hat, stands on its pedestal the swaggering statue of King William III presented by Kaiser Wilhelm II to King Edward VII on his 1907 visit to London. It was on this visit that Haldane, the German-speaking Secretary of State for War, attended a critical late-night meeting of the Kaiser and his ministers at Windsor. He could subsequently claim to be 'the only Englishman who has ever been a member of the German Cabinet'.[1]

Moving east we find the Albert Memorial, the northern tip of Alberto-polis—the stretch of land in Kensington owned by the prince's 1851 Exhibition Commissioners. Haldane had many dealings with those commissioners and their successors. At the request of Prince Albert's son, Edward, Prince of Wales, Haldane persuaded them in 1900 to make available a major part of the Imperial Institute, opened on that land in 1893, for the new headquarters of London University. A few years later he negotiated access to further land adjacent to the institute to be the birthplace, in 1907, of his beloved Imperial College.

Crossing the interconnecting road from Kensington Gardens into Hyde Park, we immediately come to the fields south of Rotten Row on which the Crystal Palace had stood at the time of the Great Exhibition. Here, on 19 July 1919, after the signing of the Treaty of Versailles, the massed ranks of servicemen and women from the British Empire and her allies assembled for the great Victory March which commemorated the formal end of the First World War. Led by Field Marshal Sir Douglas Haig, the first troops set off at 10 a.m. to wind their way north and south of the Thames

PREFACE

before the greatest crowds ever gathered in London. At noon they reached Buckingham Palace where King George V took the salute and gave a lunch for the most senior officers and politicians. That evening a magnificent fireworks display, also in Hyde Park, rounded off the celebrations, starting with the wonderfully named Special Colossal Word Device, 'Victory: Thanks to the Boys', before moving through eighty-four dazzling stages. The programme included Special Colossal Fire Portraits of the King, the Queen, Lloyd George, and Haig—but not Haldane. Yet this was the man who created the army that, reinforcing the French allies, saved Paris from falling to the Germans in 1914. In recognition of this and the nation's forgetfulness, as soon as the lunch was over, Haig made his way direct to see Haldane in Queen Anne's Gate. Haig would later call Haldane 'the Greatest Secretary of State for War England has ever had'.

Now we stride down Constitution Hill towards Buckingham Palace to reach the Queen Victoria Memorial from which George V had taken the salute. The monument was unveiled in 1911 in the presence of King George V and the Kaiser, this time making another state visit to honour his grandmother. It was on that visit that the Kaiser, together with several of his generals, invited himself to lunch at Haldane's London home, or 'the dolls' house' as the Kaiser called it. This encounter hammered another nail into the coffin of doubt as to Haldane's true loyalty in the public mind, doubt that would, in time of war, bury Haldane's reputation and political career.

But all that lay well in the future as, literally in Haldane's footsteps, we now enter the Mall. For it was here, in December 1905, in the thickest of London fogs, that Haldane stepped out of the hired brougham carriage in which he had been travelling with Edward Grey from Buckingham Palace, having received their respective seals of office as War Secretary and Foreign Secretary in the new Liberal government. Having hoped to help the driver find the way, Haldane became immediately lost. Thankfully, we can make our way more easily than he did to the south side of Pall Mall, where he eventually arrived at what was then the War Office (the site of what is now the Royal Automobile Club) to begin his long struggle for the reformation of the British army.

Further along Pall Mall a brief diversion into Carlton Gardens takes us past the home of Arthur Balfour, the Conservative prime minister who, like his Liberal friend Haldane, was one of that rare breed: the philosopher-statesman. This close cross-party friendship was to bear enormous fruit in the fields of education and defence. Immediately adjacent to Balfour's home we pass the magnificent premises now occupied by the Royal Society and the British Academy. Unusually for politicians, both Balfour and Haldane were members of each of these august academic and scientific societies.

From there we head north to St James's Square to pass the London Library. It was here that, as its vice-president, Haldane, overworked and ill, presided in the absence of its president, Balfour, at the Library's annual meeting on 6 July 1928. This proved to be Haldane's last official commitment. Shortly afterwards he made his final journey north to meet his death at Cloan.

Crossing Piccadilly, we enter the courtyard of Burlington House, the home of the Aristotelian Society, one of the leading philosophical societies of Great Britain. Haldane often debated and presented papers to the society, and was at one time its president. As we shall discover, philosophy was foundational to every aspect of Haldane's life. Taking a short cut through the main doors of the Royal Academy, we emerge onto Burlington Gardens through the building that, until 1900, housed the headquarters of London University, which owed its existence as a teaching university to Haldane. The London office of my company, Campbell Lutyens, directly faces that handsome Victorian building with its eighteen statues of celebrated men, including several of Haldane's heroes—Aristotle, Plato, Goethe, Adam Smith (whose biography he wrote), Newton and David Hume.

Heading west, once more, we resume our journey to Regent Street where we find the Café Royal. Here, Haldane and Edward Grey met over dinner and finally decided that they would join Asquith and serve in Campbell-Bannerman's government. Haldane rushed from the restaurant to tell the prime minister that he would take the War Office and lift to his lips the chalice which, for so many statesmen, had proved to be poisoned. The history of Europe in the twentieth century was written that evening.

Heading south down Haymarket and across Trafalgar Square we arrive on the Embankment, and are immediately overlooked on our right by the National Liberal Club where Haldane in his darkest hour in June 1915 was famously dined out by well over 200 MPs, each dismayed at his removal from office after the Conservatives had refused to join the coalition government alongside the 'Germanophile' Haldane.

A little further along we pass on our left the 1923 monument to the casualties of the Royal Air Force in the First World War. By establishing the Advisory Committee for Aeronautics in 1909, and chairing the committee on the creation of the Air Service in 1912, Haldane became midwife to the Royal Flying Corps and its successor the RAF.

Retracing just a few steps, we can cut through from the Embankment to Whitehall. Here Haldane is ubiquitous. Immediately adjacent to the Banqueting House we find the building which housed the 'New' War Office, opened in December 1906, where Haldane spent nearly the whole of his term of office until 1912. His rooms there are still named the 'Haldane Suite'. Proceeding south we reach Downing Street where, at number 10, Haldane sat for ten-and-a-half years in Campbell-Bannerman, Asquith and MacDonald's Cabinets. But, much less well known, we also find here the building that housed the courtroom of the Judicial Committee of the Privy Council, once the supreme appeal court of the empire. In that courtroom Haldane often pleaded as a barrister and, on becoming Lord Chancellor in 1912, he became the committee's president. It was here that he was to influence so profoundly the development of the Canadian constitution, and where his name and his judgments were to become known throughout the empire.

Returning onto Whitehall we pass the Cenotaph, designed by Haldane's favourite architect Edwin Lutyens to commemorate the glorious dead of the Great War, to reach Parliament Square. Here, together with the 'executive' in Downing Street, we find the two remaining chambers of the heart which represents British constitutional life. On its east side overlooking the river we pass the 'legislature', comprising the House of Commons, where Haldane served for twenty-four years as MP for Haddingtonshire (now East Lothian), and the House of Lords, of which he was a member for sixteen years, and over whose deliberations, as Lord Chancellor, he presided for nearly five years. On the west side we find the 'judiciary' in the form of the Supreme Court of the United Kingdom, which finally came into being in 2009, ninety-six years after Haldane as Lord Chancellor had first called for its creation in 1913.

PREFACE

At last, exhilarated and perhaps a little exhausted by our journey, we exit Parliament Square along Birdcage Walk, turn left up Cockpit Steps, and enter Queen Anne's Gate. There, at number 28, we find a blue plaque on the wall: 'Lord Haldane, 1856–1928, Statesman Philosopher and Lawyer, Lived Here', the only recognition of Haldane in a public place in Britain, despite Asquith's call for 'a statue in gold' to be raised in his honour.

This was the house where Grey came to stay with Haldane over the terrible ten weeks from late July until early October 1914 when the world crashed into war; the house from which, on hearing news of the imminent invasion of Belgium on the evening of 2 August 1914, they immediately went over to Downing Street to alert the prime minister; and the house from which Grey left the following day for the Commons to deliver the speech that roused and united the nation to enter the war. And it was also where, in happier post-war times, Einstein would come to stay as Haldane's guest on his first trip to Britain in 1921.

There are of course many other journeys that we could take in the footsteps of Haldane, not just in London, but in other cities, especially those cities around England and Wales with civic universities. Liverpool, Manchester, Leeds, Sheffield, Nottingham, Reading, Bristol and Southampton—all bear Haldane's imprint. His work was fundamental to the development of educational institutions as diverse as London University, the LSE, the University of Wales and what is now the National University of Ireland and Queen's University Belfast. Even adult education and workers' education were integral elements of Haldane's vision. No man did more to lay the foundations of our modern tertiary education system.

Many people in Britain have family or friends who have served in the army, the Territorials or the RAF, or in the Officers' Training Corps at school or university, or have been Boy Scouts. Some of us, knowingly or unknowingly, have friends serving with MI5 or MI6. Many of us have friends or family members learned in the law, or active in political life. Certainly, the research carried out by the Medical Research Council, or funded by the University Grants Committee, has had a widely beneficial impact on nearly all of us. Every one of those professions and organisations has been advanced in its development by Haldane's work and enthusiasm. Yet hardly anybody knows that, or his name.

There is often only one degree of separation between the work and achievements of Haldane and the lives of many people in Britain and also beyond her shores, particularly in Canada. Increasingly, I have felt that Haldane is to be found under almost every stone, for he had an exceptional capacity to translate well-thought-through concepts into successful practice. That is why so many of the organisations that he created and influenced are still at the centre of our life today, nearly a century after his death.

I write at a time of extraordinary debate on the constitutional structure of the United Kingdom and of the European Union; of deep divisions over the role of NATO and of the United Nations; of significant differences in international relations and styles of diplomacy. Profound issues need to be addressed in the fields of world trade, the interaction of capitalism and socialism, and the optimisation of the interdependent roles of the public and private sectors. It is understandable to feel daunted. All these issues have to be thought through by national leaders in real time in an era which is witnessing the advance of populism within the vacuum created by poor leadership and when the unremitting daily pressure on politicians tempts them to prioritise issues that are short term and immediate over those which may be enabling only over the longer term. At times like this, I believe that we can take courage from Haldane's life and approach and see in him the means of delivering successful time-tested change.

INTRODUCTION

In the summer of 1900, forty-three-year-old barrister and Liberal MP Richard Burdon Haldane was staying with Sir John and Lady Horner and their two daughters at Mells Park, the Horner family home in Somerset. Haldane's fellow guest was Raymond Asquith, eldest son of his closest political ally and future prime minister H. H. Asquith. Haldane and Raymond's father were the leading lights of the younger Liberals, the former acting as the brains of their wing of the party, the latter as their mouthpiece. Haldane could not wear his learning lightly, as his friend Asquith did. His sheer physical bulk, the slow stateliness of his movements, and his labyrinthine sentences seemed weighty with it. These characteristics, together with his preference for operating behind the political scenes and his love of German culture, meant that Haldane was never easily understood by the Great British public. It was a lack of understanding that would have serious consequences for Haldane and for the nation in the opening years of the war.

But those terrible days were far off in the halcyon atmosphere of Mells Park in 1900. 100 feet beneath the terrace of the house ran a stream which had been dammed to form a lake 'covered with waterlilies and fringed with bulrushes', a perfect spot for swimming. It was a beautiful July afternoon. At 4.30 p.m., just before tea was served, Haldane— not known for his athletic physique—suggested a bathe. The response was unenthusiastic, except from the eldest of the Horner daughters, Cicely, whom Raymond considered 'about as perfect a specimen of female beauty as I have ever seen' (although it was her sister Katharine whom he would marry a few years later). The whole party moved down to the lakeside to watch the two bathers; the spectators were 'amply rewarded'.[1] Raymond, towards the end of his stay at Mells Park, recorded the scene in a letter to a friend. With his 'uncanny gift of exact phrase', he achieves the rare feat of capturing the essence of a man so easily misunderstood.[2] Where the public could only see a suspicious gravity in Haldane's being, Raymond perceived his essential and complementary lightness:

> Haldane is an imperfect but courageous performer in the water and to see his immense but stately figure clad in a very scanty bathing dress and recklessly precipitating from dizzy altitudes into this very green and flowery pond was really exquisite: the quiet slowness and dignity with which he put himself in the most ridiculous situations proved to me more conclusively than anything else could have done the real bigness of the man—to see this vast white mass with the brain of Socrates and the shape of Nero executing his absurd antics from a thin plank which bent double under his weight and sporting fantastically in the water with a divinely beautiful girl no whit abashed recalled the sunniest days of the Roman decline. Finally he came out and after lurking coyly in the bushes for a few minutes reappeared clad in nothing but a bath-towel and a panama hat and joined us for tea on the lawn where he was soon explaining the theory and history of Buddhism—its superiority to Christianity and its weaknesses as a practical religion—to a host of local spinsters who had flocked in for food and gossip. It was magnificent. At 11–30 p.m. he left in a carriage for Bath 15 miles off having to be in the courts at 10 tomorrow and in the train all tomorrow night and the night after—on his way up and down to Edinburgh where he is pleading on Tuesday. He is a marvellous man, and never loses flesh through it all.[3]

This is a snapshot of a man who, at his death, *The Times* would describe as 'one of the most powerful, subtle, and encyclopaedic intellects ever devoted to the public service of his country'.[4] On that July afternoon he was already the most vocal member of the House of Commons in the cause of education, a champion for universities, for widening access, and for a dramatically improved state school system. He was not yet, however, the Secretary of State for War responsible for creating the British army that would fight the bloody battles of the First World War in which Raymond would die, nor yet the Lord High Chancellor of Great Britain who would help to shape the modern British and Canadian states.

Haldane has largely been forgotten today, lost behind a range of his contemporaries whose personalities are more instantly accessible and whose deeds are more easily amplified—individuals such as Lloyd George and Churchill who dominate our history books. And yet, in Haldane even Churchill met his match, as Lionel Curtis remembered:

> Winston Churchill one day ran into him in the lobby of the House, tapped him on his great corporation and asked, 'What is in there Haldane?' 'If it is a boy,' said Haldane, 'I shall call him John. If it is a girl I shall call her Mary. But if it is only wind, I shall call it Winston.' W. C. is not often repaid in his own coin.[5]

It is high time Haldane is remembered.

* * *

It is the purpose of this book to put that right. It also aims to offer an example of statesmanship that we so vitally need today. I have therefore not chosen the classic chronological structure that simply tells a story. Rather, I have chosen, in Part 1, to take deep dives into the key personal foundations of Haldane's statesmanship: the family traditions that he inherited; the emotional world in which he was grounded; the friends who supported him; the philosophy that directed him; and the economic thinking that kept him active in the pursuit of sound government. This introduction consequently limits its focus to a sketch of the early years of Haldane's life, stopping short of his entry into Parliament in December 1885 at the age of twenty-nine.

In Part 2 we turn from the more personal and intellectual themes of earlier chapters to look at the very practical ways in which Haldane built upon these foundations as a statesman—the ways in which he reformed both the educational landscape and the defences of the country, and the manner in which he allowed his philosophy to contribute to enhancing the structure of the British and, indeed, the Canadian state. I'm conscious that this thematic approach may sacrifice the clarity that a chronological approach can bring, but it should grant us an even more important perspective regarding just what Haldane achieved in each of the three major fields in which he brought his influence to bear. Given such a structure, Part 2 has its own introductory chapter that paints a picture of the political world in which Haldane operated, while Chapter 7 picks up the story of his legal and political careers from 1885 onwards. The chronology provided in Chapter 7 should therefore help to ground the three thematic chapters that follow. My hope is that our exploration of Haldane's states-manship through these years will sound a message of hope for all who despair in our present political climate. Of course, Haldane's was a unique life—'God has broken the mould,' as Lady Horner once said of him—and his times were different from our own.[6] But his selfless com-mitment to public service, his guiding fundamental principles and the techniques he deployed in his statesmanship are as relevant and as neces-sary today as they ever were.

* * *

Richard Burdon Haldane was born on 30 July 1856, within the grandeur of the Haldanes' Edinburgh home, 17 Charlotte Square. With its palatial facades designed by Robert Adam and its vast rooms, the square was one of Scotland's most enviable addresses. On his father's side, Haldane hailed from an ancient Scottish family of public servants; on his mother's, a tradition of intellectual accomplishment and legal acumen, which included the notable figure of John Scott, first Earl of Eldon, who twice served as Lord High Chancellor of Great Britain—as his great-great-nephew, Haldane, would do. Uniting the families was a strong Protestantism of a Calvinistic variety. 'Religion permeated our lives', Haldane's sister Elizabeth recalled, 'and a sense of sin and its conse-quences seemed to dog our footsteps when we remembered what it meant.'[7] But the family's summers and autumns were spent in the rejuve-nating atmosphere of Cloan, their small estate in Perthshire. Elizabeth gratefully remembered: 'The oppressive theology that was apt to over-shadow our lives was blown away by the fresh country breezes.'[8]

The Britain into which Haldane was born was, in many ways, one of the most self-assured nations on the planet, revelling in its industrial pre-eminence, imperial expansion and scientific discovery. Scotland itself—or North Britain as it was often called—not only rested content with its place within the Union, but still basked in its Enlightenment heritage. It contin-ued to lead the way in education and to produce a stream of thinkers and inventors shaping the contemporary world. Alexander Graham Bell, the inventor of the telephone, was born nine years before Haldane and only a few hundred paces from the Haldanes' front door. England had her own inventors, too, not least George Stephenson, the pioneering railway engineer. Indeed, with the railway boom of the decades preceding Haldane's birth, travel had never been easier between the two nations (a fact that Haldane was to take full advantage of once he flew the nest). The growth of Britain as an industrial power meant that, in 1850, it could boast of having the highest income level in the world.[9]

But the swagger masked a growing unrest. The opportunities for profit-making open to the few often meant a corresponding oppression of the many. Urbanisation had brought overcrowding and new health problems. The Crimean War had only just ended and had been characterised by military fiascos and appalling casualties, stirring up riots at home. Darwin would shortly publish his *On the Origin of Species*, and old religious certainties would become open for dispute. The Whigs who governed in Parliament when Haldane was born would soon be submerged within the Liberal Party, while the rumbles of organised labour could be heard as it rallied itself for an assault on the seats of power. It was into this cocktail of arrogance and anxiety, of stability and change, that Haldane was born. To navigate his way through this period of flux would require a steady head and firm principles—he was to perform the task with admirable ability.

He would also have to make his way in a family setting that was far from straightforward. His father, Robert Haldane, had lost his first wife during the birth of their sixth child (who also died), and his second wife, Mary Elizabeth, twenty years Robert's junior, was to lose her first child in infancy. Mary subsequently bore five children, the eldest of whom was our Haldane, Richard; the second, Geordie, would die at sixteen from diphtheria. Loss was part of the fabric of their lives. And for Mary Haldane's children, so too was ambition. She had marked out Richard from childhood as a future Lord Chancellor, and his siblings would each eventually attain distinction in their respective fields. John, a distinguished physiologist and Fellow of New College, Oxford, invented the gas mask, identified carbon monoxide as a source of poisoning in mines, and developed the first diving decompression tables, amongst many other achievements; Elizabeth held numerous positions of national importance and was the first woman to be appointed a justice of the peace in Scotland; William became Crown Agent for Scotland and was knighted. We will have more to say on the remarkable characters that made up the Haldane family in Chapters 1 and 2, but it is at least clear that Haldane was, from early on, destined for great things.

Haldane and his brothers received their schooling at the Edinburgh Academy, an institution founded with the support of a host of Scottish luminaries, including Sir Walter Scott, in 1824. Its purpose was to provide an education for the sons of Scotland's middle and upper classes that would rival the great public schools of England. The school had already produced many eminent men, including Archibald Campbell Tait, the first Scotsman to be an Archbishop of Canterbury, James Clerk Maxwell, 'the father of modern physics', and Robert Louis Stevenson, the celebrated writer.[10] Although the published prize lists show that Haldane won prizes for 'scholarship' every year for his last four years at the school (he was always within the top eight highest-performing pupils in his class, though never first), the Academy's diet of Latin and Greek classics did little to rouse the excitement of his natural disposition towards abstract thought and practical action. 'School was indeed never an interesting period to me,' he wrote later in life.[11]

But a vivid depiction of him as a schoolboy is to be found in 'The Edinburgh Academy Chronicle' of 1909. Haldane, by this time Secretary of State for War, had recently visited the school to review its newly established officers' training corps—a key component of the so-called Haldane Army Reforms. The 'Chronicle' records the parade and Haldane's speech, and adds the following letter written to the *Daily Mail* by an old classmate:

SIR,—I recollect the present War Minister at school very distinctly. He had then, as now, a substantial figure, and wore knickerbockers with scarlet stockings.

I daresay few would believe that Mr. Haldane was, as a boy, a very fair slow bowler, and I remember him playing for the Second Eleven of the school.

...

I have never seen him in Parliament, but his attitude in class when answering a question was almost impressive. With hand uplifted and head advanced, and eyes turned back as if searching into the depths of his inner consciousness, he would slowly and deliberately deliver himself of what he had to say. 'Solid and sound' would have been the general verdict on his character, and he is the only one of his class-fellows to rise to eminence.[12]

INTRODUCTION

Haldane formed a great allegiance to his principal master at the Academy, Dr James Clyde, a model of stoicism who instilled in him a scepticism concerning the religious authority of the Bible. Likewise, he made a life-long friendship with his contemporary John Kemp, who would go on to co-translate Schopenhauer's *The World as Will and Idea* with Haldane and 'devil' for him at Lincoln's Inn.

* * *

But it took matriculation onto the Arts course at Edinburgh University at the age of sixteen for Haldane really to become intellectually alive. Here he attended the lecture rooms of some of the country's leading scholars. William Young Sellar, professor of Humanity (that is, Latin), was to be the greatest influence, taking a personal interest in developing the young Haldane's mind and connections. Haldane would visit him in his home, meeting there some of the great literary figures from across the border, including the well-known Master of Balliol, Benjamin Jowett, and the critic Matthew Arnold. Through Sellar and his friends 'I learned ... something of the wider outlook on life which literature could give'.[13]

John Stuart Blackie, professor of Greek, also played a pivotal role in widening Haldane's outlook. For it was this eccentric professor who persuaded Haldane's parents to allow their son, still in his seventeenth year and in the midst of a religious crisis, to attend the University of Göttingen for a term in 1874. It was the start of Haldane's lifelong love of German education and literature, the place where he would meet the celebrated Professor Hermann Lotze, and where his passion for philosophical reflection would take hold. This passion grounded all of his subsequent activities, whether in the law, politics, educational reform or military organisation. It was in Göttingen that the seeds of Haldane's success as a statesman were sown; so, too, the seeds of his downfall. Forty years later, it was no boast for a British statesman to have attended a German university, let alone to have liked it. It could even mean the end of a career.

In the 1870s Haldane's career was only just taking shape. After his spell in Germany, he returned to Edinburgh to complete his studies, focusing on philosophy in particular. It paid off. Along with his first-class degree, Haldane won every major prize in the discipline, not least the Ferguson Scholarship for which students at all four Scottish universities were eligible. Yet it was the law, not academic philosophy, to which he turned for a living. Not long after the death of his father in 1877, Haldane, aged twenty-one, moved to London to read for the Bar at Lincoln's Inn. Called to the Bar two years later, with chambers at 5 New Square, Haldane specialised in conveyancing (the process of moving the legal ownership of property or land from one person to another). After a slow start and minimal financial returns, he received his big break with a request to assist the 'leader of the English Bar and the great Chancery Counsel', Horace Davey. Haldane was to 'devil' for Davey; in other words, read his briefs and mug up on the legal authorities before a case. At first, Haldane thought him 'very cynical & disagreeable but extremely clever'.[14] He went on, however, to establish a deep rapport with Davey, admiring his razor-sharp mind.[15] Davey's admiration of Haldane must have been great, too, for it was not long before the junior counsel was left to hold his own, in Davey's place, in cases as weighty as an application for special leave to appeal by the government of Quebec before the Privy Council (Haldane's first battle on behalf of the Canadian provinces) and the Scottish Petroleum case of 1883 before the Master of the Rolls, Sir George Jessel, and two Lords Justices of Appeal. In the latter case, Haldane's arguments roused the excitement of 'the great Sir George', who proceeded 'to play with me as a cat does a mouse' and 'to throw the power of his personality into the struggle'. By 4 p.m. Jessel was looking very ill. Two days later he was dead. As Haldane records in his *Autobiography*, 'My brother barristers affected to reproach me for having killed Jessel. If I had, it was indeed unwillingly, for I had the highest admiration and deep regard for that great judge.'[16]

These cases won Haldane the respect of London's major firms of solicitors, and his business quickly grew. By the time he took silk in 1890—at the age of thirty-three, 'the youngest Q.C. made for 50 years'[17]—he was earning the considerable sum of nearly £2,500 a year (roughly equivalent to £300,000 today). In his last year at the Bar in 1905, before entering government, that figure was approaching the enormous sum of nearly £20,000 (today's £2,400,000).[18] The intervening years saw Haldane establish himself as—in the words of John Buchan—'a tremendous figure at the Bar' and 'a most formidable advocate, especially in cases of constitutional law'.[19] In those days of empire, Haldane's detailed learning in the different systems of law in the British dominions—whether Buddhist, Maori,

INTRODUCTION

French, Roman-Dutch, Islamic or Hindu—brought him constantly before the judges of the House of Lords and Privy Council. He developed a particular speciality in questions surrounding the Canadian constitution, appealing on behalf of the provinces seven times before the Judicial Committee of the Privy Council between 1894 and 1904.

This command of the Bar grew concurrently with his rise as a Member of Parliament, having entered the Commons as a Liberal in 1885. The story of Haldane's political life, which commenced at that time, is reserved for Chapter 7. But before we come to Haldane the statesman, we need to understand Haldane the man. What were the conditions that made his remarkable political career possible? Haldane's achievements in education, laying the bedrock of the university and state school systems that we know today in Britain; his creation of the army that, with its French allies, saved Paris from falling to the Germans in the opening months of the First World War; his fashioning of the British state in its governmental and administrative forms; his shaping of the Canadian constitution in favour of provincial over federal empowerment—behind all this stood one human being.

He was a man acutely conscious of the weight of his ancestry, but who felt liberated by the support of three outstanding women who loved him dearly: his mother, his sister and Frances, Lady Horner. He was a man crushed by grief at the early death of his brother, and twice plunged into black despair by romantic rejection. He was a man surrounded by the widest circle of friends, including King Edward VII, a Rothschild or two, and Einstein. Such relationships form the focus of our first three chapters. The remaining chapters of Part 1 guide the reader through two key components of Haldane's rich intellectual world: his philosophical beliefs and his economic commitments. Armed with an understanding of these, the way is clear for grasping, in Part 2, the mastery of Haldane's statesmanship.

PART ONE

LAYING THE FOUNDATIONS

1

A FAMILY TRADITION

The one and only secret of happiness lies in the performance of duty in the best and most conscientious manner.

John Burdon Sanderson to Haldane, 1874[1]

Richard Burdon Haldane, a plucky thirty-four-year-old barrister, is fighting a case he knows he can't win. On the bench before him is Sir Edward Ebenezer Kay, a High Court judge in the Chancery Division. Kay doesn't much like what he's hearing from the budding legal mind and lets it be known; he treats Haldane without consideration, and speaks 'rather offensively'. This is not the kind of behaviour the well-bred Scotsman is used to. But Haldane isn't intimidated by the judge, and has the mental toughness to make a stand. Describing the action in a letter later that day to his mother, he writes that Kay 'got it back like lightning in a Burdon Sanderson & not a Haldane spirit. I lost my case—indeed it was hopeless—but he will be careful the next time.'[2]

What 'spirits' were these that Haldane was aware of inheriting? Was one quick and cutting, the other slow and courteous? Who were these Burdon Sandersons and these Haldanes with their distinctive attitudes?

Remarkably, the latter family have claimed to trace their lineage all the way back to Charlemagne,[3] and a glance at their accomplishments suggests a resourcefulness and commitment to public duty that can have few rivals.[4] We find these characteristics embodied, for instance, in the powerful Sir John Haldane (d. 1493), who was successively ambassador to the courts of France and Denmark under James III, Master of the King's Household, Sheriff-Principal of Edinburgh, and Lord Justice-General of

13

Scotland 'benorth the Forth'.[5] They are there again in John Haldane of Gleneagles (1660–1721), who sat in the last Scottish Parliament and was one of the forty-five Scottish members of the first Unionist Parliament in 1707, earning him the nickname 'Union Jack'.[6] Nor should we forget his infamous son Patrick Haldane (1683–1769), professor of Greek, then Ecclesiastical History at the University of St Andrews,[7] who went on to hold office as a commissioner valuing and disposing of estates forfeited by Jacobites upon conviction after the 1715 uprising (a role he executed with such ruthlessness that he earned the name 'the curse of Scotland'),[8] eventually rising to Joint-Solicitor-General for Scotland, a month before Culloden. Patrick's son, Brigadier-General George Haldane (1721–59), was governor of Jamaica, a position he obtained through supporting the rehabilitation of William Pitt the Elder's political career in 1757,[9] though George died of what is likely to have been yellow fever within four months of his arrival on the island. Patrick's half-brother, Robert Haldane (1705–67), took a quite different career route. Robert was the first ever Scot to command a ship of the East India Company and is said to have made £70,000 in a single voyage. Still, this did not preclude a parliamentary career. When his nephew, George, accepted his posting to Jamaica in 1758, his seat for Stirling Burghs became vacant and Robert slipped into his shoes without opposition.

Command of the sea also fell to Admiral the Viscount Duncan (1731–1804), son of Helen Haldane[10] (maternal grandmother of Haldane's grandfather) and hero of the Battle of Camperdown against the Dutch during the Napoleonic Wars—'one of the most complete victories in the age of fighting sail'.[11] If the spirit of public service, so evident in Richard Burdon Haldane, can be discerned in the preceding distinguished men (putting to one side their—at times—unpalatable self-seeking), then it is in the traits of kindness and courage that a connection between the two viscounts is to be found. As one biographer puts it: 'Duncan's reputation for coolness, courage, and daring was well deserved,' while his 'kindly, unaffected, and modest nature, noted by contemporaries, is a feature of his correspondence'. He was a man, we are told, 'reluctant to find fault with subordinates', though 'severe with those who failed in their duty.'[12] In this, we have a fine description of Haldane at the War Office. A depiction of the heroic admiral 'calm in the midst of gun and cannon fire' is still to be found hanging in the Scottish National Portrait Gallery today.[13] Behind the hero, an officer blows a trumpet, symbolising the fame Duncan would win. One searches the walls in vain, however, for a portrait of his descendant, the Secretary of State for War.

* * *

Two brothers of the Haldane line stand out above all these illustrious forebears as significant for our story: Haldane's paternal grandfather, James Alexander Haldane (1768–1851) and his brother Robert Haldane (1764–1842), nephews of Admiral Duncan. Men of the sea turned evangelists, they had, in R. B. Haldane's view, 'the making of heros [sic] in them'.[14] James Alexander (as he was known), even before the fervour of the Gospel took hold of him, certainly showed his heroic qualities. As captain of the *Melville Castle*, a ship of the East India Company, he famously quelled a mutiny on board a neighbouring ship, the *Dutton*, with a composure in the face of danger that still astonishes. The men had risen against their officers in outrage for want of supplies and were threatening to blow up the ship in protest. Haldane put a stop to the threats in a manner more reminiscent of an episode of *Hornblower* than a real-life crisis:

> The scene was appalling, and to venture into the midst of the angry crew seemed to be an act of daring almost amounting to rashness. Ordering his men to veer round by the stern, in a few moments Captain Haldane was on the quarter-deck. His first object was to restore the officers [sic] composure and presence of mind. He peremptorily refused to head an immediate attack on the mutineers, but very calmly reasoning with the men, cutlass in hand, telling them that they had no business there, and asking what they hoped to effect in the presence of twenty sail of the line, the quarter-deck soon cleared. … Two of the crew, intoxicated with spirits, and more hardy than the rest, were at the door of the powder magazine, threatening with horrid oaths that whether it should prove Heaven or Hell they would blow up the ship. One of them was in the act of wrenching off the iron bars from the doors, whilst the other had a shovel full of live coals, ready to throw in! Captain Haldane, instantly putting a pistol to the breast of the man with the iron bar, told him that if he stirred he was a dead man. Calling at the same time for the irons of the ship, as if disobedience were out of the question, he saw them placed, first on this man and then on the other. The rest of the ringleaders were then secured, when the crew, finding that they were over-

powered, and receiving the assurance that none should be removed that night, became quiet, and the Captain returned to his own ship. Next day, the chief mutineers were put on board the Regulus, King's ship, and the rest of the crew went to their duty peaceably.[15]

James Alexander's brother, Robert, also made a name for himself as a naval man, but gave this up early for a life committed to the spreading of a certain Calvinistic theology that had captured both his and his brother's minds and hearts while still young men; so committed in fact, that Robert sold his estate at Airthrey to fund a hugely expensive mission to Bengal. This mission fell through before it even got going, and once his brother had likewise left life on the high seas behind him, together they set about taking their unique, impassioned brand of Protestantism into the sleepy parishes of their native Scotland, establishing the Society for the Propagation of the Gospel at Home in 1798 and building vast preaching centres, known as 'tabernacles', throughout Scotland, both to great effect. The Congregational movement north of the border 'is to be traced to the work and philanthropy of the Haldanes',[16] as is the rise of the Baptists as a distinct denomination, due to the brothers' conviction on that issue.[17] And, according to a study on *The Church in Victorian Scotland*, 'so far as Scotland is concerned [Robert Haldane] has a good claim to be called the Founding Father of Fundamentalism.'[18] Robert even founded a school of religious thought on the Continent opposing rationalist views of Christianity, after a year spent in Geneva and two in Montauban. When R. B. Haldane visited the south of Germany long after the deaths of Robert and James Alexander, he would still be asked if he was a 'Haldanite'.[19]

Robert's primary impact came through his writing and the enormous funds he put into their enterprises (£70,000, it is estimated, between 1798 and 1810, roughly equivalent to £5,500,000 today), while James Alexander had the gift of preaching.[20] For the latter's grandson, this evangelical inheritance was absolutely central to his conception of his own mode of reaching 'the people', but this time on political issues, such as free trade and, above all, 'the gospel of Education'.[21] The number of references in his daily letters to his mother to taking on the mantle of these evangelists is quite remarkable. At a 'non-party address on the "Rights & Duties of working men"', Haldane reflects: 'I had a solemn message to these poor agricultural labourers. It is preaching the Gospel, this.'[22] Speaking at an event two years later, he makes 'the chapel resound & they said it was like my grandfather'.[23] In 1903 he sees himself as 'a sort of Evangelist, stirring people up about this Education business'.[24] Before a speech in his constituency in the same year, he is 'ready for the battle … I feel a little like James Haldane did. Very keen and full of conviction.'[25] Back in London, about to start 'out for the Midlands to speak at Wellington on Free Trade', Haldane feels 'like my Grandfather preaching the Gospel. It is a time when a fighting attitude is essential.'[26] Although by 1916 Haldane feels he has 'preached many sermons'[27] on education, he is still buzzing with evangelical fervour for the cause:

> I speak today at 4.30. Of course there are attacks on me in anticipation, but I do not mind these. I have a strong bodyguard of supporters, well organised, who think with me, and above all I have the truth on my side.

> It is like the Campaigns of Robert & James Haldane over again.

> I don't know how I shall do, but one must live by faith. At all events there is abundant public interest.[28]

The interest is so great, in fact, that Haldane finally, a few weeks later, arrives at a point of genuine clarity about the nature of his public position: 'I feel as if at 60 a new call has come to me from the people, to be an evangelical, like my forefathers, in the cause of education. I am receiving invitations to great meetings to stir them up.'[29]

The references to the Haldane brothers continue right up until the end of his correspondence with his mother, with Haldane at sixty-four likening himself, with youthful exuberance, to 'a missionary' and, at sixty-six, 'a Revival preacher' in the style of his ancestors.[30]

So, the slow and courteous manner we initially inferred from Haldane's response to Judge Kay doesn't quite seem to hit the mark for a description of the Haldane 'spirit'. It seems, rather, to be a spirit defined by a 'fighting attitude', one 'full of conviction', capable of 'stirring up' the people to the cause at hand. It is also, if his earlier forebears are anything to go by, a spirit bound by the notion of duty, both to the public and to the monarch. Such a cocktail of characteristics undoubtedly finds embodiment in Richard Burdon Haldane, but so far we only have half of the story.

* * *

What about the 'lightning' spirit of the Burdon Sandersons? We certainly don't see much of it if we look to Haldane's maternal great-grandparents; but we do see two other facets of his character neatly personified in them. As his mother, Mary Elizabeth Haldane (née Burdon Sanderson), put it: 'Sir Thomas Burdon [who was mayor of Newcastle in 1810 and 1816] was a complete man of the world. ... He was open-handed and generous, and was idolized in Newcastle owing to his liberal actions, while his wife, though attractive, was retiring and loved study.'[31] Mary's maternal grandfather, Sir James Sanderson (1741–98), as Sheriff of London then Lord Mayor on two occasions,[32] showed another aspect so marked in his great-grandson: boldness in the face of adverse public opinion and behaviour. As Mary again remarked, Sir James 'distinguished himself in the latter part of the eighteenth century by his fearless manner of grappling with the dangers and difficulties which attended the circulation of revolutionary principles in this country'.[33] He was evidently a man who would put his own well-being in jeopardy for the sake of others, for he 'lost his life, it is said, by sending Pitt [the Younger] home in his carriage after a late sitting in the House of Commons and himself returning in a damp hackney coach'.[34]

It was Sir James's daughter who married Sir Thomas's son, who took on the additional surname of his father-in-law, becoming Richard Burdon Sanderson. He, too, distinguished himself, but this time in the academic arena, winning the coveted Newdigate Prize at Oxford in 1811 and the English Essay prize in 1814. He became a Fellow of Oriel, a reward reserved for the cream of Oxford graduates, and then pursued a legal career to follow his illustrious uncles, Lords Eldon and Stowell. It was the Earl of Eldon who appointed him Secretary of Presentations. But it was this post that was to be his undoing in the worldly sense and his making, as far as he saw it, in the spiritual sense. A strongly religious young man, Burdon Sanderson was disgusted with 'the abuse of clerical patronage for political purposes',[35] which he discovered in this post, and decided to resign from his position and leave the Church of England. This decision deeply hurt his uncle, who had taken him under his wing and bore hopes of greatness for his nephew. Yet this decision, under the power of a firm conscience, shows us once again an aspect of the Burdon Sanderson spirit that can be traced down to his grandson, the statesman. According to Haldane's mother: 'My father was not one to flinch, even if the sacrifice cost him almost his life. He was devotedly attached to his uncle, and his work was congenial to him, but he felt he must give it up, cost him what it might; and he did so.'[36] His daughter's son (our Haldane, that is), who remained steadfastly silent for the sake of the government under the greatest pressure to make good his name, who refused to submit to the histrionics of those crying for compulsory service, who 'preached' the reform of the education system in the teeth of attacks from grim-faced traditionalists and churchmen; this son seemed to demonstrate again and again this spirit of sacrifice for the sake of the greater good, as he saw it, which so marked the grandfather he was named after.

But, for Richard Burdon Haldane, success in the eyes of the world and weighty spiritual duties were not necessarily to be distinguished. His trajectory towards the Woolsack (the red seat made of wool reserved for the Lord Chancellor in the House of Lords) was encouraged, in fact, by his deeply religious family, particularly his mother, who longed to see her son fulfil the office that her great-uncle had once held for so long. Even his nurse cherished hopes in this direction, as Haldane recounts in his *Autobiography*:

> When I was about six years old and my nurse had taken me on a visit to Montague Grove at Hampstead, the London house of Richard Burdon Sanderson, my maternal grandfather, she conducted me to see the House of Lords, then in recess. She persuaded the attendants there to let her place me seated on the Woolsack, and then exclaimed: 'The bairn will sit there some day as of right.' 'Perhaps so,' our Highland butler observed, 'but by that time, Mistress Ferguson, your head will be weel happit.' At all events, for the English Bar I was destined by general family acclamation, and into the spirit of the decision I entered early.[37]

It is unsurprising that Haldane's nurse felt so confident in his 'right' to this great office when we consider his mother's perspective on his chosen path. As Haldane's sister, Elizabeth Sanderson Haldane, reflects:

> Her [Mary Elizabeth Haldane's] eldest son had chosen the law as his profession, to her great pleasure, as her connexions were largely legal, and it was a special delight to her that he twice occupied the position of Lord Chancellor. It was the position her grand-uncle had held for nearly twenty-five years, and her brother had married the sister of another Lord Chancellor (Lord Herschell), so that she felt it was a sort of family possession.[38]

19

It was a connection that undoubtedly supported Haldane's ascendency. In 1904, seven years before Haldane donned his robes as Lord Chancellor, we find him writing to his mother:

> The Editor of the Times told me that the old Lord Chancellor [Lord Halsbury] had actually taken him aside to impress on him the other day that I was his only fit successor, both as Chancellor & as Speaker of the H of Lords, & that the Times should [be] supportive. The old Chancellor lays stress, too, on my being Lord Eldon's great grandnephew.[39]

These circumstances make it quite natural that seven years later Haldane should write: 'It seems strangely familiar to be in the great Lord Eldon's place.'[40]

But to what extent was Haldane actually like his famous ancestor? True, both had their houses targeted by activists of one form or another; but when we consider that Eldon was viewed as 'the epitome of resistance to all reform'[41] by the liberals of the time, we begin to realise that their hardships sprang from very different viewpoints. Haldane was fundamentally a great reformer, who would travel hundreds of miles through the night, often multiple times a week, just to speak on platforms where he felt that his gospel of a radically revamped education system or a drastically restructured British army needed to be heard. Eldon, on the other hand, staunchly opposed reform at almost every turn, whether it was the abolition of slavery, Catholic emancipation, or the revolutionary reform bills of the 1830s. Gladstone, one of Haldane's political heroes, even described Eldon as 'the great champion of all that was most stupid in politics'.[42]

And yet, Eldon and Haldane were not entirely dissimilar. Their habits of forming judgments and of working are reminiscent of each other. Eldon would look to take all sides of an argument into consideration, which meant he crept only tentatively towards a conclusion, finding countless qualifications to modify each point. It was a process tortured enough to earn him the title Lord Endless—a name given him by Jeremy Bentham, no less. While Haldane could get through a vast amount of legal work and judgments in a very short space of time, he was certainly prone to a style so involved and intricate—both characteristics of Eldon's oratory and judgments—that it could frustrate listeners, causing a 'lucid fog' to descend upon the brain.[43] A great advocate for emphasising the multiplicity of aspects that make up any feature of reality, Haldane, like his great-

great-uncle, was prone to prod and test his object of attention at lengths that only the very patient could accept with equanimity.

As a young trainee lawyer, Eldon showed a capacity for industry that few could match, working 'from four in the morning until late at night, sometimes with a wet towel round his head to keep him awake'.[44] Perhaps it is this industrious spirit that meant Haldane could write to his mother about his own experience as a young barrister in these terms, without fear that she would think him excessive: 'No briefs today. ... Since coming up [to London] one has been getting through between eleven & twelve hours reading a day & I intend to keep on doing this.'[45] Haldane's often baffling, at times unhealthy, working habits begin to make a little more sense when we bear his ancestry in mind. Haldane, at least, felt it was in the blood: 'I think you and my father have given me a strong nervous system—for I rarely tire & I require very little sleep.'[46]

Eldon and Haldane had their similarities in other respects too. Both were fiercely loyal to the Crown and developed personal relationships with their sovereigns. George III was to stress that Eldon was '*my* Lord Chancellor'. Eldon was indeed one of the principal defenders of George's authority when the first bouts of madness showed themselves. After one episode, George thanked him personally at Windsor 'for the affectionate fidelity with which he [had] adhered to him when so many had deserted him in his malady'.[47] George's successor, after initial suspicions, warmed to Eldon enough to call him affectionately 'Old Bags', after the bag which bore the Great Seal. He even turned to Eldon to reinforce his authority over his seventeen-year-old daughter, Princess Charlotte, after she had objected to her father's choice of attendants. The princess tearfully recounted that she had been compared to a 'collier's daughter' after Eldon had boldly exclaimed, in the presence of her father, that he would have locked her up if she had been one of his own daughters.

Haldane, while never reaching such heights (or depths) of boldness, was certainly one of the ministers dear to Edward VII. Even before Haldane took office, he could report that 'The King and the Prince of Wales are very well disposed to your Bear'[48] (as his mother playfully called him). Meeting Edward in his favourite German spa, Marienbad, Haldane (by this time in office) was whisked off alone with the king to a little café in the forest to drink coffee like regular civilians and discuss political events.[49]

The king, apparently, believed him the best Secretary of State in his experience.[50] Perhaps the king's regard for his minister led to the strange behaviour we find described in this letter from Haldane back to his mother:

> I spent yesterday with the King at Taplow. He & I really get on well. He was affectionate—took me out in his motor to make a call—had a photograph taken of himself & the others on the lawn in which he insisted that I should be lying on the grass talking to him. He arranged the position of my feet so that my boots might not come out of focus & appear big. In the afternoon he took me for a walk alone. I did my best to smooth over ruffles with the others.[51]

The photo in question makes Haldane appear quite absurd, and one wonders if the king didn't enjoy taking advantage a little of his loyal subject. Edward certainly felt comfortable enough with Haldane to tease him gently, on one occasion pronouncing the old, unfashionable hat upon Haldane's head to be an inheritance from Goethe.[52] But there can be no doubt about the deep bond of affection between the two men, and Haldane's letters reflecting on the loss of his king in 1910 are touching to read. As the end approaches, Haldane writes: 'He will probably be gone before I can be near, my dear King & master. It is a blow to the nation, & to me individually a personal sorrow. For I was nearer to him than others.'[53] And when the time came: 'The relation between myself and my King was not a usual one & something personal is snapped in two.'[54] Haldane was even sent for by Queen Alexandra in her first days of mourning. As Haldane recounted to his mother:

> I saw her alone in the room where he lay. She told me, as I had my last look at him, reposing uncoiffured on his bed, that he was fond of me & cared for my work for him. ... I kissed her hand & promised that I would never forget him or her. ... I stayed about a quarter of an hour with her while we stood by his side. He looked little changed, the old expression with perfect peace.[55]

Just as George III's son, George IV, turned to Eldon at a time of trial, so too did Edward's son, George V, turn to Haldane in a moment of difficulty. At the collapse of the government in 1916, George secretly called upon Haldane, who was by this time *persona non grata* in the public eye, 'for advice in the interregnum, about the constitutional position. ... Of course this is very private & I shall not go near the Palace. But the constitutional problems are grave.'[56] It is this legal expertise that brings us to the final note of similarity between Lords Haldane and Eldon, for both left distinctive marks upon the law.

Eldon, already known as 'the great luminary of the law'[57] while still a young man, is said to be 'one of the principal architects of equity jurisprudence', while Haldane was 'particularly strong ... in the uncertain area where the principles of common law and equity overlap'.[58] Haldane's own lasting impression has been left by his distinctive shaping of the Canadian constitution, having contributed to a remarkable thirty-two judgments on the country's legislative matters between 1911 and 1928. Haldane's legacy in this respect is hotly disputed, championed by some for its radical devolvement of powers to the provinces and vilified by others for its tight restrictions on the centralised federal government. There will be more to say on this later in the book, but what we can say at present is that Haldane, like his great predecessor on the Woolsack, was not simply a lawyer content to preserve the status quo. Both men sought to *fashion* the law to meet the needs of the time (though in Eldon's case, he sought to do this in a way that was consistent with his conservatism). Nor was Eldon the only ancestor to set an example in this regard. Eldon's brother, William Scott, Baron Stowell (1745–1836), was a famous judge on the Admiralty bench. According to one biographer, Stowell 'laid foundations for the international law of war which remained important into the twentieth century'.[59] Hence Haldane could write to his mother in 1921: 'The House of Lords still occupies me with Admiralty appeals—more a subject for Lord Stowell than for myself.'[60]

The final family member on his mother's side who acted as a guiding light for Haldane's life was his uncle, Sir John Burdon Sanderson (1828–1905), a scientist of international renown. Sir John was a pioneer of germ theory and experimental pathology, while also a landmark figure in the history of physiology. Someone to whom even Darwin turned for scientific aid, he was the first ever professor of his discipline at Oxford and was responsible for the creation of the Faculty of Medicine at the university. From his uncle, Haldane learnt two things. Firstly, he learnt the vital importance of scientific investigation for an understanding of life's problems and complexities. In an age when classical study was considered the summit of human learning, Haldane knew that such study alone was far from sufficient as a guide to understanding the rich variety of reality. And, because scientific enquiry was in the family, as it were, Haldane took it as entirely natural that one should have its methods and findings to hand in whatever investigation was under way. Secondly, Sir John was an early influence on Haldane's understanding of duty—that paragon of Victorian virtue. In an early letter written to the teenage Haldane in the midst of his anxieties about life's meaning and purpose, we find his uncle stating:

> The question no longer is how to make things in general better than they are but how to overcome the definite obstacles which stand in the way of progress in a given direction. In this way one is brought face to face with duty & soon learns that the one and only secret of happiness lies in the performance of duty in the best and most conscientious manner.[61]

This emphasis on the renunciation of self for the duty that lies before one is at the very heart of Haldane's approach to his vocation as scholar and statesman. As he himself put it:

> It is not in Nature, but as immanent in the self ... that we find God; and so it is that this great truth pervades every relation of life. 'He who would accomplish anything must limit himself.' The man who leads others must himself be capable of renouncing. Not in some world apart, but here and now, in the duty, however humble, that lies nearest us, is the realisation of the higher self—that self that tends Godward—to be sought. And this carries with it something more. To succeed is to throw one's whole strength into work; and if work must always and everywhere involve the passage through the portal of renunciation, be it special and even contracted, then the only life that for us human beings can be perfect is the life that is *dedicated*.[62]

In a sense, it is this emphasis on renunciation and dedication that acts as the river which unites the various streams that we have seen flowing from both Haldane's paternal and maternal forebears. Haldane's own expression of the need for these virtues, as discovered in the above quotation, is evidently moulded by his philosophical studies, which we shall come to later in Part 1, and which are unique to his historical context. But, despite the differences with his ancestors in how these ideas take shape, the conclusions are the same. The old Protestant work ethic is here reworked for an age that was beginning to reject the prior certainties of Calvinistic theology. Here again is the inherited sense of the significance of suffering for the development of one's humanity. In this way, Haldane was able to keep that most personal of bonds, the most important relationship of his life—his bond with his mother—so close and intact. He could say the things he knew she wanted to hear, about faith, about God, about service, and rest assured that he was in no way intellectually compromising himself. But as this suggests, for all his need of an intellectual framework and bedrock to make his way through life, Haldane's emotional attachments were just as, if not more, foundational to his existence.

2

THE HEAD AND THE HEART

How little life can be understood from the outside.

Haldane to Lady Horner, 1905[1]

We often set the head and the heart in opposition. The problem with presenting Haldane the man is that there is a temptation to forget the heart entirely. His obsession with matters of the mind, coupled with his unmarried state, initially suggest that we are dealing with a person for whom emotions were of little account, for whom the languages of passion and of love were irrelevant, if not unknown. His nephew, Graeme Haldane, once told the biographer Dudley Sommer:

> I doubt ... whether I or anyone else really succeeded in establishing the closest form of human friendship [with Haldane]. My uncle lived in a mental world into which it was extremely difficult for other minds to penetrate fully. To some extent he naturally lived a lonely life which could not be completely shared by anyone.[2]

Reading this we don't wonder that, when the young Liberals sought to work out a fresh social programme at the turn of the century, Haldane was viewed as the '"mind" of the new outlook as distinct from its drive & human approach'.[3] This particular emphasis of approach meant that, when Sommer's biography appeared, Harold Nicolson wrote to the author in surprise: 'I gather from your book that he was a kindly man. ... But the impression he gave to those who did not know him was of being an aloof and rather inhuman little person.'[4]

This chapter seeks to show just how off the mark we would be to accept this impression. Previous studies, in an effort to resist the image of a cold-

27

hearted Haldane, have stressed the importance of his relationship with his mother and the tragedy of his failed engagement to Val Munro Ferguson. But a careful sifting of archival material and consideration of a new body of letters, brought to light in 2010, allow us to go much further than past portraits of Haldane's character. In what follows, we will not only take a fresh look at just what his relationships with his mother and with Val reveal, but also at a number of other key relationships that are able to demonstrate more clearly than ever before just how human he was. It will also become plain that, in many respects, the impression that the head dominated with Haldane is partly a result of the influences of certain people and emotions upon his heart.

It is perhaps helpful to begin with an insight into the world in which Haldane grew up, and the characters of his parents and siblings. His early life is a fascinating mixture of extreme religious observance and homely harmony. Both the Haldane and Burdon Sanderson sides of the family insisted that the God who is revealed in Jesus Christ, and discovered in the Scriptures (narrowly and strictly interpreted), was to be the foundation of the family and its practices. For this reason, Haldane's mother, Mary Elizabeth Haldane (née Burdon Sanderson), guided by her father, refused the suitor to whom she was most attracted in her youth, because he did not possess the requisite religious commitments. This was to be a source of great sorrow for her throughout her life, despite the happiness that her later marriage brought her, particularly in her children. A further sorrow was to have a plan for her to go to London, where she might cultivate her burgeoning artistic skill in the studio of Henry Sass, abandoned as unsuitable for a young lady in her position. Despite her great fondness for her parents, her upbringing, dominated by governesses, was of the most rigid sort. Her feet were placed in stocks during lessons, while her back had to hold a backboard in place; she remembered being shut in the cellar for not showing sufficient respect to the butler, and being kept in an empty room for a day as a form of corporal punishment, with only bread and water for sustenance. And when she was forced to learn Psalm 139 for another misdemeanour (these acts were often fabricated by her governess and then reported to her parents), she developed an acute sense of sin: 'I was often kept awake by the thought of the sinfulness of my nature and with the sense that at any moment judgement might be passed upon me. I knew that I was a great sinner and that God was my judge and must condemn me.'[5]

Her sex had been a disappointment to her grandfather, who 'did not reply to the announcement [of her birth], as I was to have [been] named after him and been his heir had I been a son'.[6] When she tells the story of her father building a new family home, we are not surprised that she was surrounded by a sense of her own worthlessness:

> The Manor House of Jesmond was pronounced to be in a dangerous condition ... and it was entirely rebuilt and a new foundation stone laid. This was done to the great disappointment of my sister and myself, because our names were not placed on the stone, but only my brother's. From that time forward the fact of my being merely a daughter rankled in my mind, and during my childhood, and for years afterwards, I used to feel as if I was nobody to anybody.[7]

Hardship, then, was a given in her life, even before the many deaths she was to face as a married woman (two sons; her eldest brother and his two daughters in a railway accident; her husband; and three grandchildren in the First World War). Being denied worldly solace early in life perhaps accounts for her need to find peace in that which is beyond the world, and her consistent suggestions that temporal sorrows ought to seek alleviation in the light of the eternal. This was to give her great empathy with those who suffered and paved the way for the immense serenity she exhibited in older age, when she was famed for her ability to give comfort to the perplexed or sad and courage to the frightened. She was never harsh with her own children, and even shocked them sometimes by the merciful attitude she showed to those they had been taught by their religious teachers to consider damned.[8]

The man she was to marry, Robert Haldane, a widower with five children, found his solace, too, in things divine, but in his case the darker side of religion had a greater prominence, given the harsh Scottish Calvinism of his own father. When Robert (by profession a Writer to the Signet)[9] preached to the locals at Cloan, in a little barn built for the purpose, he preached 'the Word of God in all its strictness'.[10] Haldane's sister recollected: 'Religion permeated our lives, and the sense of sin and its consequences seemed to dog our footsteps when we remembered what it meant.'[11] This was coupled with 'a Puritan dread of pleasure—even artistic pleasure—unless it were to lead to something useful to mankind'.[12] But Robert was a good, kind man, who loved animals and a simple country life. Despite the austerity of his theology, he was devoted to his children, and in his final years came to rely on the eldest son of his second marriage. Thirty-four years after his death in 1877, Mary reminds Haldane:

> You upheld your dear father when he sorely needed support. Those times I cannot possibly forget nor how much he rested upon you. All this comes back to my memory constantly. 'One thing,' he said to me, 'I cannot face and that is Bo's [Haldane's pet name as a child] going up to London and leaving me[.'] [H]e never had to face it. He left us, before you went up to London.[13]

Mary was to survive her husband by forty-eight years, and she became the 'mainspring' of the family.[14] But some biographers have relegated the role Haldane's father played in his life to a point of insignificance. One striking feature in the letters from his mother that Haldane kept is her repeated stress on how much he cared for and looked after his father in his old age,[15] and it is surely significant that when his father dies we find Haldane writing: 'The world and life seem very real when one's father is gone, and duty becomes more and more apparent and binding.'[16] Despite the advanced age of the children from Robert's earlier marriage,[17] Haldane became, at twenty, the head of the family. Mary explains: 'You have never forgotten the first family either, who seem to have been left by their father almost to hand upon you. None of them had force of character to be able to help themselves.'[18] So we ought not to forget that Haldane loved his father, and saw himself as carrying on his responsibilities in some sense.

* * *

But this is to jump ahead. It is important to bring out a further aspect of Haldane family life, relevant to our subject, and that is the sense of the harmonious relations between all members of the family. Haldane's sister, Elizabeth, tells a story to illustrate the point:

> The only approach to a quarrel amongst us was one between Richard and John [one of Haldane's younger brothers, whose achievements we will explore shortly], over the problem of Achilles and the Tortoise, and as they were driving together on their way to a tennis party, they landed in a ditch, so excited were they over the subject. Hence they have never quarrelled

again! When we were all together at Cloan, there seemed no end to the subjects we had to discuss, between politics, science and philosophy. One's life no doubt became what the Germans call *zersplittert*, but if that does not make for efficiency (and it does not), it makes for great happiness.[19]

The difference in outlooks between the children and their parents raised, perhaps, one or two more difficulties, but even then the impression is that divisive argument and ongoing disagreement were to be avoided at all costs. Haldane's adult baptism, around the time he went to Göttingen at seventeen, is a revealing event in this respect. Although no longer a Christian in any traditional sense, Haldane consented to be baptised to relieve the anxiety of his Baptist father and mother, on the condition that he 'assented to no formula and gave no undertaking'. He would undergo the ceremony 'if, but only if, this anxiety could be relieved on terms that did not compromise me'. But the terms seem to have been broken:

My father did not, I think, realise in the least how far away from each other our minds were on foundational questions. He proposed that the ceremony should be gone through quite privately at the church to which the family went when in Edinburgh, and that no one should be present except those immediately concerned. I do not think he had taken in the importance which I attached to this undertaking. Anyhow, he seemed to have let the appointment be known, for, when I got to the church, there were present not only the minister, but a crowd of deacons and other onlookers. My mind was at once made up. To begin with I told them all openly that I would not refuse to go through the ceremony, but that I should make a definite explanation the moment it was over. I rose dripping from the font, and, facing the congregation, announced to them that I had consented to go through what had taken place only to allay the anxiety of my parents, but that now, as those present might have misunderstood, I must say something to them. It was that I could not accept their doctrines; that I regarded what had taken place as the merest external ceremony; and that for the future I had no connection with the church, or its teaching, or with any other church. I then changed my clothes and walked away from the building. There was much consternation, but nothing was said, probably because there was nothing to say. My cousin, the late Bishop of Argyll, who was present, walked after me and was very kind and sympathetic. But the incident was a closed one. It was never alluded to afterwards, and silence was preserved in our household on the subject.[20]

Haldane's later efforts to assure his mother that they believed substantially the same things, just that the form of expression was different, suggests that he did not want this rift to be viewed as ultimate, but rather that it represented a difference of opinion in how truth ought to be represented.[21] Haldane repeatedly stresses, as we shall see in Chapter 4, that a representation of truth appropriate for one generation is not necessarily appropriate for another. This dread of fundamental disagreement can be linked to the value that was placed on harmony within the family; the family was to be a place of refuge rather than quarrel. Peace and acceptance were their watchwords, the first being a sign of God's presence, the second a sign of obedience to His will (I have not been able to discover one single instance in the letters between Haldane and his mother of a voiced material disagreement).[22] This all went to the making of a very tight-knit family, with a great emphasis on the importance of 'home'. Time and again in later life, we find Haldane reflecting on the significance of home to him,[23] particularly the comforting atmosphere of Cloan.[24] It is an atmosphere beautifully evoked by a close family friend of the Haldanes, Violet Markham, writing in 1956:

> The drawing-room at Cloan, the real social centre of the family, had spaciousness and comfort of a kind as rare today as the country house itself. It was no period piece. ... [It] had a good deal to say about the past and the present of the family. ... Distinguished ancestors looked down from the walls, their portraits reinforced by engravings, sketches, miniatures old and new. ... There were framed photographs: they might be of a grandchild, or of some special occasion, or the autographed likeness of a visiting royalty. ... The latest books were to be found on the table, a variety of newspapers on another. And with its warm and friendly atmosphere it was an eminently comfortable room where couches and armchairs with chintz covers were an invitation to gossip, either *tête-à-tête* or in little groups. There were many flowers ... spread[ing] a perfume special to the room.[25]

But more than the comfort of the house, it was the family who lived or gathered there that mattered most to Haldane. In terms of supportive siblings, the three from the marriage of Robert and Mary who lived into adulthood—John, Elizabeth and William—all played key roles in Haldane's life. John was the intellectual companion, who offered the scientific counterbalance to Haldane's philosophic temperament (though

John received a high First in Philosophy at Edinburgh and his work was driven by his philosophic commitments, while Haldane sat on many scientific committees and, like John, achieved the distinction of a fellowship of the Royal Society). The pair published an essay together in an early collection of essays,[26] edited by Haldane at the age of twenty-seven and his friend Andrew Seth (later Professor Andrew Seth Pringle-Pattison), where the brothers argued from both a scientific and philosophical perspective against the pervading mechanistic worldview of the time. They also gave lectures together and frequently spoke to each other on intellectual matters, and John even accompanied his brother on the (in)famous 1912 Haldane Mission to Berlin. John, Fellow of New College, Oxford, and Honorary Professor at the University of Birmingham, has been called the 'Father of Oxygen Therapy'. His investigations into altitude and diving physiology and carbon monoxide poisoning 'led to a sea change in clinical medicine and improved safety and reduced mortality and morbidity in many high risk situations'.[27] Indeed, his decompression tables remain the basis of modern tables, by which divers are able to avoid 'the bends'. Furthermore, during the First World War he correctly identified the type and effects of the poison gas used by the Germans and designed a portable oxygen-administration apparatus for use in the field: the first gas mask. Like his older brother, he gave the prestigious Gifford Lectures, and he was president of the Institution of Mining Engineers and director of the Mining Research Laboratory at Doncaster and Birmingham. He was made a Companion of Honour in 1928 and received the Royal Medal and the Copley Medal of the Royal Society in 1916 and 1934 respectively.

As for Elizabeth, or Bay as she was known, it was she who looked after Haldane in the aftermath of a crisis, most significantly when his engagement to Val was broken off (Elizabeth herself never married).[28] It was also she who acted as hostess when Haldane was host, and as his plus-one at the many official and social events that he had, often reluctantly, to attend. Elizabeth had a fine intellect in her own right. She wrote a number of impressive studies and was a translator of Hegel and Descartes. Among many distinguished positions, Elizabeth was a manager of Edinburgh Royal Infirmary, vice-chairman of the Territorial Nursing Service, and a member of the 1912 Royal Commission on the Civil Service. She was the first female trustee of Andrew Carnegie's United Kingdom Trust and the first woman to be appointed a justice of the peace in Scotland (1920). In 1917, eleven years before her brother John, Elizabeth was made a Companion of Honour, an accolade which only sixty people can hold at any one time.

William (known as Willie), on the other hand, was very much a different breed from the rest of the siblings, with a keen eye for business and for estate management. He became Crown Agent for Scotland, was knighted, and took Haldane's private affairs, particularly the management of his money and property, in hand (as he did for many families of the 'gentry', including Frances Horner, of whom more later).

What the above paragraphs are seeking to make clear is just how much Haldane's sense of the seriousness of life, of the inevitability of its hardships, of its religious bearing, of its intellectual demands, and yet of life's warmth, of the beauty of harmonious relationships, trace their origin back to the home life of his youth. It is no surprise that it was precisely these elements that were so markedly emphasised in his philosophy, as we shall discover in Chapter 4.

* * *

We can now look a bit more closely at two of the most vital familial relationships in Haldane's life, namely those with his mother and his younger brother George, known as Geordie, who died from diphtheria aged sixteen, when Haldane was just nineteen. Thinking about this latter relationship is a good way into the former. The loss that both Haldane and his mother sustained at Geordie's death particularly united them, and it is an event which, as each reflected upon it across the years, acted as a point of convergence for many of the key emotional ties that bound mother and son together. It also raises themes central to Haldane's intellectual pursuits, and it demonstrates very clearly the point made at the outset of this chapter: that the dominance of matters of the mind in Haldane's life can be understood, in part, as a reaction to matters of the heart.

Let us take that final point first. Geordie, by all accounts, had a very remarkable character—he was highly intelligent, a gifted musician, and remained untroubled by religious doubts. He had a personality that one couldn't help loving in its simplicity and purity. Haldane was deeply attached to him, and his loss was a lifelong grief. Willie, towards the end of his life, reflected that 'his [Geordie's] death led Richard to Philosophy, I am quite sure'.[29] Now this isn't entirely accurate. Even before Geordie's death in March 1875 we find Haldane keenly engaged in philosophical questioning and enjoying the metaphysical challenges set before him by the professors at Göttingen. But what we can say is that the philosophy he was discovering seems to have become a lived reality in his time of mourning. Reflecting on his loss, Haldane writes: 'The very sadness is good for us; it teaches that the things of time are passing away, and that life has a deeper meaning than that which is apparent on its surface.'[30] It is the sadness that teaches the philosophical truth. This is linked to the ability to see the truth, which involves the ability to stand back from immersion in temporal and material things, and to see the world from a position approaching objectivity. Haldane writes to his mother on the twenty-first anniversary of his brother's death:

> This date is one we are not likely to forget. My father passed away as it were in the established order of things. Not so Geordie. It was a great part suddenly scratched out of our lives, & I think it has had a detaching effect on all of us. It will not be forgotten—the change that came this afternoon one & twenty years ago.[31]

When Haldane, in his philosophical works, speaks of rising to a 'higher standpoint', and quotes Matthew Arnold approvingly on the desire 'to see life steadily, and to see it whole', this is surely not unconnected to the 'detaching' experiences of 1875.[32]

There is a connection here with Mary's own ability to consider life's sorrow from the perspective of eternity. This is a theme that appears numerous times throughout the letters, and again we find that, in many ways, it is from his mother, not philosophical tomes, that he learns the true value of taking strength from this perspective.[33] In other words, it was not a perspective that Haldane simply arrived at out of an intellectual examination of the world; it arose out of an emotional bond.

As we have seen, Haldane was evidently extremely close to Geordie, and it was a huge blow to him when he died. For Mary it was a source of untold suffering, and it was coupled with the fact that she contracted the disease from which her son died. There was, then, a bond of suffering which united the two, but as the years progressed there was also a shared ability to think of this suffering as ultimately beneficial. The following letter from Mary to her son in 1893 is telling:

My dearest R.

You know me better than anyone on earth. You know what that blow was which fell on us back in 1875. It seemed as if the light had gone out of our selves when those deep blue eyes were closed forever.

But yet it was not so. I like your sentence so much about him. The period of perfection was sooner reached than with most of us, and now his presence seems to linger with one, that of a spirit made perfect. I often feel thankful that it was granted to me to know him. Even in life, I used to marvel at the little hold that any evil had upon him, and even wondered that he was my son, he seemed so much in advance of me.

But we must not forget recent happiness in past experiences. Sorrows bring with them results which cannot be changed otherwise. You have had your share, and I feel persuaded that if you could, you would not exchange your own life with that of others who have had no crosses. With these trials of course you have had more success than is the lot of most men; but these other rough passages in life have their own [word unclear]. All these things have drawn us into a peculiar bond of sympathy which is difficult to define. The mother rests upon her son, and the son understands his mother. It is not often so, but the circumstances of our lives have been peculiar.[34]

The trials to which Mary refers are, in addition to the loss of Geordie, the two failed romantic attachments that we will discuss later in this chapter. The point to make here is that the relationship between mother and son was no ordinary one. It is not just that they were deeply in tune with one another (and indeed, the fact that Haldane, when away from Cloan, wrote daily to his mother from his arrival in London in 1877 to her death, aged 100, in 1925 is an incredible witness to that bond); it is as if the lines between them were blurred. Each experienced the emotions and feelings of the other as if they were their own. Haldane's sufferings were Mary's sufferings and vice versa. But in their view it was not pointless suffering; ultimately, it was redemptive. Haldane expressed both aspects when he wrote about the break-up of his engagement to Val Munro Ferguson:

Of course the wound, and I feel how much it is a wound through me to you personally, is hard to bear, & the interest of life has been taken away. But this will remain so only for a time and the future has probably a great deal in store. Wisdom and strength come—as you say—through sorrow.[35]

There is a sense, then, in which Mary Haldane lived through her son. In this she somehow found meaning for her own life:

IN THE BEGINNING...

1. Haldane's birthplace, on 30 July 1856, at 17 Charlotte Square, on the west side of the square in the Georgian 'New Town' of Edinburgh. Behind the palatial facade, designed by Robert Adam, Haldane's family lived and his beloved brother Geordie died aged 16.

In the Blood

The Haldane family has a long and noble heritage, boasting of many eminent politicians, soldiers, and sailors. The family's lineage can be traced all the way back to Charlemagne.

2—3. James Alexander Haldane, Haldane's grandfather (1768–1851) (above) and his brother Robert (1764–1842) (below) were famous Scottish evangelists, whose missionary zeal was an important inspiration in Haldane's more secular attempts to spread 'the gospel of Education'.

4. Haldane's great-great-uncle on his mother's side John Scott, first Earl of Eldon (1751–1838) twice served as Lord Chancellor in the early 19th century; Haldane was to do the same in the early 20th century.

5. Sir John Scott Burdon Sanderson (1828–1905), Mary Haldane's brother, a distinguished scientist, 1870, and the first holder of Oxford University's Waynflete Chair of Physiology.

6. The childhood home of Haldane's mother, Mary Elizabeth Haldane (née Burdon Sanderson), Jesmond Towers, Jesmond, near Newcastle upon Tyne, late 19th century.

Haldane Family Country Home: Cloan, Perthshire

7. Cloan, the country home of the Haldane family, taken at the turn of the 20th century, with the Ochil Hills rising behind to the south. The two windows of Haldane's study are in the tower on the left, on the second top floor.

8. Cloan today. The house is situated one mile south of Auchterarder, in Perthshire. The estate was acquired by Haldane's father in 1851, five years before Haldane's birth.

9. The view from Haldane's study north to the Grampians, as he would have seen it.

10. The view from Cloan today north to the southern flank of the Grampians.

Haldane's Family

11. Robert Haldane (1805–1877), Haldane's father, a lawyer and Writer to the Signet c. early 1850s.

12. Mary Elizabeth Haldane (1825–1925) (née Burdon Sanderson), Haldane's mother and Robert Haldane's second wife, 1882.

Richard (1856–1928) 1874	Geordie (1858–1874) 1870	John (J. S.) (1860–1936) 1879	Elizabeth (1862–1937) 1874	William (1864–1951) 1877

13—17.

18. Geordie, John and Richard Haldane, June 1861, left to right, aged 5, 3 and 7.

19. Haldane, back row, fourth from left with arms crossed, see inset below, in his first year at school at the Edinburgh Academy, 1866/7.

1861

1866

1870

20. John, Richard and Geordie Haldane, November 1870, aged 10, 14 and 12.

21. Göttingen University in the 1800s.

22. Professor Hermann Lotze (1817–1881), who introduced Haldane at Göttingen to the life-changing philosophies of Fichte, Kant and Berkeley. His classroom was Haldane's 'Spiritual Home'.

23. Fräulein Helene Schlote, Haldane's German tutor whilst in Göttingen; it was the start of a lifetime's friendship.

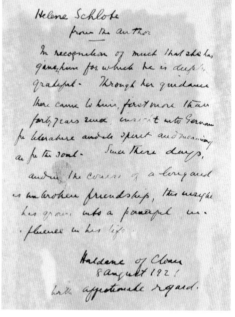

24. Inscription to Fräulein Helene Schlote in Haldane's book *The Reign of Relativity*, given by the author in 1921.

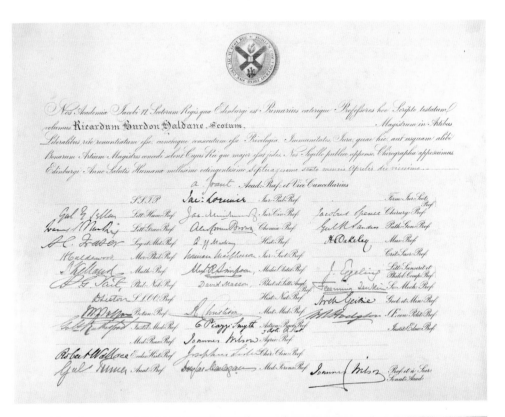

25. Haldane's diploma of Master of Arts, Edinburgh University, April 1876, signed by his favourite professor, William Young Sellar, and 31 other professors.

26. Old College, Edinburgh, early 19th century.

Haldane leaves Cloan for London

27. After the death of his father in 1877, Haldane, at the age of 21, left Scotland for London to read for the English Bar. Haldane is shown above in 1879, aged 23, with his mother, 54, Elizabeth, 17, and John, 19, at Cloan.

HALDANE'S CONSTANTS

28. Mary Elizabeth Haldane aged 80, the 'mainspring' of the Haldane family, renowned amongst famous statesmen, writers, soldiers and scientists for her immense serenity and unflinching religious faith. She was Haldane's 'source of strength', 1905.

A Protective Sister

29. Elizabeth Haldane, c. 1879, aged 17. Educated principally at home, Elizabeth shared her brothers' tutors, participating in discussions on philosophy, science and politics.

30. Elizabeth Haldane, c. 1900–10, during which period, in 1905, she wrote her '*Life of Descartes*', in recognition of which St. Andrew's University conferred on her the honorary degree of LLD.

31. Elizabeth Haldane, c. 1920–25, Haldane's sister, an influential public servant, a Companion of Honour, and the first Justice of the Peace in Scotland. She never married, and lived with Haldane in London and Scotland, looking after his domestic affairs. Her diaries show her deep concern for her brother's well-being and are a fascinating insight into the daily life of Haldane, personally, professionally and politically.

Haldane and his Dogs

32. Haldane's St. Bernard, his most beloved dog, who lived from 1906 to 1921, was the controversially named Kaiser, seen here with Haldane and Sir Ian Hamilton.

33. Kaiser, with guests at Cloan, including John Buchan on left, Haldane's brother J. S. Haldane in middle and, believed to be, Randall Davidson, the Archbishop of Canterbury. Kaiser, by his demeanour and character, 'inspired' Haldane's meditation.

34. After Kaiser's death, the labrador Bruce, the 'Black Dog', entered Haldane's life.

35. Bruce was a personal favourite of J. M. Barrie who would roll around with him on the drawing room floor at Cloan. In the Dogs' Graveyard at Cloan, there is the inscription: 'Bruce, A much loved Labrador Dog, Sir J. M. Barrie's Friend'.

36. Mary Elizabeth Haldane in her saintly old age in 1923. From the time Haldane first went to Göttingen until her death in 1925 there was rarely a day when she and Haldane failed to write to each other, when not together at Cloan.

It is worth having, to have the love of a son whose love is strong and unchanged. I cannot tell you how precious your words are to me, and how they make me feel that, after all, my life has not been a failure, as I am sometimes apt to think when I see my children doing so much that I cannot do. 'Love is the fulfilling of the law.' And love must fulfil what is lacking in the powers. It runs deep, as you know, and is yours, true & strong. There has always been a peculiar sympathy between us which makes me feel acutely your joys, as well as it has your sorrows. Parting is more or less a pain to me, but I feel … how supremely thankful I should be for our frequent meetings.[36]

This created its own burdens, of course. Her goodness of character—which impressed all who met her and won for her the admiration of prime ministers, generals and archbishops—was a goodness which meant that, for her children, their 'only anxiety was to appear before her as worthy of her great love for us'.[37] This explains, perhaps, why many of Haldane's letters to her suggest, on an initial reading, that Haldane was of a rather self-laudatory nature, as he frequently cites his triumphs and achievements, without any attempt at humility. This becomes far more comprehensible when we read of his desire to appear worthy before her. Given that Haldane was known for his distinct lack of self-aggrandisement in every other walk of life, it seems to make more sense to read the letters as an attempt to please his mother, rather than seeing them as a revelation of a hidden, over-fed pride.

But his letters were more than just an opportunity to express his achievements. They were also the context in which he could honestly express his emotions, conscious as he was of his own inability truly to articulate his feelings face to face. On his way back to London after a stay at Cloan, Haldane writes:

Dearest of Mothers,

I take my pencil to write a little letter continuing our talk of this morning. For you must never think that because I do not express myself much I do not feel very deeply my tie to yourself. It is the best thing in my life & as the years move on I prize it more & more. There is nothing to compare with—nothing so sacred as—the love of my mother for me & mine for her. Distance does not diminish it & it grows with the years.[38]

It is not surprising that Haldane greatly feared losing his mother (who lived to be 100 years and 16 days!). His language is often extreme in this respect: 'It would be nothing short of a dreadful calamity to all of us, and especially to me, if anything were to happen to you—and you will not therefore wonder that one gets fidgety.'[39] On her seventy-first birthday, he writes: 'May you long be spared to your children. They need you & are deeply attached to you. I do not know what I should do if you were not in my life.'[40] It is clear that Haldane relied on his mother. She was, as he so often said, 'a source of strength' to him and an inspiration.[41]

This dependence is particularly interesting because, after an examination of his political actions, we would surely associate Haldane with independence of thought and action; and, after an examination of his philosophical writings, as a man who relied on the 'consolation of philosophy', not human relationships, for his strength. The point that seems to emerge in reading these letters is that this very independence in public life is rooted in a dependence in private life. It is precisely because he has this source of strength behind him, in the person of his mother, that he can risk putting into jeopardy his safe political existence by the strong independent stances he took on certain matters. Time and again in their letters Haldane and his mother reflect on the importance of renouncing one's natural desires for security and prestige in order to achieve real self-development and to improve the conditions of society.[42] One ought to be prepared to risk acting in such a way that may endanger the privileges and safety offered to a 'party man', if one wants to live a fully human life. Haldane's readiness to take on the dangers of working cross-party, and even eventually to make the highly precarious move to Labour in 1924, had more to do with Mary Haldane than some might have realised.

But beyond these serious questions of what it means to live a fulfilled life, Haldane's letters to his mother were also his opportunity to express the real childlike side of his character. His mother called him her 'Bear', and he loved to play on this theme. When he receives a new dressing gown as a gift from her, he jokes: 'Indeed it is a most welcome present this new skin which the mother has given to her bear.'[43] And when Mary is in Rome on holiday, he playfully remarks: 'You must use money freely & get anything you want—or your Bear will growl.'[44] In the heat of political battle, moreover, the Secretary of State for War can maintain this light-hearted tone:

> Your letter breathes a peaceful atmosphere. That is not the atmosphere that
> your Bear is living in. As it begins to get about that there are to be large

reductions & reorganisations, the vested interests are beginning to rise & the attacks on me are commencing. But your Bear shuffles along—regardless of the insects that sting.[45]

And again: 'Your Bear is advancing on his way here—regardless of sticks & stones hurled at him. He does not mind the stings of bees if he can get his paw on the honey.'[46]

Even when the most internationally significant of events are at stake, such as Haldane's smoothing of Anglo–German relations during the Kaiser's state visit to England in 1907, he maintains the theme: 'The Foreign Office is unstinted in its expressions of gratitude. Where they were faced by a stone wall your Bear climbed over—extending his paw to the Emperor.'[47] This wonderfully boyish attitude in the letters brings out a side of Haldane's personality that we would do well to remember before we judge him as overly intellectual and oppressively serious.

* * *

Indeed, Haldane was noted by a number of his contemporaries for his wonderful sense of humour. It is worthwhile taking a brief interlude to highlight this point, as it is one that has been largely neglected in previous biographies. Haldane's letters to his friend the literary critic Edmund Gosse (a friendship discussed in the next chapter) concerning his dogs at Cloan provide ample material not only to show just how funny Haldane could be, but also the emotional significance that he invested in his pets at home.

A visitor to Cloan can to this day find in the dogs' cemetery the gravestone of two of his favourites, Kaiser and his successor Bruce. The very fact that the great St Bernard which lived so long in the Haldane household was named Kaiser is itself illustrative of Haldane's careless attitude to the danger of misinterpretation.[48] He particularly enjoyed investing his dogs with almost human qualities. There are many references to them in the letters to his mother, and J. M. Barrie was an intimate friend of Bruce. Barrie was even known to roll around with him in reckless abandon on the drawing-room floor at Cloan and on the lawn. But it is in Haldane's letters to Gosse that we see the playful side of his canine relationships played out most fully.

I quote only a small handful of the many references to them throughout the letters, but they say a lot about the man some have called 'humourless'.[49] In May 1918, Haldane writes:

I have been walking a little today & reading much. I say to my great old dog 'study', and he solemnly precedes me to an arbour in the Glen where I study Hegel while he lies at my feet meditating on the Absolute in his own fashion.[50]

And in April 1921:

I have been taking long solitary walks & am nearly at the end of all the little work I brought down. The Great Dog condescended yesterday to take a short walk with me, but he injured my feelings by intimating decisively that he preferred the company of the laundrymaid. And this although I lavish attentions on him.[51]

This was no unique instance of the 'romantic' attitude Haldane took to his dogs, particularly to Kaiser. After the St Bernard's death in August 1921, he turns to Gosse for guidance:

Now here is a question that is disturbing me. Elizabeth & my mother keep insinuating that it is not good for man to live alone, and that I ought to consider taking to myself another Dog! But grief surges up, although the gentle touch of time is softening it. I collect what I believe to be 'Forget-me-nots' (alas, I know no botany, & doubts are suggested about my faith in my choices) & lay them on his grave. I cannot bring myself to think of another companion—however, yet. My dear Dog taught me so much about the unnecessary differentiation we human beings make of space from time. I wish I had dedicated the 'Reign' [of Relativity] to his memory, but this you & Elizabeth would, I fear, have discouraged.[52]

A week later, Haldane continues:

Secondly, your wise counsel as to my dear Dog. But my doubt is whether it would not be better for his successor if he were different. Still large, but not 8 stone in weight. Otherwise No. 2 might feel instinctively that I was making comparisons to his detriment with No. 1. In so close a relationship these nuances have to be attended to. The charm of Kaiser, too, was that he returned very little of my emotion. ... I gulped down my feelings when I saw how he preferred the society of the servants' hall. I should mind this less in my bereavement if the new one were a little different. I want him to walk with me & to take care of my family of memories. I am sorry to say that the Dean [of St Paul's, known as the Gloomy Dean] showed but little of the feeling I had hoped for when I took him to visit the tomb, no consoling words such as I expected from a Minister of Religion.[53]

Eventually, by May 1922, Haldane had found a new partner, but could not let go of the thoughts of his previous love:

> Meantime I am on honeymoon with my number 2. Black & comely— young, only twenty months—full of activity & good nature. Quite intelligent. Knows how to poke open gates with his nose, & does not attack other dogs or sheep. But yet I yearn after my old love. This one will not inspire me in meditation by the suggestiveness of his demeanour or by his suspiciousness & obstinacy. For even vices become virtues in the Dog we love. However time & what the late Mrs. Ward called 'the strange but sweetly compelling power of marriage' may do much. [54]

In September that year, he admits with disappointment:

> I have been walking much with my Black Dog. But he has made me sad. He allowed himself to be rolled over in the dust of the public road by a smaller collie, just as though he had been a Greek Army. I thought mournfully of what his predecessor, the Great Dog, would have done. One terrible moment, & then eight hundred weight launched through the air on the oppressor with two front paws like prize fighters' arms, & then two vast jaws over the unhappy enemy. No wonder that even when he could hardly totter, all dogs who saw him from half a mile off fled ... I had been instructed to write a little book for the Queen's Doll's House. I wrote it on philosophy & sent it in. Now I regret that I did not choose another subject, 'The Life of a Great Dog'. [55]

It is rather wonderful to see the old War Minister and Lord Chancellor, the man who had undertaken some of the gravest activities of statesmanship of his generation, display such playfulness and humour.

* * *

But there were periods in Haldane's life when playfulness and humour seemed an impossibility—for he was not, as a young man, lucky in love.

In 1881 Haldane fell madly in love—and the adverb is not an exaggeration—with Agnes Kemp, the sister of his school friend and co-translator of Schopenhauer, John Kemp. [56] She rejected his advances. Haldane was crushed, plunging into a state of depression that, when expressed in the letters to his mother, makes for distressing reading. Things looked much brighter when, in the spring of 1890, he became engaged to Val, the sister of another close friend, Ronald Munro Ferguson (later Lord Novar, sixth

Governor General of Australia). After a few golden weeks, where he could exclaim 'I was never so happy',[57] Val broke the engagement off; once more Haldane had to face humiliation and shattering loss (it has subsequently been suggested that Val was, in fact, a lesbian).[58] As we explore these seismic events in Haldane's life, we will discover something of that genuine humanity that exemplifies itself at every turn in his letters to his mother, and once more that emotional basis upon which so much of his intellectual life was built.

For anyone who doubts that Haldane had a passionate side, there is a remarkable letter written to his mother in the teeth of rejection from Agnes, showing Haldane at his most fiery and impassioned:

> My dearest mother,
>
> I will not give her up until I find that I am powerless to make her marry me. My whole life is hers. I did not know this till Monday. I have written to her in the strongest terms, and I should hear from her tomorrow. If she says she cannot take the step of trusting herself to me, I shall reply that I shall ask her the same question six months hence.
>
> Nothing could do me any good just now: I am working hard and shall work still harder even after getting the reply I anticipate tomorrow. Forces have taken possession of my life, forces of which I knew nothing till now, forces which have bound me to her.[59]

That triple repetition of 'forces' shows more powerfully than any other phrasing in the letters just how entrapped he had become by his feelings and emotions at this time. This is not a man dwelling, to quote a translation of one of his most cherished Latin poems, 'remote, aloof / In some high mansion, built on Wisdom's hill'.[60] This is a man in the thick of life, experiencing its emotional extremes. And yet the reference to 'working hard' points to an important fact. Throughout the letters of this period, there is an almost continual affirmation of work as the remedy to his anxiety as he waits in anticipation of her final answer and his eventual misfortune.[61] It makes one realise that the fame for inexhaustibility in hard work that Haldane came to acquire is likely a consequence (at least in part) of his attempt to shut out his emotions; to keep his mind off himself and fixed on other things. That is interesting because it shows that what appears to be an almost inhuman appetite for work comes out of a truly human experience of emotional vulnerability.

It is patently clear from the letters just how vulnerable he was. The following excerpts are taken from letters over a six-month period, as he tries to deal with Agnes's rejection:

> I feel very flat & listless today, not taking an interest in any thing [*sic*], & not caring to work steadily. I do not seem to myself to be of any use to anybody.[62]

> For the last four years [since arriving in London] I have suffered periodically from depression of spirits, partly connected I think with this affair, and partly constitutional. The present has been a bad attack, but I think it is passing off.[63]

> Today it is four months since what was a terribly marked day for me the 28th February. I do not know how you have found the period but of late I seem to myself to have been passing through a valley of dark shadows. Nor is the morning in sight.[64]

> I am very well physically—I wish I could say as much mentally, but one must not complain.[65]

This final statement against complaint is surely a result of that familial attitude cultivated amongst the Haldanes, where complete acceptance of the hand one is dealt is the only respectable response to the world. It is obvious, however, that whatever acceptance there might have been on Haldane's part (and the statement does seem forced), it was of a painful, not a peaceful, character. This pain compelled him to seek a way of rising above the passing things of time:

> I will not write much. I am not overcome. I hardly expect even a ray of hope from her answer. What she is to me I know now for the first time. Do not fear for me whatever may happen.

> Henceforth my life consecrated as it has been by her influence will be above trivialities and insecurity.

> I will not leave town or see any one [*sic*] but just go on with my work.[66]

This is hardly the letter of a man who has now risen above insecurity; its rather grand tone is more suggestive of the truly disturbing feelings he is experiencing. But his pain has sent him on a mission to find a way to avoid such feelings in the future; this is certainly where his obsession with work comes in, as I indicated, and his philosophical studies play their part here too. In itself, however, the very rawness of the experience at this time steels him against the full blast of the blow that is to come from Val's rejection of him nine years later. Having gone through a genuine breakdown as a result of Agnes's refusal (Haldane actually describes the situation in these terms to his mother),[67] he is determined that nothing will touch him with such force again. Early in his attempts to win Val's hand and thinking he simply has no chance of success, he reassures his mother:

> I am realising the benefit of the ordeal of … nearly eight years ago, for I find myself strong and full of continued interest in work which is of far more than individual importance. You need have no concern about me.

> After writing once in reply to this, say nothing more of it, but have faith in the character which time & adversity have found in your son.[68]

How strong he really was on this occasion is put into question by his request for no more speech to be uttered on the topic, and a sense that Haldane's composure was not always as it seemed is something that one becomes aware of again in later events, particularly in his reaction to the press's vilification of him during the war.[69] Where perhaps the true strength and composure are found is in his sense that he has grown from past misfortunes and therefore that he can do so again. When the final cut comes from Val, and the engagement is broken, Haldane writes to his mother: 'Your boy is well & strong & he will grow through this as he has grown through other misfortunes.'[70] The fact that he had to 'grow through' the experience shows that he did not stand above it; the sorrow and the pain were real and deeply felt. The impression, then, that Haldane was somehow emotionally at a remove from life's ups and downs is misguided. What makes Haldane stand out is his ability truly to inhabit his emotions, while at the same time being convinced that in the end, as Julian of Norwich once wrote, 'all shall be well, and all manner of thing shall be well':[71]

> Today a year ago I was left alone. Well. I came back to you, & good has been the result. I can truly say that I would not be without what has passed. One gains wide knowledge in the Sanctuary of Sorrow—and a strength and experience which cannot be gained in any other way. There is no royal road to all this.

> I am older, but this year has been the richest in my life and it has been well worth living. I am very grateful to yourself.[72]

The fact that Haldane's loss brings him 'back' to his mother, as if she had lost him to Val, is telling. It hints at an important characteristic of Haldane during this affair, namely his wholehearted immersion in the object of his affection, even at the expense of his precious relationship with his mother. This intensity of attention, and the fear that it may impact his filial bond, is expressed in a remarkable letter written just after Val accepted his offer of marriage:

> My dearest Mother,
>
> Val Munro Ferguson & I exchanged the custody of our souls yesterday evening. All has come out in the best way. From the first she had known how her heart lay, but she had need [*sic*] time to make sure of herself. Now I have it all. I told her first <u>all</u> my past history—names excepted— for I felt that the secret of marriage is sincerity, and we are equally intent on seeking to place our feet in this lifelong business on rock and not in the sandy ground of mere sentiment. I do not think two people have ever begun with a high standard & aim more completely common. We had much talk about yourself and I undertook to convey her love to you. I think you should write to her at once … I believe it to be just as easy that you should meet for the first time by letter. I do not think you will ever find a difficulty with her—assuming you will be here in 10 days or a fortnight. Bay would come up here for a day next week. We will also make the beginning a gradual one & this is as well. For myself I have no doubt at all that this is the beginning of infinite gain to me. And you will not mind if for a bit at first I seem so absorbed with her that you see less of me. All this will be but temporary, and you & I both think of perma- nent goods in our lives as outweighing everything of the moment. Yet I know how keen she is that you should feel no temporary loss even.[73]

The letter reveals a fascinating ambiguity in Haldane's character, which is perhaps already evident from what has been discussed in this chapter so far. On the one side, there is the rather abstract and noble quality of the desire 'to place our feet in this lifelong business on rock and not in the sandy ground of mere sentiment'; he wants to begin 'with a high standard & aim'. But at the same time, there is the impassioned language and pos- sessiveness, as they 'exchange custody' of their 'souls', so that now he has 'all' of her heart. And having her in his possession, he submits to an inevi- table 'absorption' in her. Here, both the head and the heart have their say. And yet in this instance, it seems that the heart has the upper hand.

If her own reports are to be believed (and her alleged lesbianism put to one side), then the sense of domination in the language of 'custody' emerged as the key feature that caused Val to terminate the engagement. For Val, that custody turned to captivity. Having heard from an intimate friend of Val's, Haldane reports to his mother:

> She was—she said—dominated by my personality—no one could know what it was who had not felt it—it meant for her servitude & in fear and terror she broke the engagement off, finding herself at the moment strong enough to do so. She had found herself reduced to a condition of intellectual captivity.[74]

It is significant that the captivity is of an intellectual nature. Here a dynamic of Haldane's personality appears, which sheds light on the relationship between his mental and emotional worlds. It would seem that Haldane was indeed a deeply emotional person, but his emotions always had to pass through the prism of his intellectualised interpretations of the world. Those whom he loved would also have to face that drive within him to find a rational way of expressing reality, and because that way offered such security to Haldane, it couldn't be challenged. He was not a man to let emotions and feelings float freely; they had to be pinned down, understood, systematised. We see this again and again in his letters. He had no time for 'the sandy ground of mere sentiment'. For his mother, this all appeared quite natural and largely in tune with her own thinking. But it would appear that, for Val, this weight of thought had a crushing effect.

* * *

But there was another woman in Haldane's life, and with her there was no question of domination. This was Frances Jane Horner, Lady Horner, wife of Sir John (known as Jack) Horner of Mells, whose daughter Katharine married Asquith's eldest son, the legendary Raymond.[75] Frances was the daughter of the Scottish MP and patron of the arts William Graham. Through her father, she was welcomed into the circle of the Pre-Raphaelites, and became muse to Edward Burne-Jones, whom she met when aged eighteen or nineteen. She was the recipient of what now comprises eleven volumes of letters from Burne-Jones written between 1884 and 1898. The sole subject of several of his drawings and paintings, she appears in multiple images as Eurydice on the Burne-Jones-decorated Broadwood piano presented to her in 1879 by her father on her twenty-fifth birthday. She also appears prominently in *The Golden Stairs*, painted in 1880, and *The Hours*, painted in 1882. With such a background, it is no surprise that Frances was a lady of immense culture, with a wide circle of highly influential friends. She was even called 'the High Priestess of the Souls', a group of 'distinction, brilliance and allure' at the centre of English 'Society' life at the turn of the nineteenth century, known for their 'mutual interests in literature and art.'[76] One of the 'occasional Souls' was Haldane.[77]

It has never been denied that Haldane and Frances were very close; the tribute to her and to her husband in his *Autobiography* makes the strength of their bond very clear. In Part 2 we will see the pivotal role Frances played in Haldane's decision to enter into government in 1905; strange as it sounds, it is no exaggeration to say Frances's influence on Haldane turned the tide of European history.[78] However, the present Earl of Oxford and Asquith, a year before inheriting the title and Mells Manor in 2011, unearthed a collection of letters in a cupboard there, written by Haldane to Frances, which show a totally new side to this relationship. Though the letters are intermittent and clearly not a complete collection, they are revelatory. Their existence was obviously not a complete secret, given that excerpts from them feature in the Haldane Papers at the National Library of Scotland. But these include no mention of the person to whom the letters were written and contain none of the personal messages within the correspondence; they purely concern Haldane's day-to-day activities and political viewpoints. Evidently, the extent of their relationship was not something the public were to know about. To read the letters in their entirety is to realise that these are the letters of a lover.[79] Though we have no evidence to suggest that this was a physical relationship, and there are some indicators that it was not, it was certainly intimately romantic. Haldane's words show a wholly different side of the man from that which his fellow politicians and constituents would have known. Here is an undeniable shared passion and tenderness between two people. In these letters, where mind and heart seem so exquisitely balanced, Haldane finally emerges as the rounded man.

Frances and Haldane seem to have first met in 1893, at the novelist Elizabeth Gaskell's house.[80] On Frances's fortieth birthday the next year he gave her a gift, which shows how close they had already become. It is a pocket edition of Goethe's *Faust*, with a portrait of Goethe and a photograph of the terrace at Mells Park[81] stuck, in all likelihood, by Haldane's own hand onto the opening pages, accompanied by two handwritten extracts from Goethe's text in German. One quotation refers to a state where 'lawless promptings' and 'unholy deeds' are put to sleep to allow for the 'love of humanity' to reign in peace and direct us to God, while the other concerns the light that one finds in one's own heart when reason triumphs over darkness, bringing hope and new life. Perhaps this is indicative of the nature of the love between Haldane and Frances; perhaps it was not of the carnal, pulse-quickening kind, but a love that calmed and settled, more *philia* than *eros*.

But there is another extract, written in Haldane's hand on the flyleaf, which gives us a fuller picture of their unique bond. It is a quotation from the fourth stanza of an untitled poem written by Goethe to Charlotte von Stein, often referred to by its first line, 'Warum gabst du uns die tiefen Blicke'. This is immediately arresting because of the nature of Goethe's relationship to Charlotte: she was a married woman, and they shared an incredibly intimate bond, but one that remained, as far as we know, unconsummated. I refrain from using the word 'platonic' because to say that sexuality did not come into it would perhaps be to say too much. It was almost certainly of a romantic nature. But it appears to have remained a union of souls, rather than bodies. Indeed, Haldane's evident friendship with, and respect for, Frances's husband Jack, his stays with the Horner family each Christmas at Mells, and his frequent enquiries into Jack's health and well-being throughout the letters suggest that they did not envisage their love as disrespecting or trespassing upon the love between husband and wife.[82] The lines that Haldane quotes for Frances can be translated:

You knew every feature of my being,
Saw the purest tremor of each nerve,
With a single glance you could read me,
Hard as I am for mortal eye to pierce[83]

This tells us how exceptional Frances was in understanding Haldane, but it hints at something more. Since these lines implicitly call for the rest of the stanza to be read, we do so, and discover that the relationship is defined by its opposition to the irrationalities of lust.

You brought calm to my heated blood,
Guiding my wild and wandering course,
And in your arms, an angel's arms, I could
Rest as my ravaged heart was restored.

It is difficult not to identify the 'ravaged heart' of this poem with Haldane's own heart after the tragedy of his broken engagement. Frances, in this light, is seen as a comforter and a source of peace. Haldane appears to have found healing in her presence and through her love—'Feeling himself virtuous in your sight', as Goethe goes on to say. It is in Frances that his self-image, humiliated for a time, is restored.[84]

The peacefulness of their relationship was not always at the expense of passion, however. Indeed, the letters, commencing in 1897, begin with an episode of high drama. It is six years after Haldane's failed engagement, and Val has fallen suddenly ill and is approaching death. By this date there is already a clear emotional union between Frances and Haldane, to the extent that Frances is, for a time, deeply jealous of Haldane's ongoing feelings for Val, and Haldane is at pains to assure her of his commitment to herself. While Val lies dying, Haldane writes to Frances in the following terms:

My own soul I cannot fully analyse. But of this I am sure—that the old feeling which has surged up is only caused by the thought of her as she is now. The past & its possibilities are dead, & it is to yourself that I have permanently sent out my heart. But this solemn time brings back the past and I am deeply moved by feelings which had become but a memory.[85]

It is unfortunate that we don't have Frances's responses to these letters, but it is clear that Haldane's assurances were not fully accepted. A week later he wrote this extraordinary missive (and it reveals so much that it is worth quoting in full):

Last night I had a dream that was very vivid. I was in a strange house and knew that you were living there & I had come to seek you but I could not find you. And at last Edward [Frances's eldest son, who was to die in the war] appeared & came up to me & said 'You have hurt mother, & she is very sad'. I awoke and Kennedy [Haldane's butler] came and put your letter in my hand.

I had been very sad. Since Thursday morning the thought that was most with me was that her death had robbed me of you. I felt hard & angry. When I read that letter I put it straight into the fire. There has not been a moment in the

49

past three & a half years when if you had both come before me I should not have gone straight & unswerving to your arms. There has not been a moment in the past six days when, if I could have recalled her, it would not have been to say that the bitterness was gone, that all seemed clear that once was dark, that the memory of the past was sacred—Yet that it was not as a lover—it was not as the same person—that I stood before her, for all she had been and was still to me.

I thought you should have known this, & I felt hard & tried to shut you out. But the cloud came heavier & heavier all yesterday, & I found myself looking for your name in the old visitors [sic] book & stretching my hand in the night to feel that your ring was still there. And this morning [after Haldane received another letter from Frances] it seems that the storm has passed & the sun has broken through the clouds, & on all accounts & about everything I am just as I was & I think not of the past but of the present and of the best that is to be. Since I wrote the first half of this last sentence I have slowly read through your letter again—line by line and word by word, & I feel as though I were raised above the reach of everything on a great rock—so firm & immovable that nothing could shake it. Why did you not understand? It was right that I should tell you all I did. It was right that I should feel it. To recal [sic] the past does not mean that the present is not held for far better. Why would you not have faith when I asked you? Yes indeed—what is there to compare with your record—nothing! I owe the best I have to you & I am bound by every real tie—by the ties I love to be bound by. Did you think that I had forgotten this—that I was likely to? Sometimes it seems to me that you never understand how unlike we are in our speech, or make allowance for difference of language when we talk. It is all there—over & over again—more, if that be possible, than ever now. And today your letter has made me feel content & happy & full of the sense that life is a good thing. I feel grateful to the ruby & to the sapphires for rising up in testimony, & I shall think more of them in future. And the sapphire in the ring has been faithful too, & has looked so reproachful that I did not even dare to think of taking it off, & it spoke so that I have had to look at it every now & then.

Somehow I feel as though the past week has brought back the memory of an old world—a world where I was once very happy & which I would once have chosen beyond anything that then seemed possible to live—a world the memory of which will always be sacred & hold a place in my heart. But a world from which I am separated by a great ocean that I have no desire to cross, if I could, for I have found myself in a new world—one which is far more real & which I know to be far better—one which I could not quit without quitting the very roots of life.

What might have been I know not, but I do know and feel sure of what is.

No, you must never doubt again. Think of your supposing that what has been built up so firmly since 1893 could be swept away like this. You don't know me a bit—when you think like this. The ruby and the sapphires were much wiser. But I like to think of you trying to put me out of your heart & failing altogether and I picture you to myself sitting alone in the library at eleven at night & writing that letter, & thinking you need not send it, & then sending it on Saturday with the P.S. which was the best of all—written upside down on the back sheet—& I have been looking forward all morning to writing this letter to you and I am going to walk to the station to post it with my own hand & to send a telegram to you with one word in it—I won't write in this letter about the Asquith visit. I shall write again tonight and tell you news of it. They were very agreeable & although I found it out from him I am not in the least jealous that you have invited him to stay at Buckingham Gate![86]

The whole range of human emotion is present here, from sadness and anger to transcendent joy. What drama, what intimacy, we are privy to: the mutual vulnerability and confusion; the image of Haldane being brought to a moment of climactic choice, choosing to run into Frances's arms, despite all that had passed between himself and Val; the declaration of Frances's incomparable record in Haldane's life, constituting the very roots of his existence. Haldane was forty-one when he wrote this, but it is the language—jealous, exaggerated, dream-altering—of youthful and impassioned love.

It was to settle again in the years to come, but it was never to lose its depth. It was a love that seemed to call forth from Haldane its profession, with a startling ease and freedom of expression (and it is significant that, with the exception of his mother, Frances is the only person Haldane ever addresses in his correspondence as 'darling'):

This is just a line Darling, to tell you that I love you.[87]

I thought of you through the day & realised again & again how much I loved you.[88]

Despite the sweetness of tone, Haldane's could be a jealous love. He tells Frances in no uncertain terms that he resents the presence of other people while he is with her, and that he longs for time alone with her.[89] A physical undertone does seem to be present in some of his admissions, though we do well to remember Goethe's words above. What are the implications, for example, in this playful comment?

> The Ranee [of Sarawak] left yesterday morning. I had a dangerous success with her, judging from a letter she wrote to Gask & which E. [Elizabeth] showed me. What do you think? I believe that I am at my age to be relied on. I hope so. She is a powerful personality but a little self conscious [*sic*]. I think she knows that you & I are very close to each other.[90]

This closeness is sometimes shrouded in a sense of secrecy. We find Haldane refusing to tell his close friend and Foreign Secretary at the time, Sir Edward Grey, about why a new jacket fits him so well (Frances had evidently 'assisted in the measurement');[91] and there are hints that something is being hidden from outsiders' eyes when Haldane writes:

> And now for ourselves. I was very very happy with you, & I long for Thursday and the resumption of our talk. After all there is no place like Whitehall Court for quiet—is there. It was wonderful how much we managed to get of each other on Sunday, considering the difficulties.[92]

But the sense of secrecy must be weighed against Frances's commitment to truthfulness, which Haldane emphasises on two occasions in the letters. Frances is 'so trusted for unselfishness & truthfulness by all you come in contact with'[93] and has 'an intense sense of truth and fact'.[94] Their secrecy is therefore unlikely to be because of the clandestine nature of their relationship; it is perhaps more a marker of its sacredness for both parties. Indeed, judging by the letters, what Haldane really values is having time for 'one of our talks'. He repeatedly stresses his need for such communication, which amounted to a form of 'communion' for him.[95] She is not simply a lover; Haldane calls her 'my dearest friend'.[96] The fact that he left Frances some £5,000 in his will (roughly equivalent to £300,000 today) reflects her honoured place amongst his extensive body of friends: only his sister Elizabeth received more.[97]

One of the remarkable features of Haldane's letters to Frances, intermittent and clearly incomplete as they are, is that, from first to last, for over thirty years, the tone of profound intimacy remains unabated. It is worthwhile picking out some of the most touching moments across the years to give a sense of the constancy of that tone and the nature of that intimacy. In 1897, while Val lies dying, he can write to Frances, 'Darling I trust you to understand. ... I do not know why, but I feel very very near you & your hand touching me as I write.'[98] He consoles himself, just after Val's death, by writing: 'For the rest of life I have your love and affection and I feel you very near me. Let us look to the East dry-eyed, & hand in hand tread together the path mapped out.'[99] By October 1905 that path is already well trodden:

> More & more as life goes on with me I feel that our relationship is the largest & deepest fact in my life. The sense of this grows with me. It has become a natural one—not something at which I wonder. I should wonder now if it seemed otherwise. And it is borne in on me that with you the same thing is true. It is wonderful and makes me feel how little life can be understood from the outside. I have the deepest sense of what I owe you not only for what you have given to me, but for what you have done for me.[100]

The closeness is such that, in 1908, as Frances struggled to come to terms with the loss of her eldest son, Mark Horner, from scarlet fever, Haldane could address her: 'My own—my heart goes out to you & I am thankful that it is getting to be only hours before I may see you again.'[101] His desire for closeness to Frances, in whatever form, is obvious a few months later: 'Darling, I had come home to write to you & somehow did not think of a letter from you. Yet there was the little book[102] waiting for me & a quotation in it that I did not know. It will (the book & the quotation both) go about with me for the term of the coming year.'[103] And, just as Frances was there for him at the outset of his ministerial duties, so too was she there at their end, a refuge where Haldane—battered by the press, rejected by his friends—could unload his deepest regrets and desires: 'The little things don't matter. The blow to all my hopes for peaceful development which this outbreak of war has caused is the really serious fact, & it is that that affects me. I long to see you on Wednesday. Perhaps you may be able to get here about 5 or 5.30 so that we can be alone together.'[104] Two days later he wrote:

> I shall not forget ever how helpful you have been at this time, or how help-ful you have always been. It takes a deep tie to make such helpfulness a certainty on which one can always rest with absolute security. The tie between us is very deep drawn and close—almost more fundamentally so, if that be possible, than it ever was.[105]

By this time—1915—Haldane was already fifty-nine, and felt himself becoming an old man. Haldane liked to use this fact as a point of contrast with their relationship, which, for him, was ageless: 'I wish you & I had a day alone somewhere together. We might still manage a walk, & I am sure this would be a good & a success. The old tie is unweakened & the old light undimmed for both of us.'[106] But with age comes loss. In 1917, this loss is the death of Edward Horner, Frances's charming and only remaining son, in the Battle of Cambrai.[107] The tenderness which Haldane feels for her, so clear in these previous quotations, finds its most poignant expression at this moment: 'My heart is full—you suffer & I cannot take off your suffering.'[108] The loss only brings the constancy of their love into further relief; again and again Haldane returns to his refrain: 'No, nothing can break what is between us. Coming old age alters the form which growth gives but not the substance.'[109] And yet, as Haldane notes: 'How strange is it that you and I, so different, should so completely belong to one another. But so it is—a great elemental fact which nothing shakes.'[110] Indeed, the letters continue in this vein right until the end of Haldane's life, and it is to Frances that he sends his final message, which reads: 'Getting on. All well. Love. A little tired but going on quite smoothly. Hope to write soon. Ever yours R.'[111]

Here were two characters vastly different, but bound together by an unbreakable emotional tie. While it is vitally important to stress that bond, it is equally important to stress the difference between them, because it was through this exposure to Frances's otherness that Haldane's character was able to flower. She initiated Haldane into facets of reality of which he had previously been ignorant. At times, he was painfully aware of how alien his own way of thinking was to Frances's. Edward Horner's valiant death allowed Haldane to reflect:

> You have at all events this that you may feel proud of Edward's courage and of his fearless sacrifice for what he held high. He never held back or questioned. Now in that quality there is what is great, & we all do it reverence.

> But I wish my mind did not turn so to idealism, for it is shadowy to you and does not help you as it would [have] helped and has helped me.

But by 1924 Haldane recognised that his idealistic bent had been softened by the influence of Frances's finely tuned aesthetic sense: 'I think that you have taught me to understand and appreciate beauty more than I did. I am always discovering how little I have really known, and how much others know.'[112] This is an astonishing statement. A number of Haldane's acquaintances claimed that he liked to give the impression of omniscience;[113] how differently he appears here. One wonders if this new knowledge that Frances is able to disclose relates to the statement in the letter of October 1905 quoted earlier: 'how little life can be understood from the outside'. Both previous experiences of romantic love in Haldane's life proved unreciprocated and it is as if this held him at arm's length from a whole field of human knowledge. In his relationship with Frances Horner Haldane enters into a new realm, and it brings a sense of completion and balance to his character. In these letters we discover the head and the heart of Haldane dancing in a harmony hitherto unknown.

* * *

Many others who knew Haldane intimately were won over by this harmony, so often hidden from the public eye. To read the letters sent to Elizabeth Haldane on her brother's death is to be overwhelmed with a sense that, whatever one could say about the greatness of his intellect, it should always be balanced with the greatness of his heart. 'I have never known anyone who gave one such sense of greatness of mind and heart',[114] wrote Violet Bonham Carter. Lord Arnold, reflecting on the kind consideration Haldane showed to his younger colleagues on the judicial bench, states: 'When the whole house is paying tributes—all fully merited—to his achievements and his extraordinary mental powers I feel that some of us were granted the opportunity also of witnessing in close intercourse his big qualities of heart.'[115] The newspapers, too, often missed this quality, as Harold Begbie pointed out: 'You [Elizabeth] know of qualities in him which *The Times* has not mentioned in their otherwise praiseworthy notice—his sweetness, his glad friendliness of heart.'[116] Perhaps the best witness to Haldane's humanity is found in the testimony of the soldier and lawyer J. H. Morgan:

> I can never forget that in him I had—not even excepting Morley—the kindest friend who ever guided my faltering steps and inspired my work. I have many notes of my conversations with Morley about him. Morley was,

as you probably know, often very bitter during the war about his former colleagues and he was so autocratic in temper that one could not object, without a quarrel, to what he said. It will, I think, please you to know that, in the middle of one of his political tirades against Lord Haldane, I interjected 'I don't know. That may be. But look at his kindness of heart!' Morley melted immediately and said 'Ah! yes, there you speak truly' and went on to tell me story after story (one in particular about Lord Tweedmouth) of Lord Haldane's unwearied offices of kindness.[117]

Reading these tributes and having looked at the most vital emotional relationships of Haldane's life, we can see that—despite the reservations of some who, like Harold Nicolson, did not know him or who, like his nephew Graeme, saw his personality incompletely—we are indeed dealing with a profoundly human person. Haldane may have had a prodigious appetite for work, often of the most dry and exhausting kind; he may have lived a celibate life; he may have chosen philosophical tomes as his bedtime reading; but he also felt the highs and lows of love; he experienced the lasting loss of bereavement; he knew the gentleness of family and its steadying support; he wanted the closeness of a woman. In Part 2 we'll explore Haldane's selfless dedication to the state; but in so doing we mustn't lose sight of the struggles and joys of intimate passions and griefs that grounded him in the world. His was a form of statesmanship which we may not always relate to in each and every one of its particulars, but it was certainly not a thousand miles from our own experiences of human frailty and strength. Perhaps we can better understand some of the apparently inhuman heights scaled by Haldane when we remember that such accomplishments often arose out of the most human of depths.

3

THE COMPANY OF FRIENDS

I loved him: I cannot tell you how much: He was the greatest man I was privileged to count among my friends.

John Bigham, 1st Viscount Mersey to Elisabeth Haldane on Haldane's death.[1]

Haldane moved in practically every set. The powerful were drawn to him like a magnet—and he to them in turn. We know from our opening chapter his closeness to Edward VII, and obviously his political connections were second to none. He was on intimate terms with the Archbishops of Canterbury and York, both regular visitors to Cloan. That house, famous for its unremittingly highbrow atmosphere, saw an endless stream of the country's leading lights pass through its doors. Generals of the British army, principals and professors of the universities, famous authors, philosophers, and scientists—these were never out of place around the Haldane dining table, where they may well have found themselves sitting next to the prime minister or the Foreign Secretary.[2]

One regular guest, Violet Markham, captures the atmosphere of the place:

> Talk and discussion were at a high level at Cloan. Scientists often formed part of the company, and new and unfamiliar words like 'quantum' and 'atom-splitting' found their way into my vocabulary. Bridge was inescapable at that time in most country houses, but I never saw a card table at the Haldanes [*sic*]. In his [Haldane's] view it [bridge] had done more to destroy the intellectual life of England than any other cause.[3]

Men of business, too, had their place. Haldane loved those who could make an idea a reality; he relished the entrepreneurial spirit. He also wasn't reluctant to ask such men (for they were almost always men in those days) for the money he needed to make his own projects flourish. Our chapter on Haldane's work in education will show that very clearly, but it is not the case that Haldane nurtured these friendships simply for such utilitarian purposes. His relationships with various members of the Rothschild family are a case in point.

Famous for their banking house and their philanthropy, the Rothschilds held a dominant position in society and affairs throughout Haldane's lifetime. Governments of every party—and not just in Britain—sought to utilise the fabled Rothschild financing skills in the service of their nation. Exceptional interventions such as the financing of Wellington's army in the Peninsular War, the purchase of shares in the Suez Canal and, on the outbreak of the Great War, a whole range of essential financial and market interventions marked out the Rothschilds as a force to be reckoned with. It was not one that was going to keep Haldane at bay; quite the opposite.

Niall Ferguson, in his authoritative book *The House of Rothschild*, refers to Haldane acting as the family's legal adviser 'for many years'.[4] It proved to be a vital role. Haldane recalled that in 1889, as a thirty-three-year-old lawyer, he 'rearranged the Rothschild partnerships which had got into a very vague relation, placing the whole family at the mercy of one dishonest partner'.[5] Yet this was more than a professional relationship, far more. Haldane was particularly close with the English branch of the family, led by Nathaniel (Natty) Rothschild, the first Lord Rothschild—the first Jew to be ennobled in Britain who had not previously converted to Christianity—and his wife Emma. The visitors' book from their country home at Tring Park reveals that between 1889 and 1900 Haldane stayed twenty-one times, a record only to be exceeded by the Conservative leader and prime minister Arthur Balfour.[6] This is before Haldane had even taken Cabinet office. Another Tring visitors' book, which covers the period between 1900 and 1911, discloses a further twenty-nine Haldane visits.[7] Given this regularity, it is perhaps no surprise that at Tring, as Haldane recorded in his *Autobiography*, 'I had a room which was always reserved for me'.[8]

It was, of course, a friendship which had its practical uses. Natty Rothschild was a critical donor behind the construction of the LSE building at Clare Market, Aldwych, providing £5,000 towards the total cost of

£18,000—a gift enabled by Haldane. But his relationship with the Rothschilds went well beyond philanthropy, as an event in March 1915 shows. Haldane was temporarily in charge of the Foreign Office while Grey was on holiday, and he found himself in a difficult situation:

> It was ascertained … that a steamer had started from South America and that, although neutral, there was reason to suppose that she contained supplies intended for the Germans. There was no material to act on, and the only way was to resort to private influence [it is unclear exactly why Lord Rothschild had such influence on this particular ship]. I motored to Lord Rothschild's house in Piccadilly and found him lying down and obviously very ill. He stretched out his hand before I could speak, and said, 'Haldane, I do not know what you are come for except to see me, but I have said to myself that if Haldane asks me to write a cheque to him of £25,000 and to ask no questions, I will do it on the spot.' I told him that it was not for a cheque, but only to get a ship stopped that I was come. He sent a message to stop the ship at once.[9]

Now £25,000 has a value in today's money of around £2.5 million.[10] Unconditional support on such a magnificent scale is not easily earned. Haldane's relationship with Natty was clearly deeply grounded in mutual confidence. It was a confidence also felt by Natty's brother, Leopold, who in 1906 described Haldane as 'certainly one of the ablest men in the Cabinet, if not the ablest'.[11] And although Haldane had, by that time, ceased to act as legal adviser to the banking house, he still had his uses, as Leopold records in February 1912: 'The improvement … in our markets these last few days … [is due] no doubt mainly to the political atmosphere having been cleared by Lord Haldane's visit to Berlin … Berlin private telegrams are to the effect that our Minister of War's presence in Berlin has given unfeigned gratification.'[12]

Natty Rothschild was to die shortly after Haldane's visit to his house in Piccadilly and Haldane himself was to be ousted from office within weeks. But this did not sever his relations with the family. Natty's wife Emma, Lady Rothschild, became an ever-greater feature in Haldane's life, and their continued correspondence until Haldane's death is rich with insight into their daily lives. A typical letter, written from Cloan on 29 August 1918, demonstrates the sheer variety of personalities that Haldane was in touch with at that time:

I have been here since the 8th. I have plenty to do and time passes quickly. The Ranee of Sarawak [Sylvia Leonora Brett, wife to the last of the White Rajahs] has just left us, and the Archbishop of Canterbury is coming, but otherwise we have been very quiet. Next month various professors will arrive. I read and write most of the day.

I was very glad to see Walter [Emma's eldest son] not only take his seat but appear several times on the benches of the H.[ouse] of Lords. It is a dull place but it has a history and an atmosphere. ... Lord Morley I saw just before leaving. He and I dined with Lloyd George—a curious small party, only Winston [Churchill] as our fellow guest.[13]

Another member of the family close to Haldane was Natty Rothschild's first cousin, Constance, married to the Liberal politician Cyril Flower. Overhearing Haldane holding forth on the subject of German literature one day on the terrace of the House of Commons (probably around 1886, when Cyril Flower was made party whip under Gladstone), Constance 'begged' for an introduction and the two swiftly became firm friends.[14] Haldane would offer her advice on philosophical reading, share with her the bleakness of his feelings after his failed engagement, and tell the choicest parliamentary stories. Remembering 'his student's pale colouring, rather heavy lids, and eyes that speak of close and tiring study', Constance adds:

Haldane came frequently to our Buckinghamshire home, where he would indulge in plentiful gossip that he called 'biography'. But it would be absurd to associate his name with the word 'gossip', for he is one of the most remarkable men that it has been my good fortune to know. Besides his fine intellectual gifts [he] has always shown much and unusual kindness of heart. He never forgets old friends, and has indeed, even at much inconvenience to himself, done many a gracious act to give others pleasure.[15]

Haldane was also close to the Paris branch of the family, so much so that for many years he would spend the weekend before Christmas at the Château de Grosbois near the French capital as the guest of Prince and Princess Wagram, the latter being Lady Rothschild's sister. He certainly enjoyed the perks of his Rothschild connections. After a stay at another of their residences, this time Baron Ferdinand Rothschild's home at Waddesdon, he wrote to his host:

I do love all seemly luxury. When lying in bed in the mornings it gives me great satisfaction when a lacquey enters the rooms and asks whether I will

take tea, coffee, chocolate or cocoa. This privilege is accorded to me in the
houses of all my distinguished friends: but it is only at Waddesdon that on
saying I prefer tea, the valet further enquires whether I fancy Ceylon,
Souchong or Assam.[16]

* * *

But Haldane could foster friendships far removed from the grandeur of
public life and high finance. Perhaps the most notable friendship of this sort
was that with Peter Hume Brown, professor of Ancient (Scottish) History
and Palaeography at Edinburgh University from 1901 until his death in
1918, and historiographer-royal for Scotland from 1908. The two had met
as students at Edinburgh and were drawn together by a shared passion for
German culture and literature. Hume Brown quickly became tutor to
Haldane's younger siblings during their autumn stays at Cloan. The family
were so fond of him that his autumnal visits continued once the years of
tutoring were over; he became 'like a brother or son in our family'.[17]

Throughout the 1890s Hume Brown built a reputation as a historian—
though holding no academic post at the time—with biographies on well-
known Scottish figures, such as the humanist George Buchanan and the
Protestant reformer John Knox, alongside other works, notably a history
of Scotland before 1700. Such was his reputation that Cambridge University
Press then commissioned him to write a new *History of Scotland*, which
would eventually be published in three large volumes between 1898 and
1909. In the year that the first volume appeared, Hume Brown and Haldane
made the first of what would be fourteen consecutive holidays together in
Germany across the Easter recess. The ostensible reason for their travels
was Hume Brown's desire to assemble materials for a projected book on
Goethe—a book that was still not complete upon his death and which
eventually appeared posthumously, having been finished by Haldane and his
sister Elizabeth. The two men revelled in retracing Goethe's footsteps, visiting the sites where the great man's presence still lingered, notably in
Weimar and Ilmenau. Haldane provides a characteristic snapshot of their
adventures in a letter to his friend Edmund Gosse in May 1904:

You would have liked to sit—as I did two nights ago—on the top of the
'Schwalbenstein' rock at midnight, in the solitude of the pine forest, and

to have read by the light of the full moon the little tablet in which he [Goethe] recorded that there, on March 29, 1779 ... after seeking for it for three years, the 4th Act of his 'Iphigenie' flashed upon him, and was written in a single day of solitude. The place is simply inspiring.[18]

But their travels were more than just literary pilgrimages. It was evidently also a chance for Haldane, that inveterate workaholic and obsessive political strategist, to let off steam and live a life of scholarly leisure for a few days in the company of one whose life was removed from the vicissitudes of government. A description of their stay in Weimar in April 1899 captures the contrast in atmosphere with Haldane's life in London:

> We walk for four or five hours in the Park & read Goethe aloud. Then Peter lies on a sofa & nurses himself & reads, while I write at the book[[19]], which is getting on. We are perfectly content & happy—sleep like tops & rise before 7, English time.[20]

For all Hume Brown's intellectual accomplishments—'his spirit and devotion were those of the finished scholar', wrote Haldane[21]—there was also an element of comedy about the man known within the family simply as 'the Professor'. Again, Haldane catches something of this in his letters home from Germany to his mother. In May 1910, he remarks:

> We got here at 9 last night—a good journey & both in good form. Notwithstanding his travels the Prof. needs a courier. He is very helpless about tickets, cabs, hotels etc. But my experience as a Servant of the Crown enables me to minister to him.[22]

For Hume Brown, it was Haldane's company that meant the most to him, far more than any Goethe-related nugget upon which they might have stumbled. He wrote to Haldane after one such trip:

> Before taking up my burden I must write a line to say how greatly I have enjoyed this our last visit to cherished Ilmenau. It seems as if each successive visit were pleasanter than the last. I cannot but feel that it is to you that I owe this annual refreshment for mind and body, for though Ilmenau has many attractions, it is seeing it with you that makes it what it is in my memory and imagination.[23]

As Haldane's importance as a statesman grew, particularly in the wake of his secretive mission to Berlin in February 1912, travelling peacefully in Germany proved difficult. Their trip in the spring of that year turned out to be their last. It had got to the point where 'the Professor' was reported to be Asquith, then prime minister, in disguise, and their literary pursuits were viewed as a thinly veiled cover-up for treaty-making.[24]

Back home at Cloan, the Professor's visits were looked forward to not only by the family, but perhaps even more so by Car, often referred to as 'the little dog'—the Haldanes' counterpoint to the 'Great Dog', Kaiser. In the years immediately after Hume Brown's death in 1918, Haldane lingers not simply on his own loss but on the loss sustained by this 'little dog'. 'One misses the Professor much at this time,' he tells Frances Horner on 29 April 1919. 'He was part of our lives. Even the little dog rushes down the stairs when he hears a motor, to see if it is not the Professor arrived at last, & returns sad.'[25] A year later, and more playfully, Haldane writes to Gosse:

> I have walked most days—Kaiser will not accompany me, for he has formally joined the Labour Party, i.e. has devoted himself exclusively to the laundry-maid, whose stove suits him, and to the chauffeur who furnishes him with meals. But the little dog goes with me, as he used to do with the Professor.[26]

Haldane's idealism often gave him an air of philosophical detachment that hid a deep vulnerability. The death of Hume Brown revealed that vulnerability, and Haldane's reaction shows just how essential the Professor's friendship had become to him. Once Haldane had returned to London after the funeral, he wrote to his sister Elizabeth:

> Yes, one does not get away from the thoughts that keep flooding in. And in some ways you had him more with you than even I had. But for both of us it was a friendship as perfect as it was intimate. He will haunt the rooms and the walks for us at Cloan. I cannot realise that I shall not see him again, & so uniform was the level of the talk that I seem to speak with him all day.

> The middle movement of Chopins [sic] funeral march has a new meaning for us. Fortunately I have not to see many people just now, for I find it difficult to speak.

Such was the power of this the least showy of all Haldane's friendships.

* * *

Before we come to a friendship that was to rival the intimacy of that with Hume Brown, it is interesting to reflect on the sheer breadth of Haldane's social world, and the extraordinary part he played in events of historical significance within the lives of so many people from so varied a background. Part 2 will explore Haldane's working relationship with the well-known social reformers Sidney and Beatrice Webb, whose marriage was to have such a profound effect on the educational, economic and welfare provision of Great Britain. But we might mention here—as an example of one world in which Haldane was moving, and his hidden hand within it—that it was Haldane who made the Webbs' marriage possible.

It was always going to be a challenge for Sidney to be left alone with Beatrice, and unburden his feelings for her. To visit her under her father's roof would not be straightforward because of Sidney's humble background and socialist convictions. Haldane had a solution. With his more appropriate breeding, Haldane played the part of Beatrice's suitor and asked her father if his friend Mr Sidney Webb might accompany him on his next visit. When Haldane, late on the evening of their visit, made a point of going for a walk on his own, Beatrice and Sidney were given the chance to be alone together and have 'a conversation which they could not otherwise have had'.[27] It was the first of the Webbs' many 'intrigues' with Haldane, as Beatrice called them, intrigues as momentous as the founding of LSE and Imperial College London, which we shall examine in Chapter 8.

But the point about the breadth of Haldane's social world, and the far-reaching historical impact of his connections, is nowhere better demonstrated than by the stories of his interactions with Oscar Wilde, on the one hand, and Einstein, on the other.

Haldane had met Wilde on a number of occasions 'in the days of his social success', but had not known him well.[28] It was in the least sociable of contexts—Pentonville Prison—that Haldane really came to play a role in Wilde's life. Wilde had been confined there since early June 1895, following his famous sentencing for 'gross indecency' and a short period at Holloway Prison. Haldane, at this time, was serving on a Home Office committee investigating the organisation of the prison system. This granted him the right to visit any prison at any time and see any prisoner of his choosing. Wilde was suffering terribly from the conditions at Pentonville, where he had a cell 13 feet long, 7 feet wide and 9 feet high.

He was required to perform six hours' hard labour daily, upon a far from adequate diet. It is suggested that he lost 20 pounds in his first month. A mutual friend of Haldane and Wilde's, Lady Brooke, persuaded Haldane to visit the prison to see if there was anything that could be done to alleviate his distress. Haldane, 'haunted by the idea of what this highly sensitive man was probably suffering', immediately responded, visiting Wilde on 14 June 1895.[29] Wilde was at first unresponsive. But Haldane, placing a hand upon his shoulder, encouraged him to see the latent literary possibilities of his situation—here, at last, was a great subject for his talents. In an act that was 'an extraordinary relaxation of the prison rules', Haldane promised to get hold of books and writing materials for Wilde, who immediately burst into tears. Wilde promised to make the attempt at writing something of worth.[30]

Wilde's first request was a somewhat naïve one. It was for Flaubert's works. Haldane had to point out that Flaubert himself had been charged with indecency over the publication of *Madame Bovary*. The prison authorities were unlikely to accept such a request. At this point Wilde 'laughed and became cheerful'.[31] His subsequent requests were more sensible—the works of St Augustine, some volumes by Pascal and Cardinal Newman, Mommsen's *History of Rome*, and Walter Pater's *Studies in the History of the Renaissance*.[32]

A month later Haldane had Wilde transferred to Wandsworth Prison, where he believed conditions were slightly better and where he could monitor Wilde's progress through his friend William Morrison, the prison's chaplain. It was here, on 17 August 1895, that Wilde received his little library from Haldane, though he could only access one book a week. Three days later, Haldane visited him in person, finding him 'much broken'.[33] Haldane sent on more books, through his own bookseller, at the end of the month. These were further volumes by Pater, which Wilde was 'anxious' to have.[34] As Thomas Wright has pointed out, in his fascinating *Oscar's Books*, the pleasure which Wilde received from reading these books 'was the only subject he could discuss with equanimity' when visitors came to see him.[35]

It is no surprise he was on the edge. Wilde by this time was suffering from partial deafness and chronic diarrhoea. Haldane then persuaded the Home Secretary to intervene and have him transferred to Reading Gaol, where the air quality would be greatly improved. Meanwhile, Haldane made arrangements to ensure that Wilde's wife and children were looked after. Haldane writes: 'On his release there came to me anonymously a volume, *The Ballad of Reading Gaol*. It was the redemption of his promise to me.'[36] Reflecting on the fact that men of Wilde's class tended to die within two years of completing a sentence of hard labour, Wright even argues that it was partly thanks to Haldane's benevolence that Wilde went on to live for a further three-and-a-half years.[37]

Wilde was already well known in Britain at the time of his exchange with Haldane, but with Einstein it was Haldane's privilege to introduce the great discoverer of relativity to the British people in person. Haldane and his sister Elizabeth acted as the Einsteins' hosts during their first ever visit to London in 1921.[38] Einstein and his second wife Elsa were on their way back to Germany after a lecture tour in the United States. Haldane was captivated by Einstein's revolutionary theory, and believed that it contained philosophical ramifications of the highest order—a view that has been superficially interpreted as contrary to that of Einstein, who told Randall Davidson, the Archbishop of Canterbury, at Haldane's dining table that the theory was 'purely abstract—science'.[39] Haldane, out of office at this point, had published a dense and lengthy book entitled *The Reign of Relativity* in the same year as the visit, outlining the philosophical aspects. In a way that is almost unimaginable now, the book went through three impressions within its first six weeks in print.

Haldane's invitation to Einstein was a brave and magnanimous gesture in the context of the times, not just because the war had only recently ended, but also because of the unjust tide of ill-feeling against Haldane for his German connections—which had reached its climax in May 1915, when Haldane, as we will discover in Part 2, was ejected from government. 'It was certainly courageous of Einstein to have come so willingly to London', wrote his biographer Ronald Clark; 'it was equally courageous of Haldane to be his host.'[40]

The Einsteins were rather overwhelmed at first by their surroundings, and they found their assigned footman and Haldane's butler particularly intimidating.[41] Haldane put on a splendid dinner for his guests on their first night. Not only was the See of Canterbury represented, but also the great scientific figures of Britain, including Arthur Eddington, the Astronomer

Royal Sir Frank Watson Dyson, Sir J. J. Thomson, and the philosopher A. N. Whitehead. But the highlight of the visit was Einstein's public lecture at King's College, University of London, on 13 June—though not before Haldane and Einstein had made their way to Westminster Abbey to lay a wreath at Newton's tomb. Haldane had arranged the lecture with the principal of King's, Ernest Barker, who found himself 'terrified by the commotion' caused by the prospect of the lecture. His fears, at first, were based on a continued anti-German feeling within the nation, but these were replaced by fears at the sheer demand for tickets. Would the lecture be 'disturbed, or even prevented, by an uncontrollable crowd of would-be listeners'?[42] The fact that the lecture would be delivered in German and cover an obscure topic did not seem to perturb the enthusiastic crowd.

Order was, however, maintained. Despite the numbers, a hushed atmosphere pervaded the hall. In the silence, Haldane arose and opened proceedings with the words: 'You are in the presence of the Newton of the twentieth century, of a man who has effected a greater revolution in thought than that of Copernicus, Galileo, and even Newton himself.' The *Nation & Athenaeum* continued in its report:

> One felt the slight shock in the air. For, after all, is not Einstein a German? But Lord Haldane, smiling, wary, and implacable, drove the point home. They had to swallow it whole: the dose was not minimised, however indecent the truth might appear that the greatest scientific man the latter centuries have produced is a German Jew. One glanced at Einstein: he was patient, dreamy, looking at nothing.[43]

When Haldane changed the topic to discuss the qualities of Einstein's violin playing (evidently Haldane felt himself qualified to judge, having heard him play at Frances Horner's London home), the audience seemed to breathe a sigh of relief. Haldane believed Einstein had a better understanding of the music that he played than most first-class professionals.[44] Einstein was thrilled. The reporter gleefully noted that he was, after all, susceptible to flattery. Einstein then rose to deliver his lecture, taking relativity as his topic. The encore he received towards its end, and the long applause, suggest it was a success.[45]

In fact, the whole visit appears to have been a success. Haldane felt a little insecure about his German, having not spoken it for almost a decade, and was naturally disappointed that Einstein would not fully endorse his philosophical rendering of the scientific theory. But they seem to have clicked nonetheless. After his visit and knowing of Haldane's great veneration for his mother, Einstein wrote to Mary Haldane, isolated from events in Scotland:

> One of the most memorable weeks of my life lies behind me. Visiting this country for the first time I have learned to marvel at its splendid traditions and treasures of knowledge. One of the most beautiful experiences was the intimacy with your two children, the harmonious hospitality of their home, and the wonderful relations which unite them with yourself. ... The scientific talk with Lord Haldane has been for me a source of pure stimulation, and so has the personal intimacy with him and his remarkable knowledge.[46]

Even in the 1950s, Einstein could still recall Haldane as a 'man of kind and subtle feelings as is so rare in the case of men of quite unusual energy and working capacity. ... I never had the feeling that there was anything worthwhile for which he would not easily find the necessary time and strength.'[47]

Beyond developing personal ties, the visit had wider international consequences. Professor Frederick Lindemann of Wadham College, Oxford—later Lord Cherwell, known as Churchill's reactionary one-man think tank—had taken Einstein on a brief tour of Oxford after his stay with Haldane.[48] Following their tour, Lindemann wrote to Haldane encouragingly: 'Whatever anyone may hold about political matters, there is no doubt that international co-operation is absolutely essential in scientific questions and you have, I feel sure, done more to re-establish good relations by your reception of Einstein than anybody else could have done by years of endeavour.'[49] Haldane, greatly pleased, reported to Einstein: 'There is no doubt that your visit has had more tangible results in improving here the relations between our two countries than any other single event.'[50]

After Einstein's visit the two men kept in touch by letter, exchanging ideas and thoughts on books. But one gets the sense in reading these letters that, more than intellectual note-swapping, Einstein valued the political opportunities that came with knowing Haldane. In particular, he found in Haldane a conduit through which he could feed ideas about German reparations after the war. For example, on 30 August 1922 Einstein wrote to Haldane sharing with him an article from a German newspaper in which

EMOTIONAL LIFE

37. Val Munro Ferguson, who became briefly engaged to Haldane in 1890 before she broke off the relationship due to 'intellectual captivity', having felt herself dominated by Haldane's personality. She is pictured c. 1890 and died at the early age of 33 in 1897.

38. A young Elizabeth Haldane, Haldane's sister. She was a constant companion and confidante throughout his life's triumphs and trials, c. 1905–10.

39. After Haldane's breakdown as a result of the rejection of his first love, Agnes Kemp, in 1881 he went to convalesce with the Asquiths at their Hampstead home. This photograph of Helen Asquith (1854–1891), H. H. Asquith's first wife and mother of five children, including Raymond Asquith, was inscribed to Haldane 'with affectionate remembrances' by Asquith after Helen's early death in 1891, c. 1890.

H H Asquith 1892 by Violet Rutland

40. The drawing of H. H. Asquith (1852–1928) was made by Violet Rutland in 1892, the year following the death of his wife, Helen.

Haldane's Great Love and Influence

Frances Horner (née Graham) (1854–1940) was Haldane's closest female friend and greatest romantic love from 1893 until his death in 1928. She was the first and only woman to reciprocate Haldane's love, and she considerably influenced the course of his life, including his entry into Government in 1905. She was the second daughter of William Graham, a wealthy Liberal MP and important patron of Edward Burne-Jones. She was married to the lawyer, Sir John Horner, and lived at Mells in Somerset.

41. Frances Graham, from a drawing by Dante Gabriel Rossetti, entitled La Donna della Fenestra, 1879.

42. Frances Graham, 1875, both muse to, and correspondent of, Edward Burne-Jones. He painted and drew her in her own right and allegorically.

43. Frances Horner's photograph in a folding travelling case carried by Haldane until his death, c. 1910s.

44. Frances Graham pictured playing the cymbals on the bottom step of The Golden Stairs by Edward Burne-Jones, 1880.

Frances Horner's Home, Mells Manor

45. Haldane in the garden of Mells Manor, 1906, into which the Horner family moved from Mells Park in 1900. Haldane stayed at Mells Manor on Christmas Eve for most years of his life after meeting Frances Horner and her husband Sir John Horner.

46. The blue plaque commemorating Lord Haldane can be seen on the face of the house next to the bottom right ground floor window.

47. 28 Queen Anne's Gate, Haldane's London home from early 1906 until his death, was conveniently located a mere quarter of a mile from Downing Street and the Foreign Office, across the corner of St James's Park, and from the Houses of Parliament, across Parliament Square. Frances Horner worked with Elizabeth Haldane on its restoration. Haldane likened Elizabeth's role to that of Frances, in a letter to his mother, as standing 'in the relation of a firm Chancellor of the Exchequer to a brilliant but not cheap spending department'.

48. Haldane in old age, 1920s. On his death countless friends recalled his unfailing kindness of heart.

A COMPANY OF FRIENDS

49. Churchill and Haldane photographed with Edward and Dorothy Grey at Lord Tweedmouth's home, Guisachan, in Inverness, c. 1902. Two months after Grey became Foreign Secretary, Dorothy was thrown from a similar cart, in February 1906, and died.

50. Haldane's Social World

LAW	POLITICS	INTELLECTUAL	EDUCATION AND ECONOMICS	SCIENTIFIC
Lord Sankey	Arthur J. Balfour	Peter Hume Brown	Beatrice and Sidney Webb	Albert Einstein
Lord Birkenhead	Herbert Henry Asquith	Bernard Bosanquet	John Maynard Keynes	Lord Rayleigh
	Edward Grey		Harold Laski	J. J. Thomson

Winston Churchill

John Morley Ramsay MacDonald

SOCIETY	PHILANTHROPY	MILITARY	LITERARY	THE CHURCH

| King Edward VII | Lord Rothschild | Douglas Haig | Edmund Gosse | Randall Davidson |

    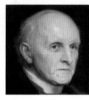

| Lady Rothschild | Andrew Carnegie | John French | Oscar Wilde | Cosmo Lang |

| Lord Esher | John Buchan | William Inge |

| Robert Baden-Powell | J. M. Barrie |

51. Haldane was a regular visitor to the Rothschilds at Tring Park both before and after entering government. After the death in 1915 of Lord Rothschild, a generous supporter of Haldane's educational initiatives, Haldane remained close to Lady Rothschild.

52. King Edward VII (1841–1910), photographed in colour for the first time, by Lionel de Rothschild at Strathspey in 1909.

53. Haldane in front of Balmoral, 1910. King Edward VII viewed Haldane as his best Secretary of State.

June 10th. 1903.

INVITED	ACCEPTED	REFUSED
The King & Queen	The King & Queen	
Princess Victoria of Wales	Princess Victoria of Wales	
Duke & Duchess of Marlborough.	Duke Duchess of Marlboro'	
Marquis & Marchioness of Lansdowne	Marquis & Marchioness of Lansdowne.	
Earl & Countess of Gosford.	Earl & Countess Gosford.	
Earl & Countess Carrington	Earl & Countess Carrington	
Earl & Countess of Crewe.	Earl & Countess of Crewe.	
Earl & Countess de Grey	Earl & Countess de Grey	
Viscount & Viscountess Churchill	Viscount & Viscountess Churchill	
Sir E. & Lady Helen Vincent	Sir E. & Lady Helen Vincent	
Lady Suffield	Lady Suffield	
The Portuguese Minister	The Portuguese Minister	
Lord Revelstoke	Lord Revelstoke	
Mr. A. Chamberlain	Mr. A. Chamberlain	
Mr Haldane	Mr. Haldane	
Mr. Morley	Mr. Morley	
Mr & Mrs Leopold de Rothschild	Mr & Mrs Leopold de Rothschild	
Mr. J Ward.	Mr J. Ward	
Mrs Behrens	Mrs Behrens	
Lord and Lady Tweedmouth		Lord & Lady Tweedmouth
Lord Rosebery		Lord Rosebery
Mr Balfour		Mr Balfour

29. accepted with 4 at home, made a total of 33.

54. A page from Lady Rothschild's book containing the names of the guests at a dinner at Tring Park for King Edward VII and Queen Alexandra, which Haldane attended on 10 June 1903. The King ensured that Haldane was included regularly in his friends' house parties.

55. Haldane and Albert Einstein photographed in June 1921 on the back steps of 28 Queen Anne's Gate where, with his wife Elsa, Einstein stayed as Haldane's guest. It was Einstein's first visit to Britain and Haldane's invitation was brave in the context of the unjust ill-feeling which Haldane suffered for his German connections.

56. Haldane and Einstein seated inside 28 Queen Anne's Gate where, famously, Haldane gave a great dinner to which the Astronomer Royal, the Archbishop of Canterbury and other distinguished scientists and philosophers were invited.

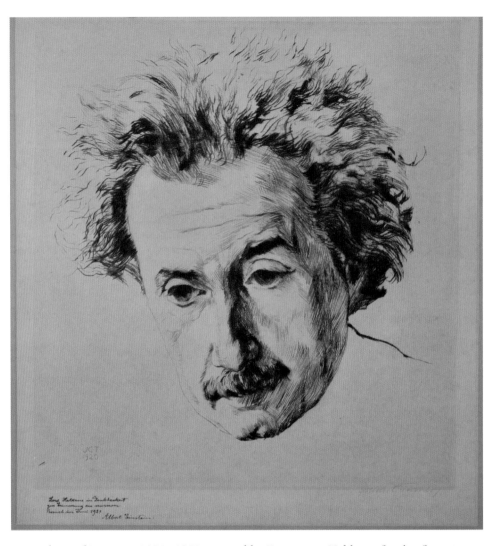

57. Etching of Einstein (1879–1955), signed by Einstein to Haldane after his first visit to Britain.

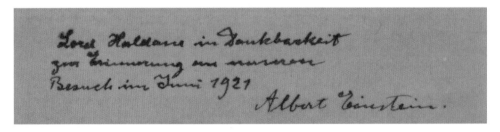

58. Inscription (in German) on the above etching by Einstein to 'Lord Haldane in thankfulness of the memory of our visit in June 1921'.

59. The inscription by Einstein to Graeme Haldane, Haldane's nephew, in a copy of '*The Theory of Relativity*' thanking him for his help during his stay in London with Haldane.

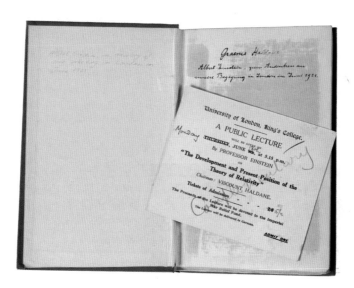

University of London, King's College.

A PUBLIC LECTURE

WILL BE GIVEN ON

~~THURSDAY~~, JUNE ~~9th~~, at 5.15 p.m.

Monday **13th**

By PROFESSOR EINSTEIN

ON

"The Development and Present Position of the Theory of Relativity"

Chairman: VISCOUNT HALDANE.

Tickets of Admission   -   -   -   ~~2/6~~ 5/=

The Proceeds of the Lecture will be devoted to the Imperial War Relief Fund.

The Lecture will be delivered in German.

ADMIT ONE

60. The ticket used by Graeme Haldane, for the public lecture at King's College, London, given by Einstein and chaired by Haldane. Haldane opened the proceedings with the words: 'You are in the presence of the Newton of the 20th century'.

Company of Friends: Literary

Haldane's closest male personal relationship outside family and politics was with Edmund Gosse, the writer and critic who became Librarian of the House of Lords. Their friendship was built upon the foundations of a mutual love of literature. From the early 1900s until their deaths in 1928, Haldane and Gosse saw or wrote to each other regularly. Haldane's letters to Gosse provide profound insights into Haldane's life and thinking. Haldane was also very close to the writers John Buchan and J. M. Barrie.

61. Portrait of a youthful Edmund Gosse (1849–1928) painted by John Singer Sargent, 1885.

62. Cartoon by Max Beerbohm of a meeting of the Academic Committee of the Royal Society of Literature, established in 1908 by Edmund Gosse with Haldane's support. Haldane is pictured to the right of centre in lawyer's robes with the moustachioed Gosse to lower left of centre.

63. Cartoon by Max Beerbohm of the unveiling of the bronze bust of Edmund Gosse in 1909. Haldane is pictured at the right of the group behind Gosse's left elbow.

64. The bust now stands in the London Library, of which Gosse and Haldane were both vice-presidents.

The

Ballad of Reading Gaol

By

C. 3. 3.

Leonard Smithers
Royal Arcade London W
Mdcccxcviii

65. Haldane was the first visitor to Oscar Wilde (1854–1900) in Pentonville prison in June 1895. He arranged for books to be sent to Wilde and encouraged him to write of his prison experiences. Wilde promised Haldane to write something of worth.

66. The first edition copy of 'The Ballad of Reading Gaol' 1898 written by Wilde under the pseudonym C.3.3. was sent 'with the compliments of the author' to Haldane in 1898. Haldane viewed this book as the redemption of Wilde's promise.

Company of Friends: Political

67. H. H. Asquith c. 1915, who served as Prime Minister between 1908 and 1916, described Haldane in that year as 'the oldest personal and political friend that I have in the world'. They met in 1881, working together as young barristers. Their relationship was to fade in later life, as Haldane moved to the Labour Party in pursuit of the cause of education.

the industrialist and journalist Arnold Rechberg contended that it would not be possible for Germany to fulfil its reparation payments as demanded by the Treaty of Versailles due to its economically weak position. He proposed that German and French industries should unite to form a close community of interests. To make this a reality, German payments to their principal creditors, France and Great Britain, could be converted by French and British industries into participation in German industry. Thirty per cent of the share capital invested in Germany's large-scale industries should then be transferred, Rechberg argued, to the creditors' governments, who would then transfer those shares to their own large-scale industries.[51] Einstein wrote to Haldane: 'As this plan seems to me so reasonable and naturally suitable, I dare to request that you consider this proposal yourself and in case of approval apply your great authority in support of it.'[52]

Haldane replied favourably, and likewise sought to utilise the power of Einstein's name to see if the idea (though not a particularly new one) would gain traction. 'It would be an advantage if I may share your name with Mr [A. J.] Balfour, as a private affair and not for the public sphere,' wrote Haldane. 'You have personally very great fame in these lands, and I would very much like to be able to say that I had heard about the article from you.'[53] Haldane also visited the Foreign Office and the Treasury on Einstein's behalf, but was warned by Sir Basil Blackett, permanent adviser about the reparations procedure, that such an idea had to come spontaneously rather than as an imposition from government.[54]

To have experienced encounters as diverse as those with Wilde and Einstein, to have engaged so actively and politically on the behalf of personalities operating in such widely divergent fields, would have been remarkable for most of Haldane's contemporaries. But for Haldane himself there is almost something natural about it. His social and political nets were cast staggeringly wide, but that was only a reflection of the breadth of his own polymathic interests, and indeed of his likeability.

* * *

But we now return to friendships of a more intimate nature. One that stands out and even rivals Haldane's closeness with Hume Brown was his friendship with literary critic and writer Edmund Gosse. In many respects his relationship with Gosse was, with the exception of that with Frances Horner, the most unusual and the most spiritually intimate of all Haldane's friendships. Initially they were brought together by their mutual love of literature, and Gosse's 1904 appointment as librarian to the House of Lords was the catalyst to an ever-deepening friendship that would last until Gosse's death in May 1928, just three months before Haldane's.[55] But, even as early as 1905, Gosse could call 'the play of Haldane's intellect … the most wonderful fact in my daily life'.[56]

Gosse had 'a genius for knowing people' and was widely conversant with the leading authors of his time, at home and abroad, especially in France.[57] His appointment as the inaugural Clark Lecturer in English Literature at Trinity College, Cambridge in 1884 was supported by Matthew Arnold, Robert Browning and Tennyson.[58] He was one of the few Englishmen to be elected an honorary member of the Académie Française, and was awarded a clutch of honorary doctorates by universities, including the Sorbonne. Gosse was a friend of André Gide, and was the first man to introduce the great Norwegian playwright Henrik Ibsen to English readers. He was also a voracious columnist, particularly for the *Sunday Times*.

The letters from Haldane to Gosse reveal Haldane at his most lyrical and playful. When they were not speaking in person—which was often—they were constantly writing to each other, exchanging views on literature and commenting admiringly on each other's writing. It is in these letters, more than anywhere else, that we get a sense of Haldane's literary sensibilities. When Gosse, for instance, published a book featuring an appreciation of Charlotte Brontë, sister to Haldane's beloved poet Emily, it elicited the following response: 'You have estimated our Charlotte at just her level. It was not indeed a character adapted to "padded sofas" and Berlin wool work. Pain, resistance and, I suspect also, tingling passion, were the material of that little soul.'[59]

The book *Father and Son*, which Gosse wrote in 1907 and for which he is most renowned, has been described as the first psychological biography. It was met with enthusiasm by many critics, not least Haldane: 'Now I have nearly finished it, and am delighted. It is the most delicate piece of work of the kind that I have known since the "Souvenirs de Enfance et de Jeunesse"—one of my old favourites. I sit up over it late at night and cannot lay it down. When we meet I will tell you how it has moved me and why!'[60] Indeed, Gosse's writing facility was something that Haldane greatly envied, and he turned to Gosse regularly for editorial assistance with his own writing. In 1919, after sharing the draft of an article with Gosse, Haldane writes: 'You are indeed a friend in need. I have recast the article exactly as you prescribed, and I think it reads much better. I am shockingly deficient in technique as a writer and speaker.'[61]

Given this self-evaluation, it is not surprising that Haldane drew heavily on Gosse's insight in the preparation of a speech that was perhaps the most important of his later life, namely the address he gave to the special joint meeting of the American Bar Association and the Bar Association of Canada in Montreal on 1 September 1913 entitled 'Higher Nationality: A Study in Law and Ethics'—a speech we shall explore in detail in Chapter 10. Gosse recalled Haldane's meticulous preparation. Haldane, he tells us, began writing 'what became "Higher Nationality" at Cloan towards the end of February [1913], and submitted to me his first draft. I found very considerable fault with the form of it, and he re-wrote it, no fewer than five times.' He continues:

> In the course of the many interviews we had on the subject, at 28 Queen Anne's Gate, and here at my own house, I was struck by the modesty and docility of the Lord Chancellor, who considered every one of my objections, and put nothing aside without attention. He was intensely desirous to produce an essay of real weight, capable by its form of pleasing the Americans and by its theme of awakening international reflection.[62]

But literature, not the challenges of international relations, formed the real bond between the two men. In 1908 they even established the Academic Committee of the Royal Society of Literature together, an attempt to create a British equivalent to the Académie Française. The committee was considered 'a body consisting of the foremost literary men in England',[63] including Robert Bridges, Joseph Conrad, Thomas Hardy, Henry James and W. B. Yeats. When at Cloan, Haldane delighted in keeping Gosse up to date with his reading. 'I got here on Saturday morning', he wrote in the summer of 1916, two years into the war, 'and began a holiday by sitting down to reread an early Victorian novel. I chose "Martin Chuzzlewit" and am now spurred on to finer reading. It was like the soup at dinner, an indifferent but appropriate preliminary.'[64] Haldane evidently relished the chance to forget, even if just for a short time, the seriousness of the international situation and lose himself in the world of letters. And so, with a light heart, he upbraids Gosse that November: 'How naughty of you to say what you did about Goethe and Heine! But I say nothing.'[65] A week later: 'Why have I no word from you? Can you have revolted at my gentle reproach about the Great Goethe? If so let his spirit depart, for he must not separate you and me.'[66]

Haldane's literary reflections to Gosse demonstrate his enormous range and thoroughness. It is not just that he is reading Hardy and Dickens, books on the philosophy of mathematics, Hegel and biographies in German—he is, for the most part, rereading them. Yet these literary endeavours were not all for personal satisfaction. In 1925, at the age of sixty-nine and despite ill health, Haldane broke his holiday at Cloan to address the Brontë Society, of which he was president. 'Here am I', he enthuses to Gosse on his return to Cloan, 'not a penny the worse for eighteen hours of travelling between Haworth and here. I think my sciatica or rheumatism is slowly quieting down. I was able to speak for 40 minutes. I began standing, but had to ask them later to let me sit. I was steeped in the subject and was not using notes, so there was no embarrassment. A fine local gathering—severe Yorkshire. It would not have done not to have gone—tho' it was a little of an effort. In the end it seems to have done me good.'[67]

Haldane also turned to Gosse in the thick of his political duties, some-times to talk through the greatest political and social upheavals of their times, sometimes simply to let out a little boast—for Haldane knew that Gosse, unlike others, was receptive to both. Gosse loved to feel close to the action, and he enjoyed basking in others' glory. As Arthur Benson once cuttingly remarked: 'He [Gosse] is only on the fringe of the real thing, of course, but does not know it.'[68] Where some might detect a touch of self-aggrandisement in Haldane's stories, Gosse felt the tingle of proximity to power. For example, in the autumn of 1908 Haldane was not yet a long-standing habitué of royal hospitality, and it is rather endearing that his relationship with Gosse enables him to write a little breathlessly from Balmoral of his interactions with Edward VII. 'Yesterday my Royal Master opined that I could not show prowess in the sports of this domain—so I went out and caught fourteen trout for his breakfast. He was as unbeliev-ing as the disciple, and was relieved to find that I had caught them with worms.'[69] The admission of the worms—no angler's boast—reminds us that Haldane was still self-aware enough, despite his exalted company, not to take himself too seriously.

Whenever Haldane was in London, and struggling with the weight of ministerial responsibility, he sought out Gosse's company. Sometimes they would go walking together, once for a five-hour trek over Ashridge Common,[70] or they would be in the House of Lords library. But more often than not they were at each other's houses. On 29 July 1914, with the country suddenly trembling on the brink of war, Gosse received an urgent letter from Haldane. 'Will you—if you are free—dine alone with me tomorrow night (Thursday) at 8.15?'[71] Haldane needed Gosse as a patient confidant and interlocutor. On 2 August Gosse paid another visit, the record of which provides a remarkable insight into the comings and goings at 28 Queen Anne's Gate at this most pivotal moment in world history—a moment explored more fully in Chapter 7. At this time the Foreign Secretary, Edward Grey, was staying with Haldane. Gosse, finding himself so close to the central protagonists of international affairs, struggled to keep his feet on the ground, as his letter to Earl Spencer on the following day made clear.

> What days these have been! Yesterday, Haldane telephoned for me to come and cheer him up in the interval between the Cabinet meetings. At the door Grey was showing Cambon [the French ambassador] out—such an aged, and drawn, and flushed Cambon! Grey was perfectly calm, but grave to solemnity, and it was he who told me that the Germans had seized Luxembourg. I found Haldane very depressed, but resolute, and all the finer part of his theoretical intellect exposed. He is at his very best at the moment when it is not detail, but a wide and even imaginative grasp of situations that is required. I urged him to lie down and rest, but he refused altogether, saying that to talk was the only rest possible. I stayed an hour and a half. Meanwhile Grey took the motor and went off to the Zoo, to spend an hour among the birds. Was that not characteristic? At 6 Lichnowsky [the German ambassador] called for a few words with Haldane before the Cabinet at 6:30, so I vanished down the back staircase.[72]

Three weeks later Gosse again wrote to Spencer:

> I have seen very few people, except, almost daily, Haldane. He has been here [Gosse's home at 17 Hanover Terrace] often, walking with me in our leafy enclosure, sharing our Spartan meals. He has come out very splen-

didly, with a new and revised sense of intellectual command, totally disinterested, accepting without a murmur the fact that his plans and schemes have been swallowed up and completed, without a complaint of the ingratitude of a vain population. I was able to be of slight use at the psychological moment, in telling him exactly the hour when it was needful that he should have a frank understanding with Kitchener [the new Secretary of State for War]. It was a wonderful chance—I overheard a conversation not intended for my ears. Some day I will tell you how wonderfully it turned out.[73] Kitchener is rather splendid; he moves about like a thundercloud, alarming, reposeful too; he has tremendous shortcomings, but he is the national mascotte and Haldane is there to mollify his severities and to urge the humanities. Kitchener is perfect with Haldane, and seems to appreciate his worth, the more no doubt because Haldane, with delicate tact, avoids all self-prominence, gives K.[itchener] all the credit.[74]

But Gosse was soon to be able to help Haldane in other, more personal ways. On 14 December 1914 Haldane sent him a damaging article that Professor Oncken of Heidelberg had written. It told of an occasion in which Haldane had apparently referred to Germany as his 'spiritual home', and it would trigger one of the most painful episodes of Haldane's life. To this day Oncken's article lies close to the roots of Haldane's tainted public reputation. As we shall see in Chapter 7, certain loud sections of the press were disposed to find in Haldane a traitor and a shame to the nation. With these fateful words—'spiritual home'—his enemies found the proof, or so they thought, that assured them of their instinct. In the weeks that followed publication of the article, the flood of vitriolic articles mounted. But unlike a number of Haldane's closest political allies after his ejection from government, Gosse refused to remain silent. At last his literary skills could be deployed in the service of a friend and of justice.

On 9 January 1915 Gosse wrote a carefully crafted letter to the *Morning Post* which sought to place Haldane's comments in a historic—indeed literary—context, and in so doing to set the record straight. Oncken had been introduced to Haldane at a dinner given by Mr and Mrs Humphry Ward on a visit he had made to Britain in 1912. Looking back on that visit two years later, Oncken chose to write tendentiously, and in the vastly changed circumstances of war, that Haldane had told him that evening about the place Germany held in his heart—it was, in fact, his 'spiritual home'. Gosse took pains to point out, however, that Haldane's comment referred principally to the atmosphere in the classroom of Professor Lotze in Göttingen, where some forty years previously Haldane had studied. Reminding the reader that Robert Browning had also found in Lotze a profound spiritual influence, Gosse comments:

> But what created emotion in an English poet of one generation and in a Scotch statesman of a later one was not German feeling in general, nor the brutal presumption of a governing class in Germany, but the sweet humanity of a single German philosopher, who was a stranger and a foreigner to the mass of his own countrymen. Surely this has only to be realised to put an end to the absurd misrepresentation of a phrase which might now be relegated to oblivion.[75]

Haldane wrote the same day in gratitude: 'My dear Gosse, Splendid! How quick you are. You have rendered me a great service. Your letter is full of tact. It has the characteristic delicacy of the "Gosse touch". It ought to do great good.'[76] But the libellous damage had already been done and, despite the good that Gosse's letter no doubt achieved, a direct line of causation can be drawn from the Oncken accusation to Haldane's exclusion from the coalition government on its formation in May 1915.

But Gosse meant far more to Haldane than just a defender of his reputation. Gosse was a man to whom Haldane could express his humblest concerns, his love of literature, his passion for his dogs, and his most dramatic political adventures. According to Gosse's biographer, the closeness of this friendship is 'impossible to over-emphasise'.[77]

* * *

The steady ripening of Haldane's friendship with Gosse as the years progressed stands in contrast to the two most vital friendships of Haldane's life from a political perspective, namely his friendships with H. H. Asquith and Sir Edward Grey, the future prime minister and foreign secretary respectively. It was with these two men that Haldane formed such a powerful triumvirate both in and out of office, driving forward the Liberal imperialist cause. It was through their friendship and political affinities that the agreement known as the Relugas Compact came about, the breakdown of which led Haldane to the War Office. It was their interactions that directed much of the country's foreign policy as it advanced unknowingly towards the First World War. We will explore that story more fully in Part 2, but what were the bonds uniting these three men?

Haldane entered the House of Commons at the same time as Grey in the election of December 1885. Grey was just twenty-three when he became member for Berwick-upon-Tweed; Haldane was twenty-nine. Asquith, through Haldane's introduction of him to his own adjacent constituency of East Fife, joined them in Parliament the following year at the age of thirty-three. Haldane and Asquith first met as two briefless barristers at dinner in Lincoln's Inn in 1881, after which 'a great friendship' arose between them.[78] Indeed, Roy Jenkins believed that Asquith's relationship with Haldane was the closest friendship that Asquith ever developed with any man.[79] In some respects, we might not be surprised at this. Both hailed from deeply religious families; both were fiercely intelligent (Asquith had had a glittering Oxford career); both were passionate about Liberal politics; both struggled to get their legal careers off the ground; both, in the end, found themselves leaders at the Bar. Yet in other respects they were strikingly different. Asquith had little time for the abstractions of metaphysics; he was intent on reaching the highest seats of political power, using the law as a vehicle to advance his ambition; he was eloquent and lucid in speech, though no great political thinker of originality. None of these things could be said of Haldane. This balance of difference and similarity meant that there was little sense of rivalry—despite the occasion in 1899 when Haldane gleefully reported to his mother that he'd had 'a fight in the Courts with Asquith, whom I defeated with slaughter'.[80]

As young men they saw each other almost every day, dined together once or twice a week, and went abroad together each Easter. Haldane was a regular visitor to the Hampstead home of Asquith, his first wife Helen, and their children. Their second child, Herbert, recalled one such visit and an incident which could well have changed the course of history. It was a summer evening in the mid-1880s. Herbert and his older brother Raymond were playing cricket with their father, while Haldane 'stood talking to my mother in the deep field, and now and then stooped to throw in a ball which had been discharged to the boundary'. After the game, 'my father and Haldane, his hands locked behind him and his head slightly bowed, deep in discussion, walked up and down the path beneath the old wall of mellow brick that formed the boundary of our ground'. Only a few hours later this entire wall collapsed, 'covering with lumps of debris and splintered bricks the whole length of the path on which Haldane and my father had been walking'. Herbert reflects:

> It is curious to look back out of what was then the remote future at those figures on the lawn, my mother in her sun-bonnet, and Haldane, who in the eyes of childhood was already magnified, a hero of giant girth ... and my father, a young man scarcely known to the world, with a slender figure and slightly ascetic aspect, a wide brow, a firm mouth, a humorous but faintly sardonic smile, and a clear, searching intelligence. ... It is curious also to reflect that, in the strange web of circumstance, the collapse of that wall a few hours earlier might have changed the course of history and that the error of some unknown Georgian architect might have destroyed at a single blow the Prime Minister of 1914 and the creator of the British Expeditionary Force, including in its possible results the fall of Paris, with all its consequences for Europe and the world.[81]

Haldane would not just pay social visits to the Asquiths in Hampstead. Four years into their marriage, in 1881, Haldane even went to convalesce with them, after suffering a breakdown—explored in Chapter 2—as a result of his rejection by Agnes Kemp, the sister of his school friend and later colleague John Kemp. It was to Asquith, not known to outsiders for the warmth of his humanity, and Helen that Haldane turned. It would not be many years before Asquith was mourning his own loss, after Helen died from typhoid fever in 1891. Haldane remembered her as a beautiful and simple spirit.[82] Three years later, he was best man at Asquith's second marriage to Margot Tennant at St George's, Hanover Square.

Not particularly beautiful, and certainly not simple, Margot would prove to be a staunch supporter of Haldane, but when Asquith's early seriousness was compromised by a fondness for drink, bridge and high society, Haldane felt that Margot was partly responsible. His following comments to his mother in March 1917, when Asquith was leader of the opposition, are characteristic:

> The Dardanelles Report is in every one's mouth. Poor Asquith is much criticised. He had a very difficult task & people are not very fair. But the household arrangements at Downing Street [when Asquith was prime minister], and the social arrangements there made things more difficult than they ought to have been. The unfortunate Margot is responsible for a good deal of the want of concentration.[83]

The relationship with Grey was of a subtly different hue. Haldane had worked with Edward Grey's uncle, Albert Grey, later Earl Grey, as a young Liberal on the Albert Grey Committee—the private discussion group of prominent Liberals, out of which came the 'Eighty' Club (see Chapter 6). This Grey family connection is likely to have assisted Haldane in developing his relationship with the young Sir Edward after he entered Parliament. Representing Scottish and Border constituencies respectively, Haldane and Grey, along with Asquith, travelled and operated in some proximity. Haldane found himself in constant and intimate communication with Grey and his wife Dorothy. Despite their different backgrounds and private interests (the Greys were country people through and through), they held the same views on most subjects.[84] The contrast in physical appearance between the two men was likely to arouse mirth in some circles, with Haldane's 'porky presence' comparing rather unfavourably to the handsome features of Grey and his lithesome sportsman's body (he was a gifted real tennis player).[85] Opposites attract of course, and Haldane would frequently visit Fallodon, the Greys' Northumberland home, while they were regular visitors at Cloan, as were the Asquiths.[86]

The intimacy between Haldane and the Greys went beyond merely political interactions. Writing to his sister Elizabeth on 30 October 1890 Haldane talks of all that he has learned in the months following the breakdown of his engagement to Val Munro Ferguson. Philosophical as always, he refers to being much richer for what has happened, before going on to observe: 'And you and the Greys, too, who have looked on so very near, have gained and learned in the work of helping a fellow creature.'[87] Haldane himself would, in turn, come to their aid.

Their ambivalent commitment to political life, seeking to balance the call to public service with the much stronger call of the countryside, caused the Greys much distress. The following letter written to Edward by Dorothy in the early summer of 1893, his first year in office as parliamentary under-secretary for foreign affairs, reveals both Grey's lifelong antipathy to office and something even at that early stage of the influence of their friendship with Haldane. This letter, unlike her others, was copied out in Grey's own hand, eight months after the death of his wife. He notes that she wrote it in their London house, and sent it down to him at the House of Commons:

I want to write to you: first about the Hudson book.[88] I have read a good deal: it touches very fine notes of feeling for nature. I felt first sad because it was such a long way off from what we are doing: then the feeling stole over me of being very faithful to the holy things and very firmly separated from towns. I read on and on and old Haldane [thirty-six years old to Grey's thirty] came in in the middle. After the usual commonplaces I sort of let out, and we talked from 5 to 8 and the result is that he has gone away saying 'I understand at last. You must not stay in politics. It is hurting your lives. It is bad.' I piled up my feeling to hurl at him and among other things said that if we went on crushing our natural sympathies we should probably end by destroying our married life, because the basis and atmosphere of its beauty would be taken away and it would die. This seemed to strike him in an extraordinary way. He said he had felt in himself how much your unhappiness in office made it difficult to talk to you or be intimate, and that he had been feeling there was no spring or heart in either of us. Then he said many nice Haldanesque things and reproached himself for not having understood before our passion for the country. Then we talked for a long time, he arguing in favour of giving up politics and I against it, and I believe he had the best of it. I was quite touched by him; we must be nice to our Haldane. He thinks now that it would be quite reasonable if you resigned at once, though I told him we had no idea of that. I wonder if you will see him in the House tonight and what he will say to you. He told me he had had a talk with you today which had been nicer than of late. It's funny to write and tell you all this but I may be gone to bed when you come. I shall read more Hudson tonight and store it up for you like honey.[89]

Haldane, Grey's biographer tells us, 'had clearly been carried off his feet by the suddenness of Dorothy's onslaught but he soon recovered himself'. The following year, in October, we find Haldane writing to Dorothy with a different perspective:

The one blow that I should feel a heavy and even crushing one would be that Edward should leave politics. For me it would rob the outlook of much of its hope and meaning. I think his presence is of the last importance to the Liberal party. And how much I believe in that Liberal party and in the work we have to do, you know. All I ask is that you should not come to any decision just now, and that I do ask on personal as well as general grounds. If only Edward was in Rosebery's place [the prime minister], I should feel sure of what I only hope for now. We are all soldiers in a great struggle, and cost what it may to our feelings let us storm the breaches, that have been made visibly in the opposing barriers. It is a religious question with us.[90]

But for comradeship with Haldane, it is likely that Grey would have left politics during the long discouraging period of Liberal divisions and impotence. As far back as 1890 Grey had written to Haldane:

> Your influence will always be greatly indirect, and it will be your privilege never to be able to measure it. If it were not for you I do not think I should have even the hold on public life which I have now. There are others too more worth influencing. I should say, for instance, that Asquith owed some of the very best of himself to you; in knowing you both I feel as if it was so.[91]

It is clear that the three men were united in quite profound ways. It is therefore perhaps not surprising that their personal characteristics should intertwine with each other in effective political ways. Haldane was the hard worker, the thinker, the man who could develop coherent, grounded policy and strategy. Asquith, though less of an original thinker, had a great gift of speech, was wise, and his abilities in debate made him popular with more senior politicians. Grey, by contrast, was in Haldane's opinion advanced in his views and of a very independent mind in the best Whig traditions. Haldane correctly pointed out that the whips could not count on Grey as they could on Asquith. Grey was much more his own man; his attachment to office, his political career, was always something he viewed with ambivalence.

The three men made a powerful combination, and it is not surprising that the Cabinets in which they served were some of the most famous in British history, if not always for the right reasons. But behind the tragedies of war, there were more personal tragedies in their years of power. Less than two months after her husband had been appointed Foreign Secretary, Dorothy Grey was thrown from a dog cart in a Northumbrian lane on 1 February 1906 and died in the early hours of 4 February without regaining consciousness. Grey wrote immediately to Haldane from Fallodon:

> Dear Richard,
>
> It is over, and we are companions in sorrow now until life ends. I shall feel the need of friends, a thing I have never felt while I had her love every day and could give all mine to her. If I could realise at once all that this means I could not live, but I suppose nature will dole out to me just the suffering every day which I can bear. My best chance is to begin work again at once, and I have told them to begin sending F.[oreign] O.[ffice] work to me

tomorrow. Will you have me in your flat if I come to London next week and have all my things moved down from the flat above?[92]

The reference by Grey to being 'companions in sorrow ... until life ends' refers to the sorrow that Haldane continued to feel over the breakdown of his engagement to Val Munro Ferguson and her subsequent death in 1897. Writing to his sister Elizabeth on the same day from Lord Rothschild's home at Tring Park, Haldane says: 'Lady Grey has passed away. I have telegraphed that I will go to him [in Northumberland]. But I think that he will stop me and propose to come to me. He [Grey] wrote "I think I must turn to you".'[93]

Whitehall Court, just behind the Old War Office Building, was where Grey and Haldane each occupied a flat, Grey's above that of Haldane. By 7 February Haldane had asked Grey to make his home with him, cancelling his engagements to devote his evenings to his shattered friend. Writing to his mother on 16 February, Haldane says: 'E. Grey is splendid—his attitude is one of thankfulness for all the happiness he has had';[94] but these were sentiments to comfort his mother, for Grey's feelings oscillated between thankfulness and despair. Seeking to immerse himself in work, Grey himself writes on 22 February to another close confidante: 'I feel like a prisoner in a cell who beats his head against the walls; but these fits pass or cease at any rate while I do my work.'[95]

Grey stayed with Haldane at Whitehall Court until the day he wrote the above words. Not long after, he moved into a house at 3 Queen Anne's Gate, which Dorothy had found, while Haldane, with the help of his sister Elizabeth and Frances Horner, moved into number 28 in the same street. Once more the two friends—now both alone—were physically proximate. Haldane's closeness to Grey, unlike that to Asquith, was to remain unbroken as the storm clouds of war gathered around the Cabinet and the nation.

Chapter 7 will tell the story of how Haldane, Grey and Asquith came through those storm clouds, the latter two retaining their positions of power, while Haldane was effectively abandoned. We will see how a 'wound which never quite healed'[96] opened up as a result of Asquith's handling of Haldane's exclusion from government and his subsequent reluctance to clear decisively Haldane's name in public. But we will also see something of Haldane's remarkable ability to rise above recrimination and injustice, writing to Margot the day he left office on 24 May 1915: 'I am very happy. I have my individual work & another life besides for which there has been little room for ten years. I am content & consider that I have been a most fortunate person.'[97] These are the words of a man who, according to his great love Frances Horner, 'seemed unattainable of anything but a sort of unconquerable serenity'. 'I never heard a small or unkind word from him', she wrote.[98] The extent to which this attitude was built into Haldane's DNA or arose out of a hard-won intellectual and emotional struggle is an intriguing question. Given what we discovered in our last chapter, the latter is more likely. What is clear, as we shall now go on to see, is that Haldane possessed a philosophical outlook in which serenity was the logical response to the universe. His friendships were, for the most part, lasting and a great comfort in time of trial, but as his relationship with Asquith showed, they were not always so. Haldane's philosophy was his defence against the vagaries and chances of time.

4

A PHILOSOPHY FOR LIFE

Some one, I think it is Goldsmith, has written that philosophy is a good horse in the stable, but an arrant jade on a journey. This was not true of Haldane's philosophy. He found it a real support in the trials and storms of life. When these beat upon him, he had the large view that transcends consideration of personal fortunes.

Viscount Grey of Fallodon, 1928[1]

Stephen Hawking and Leonard Mlodinow's 2010 book *The Grand Design: New Answers to the Ultimate Questions of Life* opens with a startling, controversial claim:

> Living in this vast world that is by turns kind and cruel, and gazing at the immense heavens above, people have always asked a multitude of questions: How can we understand the world in which we find ourselves? How does the universe behave? What is the nature of reality? Where did all this come from? Did the universe need a creator? Most of us do not spend most of our time worrying about these questions, but almost all of us worry about them some of the time.

> Traditionally these are questions for philosophy, but philosophy is dead. Philosophy has not kept up with modern developments in science, particularly physics. Scientists have become the bearers of the torch of discovery in our quest for knowledge.[2]

This is a fairly drastic assessment of philosophy's usefulness today. Yet there is good reason to begin our study of Haldane the philosopher with such a damning judgment, for it represents the kind of attitude, by no means non-existent in his own time, that Haldane spent his life fighting against. It claims the superiority of one discipline over others, and advocates a specific way of looking at the world as the *only* way to look at the world.

Haldane, on the other hand, was adamant that 'to see life steadily, and to see it whole'[3] required quite the opposite approach. For him, any adequate understanding of the world, with its multitude of differing aspects (scientific, moral, aesthetic, religious etc.), demanded a plurality of perspectives and disciplines. Haldane, as we shall see, not only viewed philosophy as one of those important perspectives; it was his philosophical training that taught him the need for this plurality.

The Hawking and Mlodinow quotation is relevant in another sense. Taking this attitude to philosophy as their starting point, they go on to suggest that there might be a scientific theory (M-theory, which is more like a set of theories) that can answer all the questions posed. They claim that all our difficulties can be resolved into its terms; hence the redundancy of philosophy. One great irony, to which Haldane would have been particularly sensitive, is that the two scientists invoke an understanding of human perception (which they call 'model-dependent realism') that philosophers have long debated under different guises. More astonishingly still, their form of realism represents a view that comes very close to what Haldane himself advocated as a philosopher a hundred years previously! As one critic wryly ends his review: 'Dare I say that it may be the oracular Professor Hawking who is failing to keep up with the philosophers and the theologians, rather than the other way round?'[4]

So the issues Haldane battled with a century ago remain contemporary issues. Even more importantly, the philosophy Haldane used to combat this Hawking-esque perspective was not content to remain concealed in an ivory tower. It was an intellectual endeavour that radically shaped his political life—indeed, every aspect of his life. We cannot understand his statesmanship without it.

* * *

But before we outline Haldane's philosophical vision, it is worthwhile exploring briefly the intellectual path that took him to philosophy. We have already seen the wide-ranging interests of the Haldanes and Burdon Sandersons, encompassing religious studies, scientific investigation, the law and politics. The religion of his parents was, until Haldane's sixteenth year, the dominant factor in his intellectual life. But by the time he reached sixteen he had begun to think that the intellectual foundations of that religion were unstable. As he wrote: 'It was religion of a somewhat emotional type, stimulated by a wave of feeling which at that time was pervading Scotland. But presently questions forced themselves upon me. Was the basic foundation of such feeling reliable?'[5] Haldane's youthful response was characteristic of how he would deal with all subsequent unsettlement: 'I began to read copiously.'[6] He was unable to find the depth of reflection he was looking for in the established religious authors. Far more stimulating were the revolutionary writings of David Friedrich Strauss and Ernest Renan, which put easy assurances of Jesus' divinity into question. Believing things on the basis of religious authorities was no longer an option for Haldane—he needed logical reasoning. Philosophy became his refuge. For a time he could not work himself out of his muddle. Everything he had known and been taught about life's great questions was up in the air. He kept these deeply disturbing thoughts from his parents, who were considering sending him to Balliol College, Oxford, to continue his studies. They were, however, suspicious of the Anglican influence in Oxford at that time and, at the instigation of Edinburgh's eccentric professor of Greek, John Stuart Blackie, it was decided that instead the young Haldane ought to have some months at the University of Göttingen, before returning to his studies in Edinburgh. If Haldane's parents thought the Anglicanism of Oxford might have threatened the religion of their son's youth, they evidently had no idea what intellectual temptations were lurking in Germany.

Haldane arrived in Göttingen in April 1874. At first, he longed for home in what seemed a topsy-turvy world. 'In the grey of the dawn [on his first morning] what particularly distressed me was to see a woman and a dog drawing along the street a cart containing a man and a calf. I felt these were odd and unfamiliar people among whom I had come to live.'[7] Quickly, however, he found his footing. Armed with a letter of introduction from Professor Blackie, Haldane went to meet Göttingen's most famous philosopher, Professor Hermann Lotze. Here he encountered a perspective strikingly alien to that of his parents.

There were many famous figures in Göttingen during the brief period of Haldane's studies there. But, as he told a group of Welsh students years later, 'the figure that stood out above all the others was that of my old master, Hermann Lotze'.

I had the privilege, boy as I was, of seeing him often in his study as well as of listening in his lecture-room, and to the end of my life I shall hold the deep impression he made on me—of a combination of intellectual power and the highest moral stature. It seems to me but yesterday that he used quietly to enter the lecture-room where we students sat expectant, and, taking his seat, fix his eyes on space as though he were looking into another world remote from this one. The face was worn with thought, and the slight and fragile figure with the great head looked as though the mind that tenanted it had been dedicated to thought and to nothing else. The brow and nose were wonderfully chiselled, the expression was a combination of tolerance with power. The delivery was slow and exact, but the command of language was impressive. Our feeling towards him as we sat and listened was one of reverence mingled with affection.[8]

Haldane's recollection—his meticulous focus on the face, the figure, the head, the brow, the nose, the expression of his teacher—emphasises the way in which Lotze, in Haldane's eyes, *embodied* the pursuit of truth and the desire for knowledge. In the intellectual realm, he set the pattern for Haldane's life. Lotze showed him that philosophy could be more than a helpful resource for getting through life's muddles; it could be lived, it could be a vocation.

It is no surprise that one of the first books Lotze recommended to Haldane for reading was Johann Gottlieb Fichte's *The Vocation of Man*. The book had a profound impact on Haldane, with its stress on the importance of acting in accordance with one's conscience,[9] of the attempt to see into the 'most secret core' of nature[10] and of eradicating inequality. Every human being, according to Fichte, is called to such a life. It is also likely that Haldane read Fichte's accompanying lectures on the 'Vocation of the Scholar', in which that vocation is described as 'the supreme supervision of the actual progress of the human race in general and the unceasing promotion of this progress'.[11] This involves an absolute dedication to the truth. 'I am a priest of truth,' wrote Fichte. 'I am in its pay, and thus I have committed myself to do, to risk, and to suffer for its sake. If I should be pursued and hated for the truth's sake, or if I should die in its service, what more would I have done than what I simply had to do?'[12] These ideas—that each of us has a purpose in the world, and that the scholar's is one of the most vital—seem to have had an intensely restorative effect on Haldane. We do not know if he accepted all he read in these texts, but it clearly appealed to him that one could give one's life to something that wasn't dependent on historical revelation and didn't require membership in a limited human community—both key aspects of the Christianity of his childhood. The idea, moreover, that the philosophical task could be bound up with the very fate of humanity and history was revelatory. Here was an activity that could give Haldane's life a point, and a grand one at that, even in a world where, for him, religious observances had become redundant.

* * *

This talk of philosophy as a life's vocation bound up with world history is likely to sound strange to us today. If you know anything about 'analytic philosophy'—the most dominant philosophy in Britain and America in the second half of the twentieth century—you will know that it very often approaches philosophy as a technical tool for problem solving, with a narrow focus on logic and language. It is certainly not designed to elevate the spirit in the manner of Fichte's writings, and it offers a somewhat reduced vision of the philosopher's task. The philosophy that appealed to Haldane—broadly captured under the name 'Idealism' and which we will explore below—was to suffer drastically at the hands of well-known thinkers such as Bertrand Russell, G. E. Moore, Wittgenstein and A. J. Ayer in the decades leading up to the Second World War. This was not simply based on their refutations of Idealism's arguments. A range of historical factors contributed to the downfall of the philosophy so dear to Haldane, not least the tragedies of the First World War.[13] All the grandeur of Idealism—its tendency to tie every dimension of the world into a system, to see history unfolding in a positive progression, to raise the state to a privileged position, to give human minds an almost godlike character—all this was cast aside in a cynical, post-1918 world. In such a context, any exalted role for the philosopher seemed out of the question. It was now the scientist who had the keys to reality—a view that still prevails today, as the Hawking/Mlodinow quotation demonstrates. On the Continent things were different,[14] but in Britain it came to be a mark of philosophical acumen to downplay the philosophical task and to see it very much as a handmaiden to the sciences. As the leading analytic thinker Professor Gilbert Ryle once contemptuously, and rather pompously, put it:

> I guess that our thinkers [British as opposed to Continental] have been immunized against the idea of philosophy as the Mistress Science by the fact that their daily lives in Cambridge and Oxford colleges have kept them in personal contact with real scientists. Claims to Führership [Ryle was writing in 1958] vanish when postprandial joking begins. Husserl [an archetypal 'Continental' philosopher] wrote as if he had never met a scientist—or a joke.[15]

With this privileging of 'real scientists', a corresponding narrowing of the philosophical endeavour ensued. Importantly for us, the idea that the philosopher could also be the practical man of action in public life was dispensed with. In Haldane's time, the possibility of the philosopher-statesman was a real one; indeed, he was one himself. A philosophical education, as it was in the latter decades of the nineteenth century when Idealism reigned supreme, could inspire a young man or woman with the hope that their actions could have world-changing consequences; it could assure them that there was a deep bond uniting all human beings (Hegel called it *Geist*); it could tell them something about the liberating effect of living as a responsible citizen within society. This understanding of what a philosophical education should provide was already on the wane in the years before 1914, as 'Realism' began to take root in the English universities—a view not easily summarised, but which fiercely repudiated the Idealist claim that thinking affected the reality of the thing that was being thought about. The notable Oxford philosopher R. G. Collingwood considered the whole bent of the Realist school to be one that undermined the earlier vision of philosophy as a possible guide to life. Writing in the ominous year of 1938, and reflecting on the rise of Realism in his own Oxford days before the First World War, Collingwood pronounced a damning judgment on the political and social ramifications of Realism:

> The pupils [of the Realist school], whether or not they expected a philosophy that should give them ... ideals to live for or principles to live by, did not get it; and were told [by their teachers] that no philosopher (except of course a bogus philosopher) would even try to give it. The inference which any pupil could draw for himself was that for guidance in the problems of life, since one must not seek it from thinkers or from thinking, from ideals or from principles, one must look to people who were not thinkers (but fools), to processes that were not thinking (but passion), to aims that were not ideals (but caprices), and to rules that were not principles (but rules of

expediency). If the realists had wanted to train up a generation of Englishmen and Englishwomen expressly as the potential dupes of every adventurer in morals or politics, commerce or religion, who should appeal to their emotions and promise them private gains which he neither could procure them nor even meant to procure them, no better way of doing it could have been discovered.[16]

The cataclysmic events of 1914–18 only made it more difficult for Idealist philosophy to thrive. The optimism that had characterised its outlook would take a long time to claw back.

In fact, it has yet to do so. We still live in the wake of the horrors that scarred the history of the twentieth century, and the twenty-first has not been without its own. As we turn to Haldane's philosophical outlook, in itself so optimistic, it may well seem alien and hard to reconcile with our contemporary view of the world. You may well be inclined to raise a sceptical eyebrow and question its relevance. On the other hand, our present national and international ills may create in you a longing for a restored optimism, in which case you may find the seeds of hope in what follows. Either way, if we want to know what fuelled Haldane's remarkable commitment to public service, if we want to know what underpinned every activity of his statesmanship, then we have to know at least the basics of this philosophy. If his philosophy is outdated (though some would now question this), then the achievements resting upon it are most certainly not.

* * *

Returning, then, to those transformative months in Göttingen, we find Haldane blossoming under the guidance he was offered there. Beside Fichte, Lotze also set him reading the great German philosopher Immanuel Kant, and the famous Irish thinker George Berkeley[17]—the latter having a particularly strong impression on Haldane for his astonishing demonstration of the foundational role of the mind in the perception of objects. The subtleties and complexities of these thinkers fascinated Haldane, and indicated to him a whole new way of existing. Instead of the rigid dogmatism pervading his earliest years, he discovered the excitement inherent in the pursuit of knowledge:

I had now become emancipated from religious depression, and my attention had become concentrated on a search for light about the meaning of God, Freedom, and Immortality. Lotze's influence had set me to pursue the search in a new spirit, and with a fuller consciousness of the vast theoretical obscurity in which these subjects were buried.[18]

Alongside this new passion for philosophy, Haldane developed a love of German literature under the guidance of his tutor in this subject, Helene Schlote—'one of the most accomplished women I ever came across'.[19] This remarkable lady 'knew her Goethe as only a scholar could',[20] and it was at this time that Haldane's love of Germany's great intellectual hero was formed. With the exception of the war years, Haldane kept in constant touch with Helene until her death in 1925, and even provided her with funds during the lean years of German reconstruction. In her copy of *The Reign of Relativity*, handed back to Haldane by her family after her death, there is a dedication in Haldane's hand that demonstrates the lasting impact of his time in her company. It reads:

Helene Schlote,
from the author

In recognition of much that she has given him for which he is deeply grateful. Through her guidance there came to him, first more than forty years since, insight into German literature and its spirit and meaning for the soul. Since these days, and in the course of a long and unbroken friendship, this insight has grown into a powerful influence in his life.

Haldane of Cloan.
8 August 1921
with affectionate regard[21]

Haldane returned from Göttingen to Scotland mentally and physically transformed. Gazing upon the image of the rotund lawyer in later years, it is hard to believe that he stepped off the ferry in Leith gaunt, moustachioed and long-haired; but so it was. It was the physical manifestation of his new dedication to the life of the mind.

His studies at Edinburgh increased in intensity, though he was fortunate to be surrounded by friends of equal fervour, in particular Andrew Seth, who would later be known as Andrew Seth Pringle-Pattison, professor of Logic, Rhetoric and Metaphysics at St Andrews. Accompanied by a new-found artistic sensibility (Shakespeare, Wordsworth and, as we have seen,

Goethe were revealing their greatness to him), Haldane became immersed in the groundbreaking idealist thinkers of the day, especially James Hutchison Stirling, Edward Caird and T. H. Green. This immersion established Haldane as an early member of those who came to be known as the British Idealists.

Green, more than any other perhaps, was responsible for the rise of this movement. He was an Oxford philosopher, and so Haldane did not directly study under him (though Asquith did),[22] but his emphasis on the social responsibilities of the philosopher, his reworking of the Christian tradition into a form of thinking compatible with the latest German intellectual trends, his belief that human fulfilment and freedom could be found in the active exercise of one's citizenship within the state—each of these would mark out Green as a philosophical master worthy of Haldane's discipleship. When Haldane and Seth came to edit their first book-length foray into philosophy, *Essays in Philosophical Criticism*, in 1883 it was dedicated to Green's memory.[23]

The constellation of thinkers that contributed to the book, such as Bernard Bosanquet and Henry Jones, were to become not only the leading lights of the next generation of British philosophers, but also close associates of Haldane. In most of his philosophical publications that followed, Haldane's construal of reality found its resonances in the work of these contemporaries, and in some cases took its cue from them. Indeed, their vision shaped his practical politics. Haldane's focus on education as the bedrock of a liberating and contributive citizenship (and, therefore, a healthy state) is absolutely in line with Green and his followers;[24] so, too, is his view of history as an unfolding of the spirit within the world and his understanding of individual freedom as compatible with state intervention (a topic to which we shall turn later). In other words, Haldane's youthful engagements with Green and those who took up his mantle place him very much within the mainstream of British Idealist thinking. Originality was never the great hallmark of Haldane's philosophical contribution; his exposition of the content of that thinking was, however, noted for its clarity and persuasiveness. On Volume 1 of the book that was to appear as a result of Haldane's 1902–3 Gifford Lectures at the University of St Andrews, W. Caldwell of McGill University wrote: '*The Pathway to Reality* will easily take its place in the general literature of the day as one of the most readable presentations of the idealism of the nine-teenth century.'[25] More importantly, no other philosopher of this school brought Idealism's insights into the actual composition of the state to a greater extent.[26] It should be added that Haldane's philosophical thinking was not, for the most part, derivative of his fellow Idealists. He was a great reader of the original sources upon which the whole edifice of Idealist thinking was based. Indeed, he was even a translator of those sources, publishing with his old school friend John Kemp the first of a three-volume translation of Schopenhauer's *The World as Will and Idea*[27] in the same year as *Essays in Philosophical Criticism*. But it was the thought of Georg Wilhelm Friedrich Hegel that most enthralled Haldane. Haldane considered him 'the greatest master of abstract thought that the world has seen since the day when Aristotle died'.[28] We will look later in the chapter at why he thought that this was so.

We should note one final point about the student days in which Haldane's first philosophical sensibilities were formed. What is striking when we consider Haldane's approach to his studies is the single-minded devotion with which he pursued them and his remarkable ability to absorb and process this vast range of challenging authors, in both German and English. In 1875, a year after his semester in the shadow of Lotze, Haldane—still a matriculated student at both Edinburgh and Göttingen—travelled to Dresden, where, he tells us, 'I went because I wanted to read Philosophy in peace, and where I had no friend except the Professor of Philosophy in the Dresden Polytechnic'.[29] It is a comment that seems to sum up Haldane's attitude at the time: a total absorption in the quiet con-templation of the foundations of reality. It stands in stark contrast with the stress and business of the London life that was soon to come upon him. But we should not be too quick to place this early commitment to a secluded life of the mind as somehow in tension with what was to come. It is likely that Haldane saw it as a kind of preparation, a bulwark against the inevitable fluctuations of future success and failure, a grounding in the values and eternal verities which made sense of the social and political actions that would form his public life. And well grounded he became. Upon the completion of his studies at Edinburgh, Haldane swept the board of university prizes, winning the Bruce of Grangehill Medal in Philosophy, the Gray Scholarship and the Ferguson Scholarship in Philosophy of the four Scottish universities. Haldane's talent was obvious, but what did he actually believe?

* * *

Trying to summarise Haldane's philosophical views is no easy thing; nor is it something of which he himself would have entirely approved. He believed that philosophy was a lifetime's work and that its results were achieved through diligent systematic study.[30] Yet he, too, found himself summarising the products of his own systematic reading, time and again reiterating his central philosophical tenets in articles, talks and books. Though it is true that he was once accused of creating a 'lucid fog' when he spoke in public,[31] there are certain notions which are readily grasp-able for each of us and vital, as I have said, to any understanding of his life and statesmanship.

It might seem sensible to begin by asking what, for Haldane, was the purpose of philosophy. On his terms, one key function of philosophy was its ability to recover and harmonise all the many differing viewpoints within the world,[32] including the differing viewpoints of science and phi-losophy which began our discussion. Haldane argued that if we consider the workings of the mind closely and carefully enough—with philosophi-cal rigour, that is—we discover that all individual views of the world sim-ply represent what he called different 'categories' or 'degrees' within real-ity, which are determined by the purposes we have in mind when we engage with the world before us. This may sound strange, but consider this book in your hands. Most likely, you currently see it as something that gives you information about an Edwardian statesman, as you are reading the book with the view to find out more about this man named Haldane, and so you focus on the words on the page and their meanings. Consequently, you are paying attention to very few aspects of the rich, complex world before you. You are unlikely to be concentrating on the quality and make-up of the paper or the measurements of the margins. But imagine you were to look at the book with a view to painting it, perhaps as part of a wider self-portrait. All of a sudden you see the book differ-ently. You no longer seek to absorb the meaning of the words on the page, but notice the shadow that falls on the paper, the curves and lines of the typeface, the way the book contrasts in shape and colour with the desk behind it. This experiment can be repeated with numerous other modes of engagement—as a copy-editor, a book-binder, a translator, and so on. The point is that in each of these cases the book is seen differently depending on the purpose with which one approaches it. In each case, what is seen is real, and has just as much validity and truth as any other perception. No one, therefore, can claim to have exhaustively observed the book.

This view allows multiple versions of reality to co-exist without being in tension, and it again accords with some of the latest science. Take Hawking and Mlodinow's model-dependent realism: 'According to model-dependent realism, it is pointless to ask whether a model is real, only whether it agrees with observation. If there are two models that both agree with observation ... then one cannot say that one is more real than another.'[33] We do well to think through the implications of this for today, but Haldane's rendering of this point had important consequences in his own context. If this is a true way of understanding human interaction with the world then there is no contest or tension between the differing view-points, say, of the scientist, the philosopher, the religious person. Each viewpoint is simply a representation of the different purposes with which they approach reality. In Haldane's time, when certain scientists were claiming (as some still do today) that their way, and their way only, allowed for a true understanding of reality, this philosophical insight served as a helpful rebuttal. Some, for example, argued that all reality could be understood in terms of what is called mechanism, where reality can be reduced to physical and chemical processes. Haldane used philosophy to fight strenuously against such a view, and for good reason. Not only did this make a mockery of the religious views of his forebears (I sometimes wonder if Haldane's philosophy is, in part, a veiled defence of his parents' piety), but it also went against the physiological findings of his brother, who discovered that organisms behave in ways that defy such reduction-ism. In line with his philosophy, Haldane did not consider mechanism as simply wrong; rather, it was right, but only up to a very limited point. Yes, physical and chemical processes were a key part of reality, but what about the many other valid aspects of existence? What became of the moral aspect of the world, or the aesthetic, or the religious? Were these all to be placed on the scrapheap as redundant and illusory? Haldane's emphatic response was no. He wanted to confirm that what he called 'the world as it seems' to the good person, the artist and the religious person is the world that we live in—just under different aspects, which are determined by the different purposes of each person. He was firmly against the attempt to reduce reality to one aspect. The biologist who reduces everything to physical processes simply sees one aspect of the world—valid as far as it goes, but in no way exhaustive. Each viewpoint is relative to the purposes and position of the person viewing the world.[34] No person can claim an absolute knowledge of anything. This is the reason Einstein's revolutionary theory of relativity—where spatio-temporal measurements are relative to the standpoint of the observer, and yet maintain their reality despite differing measurements—was so important to Haldane as a philosophical tool. It was the scientific manifestation of his wider philosophical principle.[35]

This deeply affected Haldane's understanding of what constitutes 'the truth'. For Haldane, truth must encompass the whole range of differing perspectives on that which is under consideration. Truth is not to be determined simply by our standard scientific measuring equipment. This can be crucial, but there are so many other forms of truth, before which such equipment stands helpless. It is worthwhile quoting, in this respect, a lengthy section from the first volume of Haldane's *The Pathway to Reality* (originally his Gifford Lectures at the University of St Andrews). When we remember that these words were taken down by a copyist as he lectured from notes, it is possible to hear something of the living voice of Haldane in this passage:

> There is a form of truth which deserves the name just as much as the truth which measurement gives us, and that is the truth which we recognise in the perfection, say, of a great poem, of Shakespeare's Hamlet, of Milton's Lycidas, of Wordsworth's 'Lines written near Tintern Abbey'— or the truth which we recognise when we say of a great picture that it is inevitably painted as it is, and not otherwise—the truth which we find when we look at the expression on the face of the Virgin in one of Raphael's Madonnas, the consciousness of her great calling as the Mother of God, and the profound feeling with which that consciousness has filled her mind. Or take a sunset by Turner. There, again, we feel that to him Nature looked at that very instant as he has shewn her, and not otherwise, and that before us we have, in the deepest sense of the word, Truth. Or again, if we turn to the sphere of action, we find the truth in the

conduct of the men who charged at Balaclava, and who preferred duty to life; in the justice of Aristides; or in the character of Socrates; or in the surrender of self to God as manifested in the life of Jesus; or in the suppression of the will to live as shown through the career of Buddha. In all these facts there is that which appeals to our minds, to reason as well as to feeling, as indubitably the truth, and the truth in a sense which compels assent just as much as did the results we arrived at when we applied the balance, or the measuring rod, or the chronometer.[36]

If truth is so multifaceted, then it seems difficult to claim that the *complete* truth about anything can ever be finally attainable. Truth is something we move towards, but never totally grasp. The mind is ever dynamic, as it looks to gain fuller, more comprehensive understandings of the objects before it. In the case of the book in your hands, it is clear that once we have consulted you as a reader, we have only got a very limited notion of the book. As we go on to consult the artist, the copy-editor, the bookbinder, the translator, we discover that the truth of the book has developed and expanded.

The implications of this view for Haldane's statecraft are significant. When faced with a difficulty—say, the reorganisation of the army—his style was always to consult others, in this case the army's senior officers, each with their own specialist knowledge, adding new perspectives to his own, building a fuller picture of the problem and its possible solutions. His predecessors at the War Office, as we will see in Chapter 9, failed precisely because of their unwillingness to take this range of views seriously, clinging obstinately to their own ideas of what the army should be. But Haldane was wise enough to know he could never be in sole possession of the 'true', complete view of things. As he says: 'Reality is more than what in each case it has been taken by abstraction to be, and if it is so no single order of conceptions is adequate to complete explanation.'[37]

This tolerance—indeed, welcome—of others' conceptions of reality is also part of why Haldane worked so well with others, both within and outside his own political party. His friendships with leading Conservatives, for example, were key to his success as a statesman, and this is undoubtedly connected to his philosophical wariness about branding one view of reality 'right' and another 'wrong'. He was once accused of 'wanting to please everybody';[38] but it was more that he could see in almost every position something of value and wanted to foster that for the good of whatever cause was in question. Haldane himself saw the value of his philosophical training in this respect, as the following story, told by his friend Violet Markham, amusingly reveals:

> A Royal Commission, of which Philip Snowden was chairman, had been set up to discuss methods of entry, advancement, retirement and pensions for the Civil Service. Lord Haldane was one of the witnesses. After his examination he was about to leave the room when Snowden, whose acidity of speech was notorious, suddenly stopped him with the words, 'One minute, Lord Haldane; I want to ask you a question. Did you ever find that the study of philosophy was of any practical use to you when you were Secretary of State for War?' Haldane, with his hand on the door-knob turned and replied without a moment's hesitation: 'Well, Mr Snowden, my knowledge of philosophy, such as it is, taught me to lay my mind parallel to that of others; it taught me how to reconcile the opinions of my civil and military colleagues; and at times, Mr Snowden, at times, it made me patient when confronted with ignorance'. With these words the door quietly closed behind him.[39]

Haldane's political speeches are noted for their respect to his opponents, and his disagreements tended to arise not because he saw a direct clash between his 'truth' and his opponent's 'truth'. Rather, Haldane usually considered the fault of his opponent's position to lie in his or her limited view of the whole host of factors that needed to be taken into account; it was not that the position was simply 'wrong'. Haldane's claim to be in possession of a more reliable perspective rested on a belief in his having considered more of the key factors in question, building up a fuller understanding of the issue. It is a style of argumentation unfashionable today, given our penchant for polemics, but it is surely one from which we could learn.

* * *

Haldane's holistic vision, which sought to reconcile the many perspectives on the world, is informed by his lifelong immersion in the writings of the German philosopher G. W. F. Hegel (1770–1831), who is notoriously difficult to read and understand. Haldane 'once told Prof. J. H. Morgan that he had read Hegel's *Phenomenologie des Geistes* nineteen times'.[40] We won't get bogged down in the intricacies of the Hegelian system in this book, but we can at least comment on a central dimension of Hegel's thought, which enthralled Haldane, and towards which the above observations point. In expressing this thought, I draw upon Haldane's own reading of Hegel—something worth pointing out, given the immense variety of interpretations that exist. The seasoned philosophers amongst you will likely find fault in the simplicity of my presentation of his thinking here, but it is hard to approach this any other way if the ideas are to have a wide audience. For the subtleties and nuances of the arguments, Haldane's own books will amply provide more detail.[41]

Put simply, as Haldane understood him, Hegel considered mind to be at the foundation of reality—the reason he is known as a thinker within the Idealist tradition. For anything to be an object before you, your mind must play a constitutive part. Drawing on my previous example, for this book to be a book your mind has to make innumerable abstractions or distinctions. It has to distinguish paper from finger, desk from binding, colour from colour and so forth. This is all the work of the mind, according to Haldane's reading of Hegel. The book only becomes an object because of the mind. Objects do not, therefore, exist in and for themselves. That is not to say Hegel or Haldane would think that the book doesn't exist, that it is not real. The objective world is there, but it must always be considered as inseparable from your own subjective side. In other words, the world must have an objective side for your mind to work upon, but that objective side can never be considered as totally independent.

Haldane tried to avoid speaking of 'individual minds' or 'a mind', preferring simply 'mind'. This is to stop us thinking that mind is just another object within the world, which each of us possesses individually. For Haldane, again drawing on Hegel, mind is more akin to a process of distinguishing, abstracting, or judgment-making; a process in which we all share.[42] Surprisingly, it is here that God comes in. For Haldane, because mind is not an object in the world and because it undergirds all reality, he thinks of it as coterminous with God. But not a God as traditionally conceived by the Abrahamic faiths; a God, rather, that is totally immanent within the world. God is in no sense transcendent. The divine is within us, not beyond us. Avoiding the complexities of exactly how Haldane makes this identification of mind with God, the important thing for us to understand is that he believed, for serious philosophical reasons, that mind is unimaginably powerful; that God can be found if we look into our own selves; that all our actions, however humble, can connect us with God and God's realisation in the world.

For Haldane, the Hegelian claim that 'the spiritual alone is the real' was one of life's most vital truths. So important was it that he had it inscribed in the original German into the wood of his bookcase in the library at Cloan.[43] This conviction may again smack of anti-Realism, but that is not what Haldane had in mind (no pun intended!). Rather, he wanted to suggest that the universe is more than just matter and energy,[44] that it is in some sense underwritten by Spirit (*Geist* again), and that what is required for a truly fulfilling life is the attempt to live according to that Spirit. For Haldane, that attempt is characterised by a desire for 'the highest in quality and range',[45] which means self-renunciation in the cause of others (putting others before oneself, that is) and in the execution of one's duties. In this way, one transcends crude or material desires—fame, wealth etc.—and lives on what might be termed a spiritual plane. Paradoxically, we discover ourselves more fully by means of self-renunciation, as we encounter what is best and what is highest in us. It is a fundamentally humanising endeavour.

The striving for what is higher leads to an encounter with the Infinite. But such an encounter, cast in a Hegelian light, entails a paradox. It is only when we have accepted that our striving will never terminate in some perfected ideal (in God, in truth completely comprehended) that the ideal is encountered. To accept the impossibility of encounter, but to continue striving at the highest pitch—that is when we discover what is true and divine. Haldane states: 'It is in the quality of the struggle to attain it, and not in any finality we suppose ourselves to have reached and to be entitled to rest on, that truth consists for human beings.'[46] The consequences of this insight were momentous for Haldane's statesmanship. The immense industry of the man; the continual struggle for the best on behalf of others to the detriment of his own health and comfort;[47] the apparent serenity in the face of troubles—these can all be accounted for when we consider the philosophy that underpins his political activity. As Haldane once tellingly observed: 'It is the man who accepts his obligations to those around him, and who does his work in

99

his station, whatever that station may be, with indifference as to the consequence to himself and without thought of what may happen to him individually, who makes the real impression.'[48]

Haldane's exalted understanding of the human mind also helps us understand why he was at such pains to emphasise the power of thinking—it was at one with the divine! He had a profound faith in the capacity of thought to solve a problem, even the most intractable. Reflecting on his chairmanship of the Committee of Imperial Defence while in Cabinet in 1924, he comments in his *Autobiography*: 'The maxim I ventured to commend to them [the chiefs of staff of the three armed services] was based on old War Office experience, and I offered to have it put up in letters of gold. It was that "Thinking Costs Nothing."'[49] Haldane's success while Secretary of State for War lay in his ability to step back from the immediate confusion of things, consider the purpose for which the army was in existence, establish the principles upon which that purpose could be achieved, and then reorganise on that basis. His constant refrain at this time was 'think before you act'. This insistence was irreducibly tied to his study of Hegel. Haldane draws the link in his *Autobiography*:

> From an early stage I began to study the great principles on which Continental military organisations had been founded, as set forth by Clausewitz, Bronsart von Schellendorff, and Von der Goltz, with the description of Napoleon's mind in Yorck von Wartenburg's book, written from the standpoint of the German General Staff. ... But these works merely illustrated the necessity of careful thought before action. This was the lesson which I had learned early [as a philosophy student], and to apply it to the new question of Army reorganisation was a natural step. When the Army Council asked me one morning again for some notion of the Army I had in mind, my answer to them was, 'A Hegelian Army.' The conversation then fell off.[50]

Despite the classic complexities associated with the word, I don't think there is anything particularly complex in what Haldane means by 'A Hegelian Army'. All the indicators suggest that this, for Haldane, meant an army organised on rational principles, orientated towards a rational goal, with each part organically related—all of which could be accomplished if the best military and organisational minds could be dedicated to the task, which is precisely why Haldane gave pride of place to the General Staff.[51]

Just as importantly, Haldane's identification of mind with God gets to the heart of why he cared so much about every class within society. He genuinely believed in the equal dignity of every human being. If minds were not objects in the world, which could, as it were, be lined up next to each other; if they all, instead, represented degrees within the one divine mind, then the possibility of denigrating some person or class of people as unimportant or worthless was out of the question.

* * *

But Haldane didn't just focus on Hegel's understanding of mind—though this is what comes up most prominently in his philosophical books. His understanding of the state is also deeply indebted to his philosophical hero. Indeed, fashioning a proper understanding of the state was crucial in seeking to honour the insight into the equal dignity of human beings mentioned above. We will look in Part 2 of this book at the way in which Haldane's philosophy of the state worked itself out in practice, but it is appropriate to outline the philosophical side of it here.

Freedom is the dominant principle underlying Haldane's concept of the state. The obvious question to ask is how the state—a word so evocative of monolithic, overbearing control—can possibly foster freedom. As the great Genevan philosopher Jean-Jacques Rousseau once put it: 'The problem is to find a form of association which will defend and protect with the whole common force the person and goods of each associate, and in which each, while uniting himself with all, may still obey himself alone, and remain as free as before.'[52] According to Haldane's philosophical ally Bernard Bosanquet, one can trace from Rousseau—through Kant, Hegel and Fichte—a concern to establish the whole of political philosophy upon the notion that freedom is the essence of human nature.[53] It would make sense, therefore, if the state allowed for that essence to be expressed to the fullest degree. But surely this can only lead to anarchy? The British Idealists—who, as you will remember, could count Bosanquet and Haldane within their number— drew particularly on Hegel here to show that this assumption was misplaced. According to Hegel, the state or, in the following quotation, the 'universal' is what makes freedom possible:

The state is the actuality of concrete freedom. But concrete freedom consists in this, that personal individuality and its particular interests not only achieve their complete development and gain explicit recognition for their right ... but, for one thing, they also pass over of their own accord into the interest of the universal, and, for another thing, they know and will the universal; they even recognize it as their own substantive mind; they take it as their end and aim and are active in its pursuit.[54]

Haldane, whose debt to T. H. Green's reading of Hegel is apparent throughout his reflections on the state, put this in his own unique way:

Knowledge is power, but knowledge must not be merely abstract and material; it must be knowledge of those things that are high and spiritual, a knowledge that tells men and women that the State is largely their own lives, and that their own lives are a trust to be carried out for the benefit of those around them as well as for themselves.[55]

What seems to be implied is that notions of freedom which focus on self-satisfaction at the expense of others are not really representative of freedom at all; or if they are, then they are representative of the most undeveloped form of freedom and are deeply deficient. It is only when we begin to will in common with others that we begin to discover 'concrete freedom'. It is in this context that rights develop (and therefore duties too); that we are able to create conditions—in the form of schools or healthcare systems, for example—capable of catering for our needs as human beings; that we can pursue our ends without the continual disruption and derailment that comes from a multitude of other competing ends. In short, when we will in common with others we find we are able to be ourselves more fully. By the British Idealists' account, the ability to be oneself, and to be oneself with and for others, *is* freedom.

If the state is the manifestation of that communal willing then we could say with Haldane's fellow Idealist, Henry Jones, that the state and the citizen are like the concave and convex sides of a circle; both 'share the same destiny. ... The state exists to provide the conditions and means for the development of citizens.'[56] But given the great mass of people that make up a state, how is it possible for those needs for development to find expression? In answering this question we come to one of the vital philosophical terms of the time, a term much admired by Haldane but today fallen out of use: the General Will (*volonté générale* for Rousseau; *der allge-*

meine Wille for Hegel). In Rousseau's conception, as Haldane acknowledges, the 'General Will ... represents what is greater than the individual volition of those who compose the society of which it is the will'.[57] It is the will that represents the best interests of the people as determined by the people as they will together, in opposition to any individual person's purely self-interested or selfish will. It is to be distinguished from a simple 'aggregate of voices',[58] which may flare up from time to time, while not according with the best interests of the community. This would be more like 'a numerical sum of individual wills'[59] (Rousseau's *volonté de tous*, 'the will of all'), and would lack that sense of a will which rises above 'our ordinary habits of mind', such as the General Will often does. This will is particularly evident in times of national crisis, Haldane claims. In these times, it is not unusual to see a nation pulling together in remarkable ways, willing and performing acts of heroism or sacrifice that would, in less extreme circumstances, never cross the minds of the men and women who make up that nation. But, for Haldane, even in less extreme times, the General Will is still operative, just perhaps less easy to discern.[60]

We can make it sound less grand and perhaps more accessible if we simply see it as a manifestation of public opinion. This appears to be how Haldane conceptualised it, switching happily between the terms General Will, general opinion and public opinion. For most of us today this doesn't sound like much of a clarification. The enormous diversity of opinions and the compromised nature of the channels through which we discover those opinions appear to obliterate any chance of uncovering an analysable public viewpoint. But Haldane, returning to his favourite theme of 'mind', counters this both by pointing out the significant identities that exist between minds and by providing examples which reinforce the existence of a working public opinion, while admitting the immense difficulty in uncovering what exactly that opinion is.

On the identities between minds, Haldane would remind us of the almost infinite number of concepts we share uncontested which allow us to communicate meaningfully with each other. When we speak to another person about a table, or a chair or a mirror, and indeed most objects in the world, we are confident that we shall be understood because of the identities in our thinking about these things. Yes, there will be some divergence in our concepts when we first think of certain objects—whether the table is round or square, or made of wood or metal—but the chances are that the similarities are greater in number: that it has legs, is a solid structure, can balance things, is an accessible height, belongs in a variety of settings etc. These identities in thought show us that our minds are not atoms, cut off one from the other, but are attuned to the same world and, sharing the same systems of thought, are in unison about much of that world. If such is the case, what is to stop opinions cohering in the same way and forming something of a 'general' manner? 'If minds are no longer thought of as exclusive things', writes Haldane, 'with separate spatial and temporal positions, the doctrine of a general will becomes less difficult.'[61]

As for examples that illustrate the existence, admittedly difficult to decipher, of an operative public opinion, Haldane points out, in an article of 1896, the way in which the nation had witnessed 'great changes in public opinion' as a result of 'the failure of a potato crop, the perpetration of atrocities in the East, the return of an Irish party with preponderating numbers'.[62] He also draws attention, in a much later piece of writing, to the obvious case of national elections as a means of seeing public opinion at work, but is happy to concede that this raises a host of ambiguities (which we would do well to bear in mind when considering the history of Brexit) and that it takes a great statesman to get at what is essential within that opinion:

> It is not enough to say that in the ballot boxes a numerical majority of votes for a particular plan was found. For it may have become obvious that these votes did not represent a clear and enduring state of mind. The history of the questions at such an election and the changes in their context have therefore to be taken into account. A real majority rule is never a mere mob rule. The people is not a simple aggregate of momentary voices but is a whole, and it is this character that governs its manifestations of opinion. Representative and responsible government is thus a complicated and difficult matter, and, if it is to be adequately carried out, requires great tact and insight, as well as great courage; qualities which the people of a country like our own have become trained to understand and to appreciate. No abstract rules for interpretation can take the place of these essential qualities of character in the statesman.[63]

These qualities were important to Haldane because he found in public opinion the true source of sovereignty, and so deemed essential the existence of those capable of discerning its character and movements. It is, of course, a major claim to say that sovereignty resides in public opinion. Surely, in a case such as the Great Britain of Haldane's time, it was in the sovereign (the name seems to give it away), or at least in his or her government ministers, that sovereignty inhered. Haldane argues to the contrary because the existence of a monarchy depends on the acceptance, usually tacit, of the public, and this acceptance is even more crucial in the case of a government, which relies on the consent of the governed in a very evident fashion.[64] We know from history that when a sovereign or a government fails drastically in the eyes of the people dramatic upheavals are possible and the true source of sovereignty, in Haldane's view, reveals itself. The French Revolution is an extreme case in point.

In this light, it becomes clear just how important it is for the state to advance the interests of the citizens who make up that state. As Hegel commented: 'The state is actual only when its members have a feeling of their own self-hood and it is stable only when public and private ends are identical.'[65] One way to ensure that private ends are expressed in a way that is in keeping with the best interests of the whole is to decentralise governmental structures and devolve political power in an attempt to resist the imposition of top-down decisions. Again, Haldane was not unique in advocating such dispersal of power. Hegel had argued, despite at times promoting a strong centralised state,[66] that 'the proper strength of the state' lies in the outworking of the interests of local associations, as manifestations of individual wills working and willing in common with others.[67] Likewise, though disagreeing with Hegel and his followers on the possibility of a General Will,[68] the group known as the British Pluralists— notably Frederic Maitland and Haldane's close associate Harold Laski— saw in associations and local group life signs of communal willing. For the Pluralists, the balanced co-existence of such groups was the key to a well-ordered society.[69] Above these perspectives rose the distinctive voice of Mary Follett, the organisational theorist much revered by Haldane.[70] Haldane's preface to Follett's *The New State* is a powerful example of his ability to hold a range of opinions in harmony, where the best in Monist and Pluralist thinking—the former seeing state power as inherent in one source, the latter in many sources—is gathered up into a distinctive standpoint. Follett is viewed as prophet and ally. 'The cardinal doctrine of her book is that the state is what its members make it to be', observes

Haldane.[71] The practical consequences of that doctrine struck Haldane as particularly important; he quotes Follett as follows:

> Neighbourhood education and neighbourhood organisation is then the pressing problem of 1918. All those who are looking towards a real democracy, not the pretense of one which we have now, feel that the most imminent of our needs is the awakening and invigorating, the educating and organising of the local unit. All those who in the humblest way, in settlement or community centre, are working for this, are working at the greatest political problem of the twentieth century.[72]

Where Follett markedly differs from the pluralists is in her belief in the perniciousness of balancing power and wills.[73] This puts competition at the heart of the state, as each group competes against the others to have just the right amount of power that is their due. Follett, on the other hand, believed that the will of each human person and group could find its completion, and therefore freedom, in harmonious relationships with other human wills.[74] This may be overly idealistic on the practical level—though Follett evidently didn't think so—but we can at least see that she was driving at a much more positive kind of relationship between individuals and between groups than was the case with the pluralists, who were more likely to stress the difficult realities of living and working together.[75] In everything we read by Haldane we see shining through a similar positivity to Follett's and a similar emphasis on the importance of the individual's place within the whole.[76] Yet, Haldane's realism is perhaps more evident than hers. His statement on equality is characteristic and is likely to be indicative of his attitude regarding harmonious relationships between human wills: 'How is equality to be realized? The fact that it can never be obtained, that the natural differences in the intellectual and moral capacities of individuals render it a goal never to be reached, does not in the least diminish the obligations to strive after it.'[77]

* * *

Chapter 10 will show how Haldane's insights into the nature of the state worked themselves out in practice. We can now step back and ask ourselves whether all this philosophising alienates us from the Haldanean approach or whether it draws us to it. If you find yourself in the former camp, then it is worth bearing in mind that Haldane's passion for philosophy did not cancel out a love of literature, particularly poetry. In fact, he believed that the best poetry offered another route into the findings of philosophy:

> Of God we can have no pictorial vision. ... The symbols of art and religion enable us to have a vivid sense of his nature. We require their constant aid, even if we cannot ask them for a satisfying view of the foundations of the real [as we *can* do with philosophy, Haldane suggests]. If we have that aid we can find him in the objects of our daily experience.[78]

Haldane's philosophical books are packed with quotations from his favourite poets, most notably Goethe, Robert Browning, Wordsworth and Emily Brontë. He saw this as a way of allowing his readers flashes of the deeper insights he had achieved through long philosophical study. Poems take us to the heart of the matter in a direct fashion. He loves to quote, for example, Wordsworth on the

> Sense sublime
> Of something far more deeply interfused,
> Whose dwelling is the light of setting suns,
> And the round ocean and the living air,
> And the blue sky and in the mind of man;
> A motion and a spirit that impels
> All thinking things, all objects of all thought,
> And rolls through all things.

Having given these lines from 'Tintern Abbey', Haldane exclaims: 'Ah! In the poets, when at their best, we have the discernment of what has been the last, and perhaps the highest, result of the greatest speculative thinking in the history of Philosophy.'[79] He was often found quoting Emily Brontë's 'Last Lines', as one of the greatest examples of how death should be met and of the relationship between God and the human person.

> No coward soul is mine,
> No trembler in the world's storm-troubled sphere
> I see Heaven's glories shine,
> And faith shines equal, arming me from fear.
>
> O God, within my breast
> Almighty, ever-present Deity!

Life that in me has rest
As I—undying Life—have power in Thee.

Vain are the thousand creeds
That move men's hearts, unutterably vain;
Worthless as withered weeds,
Or idlest froth amid the boundless main,

To waken doubt in one
Holding so fast by Thine Infinity,
So surely anchored on
The steadfast rock of immortality.

With wide-embracing love
Thy Spirit animates eternal years,
Pervades, and broods above,
Changes, sustains, dissolves, creates, and rears.

Though earth and man were gone,
And suns and universes ceased to be,
And Thou wert left alone,
Every existence would exist in Thee.

There is not room for Death,
Nor atom that his might could render void,
Thou, Thou art Being and Breath,
And what Thou art may never be destroyed.

Haldane, who quoted the lines in his third Gifford Lecture at St Andrews in 1902, said of the poem: 'Certainly speculative poetry has rarely reached a higher intellectual level than in this dying outburst. It contains the teaching of Aristotle transferred from the abstract to the concrete.'[80] Violet Bonham Carter, daughter of H. H. Asquith, fondly recalled: 'I have vivid memories of walks with him [Haldane] at Cloan up steep and heathery hillsides. While I panted breathless in his wake he ambled rapidly ahead reciting Goethe and Emily Brontë without a pause for word or breath. The line "Changes, sustains, dissolves, creates and rears" still conjures up for me the vision of Haldane's back topping the sky-line.'[81]

The poem's reference to death is enlightening because it hints at Haldane's apparently fearless attitude to this event, and again resonates with a feature of his statesmanship. The serenity that characterised Haldane's approach to politics (his adversaries sometimes confused it with smugness) and the sense of repose he maintained throughout most of the war were dispositions forged by a belief that even the most terrifying eventualities—death included—were not to be considered as ultimate. They had only a relative importance. In the final analysis, they remained abstractions of mind. 'Death', Haldane once commented with scriptural relish, 'loses much of its sting and the grave of its victory' when we consider it in these terms. He explains further:

> The contrast, after all, between life and death is a contrast which is made within self-consciousness. Self-consciousness is not itself an event in time. It is that within which the world of events in time falls. This does not mean that the contrast between life and death does not exist. It does exist, but it presents its appearance of finality only for a comprehension which is not complete, and which therefore corresponds only to a degree in reality.[82]

This is one reason why, for Haldane, education was so crucial. We shall look at his understanding of education fully in Chapter 8, but we can point out here that he gives the topic primacy precisely because he considers it to be that which facilitates the mind to progress towards an ever more comprehensive vision of reality, one which does not become stuck on one degree. Of course, he was also deeply aware of the economic importance of an educated public; this was part of why he laid stress on options for technical vocational and scientific training, as well as a broader humanistic education. But on an even more fundamental level, he knew—from personal experience—that a good education could provide the resources by which one could rise above the troubles and tragedies of the everyday. This was not only the path to a calm, strong, courageous and successful person; this was the path to a nation's prosperity too. No wonder he poured his energy into the cause of education for men, women and children of every class within society. To be educated is to be given the opportunity for emancipation from those blinkered views that keep us from truly realising our potential.[83] It does not guarantee such emancipation, of course, but it does make it more readily attainable.[84]

To talk philosophically of rising above the circumstance of the everyday should not, however, blind us to the fact that Haldane's desire to transcend daily trials is deeply rooted in his own familial and emotional experiences. In other words, it does not arise purely from philosophical reflection. On

109

the one hand there was the resignation to divine Providence that was a trademark of his family's Calvinism. As Stephen Koss notes: 'The resigned acceptance of personal and professional misfortune was an integral part of the religious ethic that dominated Lord Haldane's life by its influences, if not by its formal doctrines.'[85] The Haldane family single-word motto— 'Suffer'—is therefore entirely apt. As we have seen, the loss of his brother Geordie, and two failed romantic endeavours, were critical in the formation of Haldane's approach to the sorrows of existence. Philosophy helped him construct an intellectual framework to deal with such sorrow, but it was not necessarily philosophy that convinced him of the importance of doing so. In other words, he felt loss and pain deeply, and this may have compelled him towards intellectual coping mechanisms (though he clearly had a natural propensity towards philosophy, too). As we saw in Edward Grey's words at the opening of this chapter, Haldane found in philosophy 'a real support in the trials and storms of life. When these beat upon him, he had the large view that transcends consideration of personal fortunes.' Grey goes on to add: 'His philosophy supported him also in times of personal grief or physical pain.'[86] Indeed, Haldane told his mother in 1890, 'I begin to realise that we as a family feel things more than other people. This was so with yourself and my father, and it has descended.'[87] The emotional world that we explored in Chapter 2 should not be forgotten as an important component of his engagement with philosophy. The most abstract of Haldane's thoughts were always based in the concrete world of human interaction. In the next chapter, we will discover that it is precisely in this concern to do justice to the challenges and possibilities of everyday life that his economic thinking was based.

5

WEALTH AND THE NATION

Economic activity should always be carried on consistently with the greatest social purposes, and its rewards should be, as far as possible, rewards for real service rendered whether by hand or by brain.

Haldane, Introduction to Mary Follett's *The New State*[1]

In March 1874 Haldane wrote a letter on the nature of his emerging philosophy of life to his illustrious uncle, John Burdon Sanderson. For a young man, still only seventeen years old and about to depart his native land for the University of Göttingen, it is remarkably mature:

It is just at that period of life at which I have now arrived that one first begins to know a little, though a very little, of the world and of himself. Even this small insight into the nature of things was with me, though I know it to be very superficial, sufficient to bring on an attack of the malady, so prevalent among human beings, disgust with the world and after that with self. This for a time gained ground with me and even, I must admit, caused me to wish that I might be fortunate enough to quit the stage before coming in contact with the realities of what seemed an uncomfortable and heartless world.[2] Here it was that the path was made rather clearer by my getting hold of John Stuart Mill's autobiography,[3] for reflection upon this and one or two other biographies has shown me that selfishness lies at the bottom of this view of life. Surely one must have a part to play, however humble it may be, in society, and he can only fulfil his duty by thinking of mankind as a whole, and not merely of himself. I can honestly say that I have derived consolation from this, and believe, moreover, that it is my duty not so much to lament the imperfection of any theory of life I can form, but to try to do what little I see and feel to be right, as well and disinterestedly as possible.

Haldane professed himself glad to have made up his mind upon the law as his future profession, 'as it would seem to be one salutary to myself, and where abundant opportunities occur for doing a little for humanity'. Haldane continues:

> I feel the good effect of having a definite object before me, and just think the sooner I come in contact with life through it, the better. Philosophy especially concerns me, but all manner of culture, both scientific and literary, seems necessary to the attainment of my ideal, to be as far as I can a good and useful example to humanity.[4]

We must, of course, pitch the whole of Haldane's subsequent professional and public life in the context of this desire; but as we come to consider his economic thinking and his interactions with the business world they take on a pronounced relevance. Profit-making and the amassing of wealth were of little value to him. Rather, the idea of disinterested service to others was his liberation and modus operandi. And it was in light of this idea that the relations of capital to labour, tariff reforms, the interactions between the private and public sector, and the many other economic and business considerations that Haldane tackled presented themselves. His aim was emphatically not 'simply to provide the best conditions for the operation of the Darwinian process of survival of the fittest to produce and accumulate'.[5] He resisted to the end a form of individualism which saw human beings as little more than what he called 'wealth-producing animals' in competition with each other.[6] But he knew that a sound financial footing was necessary for any state to flourish, and he poured a vast sum of his energy into keeping Britain at the forefront of good, sane economic thinking.

It was a sanity much needed. When he arrived in London three years after having written to his uncle with such high ideals, the capital was awash with discontent. After the relative gentility of Edinburgh's New Town and the quiet of the Ochil Hills at Cloan, he rapidly came face to face with poor public health and poverty, the great human difficulties facing the working classes, and the extraordinary contrasts in quality of life between, and even within, the different boroughs of London. Evidently, an unqualified capitalism had become deeply problematic. Socialist thinking was taking root in ways that many of Haldane's peers found threatening, as the established class system began to crack under the burden of a demographic that had found its voice. The emergence of the trade unions and a nascent Labour Party were beginning to dislodge a complacent Liberalism and anger an entitled Conservatism. Haldane, through his growing friendships with the likes of the socialist Webbs on the one hand and the Conservative A. J. Balfour on the other, found himself playing—as he would so often throughout his long career—the constructive mediator.

* * *

But to play mediator Haldane had to know the intellectual nuances of each side, and he was never one to remain ignorant for long. Property law was one contested area that he swiftly mastered. He became an expert in conveyancing, so much so that, in April 1882, the Lord Advocate, J. B. Balfour[7] (not to be confused with the Conservative prime minister A. J. Balfour), wrote to the Council of the Incorporated Law Society, together with William Barber, Haldane's pupil master of 1877/8, recommending Haldane as a candidate for the lectureship on Real Property Law and Conveyancing which had become vacant.[8] His knowledge is reflected in his early intervention as an MP in the debates on the economic importance of the Irish Land Act of 1887, where he characteristically brought to bear his professional work in the law upon a practical political economy for Ireland. It is clear that he understood the importance of sound property law as a central pillar of a healthy society, but he was not convinced that the ownership of private property was an unmitigated good. As we will see in our analysis of Haldane's Land Bill of 1892 later in this chapter, he was quite aware of the damaging effects of private property situated on the edges of growing towns and cities when it prevented local councils from responding to the demand for workmen's housing and local amenities. Nationalisation of the land was, in his view, clearly impractical, but a middle course could be sought, allowing compulsory purchase of land in necessary cases. This balanced thinking was early informed by voracious reading. We know for sure that Haldane was reading Henry Sidgwick's new book *The Principles of Political Economy* in the late spring of 1883, and it is likely he was familiar with Henry George's highly influential *Progress and Poverty* (1879), in which George argues, as Haldane would go on to do, that the economic rent (any unearned income) of land should be shared by society.[9] Indeed, the breadth of Haldane's reading must have been exceptional if we believe his revelation to his aunt Jane in October 1884: 'Politics have kept such a possession of me that I have been averaging a volume a day of biographies and histories since I came up.'[10]

This reading would prove to be very useful by the time Haldane began his political career. The economy was in 'the trough of a business slump' when he entered Parliament in 1885.[11] Thirty-eight out of fifty chambers of commerce, from which information had been requested by the recently appointed Royal Commission on the Depression of Trade and Industry, had responded by saying that the industries in their areas were in significant distress. With trade union unemployment itself at over 10 per cent, angry demonstrations took place across the country, and these continued intermittently for two years. Riots in February 1886 in Trafalgar Square resulted in shops in Pall Mall and Piccadilly being robbed in broad daylight. The public were at once fearful of revolution and concerned at the conditions suffered by the 'underclass' of casual labourers in many of the big cities.

Haldane did not remain aloof. A year after the riots, on 13 November 1887, another attempt was made to hold a meeting in Trafalgar Square, this time in defiance of an order made by the commissioner of police—a day that came to be known, as have other days, as 'Bloody Sunday'. John Burns, who would subsequently sit alongside Haldane in Campbell-Bannerman's 1906 Cabinet, and the Liberal MP Robert Cunninghame Graham had been invited by the Social Democratic Federation to speak to the protestors. The two men tried to address the meeting in an angry atmosphere of police restraint and vicious street fighting. Haldane had got to know Graham through his visits to the impoverished regions of south and east London. After Burns and Graham had been arrested on a charge of incitement to disturbance, later reduced to unlawful assembly, Haldane would not leave Graham in the lurch, despite his feeling that the two accused had acted foolishly. He stood bail for him. At the subsequent trial at the Central Criminal Court, Asquith appeared for Graham and Burns, and Haldane gave evidence on their behalf.[12] But the men were both convicted and sent to prison for six weeks. Asquith's son Herbert recalled that this incident first brought Asquith to public attention as an advocate, and pointed out the sequel to this case, five years later, when the young counsel had become home secretary.[13] Asquith then ordered that Trafalgar Square might be used for weekend and bank holiday meetings in daylight, thus embedding the subsequent practice of free speech in Trafalgar Square.

Haldane was not one to wash his hands of those who adopted a radical stance. His involvement with the Workers' Educational Association, his visits to Canon Barnett at Toynbee Hall, and, perhaps most significantly, his lifelong friendship with the social reformers Sidney and Beatrice Webb were characteristic of this. Each of these contacts shared that most admirable of qualities to Haldane: the ability to take real, if incremental, steps towards radical change within the realms of practical educational, social and political action. A further attractive aspect about the Webbs was their desire to root their arguments and practices in sound data; in fact, it was this desire that lay behind the creation of the London School of Economics, and it is no wonder that Haldane wanted to play a part in that process. For Haldane the statesman, a mastery of political economy was essential if the challenges of the day were to be met. Bearing in mind the atmosphere of tension between capital and labour that gripped the country; Haldane's own position of tension between the great figures on both sides of the debate; and his passion for building an educated public, capable of thinking through and beyond the complexities of the issues involved—remembering all this, we are not surprised that Haldane should turn, as the tensions grew, to a close study of the greatest thinker on political economy that Britain could boast of, publishing his *Life of Adam Smith* in 1887. It was his first sole-author monograph. At thirty-one years of age, Haldane was returning to first principles.

* * *

Haldane set out to investigate a number of foundational questions. What is the nature of economic activity? What are the building blocks of capitalism? What can the state do to enable growth and investment whilst ensuring an appropriate social responsibility? In choosing to study Smith (1723–90) and to make him the subject of his first full-length book, Haldane was both typically thorough and far-sighted and, as in all of his enthusiasms, character-revealing. We find revealed here the principles underlying the economic foundations of the state and society that were to be such an inspiration to Haldane. Indeed, the sweep of Smith's grand vision was to influence Haldane throughout his life.

It was no mere accident that Haldane selected Smith as his subject. He agreed with Thomas Carlyle on the importance of 'hero worship', and chose his own heroes carefully.[14] Upon their thinking he built his own. The book was also a form of homage to Haldane and Smith's Scottish roots. Smith's birthplace, Kirkcaldy, is, as the crow flies, only a dozen miles from Haldane's birthplace in Charlotte Square, Edinburgh, close enough indeed for David Hume, when writing to his friend and confidant Smith from his new house in the Old Town of Edinburgh, to say how glad he was 'to have come within sight of you, and to have a view of Kirkcaldy from my windows'.[15] Haldane's Perthshire home Cloan in turn was only 20 miles north-west of Kirkcaldy. The lives of both Smith and Haldane were embedded in strong and supportive matriarchal homes. Neither man married and both were devoted to their mothers, Smith sharing a house with his mother for sixty-one of his sixty-seven years and Haldane for sixty-nine of his seventy-two. Both had a deep interest in moral philosophy, Smith occupying the chair of Moral Philosophy at Glasgow whilst Haldane was offered that chair at St Andrews in 1905, after delivering the Gifford Lectures there (though he sensibly but reluctantly turned the offer down). Both were passionately wedded to the cause of the education of society, Smith as the thinking political economist and Haldane as the practising political philosopher.

In February 1792, two years after Smith's death, William Pitt the Younger hailed the Scot's 'extensive knowledge of detail and philosophical research' as that which would 'furnish the best solution to every question connected to the history of commerce or with the systems of political economy'.[16] The Nobel Laureate Amartya Sen, commenting 226 years later on Jesse Norman's excellent 2018 book *Adam Smith: What he Thought and Why it Matters*, declared that Smith's insights can help us solve some of the most difficult social and economic problems of our contemporary world. This astonishing sense of Smith's abiding relevance was not missed by Haldane, but he regretted that Smith's work was not better known and that the records of his life were so meagre. This was another reason why he set out to bring Smith's life and work alive. Haldane desired, in other words, to make his hero our hero—using this word quite explicitly.[17] His admiration was plain to see: 'No man in modern times has said more with so much effect within the compass of one book.'[18] Yet Haldane lamented that 'as we become removed by an ever-increasing distance from the prejudices and opinions which Adam Smith once for all shattered, their magnitude and importance appear to grow smaller'. He recognised that even the battle between free trade and protection would 'never again be fought on the ground from which Smith drove his opponents',[19] yet the relevance of his approaches in Haldane's own setting remained. The future was to prove Haldane right. In 1903, fifteen years after the publication of Haldane's *Life of Adam Smith*, Chamberlain would split the Conservative Party over protectionism. It was arguably the greatest issue of the day, and paved the way for the Liberal victory of 1906, their subsequent nine years of government, and Haldane's own years of office.

Haldane held that one of the secrets of the great popularity of *The Wealth of Nations* was the concrete quality through which the author united in himself two powers which do not often go together: the power of abstract thinking, and that of grasping facts with a keen interest in them merely as facts. Smith 'had a perception that abstract propositions, however carefully stated, can express only one aspect or side of things, and are therefore wanting in truth, a quality which belongs to what is concrete alone'.[20] Haldane shrewdly observed that abstractions are useful servants, but bad masters. Smith's digressions, sometimes long-winded but always profitable, into discussions of 'those real details of commerce and politics which are so rarely subjected to any scientific treatment' were a principal merit of the book.[21] Haldane—that expert negotiator of messy practicalities and therefore an expert in making things happen—was naturally in sympathy with such an approach. He asserts that 'it cannot be too constantly borne in mind that political economy is not politics; that in politics we are bound to take into account the whole of the springs of action, and that so certainly as we proceed by the method of political economy, looking at one aspect only at a time, so certainly shall we come to political grief'.[22] This is remarkably pragmatic and down-to-earth for a young MP only two years in the House of Commons. One can't help feeling that this—what shall we call it?—realism lies at the heart of so much of Haldane's later political success. Haldane's friend, the much older John Morley, was to make roughly the same point in different words when he wrote: 'Improvisation has far more to do in politics than historians or other people think.'[23] Haldane, devoted to the German Idealists, was indeed a great lover of systems; but he was also a disciple of Smith, master of the concrete and the real, and so he knew that if one failed to show flexibility when facing the unpredictable, through intransigent loyalty to a system, then the system would be proved pointless in any case.

Haldane's later reflections on the budget of 1902 serve as a good example of this realism and adaptability. In a speech in the House of Commons that April, he gave the following reason for rejecting indirect taxation (VAT would be a modern example of such a tax):

> There may be times when, from the necessities of the case, you must resort to indirect taxation upon the food of the people. I am no dogmatist or fanatic in these matters, but I for one would consent to such a duty only with the greatest reluctance. I should only consent after there had been a most careful preliminary inquiry to show not only that such taxation was absolutely necessary, but on whose shoulders the burden would fall. Many people in this country live on the narrowest margin of subsistence, and a tax of this kind falls on the poor of this country with a weight which has no parallel in any other tax. Have the Government made such exhaustive inquiries that they are enabled to say that they have got adequate knowledge on this topic?[24]

For Haldane, if one is going to make an argument for a particular tax it must not be built on fancy or on an idealised conception of things; it must be rooted in reality, and its consequences have to be thought through to the end—indeed, they must be thought through in relation to the whole spectrum of society. Haldane wanted the government to exercise its powers in a way that responded responsibly to what the nation was actually capable of delivering. It was inappropriate to impose a theoretical solution to a problem, if that solution was removed from the practical facts. The government must determine the actual parameters for action, before implementing policy.

Alongside a respect for the concrete realities of the day, we find in *The Wealth of Nations* a number of key doctrines that Haldane kept close to his heart during the years in which he influenced the political and social policy of Britain. Pre-eminent in importance was the theory of the division of labour—allowing for specialisation in particular tasks—and the galvanising force of trade as the cornerstone of economic growth.[25] The greater the size of the market, the greater the opportunity for capturing the benefits of the division of labour. Free trade was part of keeping the market as wide as possible. But Haldane saw that it carried with it dangers which had to be balanced with the benefits. Whilst it benefitted the poorer classes through reductions in food prices it also put a downward pressure on wages to provide a competitive edge to home manufacturing in relation to overseas competitors. For Haldane, and to some extent for Smith too, the doctrine of free trade had to be balanced with other complementary and, where necessary, mitigating policies. The rights of the workers; their hours of employment; their health, education and social conditions; the split of economic value between the wage earner and the capital provider; and the welfare of the community through such provisions as the poor laws—each of these were to be central themes of his life, and the implementation of free trade had to be thought through in relation to them.

Haldane also places focus on Smith's views on individual liberty and the roles of the sovereign and of the state. Smith emphasises the importance of natural liberty, in a manner that is perhaps different from the more collectivist utterances that we often find Haldane making.[26] In Smith's view, each of us, so long as we do not violate the laws of justice, should be left perfectly free to pursue our own interest in our own way, and to bring both our industry and our capital into competition with those of any other person, or group of people. 'The sovereign should be completely discharged from any duty directing or superintending the industry of private people towards employments considered most suitable to the interests of society.'[27] The individualism of Smith, however, is not dogmatic—it is rather the result of a close study of actual men and things, where experience shows that the affairs of the world were generally best managed when the people whom these affairs concerned were left as much as possible to their own devices. This system of natural liberty meant that the sovereign or the state had, in Smith's view, to attend to only three duties, which Haldane summarises as follows:

> First, protecting society from violence and invasion of other independent societies. Secondly, to protect every member of society from the injustice or oppression of every other member of it, not least through establishing good justice. Thirdly, the duty of erecting and maintaining certain public

works and certain public institutions which it can never be in the interest of any individual, or small group of individuals, to erect and maintain, because the profit could never repay the expense to any individual, or small number of individuals, though it may frequently do much more than repay it to a great society.[28]

As we will see in our chapter on the state, Haldane's view on intervention goes something beyond these limitations, but it is striking that the three aspects outlined here are precisely the three realms of influence that he was to dominate in his years of political responsibility: security, law and social infrastructure. In preparing the armies of the nation as Secretary of State for War, in his legal work as a lawyer, parliamentarian, legislator, Lord Chancellor and judge, and not least in his tireless work as one of the main creators of the modern university structure of the United Kingdom, we find the not-so-invisible hand of Adam Smith at work.

The Wealth of Nations concludes with Smith's thinking on how the revenue to support the role of the sovereign should be gathered. Here again we find further constituent elements which were to influence the political creed of Haldane. Smith quite clearly assists Haldane as he seeks to address the following issues: which parts of expenditure should be defrayed by the general contribution of the whole of society and which by only some subsidiary section of beneficiaries? By what methods should these contributions be levied? And, finally, under what circumstances should encumbrances on the general revenue or the national debt be created?

Smith delves deep into the division of taxation between rent, profits and wages, concluding with four central maxims.[29] First, every subject should contribute in proportion to his capacity. Haldane agreed with this and his promotion, for example, from very early in his political career of the taxation of the 'unearned increment' is a reflection of Smith's thinking. Where there was an increase (or increment) in the value of land as a result of a growing population in its vicinity, Haldane believed the owner of the land ought not to benefit from that increase (a point that will be expanded upon shortly). On the contrary, he advocated that it was right that the whole of that increment should be due to the community itself. Haldane's daring but unsuccessful Local Authorities (Land Purchase) Bill of 1891 and 1892, seeking to give councils power for compulsory acquisition of land and powers to deal with the unearned increment, has its roots—surprisingly—in Smith's thinking.[30] Yes, it embodied principles of socialism too, with its emphasis on a fair redistribution of wealth, but it is in fact a brilliant example of Haldane's ability to take the best from two different schools of thought and fashion therefrom an original policy proposal that could appeal across a spectrum of political viewpoints.

Secondly, Smith underlined his belief that tax should be certain and not arbitrary. Smith's precepts are echoed in Haldane's thinking on this issue. Smith found the Land Tax offensive in so far as valuations of equivalent land in different parts of the country were often dissimilar. Haldane once again agreed and fought to rectify this, especially in Ireland, taking on the landlords within his own party as well as within the ranks of the Conservatives. Thirdly, Smith advocated that every tax should be levied in the way that is likely to be most convenient for the contributor to pay; and, finally, that every tax ought to be designed to minimise the costs incurred in gathering it. Convenience and efficiency of tax collection, as with efficiency in all other matters of government, were core beliefs of Haldane. The significant changes that the Liberal governments of 1905–15 famously instigated in income tax, death duties, excise duties and the payment of national insurance reflected these underlying principles.

* * *

Haldane's Local Authorities (Land Purchase) Bill of 1891 and 1892, just mentioned, is worth expanding upon further. Indeed, according to historian Colin Matthew, it was 'the most radical, most substantial, and best organized attempt at legislation' that arose from the group with which Haldane most readily identified in the days before he joined the famous Liberal Cabinets of the early twentieth century.[31] It shows how Haldane built upon Smith's thinking, while also incorporating the best insights of socialism.

The Bill was orientated to release working-class citizens from the unjust consequences that accrued through private ownership of land. Haldane was deeply troubled by the fact that the value of privately owned land on the borders of expanding towns and cities was rising at perilously fast rates in conjunction with the demands of a growing population: the 'unearned increment'. There might have been no special improvements to a piece of land to justify an increase in value in itself; but its situation may have become such that the local council, desirous to buy up land to meet housing demands and provide essential amenities, was at the mercy of the landowner. In such a position, the landowner was capable of naming a price astronomically higher than that for an equivalent piece of land in a not-so-desirable location (bear in mind that we are speaking of land that had been bought at a time when it was still a considerable distance from the nearest urban development or was near a development that had a steady population). As Haldane saw it, the difference in price was not due to the owner, but due rather to the population who sought to expand into that space. It was the latter's hard work that accounted for the growth in industry, and therefore population, in that area; the landowner could just as well have sat there twiddling his thumbs. Drawing on recent precedent set by railway companies, Haldane's proposal was a simple one:

> We may fairly say that in the days that are to come, if a special growth in value is caused by a movement of population, that growth is to belong to the population that created it. The municipal authority may have power to purchase the land, as it wants it, compulsorily, just as a railway company can. But it may have more than this. It ought to have power to purchase in the future on the footing of paying nothing for any special value which may be its own creation, and which the law has declared should no longer be recognized as the property of the landowner.[32]

The suggestion was, as Matthew admits, a 'daring' one in 1892, and even within the Liberal Party there were those who perceived it as a socialist or Fabian move.[33] But it was in fact a proposal that paid full attention to the realities of the situation, seeking a solution to a problem within the boundaries of the genuinely possible. It was no good, Haldane claimed, calling for the nationalisation of the land, as many radicals were doing:

> The truth is, that the title to land in this country is inextricably interwoven with the title to moveable property, and the consequence is that no sudden interference, on a large scale, with the one could take place without serious interference with the other. If the banks came down, so would the manufactories and other institutions which organise employment among working people.[34]

And yet, Haldane was no fatalist: 'Between the expropriation of all private landlords and the expropriation of none, is the practical course of expropriation with a free hand wherever desirable.'[35]

The Bill in which this 'practical course' was embodied failed, however, to pass through the House; the smell of socialism was still a little too strong upon it. But it clearly indicates a central facet of Haldane's thinking on economic matters: the state has a responsibility to put labour and capital on a more equal footing;[36] it ought not to prioritise 'property owners of whatever class', but must seek 'to better the condition ... of those who have needs more pressing than that of property'.[37] The state, according to Haldane, must operate on the principle that 'when public interests conflict with private ownership of property, the latter must yield to the former, subject to the condition of the private owner receiving the money equivalent of what he gives up'.[38] This is equality with an edge. He knew that it could not be achieved by pleasing everyone; some would have to suffer. But Haldane had the wider outlook. The pain involved in letting go of property paled in comparison to the suffering of working men and women lacking proper housing and without the amenities that make life human. The latter bore the burdens of profit; they did not reap its rewards. Haldane wanted to see those rewards far more evenly distributed.

Yet Haldane was not a socialist, despite what some of his peers may have thought (and what the posthumously named Haldane Society for Socialist Lawyers suggests). He was just too practical to believe that a socialist regime could function. The state needed to give free play and incentive to individual initiative and enterprise—to deny this would be to deny a basic and highly potent force within human nature. Where Haldane differed from many traditional capitalists was in his desire to see that those rewards remained just, and did not unduly burden those who either lacked initiative and enterprise (often as the result of a deficient education system or the chance of birth) or operated beneath the entrepreneur as employees.[39]

* * *

Another occasion to shine light on Haldane's economic thinking arises when we look at his reaction to the crucial event in 1903 when, on 15 May, Joseph Chamberlain, Colonial Secretary in Balfour's Conservative and Unionist government, made his unexpected and controversial Birmingham speech in favour of empire trade preference. Chamberlain believed that such a policy would significantly bolster the unity of the empire (he was not in fact principally concerned with increasing revenue), and thereby offer 'the best solution to the major social and economic problems of the day'.[40] His policy was summed up by Haldane in a 1903 speech repudiating the Protectionists' arguments, called 'A Leap into the Unknown'. To show the apparent inconsistencies of their arguments, Haldane states: 'we are to establish a protective duty on articles of food which this country imports, and which the Colonies in any degree supply, with remission for the Colonies. ... We are to give the Colonies Free Trade, but the Colonies are not going to give the mother country Free Trade.'[41] It was clearly a provocative proposal to a nation that, despite growing competition from the likes of Germany and the United States, was still the strongest industrial power in the world. Would the leap into the unknown be worth it?

Thus Chamberlain sparked the momentous tariff reform debate, which pitted the free traders against those who advocated protectionism, and which was, as we have seen, to change the face of the early-twentieth-century political landscape. The prime minister, Arthur Balfour, sought to head off the split that rapidly emerged in the Cabinet and the country and, despairing of what he was hearing from Treasury officials, in his search for objective advice turned to a young economist, Percy Ashley—a figure who would prove to be vital to Haldane as he came to form his own opinion on the matter.

By the autumn of 1903 Balfour had produced a paper which acknowledged that the protectionist policies of certain of Britain's trading partners required the country to reconsider the case for free trade, arguing for some 'liberty of fiscal negotiation'.[42] In due course Balfour went further, and accepted the theoretical case for preferential tariffs; but, in his view, they were still not within the realm of practical politics. This satisfied no one, and after Balfour accepted the resignations not only of Chamberlain but of three of his more intransigent pro-free trade opponents, the fat was in the fire. Just as with the Brexit debate, much of the argument became deeply polarised. Simplified propaganda such as 'Tariff Reforms means Work for All' and the propositions of the 'Free Fooders' took hold. It was not a straightforward party split, however; the Conservatives and Liberal Unionists, who made up the so-called Unionist Party, were internally divided within their own camps.[43]

As Haldane observed, 'sides were taken violently, and families were divided. … There was as much bitterness within the ranks of the Conservative party as there had been, seventeen years before, within the ranks of Liberalism about Home Rule.' Yet the biographer of Adam Smith went on to observe that the split was not over any new issue. Its economic and imperial aspects had been debated many times. What had changed was that, with Chamberlain, 'a protagonist of the first order had come on the scene, a minister of commanding personality and great energy'. As a result, 'people could talk of nothing but the fiscal question and its bearing on colonial policy'. Haldane, clear-sighted as always, pointed out the inevitable outcome of this excitement, indeed hysteria:

> The British public took its usual course. It delights in the spectacle of a strong man fighting, and it showed its pleasure in rounds of applause. But this could not continue. In its heart the public hates everything sudden, especially when it takes the shape of an abstract proposition. What was put before the country, the eloquence and the energy of the protagonist not-withstanding, was propounded both suddenly and in an abstract form. People began to ask about the cost, and then to grow suspicious and sulky. … At first the prejudice had been unduly for the policy. Later on it became markedly against it.[44]

So what did Haldane, though still a backbencher, do? As judgment on the issue was yet to be made, he set out to establish the facts. He believed that much good had arisen from men and women being forced to think 'as closely as they are capable of doing' on such an important subject. 'The difficulty of counting the cost of a sweeping change in economic policy became every day more obvious.' What was needed was the fullest possible information on which to judge the merits of the opposing factions. Haldane himself concluded that he wished to make 'as unprejudiced a reconsideration of the fiscal question as a politician is capable of'.[45] As Balfour had done, he accordingly turned to Percy Ashley, who had a more detached position than himself. As early as December 1901 Haldane had begun to engage Ashley as 'a sort of political secretary—not for writing letters,' he clarified to his mother, 'but for looking things out for me. He is a very clever young political economist. … He knows German & French well & has travelled a good deal. I think he will help me a good deal & I can talk over speeches with him.'[46]

Help him he did. Following Chamberlain's bombshell, Ashley and Haldane spent some twelve months in discussion and joint reading, and collected a mass of material on the issues. This included detailed studies of how Germany, the United States and France had addressed the questions of free trade and protectionism in their own particular circumstances through the nineteenth century. Ashley used the material to lecture at the London School of Economics in the Lent and Summer terms of 1904, and Haldane proposed that he should publish his lectures in book form as *Modern Tariff History* in the autumn of that year. Haldane wrote a seventeen-page preface, and they celebrated the completion of their work by spending a week together at Cloan in late September.

Haldane referred in his preface to the work of Adam Smith, Friedrich List and others in this field, but professed that the public had grown discontented with arguments of the past.[47] This was itself a profession that owed much to Smith. In his *Life*, Haldane is anxious to emphasise that his hero set himself to investigate the concrete facts of his own day, and that these must always govern whatever system of political economy one might look to adopt. It was precisely this return to concrete facts that *Modern Tariff History* set about doing. Haldane and Ashley were able to demonstrate that the political, economic, and geographical particularities of each country examined in the book—Germany, the United States and France, 'those states which are most frequently compared with the United Kingdom'[48]—were the paramount factors determining their own tariff systems; in other words, abstract theories, though useful, were not of the first importance. By looking closely at the reasons behind each country's protective duties, the book served to show those who would draw a straight analogy between Great Britain's policies and those of its foreign counterparts how misleading such an approach would be. Each of the three countries analysed in the book had markedly different histories, needs and conditions of development.[49] Germany, formed as it was from a collection of small states with their own individual tariff arrangements, based its national unity on internal free trade in exchange for external protection for the new nation. Home food supply had to be adequate in case of war, hence agriculture had to be fostered and protected. Yes, the Germans might have studied the doctrines of Adam Smith, but the absence of command of the seas and their own particular geographical and social limitations and possibilities dictated how their wealth might best be procured and distributed. Haldane reminded his readers that a protectionist writer like Professor Adolph Wagner in Germany admitted that it is 'despite commercial disadvantage' that the country ought to restrict the liberty of trade in order to bolster its agriculture and thereby ensure the safety of its empire.[50]

In the United States, by contrast, tariffs had been a major source of government revenue, but at the cost of affording undue protection from free competition which allowed, under the trust system, huge monopolist organisations to develop. The resulting higher prices both damaged the interest of consumers and led detrimentally to higher costs of production in industries such as shipbuilding. Ashley and Haldane concluded that the United States' experience was of an exceptionalist nature—with its lack of interest in questions of national defence (how times have changed!) and with a vast and growing home market—and therefore of little economic relevance to understanding the issues in Britain in 1904.

Ashley and Haldane's study of France was to prove more interesting. They drew attention to France's history of protectionism, despite the nation having a substantial seaboard with which a great foreign trade might have been associated and which they believed could have led to significant development of her home industries. From their examination it would appear that, possibly with the exception of her agricultural industry, France would have been better off for much of the nineteenth century under a free-trade system; though Haldane adds that he speaks only 'so far as a foreigner may presume to form an opinion'. Despite their 'great intelligence, industry and adaptability' and their access to large supplies of raw materials, the French found such advantages hampered by the dulling influence of protective tariffs and the taxation on many of their materials. Haldane observed in his preface that France was not hampered by the geographical conditions that played their part in influencing the rulers of Germany to subordinate considerations of economic development to those of national defence. The issue in France was one of class. The 'class influence of the manufacturers on her politics has been immense, and she has had to pay for this. Her history is a striking illustration of the tendency of a protective system to get the upper hand, and, having got it, to keep it.'[51]

The conclusion for Great Britain which Haldane drew from the research undertaken and summarised by Ashley was not that there was no need for tariff reform. But he reached the view that 'In the case of a small island with a great seaboard, and a great national capacity for command of the sea, protective remedies seem to me to be no remedies.' He recognised the difficulty of bringing the 'loose jointed' (in both geography and constitution) subjects of the empire within an economic ring fence, such as the geographical conditions of Germany and the United States had made possible. On the contrary, he believed that 'the history of cohesion of the Empire rested on just this looseness of jointing; never on mechanical devices, but always on the simple co-existence of common purpose and sentiment with the most complete local liberty'. When Haldane came to consider the extreme difficulty of avoiding the friction arising from the want of local liberty, which every tariff system tends to bring with it, and the impossibility of counting the economic price that must be paid if Britain were to part with the existing liberty of buying and selling, he felt deep misgivings about introducing a new tariff. 'Its risk is tremendous, and what is risked is nothing short of the cohesion of the Empire. Surely the burden of proof rests heavily on those who invite us to leap with them?' Invoking the appeal *Vestigia nulla retrorsum!* (No backward steps!) he concludes his preface to Ashley's book with the resounding appeal that:

> For the sake of the Empire, as well as our own sakes, we must seek to develop the wealth of the islands which form the centre of the Empire, and to expand their commerce. ... If we would remain ahead of our rivals, we must continue to be ahead of them in the quality of what we make. No tariff can keep out that quality which is the key to quantity.[52]

* * *

And yet, as we have seen, Haldane was clearly far from being a straightforward capitalist. His views on nationalisation of the coal-mining industry illustrate the refinement of his thinking on this issue. The pressure towards nationalisation had been growing with the rise of the labour movement and in light of various ventures that had proved public ownership successful.

Until the middle of the nineteenth century, capitalism in Britain operated on a relatively unbridled basis. But a series of Factory Acts limiting the hours of work and improving terms and conditions of employment gradually came into force between 1843 and 1901, and Gladstone's Regulation of Railways Act 1844 set the pattern for regulation of natural monopolies. Whilst transport, with the important exception of roads, was largely the remit of the private sector, with canals, railways and docks being typically built and owned by companies that sought to make an economic return for their shareholders, the role of the local authorities in utility development and ownership was increasingly recognised. In 1856 Joseph Bazalgette was appointed chief engineer of the Metropolitan Board of Works, and the sewage problems of London were for the first time addressed on a comprehensive scale.

But, as R. H. Tawney pointed out, even by the time of Campbell-Bannerman's premiership (1905–8), the government did not own or administer any businesses (with the exception of the Post Office and a handful of naval and military establishments); nor did it concern itself with the vexed question of how to organise industry or market its products.[53] The course of trade was left to itself; business enterprises enjoyed a remarkable freedom. This was based upon the assumption—informed no doubt by the thinking of Adam Smith—that profit-seeking entrepreneurs, if left unrestricted, would make use of the national resources in the most effective manner. And it was thought that competition would ensure that the consumer remained safe from exploitation.

Following the start of the First World War, however, the disruption of supplies of certain products typically sourced from Germany called for central action. Haldane was quickly enlisted to chair a government Chemical Products Supply Committee to consider and advise as to the best means of obtaining for the use of British industries sufficient supplies of chemical products, colours and dye-stuffs—kinds hitherto largely imported from countries with which Britain was then at war.[54] The 'not very successful national dye company' which resulted only served to show up a dangerous 'lack of urgency in scientific matters' within government.[55] Members of the Royal Society and other learned societies consequently urged for 'Government assistance for scientific research for industrial purposes'.[56] Haldane, along with the president of the Board of Education, Joseph Pease, was responsible for a White Paper issued by Arthur Henderson, future leader of the Labour Party, in May 1915, outlining a 'permanent organization for the promotion of industrial and scientific research'.[57] This was formalised by an Order in Council on 28 July as a committee of the Privy Council. Six Cabinet ministers, as well as Haldane, Pease and Arthur Acland, were appointed as the initial members of this new committee. On 1 December 1916 the committee was reorganised into a separate Department of Scientific and Industrial Research, with its own minister—a foreshadowing of the even more radical and still unrealised proposal for a Department of Intelligence and Research made in the 1918 Haldane Report on the Machinery of Government.[58] The new department encouraged 'scientific and industrial research in its own laboratories, in universities and through research associations in industry'. These associations were 'probably the most successful development in the progress of DSIR'.[59] In 1919 there were just nine such associations. By 1962 there were fifty-two. The department was eventually abolished by the Science and Technology Act 1965, with many of its responsibilities passing to the new Ministry of Technology and the equally new Science Research Council.

Returning to the situation that prevailed during the First World War, many industries became subject to government control of one form or another. The railways, for instance, had been run throughout the war as a consolidated national service rather than as a series of private profit-making agencies—an experiment which was 'widely held to have vindicated itself triumphantly'.[60] So much so that in 1919 a Bill was introduced for the establishment of a Ministry of Ways and Communications, with powers to buy up all railways, canals and docks. Whilst this plan was abandoned in 1921 in the struggle between 'the good fairy Reconstruction and the bad fairy Bolshevism',[61] the 130 railway companies of pre-war days were by government decree grouped into four regional private-sector monopolies: the London and North Eastern; the London Midland and Scottish; the Great Western; and the Southern. Safeguards for the community were maintained by means of a new Railway Rates Tribunal. Mechanisms were also put in place to deal with labour disputes—though this was not always effective. Public ownership was off the agenda until the aftermath of the Second World War.

Paralleling such proposals for government-imposed amalgamation, there was also an acceleration of private industrial mergers, a trend which had become more prevalent during the war. By 1919 the forty-three chief banking concerns of 1914 had been consolidated into five very much larger banks with a commanding hold on trade and industry.[62] Even in 1918, the degree of such combinations had excited the attention of the government, which then appointed a Committee on Trusts to investigate them. A minority report concluded that some industries had gone so far in this process of combination that the time had come for public ownership. As historian Arthur Marwick pointed out, it appeared that the collectivists were starting to have it both ways, advocating that highly fragmented industries should be nationalised because they were inefficient, whilst highly concentrated ones should be nationalised because they were a menace![63]

Come the end of the war this was all to change. The slump in wages and output that followed the completion of hostilities, exacerbated by rising unemployment, meant that the post-war debate on governance, profitability, social purpose and responsibility of corporations became a matter of increasingly wide political and public interest. There emerged a greater awareness of the fundamental rights of workers and the obligations of companies towards them. A classic case in point was the situation of the coal-mining industry.

The threat of a national miners' strike in February 1919 resulted in the government establishing a Royal Commission on the Coal Mines to enquire into the nature of ownership and operation of that industry. An essential feature of the miners' demands was a plea for nationalisation of the mines. It became relevant therefore to enquire into the general problem of organising the coal-mining industry upon a national basis. Twelve commissioners were appointed, four by the government, four by the Miners' Federation of Great Britain, two of whom were agreed between the government and the miners (R. H. Tawney and Sidney Webb), and three by the coal owners. The chairman, Lord Justice Sankey, was—you will not be surprised to hear—a great friend of Haldane.

In the event that the commission recommended nationalisation, it would be essential to recruit a civil service fit for purpose under a dedicated minister with oversight of that industry. The commissioners turned to Haldane, out of office now for four years, for evidence. As the prominent left-wing political theorist Harold Laski writes in the introduction to the transcript of Haldane's testimony to the Royal Commission—which, in view of its importance, Laski and R. H. Tawney arranged to be published as a separate pamphlet in 1921[64]—there were several reasons for that choice. Haldane had given evidence before the Royal Commission on the Civil Service in 1912, evidence which Laski avowed was generally admitted to be the most illuminating discussion of the problem of personnel in government. Secondly, Haldane's service for six years as Secretary of State for War provided experience not merely of ordinary civilian government officials but also the role of technical officials connected with a great department of state. But thirdly, as chairman of the Machinery of Government Committee, which reported in 1918, Haldane had only recently surveyed the whole problem of government organisation. Few, if any, men in Britain could be considered so competent to discuss the technical issues in the coal mines debate, which was effectively putting private enterprise on trial.[65]

We might speculate to what extent Laski, by means of such a publication, was also giving public praise and recognition to a man who had not only been unjustly vilified before and throughout the war, but had also played a crucial part in Laski's own rise to a position of intellectual importance. For in March 1920, while Laski was still a young academic at Harvard, Haldane was the principal enabler of his appointment to a lectureship at the LSE, where Haldane was a governor and 'perhaps the most important patron'.[66] The two men were to develop an extremely close relationship once Laski returned to England. Laski dined almost weekly at Haldane's London home and worked closely with him in the cause of adult education. It has even been suggested that Haldane's shaping of the Canadian constitution, as explored in Chapter 10, owed much to this friendship and Laski's pluralist understanding of the state.[67] Through Haldane, Laski was admitted into some of the country's most influential political and social circles.[68] It is also no surprise that Laski should want to publish Haldane's evidence to the Coal Commission, given the view of Laski's closest confidant, the much older famous US Supreme Court Justice Oliver Wendell Holmes, who wrote to Laski in March 1920:

> I have read the three volumes of evidence before the Coal Commission. The *chef d'oeuvre* of the piece is Haldane's evidence on the organization of the civil service. I like to see a man who throws overboard outright the whole system of mechanical panaceas and takes the straight road on the old paths of initiative, courage and knowledge as the roots of effective government.[69]

INTELLECTUAL FOUNDATIONS

68. Georg Wilhelm Friedrich Hegel (1770–1831), Haldane's greatest philosophical hero and inspiration, whose thinking was core to Haldane's statesmanship. Texts from Hegel's notoriously difficult writings were carved into an oak mantelpiece and bookcase at Cloan.

Early Inspiration

Haldane was released from youthful religious angst by the philosophical works he was introduced to in Göttingen, particularly the writings of Johann Gottlieb Fichte (1762–1814) and Bishop Berkeley (1685–1753). The portraits below are taken from the same book of *cartes postales* as that of Hegel (previous page) assembled by Haldane featuring images of his intellectual heroes. Haldane would become a prominent philosopher in his own right, even receiving an offer of the chair of moral philosophy at St Andrews University after delivering the prestigious Gifford Lectures there between 1902 and 1904.

69. Johann Gottlieb Fichte

70. Bishop Berkeley

71. The graves of Fichte (the gravestone and monument on left) and of Hegel (the cross and gravestone in middle) at the Dorotheenstadt cemetery in Berlin. The Kaiser was bewildered that Haldane took time on his 1906 visit to pay his respects at their graves.

72. The philosopher T. H. Green (1836–1882) made the insights of Haldane's philosophical heroes profoundly relevant to a budding statesman, with his emphasis on engaged citizenship as a means to self-fulfillment.

73. It is not surprising that Haldane chose Green's work as the stable support upon which to lean in this portrait, c. 1902.

74. Adam Smith (1723–1790) was the subject of Haldane's first sole authored book. Smith was himself a philosopher, but Haldane was more impressed by his revolutionary economics, which were to guide Haldane across a lifetime's commitment to practical politics.

75. John Maynard Keynes (1883–1946) served as
Secretary of the Royal Economic Society during
many of the years 1906–28 during which Haldane
served as its President.

76. Harold Laski (1893–1950), an
internationally prominent left-wing
economist and political theorist.
Haldane was intrumental in securing
Laski's dominant place in public life.

77. Haldane's dedication to the most demanding intellectual pursuits was never divorced from his devotion to literature. His admiration for the work of Johann Wolfgang von Goethe (1749–1832) meant he was always 'urging the humanities', as Edmund Gosse said of him.

78. The poetry of Emily Brontë (1818–1848) was of great importance to Haldane. The works of her *Last Lines* were constantly on his lips. He considered them to be one of the most profound artistic presentations of his central philosophy.

79. The poetry of Robert Browning (1812–1889) (left) and that of William Wordsworth were also considerable influences on Haldane.

A Meritorious Intellect

80. John Morley (1838–1923), who like Haldane was awarded the Order of Merit, served in Cabinet with Haldane from 1905 to 1914. Profoundly intelligent, Haldane called him 'the most interesting personality I ever knew'. He was painted by John Collier in 1913.

The key issue which Haldane was asked to address during the evidence hearing was that of the composition and recruitment of the civil service to which the coal-mining industry would be responsible in the event that it was to be nationalised. In Laski's introduction to the reprint of Haldane's evidence, he asserts that 'it has become obvious that the primary services upon which the modern state depends—mines and railroads—can no longer be left to the free play of private competition'.[70] Workers lacked the motivation to keep efficient production at an adequate level.

Yes, the profit-seeking motivation had allowed for an 'unprecedented' increase in wages and working hours had been significantly reduced. But this clearly was still not sufficient to keep workers invested in the success of the enterprise. They demanded that services 'so fundamental to the national life should be run by those who, from the lowest to the highest, have a part in their organisation'.[71] But equally it was clear from the experience of war production that the transfer of such industries to the control of a government department was impractical. Such a department would be unsuited to the special technical needs demanded by an industrial service like the mines. The Civil Service, being hierarchical in nature, did not breed in its members the initiative, flexibility or inventiveness necessary for a nationalised industry. Nor, Laski felt, would it elicit creativity in the mass of the workers. Without such a motive, industrial well-being was unachievable.[72]

Could a new attitude be developed? This is where Haldane came in. He was clear at the outset of his evidence that he was not there to address the question of whether there should or should not be nationalisation of the coal industry. He set out, rather, to tackle the question of whether it is possible 'to train a body of civil servants fit for rapid and efficient administration'.[73] Fundamental to that quest was his understanding of the need for separation of functions, which he had gained at the War Office—Smith's division of labour again. He detailed the critical difference there between the skills required by the commander in the field and those of the administrator. He believed that some of the administrative requirements of the army were of an equal complexity to those pertaining to civilian business. But administrative skills had to be taught—education, as always, was the key—and he explained at length how he had set up with Sidney Webb, himself a member of the Coal Commission, the training of forty administrative army officers each year at the London School of Economics, where 'they were taught things which they never could have learned in the army'.[74]

He saw no fundamental difference between the capabilities of men in any profession. Some had the qualities of courage, taking the initiative and assuming responsibility, and these were to be found both in the army and in the business world. But it was more difficult to find these people in the Civil Service, where rules and seniority were much more relevant to promotion than selection on merit. He believed that with the best class of men the motivation to distinguish oneself in the service of the state could be just as potent as that of 'the great impulse in the business world, namely, the desire to make a fortune'.[75] It was this realisation that the administrator needed to be trained and that the administrator's role was equally as important as that of the officer in the field that lay at the foundation of the transformation effected in the British army.

Haldane also explained the need to identify the right kind of competence in the minister who would lead a great department, one who would have responsibility and authority and the ability to command the respect of the House of Commons. He identified another problem for resolution. 'The difficulty here is that people [ministers] are chosen for their powers of talking in Parliament rather than administration.'[76] For Haldane, both were critical. The minister must have expert knowledge, and that can only be acquired by surrounding himself with experts and by having an advisory council. He must listen to these experts and to his advisory council, but he must never be subservient to them. The minister must be solely responsible and accountable to Parliament for final decisions.

But advisers were still essential. Haldane believed that the minister should be very conscious that these members often had expertise very much greater than his own and that he would be wise to let himself be guided by them, although he must categorically not be encouraged to place responsibility on them. He advocated the fullest possible degree of consultation with such experts, but believed that 'the true kind of council meets formally very seldom, but it is meeting always in reality'. He continues in true Haldanean style:

> The Minister ought to live with it [the council]. He ought to sit in the room with it, smoking cigars with it, lunching with it, taking tea with it, dining with it, and being with it until all hours in the morning. Its members ought

to be his guides, philosophers and friends, and they ought to understand one another and feel that the best thing in their interests and in his interests is for him to say at the end of their deliberations: 'I will take my own way about it, but you will know it is in harmony, not only with the letter, but with the spirit of what you have been thinking.'[77]

It is vintage Haldane: very full-on, but so human. In his disregard of a pedantic officialdom and his endorsement for working patterns which encourage a genuine cross-fertilisation of ideas, the vision that Haldane presents here remains strikingly fresh. He seems to see into the heart of what makes for effective teams and leadership; he is wonderfully dismissive of superficiality. 'That is what I call getting rid of red tape and making the thing work.'[78] Haldane's realism, his ability to see beyond mere ideas and into the practical facts that must precondition the existence of those ideas, hits us once again:

> The whole future of the success of nationalization … seems to turn on the getting of capable men. Then it is easy; but if you do not get a man who is capable, the best thought-out scheme of nationalization in the world will not work. Therefore, you want to get capable men as managers—someone who will work with the men as I suggested the Minister should work with his Council—that is to say, live with them and make them feel that he is one of themselves and make them love him just as the soldiers love the competent company officer who, while he commands them, will sacrifice himself for them if necessary.[79]

He believed passionately that the civilian servant of the state could be as proud a position as that of the man who served in the army and the navy, and that for this to be the case there must be 'public spirit, public honour and public recognition'.[80] Haldane thought that the state should pay good salaries and that the state official had hitherto been 'the patient beast of burden who has been underpaid'.[81] But that did not mean that good salaries had to be of a level that would allow for opulence. Senior military personnel 'live on what the rich man often calls very little indeed, but their reward comes to them in another way. They have social advantages which he has not. They are rewarded by the public, by honours, and by positions which tell.'[82] There was no reason, in Haldane's mind, why this could not be the case for those who served other branches of the state.

* * *

Haldane had a particular interest in the interaction of macro- and micro-economics with national growth and business enterprise. The foundation of the London School of Economics and Political Science was to become an important contributor to understanding this relationship. But the Royal Economic Society[83] (RES) was also an organisation to which Haldane was drawn at a time of considerable—indeed, revolutionary—thinking in economic affairs and policy. John Maynard Keynes's work lay at the heart of that revolution. Haldane was elected president of the RES in 1906 within months of his appointment as Secretary of State for War. There could have been no greater demonstrator of Haldane's belief in the importance of the science of economics than the fact that he remained president until his death in 1928. Whether that long period of Haldane's presidency was wholly desirable for the development of the science of economics may be judged by the change of rules brought in immediately after his death which imposed time limitations on office. But his lengthy tenure underlined the central importance which Haldane ascribed to the role of the developing science of economics in society, both theoretical and applied.[84]

There must have been many occasions on which Haldane and Keynes interacted at the society, as Keynes was its secretary at the time of Haldane's appointment and he (Keynes) doubled up this role from 1911 onwards by becoming editor of its principal publication, *The Economic Journal*.[85] Haldane presided at the society over the period of Keynes's initial challenge to Alfred Marshall's classical economics. Keynes's *Economic Consequences of the Peace*, published in 1919, with its emphasis on the growth of the demand side of the economy, was the forerunner of a revolution in economic thinking as great as that of Adam Smith.

The interplay of economics with national affairs was a constant concern for Haldane. We have seen it in his early espousal in the 1880s of the taxation of the unearned increment and of land taxation policy in Ireland. We see it again in 1907 in Haldane's inaugural presidential address to the International Congress of the RES, when he dwelt on the international brotherhood of science and, in particular, the science of the state.[86] What we find here is a summation of one of the key points from the biography of Adam Smith that first launched Haldane into the world of economics, but with a new international dimension. In his address, he praises Smith as a man who had 'profoundly freed his mind from every kind of narrowness'.[87] He reminds the delegates that Smith saw that no economic science was perfect for the purposes of the state unless it was set in the context of its times. Smith himself recognised that there might be circumstances in which his doctrine of commercial freedom would not apply. Drawing on his experience working with the military—an advantage he was without in 1887 when he wrote his biography—Haldane goes on to say that the relationship between the economist and the statesman was analogous to the General Staff and army commanders; the role of the economist was to work out principles and plans for the statesman. But the economist's reflections are not enough on their own. The statesman must balance the many particular circumstances of his time and keep forever in mind that the management of human affairs requires the art of dealing with human nature. An understanding of the relationship between capital and labour can only get you so far!

Haldane argued that the science of economics, as with all other sciences, was becoming more and more specialist. Recalling, as he often did, Goethe's dictum that 'he who would accomplish anything in this world must learn to limit himself', he was able to emphasise to this great international gathering the value of their different minds, attainments and specialised work, but all converging upon a broad common purpose. Economics was no longer seen simply in the context of the question 'how shall we make our own nation more prosperous?' Haldane's address reveals a man who is now asking, 'how can the science of economics contribute to the healthy functioning of the world?'

The RES was the platform for further Haldanean contributions to economic practice and theory. In 1925 the society hosted a discussion on the great question of the national debt at its annual meeting.[88] Haldane was in the chair. Hugh Dalton—elected that year as an MP for the first time and to go on to become Chancellor of the Exchequer from 1945 to 1947 in Attlee's post-war Labour government—opened the discussion. The question being debated was whether it was desirable, and if so at what speed, to seek to pay off or reduce the outstanding national debt. Dalton advocated measures which he believed could repay the whole national debt within thirty years, claiming the inter-generational high ground by stating that the most important duty of the state is 'to protect the interests of the future against the demands of the present'.[89] He believed that nearly all of the money paid to the holders of war loans would be reinvested.

Keynes, who spoke next, disagreed. He saw only two reasons which would merit expediting the repayment of debt. The first was to allow for the raising of funds on behalf of public bodies which might require new capital for productive purposes. Not seeing the demand for such stimulus in 1925, he believed that the reduction in debt would simply stimulate the flow of capital into the hands of public bodies abroad. The second reason would be to stimulate the amount of national savings, a policy advocated by Dalton. But Keynes believed that by no means all of the money taken from the taxpayer to fund the repayment of debt would be saved. He could not see at that time that the need for additional savings was urgent enough to justify heavier taxation in order to bring about its heavier stimulation. He decried the attraction of compound interest applied to the reduction in debt and contrasted that 'aesthetic' outcome against the effects within the community; he preferred to see the operation of compound interest working to benefit the community at large. He feared that the increase of taxation that would be necessitated would hold back the general progress of the community. He wanted to see the national debt being reduced, as after the Napoleonic wars, by the general progress of the community, not a Sinking Fund. This was a preview of the Keynesianism of the General Theory which he was to publish in 1936.

It fell to Haldane to sum up the debate. Stressing both the political and economic dimensions of the issue, he believed that the answer to the question depended to a considerable extent on what view was taken of the future of the country:

> If this country is doomed never to recover itself, its industry never going to improve, if we are to the end of our advantage and the prospects that we had in the days of the industrial revolution are all gone, then I agree we had better pay off [the debt] as fast as we can to keep the peace with our creditors. But if, on the other hand, you take the view that we are no worse off than we have been before, that we have got the old stuff in our people, if you take the view that, as put forward in another connection, what you get out of the earth is according to what you have put into it, because of new methods of science and new means of production, then you must remember, with your past experience, to take care to burden industry when it is in a difficult position as little as you can, and to proceed very cautiously in the repayment of your debt.[90]

Haldane went on to admit that the future was uncertain, despite many people seeing the prospect of the League of Nations pointing to a long period of peace in which to reduce debt. Haldane of course hoped for such a period of peace but 'as a student of history and in particular the history of the origins of wars', he was not overly sanguine.[91] 'Of course we should all like to get rid of the National Debt,' he exclaimed, 'but if we cannot, is that a thing which should lead us to despair if we believe in the future of our people—if we believe in the progress which is being made in education, in the outlook of youth, in the rise of the democracy, and in the consequent prospect of greater production and of more industrial power?'[92]

There was no need to rush the repayment of the national debt; it was possible that this would create worse conditions for industries. He concluded stirringly with the words: 'Let us then have courage, let us have faith, and let us put our full energies into developing the productive capacity of this nation.' Haldane understood that progress could never be achieved without hope; to instil hope was his constant aim. He was more than aware of the horrors and depravities of which human beings were capable; the war had only ended seven years previously (and another was only fourteen away). Yet Haldane never lost a sense of confidence in the human capacity to transform a dismal situation into one of success.

But there weren't many of Haldane's calibre to catalyse the latent potential within the nation. The first—minority—Labour government, in which Haldane served in his old role as Lord Chancellor, fell at the Conservative victory in the general election of November 1924. In April 1925 Churchill took Britain back onto the Gold Standard at its unsustainable pre-war parity. This was a body blow to the already hard-hit mining industry and laid the foundations of both the miners' and the general strikes of 1926. Lloyd George became leader of the Liberal Party in October 1926 on the resignation of Asquith, and developed ambitious plans for government economic intervention. These plans threatened not just the Conservative Party but also the Labour Party's position as the official opposition.

Lloyd George published his yellow book *Britain's Industrial Future* in early 1928, just a few months before Haldane's death that August, containing exhaustive proposals for dealing with Britain's grave unemployment situation. In March 1929 this was followed by his sixty-four-page pamphlet 'We Can Conquer Unemployment', setting out specific remedies. On the international front, focus was placed on an ever-increasing freedom of trade. At home, efficiency of British industries and a programme of national development became paramount. But Lloyd George went further. He pledged that within two years of adopting a new, detailed policy of investment in a national system of roads and bridges, of housing, of telephone and electrical development, of land drainage and, in London, passenger transport, unemployment levels could be brought down from the December 1928 level of 1.5 million to the 'normal' level of less than 1 million.

Within two months of the publication of Lloyd George's pamphlet, Keynes and H. D. Henderson, respectively the chairman and editor of *The Nation*, produced a forty-four-page analysis of the Lloyd George programme entitled 'Can Lloyd George do it? The Pledge Examined'. It reviewed the proposals and contrasted them to the economic policy of recent years which had 'been dominated by the preoccupation of the Treasury with the departmental problem of debt conversion'. It damned the belief of the Conservative government that the less it borrowed the better the chances of converting the national debt into loans carrying a lower rate of interest. 'In the interests of conversion, therefore, they have exerted themselves to curtail, as far as they can, all public borrowing, all capital expenditure by the State, no matter how productive and desirable in itself. ... To all well-laid schemes of progress and enterprise, they have (whenever they could) barred the door with, No!'[93]

Keynes and Henderson then went on to say:

[It is] no accident that the Conservative government had landed the country in the mess where we found ourselves. ... Negation, Restriction, Inactivity—these are the Government's watchwords. Under their leadership we have been forced to button up our waistcoats and compress our lungs. Fears and doubts and hypochondriac precautions are keeping us muffled up indoors. But we are not tottering to our graves. We are healthy children. We need the breath of life. There is nothing to be afraid of. On the contrary. The future holds in store for us far more wealth and economic freedom and possibilities of personal life than the past has ever offered. There is no reason why we should not feel ourselves free to be bold, to be open, to experiment, to take action, to try the possibilities of things. And over against us, standing in the path, there is nothing but a few old gentlemen tightly but-toned-up in their frock coats, who only need to be treated with a little friendly disrespect and bowled over like ninepins![94]

We might wonder, then: was Haldane a Keynesian or was Keynes a Haldanean? If only Haldane could have lived just one year longer to hear the political economist speak out so strongly in the service of the state.

In the end, everything we have explored in this chapter comes back to two basic claims that Haldane seems to make at every turn: base your economic and business plans on what is actually possible, but never be blind to the sheer enormity of what is actually possible! The 'true leader' is the one who can, in Haldane's words, 'fill the minds of those who hear him, even of such as are in the depths of national despair, with the sense of the greatness of which human nature is capable'.[95] As ever, when it comes to Haldane, the idealist is the realist and the realist is the idealist. Study your facts—study, study, study. They will show you your limitations and your potential. And once you have grasped the nature of both, set to work—and work, and work, and work. That, according to Haldane, is how you change the world.

And change the world he did, as we are about to discover.

PART TWO

BUILDING THE STATE

A BRAVE NEW WORLD

A powerful and beneficent personality, a great citizen, above all a loyal and generous colleague.

Beatrice Webb on Haldane[1]

Haldane was a man irreducible to one sphere of activity, one political party, one tradition. Beatrice Webb, the social reformer whose words form the epigraph for this chapter, once wrote of him:

> Plenitude, mental and physical, seemed to me his dominant feature, lead- ing to a large intake and a like output. A big head on a bigger body—gen- erous expenditure on the good things of life, not least among them choice edibles and the accompanying portions and potions of nicotine and alco- hol, also of select quality; long hours of work; endless documents and books mastered and remembered; a multitude of interests, and an ever- widening circle of friends and acquaintances, extending from Emperors and Kings, distinguished diplomatists, and famous men of science and learning, to representative manual workers and scientific administrative experts of all sorts and kinds; any adequate picture of his life would entail a large and crowded canvas.[2]

Our brushstrokes in Part 2 begin with the background, particularly the political setting, that will help us to make sense of Haldane's contribution to the life of the state. The major parties were not the major parties we know today; their debates were not (with certain significant exceptions) the debates of our day. When Haldane entered Parliament in 1885 the Labour Party didn't exist, women couldn't vote in national elections, and MPs received no income for their work. It would take another twenty- seven years before electric lighting was installed in the Commons. A taxi to Parliament would have involved a horse. It is, in many respects, an alien world. Some things remain the same, of course. Antipathy between parties, the struggle between rich and poor, the suspicion of growing world powers—these were as well known then as they are now. So, before we come to Haldane the statesman, we have to know something of his setting, at once so foreign and so familiar.

Given his thirty core years of service to the Liberal Party (1885–1915), it may be sensible to start by asking what it meant to be a Liberal in the days of Haldane's public life. And yet a definition is far from straightforward. The Liberals were an amalgam of Whigs, Peelites (progressive conservatives following Sir Robert Peel) and Radicals that emerged in the 1860s to champion free trade in opposition to protectionist Conservatives. At their head was the dominating figure of William Ewart Gladstone, who would hold prime ministerial office no less than four times across four decades. His was a Peelite brand of Liberalism—characterised by a strong moral determination to strengthen the existing social order while correcting its abuses. Gladstone's name became synonymous with Liberalism,[3] but the party was still uncomfortably pulled between the two poles of the past and the future, represented by the old-fashioned Whigs on the one hand and the rising spirit of socialism and organised labour on the other. Part of the Liberals' strength was their potential to hold within themselves the principles of both. Given the latent fault lines between the concerns of these two political approaches, however, this was also their weakness.[4] The Whigs, despite their great achievements in the cause of freedom (the abolition of the slave trade in 1807 and the Great Reform Act of 1832, for instance), had nevertheless been a party of the landed classes, who sought to represent the interests of the underrepresented and disenfranchised, as opposed to the Conservatives, who championed the interests of the established Church, landowners, and those in possession of capital. Most of the men who represented labour were, like the Whigs, dedicated to the cause of liberty, but they more narrowly sought the liberty of one particular section of society—the liberty of working men, as expressed in their rights and well-being—and it is out of their ranks that many of these leaders sprang.

Haldane lived this tension between Whigs and labour. In a sense, his life followed a trajectory from one to the other, and his final political office was to be Lord Chancellor in the first ever Labour government in 1924 (the Labour Party itself having been founded just twenty-four years previously). But he couldn't escape a continuing conflict between his Whiggish background and his commitment to the cause of the working classes. He himself was of the upper-middle classes, but he cared passionately for freedom, not least the freedom of labourers. He spoke out on their behalf continuously—for affordable, clean housing, for free and continuous education, for humane and satisfying working conditions. The platform for such vocal support was, in the first decades of Haldane's political life, an organisation known as the 'Eighty' Club. His intense devotion to the work of the club, which he had helped form shortly after Gladstone's success in the 1880 general election, is a reflection of the tensions Haldane embodied and the direction in which he hoped to move the Liberals. Built upon the remnants of the Whiggish Albert Grey Committee, it sought to promote political education and organisation. The club consisted of 'a number of gentlemen' willing to volunteer in speaking on political subjects.[5] If its roots were in Whig politics, the topics that the club's representatives covered on public platforms and in their regular published pamphlets show the Liberals' concern to address the issues of the day most pressing to the working classes: social reforms, housing, education, leasehold enfranchisement, eight-hour working days and socialism were some of the club's leading topics of discussion. With John Morley and Lord Kensington, Haldane was an inaugural committee member and, from February 1881, its first honorary secretary for two years. In fact, writing with blunt honesty to his mother in February 1882, the twenty-five-year-old Haldane could say: 'We [the 'Eighty' Club] have really done a very great deal, & I may say that I have arranged & got up the whole of it.'[6]

Gladstone became president of the 'Eighty' Club in 1884. After his successful election as a Member of Parliament in 1885, Haldane became a vice president of the club, to be joined later in that role by his two great friends, H. H. Asquith on becoming an MP in 1886 and Sir Edward Grey in 1889. The club was therefore backed by some of the most powerful political personalities of the day and energised by the up-and-coming talent within the party, many of whom would come to embody what was known as the New Liberalism—which Haldane defined as a movement for those who esteem 'a progressive policy in social matters more highly than anything else.'[7] It was in the context of the 'Eighty' Club that Haldane hoped, in his early political years, to persuade the developing labour movement that the Liberal Party could deliver on its concerns—that no separate, new party was needed to fulfil their desires. With the founding of the Social Democratic Federation in 1884, the Independent Labour Party in 1893, and the Labour Representation Committee in 1900 (which was, in effect, the founding of the Labour Party as we know it today), it was clear that the battle was being lost. The socialist impetus behind these developments was still deeply unsettling to the Liberal heartland, and for all the rhetoric about the labourer's emancipation, mainstream Liberalism couldn't bring itself to go to the lengths of those at the vanguard of the labour movement.

Haldane, however, knew where the future lay. As early as 1892 he suggested a Ministry of Labour, headed by Arthur Acland, within the Liberal government. Acland had previously organised the Oxford Extension Lectures, connecting him to the industrial classes of northern England, and had served since 1885 as MP for the Yorkshire town of Rotherham. He was well known, therefore, by labour representatives and deeply knowledgeable of their concerns and worldview. Haldane accordingly wrote to the party's chief whip:

> Why should not the opportunity be taken of doing what would at once be useful and popular, making the labour department of the Board of Trade a reality by putting it under his [Acland's] charge and extending its functions? ... The minister in charge of the labour department would have abundance to do and Acland's large experience in settling industrial disputes and getting at the minds of the working people would enable him to develop the functions of his office from the very first.

An original idea, but Acland, despite his working-class connections, came from the traditional ruling classes. Surely, we might think, a man from within the ranks of the labour representatives should hold such a position. But Haldane had already thought the whole thing through:

> He [Acland] is in a unique position. [Thomas] Burt, for example, is regarded with an approach to hostility by the Labour Party, and there is probably no man within their ranks whom their jealousies would permit to fill the most prominent position in the Labour sphere. ... But in Acland there is no sense of rivalry. They look on him as a highly educated outsider

who has devoted his life to the study of the relations of capital to labour. I am aware to talk of a Labour ministry is to suggest what is easy to speak of and difficult to do, but if some step towards it could now be taken I feel sure that it would strengthen Mr. Gladstone's position both in the Constituences [sic] and in the present House of Commons.[8]

The idea for a Ministry of Labour was one that would take twenty-four years to materialise.[9] But despite party sluggishness, Haldane did not wait around in mastering the most progressive thinking. Very early in his political career he established friendships and working relationships with the likes of Sidney Webb—'that pioneer of the welfare state'[10]—and Beatrice Potter, soon to be Beatrice Webb. As leading members of the Fabian Society, founded in 1884, the Webbs were committed to advancing the socialist cause through gradual legislative change (and also, unfortunately, partly through eugenics, though Haldane played no part in that campaign).[11] In looking for gradual change, the Fabians attempted to repudiate 'the common assumption that Socialism was necessarily bound up with Insurrection on the one hand or Utopianism on the other, and we set to work to discover for ourselves and to teach others how practically to transform England into a Social Democratic Commonwealth'.[12]

What bound the Webbs with Haldane was, according to Beatrice, 'our common faith in a deliberately organised society: our common belief in the application of science to human relations with a view to betterment'.[13] Before entering office, Haldane sought to put this faith into practice through a brand of Liberalism known as Liberal Imperialism. This was a political approach that both stressed the core values of the New Liberalism—esteeming a progressive policy in social matters more highly than anything else—while at the same time, unlike the majority of New Liberals, championing the empire (not with a view to British world domination, as we shall see later, but rather to developing mutually beneficial economic co-operation). The Liberal Imperialists also backed a programme of 'National Efficiency' (as did some Conservatives and some socialists, including the Webbs) that sought a more rationally organised, more scientific state, one that was based on the German example as distinct from the traditional laissez-faire British approach. The Liberal Imperialists looked to the Earl of Rosebery as their head, and counted within their number the likes of Grey, Asquith, and Ronald Munro

Ferguson (later Lord Novar, and the brother of Val, Haldane's one-time fiancée). But Haldane was their principal policy-maker. Under Haldane's lead the Liberal Imperialists sought to learn from the Webbs' careful studies of poverty, its impact and its possible reversal, and bring their conclusions to bear upon Liberal policies. By Beatrice's account, 'Haldane was the only one who approached to a Socialist or remained a true collectivist. The others could more properly be termed "radical reformists".'[14] But Haldane's hopes that connections with the Fabians would enliven the Liberals with the most progressive thinking of the time were not to be realised. As he put it:

> I never belonged to the Fabian Society, but was always very much in contact with Sidney Webb, and I brought some of his ideas into the consultations which Asquith and Grey and I used to hold about the future of Liberalism. If these ideas had been more studied in the days of Campbell-Bannerman [Liberal leader from 1899, prime minister 1905–8] and before that, the fading away of the Liberal Party might, I think, have been averted, and a party still more progressive in spirit might have grown up, not of extreme views, but as a body of thinkers among whom Labour and Liberalism might have come to dwell under a common roof, a roof sheltering them as the real and united alternative to the Conservative Party.[15]

The Fabians themselves bore some of the responsibility for the failure of this vision to materialise. Their manifesto of 1893 was a clear call for a separate Labour Party anchored in the trade union movement. To Haldane, who had begun to see a gradual 'modification' of the 'Liberal machine', the publication of such a manifesto was a 'heavy blow'.[16] The progress the Liberal Imperialists were making in persuading the older generation of the Liberal Party to embrace a number of key Labour principles had been drastically compromised. Nevertheless, the Webbs did not abandon those in sympathy on the liberal side, particularly as the years following the manifesto's publication made it plain that support from one of the major political parties was still necessary if their reforms were to be realised. As Keir Hardie, writing in 1905, pointed out, 'At the General Election in 1895, the Independent Labour Party put forward twenty-eight candidates, none of whom were returned.'[17]

The founding, in 1902, of the 'Coefficients' dining club saw the Webbs once more making a concerted effort to work with Liberals of advanced views, notably Haldane and his fellow Liberal Imperialist friend Edward Grey. Sidney Webb was clearly impressed by their continued resistance to both an old-fashioned Gladstonian Liberalism and a facile jingoism, praising them and their colleagues Asquith and Lord Rosebery in a famous article of 1901 for their 'courage to cast off the old clothes'.[18] Alongside Haldane, Grey and Webb (though not, interestingly, Beatrice), the broad-church club's other founder members included the founding director of the LSE, Professor W. A. S. Hewins, his soon-to-be successor H. J. Mackinder, the militant imperialist and Germanophobe L. J. Maxse (who would become one of Haldane's fiercest critics), the philosopher Bertrand Russell, and the writer H. G. Wells. The club's express purpose was to promote and think through the cause of 'National Efficiency' (explored in Chapter 10), with Haldane hosting its first dinner in his flat at Whitehall Court in December 1902. But despite the impressive range of topics discussed by the group across the years[19] and an expanding membership that would take in figures from both ends of the political spectrum,[20] the club remained largely ineffective in bridging the Liberal–Labour divide, and Fabian thinking continued to operate at a distance from the centres of political power.

If Fabian thinking was still on the margins, how did it win out? According to Haldane's sister, Elizabeth, it was not simply Liberalism's failure to learn from the latest socialist thinking that accounted for the party's later demise (the last Liberal government in Britain ended in 1915). Even those such as her brother, who sought to bring the two approaches under one roof, were already undermined in their attempt simply by means of their background, 'for despite all we said on platforms, we were not "of the people," nor did we truly understand their needs. We were in great measure Whigs still.'[21]

There is an argument along the same lines that says that the whole set-up of Haldane's life put him at a remove from those whose views he sought to express. Again, it is Beatrice Webb who, early in her working relationship with Haldane, makes the point:

> As for Haldane … he is a large and generous-hearted man, affectionate to his friends and genuinely enthusiastic about the advancement of knowledge. But his ideal has no connection with the ugly rough and tumble work-a-day world of the average sensual man, who is compelled to earn his livelihood by routine work and bring up a family of children on narrow

means. Unmarried, living a luxurious physical but a strenuous mental life, Haldane's vital energies are divided between highly-skilled legal work and the processes of digestion—for he is a Herculean eater. He finds his relaxation in bad metaphysics and in political intrigue.[22]

Webb makes a related point elsewhere:

> Where we differed was in the orientation of political power. Haldane believed more than we did in the existing governing class: in the great personages of Court, Cabinet and City. We staked our hopes on the organised working-class, served and guided, it is true, by an *élite* of unassuming experts who would make no claim to superior social status, but would content themselves with exercising the power inherent in superior knowledge and longer administrative experience.[23]

Webb's point is insightful, but not in the way she intended it. There is, as Haldane the philosopher would have said, a 'confusion of categories' in her words. Haldane's belief in the existing governing class was a belief in the channels through which real political developments could be made *given the existing structure of things*. To compare this to the Webbs' own 'hopes' for how things might be is unfair. Haldane's own hopes were very much *not* in the existing state of play—he was clear, for example, that he wanted to see an 'elite of talent' rise up to replace the hereditary peers,[24] and his willingness to enter the first Labour Cabinet, whose make-up was far from traditional, shows a remarkable openness to the new. If Haldane continued to put faith in 'Court, Cabinet and City', it was a faith founded in their elasticity, their ability to change, as they reflected and embodied public opinion—which, according to Haldane, was the ultimate source of sovereignty.[25] If we remember this qualification, Webb's point is important because it actually shows Haldane's fundamentally democratic instinct, as opposed to Webb's instinct, which was essentially to become what the historian Colin Matthew, in another context, has called 'the captive of an interest',[26] that of the working class. Haldane's belief in both Court and Cabinet was nothing less than a belief in constitutional monarchy (which keeps the monarch politically neutral) and parliamentary democracy (which attempts to ensure the actual sovereignty of public opinion): another instance of Haldane's irreducibility to one faction or interest.

Haldane bridged the gap between the dying Whigs and the emerging Labour in his ability to own his own privileged past while embracing a democratic future. There were certainly a good number of people, including the Webbs, who decided to renounce the style of living that had characterised their inheritance in the cause of a more socially democratic society. Beatrice Webb's dinners were said to be 'exercises in asceticism',[27] as she attempted to live a life in solidarity with the poor. There were the young Oxford graduates, men such as William Beveridge and R. H. Tawney, inspired by T. H. Green's vision of radically engaged citizenship (see Chapter 4), who lived and worked at Toynbee Hall, a place specifically designed to allow future leaders to dwell alongside the impoverished inhabitants of London's East End. This would provide an insight into societal conditions that no amount of theory could bring. Haldane, however, did not attempt to live like 'the working man', let alone embrace the conditions of the unemployed.

The tone is set by the very manner in which Haldane entered politics. It was admittance, in 1878, to the exclusive world of the London gentleman's club Brooks's—the traditional stronghold of upper-class Whiggery, and a far cry from Toynbee Hall—that represented Haldane's first step upon the political ladder. Moreover, it was an aristocratic relative, Robert Haldane-Duncan, third Earl of Camperdown, who secured his place for him. As Haldane told his mother at the time: 'He [Camperdown] is to propose me & Lord Stair is to second my name. ... It is really an incalculable advantage to me to have him thus backing me up. I am committed to Whig politics somewhat prematurely it is true, but this would have been so at any rate.'[28] Throughout his life Haldane maintained a manner and ways which were undeniably patrician—his double-pronged silver cigar forks spoke for themselves.[29] He was undoubtedly a great lover of food and wine, said to possess 'the finest cellar and the best table in Scotland'.[30] In fact, when his twenty-one-year-old nephew Graeme Haldane arrived as a student at Trinity College, Cambridge in 1919 his uncle insisted on financing a small wine cellar for his rooms.[31] This is hardly the behaviour of a Keir Hardie.

But if Haldane's eating habits were far from puritanical, his work ethic was decidedly Protestant.[32] He found in work a kind of justification for, and a sanctification of, his own existence. Work validated him (it also distracted him from his turbulent emotions, as we discovered in Chapter 2), and so he filled up almost every hour with it. Almost. Dining was for him the exception. It was the setting for his relaxation, where his 'strenuous' hours of work were relieved by the consumption of 'choice edibles'. Denied (or denying himself) the other home comforts of married life and the space of free evenings and weekends, Haldane's love of the table is surely a forgivable foible, if it is even that. We might see it in a rather different light if we remember (notwithstanding what has been said about relaxation) that it was at his dinner table that Haldane *got things done*. This was the setting for that key Haldanean technique for political success: bringing miscellaneous groups of people together in an informal, convivial atmosphere, where professional, daytime rivalries are set aside as the wine takes hold, to be replaced with late-night plans for collaborative, transformative action. Finally, we have to remember that, despite traditional, epicurean delights, Haldane did not remain aloof from the springs of radical change that would affect the lives of the poorest in society. He was not a socialist, but he did work closely with those on the left, helping to found the London School of Economics (essentially a socialist endeavour, see Chapter 8), promoting the careers of leading socialists (Harold Laski in particular), dining at Toynbee Hall with its founders, lecturing at the Working Men's College and at the St James's and Soho Radical Club, actively supporting the Workers' Educational Association, and meeting regularly with the labourers within his constituency. And he did, of course, serve in the first Labour government.[33]

Bearing all this in mind, Beatrice Webb couldn't help but form an overwhelmingly positive view of Haldane, which she made explicit in her second volume of memoirs, *Our Partnership*:

> As lawyer, politician and administrator, R. B. Haldane came to be recognised as one in the first rank. ... But it was pre-eminently as a big public personage, in some ways the biggest and most genial of his time, that he will be remembered by those who knew him. ... He had a notable gift for manipulating his fellow-men and for the organisation of business; for getting the best out of his subordinates; mainly because, whilst being somewhat cynical, he was always good-humoured and considerate, tempering rebuke and approval with kindly humour. Thus, it was in personal intercourse that he excelled; in successful intrigue, always for public and not for private ends. About Haldane's personal disinterestedness there can be no doubt. He loved power, especially the power of the hidden hand; or shall I say of the *recognised* hidden hand? But he frequently sacri-

ficed his own prospects if he could thereby serve a friend or promote a cause he believed in. To sum up my memories: a powerful and beneficent personality, a great citizen, above all a loyal and generous colleague. [34]

* * *

Such is the record of Haldane by one of the leading socialist thinkers of the day. And yet, throughout his life, Haldane, truly irreducible, maintained a close circle of friends within the Conservative Party. This, too, was a party on the move, and not into the past. Haldane stated their differences from and similarities to the Liberals succinctly in 1896:

> If Liberalism is associated with Home Rule, Conservatism is associated with the special championship of the interests of Church, Land, and Capital. For the rest, in the matter of the treatment of social problems, the distinction between the Liberals and Conservatives is one of degree rather than of kind. There is no greater delusion than that which a few years ago was current among a good many people, that we were approaching a period when the difference between the two parties would turn on economic principles, the Conservatives remaining free from any taint of Socialism. [35]

Home Rule for Ireland—governed from London since 1801—was indeed the defining measure of Liberalism once the Liberal Unionists split from the party in 1886, rebelling against Gladstone's desire to appease Irish nationalists through granting self-government (though still within the context of the United Kingdom). Haldane was not one of the rebels. He believed in the course Gladstone had set upon because he believed in freedom and because he knew that anything short of devolved self-government would fail to meet Irish demands. [36] Furthermore, by the time the Liberals won the 1892 general election they were reliant on Irish MPs to make up their majority. According to Haldane, 'Only one thing was evident, having regard not only to our convictions but to the composition of our majority. It was that we must introduce a Home Rule Bill.' [37] This had its benefits for Haldane's political career, as the battle over the finer points of the legislation brought his legal knowledge into high demand. 'My training in the learning of the Canadian Constitution gave me an almost unique opportunity in the House of expounding and defending the Bill, and of this opportunity I made ... full use, with the general assent and good will of the

Commons.'[38] The problem, however, was that the storm over Home Rule kicked the prospect of legislating for progressive social reforms, about which Haldane was passionately concerned, into the long grass. It was also a Bill that would evidently be demolished in the overwhelmingly Conservative Lords.

Gladstone's failure, followed by the brief and ineffectual premiership of Lord Rosebery, meant that it was not long before the reciprocated sympathies of Conservatives and Liberal Unionists were cemented in the coalition government of 1895 (to this day, the official title for the Conservative Party is the 'Conservative and Unionist Party', but for ease I shall simply refer to them as Conservatives). The Conservative leader, Lord Salisbury, then recognised the need for 'an extra tinge of Liberalism' in Conservative policies.[39] As Haldane said in 1896, 'This taint [socialism], if taint it be, has deeply penetrated their [the Conservatives'] policy, as it has done that of their opponents, and there is no champion of non-interference, however stiff-necked he may have been, who has not become infected with it.'[40] But the 'taint' was there even earlier than that. Already in 1885 Gladstone was complaining about the 'leaning of both parties to Socialism which I radically disapprove'.[41] Even Salisbury in his Oxford Union days and his first election address at Stamford sounded a note for state intervention.[42] By 1891 he could say that his Conservative Party had 'always leaned—perhaps unduly leaned—to the use of the State, so far as it can properly be used for the improvement of the physical, moral and intellectual condition of our people'.[43] Salisbury had always supported factory legislation, had sought improved treatment of paupers, and had even been accused of 'State socialism' in response to an article of 1883 recommending the intervention of quasi-public bodies in the improvement of housing conditions for labourers and artisans.[44] To find him legislating, with a 'Liberal tinge', in 1887 and 1891 on land purchase in Ireland is not, therefore, entirely surprising. Haldane was not wrong to see the presence of socialist principles as pervasive, and it was characteristic of him to alight upon that which unites parties rather than divides them.

It was upon the foundation of united principles that Haldane sought to build working relationships with Conservatives. Haldane was fundamentally a principle, not a party, man. There will be plenty to say in Chapter 8 on his close collaboration with and support for A. J. Balfour, Leader of the

House of Commons from 1891, and, as prime minister, of the Conservative and Unionist administration from 1902 to 1905. We will see that the success of the University of London Act 1898 was deeply indebted to Haldane's ability to get Balfour on side, as it was really only the latter who could give the Bill fair passage through Parliament. When it comes to Balfour's 1902 Education Act—which allowed public funds to be spent on Church of England schools as part of its attempt to unify primary and secondary education in England and Wales—we shall see a different dynamic emerge, one in which Haldane stands as a lone voice of support from the opposition benches: a stance that was shockingly contrary to the convictions of the Liberal heartland. When Haldane felt that a transformative educational principle was at stake, there was no amount of party grievance that could make him back down; he would vote with the Conservatives every step of the way.

* * *

He would do the same on certain imperial questions. This was certainly the case when it came to the Second Boer War (October 1899 to May 1902)—a conflict between the British Empire and two Boer states over the empire's power and influence in South Africa. Though a Liberal, Haldane supported the Conservative government's approach to the war, not out of any belief in the glory of the cause, but as 'the least of two terrible evils'.[45] His initial survey in June 1899 of the prospect of war suggested otherwise: 'I am pretty sure the Govt do not wish to fight in the Transvaal—there is no justification for it, & they know that. Chamberlain's speech [Chamberlain was Secretary of State for the Colonies at the time] is bluff, & nothing more.'[46] But when President Kruger's refusal to grant full voting rights and representation to British subjects living in the Transvaal escalated in September 1899 to the point of issuing an ultimatum that all British troops were to evacuate the Transvaal border within forty-eight hours, Haldane felt Kruger had brought the conflict upon his own head.[47] In November 1900 Haldane's view was further shaped by an encounter with Adrian Hofmeyr, an Afrikaner who happened to support the British cause, who told Haldane 'clearly that the Boers meant war, and that its coming was only a matter of time. This, he says, the talk he had with the Boer officials while in prison at Pretoria made him certain of.' It is in light of this information that Haldane tells his mother, 'It is a lamentable miserable business, but the least of two terrible evils; that is my conclusion about it.'[48] Just what exactly the other terrible evil was is unclear here, but the context suggests that he means something like British limpness in the face of unjust aggression and the repression of British subjects. According to his *Autobiography*, Haldane believed that if Britain failed to fight in such circumstances it would have meant placing the country 'in a position of danger from the rest of the world'.[49]

The question of the justness of this war dominated headlines at the time, as did the British use of concentration camps in South Africa. Haldane was supportive of these camps. We should be aware, of course, that such camps were not intended for the purpose of extermination, as the Nazis would later design them, but they were nevertheless hotbeds for disease and malnutrition. Death rates were staggeringly high.[50] Haldane's own brother, the physiologist John Scott Haldane, having read the reports of Emily Hobhouse after her visits to the camps, was outraged by the conditions there. So much so that he went to see his brother, Richard (our Haldane), 'and said that there were things in Miss Hobhouse's report which indubitably showed that there was something very seriously wrong. R. B. H. [our Haldane, again] after listening to it said: "Go and see Chamberlain, he's a very sensible fellow" ... the result was that orders were sent out for the effecting of improvements.' The entry for J. S. Haldane in the *Oxford Dictionary of National Biography* states: 'During the South African War [J. S.] Haldane's influence was largely responsible for the improvements of the inadequate diet at first provided in the concentration camps and thus abolished a serious menace to health.'[51]

J. S.'s brother, our Haldane, was clear in his condemnation of the camps' unsanitary arrangements. During a Commons debate in June 1901, Haldane joined with pro-Boer members of the House to denounce the appalling conditions: 'They [the pro-Boer members] hate these evils; we hate these evils. They would fain have an end put to the miseries which these unhappy women and children are undergoing; we all desire to see that done as quickly as possible.'[52] But the *principle* of the camps—bringing women and children together into an area away from military activity—was one that Haldane saw as unavoidable if Kitchener's 'scorched earth' policy was to be followed. That policy, which involved the destruction of the evacuees' houses and farms in an attempt to shut down the Boer guerrilla fighters' supplies and networks, is a tough one to swallow for anyone who would want to glorify British military history. The Liberal leader, Campbell-Bannerman, famously described such tactics as 'methods of barbarism',[53] and they were widely condemned from Liberal benches. Haldane put matters rather differently. 'War is always a horrible and terrible thing—you will never make it otherwise than miserable.' Is this Haldane excusing the atrocities? His reference, in the same debate, to 'policies in connection with farm-burning and other matters which enlightened opinion has probably agreed were mistaken' appears to us now as too weak a statement on the issue. He follows this with the following assessment:

> Blunders of that kind have been made, and they always will be made in a great military campaign, because of the want of organisation which it produces. Still, I see nothing to lead me to question the desire of everybody, from the generals in the field to His Majesty's Ministers, to conduct the warlike operations in South Africa with as much humanity and as little cruelty as possible.[54]

It must be said that Haldane's habitual desire to be fair to all sides of the debate leads to a strange contradiction here. On the one hand he condemns (though not strongly) farm-burning, while on the other he has no doubts about the generals' sense of humanity—but farm-burning was not a 'blunder', it was an essential element of the scorched earth policy. Part of Haldane's ambivalence came from his friendship with a controversial colleague, Sir Alfred Milner—then governor of the Cape Colony and high commissioner for Southern Africa. John Buchan, a former staff member of Milner's, writes in his memoirs:

> What chiefly attracted me to him [Haldane] was his loyalty to Milner. Milner thought him the ablest man in public life, abler even than Arthur Balfour, and alone of his former Liberal allies Haldane stood by him on every count.[55]

Milner, initially at least, supported the use of concentration camps, so we should not be surprised to find Haldane saying to his critical Liberal colleagues, 'Before I pronounced against concentration I should like to know what other methods are open. I have listened in vain to the speeches on this side of the House for an alternative suggestion.'[56] Haldane's position may have undergone an alteration when, six months later, in December 1901, he received a letter from Milner admitting that the camps, despite all planned improvements, 'will remain a bad business, the thing, as far as I am concerned, in which I feel that the abuse so freely heaped upon us for everything we have done and not done is not without some foundation'.[57]

In 1925 Milner openly identified as a 'British race patriot', to whom the greatness of the empire reflected the greatness of the British race, a belief that was already operative while he was in South Africa.[58] According to one biographer, he fell 'prey to a facile "racialist" interpretation of the issues between Boer and Briton in the Transvaal'.[59] Haldane seems to have seen matters in racial terms, but not—like Milner—in terms of racial hierarchy. On 7 December 1899 Haldane tells his mother: 'Last night I dined with Arthur Balfour ... the talk was mostly on the war. I was the moderating influence—as I am not against the Boers but only against what they have been doing.'[60] During a debate on peace negotiations in the Commons in March 1901, his views on the racial element become clearer:

> We have got to realise and bear in mind the peculiar difficulties of the position. I believe that not only in Cape Colony and Natal, but in the two late Republics, the majority of the white inhabitants are not of British blood. If that be so, we have got to consider the point of view of the Afrikanders, and how we can conciliate the Boers as well as the people of British blood who take up a strong attitude on this matter. The business of His Majesty's Government is to hold the balance evenly between the two contending factions in South Africa, and to make it perfectly clear that there is to be no racial ascendency of Boer over Briton or Briton over Boer.

But Haldane also appears to have believed that Milner's aspirations were not in the direction of pushing the superiority of the British 'race':

> I think there has been a good deal of indiscreet blame of Sir A. Milner. I believe that, whether rightly or wrongly, Sir A. Milner is actuated by the highest motives, and is the very last person to allow himself to be made the tool of any faction at the Cape, or to support any ascendency of Briton over Boer, any more than Boer over Briton.[61]

Milner, however, had written to Haldane on 21 January that same year: 'I am all for the most forebearing and generous treatment of the Boers when they are once completely beaten—if only because that is the sole means of absorbing & ultimately getting rid of them as a separate exclusive caste.'[62] This is not an attractive outlook, and it seems hard to reconcile with Haldane's judgment concerning Milner's 'highest motives'. Was Haldane being disingenuous? Or did he believe that the 'absorption' of the Boers was an honourable intention? Perhaps Haldane read Milner's words, however poorly expressed, to mean that he desired to see Boer 'exclusivity' done away with in the hope that a more united community might emerge. This latter interpretation is the most charitable, but, even if it is accurate, Haldane must still have known that such unity ought, in Milner's eyes, to be centred and rooted in British values and practices.

It is certainly true that Haldane is difficult to pin down on issues surrounding the South African conflict. He supported the generals, but he condemned farm-burning; he saw no alternative to the concentration camps, but he wanted an end to their miserable conditions; he backed the racial supremacist Milner, but he was not against the Boers. Each of us will have to decide for ourselves whether these represent the unjustifiable contradictions of a politician too keen to please everyone; or the shrewd 'refinements' of a statesman seeking to hold in balance the many differing strands of a complex situation; or a typically Haldanean attempt to be firm on principles but realistic and flexible on practices.

These tensions are of a piece with Haldane's later decision, in March 1904, to abstain from voting in a Commons division on Chinese labour in the South African Rand mines—a policy adopted by Milner which utilised unfree labour from China in an attempt to offset a significant shortfall in the mining industry's rate of production. This was condemned as 'Chinese slavery' by the Liberals, and the outcry became particularly acute when incidents of flogging reached the ears of the British public. Haldane remained aloof from mainstream Liberal opinion, and once more took up his ambivalent stance: 'There have been abuses in the compounds of the Rand which can and must be remedied, but these abuses are being grossly exaggerated by our people for party ends.'[63] John Buchan recalls:

> I once accompanied him through his constituency of East Lothian when he was defending Milner's policy, including Chinese labour on the Rand. I came out of the hall with two old farmers. 'Was he for it or against it?' one asked. Said the other, 'I'm damned if I ken.'[64]

The future Liberal Foreign Secretary Sir Edward Grey, at one with Haldane in almost all matters, was equally baffled by his position on this issue. It was precisely because he knew the accuracy of Haldane's moral compass that the decision to abstain from condemning the policy appeared so unusual. 'Isn't Haldane curious?', Grey wrote to his wife Dorothy on 23 February 1904. 'He has so often differed from the party by rising into idealism above it, and now on Chinese Labour he has thrown ideals aside, and followed the narrow practical point that without Chinese Labour there will be a deficit in the Transvaal Revenue. But he is the same dear old Haldane.'[65]

The imperialist theme was one of the most dominant of the time. Campbell-Bannerman's comment on the 'barbarism' of British military policy was at one with the views of those known as 'Little Englanders'. In their view, Britain had no business interfering on the international stage; the country should concern itself with pressing social matters at home and direct its wealth to solving these, not to global economic and geographical expansion. What they saw as the 'morally detestable'[66] character of British behaviour in South Africa only served to sharpen their stance against imperialism. Haldane, as the mastermind behind the Liberal Imperialists, represented a very different view. This group of men believed the flourishing of the empire to be an essential aspect of prosperity at home. Imperial ties, or 'silken bonds' as Haldane called them, were the foundation of successful trade, and so of a thriving economy, and they carried with them a certain prestige amongst other nations, which both encouraged further trade deals and ensured Britain a seat at the table on all questions of international importance.

The British Empire was indeed the largest empire ever to have spanned the earth, with a staggering 412 million people under its rule at its height in 1913.[67] Nevertheless, the 'Lib Imps', as they were known, held to a fairly moderate form of imperialism. None within their number would go to the extremes of a Cecil Rhodes, for example, who famously exclaimed, 'I would annex the planets if I could.'[68] They were in favour of timely self-government for the dominions, and sought a unity in spirit rather than in imposed laws. Their ideal approached something closer to today's Commonwealth. Haldane's stance on Home Rule was simply an extension of his imperialism:

I was opposed to the rigid bonds of Imperial Federation and Imperial Preference. I believed that if we only gave free rein to the Colonies they would rally to the Empire. ... We [the Lib Imps] were strong Home Rulers because we held that it was only by giving Ireland freedom to govern herself [though still as part of the United Kingdom] that we could hope to satisfy her. But we felt not less the necessity of studying how the sense of liberty might be made to reach Canada, Australasia, and even India.[69]

Of course, one can remain critical of this position, for even if that 'sense of liberty' could be achieved in places such as Canada or South Africa, it would be felt, in the main, by the white settlers whose ancestors had colonised those countries in the first place. Haldane's views on the eventual governance of South Africa illustrate the point—it is the concerns of Boers and Britons, both white settler communities, that dominate. But it is at least clear that he had a respectful awareness of indigenous communities. His work at the Bar made this inevitable.

I remember ... one fortnight within which, towards the end of my time [at the Bar], beginning with a case of Buddhist law from Burmah, I went on to argue successively appeals concerned with the Maori law of New Zealand, the old French law of Quebec, the Roman-Dutch system of South Africa, the Mohammedan law and then the Hindu law from India, the custom of Normandy in a Jersey appeal, and Scottish law in a case from the North.[70]

The maintenance of these legal systems was close to Haldane's heart, and there is never any sense in his writings or speeches that he seeks to impose British models on other nations. Haldane's philosophical studies encouraged a sense of openness to other cultures. His respect for the ancient Indian philosophical tradition captured in the Upanishads,[71] and his correspondence with Indian philosophers, both of which flourished in his later years, suggest an attitude that is out of sync with common caricatures of the imperialist. Although he writes very much in the context of British rule in India, there is a passage towards the end of his *Autobiography* that takes us close to his true sensibilities:

I have never been in India and am not likely now to go there. But in my later years I have studied her philosophical literature, and I have had many native friends there, some of them men of learning who have been thorough students of our own thought as well as their own. There is in Bengal particularly a philosophical outlook which has moulded even Indian politi-

cal aspirations, among Mohammedans as well as among Hindus. The expo-
nents of this outlook have come to talk with me in London and in Scotland
for years past. We seem hardly to realise how much of a suggestive spirit of
their own they have to bring to us [that is, an inspiring spirit that can bring
ideas to other cultures], a spirit which may not always assume a very practical form, but yet is one that ought to be taken into account at every turn
by those responsible for seeking practical reforms in the system of [British]
Indian government. For want of knowledge [on the British side] has
brought in its train want of sympathy. Without such sympathy we may well
continue to succeed in 'policing' India, but it is difficult for us to gain the
confidence of the Indian people.[72]

So we should not gloss over Haldane's belief in empire, nor should we
totally reinterpret his imperialism to make it mean its opposite. While
admitting shortfalls in Haldane's vision, we can see that he did, as the
above quotation shows, go beyond the standard positions adopted within
the debate. We can see in Haldane an earnest desire to create a consensus
across nations, formed not by means of a Milner-like absorption of foreign
cultures into British culture, but by a mutual sense of exchange, where
Britain has just as much to learn from her dominions as she has to contribute to them.

* * *

Management of the empire was intimately connected to the approach that
Britain took to foreign policy. After the South African crisis, it was Russia
that first dominated Britain's foreign concerns. The development of
Russian railways in Central Asia raised worrying question marks over the
security of British rule in India, and Balfour, who was Conservative prime
minister at the time, became obsessed with mitigating the apparent
threat. He considered the army's primary function to be 'the protection
of the outlying portions of the Empire, and notably India',[73] and he
devoted over half of the meetings of the Committee of Imperial Defence,
which he established in 1904, to the safeguarding of India.[74] The Foreign
Secretary, Lord Lansdowne, sought diplomatic accord with the Russians,
spending much of 1903 in reaching out to St Petersburg, only to come up
against a brick wall. Meanwhile, closer to home, colonial tensions with
France—particularly relating to Morocco, Newfoundland and Egypt—
began to defuse in the wake of King Edward's successful trip to Paris in

A BRAVE NEW WORLD

81. William Ewart Gladstone (1809–1898), the driving force behind the Liberal Party at the time of Haldane's entry into politics. Although Haldane searched always for a more progressive liberalism, he kept this photograph of Gladstone on his desk until his death.

Social Policy and Education: Sidney and Beatrice Webb

82. Haldane worked intimately with Sidney (1859–1947) and Beatrice Webb (1858–1943) in the causes of social progress and education. Photographed c. 1895, around the founding of LSE, their work with Haldane started 10 years previously and lasted until his death.

83, 84. A book inscribed in 1901 by Beatrice Webb to Haldane with the words 'Law is the Mother of Freedom', words that he would have particularly appreciated. The Factory Acts gradually improved the regulation of working conditions, a cause close to Haldane and the Webbs' hearts.

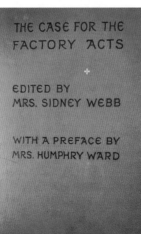

THE CASE FOR THE
FACTORY ACTS

✦

EDITED BY
MRS. SIDNEY WEBB

WITH A PREFACE BY
MRS. HUMPHRY WARD

R B Haldane
to
Beatrice Webb
July 1901.

Law is the Mother
of Freedom.

85. The portrait of Sidney and Beatrice Webb in 1928 by Sir William Nicholson hangs above the mantelpiece in the Founders Room of The London School of Economics.

86. After Haldane's death the Webbs insisted that the portrait of Haldane by Sir Arthur Cope should hang next to theirs as a co-founder. It is a copy of the protrait painted in 1914 and presented to the Privy Council by the widow of Sir Ernest Cassel, which now hangs in the Supreme Court.

The Rise of Labour

Haldane's political life embraced the waning of his family's Whig traditions and the ascent of organised labour. Haldane was vocal in advocating a reconcilion of these two approaches as a unified alternative to the Conservative Party.

87. Keir Hardie (1856–1915), photographed in 1908, a founder of the Labour Party, who served as its first parliamentary leader between 1906 and 1908. Despite Haldane's progressive attitude to social questions, he never quite fitted into the new world of socialism.

88. Archibald Primrose, 5th Earl of Rosebery (1847–1929), the putative head of the Liberal Imperialists, whose policies sought to balance the concerns of working men by benefitting both Britain and her Dominions. The portrait is by Sir John Millais, 1886.

Cross-Party Man

89. Haldane was able to reconcile his left-leaning Liberalism with many friendships among the Conservatives and a strong sympathy with certain of their policies. His close working relationship with the Conservative Leader and sometime Prime Minister A. J. Balfour (1848–1930), another philosopher statesman, was critical in advancing Haldane's educational and military causes. The portrait was painted in 1908 by John Singer Sargent.

90. The triptych of (left to right) A. J. Balfour, W. E. Gladstone, and Thomas Carlyle, which sat on Haldane's desk. The breadth of views they represent reflects Haldane's own broad range of sympathies.

91. The British army's engagement in the Second Boer War was one of the most heated political topics at the turn of the 20th century. Haldane largely supported the Conservative Government in its approach to the conflict, to the disbelief of many of his Liberal colleagues. His stance may well have been shaped by his friendship with Sir Alfred Milner (1854–1925), governor of the Cape Colony and high commissioner for Southern Africa.

92. Joseph Chamberlain (1836–1914), one of the key instigators of the Second Boer War. He served as Colonial Secretary in Balfour's Conservative and Unionist Administration, and sparked the famous tariff reform debate. This was to split his party and lead to the landslide Liberal victory of 1906 and, by extension, Haldane's membership in the Cabinet.

Suffragists and Suffragettes

The rights of women was another dominant debate during Haldane's years in public life. Haldane was a vocal supporter of the cause, sponsoring three private members' bills in 1889, 1890, 1892 which proposed the enfranchisement of certain classes of women.

93. Emmeline Pankhurst (1858–1928), leader of the suffragette movement. 'Deeds, not words' was their motto. Haldane firmly deprecated their militant measures, yet believed in the principle of women's suffrage and the suffragist movement. Nevertheless, the suffragettes disapproval of the Liberal Cabinet's lacklustre attitude to the issue led them to vandalise ministers' homes, including Haldane's. Photographed in 1905.

1903 and President Loubet's 'reciprocal goodwill visit' to England shortly afterwards.[75] Cordial relations were cemented with the signing of the Anglo-French Entente in April 1904, otherwise known as the Entente Cordiale, in which the French acquiesced in British dominance in Egypt in exchange for control in Morocco. This signalled the end of Britain's 'splendid isolation', and the beginning of a co-operation that was to have world-changing effects.

* * *

These were the years, too, in which the tide of the women's suffrage movement rose and in which controversies over the House of Lords threatened to destroy the very foundations of the constitution. Haldane was not outside such debates.

Gladstone's Liberal ministry of 1880–85 culminated in two crucial pieces of legislation: the Representation of the People Act of 1884 and the Redistribution of Seats Act of 1885. The former tripled the electorate by granting votes to agricultural labourers, ignoring for the first time the age-old claims of wealth and property. With voting now based on rights, it was only a matter of time before the cry for women's suffrage would reach a crescendo. It was a demand that had been on the scene at least since Mary Wollstonecraft's groundbreaking 1792 publication, *A Vindication of the Rights of Woman*. The Chartists of the 1840s and the Liberal intellectuals of the 1850s and 60s, such as Harriet Taylor Mill and her celebrated husband John Stuart Mill, advanced the cause. By 1865 women's suffrage committees began to form and petition Parliament. Although women taxpayers were granted the right to vote in municipal elections in 1869, it would take until 1918 for a major women's suffrage Bill to pass through both Houses of Parliament (the Representation of the People Act 1918, which allowed votes to all women over thirty). It is not surprising that between these events a radical wing, known as the suffragettes, would emerge, headed by Emmeline Pankhurst and her daughter Christabel. Haldane had sponsored private member's Bills in 1889, 1890, and 1892 that proposed the enfranchisement of women who were heads of households, ratepayers and property owners. The 1892 Bill was unsuccessful by a narrow margin of twenty-three votes on its second reading, and all seven suffrage Bills between the Liberal victory of 1906 and the start of the war failed to make it through Parliament.

The rising tide of militant action by the suffragettes in response to these repeated defeats caused Haldane alarm. Although personally a supporter of women's votes, he found himself, as a member of the Liberal government, heckled at meetings, and the windows of his London house were broken. He considered such tactics to be an impediment to real legislative advancement, alienating even those, such as himself, inclined to agree with the principles for which the suffragettes fought. Haldane was asked about their actions upon his arrival in the United States in August 1913 (he was there, as Lord Chancellor, on his way to address the special joint meeting in Montreal of the American Bar Association and the Bar Association of Canada), answering: 'You are fortunate to have no militant suffragists in America. ... Personally I am in favour of the cause of the suffragist, but the methods of the militants have delayed equal suffrage in England for many years. I very much disapprove of their methods.' He expanded later in his trip, 'I am in favour of the female force in life ... I have no doubt that in England women will at length get measures in their favor.'[76]

He would see that he played his part in making sure that it was so. The Haldane Report of 1918 on the Machinery of Government, for instance, was radical in its recommendations regarding women in the Civil Service. They were not to be debarred from certain positions simply because of their gender, and, with regards to their payment, the committee members—who included Beatrice Webb—were 'of opinion that no discrimination can properly be enforced merely on the ground of sex':[77] both radical proposals for their time. Haldane was evidently thrilled with this development, writing to his sister Elizabeth:

> I got my paragraph accepted with a trifling verbal alteration. But better still we agreed on a splendid and full paragraph in the opening part of the Report, insisting on the Civil Service being thrown completely open to women & on them being fully employed even in the highest posts. Morant, Mrs Webb & I persuaded Sir G. Murray to agree to sign. He may add a separate note of his own, but this is a big step forward.[78]

The former Cabinet Secretary (the most senior Civil Servant in the UK) Lord Robin Butler was surely right when he hailed Haldane—in 2018, a hundred years after the report's publication—as 'the ground-breaker on the role of women in the civil service'.[79]

Haldane's attitude to equality of the sexes was no doubt shaped by the beliefs of his remarkable mother, Mary Elizabeth Haldane, captured in this extraordinarily brilliant letter to the editor of *The Times* in February 1909:[80]

Sir,

Will you permit a constant reader of The Times to add a few lines to what has recently appeared in your columns on the question of Woman Suffrage?

I am now in my 84th year, and have paid rates and taxes since my widowhood for upwards of 30 years.

During that period I have had, roughly speaking, 40 men in my service, all of whom have had the opportunity of exercising their influence on the government of our country. I have three sons, all of whom have not only served their country with distinction, but have also attained to positions of pre-eminence in their different professions.

Until they reached manhood and were able to exercise their right of voting, I had no direct or indirect means of expressing myself as a citizen of the Empire which I was training my sons to serve. Although I have exercised my right of voting for school board and county council, I have never had an opportunity of expressing my views on the laws these bodies are appointed to administer.

Though I am aware that there are foolish women as well as foolish men … I have not during my long life come in close contact with either.

On the other hand, I have had a very extensive acquaintance with women of all classes who have served their day and generation nobly, and whose inclusion on the roll of voters would have been not only an honour but a strength to their country.

I am, Sir, your obedient servant,

Octogenarian

* * *

The democratic instinct of his mother is to be seen once again in Haldane's attitude to the reform of the House of Lords, which we will explore in Chapter 10. It was an issue that came to a head because of Chancellor of the Exchequer Lloyd George's revolutionary 'People's Budget' of 1909, which he described as a 'war budget' because it would 'wage implacable warfare against poverty and squalidness'.[81] Spirits, estates and higher incomes would be hit with direct taxes, including the 'supertax', which would see incomes over £5,000 a year (today's £600,000) paying an additional 6d. in the pound.[82] There would be land taxes, too. The budget would raise money to meet the staggering cost of the new old-age pensions (£16 million; equivalent to £1.9 billion in 2020)[83] and, less progressively, the new dreadnought battleships. But it was principally orientated to a vast improvement in public works and social welfare, and it was the rich who would meet the burden of the costs. Not only was there more than a 'taint' of socialism about it, the budget was a clear rejection of the tariff reformers' ideals. The latter were convinced that tariffs on imports could raise the necessary money. Why plunder the pockets of any segment of society, if such an option was available? In response, the Liberal free traders pointed out that tariffs could only mean the rising cost of imported food, and it would be the poorest in society who would suffer as a result.

The Lords, a deeply Conservative body, were only going to come to one conclusion about such a Bill. And yet it had significant public backing (particularly in the north) and it was established practice, moreover, that money Bills received fair passage through the Lords.

In this case, the Lords would only pass the Bill if the government had the mandate of the people, and a close-fought general election ensued in January 1910. The Liberals were returned, but could only maintain a majority with the support of Labour and Irish Parliamentary Party members. The budget was duly approved on 27 April in the Commons, and the Lords gave their assent the following day. However, the government feared future disruption from the Upper House and decided to go to the people on the platform of reform of the overarching power of the Lords. The Liberals were once again returned, with the critical support of the Irish. The prime minister, Asquith, then placed two options before the Lords for reform of their House. The first option was that they approve the 'veto policy', which meant that a suspensory veto would replace the Lords' absolute veto. This would allow a Bill that had passed in three successive sessions in the Commons and within the lifetime of the same parliament to receive automatic royal assent, even when the Lords had thrown it out. The other option was to accept a mass creation of Liberal peers, to which the king had reluctantly agreed if the recalcitrance of the Lords continued. The unbearable thought of such an indignity led the Lords to accept the veto policy, which became legislation with the signing of the Parliament Act in August 1911—a constitutionally groundbreaking Act. Haldane was intimately connected with its creation and, after being elevated as War Secretary to the House of Lords in March 1911, was able to assist in steering the legislation through the Upper House. Referring to 'the Parliament Bill', he wrote to his mother from Germany in May 1910: 'I drew the preamble with my own hand, & converted the Cabinet to it.'[84] Alongside the 'veto policy', the Act also made provision so that money Bills could be delayed in the Lords no longer than a month and for the reduction in the length of parliaments from seven to five years. At long last, the democratic power of the Commons over the inherited power of the Lords was enshrined in law.

Haldane wanted reform of the second chamber to go much further, but it was still a step in the right direction.[85] As we go on to explore Haldane's achievement in the service of the state later in the book, it is important to be aware of the background tensions at play between the two Houses. The Parliament Act was the culmination of a long-standing tug of war that had seen the Liberal government frustrated time and again in its attempts to pass its more progressive measures, from Home Rule to women's suffrage. Indeed, Haldane's historic Army Reform Bill of 1907 was the first major piece of legislation that the Campbell-Bannerman ministry managed to get through both Houses. One of the primary reasons for its success was Haldane's cross-party connections; he liaised with Balfour before introducing the Bill to ensure that the Conservatives would give it sufficient time in the Commons.

But how did Haldane come to command such influence within Parliament and amongst his political peers? As we go on to tell the story, in the next chapter, of Haldane's life from the time of his election as an MP, we'll find the answer to this question. We'll also discover the disturbing circumstances in which that influence was lost and how Haldane, after many trials and great personal cost, eventually won it back again.

A MAN FOR ALL SEASONS

I am certain that I am not using the language of exaggeration when I say—what can be said of no one else—that both as War Minister and as Lord Chancellor he [Haldane] has reached the highest standard that this country has known.

H.H. Asquith to Sir Edward Grey, 27 May 1915[1]

Clearly, as the last chapter showed, Haldane was in the thick of almost every major political debate of the day. But a number of those debates—particularly those concerned with tariff reform, military affairs, international relations and education—were to enter into his career more profoundly than others. Returning to Beatrice Webb's image of the 'large and crowded canvas' that would have to make up 'any adequate picture' of Haldane's life, it is at this point that background meets foreground and we can begin to paint the main events that went to the making of Haldane the statesman. Given the enormous range of his life, our brushstrokes will have to remain very broad indeed. Later chapters will fill in the detail.

From 1885 onwards Haldane was juggling his practice at the Bar with a very active parliamentary life as MP for the Scottish constituency of Haddingtonshire (later renamed East Lothian). He sat on endless committees, including the commission into the Featherstone 'Massacre' of 1893 and the Explosives Committee of 1900–4, established at Haldane's suggestion as a result of British failures in the Second Boer War. This latter committee made a decisive contribution to the development of the army's fighting capacities, and the experience Haldane gained through it was a vital building block in his later competence as War Secretary. Meanwhile, he maintained his searching philosophical enquiries, delivering the prestigious Gifford Lectures at the University of St Andrews in 1902–4, which were then published as a two-volume work under the title *The Pathway to Reality* (St Andrews also offered him the chair of Moral Philosophy, but he reluctantly turned this down). As there was no income to be had from work in the Commons, and as this made a sizeable dent in his time, Haldane made the brave decision in 1897 to go 'Special'. This meant that he would not appear in any court of first instance without a special fee of 50 guineas in addition to the normal fee. But this only seemed to raise demand, and his legal prestige: 'towards the end of my life as a "Special" my chambers were a spectacle. The floor of the clerk's room was strewn with briefs. It was a question only of which one should take and how many had to be rejected.'[2]

* * *

One of Haldane's most famous cases was one that he lost. This was the Scottish Church case of 1904, known as the 'Wee Frees' case, which provides an illuminating insight into Haldane's style at the Bar—at its best and worst. Haldane considered the case as 'probably the greatest litigation of its particular kind which ever occurred in our history'.[3] The issue concerned the union of the Free Church of Scotland with the United Presbyterian Church in 1900 to form the United Free Church of Scotland. Dissenting members of the Free Church claimed more than £2 million of the Church's money on the grounds that the union of the two Churches was invalid. They argued, firstly, that a change in the doctrine of predestination arising from the union meant an undermining of the original constitution of the Free Church. They also contended that the Church's trust deeds were for those who held to unalterable doctrines, rather than those who belonged to a developing tradition.

Haldane acted on behalf of the new United Free Church and, against the first point of grievance, chose to argue that the doctrine of predestination was not undermined by the doctrine of free will that was now part of the new statement of belief. He gathered a mass of theological material, and even marshalled the vast scriptural knowledge of his mother, who provided him with a list of all the New Testament texts that showed the validity of both doctrines. On this, he won his point, but not without much consternation from some of the judges. The librarian of the House of Lords, Haldane's great friend Edmund Gosse, amusingly recreated the atmosphere of the courtroom in his diary:

> The Chancellor [Lord Halsbury], manifestly hostile to the Free Church's position, is red with effort, mental and physical, of finding holes in Haldane's polished armour. Lord Alverstone, perfectly blank, with glassy eyes, is an evident Gallio, to whom all this ecclesiastical metaphysic is unintelligible and insane. Lord James of Hereford chafes under it, constantly snapping out, 'I say it without irreverence but,' or 'Well, well, Mr Haldane, but in the name of common sense——', and Haldane, flapping back the side of his wig, replies, 'My Lord, we deal not with the dictates of common sense, but with a mystery.' Lord Robertson, who probably knows more about it than anybody, remains perfectly still. Lord Davey [for whom Haldane used to 'devil'], with his parchment face puckered up, searches for verbal solecisms. And Haldane, bland, tireless, imperturbable, never taken at a disadvantage, always courteous, always ready, pushes on in faultless flow of language, turning the whole thing into a supplement of his own 'Pathway to Reality'.[4]

Haldane subsequently lamented that the Law Lords had not been Scotsmen, to whom his arguments—he believed—would have seemed clear as day. Nevertheless, the judges accepted his point eventually.

But on the question of the trust deed, despite a previous unanimous decision from the Scottish Court of Session to the contrary, the judges of the House of Lords held that its terms did in fact require an unswerving allegiance to a rigid body of doctrine. The public anger at the decision was intense. Surely the trust was intended for the Church, who were free to choose how its doctrines might develop or even change—precisely the point Haldane had argued. The contrary view of the Lords had cruel consequences, stripping the United Free Church of all its property, including—as Haldane pointed out—'what had been contributed by the very men who were defenders at the Bar'.[5] Worse still, it condemned them to pay the costs of the litigation personally.

Haldane, however, refused to let such an injustice stand. He rallied the leader of the United Free Church, the aged Principal Rainy—'almost stunned with grief'—and persuaded him to start a subscription at once. 'I said to him, "Let us begin the effort on the spot. It is worth the sacrifice even of your life … I am not a member of the Church, but I feel this so strongly that I will begin the list with £1000 [today's £120,000],[6] which I can well do, considering the fees I have received."' Within hours the total had reached over £150,000. Haldane then moved up a gear, deploying all the weight of his powerful contacts, and sought an Act of Parliament to address the situation:

> I saw Mr Balfour—at that time Prime Minister; he was most sympathetic and helpful. Lord Dunedin, who was then Scottish Secretary, Lord Balfour of Burleigh, and the Archbishop of Canterbury were equally keen, and I went down to Hatfield and spent the weekend with Mr. Balfour there to explain to him the facts. Parliament came to a practically unanimous decision to pass the Bill which put the matter right.[7]

* * *

This energising of networks was typical of Haldane. It was through such means that he succeeded in most of his successful political endeavours (mental and physical effort—which he exerted in abundance—was not enough). Nowhere was this more evident than in his cross-party endeavours in the cause of educational reform, as we shall see in Chapter 8. Education was one of the dominating themes of Haldane's pre-government days while the Conservatives were still in power, particularly the formative roles he played in restructuring the University of London, the founding of the LSE and Imperial College, and the development of the legal foundation of the civic universities. As will become clear, it is unlikely that he would have achieved any of these without bringing Conservative leaders onto his side, and securing big names to back his causes.

One of Haldane's other major political endeavours of this time was acting as lead policy-maker for the Liberal Imperialists. Although they failed in some of their key objectives (reinstating Lord Rosebery as leader of the Liberals, for example, or winning the fight for 'National Efficiency'), the 'Lib Imps' played a significant role in offering constructive critiques and alternatives to government policies and did a lot to widen awareness within the Liberal ranks of the emerging labour movement. Haldane, more than any of his colleagues, showed the way in which socialist principles could be balanced and even brought into harmony with classical Liberal doctrines. In the end, however, he failed to persuade the main body of the party that such balance and harmony was necessary to avoid a mass exodus of traditional Liberal followers to the newly emerging Labour camp. If they had listened to his plea, perhaps 'the strange death of Liberal England' would not have occurred.[8]

Haldane's imperialism was intimately connected to another major debate of his time, one that continues to dominate political discourse and international relations today: free trade versus protectionism. In Haldane's day, the former policy was largely championed by the Liberals and the latter by a sizeable contingent of Conservatives. Chapter 5 looked at this debate in detail, and Haldane's position within it, but it is important to flag it here as a factor that entered—at least after Joseph Chamberlain, Secretary of State for the Colonies, began his campaign for imperial protection in 1903—into almost every aspect of political life. It ripped the Conservative government in two and it dramatically turned the tide in favour of the Liberals, leading ultimately to their landslide victory in January 1906 and their subsequent nine years in government, before entering into the wartime coalition that would see Haldane ousted from the Cabinet. Given the decisive role that the Liberal government would play in shaping the outcome of events that led to the First World War, it could be sensibly argued that the tariff reform debate had much wider and more profound ramifications than the name suggests.

* * *

Haldane, along with his two closest political friends, H. H. Asquith and Sir Edward Grey, was to play a major part in this distinguished pre-war Liberal ministry and the build-up to war. And yet they very nearly didn't enter that ministry at all, due to their famous—some might say infamous—agreement known as the Relugas Compact. This was an agreement forged between the three friends at Relugas, a fishing lodge on the River Findhorn in the north-east of Scotland where Grey was staying in the autumn of 1905, just a few months before the dissolution of Balfour's government. Having abandoned an earlier attempt to wrest the party from Campbell-Bannerman's leadership, which would have allowed the principles of Liberal Imperialism to take centre stage, the triumvirate of Haldane, Grey and Asquith sought an ascendancy of their views in other ways.[9] In essence, it was agreed that CB (as Campbell-Bannerman was known) was unfit to bring their progressive policies to fruition if he led the Liberals in the

Commons, and they feared that the likes of Chamberlain in opposition would capitalise upon this to undermine public confidence in the party. In their view, CB leading in the Commons could only mean the failure of a free-trade ministry.[10] If, however, CB would take a peerage and lead from the Lords, allowing Asquith to lead in the Commons as Chancellor of the Exchequer (where he would in effect have prime ministerial power), with Grey as his Foreign Secretary and Haldane in the Lords as Lord Chancellor, then the approaching rift could be averted. In order to ensure that such an arrangement materialised, the three men decided to act in concert and, despite their protestations to the contrary,[11] effectively put a gun to CB's head: unless he agreed to take a peerage and grant Asquith, Grey and Haldane their desired posts, then all three would refuse to take office and deprive the Cabinet of the support of this vital wing of the party. In terms of Haldane's claim to the Lord Chancellorship, Grey believed that CB might be further swayed by the fact that the 'highest legal authorities on the Superior Court' backed Haldane. 'Our Lord Chancellor should be a man who has their legal respect', Grey told Asquith, '& I affirm that they are all Haldanites except Alverstone [then Lord Chief Justice].'[12] Grey also said at this time that Haldane's appointment as Lord Chancellor 'was the only office about which I felt there should be no compromise'.[13]

Having decided upon their course of action at Relugas, the question now was how to persuade CB to agree to their plan. Accordingly, Haldane sought the king's blessing for their manoeuvrings, which he obtained—subject to the king's stipulation that CB should be handled sensitively. Already a frail man by this stage, CB was initially receptive to the idea of going to the Lords, particularly as the king encouraged him in this direction. But upon consulting Lady Campbell-Bannerman, who was of strong character, his attitude became one of 'no surrender'; he was to lead in the Commons. Asquith quickly rescinded his pledge to his two friends, feeling obliged to take up the Exchequer. His argument, as he expressed it in a letter to Haldane on 7 December 1905, rested on the fact that, although the Liberals had come to power on the dissolution of Balfour's government, the general election remained ahead of them and not behind them—a situation that they had not originally envisaged at Relugas:

> I stand in a peculiar position which is not shared by either of you. If I refuse
> to go in, one of two consequences follows: either (1) the attempt to form a

Govt is given up (which I don't believe in the least would now happen) or (2) a weak Govt would be formed entirely or almost entirely of one colour. In either event in my opinion the issue of the election would be put in the utmost peril.[14]

The consequences of Grey and Haldane refusing were not so severe, and they stuck to their guns—initially, at least. Grey was offered the Foreign Office but refused, Haldane the Attorney-Generalship. CB had already offered the Lord Chancellorship to his friend Sir Robert Reid. Determined to stand resolute with Grey, and certainly unwilling to take up the Attorney-Generalship, Haldane was set to refuse, too, but not before calling upon that most intimate of friends, Lady Horner. It was due to her more than to anyone else, so Haldane later claimed,[15] that the careers of these two men, and therefore the course of history, changed. Her argument was thus: 'You told the King that you would not leave him in the lurch—besides this you are making a real risk for the Free Trade cause. There may be a very heavy reaction against the weak Government which is going to be formed, in which Free Trade will perish.' When Haldane asked, 'How can one join a Government which is almost bound to be weak and discredited from the beginning?' she answered, 'The better for you to be a member of it—the worse for the King and the public who cannot escape from it.'[16] It was a moral argument, one that was bound to disturb the acutely conscientious Haldane.

Grey was staying with Haldane in his flat at Whitehall Court at this time (as he would after the death of his wife in 1906 and again, at his home at 28 Queen Anne's Gate, nine years later, in the terrible weeks leading up to the outbreak of war). When Haldane returned there from Lady Horner's, he found Grey 'reposing on the sofa with the air of one who had taken a decision and was done with political troubles'.[17] Grey was no doubt thinking that all was for the best. He could return to the quiet of his beloved Fallodon, and Haldane could continue to earn the enormous sums he had been making at the Bar. But after Haldane related to him his concerns from an ethical angle, Grey became much disquieted. The two men talked further over dinner at the Café Royal. Finally, Grey told Haldane, 'You may do what you please.' Haldane, who had heard that the king desired him to take the War Office, thus decided to go to CB and say he would take this most undesirable of posts ('beastly' was Grey's word for it; CB, a good Scot, called it the 'kailyard') and that Grey would take the Foreign Office if offered the chance once again. So it transpired, and another step towards tragedy—and, some might argue, victory too—was taken. As Lady Horner was later to comment, 'I used to think that if Asquith were Prime Minister [as he would become on CB's death in 1908], Grey Foreign Secretary, and Haldane Lord Chancellor [as he would be from 1912], all would be well in the world, and so it was for a time, before the shattering years broke on us.'[18]

* * *

Those shattering years of 1914–18 were a long time in the making. Pre-war British foreign policy and defence are critical elements in the Haldane story, particularly in terms of Britain's relations with Germany.[19] It was on the basis of Britain's improved relations with France and in light of growing tensions between France and Germany over French influence in Morocco (the First Moroccan Crisis of 1905) that the deeply controversial 'military conversations' between Britain and France got under way. These commenced in January of Haldane's first year at the War Office (1906) after Foreign Secretary Grey urgently inquired of Haldane as to what preparations had been made on the British military side in the event of a German invasion of France. The conversations were approved by Prime Minister Campbell-Bannerman (the exact date is disputed), but they went ahead without full Cabinet knowledge—a secrecy that lasted until 1911. The joint plans, which these conversations enabled, for the defence of France in the face of possible German aggression have been viewed by some (including Haldane) as the basis upon which Allied victory was achieved, and by others (such as David Owen) as one of the key, yet unnecessary, catalysts for conflict.[20]

With relations now blossoming with France, a combination of factors led Britain ineluctably into an understanding with Russia. The threat to India was radically reduced as a result of Russia's defeat in the Russo-Japanese War of 1904–5, and France had been in the Dual Alliance with Russia since the early 1890s. By signing the Anglo-Russian Entente in August 1907, which would secure the Triple Entente between the three countries, Britain now had a bulwark against a growing German threat.

British intelligence reports suggested that Germany's 1900 Naval Law was not orientated to the creation of a fleet destined for operations in far-flung waters. Yet, unlike Britain, naval power for Germany had little to do with the protection of home supplies, as most were imported by land. Why therefore build up so powerful a fleet so close to home? By October 1902 Lord Selborne, First Lord of the Admiralty, felt he had found the reason: 'I am convinced that the great new German navy is being carefully built up from the point of view of a war with us.'[21] When the British Navy began to build her famous dreadnought battleships just a few years later, Selborne's view became more of a reality as Germany embarked on its own ambitious naval armament scheme. The arms race was on.[22]

In the British Foreign Office, the answer was clear as to where the blame should lie for the origins of this arms race. A culture of Germanophobia was on the ascent, and it too would play a central role in escalating international tensions. Francis Bertie, assistant under-secretary and subsequently ambassador to Italy, then to France, was the ringleader. With the likes of Louis Mallet, Eyre Crowe, and Charles Hardinge (a confidant of the king who would eventually become Viceroy of India) around him, both the Foreign Office and the Diplomatic Service came to adopt a stance in which all German activities and motives were viewed with suspicion, if not hatred.[23] To Bertie, Germany was 'false and grasping and our real enemy commercially and politically'.[24] Hardinge, writing in 1906 as permanent under-secretary, could say: 'It is generally recognised that Germany is the one disturbing factor owing to her ambitious schemes for a Weltpolitik and for a naval as well as a military supremacy in Europe.'[25] It was not an atmosphere in which a man of Haldane's background and proclivities would be considered welcome. This was especially the case once Grey had become Foreign Secretary on the rare occasions on which Haldane would take over from him, to allow Grey a few days' holiday.

Haldane's involvement in diplomacy with Germany in his capacity as Secretary of State for War did not help matters. By 1907 he could claim to have been 'the only Englishman who has ever been a member of the German Cabinet', having attended a critical late night meeting of the Kaiser and his ministers during the Kaiser's state visit to Windsor that year.[26] In 1911 Haldane even had the Kaiser and a number of his generals to lunch in his London home.[27] But it was Haldane's so-called 'mission' to Berlin in February 1912, while still War Secretary (he became Lord Chancellor in June that year), that was the most notoriously controversial event.

* * *

Tensions between Britain and Germany had risen to fever pitch in the wake of the Agadir Crisis of 1911. This had been brought about by Germany sending a gunboat to the port of Agadir in Morocco in the midst of a native rebellion against the sultan, which the French—who had come out of the First Moroccan Crisis with a sense of imperial primacy in that country—were assisting in suppressing by sending 20,000 troops into the city of Fez, where the sultan's palace was located. This level of French military presence was unacceptable to Germany, as they believed it would jeopardise whatever imperial claims the Germans did have in Morocco. The sending of the gunboat *Panther* was meant to convey a signal to France that it ought to back off. Discussions ensued in which Germany expressed its willingness to allow French control in Morocco in exchange for German expansion in the French Congo. But this was viewed by Britain as a threat to British interests in sub-Saharan Africa. The Chancellor of the Exchequer, David Lloyd George, in a speech at the Mansion House in July 1911, provocatively proclaimed that peace on these terms would be 'a humiliation intolerable for a great country like ours to endure'.[28]

It was in this context of heightened tension, where even moderate German papers were calling for a 'preventative' war, that the British Cabinet received an invitation from the Kaiser 'for an exchange of views … of a personal and direct kind'.[29] Haldane—who had been elevated to the peerage in 1911 as Viscount Haldane of Cloan—was the natural choice. His understanding of the German character, his knowledge of the language and his cordial relations with notable German statesmen made him ideally suited to travel to Berlin on the government's behalf. Discussions were to be informal and non-binding, although the purpose of Haldane's trip was to be concealed from the public and a cover story provided: an investigation into scientific matters with biologists at the capital's university. To lend credibility, his brother John, the Oxford physiologist, accompanied him as his private secretary.

In the course of his visit Haldane met with a number of eminent figures, but most notable were his discussions with the German Imperial Chancellor Theobald von Bethmann Hollweg and a meeting with Kaiser Wilhelm II and the naval minister, Admiral von Tirpitz.[30] Haldane encountered a willingness on the part of the German Chancellor to find a formula that would balance the concerns of both nations—that is, one that would reduce the speed of German naval arms expansion while providing a guarantee from the British that they would not take part in an unjust attack upon Germany. But in the Kaiser, and especially in von Tirpitz, Haldane encountered a less compromising spirit that was keen to assert the German right to build up its fleet at whatever pace it wished. Although Haldane left Berlin in an optimistic spirit—'There is at least the chance of the greatest event there has been for some time in the history of the world', he told his mother—it soon became clear that the peaceful inclinations of 'the good Chancellor' Bethmann Hollweg were being overrun by the militaristic faction led by von Tirpitz, for the Germans' new and ambitious Fleet Law went ahead as planned.[31] In such a context, the search for a formula became futile, and Britain felt bound 'to respond by quietly increasing our navy and concentrating its strength in northern seas'.[32] The arms race continued.

Haldane's mission to Berlin both extended a friendly hand to Germany *and* refused to give in to German desires for professions of neutrality and compromises on British naval dominance. But the facts of the trip were so shrouded in secrecy, both at the time and throughout the war, that the public inclination to equate Haldane's German connections with acts of treachery (explored a little further on) was only strengthened. By the time war came it was widely believed that Haldane had really been to Berlin to sell Britain out.

* * *

There is a strange irony to the suspicions that surrounded Haldane's feelings for Germany, however. For despite his period at Göttingen; despite his annual holidays to Germany with his friend and Goethe scholar Professor Hume Brown; and despite his praise of the German systems of education and industry—despite all these, Haldane, as Secretary of State for War, along with Grey, as Foreign Secretary, was doing more than any other member of the Liberal Cabinet to prepare Britain to meet the threat posed by Germany in the event of an outbreak of aggression on the Continent. Indeed, according to many of his contemporaries the success he achieved in these preparations was his crowning achievement during his years at the War Office (1905–12). Haldane was the minister responsible for the creation of the British Expeditionary Force (BEF), the Territorial Army, the Special Reserve, the Officers' Training Corps, the Imperial General Staff and the Royal Flying Corps. Each of these bodies, the BEF in particular, would eventually play a key role in assisting the French in their successful defence of Paris against the Germans in the opening months of hostilities in 1914.[33]

If Haldane did indeed 'save the state', as his successor at the War Office claimed upon his death, it was not because the forces he had created had won the war.[34] Rather, they played a crucial role in stopping the Germans from winning the war in those opening months of the conflict. Such a role redounds to their honour, and to Haldane's. It was why Field Marshal Haig, who had worked closely with Haldane before the war as Director of Military Training and then as Director of Staff Duties, could inscribe in the copy of his Despatches that he gave to Haldane after the war: 'To Viscount Haldane of Cloan—the greatest Secretary of State for War England has ever had.'[35] As we shall see in Chapter 9, this opinion was by no means exclusive to Haig. But Haldane's cultural attachments and diplomatic outreach to Germany meant that broader public opinion, unaware of the realities of his work at the War Office, would fail to reach Haig's conclusions, both before and, even more so, during the war.

* * *

Haldane became Lord High Chancellor of Great Britain four months after his mission to Berlin in 1912, finally reaching the position that his mother, by this time eighty-seven years old, had marked out for him as a child.[36] 'I feel at peace and at rest in this new position,' he wrote to her eight days after assuming office, '& I feel that it is the place you have always desired for me. I know I have your prayers in these great responsibilities.'[37] Haldane was to do much good work as Lord Chancellor—a role that kept him within the Cabinet, and placed him at the head of the judiciary in England and Wales and as the Speaker of the House of Lords, alongside many other responsibilities. His tenure was notable for the part he played in laying the foundations of what would become the Law of Property Act 1925 and his transformative presidency of the Judicial Committee of the Privy Council that would shape the future of Canada. As Haldane's successor to the Lord Chancellorship, Lord Birkenhead, said of him later in life, 'His [Haldane's] work on the Judicial Committee has been beyond all praise, so that no name throughout the British Empire is more respected than that of Lord Haldane.'[38]

In addition, Haldane made a significant impression on the development of a spirit of international relations with his 1913 Montreal speech at the special joint meeting of the American Bar Association and the Bar Association of Canada on the topic of 'Higher Nationality'. Spanning his period as Secretary of State for War and Lord Chancellor, Haldane was also, between 1909 and 1913, chairing the Royal Commission on University Education in London—a job that brought him immense satisfaction. But the peace he reported feeling to his mother in 1912, now that he was in the office destined for him, was not to last.

His sister Elizabeth's diary entries in the days running up to the outbreak of war offer an extremely personal insight into events and conversations from that time. Having been at Cloan when war was declared, Elizabeth travelled back to London on 6 August. On 8 August she recorded the events of the previous fortnight:

> Sir E.[dward] G.[rey] was staying with R.[ichard, i.e. Haldane] from the 27th [of July] and he and R. passed through a time of mental strain amounting to torture. Both strained for peace. To R. it was a personal sorrow of the greatest magnitude to come to war with a power like Germany. He was engaged on a very big and arduous case (Olympic v. Hawke) and terribly overwrought with this and the Cabinet on his mind. The country seemed divided, and ten of the Cabinet were against war and ready to resign. Then came the advance on Belgium, a friendly Power, whose rights we were bound as one of her guarantors to respect. To E.G.'s mind this settled matters. He went on Sunday 2nd August to Downing Street with R. and Lord Crewe who had been dining at 28 [Queen Anne's Gate]. There he found the P.M. [Asquith] and ladies playing Bridge. Lord Crewe said it was like playing on the top of a coffin. They waited till they had finished—about an hour.[39]

It is a remarkable depiction. Here are the Foreign Secretary and the Lord High Chancellor of Great Britain living under the same roof, watching their efforts towards peace, unremitted since entering office in 1905, crash around them, plunging the nation into a war that it was by no means certain of winning. Meanwhile, at Downing Street, the prime minister is playing bridge, like one 'playing on the top of a coffin', as Crewe put it. We can only wonder what Haldane and Grey thought at this moment. Did they share Crewe's disapproval? Perhaps it was this hour of levity that Haldane had in mind when, in the final year of his life, he wrote of Asquith that 'London Society came ... to have a great attraction for him, and he grew by degrees diverted from the sterner outlook on life which he and I for long shared. ... In his earlier political days he was a very serious person.'[40]

There could be no question of cards with Haldane and Grey, but Elizabeth's diaries continue to give the most human of details:

> Sir E. Grey looks older. He and R. came through a terrible time, but he spoke most gratefully of having been with R. all that time and of the help it had been. He is wonderful. Both had suffered from indigestion, whether owing to Mrs. Prunier's rich cooking or their anxiety, I know not. They could not sleep and the weight of responsibility weighed them down. To R. the war is a really <u>personal</u> sorrow.[41]

How could it have been otherwise? It was war with Germany, the country in which Haldane's intellect had been formed, where his youth had experienced its greatest transformation, where he had continued to holiday most years, where he had a wealth of friends and contacts. With no other country did he long more for Britain to develop a happy and prosperous relationship. Speech after speech, article after article, hammered home the point. His exhausting efforts to build strong relations with the country's leading figures, notably with the Kaiser and with German Chancellor Bethmann Hollweg, were in vain.

After the outbreak of war, these continental intimacies, as I have indicated, were to prove a further blow on top of an already painful wound. They provided the basis for a press attack—which had already been gathering momentum before war was declared—as vicious and as unjustified as any recorded in British history. The allegations ranged from the clearly ludicrous to the seriously damaging. Haldane was said to be a spy; the

Kaiser was his illegitimate half-brother; he kept, apparently, a secret wife in Germany.[42] More plausibly but no less fallaciously, he was also accused of weakening rather than strengthening the Army, of seeking secret agreements with the Germans during his 1912 Berlin mission that would undermine British interests, of covering up the contents of a private letter from an influential German businessman on the eve of war, and of wanting to release fewer troops to the continent than Britain was capable of doing.[43] The attacks came from a range of newspapers, most notably those owned by Lord Northcliffe (*The Times* and the *Daily Mail*), who had never quite forgiven Haldane for failing, so Northcliffe claimed, to heed his advice on meeting the military threat from the air while Secretary of State for War.[44] Edmund Gosse reported to Haldane in October 1916—almost a year and a half after Haldane left office—that Northcliffe had given a lunch for prominent journalists at which he made a speech 'entirely directed against you. After the bitterest diatribes he adjured all those newspapermen to see to it that you never regained political power. ... He told them that there was a campaign afoot to reinstate you, but that they must all combine by all means known to them to defeat it. He assured them that you were the greatest enemy to the English State.' Northcliffe insisted that the role of the journalists should be 'perpetually to insinuate into the public mind suspicion and hatred of Lord Haldane, so that the moment there is any question of his reappearance in public life, public opinion may automatically howl him down'.[45]

It should be noted, however, that the offending papers were 'either among the highest of the high Tory or the most scurrilous of the gutter press'.[46] A large proportion of the journalists involved were also personally acquainted with Haldane; as Stephen Koss puts it, 'It appears quite obvious that these individuals persecuted him not out of ignorance but out of first-hand appreciation of his vulnerability.'[47] Their attacks did not fall on deaf ears. 'On one day,' Haldane recounted, though he does not give the date, 'in response to an appeal in the *Daily Express*, there arrived at the House of Lords no less than 2600 letters of protest against my supposed disloyalty to the interests of the nation.'[48] The vitriol knew no bounds. One columnist for the *Express*, Arnold White, informed his co-conspirator Leo Maxse that the Conservative leaders were 'anxious to be present in Whitehall or St. James' Street when the plump body of the Member for

Germany swings in the wind between two lamp posts'.[49] Until 1918 special detectives frequently had to guard him 'due in large part to the seriousness of threats against his life'.[50]

As the attacks intensified with the outbreak of war, it was not just Haldane who was aggrieved. Margot Asquith, the prime minister's wife, records in her diary a snippet of conversation between herself and John Morley at a Downing Street dinner party on the evening of 19 May 1915, the day that the Liberal government sat in Parliament for the last time. Morley—whom Haldane, at the end of his life, described as 'the most interesting personality I ever knew'[51]—had resigned his Cabinet position upon the government's decision to enter the war. Margot wrote: 'I turned to Morley who is so delicious on books & so childish on war. I said how miserable I was at the anti-Haldane campaign—a man to whom we owed our entire fighting forces. I said it was scandalous to think such a man sd. be hounded out by a low Press intrigue. Morley astonished me by saying if he were Haldane he wd. never stay in a cabinet that was making war with old friends of his like the Germans—a more grotesque suggestion was never made!'[52]

Grey felt Haldane's plight keenly. He expressed his views on the matter to Lord Derby on 25 January 1915 with a disgust that is only just held in check by convention:

> I cannot express to you how indignant I feel about the attacks on Haldane. To him specially, more than to the whole of the rest of the Cabinet put together, it is due that, when the war broke out, we had the Territorials at home and an Expeditionary Force to send abroad. ... To Haldane's opinion as ex-Minister for War, under whom the Force had been created and organised, it was due—more than to any other individual member of the Cabinet,—that the decision was taken to send the Force to the Continent on the outbreak of the War. To Haldane and those who worked under him in the War Office when he was there as Secretary of State for War, it was due not only that we had an Expeditionary Force to send abroad, but that we had artillery, ammunition, and other equipment for it, which enabled it to be the efficient Force it has proved itself to be, as well as to stand the strain of a continuous expenditure of artillery ammunition lasting over many weeks: an expenditure more continuous than had been anticipated even by any Continental Army. ... I hear you spoke to Mrs. Asquith in a friendly way of Haldane, so please do not take the somewhat downright tone of this letter as being intended to convey any reproach to you person-

ally, though it is mild as moonshine compared to what would happen if I could get one of the real authors of the attacks upon Haldane alone in a room with me for ten minutes. There is a more than Prussian injustice in selecting him for attack.[53]

We can only imagine the indignation Grey felt when, four months later in May, Asquith made the decision to appoint a new Lord Chancellor to replace Haldane in the coalition government (the coalition had become necessary after confidence in the Liberals had been undermined through their supposed mismanagement of the war, not least the Dardanelles campaign). Grey even threatened resignation if Haldane was left out, but was persuaded to remain for the national interest as the war was ongoing. Haldane's exclusion had been one of the Conservatives' conditions of the coalition (the other being the removal of Churchill from the Admiralty).[54] Haldane, who was suffering from ill health at the time, rationally put it down to the public clamour that had arisen around his name, which would compromise public confidence in the government and distract from the business of winning the war.[55] But Asquith's biographer, Roy Jenkins, sees it as 'a veto of pure prejudice' by those within the Conservatives who had come to accept the smears of the press.[56]

* * *

There are differing interpretations of Asquith's behaviour in these circumstances. It is claimed that he fought hard for the retention of his old friend, but many of those reflecting on matters from a distance felt that his efforts fell short of what they ought to have been. Jenkins writes:

> Had he insisted upon the retention of Haldane the whole coalition scheme might have collapsed and the country, at a most critical stage, been left in political confusion. Even so it was exactly the sort of issue on which Asquith might have been expected to be at his best, where his disdain of clamour, intolerance and prejudice should have given him a rock-like firmness. But he was not. He capitulated, sadly and self-critically, but relatively easily.[57]

At the time, Haldane believed that both Asquith and Grey were 'struggling hard' on his behalf, telling his mother, 'The Unionist leaders admit the injustice, but they have a turbulent tail behind them who have been inflamed by slanderous newspapers. And unity is the first and essential consideration.'[58] It is possible, however, that Haldane was just protecting his mother's feelings. Asquith's wife, Margot, and his daughter, Violet, saw this moment as one of the hardest of Asquith's political and indeed personal life—the man who never shed tears wept.[59] On 21 May 1915 Asquith met with Haldane to break the news to him that the Conservatives would not be moved in demanding his absence from government. Margot records in her diary: 'H[enry Asquith] was more shattered by his talk to Haldane this afternoon than by anything else in this crisis.'[60] And yet, it appears that when the final decision was made to leave Haldane out, which seems to have been around the 24 May, Asquith failed to write to Haldane expressing his sorrow.[61] Asquith's first biographers write that 'the omission inflicted a wound which was never quite healed'.[62] Jenkins considers it 'the most uncharacteristic fault of Asquith's whole career'.[63] Certainly, Margot was not slow to pick up the pen as soon as the decision was made.[64] Asquith may have been distracted at this time by heartbreak at the hands of his daughter's friend Venetia Stanley, to whom he had been dashing off letters of the most politically sensitive nature, frequently in the midst of Cabinet meetings. The sudden loss of her affections may account for Asquith's uncharacteristic behaviour—not least his failure to write to Haldane.[65]

Haldane received the Order of Merit from King George V upon relinquishing his seals of office as Lord Chancellor, an award in the form of a personal gift from the monarch, rarely given to government ministers. It was a handsome gesture of support and solidarity from a man whose family was also under pressure for their German connections, but it was of little real comfort. Many letters were received by Haldane which lamented his departure. Winston Churchill, who reproached himself for not visiting, wrote:

> I trust the vile Press campaign of which you have been the object will not prevail against the loyalty of your life-long friends. I am so short of credit at the moment that I can only make an encouraging signal but you must take the will for the deed. I cannot tell you how grateful I am for your unfailing kindness to me.[66]

And a little later Lord Esher, who had served on the Committee of Imperial Defence for the whole of Haldane's period of service, could write:

I'm just back from GHQ [France]. I must write a line to say how disgusted I feel with the base ingratitude of our country towards one who more than any living Englishman prepared for this appalling war. Everyone who knows the facts acknowledges that without your fine preparative work we should have been powerless on land till now against Germany. The wretched people at home know not what they say or do. The army knows.[67]

Nevertheless, Haldane took Asquith's decision and silence with a graciousness that astonished those around him. On 24 May he wrote to Margot:

The only important thing is to secure a Cabinet which thoroughly commands the confidence of the whole nation—& I could not fulfill this condition. I knew it & told HHA [Asquith] so from the first. He has been affection itself to me & I shall never forget the way he took it & the tenderness he showed.

I am very happy. I have my individual work & another life besides for which there has been little room for ten years. I am content & consider that I have been a most fortunate person.[68]

All of Haldane's correspondence from this time has a similar tone. But behind the appearances of calm and recollection, it is possible to see glints of a more vulnerable side. Indeed, Sir Almeric Fitzroy, Clerk of the Privy Council, saw him immediately after he had received the Order of Merit, and thought he 'seemed thoroughly broken'.[69] Beatrice Webb records in her diary rumours that 'Haldane was a wreck'.[70] Haldane's sister, Elizabeth, who lived through these experiences alongside her bachelor brother, represents a view of things in her diary for 29 May, covering the previous two weeks, that is likely to capture some of the private opinions of her brother:

P.M. never takes trouble to consider and discuss things, no staff work. R. can't get at P.M. during the day as busy hearing appeals, then at night playing bridge and no talk, frivolous people at hand. Pressing people like Winston and L.[loyd] G.[eorge] do the things they want and afterwards get his assent. P.M. excellent if you get hold of him to explain, but is bored. Immense powers of speech, expression and acuteness of mind, but lack of imagination and concentration on his work. R. blames atmosphere produced by Margot and Violet and their surroundings. Never sends for R. to discuss matters he knows of—A. is a bad judge of men. E.[dward] G.[rey] curiously self-centred, will not go outside own work, and F.[oreign] O.[ffice] rather jealous of interference of outsiders. Reluctance to

publish Berlin interview [i.e. the 1912 Haldane Mission discussions].
Tyrrell wanted it published but PM said to E.G. it would bring up new
questions and better not. Personally can't help wondering if P.M. did 'fight
like cats or lions', as Margot says, with Conservatives over R. Perhaps he
did, but feel anyhow R. would not have behaved so to his friends.[71]

Indeed, Haldane, at the close of his life, seemed to have his own doubts
about Asquith's handling of Conservative demands: 'I was not sure that he
[Asquith] would not have done better if he had displayed more of an iron
hand in maintaining his position and that of his colleagues.'[72] It is hard to
tell just how grieved Haldane was in his heart at the inability of his oldest
political friend to withstand capitulation to Conservative pressures. It is
true that Asquith did subsequently seek to make good Haldane's name. He
wrote a letter to Grey on 27 May 1915 on the subject, which he considered publishing:

My dear Grey,

I have received your letter of yesterday. Like you, I more than doubted
whether I could find it possible to sit in a Cabinet in which Haldane was
not to be included. He is the oldest personal and political friend that I have
in the world, and, with him, you and I have stood together amidst all the
turbulent vicissitudes of fortune for the best part of 30 years. Never at any
time, or in any conjuncture, have the three of us seriously differed; and our
old and well tried comradeship has been cemented during the last 10 years,
when we have sat and worked together in the Government.

I agree with everything you say as to the injustice and malignity of the attacks
to which, since the war began, he has been exposed. They are a disgraceful
monument of the pettiest personal and political spite. I am certain that I am
not using the language of exaggeration when I say—what can be said of no
one else—that both as War Minister and as Lord Chancellor he has reached
the highest standard that this country has known.

He is far too big a man to care for the slings and arrows of the gutter-boys
of politics. And he takes with him, in his retirement, the respect and gratitude of all whose good opinion is worth having, and the profound affection
of those who, like you and me, know him best.[73]

In the end, Grey and Asquith were persuaded not to publish their letters. A
'wise public servant' had informed them: 'I fear publication might only
revive controversy, and would also lead to party recrimination.'[74] On 1 July,
however, the National Liberal Club gave a dinner in Haldane's honour at

which Haldane spoke—not of himself, but in defence of General von Donop, who, as Master General of the Ordnance, had been accused of failing to provide adequate munitions for British forces. Haldane's speech was followed by Lord Lincolnshire, the chairman of the meeting, reading a letter from Asquith written specially for the occasion. Once again, Asquith recalls the length and depth of their friendship, and stresses: 'I should wish my countrymen to realize that it is more due to him [Haldane] than to any other man that our army was ready to undertake the mission to which it has been called.'[75] Haldane wrote to Asquith subsequently to tell him that his 'very generous tribute warmed my heart. ... Passing clouds do not dim the memory of years of friendship.'[76] But Asquith did little else to clear Haldane's name and refused to express a strong opinion on the matter publicly. It evidently hurt Haldane. His attitude is captured in a letter to his mother, written six months after leaving office:

> Last night Lord Knollys [former private secretary to the king] came in and dined with me alone. He tells me that the King is now expressing himself with indignation at the attacks in the press. ... Also that the P.M. [Asquith] is at last expressing himself to people very strongly, & even proposed that I should have a statue in gold for preparing the nation for the war. Let them talk away. I rely on your [scriptural] texts.[77]

Relations would not improve when Asquith (and even Grey) refused to publish the official documents concerning the Berlin Mission of 1912.[78] The prime minister felt that the details included facts not suitable for public knowledge while conflict raged.[79] Haldane thought his fears misplaced given that recent German publications had already given a full account of Haldane's 1912 visit.[80] A number of friends and colleagues urged Haldane to make his own public defence of his actions, but he believed it ill-judged to do so. 'This is no time for airing private grievances,' he told Sir George Prothero, 'it is inevitable in a time like this, that there should be hasty judgements and injustices. If I set an example others will follow and there will be division and controversy when there should be unity. It is for the Government to decide when publication is in the public interest, the decision cannot rest with me.'[81]

The 'wound which was never quite healed' is likely to have been a combination of the factors explored above—it was not just Asquith's epistolary silence. It was the cumulative effect of seeing his friend fail to stand by him, followed by his failure to make a strong public defence of Haldane's record, and finally his refusal to publish the official documents that would rebut the press's many false allegations. Haldane never spoke of Asquith with the same sense of closeness and fondness again; one can *feel* the distance in his subsequent communications with and about the man who had once been his closest ally. Nonetheless, Haldane never quite dismissed his affections for Asquith, and when the latter fell from power himself in December 1916, Haldane wrote to him of his 'unbroken affection'.[82] Three days after Asquith's retirement from public life in October 1926 (both men would be dead within two years), Haldane concluded a letter of well-wishing with these words:

> I often take my walks here [Cloan] along the paths where I can recall our talks of over forty years since, on what could be made of the future. There have been changes in our outward relations, but none that have transformed the old inwardness. The days that were, and under other forms still are, I never forget.[83]

Even after his exclusion in May 1915, Haldane was not going to shrink into the shadows. He might have no longer been in government, but he could still serve government. His close friend the literary critic Edmund Gosse dined with him at Queen Anne's Gate on 2 August 1915, and heard of what Haldane called his 'adventures' since leaving office.[84] Gosse's record of Haldane's 'adventures' can still be found amongst Gosse's papers now kept at the Brotherton Library in Leeds.

> He [Haldane] went over [to St Omer in France] on Friday, on a secret mission from Ld. Kitchener [Secretary of State for War] to Sir John French [commander-in-chief of the British Expeditionary Force], and was at the Head Quarters when a German Taube tried to drop bombs on the house. He stood in the street with the generals, and watched the fight between the Taube and the anti-aircraft guns. He also drove along the line, through St. Eloi, Lens to Bethune, and was under fire several times. His mission was an entire success, French put his arm round him, and was as affectionate as a brother, and actually consented on Sunday to be smuggled off secretly to England to meet K.[itchener] of K.[hartoum]. Haldane and French travelled, muffled up, in the cabin of the steamer, and neither was noticed by anybody. French motored to town, had a rapid and most satisfactory interview with K. of K., entire harmony was resumed, and he went straight back to St. Omer.[85]

Reputational issues continued to concern Haldane even if he affected a disdainful insouciance in public. But to his close friends he could be more honest about his worries and he welcomed efforts to set the record straight. When, in 1917, the *Manchester Guardian* published a series of articles defending the former War Secretary's record[86] (these followed the equally significant defence that appeared in Harold Begbie's 1916 publication *The Vindication of Great Britain*), Haldane's gloss on the analysis is revelatory of his pre-war approach to foreign policy. He wrote to Gosse:

> It is quite true that I do not, even now, in the least realise that the German Govt. treacherously and consciously deceived me in 1912. I do not believe they thought of doing anything of the sort, that is to say that the personages with whom I had to do thought of it. You must reflect that if I was deceived as to [German Chancellor] Bethmann Hollwegs [*sic*] and the Emperor's intentions in 1912 then so was Jules Cambon and every Ambassador in Berlin, including our own. The Germans have had fits. They and the Russians had an anti-English fit in 1904; just before which the French had one. The history of foreign politics is a history of kaleidoscopic changes. The purpose of those concerned with affairs is to try to get a good purpose and to preserve its continuity. I hoped that I had succeeded in doing so then, and to a large extent I am quite sure that I did. Only the good mood did not endure long enough. I was far from certain that it would—either in 1906 or 1912, and therefore I threw all my strength into building up an Army which could mobilise more rapidly even than that of Germany. And if I had the same situation to face again I should take the same course, only trying to do what I did more efficiently, and screwing up my Colleagues tighter on military and diplomatic matters.
>
> In a short time after peace is made all these things will be plain, and people will see what the situation really was. That is what I believe, and if I were to put on a white sheet and gabble the prayer of an insincere person, I should only lose the respect of my friends, and of a growing multitude. No, dear G. you cannot deflect me from an uncompromising course. I prefer to be out of office for the rest of my life to departing from what I am convinced is the truth. So turn a cold shoulder to the inhabitants of Greater Pedlington [the home of *The Times*] when they look askance. This business has to be fought out and I am pretty confident of the ground.[87]

The newspaper articles were to be a turning point in building the general public's appreciation of the real nature of Haldane's influence on pre-war discussions between England and Germany. Edward Grey came to visit

Haldane at Cloan in September 1917, and Haldane records that visit in a letter to Gosse:

> Edward Grey has been here for two days and has just left. It was a very pleasant visit. We talked frankly. He had read the M.[anchester] Guardian view and endorses it. ... He said, with some emotion, 'I [Grey] was over-praised and then deposed. You [Haldane] were attacked bitterly. And yet all I did to save Europe was not comparable to what the nation and the world owes to your military reorganisation. It saved Paris and it has saved the war!'[88]

When Grey visited again a year later, Haldane once again wrote Gosse a highly revealing letter, shedding light not only on our earlier discussions concerning the collapse of the Liberal Party, but also Haldane's view of pre-war British diplomacy:

> Edward Grey left this morning after a delightful visit. ... Our talk was a good deal of the past, & I felt that he & I were two old men with our lives mainly behind us. He thinks, as I do, that the Liberal party is dying. He reproaches Margot a little. But the person really responsible is Asquith. There need have been no great Labour party shaping for the birth. And I have the feeling, for which I do not look particularly to Asquith as its cause, that we need not have tempted the Germans to war by our indolence. But that is a large question.[89]

* * *

Whatever Grey, Asquith or the *Manchester Guardian* may have said about the importance of Haldane's work at the War Office, no vindication of his efforts matched the impact of the tribute he received after the war from Field Marshal Sir Douglas Haig, commander-in-chief of the BEF from 1915 until 1919. Haig's actions and words were relevant above all others because at that time he was widely considered a national hero—the man who had brought Britain triumphantly through the war. There was no person in the whole empire whom the British public were more willing to listen to and respect. In Haldane's old age, as he wrote his autobiography, he—or his sister Elizabeth, who edited the manuscript after his death—merged Haig's tribute into one event, but it was in fact two distinct moments.[90] The first came on 19 July 1919, the day of the Victory March celebrating the Allied achievement, when Haig rode up the Mall at the head of the troops to receive the salute from the king in front of Buckingham Palace. Once the post-march lunch was complete, Haig insisted—despite being thick with a head cold—that he make one visit before going home. Haldane sat alone in his study at 28 Queen Anne's Gate while the crowds celebrated outside. Knowing how much harder victory would have come without Haldane's critical work, Haig made his way to Haldane's door to offer the thanks that had been so lacking from the nation at large. Haig wanted to 'tell him that he should have been present to share the cheers and gratitude of the people ... for the work he had done for the Army which had never been properly recognised or even partially recognised'.[91] In December that year Haldane received from Haig an inscribed copy of his published Despatches. Turning to the opening page he read the inscription: 'To Viscount Haldane of Cloan—the greatest Secretary of State for War England has ever had. In grateful remembrance of his successful efforts in organising the Military Forces for a War on the Continent, notwithstanding much opposition from the Army Council and the half-hearted support of his Parliamentary friends.'[92] When this became public, many of Haldane's critics fell silent.

* * *

But Haldane did not spend his time out of office waiting for the truth of his pre-war record to become clear. He still had a multitude of judicial, philosophical, educational and political tasks in hand. He continued, for instance, to act as the pre-eminent interpreter of the Canadian constitution. Between 1911 and his death in 1928 Haldane heard no less than thirty-two Canadian appeals as a member of the Judicial Committee of the Privy Council, delivering nineteen of the committee's judgments. He chaired the Royal Commission on University Education in Wales between 1916 and 1918, which would transform the structure of the University of Wales. From 1917 to 1918 Haldane also chaired the highly significant Machinery of Government Committee reporting to the Ministry of Reconstruction, the conclusions of which are often referred to as the Haldane Report. If Haldane's name appears in newspapers today (though this is a rarity), it is likely to be in connection with the 'Haldane Principle', which is said to have its seeds in this review of governmental structures.

That principle essentially promotes independence for scientists in deciding where government funding of science ought to be focused so that the process remains free from politicians and political agendas. This principle finally became enshrined in law in 2017,[93] ninety-nine years after Haldane's original report. As we shall see in Chapter 8, there is a debate about the exact origins of this principle, but the report's insistence on building policy based on evidence and research was—and still is—a groundbreaking moment in British governmental thinking. Indeed, it has had a 'pervasive but largely unrecognised influence throughout the English-speaking world'.[94]

The Haldane Report was ahead of its time in more ways than one. Alongside its revolutionary approach to the role of women in the Civil Service, mentioned in the previous chapter, it also recommended reorganising the Cabinet according to the nature of the service which is assigned to each department rather than the classes of person they affected. This consequently involved recommendations for a Ministry of Health, which would come into being a year later, and a Ministry of Education, which was eventually created in 1944. Similarly, the report made recommendations for a Ministry of Justice, with its own minister, a party-political-neutral Speaker of the House of Lords, a Supreme Court whose judges would be without political affiliation, and a redefined role for the Lord Chancellor as legal adviser to the Cabinet.[95] As evidence of just how advanced these 1918 recommendations were, the role of presiding officer, Lord Speaker of the House of Lords, was created in July 2006, a Ministry of Justice in May 2007 and a Supreme Court in October 2009.[96]

Haldane was ahead of the curve in other ways, too. In 1921, as we saw in Chapter 3, he published a book entitled *The Reign of Relativity* and welcomed Einstein to his home in London, acting as the physicist's host on his first trip to Great Britain—a courageous show of friendship to a German in the context of the times. Haldane continued to work on the union of the Churches in Scotland, chairing an Expert Committee into the reforms which successfully brought about the union of the Established Church of Scotland and the United Free Church of Scotland. This, along with his earlier 1904 work on behalf of the latter denomination, and despite his own distance from traditional confessions of faith, marked

A MAN FOR ALL SEASONS

94. Haldane entering Parliament Square from Whitehall in 1914, home at that time as now to both the House of Commons and the House of Lords, but today also the home of Haldane's long-anticipated Supreme Court of the United Kingdom.

Society Connections

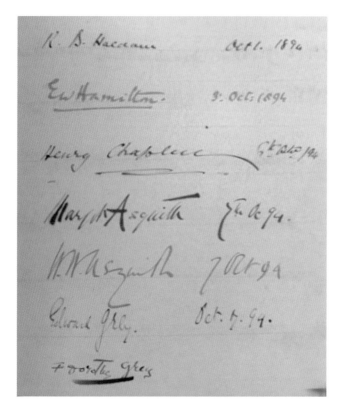

95. The Visitors' Book at Dalmeny, the Scottish home of the fifth Earl of Rosebery, recording the visits in October 1894 of his fellow Liberal Imperialists, Haldane, H. H. Asquith (and his second wife Margot, née Tennant) and Edward Grey (and his wife Dorothy, née Widdrington).

96. Lady Desborough's house party at Taplow Court 1908. King Edward VII (centre), arranged Haldane's feet (right foreground) to avoid their appearing over-large in the photograph. The reaction of Haldane's fellow guest, in close-up opposite, is noteworthy.

97. Haldane in relaxed mood c. 1908, photographed, unusually, with a shotgun. He rarely shot.

Campbell-Bannerman Government

President Board of Agriculture, Earl Carrington
Secretary for Scotland, Mr John Sinclair
Lord President of the Council, Earl of Crewe
Home Secretary, Mr H. Gladstone
War Secretary, Mr. Haldane
President Board of Trade, Mr Lloyd George
Postmaster-General, Mr Sydney Buxton
President Board of Education, Mr Augustine Birrell
First Lord of the Admiralty, Lord Tweedmouth
Chief Secretary for Ireland, Mr Bryce
Chancellor of the Duchy of Lancaster, Sir H. Fowler

The Liberal Cabinet, 1905

Lord Chancellor, Sir Robert Reid
Foreign Secretary, Sir Edward Grey
Colonial Secretary, Earl of Elgin
Prime Minister and First Lord of the Treasury, Sir Henry Campbell-Bannerman
Secretary for India, Mr Morley
Lord Privy Seal, Marquis of Ripon
Chancellor of the Exchequer, Mr Asquith
President Local Government Board, Mr John Burns

98. By persuading Asquith, Grey and Haldane to join his Cabinet without being forced by them to lead from the Lords, the new Prime Minister, Henry Campbell-Bannerman, (99. below) (1836–1908), succeeded in uniting the wings of the Liberal Party.

100. Photograph of King Edward VII and Haldane inscribed in Haldane's hand, 'A snapshot at Marienbad, 26 Aug 1906, given to the King who sent it to R.B.H.' Haldane had this photograph framed and hung on the wall of his study at Cloan. His warm relationship with the King was an important element to his success as Secretary of State for War.

Leading Liberals

101. Herbert Henry Asquith (1852-1928), painted in 1908 as Chancellor of the Exchequer
in the Liberal Administration of Campbell-Bannerman. After succeeding in 1908 as Prime
Minister, he failed to include Haldane in his May 1915 coalition government.

102. Sir Edward Grey (1864–1933) served as Foreign Secretary from December 1905 until December 1916. The merits of his pre-war diplomacy, with which Haldane was associated, are still hotly debated. Portrait painted in 1925 by Sir William Orpen.

103. David Lloyd George (1863–1945), painted in 1911 by Christopher Williams as Chancellor of the Exchequer, became Prime Minister in 1916. He had a love/hate relationship with Haldane—in army spending critical, in education passionately supportive.

104. Winston Churchill (1874–1965), Home Secretary between 1910 and 1911, before being appointed First Lord of the Admiralty (after a battle with Haldane). Churchill and Haldane became co-operative colleagues and good friends. Ernest Townsend, 1915.

105. A portrait of Haldane, painted in his Privy Council dress uniform, by George Fiddes Watt, in 1908, whilst Secretary of State for War.

106. Signed photograph of Kaiser Wilhelm II presented to Haldane at a lunch held at Queen Anne's Gate in 1911 for several generals in the German army to which the Kaiser invited himself. The Kaiser described Haldane's home as a 'doll's house'.

PUNCH, OR THE LONDON CHARIVARI.—February 21, 1912.

TURNED TURTLE.

The War Minister. "A LITTLE MORE OF THIS AND HALDANE'S OCCUPATION'S GONE!"

107. 'Turned Turtle': Haldane caricatured in *Punch* as an emissary of peace in February 1912 at the time of his 'secret' mission to Berlin to meet the Kaiser, Admiral Tirpitz and the German Chancellor, Bethmann Hollweg.

North of the Zambesi
Mozambique — Egypto — Egido.   Maps.
Timor Island.

1. Navy.
1ª Bagdhad Railway
2. Persian trade
3. Africa.
4 Asia Minor (anatolia)

1 To make a new friendship without abandoning
   old friendships & to carry these into
   the new friendship
2. To agree that neither country will from whatever
   make a
   unprovoked attack on the other
3. To secure that the proportionate superiority of G.B.
   naval supremacy
   shall remain as at present, + to keep down
   & if possible to reduce the cost to both countries
   of maintaining this proportional strength
4. To discuss in a friendly spirit trade commercial
   and territorial relations, so that the two countries
   may work harmoniously together in the different parts of
   the world.

108. Negotiating aide memoire written by Haldane (1912) and found by the author in
his personal papers at Cloan, inserted into a document entitled 'Secret Agreements with
Germany' [relating to Portuguese Possessions in Africa]. It was used by him in the
exploratory discussions with German Government representatives during his Berlin
mission.

Haldane Ennobled and Lord Chancellor

109. The Grant of Arms to Haldane as Viscount Haldane of Cloan dated 27 March 1911, on being raised to the House of Lords, whilst remaining Secretary of State for War.

110. Haldane's coat of arms with the family motto, 'Suffer'. Richard Haldane, his great-nephew, interprets the motto as 'Be Tolerant'.

111. The Order of Merit, presented to Haldane by King George V on surrendering the Lord Chancellorship in 1915.

112. Haldane as Lord Chancellor opening the law courts in 1913.

113. An impression of the Great Seal of the United Kingdom, kept by Haldane during his two periods of office as Lord Chancellor.

114. The Lord Chancellor's Purse in which Haldane kept the Great Seal of the United Kingdom.

115. Haldane in his 'working day' clothes worn when presiding over the House of Lords, 1912. As Lord Chancellor on the outbreak of war his position in government was increasingly insecure as attacks upon him mounted for his supposed German sympathies.

116. Grey and Haldane on their way to a Cabinet meeting shortly before war was declared. Grey lived with Haldane in his house at 28 Queen Anne's Gate for ten weeks from just before the outbreak of war until October 1914.

NATION CALLS FOR LORD KITCHENER

IS LORD HALDANE DELAYING WAR PREPARATIONS?

WHAT IS HE DOING AT THE WAR OFFICE?

Friendship with the Kaiser: Lord Haldane (left). Meanwhile Lord Kitchener (centre) was recalled to London

WHAT is the Lord Chancellor doing at the War Office? Lord Haldane is, as everybody knows, an excellent and admirable Lord Chancellor, a great lawyer, and an extremely fluent and voluble orator, but why is he occupying himself at this moment with affairs that have nothing to do with the Woolsack?

We had news on Monday that Lord Kitchener, without doubt the greatest available military organiser, had been suddenly recalled to London when on board a Channel steamer. And it was generally believed and hoped that it was the intention of the Government to ask him to take charge of the War Office in this great crisis.

Public opinion, which is strongly in favour of the adoption of this course, was pleased and satisfied, and it was everywhere supposed that at last we should see the right man in the right place.

But the fact is that for the last two days it is not Lord Kitchener nor even Mr Asquith, the Secretary of State for War, who has been presiding at the War Office, but Lord Haldane. Mr Asquith is, of course, very fully occupied with matters of the gravest importance, and it is explained to the few people who know of Lord Haldane's presence at the War Office that the Lord Chancellor is 'assisting Mr Asquith'.

The fact is that he has been gently but very firmly assuming control of the military preparations. It is feared that he is delaying them.

It is very freely rumoured that at Sunday morning's Cabinet meeting Lord Haldane was bitterly opposed to any war preparations at all.

His well-known friendship with the Kaiser and his admiration for all things German — a sympathy begotten of his German education — led him, no doubt, to believe that German aggression was impossible, and it was not till the afternoon of that day, when news had been received of the German attack on Luxembourg, that he became very reluctantly convinced that Germany meant business.

OFFICIAL DENIALS

Naturally the Lord Chancellor's activity at the War Office led to the belief that it was intended to make him Secretary of the State for War when Mr Asquith relinquishes that office, which he only assumed temporarily when Colonel Seely resigned.

It is generally understood that the Prime Minister, burdened as he is with the chief responsibility for British policy and the general supervision of all departments, will not continue to hold the office much longer.

To allay public anxiety, which has been much increased by the news of Lord Haldane's presence at the War Office, two official denials were issued last night.

The Press Association was 'officially informed that there is no truth in the report that Lord Haldane is going to the War Office either as Secretary of State or to assist Mr Asquith'.

The Central News was also officially informed that it was not true that Lord Haldane would take over temporarily Mr Asquith's duties.

If these official denials are true we can only ask again: 'What is the Lord Chancellor doing at the War Office?'

British Ultimatum to Germany

MR ASQUITH'S STATEMENT

BY OUR PARLIAMENTARY REPRESENTATIVE

House of Commons

THE familiar low, deep, inspiring cheer in which the House extends its cordial welcome to a Minister in hours of crisis greeted the Premier as he rose and spread out foolscap sheets

passage in which Germany gave the assurance that she would 'under no circumstances whatever annex Belgian territory', and the cheers rumbled deep and low when members heard the answer of Great Britain: 'We cannot regard this as in any sense a satisfactory communication.'

The final phrase — 'we have asked that a reply may be given before midnight' — came rapidly, without emphasis, with a little impatient toss of the head, and the Premier, folding his foolscap, dropped back into his seat. A roar of cheering

The King sent the following message to Admiral Sir John Jellicoe

AT THIS grave moment in our national history I send to you, and through you to the officers and men of the fleets of which you have assumed command, the assurance of my confidence that under your direction

---

117. A page from the *Daily Mail* of 5 August 1914, showing Haldane and Lord Kitchener arriving at the War Office and attacking Haldane's suitability to resume office as Secretary of State for War, a post assumed by Kitchener on Haldane's recommendation to Asquith.

118. Field Marshal Sir Douglas Haig, later Earl Haig of Bemersyde (1861–1928), on the Victory March in London on 19 July 1919. After leaving Buckingham Palace and before returning home he visited 28 Queen Anne's Gate to pay his respects to Haldane.

119. Haig inscribed a copy of his *Despatches* to Haldane: 'To Viscount Haldane of Cloan—
the greatest Secretary of State for War England has ever had. In grateful remembrance of
his successful efforts in organising the Military forces for a War on the Continent'.

120. Drawing of Ramsay MacDonald (1866–1937) by William Rothenstein, 1923, shortly before he turned to Haldane to help him form the first Labour Government.

121. Haldane (front row, fourth from left and inset, above right) returned as Lord Chancellor in Ramsay Macdonald's first Labour Government. The only Cabinet member with previous experience of office, he was also appointed Leader of the House of Lords.

Haldane as one of the great unifiers of the Churches in Scotland—much to his mother's joy.[97]

Political office, however, was still not out of the question.

* * *

It had become clear by December 1923 that the king was likely to call Ramsay MacDonald to form the first ever Labour government within a month, and in preparation MacDonald sought out Haldane for advice in forming a ministry, along with the offer of the presidency of the Board of Education. Haldane had been gradually drawn towards Labour on account of the Liberals' failure to take education with the full seriousness that he thought it deserved. Labour's plans for education, on the other hand, showed the kind of idealism that Haldane longed to see amongst his former Liberal colleagues. But Haldane was inclined to decline MacDonald's offer to head up Labour's attempts at educational reform, believing his usefulness to lie elsewhere. Not only did he want to return as Lord Chancellor, he also felt it would be best if he led the Labour Party in the House of Lords, given his comparative wealth of experience in that House over that of his colleagues. Not content with these responsibilities, Haldane—by now sixty-seven years old, walking with a considerable stoop, and suffering from diabetes—also believed he could offer the steady hand needed to preside over the Committee of Imperial Defence. He saw the 'general policy' offered by the committee to be 'more fundamental' to the security of the nation than what could be achieved at the War Office or Admiralty or by presiding over the new Air Force. And yet, in Haldane's view, the organisation was only 'nascent' as it presently stood. As he told MacDonald, when laying out his conditions for taking office, 'close handling [of the CID], by a Minister with sufficient position, would give confidence right through the Services and the country, and strengthen the new Government'.[98] On top of such weighty responsibilities, Haldane also hoped to play his part in enacting some of the reforms that his 1918 Machinery of Government report had recommended.

MacDonald came to Cloan early in January 1924 to talk through Haldane's suggestions, and immediately after his departure Haldane sent a letter to Gosse marked 'SECRET'. It contained the following update:

The Black Dog [Haldane's Labrador, Bruce] is just about to see R.[amsay] M.[acDonald] off the premises. The latter has been agreeable and interesting. I defined my conditions closely. The Black Dog, who was present at some of the conversations, and with whom I took close counsel, showed no dissent, but looked only languidly interested. I have agreed things with R.M., but have told him that he goes to London quite free, for I do not care for office. This has made him keener than ever and he has gone to propose my plans to his Colleagues. We have gone searching over all the Cabinet Offices and of course it is not all settled yet. He will, I think, keep the F.[oreign] O.[ffice.] I may be L.[ord] C.[hancellor] under my own, reformed, plan, free of judicial daily duties, and devoting my time to supervision of the whole machine along with R.M. If things were to go well, I think we might make a great affair out of what I worked out during the last ten days, and out of what he has now approved. He is quick at the uptake and I get on with him excellently. But he is terribly new to affairs, and the colleagues are much worse.

Still, if it comes off, I do not despair of being able to interpret to the country a new order of things which is bound to come anyhow, and which will not be so very different from the old, but will form a further step in the self-evolution of the people. There is no cause for alarm. But will R.M. get his chance? I am not sure, and this makes him gloomy for he talks, at least, as though he had begun to lean on me. I shall hear from him about the middle of the week. Until then nothing definite. I have told him that he and I are quite free and that I, for one, shall feel relieved if I remain so. All this is very secret. Keep it to yourself strictly.[99]

MacDonald did get his chance, but not for very long. The Labour ministry lasted from 22 January 1924 until 4 November the same year (though MacDonald got his chance again five years later). There was not much time for Haldane to accomplish his ambitions, but his re-emergence into the public eye was profoundly significant.[100] The man whom some had hoped to see swinging 'in the wind between two lamp posts' nine years earlier for his apparently treacherous behaviour was once again one of the highest-ranking great officers of state.[101]

In the closing years of his life Haldane continued to provide unremitting service in the many spheres he had come to dominate. When Baldwin formed his Conservative government in 1924, Haldane became leader of the opposition in the Lords. His judicial work carried on, and philosophical tracts continued to appear.[102] In addition, he continued to serve as chancellor of Bristol University (1912–28), and as president of the Royal Economic Society (1906–28) and of Birkbeck College (1919–28), which, between 1929 and 1984, held an annual Haldane Memorial Lecture in his honour, often given by public servants and academics of the highest international standing. His appointment as chancellor of the University of St Andrews came just two months before his death, so the great university at which he had delivered his Gifford Lectures some twenty-six years before sadly missed the full benefit of his powers.

Haldane died of heart failure at Cloan on 19 August 1928, aged seventy-two. Shortly afterwards John Buchan wrote to Haldane's sister, Elizabeth: 'No man ever served his generation more nobly, and our children will recognise that better than we do.'[013] The dean of St Paul's wrote in a similar vein: 'There can be no doubt now that the country knows what it owes to him, and will give him a niche in the pantheon of its most distinguished servants.'[104] Sadly, these prophecies are yet to come true.

8

EDUCATION, EDUCATION, EDUCATION

If I could arrange the Government of this country as I liked, I should hand over to Lord Haldane for the next ten years the whole of the educational system of the United Kingdom. He should be absolute dictator to do what he liked with it, and he should have all the money, within reason, that he asked for.

F. S. Oliver to John Buchan, 1916[1]

No man in British history has done so much for so many university institutions.

Sir James Fitzjames Duff, 1961[2]

At seventeen, Haldane was riddled with anxieties. His early reading in philosophy and the writings of radical theologians had shaken his faith in the foundations of the Christianity espoused by his pious parents. In time, as we have seen, he found a way out of his impasse, discovering new philosophical worlds, which taught that the faith of his family could co-exist peacefully with newer forms of thought. But it was not his reading that lay at the root of his emancipation. It was an encounter with what Haldane, following Carlyle, called 'a Great Man'.[3] Given the role he played in saving the youthful student from intellectual despair, it is not surprising that Haldane even considered this small German academic—Professor Hermann Lotze—a hero.

It is worthwhile reminding ourselves of the powerful impression Lotze made on the young Haldane:

To the end of my life I shall hold the deep impression he made on me—of a combination of intellectual power and the highest moral stature. ... The face was worn with thought, and the slight and fragile figure with the great head looked as though the mind that tenanted it had been dedicated to thought and to nothing else. The brow and nose were wonderfully chis-

201

elled, the expression was a combination of tolerance with power. The delivery was slow and exact, but the command of language was impressive. Our feeling towards him as we sat and listened was one of reverence mingled with affection.[4]

Haldane's lifelong insistence on living at 'a high level', of honouring quality over quantity, can be traced back to this early encounter in Göttingen, and is partly responsible for his outstanding achievements. That it comes from an educational setting—that of the university—is highly significant. Haldane believed that, armed with an encounter with an inspiring teacher, there was no limit to what one was capable of doing:

> In the pursuit of learning, not less than in the management of the affairs of nations, stress ought to be laid on hero worship. Nothing is more stimulating to him who is striving to learn, nothing increases his faith in what is possible, so much as reverence, though it may come only through books, for the personality of a great intellectual and moral hero.[5]

Haldane's personal experience led him to believe that it was the university, more than anywhere else, that could enable one to develop this reverence; and, of course, to get to university one ought to have gone through a thoroughly good school system that would lay the bedrock of a sound general knowledge upon which one's specialist studies could build. Small wonder, then, that Haldane dedicated himself across a lifetime to creating the educational infrastructure that would make this encounter with a hero of learning possible for the men and, importantly, women of Britain. Indeed, the encounter with a Great Man or Great Woman that such an infrastructure would facilitate would inevitably lead, so Haldane thought, to a *Great* Britain. And so, forty-seven years after that life-changing time in the presence of Lotze, Haldane could write: 'I have lived for universities. They have been to me more than anything else.'[6]

This chapter takes a close look at his passion for education precisely because it dominated his political career right from its very beginning. From his entry into Parliament in 1885 until taking his first political office as War Secretary in 1905, it was as a champion of a radically improved education system that Haldane was best known. As we will see, he felt a calling in its cause, one that would stay with him until his very last days.

* * *

Haldane's passion was fuelled by a vision. His early encounter with Lotze convinced him of the possibility of a nation led by a highly educated elite:

> In close spiritual contact with such figures [educational heroes] he [the student] gains the inspiration which will in his own way make him a leader in some circle which may be great or may be small, but which will look to him who is thus inspired as a leader.[7]

Creating such a leader was key:

> The first purpose of a nation—and especially, in these days of growth all round, of a modern nation—ought to be to concentrate its energies on its moral and intellectual development. And this means that because, as the instruments of this development, it requires leaders, it must apply itself to providing the schools where alone leaders can be adequately trained.[8]

This was an elite very much distinct from a hereditary aristocracy. It was an aristocracy of the mind, which any young man or woman could contemplate entering if they had the ability to pursue an education beyond school. Haldane insisted on 'equality of opportunity in education as something that should be within the reach of every youth and maiden'.[9] It was radical stuff. Far from reinforcing class divisions by linking education to wealth, Haldane wanted 'to break down the class barrier by making provision for enabling the youth of eighteen to go on, if he is fit to do so, and to qualify himself more highly'.[10]

Haldane was clearly influenced in this respect by the thinking of T. H. Green, who wrote: 'If the people are to be made scholars, the scholar must go to the people, not wait for them to go to him.'[11] The work of the Workers' Educational Association (WEA), founded in 1903 by Albert Mansbridge (a personal friend of Haldane's) and pushed to exceptional levels by the likes of R. H. Tawney, was the principal means through which such a movement of knowledge could take place. The WEA established courses given by university lecturers in mining and industrial districts. Haldane's early public insistence on the ability of education to solve social problems was in fact used by Mansbridge in one of the articles that launched the association.[12] Once it was off the ground, Haldane was a vocal advocate of their campaign to make the world of the university more porous, helping to launch the Edinburgh and Dundee branches and to organise a series of WEA lectures across 1907–9 in Westminster Abbey and the Royal Gallery of the House of Lords, taking the chair for the lecture on 'Democracy'.[13] The evidence he heard during two royal commissions on university education, which we shall look at later, confirmed his belief in the importance of adult education, and the work of the WEA in particular. Spurred on by what he heard, Haldane was one of the first peers to bring this vibrant new movement to the notice of the House of Lords, referring regularly to it in his speeches before their Lordships. What he called the university 'atmosphere'—the sense of excitement and inspiration that he captures in the description of Lotze's lecture room—was of enduring appeal to Haldane, and he never failed to believe in its transformative capacity and in making it available to as many people as was practically possible:

> I am not suggesting that you should contemplate the time when the working man will enter the walls of the university. He will do so, I hope, but he cannot do so in more than small numbers. I am contemplating a time when if Mahomet does not come to the mountain, the mountain will go to Mahomet. I am looking forward to the universities, through extra-mural work [that is, beyond the physical walls of the universities], reaching every district that requires it, training a new class of university tutor and, armed with that organisation, extending their beneficent work to the colliery district, the pottery districts, and the factory districts all over the country. Until you do that you will not have completed your system of giving educational opportunities, nor will you have laid the foundations of that tranquillity which you can only attain when you have got rid of class consciousness.[14]

In this sense Haldane remained, in the words of two deeply knowledgeable commentators, Lord Ashby and Mary Anderson, 'a very patrician sort of radical'.[15] Mass higher education on today's scale would not have appealed to him; he felt that the doors of the university ought to remain narrow portals for the gifted. What did appeal, however, was the prospect of taking higher education to the masses, adapting the provisions offered by universities so that something of their life—their pursuit after truth and lust for knowledge—could find a place beyond their walls. A 'patrician' vision still, perhaps, but the word radical is not exactly inappropriate, particularly when we remember the context. Take the figures for 1916. At that time, as Haldane pointed out to the House of Lords, a staggering 90 per cent of young men and women received no formal education beyond the age of fourteen, and most of the other 10 per cent were male and from the middle and upper classes.[16] In England and

Wales 5.35 million of the 5.85 million young people between sixteen and twenty-five received no formal education whatsoever.[17] Not only did Haldane campaign for a dramatic increase in education, thinking outside the traditional framework of inward-looking institutions to achieve this, he also declared that that increase, if it were to be within institutions, ought to be based on ability not wealth, and that both sexes should be entitled to pursue the road of learning. He was also radical simply by talking about education. Few people, let alone politicians, seemed concerned by the subject (though we should discount the Scots in this, who had a more impressive educational tradition). It is hard to imagine a contemporary politician claiming, as did Haldane in 1910: 'What we have got to do is to make our people interested in education, and before we can accomplish that we have to make education interesting.'[18] Tony Blair's cry of 'Education, Education, Education' would have won no elections in that decade.

The Scottish educational tradition just mentioned is surely relevant to Haldane's radical stance on the subject. The University of Edinburgh, where he spent most of his university career, was noted, along with its other Scottish counterparts, as distinct from its English cousins by the fact that the former welcomed the sons of farmers, tradesmen and labourers in a way that was barely known in the south.[19] Yes, many parents of these students had to scrimp and save to make the experience possible, and the presence of this social class was still small, but it was at least a common enough phenomenon for the likes of Haldane to have sat comfortably next to such peers in the lecture rooms of Edinburgh's Old College. This breadth of access was enhanced with the foundation, in 1901, of the Carnegie Trust for the Universities of Scotland, of which Haldane was a trustee, and which sought to remove any financial barriers for those desirous and capable of a university education. By 1910 it 'covered the costs of tuition fees for half the student body of the universities of Aberdeen, Edinburgh, Glasgow and St Andrews'.[20]

The Haldanes were on friendly terms with the Carnegies. The first mention of the connection comes on 16 June 1887, when Haldane writes to his mother:

I saw Mr Andrew Carnegie last night. He has taken Kilgraston [a house some miles from Cloan] & looks forward to seeing us. His wife will go there I fancy soon. You should call, as they will be pleasant neighbours—radicals & republicans invested with the respectability of fifteen millions of a fortune. I did not see her, but I like him.[21]

Carnegie would go on to open the Auchterarder Library and Institute, only a mile from Cloan, in September 1896. Haldane was of course present. His mother Mary travelled to the event in the same carriage as Carnegie, while his sister Elizabeth presented Carnegie with the gold key to open the door of the institute. Elizabeth would go on to become one of the original trustees of the Carnegie United Kingdom Trust, established in 1913, which widened the field of Carnegie's philanthropy beyond Scotland and, though not in all cases, beyond education (in the early years the trust did focus on the building of libraries and on adult education). Carnegie's commitment to education was remarkable, but it was of a piece with the Scottish culture of wide educational access; a culture that was already well known to Haldane in his own student days.

This culture was a far cry from the Oxford and Cambridge of the 1870s, which largely remained a preserve of the noble and the wealthy. At Edinburgh there was a 'community of Scottish students where distinction depended on intellect, not birth', and Haldane carried this tradition with him.[22] Haldane's radical credentials north of the border were not quite so startling, therefore. Yet, by seeking to bring the life of the university beyond its physical walls and, as we shall see, by advocating a syllabus far more up to date than that of any Scottish seat of learning, he could still proudly proclaim himself to his fellow countrymen as a progressive on the issue.

In the south, Haldane was on a war path. On the one hand, in his younger years (before the founding of the WEA) this meant becoming a teacher of sorts for those whose circumstances did not permit exposure to university teaching. He gave lectures at the Working Men's College and at the St James's and Soho Radical Club, speaking on topics as wide as the history of moral philosophy and the socialist theories of Marx and Lassalle. On the other hand, it meant getting himself into positions that allowed him to influence educational policy and the structure of teaching institutions. Initially, he joined the Council for the Workers' Education League and, between 1891 and 1899, that of University College, London, and he carved for himself a position within the Liberal Party of the 1890s which allowed him to focus on the extension of university education (along with women's suffrage and housing). Influence, of course, also works outside official channels, and Haldane was careful to stake a place within social circles where his strong beliefs could be brought to bear on those who had the power to put them into action, or at least *fund* them into action! Haldane's friendships with the likes of the Rothschilds and Ernest Cassel were certainly helpful in this respect. At the other end of the spectrum, his close relationship with the socialist reformers Sidney and Beatrice Webb was very much orientated to renewing the British educational land-scape. And between the philanthropists and the progressives there were the university representatives themselves, for whom Haldane always had a spare cigar and a space at his richly endowed dining table.

* * *

The fruit of this powerful combination of official and private influence is clearly evident if we examine Haldane's first major educational achieve-ment—the reformation of the University of London. In 1894 the univer-sity in the capital of the British Empire had no teachers and no students. It was composed solely of examiners and candidates. Graduates were eligible for the governing body, but the teachers at the institutions where students were educated for London degrees were excluded. They therefore had no control over the exams or the syllabus. There was growing unrest over the situation, but there was also strong opposition to change from those who had gone through the system themselves. Haldane was firm in his belief that London deserved a university 'fit for the metropolis of the Empire', which would attract the best students from around the globe.[23] As things stood, 'The real purpose of University training, the development of the mind in the atmosphere of the teaching University, where teachers and taught could come into close relation, was lacking.'[24] It was really Sidney Webb, however, who worked out what such an institution should look like.

The two had already worked together in the creation of the London School of Economics and Political Science (LSE), where Haldane was ini-tially involved in his capacity as legal adviser[25] as Webb tried to decide how to handle Henry Hunt Hutchinson grand endowment for socialist educa-tion and economic investigation.[26] In July 1894 Hutchinson, a solicitor and Fabian from Derby, had ended his own life in his early seventies, leaving some £10,000 to be applied 'at once, gradually and at all events within ten years to the propaganda and other purposes of the said Society [the Fabian Society] and its Socialism, and towards advancing its objects in any way they deem advisable'.[27] It was Haldane's professional opinion that allowed Webb and his fellow trustees to use the funds with a relatively free hand, the funds not strictly being bound, according to Haldane, to the Fabian Society as it was precisely constituted and operating at that time. Haldane's legal opinion allowed the trustees to give a large share of the money to the founding of a centre of learning that did not explicitly propagate socialist teaching. Webb was confident to pursue this course because he believed that the study of the facts of economics would lead ineluctably to a profession of socialism.[28] So, for the LSE, it was Haldane's legal knowledge that had opened the door to a successful educational venture. His role was such that historian Jill Pellew has called Haldane and Webb 'the founding fathers of LSE and [for reasons we will discover later] Imperial College.'[29]

In the case of the University of London, it was Webb (also chief of the Technical Education Board of the London County Council) who worked out an ingenious idea whereby the traditional function of that university—examining external students—could co-exist with a teaching university that granted power for making decisions on the syllabus and exams to those who taught. This was achieved by creating two distinct governing bodies. One council was devoted to the university's role as imperial examiner, and the other was an academic council which made decisions on teaching matters. Each council reported to a senate that comprised figures representative of both interests. Webb also devised a plan to create a new status of teacher—what he called a 'recognised teacher'. Such a title depended on distinction and seniority, and was open to those who taught at any higher educational institution within a 30-mile radius of London. This was 'a device to incorporate into one system the best of all tertiary education in the metropolis, to create a new pattern of university which would cater for the traditional and the new studies, for external, evening, part-time and full-time students; in a word, to put all higher education in London under one immense umbrella'.[30] This new face of the university was encapsulated in the University of London Commission Bill of 1897, which would eventually become the University of London Act 1898. But it was a long struggle to get there.

Enter Haldane—the principal negotiator. He was in his element. Though he supported those who argued that the university ought to become a teaching university, Haldane's long training at the Bar and his political catholicity gave him a remarkable ability for speaking to those who held divergent views and convincing them that, really, he was on their side too. John Buchan put it this way:

> What he had in a full degree was the gift of persuasion, the power of wearing down opposition by sheer patience and reasonableness; and he had that chief of diplomatic talents, the ability to read an opponent's mind and shape his argument accordingly. ... To differ from him seemed to be denying the existence of God.[31]

There were many setbacks. The bishops killed the first attempt in 1896, and then the Bill ran out of time in the Commons the following year. More importantly, there were just so many viewpoints to be balanced. But Haldane remained calm—he spoke to the right people in the right place, he acted as soon as a window presented itself, and he knew exactly what level of compromise was appropriate without ruining the Bill itself. One would think that a man 'enjoying a huge practice at the Bar'[32] would have run a mile from the extra responsibilities involved in seeing through a piece of legislation of this size. But Haldane approached the task with boyish enthusiasm, evidently relishing having a finger in every pie. He wrote to Almeric Fitzroy, clerk to the Privy Council, in July 1897:

> I still have hopes of the negotiations. A month ago I got the Convocation party to agree to accept the Bill if the enclosed amendments were inserted. I took them at once to Lord Herschell [chancellor of the university]. He was favourably disposed towards them. The delay has been with the Senate party, but I understand that Ld Herschell has convened a meeting of their representatives for Monday. If they will agree to the substance of the amendments & the Lord President is disposed to adopt them in the H. of Lords, I think I can get the Bill accepted in the Commons with very little discussion. Mr Balfour tells me he can find time on this hypothesis. ... The important thing is to proceed without delay.[33]

Though Haldane lacked any formal role in the process, his presence amongst the concerned parties was ubiquitous, and he was seen by the highest authorities as the man who could broker a deal. Hence Professor William Ramsay, the discoverer of argon and future Nobel Prize winner, could write to the physician William Allchin in January 1897: 'Things are taking a new dev[elopmen]t wh[ich] it is imp[ortan]t—most imp[ortan]t— you should know of. Mr Haldane is negotiating & I should be glad if you c[oul]d meet with him if poss.[ible] & talk over the matter.'[34]

The fact that the Liberal Haldane was in cahoots with the Conservative Balfour was critical. It was primarily Haldane's ability to get Balfour, then Leader in the Commons, to take up the scheme as a government measure that gave it fair passage through the House. It is fascinating to see Haldane orchestrating things behind the scenes, indicating to Balfour when a favourable wind arose by reassuring him that the Bill was now backed by the necessary parties:

> From letters I have seen I gather that the Senate stands in its approval of the Bill as arranged, and that the majority of Convocation take the same view. ... The real opposition comes from Dr Collins and Fletcher Moulton. I do not think that they can get any substantial support in the House, for the Bill is strongly supported by Herschell, Bryce, Acland, Stuart, Cozens-Hardy, and all are leading people ... Lubbock [MP for the University] is of course in two minds, and he will have to make some show of opposition but I believe he would be heartily glad to have the matter disposed of. ... Dillon says his Irish will not oppose and I think I can do something with Healy— whom I saw before the House rose.[35]

Two months before this the social reformer Beatrice Webb could write in her diary: 'If [the Bill] goes through it will be due to Haldane's insistence and his friendship with Balfour—but the form of the Bill—the alterations grated on the Cowper Commission Report are largely Sidney's...'[36] G. R. Searle puts the relationship this way: 'The fact was that the Webbs needed Haldane very much more than he needed them; nearly every single important contact which they made in the opening years of the century was obtained through an introduction from Haldane.'[37]

Haldane didn't always remain behind the scenes, and it wasn't simply his friendship with Balfour and other 'leading people' that gave him political weight. By December 1897, with the Bill having run out of time the previous August, Haldane had refined it still further and called a conference of the interested parties together in the senate room of the university. The parties agreed upon Haldane's redrafting. Then, early in the new year, the Bill passed through the Lords without a hitch. In June 1898 it came up for debate at its second reading in the Commons, and at last Haldane entered the spotlight.

Haldane certainly heightened the drama in his *Autobiography* when he set the scene for his speech on this occasion. Specifically, he claimed that the attack from Sir John Lubbock, Member of Parliament for the University, *preceded* his [Haldane's] speech, when in fact it followed (only two Members attacking the scheme before Haldane rose), and Sir Charles Dilke, who apparently 'attacked it fiercely', did not, on this particular occasion, speak at all.[38] But Haldane's dramatisation is understandable. His contribution to the debate was a unique moment of public, lyrical prowess in a career otherwise dominated by backstairs manoeuvrings or, when he did speak, overlong speeches creating the famous 'lucid fog'.[39] And others, on both sides of the House, attested to the greatness of his words. Let us hear Haldane's account of it to catch the tenor of the excitement and the forceful clarity with which he spoke:

> There was at once a storm [when the Bill was read]. ... For some time in the course of the discussion not a speech was made in its favour, and the prospects of the Bill seemed hopeless. I sprang to my feet when an opportunity at last offered, and I spoke for once like one inspired. I told the House of Commons of the scandal that the metropolis of the Empire should not have a teaching University to which students from distant regions might come as to the centre for them of that Empire. I showed how far we were behind Continental nations, and what a menace this was to our scientific and industrial prospects in days to come. I knew every inch of the ground, and displayed its unsound condition. We were far away from the days in which a step forward had been made by calling into being the Examining Body named London University, a creation which had given degrees by examination to those whom the Church had in the old days shut out from University status. That reform was in its time a most valuable service to the State, but it was a service which had become superseded in the light of new standards in University education which demanded much more. The effect of this speech was great.[40]

Whatever Haldane may have done to heighten the drama of the occasion in his retelling of it, this final claim was no exaggeration. Joseph Chamberlain—not always a friend to Haldane—told him it was 'almost the only case he had seen of the House being turned round by a single speech'.[41] Indeed, the second reading of the Bill was carried without a division. Next day, Asquith—Haldane's oldest political friend, former Home Secretary and future Liberal prime minister—wrote:

> My Dear H.—Before the impression at all fades I should like to tell you how greatly I rejoiced in the brilliant and conspicuous success of your London University speech last night.
>
> It is the best thing of the kind I have ever heard in the H. of Commons, and in my experience I have never known a case in which a single speech converted hostile and impressed indifferent opinion in the House.
>
> The result must be some compensation to you for months and years of unthankful work, and to me, as you will believe, it had all the pleasure of a personal triumph.—
>
> Always affectly. Yours,
>
> H.H.A.[42]

It would seem fair, then, for Haldane to stake his rightful place at the forefront, not just the rearguard, of London University's reform. As Ashby and Anderson put it: 'Although built on inaccurate detail, Haldane's claim to have tipped the balance [by means of his speech] was well enough founded.'[43]

After this brief, but triumphant, stint in the limelight, Haldane faded once more into the shadows, naturally to much effect. For just as the Bill appeared to be gliding through the Grand Committee stage after the debate, near disaster struck and there was only one man to fix it. Essentially, the Irish Members decided to rebel against the scheme on account of the fact that no adequate provision had been made for the university education of Catholics in Ireland. To them, this was far more pressing than the London question. Here was an opportunity to put a gun to the government's head. Either something was done about the situation in Ireland or else the Irish would block the plans for London. Once again, when faced with adversity and a seemingly intractable problem Haldane showed himself delighted. He plunged into talks with Balfour; with Michael Hicks-Beach, Chancellor of the Exchequer; with C. T. Redington as the head of the education system in Ireland and vice-chancellor of the Royal Irish University; with Christopher Palles, Chief Baron of the Irish Exchequer, who could consult the bishops; with Sir Francis Mowatt at the Treasury; and with John Morley, former Chief Secretary for Ireland.

Having prepared the ground, in particular having been assured of the government's support and funding, Haldane travelled to Dublin in October 1898 to negotiate with the key churchmen there, Archbishop Walsh and Cardinal Logue. The idea was to create two teaching universities—one based in Dublin, one in Belfast—which were *de jure* the same but *de facto* run on denominational lines, since the university in Dublin would be governed mainly by Catholics while the university in Belfast would be governed mainly by Protestants. By the time Haldane arrived in Ireland resolution between the parties had already been achieved on the principle of such a set-up, but no definite plans had been made. Haldane's job was to clarify the details of such an idea and to translate them into a Bill and appropriate charters. But Haldane had been warned by Archbishop Walsh that Cardinal Logue remained hostile to such a plan. He was advised to travel secretly to Armagh to visit the cardinal, being sure not to make his journey public. In his *Autobiography*, Haldane tells the story, clearly much tickled by the intrigue of the situation and by its surprising outcome:

> My instructions were—not to give my name to any one on the way, because there were so many people watching, and to change at a small junction and proceed to Armagh by an unusual route. ... When I got to Armagh, I was to leave my luggage at the station and to go on foot in the darkness to the Cardinal's residence, *Ara Coeli*. I was to inquire the way from women rather than from men, as they were less likely to identify me. I thought all this somewhat unnecessary, but I did what I was told and reached the villa which served as the Cardinal's palace. I knocked at the door. ... I was received by the Cardinal himself, scarlet-clad in full canonicals. After he had talked to me most courteously, saying that he was the friend of my plan, as to which he added that he knew that another section of the Hierarchy led by some one else was an unfriendly one, I was able to tell him in reply that I had the approval of the Archbishop of Dublin to the plan, expressed on paper. 'Then,' said the Cardinal, 'I approve also.'
>
> Feeling that my work was done, I was about to say 'Good night,' with a view to waiting at the station to catch the midnight train for Kingston. ... But the Cardinal said that, although the rules of the Church prohibited him, much to his regret, from entertaining me properly, still the rules of the Church were not so inhuman as to force him to send me away hungry. A little was permitted. He opened a door, and there was a table with two chairs, and on the table an enormous dish of oysters flanked by a bottle of champagne.[44]

213

Haldane had indeed achieved results. By November the Bill and charters were complete. But for a lack of courage on the part of Balfour's colleagues, the Bill would likely have become an Act shortly after. A small majority of the Conservative Cabinet had thrown it out, but the need remained. Ten years later, when Augustine Birrell became Chief Secretary for Ireland and complained of the appalling state of university education there, Haldane (who was now in charge of the War Office) asked whether he had seen the scheme drawn up in 1898. He had not, and Haldane provided Birrell with his own copies. The Church parties on both sides remained enthusiastic, and shortly afterwards the Bill passed smoothly through Parliament, allowing for the creation in 1908 of the National University of Ireland (with three constituent colleges in Dublin, Galway and Cork) and Queen's University Belfast. On the back of this transformative education Bill, alongside Birrell's name, stood the name of the Secretary of State for War, R. B. Haldane.

The passing of the University of London Act 1898, which Haldane ensured by his willingness to act on Ireland's behalf, was not the end of his involvement in educational reform in the metropolis. In fact, his involvement went well beyond reform; it also included the physical relocation of the university itself. According to J. Mordaunt Crook, 'It was Haldane, as much as anybody, who engineered the removal of the University's headquarters in 1900 from an annexe of Burlington House to a section of the Imperial Institute.'[45] Though Haldane 'engineered' the move, it was the Prince of Wales, the future King Edward VII, who had the idea. It is a testimony to the position Haldane held in educational matters that the prince sent for him especially to make his plan a reality. 'You alone', said the prince, 'can get over the opposition to a plan which will deliver the Imperial Institute and be good for the University.'[46] The Imperial Institute, originally designed in 1888 to showcase the commercial and industrial products of the colonies, was on the brink of insolvency and was considered a 'useless white elephant'.[47] The presence of the university within its walls would rejuvenate the institute while acknowledging the new stature of the university itself. In fact, to locate the university within the heart of 'Albertopolis' (as this part of South Kensington is known on account of Prince Albert's developments there) was suitable both geographically, for there was a capacity to expand the premises, and symbolically, for it had a specifically imperial dimension—precisely what Haldane wanted the university within the empire's capital to have. This expansion and dimension were embodied in the new college that Haldane now set about to establish in the heart of these new surroundings: what we now know as Imperial College London.

* * *

Before we come to Imperial's establishment—an endeavour which owed so much to the educational example of Germany—it is worth recognising that Haldane was not solely focused on the value of university training. His studies of Germany had shown him that education in the context of industry was just as valuable to the prosperity of the nation. The loss of British scientific expertise caused him particular pain. Towards the close of the nineteenth century Britain clearly lagged behind Germany and the United States in the steel and chemical industries, in synthetic dyes, in optical glass, and in a range of the more sophisticated electrical goods and other products 'which called for a high level of precision in their manufacture'.[48] Only a few decades earlier, Britain—the country that had inaugurated the Industrial Revolution—had had no real competitor in these areas. To find itself in a state of dependency on other countries was not just worrying for the economy, it was perceived as a humiliation for the nation.

Haldane identified the root of the problem as lying in Britain's defective system of technical education and scientific research. To correct it would require the adoption of new techniques and approaches across the whole political, educational, scientific and business spectrum. Speaking to an assembly of Liverpool businessmen in October 1901 on the difference in educational practices between Germany and Britain and the effects on their respective business activities, Haldane made a forceful case for the kind of transformation needed. He pulled no punches. If the British middle classes remained passive in the face of the ever-closer integration of science and business in Germany, then he predicted economic ruin. With rhetorical flourish, he exclaimed: 'They [the British middle classes] have been forced to realise that courage, energy, enterprise are in these modern days of little more avail against the weapons which science can put into the hands of our rivals in commerce than was the splendid fighting of the Dervishes against the shrapnel and the Maxims at Omdurman.'[49]

He took the German brewing industry as his illustration. Over a period of thirty years, German beer exports had grown from nothing to almost as great in value as Britain's. How had this been achieved? For nearly ten minutes Haldane, master of his brief, expounded in detail how two particular brewers had visited Britain in the early 1860s and studied its native skills. They found them to be greater and more successful than German techniques. Returning to Germany, the brewers realised that there was 'more still to be learned from science'. Accordingly, the Brauerbund was formulated in 1862 to promote the common interests of German brewers. It established scientific stations and brewing schools with classrooms and laboratories. Each school had its own experimental maltings and a brewery. Teachers were of the highest calibre. It was just the kind of project to get Haldane bursting with admiration.

He described the one-year course of study at one of these schools in Weihenstephan, attendance at which would provide exemption from one year of military service—a salutary example of the state and business in Germany working co-operatively. Quoting a paper by a chemist named Dr Frew, which had been delivered before the Society of Chemical Industry, Haldane rattles off the winter term's curriculum: 'lectures on physics, general machinery, brewery machinery, inorganic chemistry, botany (with special reference to yeast), hops, brewing practice, attenuation theory and control of work, book-keeping, the theory of exchange, and taxation of beer'. In addition there were 'practical courses in the chemical laboratory and in the use of the microscope, besides practical work in the maltings and brewery attached to the school'. All this was followed, in the summer, by more lectures on 'organic chemistry, fermentation chemistry, zymotechnical analysis, barley, brewing, faults in working, pure yeast culture, architecture[!], and theory of exchange'. Continuing his quotation, 'the student may also, if he so wishes, hear lectures on law, outlines of political economy, commercial geography and distilling, but these are not obligatory'.

If the audience were not already exhausted by this panoply of activity they would have been delighted to hear that, endowed with all this training, the aspiring young brewer then goes on to practice 'for a year or two in different breweries, so as to get the maximum of experience, or else he may take the position of brewer in one of the smaller factories'. His ascent up the ladder then—at last!—commences, from the position of 'maltster, foreman in the fermenting room, or washroom-man in one of the larger breweries'. All of this is directed to his ambition, namely to be 'chosen as brewer or brewing director in one of the large breweries'. Only at this point does Haldane wrap up Dr Frew's exact descriptions; he is clearly enthralled by this vision of rigour, of long years of intellectual and practical labour, of a youth willing patiently and systematically to build a career, of an industry that makes such educational demands on its members.

In providing this detail, Haldane sought to illustrate how the industrial life of Germany was in close contact with its academic life. Evidently, so Haldane claimed, those involved in German commerce felt a strong need for education of a university type in order to produce the teaching and organisation of their own technical schools. He saw 'throughout the industrial world of Germany science being applied to practical undertakings by men who have been trained in the universities or high technical schools or at least under teachers produced by those institutions'. The brewing example could be found across a multitude of sectors. In a 'wake-up' appeal, he observed that in 'electrical engineering, in the manufacture of chemicals, in the production of glass, and of iron and steel, and of many other articles for which Britain used to be the industrial centre, we are rapidly being left behind'.

As a final example of 'the professor coming to the aid of industry', Haldane gave his Liverpool audience an illustration which was to take on a particular importance come 1914. He pointed to the fact that in Germany, as in Britain, the manufacturers of dynamite, nitro-powders and other explosives were rivals, though prices were often regulated by mutual arrangement of groups and trusts. But 'while the rivalry of the Englishman is without stint, the German knows a better way'. Such manufacturers were cognisant of their dependence on what Haldane calls 'high science' and that such science 'cannot be bought by the private firm or company'.[50] Knowing this, they chose to make a move deeply at odds with the British competitive instinct. They jointly subscribed around £100,000[51] (which in 1900 was the equivalent of today's £12.4 million) to found what they called their Central-Stelle, which was then maintained by their subscriptions of around £12,000 a year. The Stelle was presided over by a highly distinguished professor of chemistry at the University of Berlin, who had a staff of trained assistants under him. To this organisation, as they arose, were referred problems faced by the subscribers in their individual work—the same principle, as we shall see, that Haldane implemented in his creation of the Advisory Committee for Aeronautics eight years later.[52] The fruits of the research then carried out at the Stelle were communicated to all subscribers. Haldane believed that the keen interest which the great German manufacturers of this sector took in this organisation enhanced the development of more effective and efficient products. These were used in competition with British products in important markets such as South Africa, where they were fundamental to the life of a vast mining industry.[53]

In sum, what was needed was a radical shift in the British attitude. Thinking on one's feet was all very well for certain situations, but not when it came to remaining ahead of the industrial curve. Thinking in advance—that most Haldanean of principles—was now, more than ever, absolutely essential. In addition, another Haldane principle was needed: thinking in co-operation. It was no good for British businesses to remain solipsistically turned in upon themselves, seeking a way out of their decline by means of their own limited resources. An outward turn was needed, a turn towards scientific experts and centres of learning, where the latest, most advanced technologies and techniques could be found.

* * *

The founding of Imperial College London was aimed at providing exactly this centre of learning in Britain. Haldane had first become obsessed with the idea of creating such an institution after his 1901 visit to the Technische Hochschule at Charlottenburg in Germany. The Hochschule, along with nine other polytechnics, represented Germany's new push for higher standards in technological and scientific training. It was, to Haldane, 'by far the most perfect University I have ever seen'.[54] Charlottenburg was the epicentre of the most up-to-date scientific investigation, its rooms packed with young scientists on the make, taught by the nation's leading professors, with all the cutting-edge equipment the country could afford. As Haldane repeatedly pointed out in his public addresses, the educational provision for such investigation lay behind the highly lucrative developments in German industry in recent years, developments which were now putting Britain's pre-eminence in this area at risk.[55] If Britain failed to act quickly in establishing her own centres of scientific excellence, her dominance would soon be at an end.[56] Not only was Haldane clear-sighted enough to make this judgment, which many of his more complacent colleagues in Parliament seemed to think unimportant, he was also clever enough to realise (along with Robert Morant at the Board of Education)[57] that the materials for such a centre were ready to hand—they just needed the correct organisation. Those materials were the Royal College of Science, which included the School of Mines, and the Central Technical College of the City and Guilds Institute of London. By merging these institutions and buying up further land from the 1851 Exhibition commissioners, something on the scale of Charlottenburg was possible. But it was possible only if a lot of other factors slotted into place, and, once again, it was Haldane and Webb who ensured that they did. Ashby and Anderson set out the sheer scale of the project that confronted these tried and tested collaborators:

> To turn the idea into reality required money, government consent to surrender its colleges in South Kensington, co-operation from the City and Guilds, agreement on the part of the 1851 commissioners to release land, and negotiations with the University of London so that any London Charlottenburg would not be separate from the University, as the German polytechnics were, but associated with the University, to comprise a focus for science and scholarship in the Empire's capital.[58]

When it came to finance, Haldane knew exactly where to go. He had heard of the 'Randlords' (men who had made their fortunes in the diamond fields of South Africa) Julius Wernher and Alfred Beit as 'public-spirited men of German origin ... impressed with the necessity for this country of German scientific training'.[59] Their wealth was enormous. Beit was even said to have been the richest man in the world in the mid-1890s, with shareholdings of £10 million.[60] Haldane had also heard that their company, Wernher, Beit & Co., were considering a very large donation to University College, London, in the cause of applied science. As ever, he was swift to act. His timing was critical, as is clear in a letter to Sidney Webb on 9 May 1902:

> I saw four London partners of W.[ernher] B.[eit] & Co this afternoon & had an hour with them. It was just in time. There had been no talk of a million—but they were pondering giving £100,000 to U.[niversity] Coll[ege].

This I have *stopped*. They will give £10,000 only. But I have undertaken to prepare a scheme for a Committee or body of Trustees to begin our big scheme. They will give us £100,000 to start it, & help us to get more. The partners are keen to do something. Could you come at 5.30 on Monday to the H of C—& you & I will talk over the scheme of such a Committee, to be independent of, but to work along with the University Authorities. If I can get Rosebery and Arthur Balfour to serve on it I think we may get a million. I believe W.B. & Co. will give much more than £100,000 really. Will you think out the outline of such a scheme.[61]

Haldane was now able to pull together his large network of powerful friends to act as supporters of the scheme. He knew how hard it was to make a scheme 'drive rapidly without the co-operation of the great personalities'.[62] Soon he could count Balfour, Rosebery and the Duke of Devonshire (Lord President of the (Privy) Council) as his allies. Likewise, Sir Arthur Rucker, principal of the university, and Sir Francis Mowatt, member of the 1851 commissioners and permanent head of the Treasury, were on board. Behind them all stood Almeric Fitzroy, clerk to the Privy Council, who actually drafted the key decisions that needed to be made.[63] With this support, the plan began to take shape: the commissioners were keen to release the land; the Rhodes Trust, through Beit, was willing to give more than a hand; and the London County Council (LCC) was open to providing a maintenance grant.

To secure the last of these, Haldane deployed a typically ingenious manoeuvre: he got Rosebery—one of the 'great personalities'—to write to the LCC, but he asked Webb, who was himself a member of the LCC, to draft the letter! Once again, Charlottenburg was used as evidence of what was possible: 'From its portals', says the letter, 'there issue every year some 1200 young men of 22 or 23 years of age, equipped with the most perfect training that science can give'.[64] But of course the Hochschule was not cheap. The letter points out that it cost more than £500,000 to erect and £55,000 a year to run. In response, there followed a promise in July 1903 of £20,000 a year from the LCC to help make a London Charlottenburg possible.

By October of the same year Haldane had produced an anonymous document outlining the scheme. It detailed the dream of bringing together, under the university, the existing institutions of science and technology in South Kensington, and it set out what was needed to make that dream a reality: the funds and the agreements between the various parties involved. Morant, permanent secretary at the Board of Education, was handed the document and then charged to set the cogs of the relevant administration in process. There was already a committee proposed to review the School of Mines, and Morant suggested that it ought now to expand its intention in order to review all the colleges in South Kensington. Mowatt, having just left the Treasury, was made chairman, and Webb was also asked to sit on the committee. Haldane was content to operate behind the scenes. But not for long. Mowatt fell ill in December, and Haldane, despite the many burdens of his legal and parliamentary work, offered to take the chair. As he wrote to Morant from Cloan on New Year's Eve 1904: 'I will *make* the time if it seems good to you.'[65]

The committee, under Haldane, set about reporting on what stood in the way of the scheme summarised in Haldane's anonymised memorandum and how these obstacles could be overcome. The first report, agreed and signed in February 1905 (but not released to the press), saw clearly that the transition of ownership of the Royal College of Science from the Board of Education to the university was no easy matter; it identified the challenges of governing a partnership of colleges; and it recognised the need to include the activities of the schools of scientific training within the broader work of the university, while at the same time providing for the type of autonomy that the new institution would desire. This issue of not separating applied science from traditional university courses was vital to Haldane and one of the rare issues on which he openly criticised the German system. As he said in his talk on 'The Civic University' in 1912:

> In Germany the Technical Colleges have been sharply divided from the University and given a separate existence. This is partly due to the division and separation in character of the great secondary schools in Germany. The resulting separation of the Technical College has been deplored by some of the most distinguished authorities on German Education, notably by the late Professor Paulsen. If this be a thing to be avoided, we have avoided it. We have made our start by treating education as a single and indivisible whole— and by trying to keep the different kinds of students in one organization.[66]

Whether he would still criticise Germany today for its continued separation of vocational and technical education from the more traditional gymnasium and university paths is an interesting question, particularly as Britain now lags far behind Germany in the opportunities and support it can offer to those pursuing the former route. But for Haldane, all aspects of education were organically related, and he wanted that to be reflected in Britain's educational institutions. This meant he had to tread carefully. It was wonderful that there were institutions ready to hand to form a new college, but because they were already in existence they knew what it was to be independent from university bureaucracy, and there were plenty who shuddered at the thought of surrendering such independence. Full integration into the university would take time to achieve. But other matters were moving quickly. It was only a month after the first report was signed that Haldane heard that the government was willing to relinquish the Royal College of Science, including the School of Mines. And by June 1905 the Treasury had pledged to contribute £17,000 a year, which then increased to £20,000 in November.

The first report was cleverly released to the press only in June, once its objectives were already achieved. The papers were full of admiration. Haldane was in the limelight again, hailed now as the creative force behind the proposed college, with Webb (unfairly) only a shadowy figure. But it is true there was something unique about Haldane's role. Jill Pellew has put it this way: 'Projects of this nature involve considerable team work but need a motivator with vision—a role that Haldane undoubtedly played.'[67]

But there was still much to do. Haldane and his committee met with the representatives of the university in July and secured their support for the scheme. Further support was forthcoming from the City and Guilds, helpfully chaired by Haldane's old friend Lord Halsbury. Tension remained evident in so far as the university pushed for the new college's full and immediate incorporation into its own body, while the City and Guilds made a condition of their joining that they retained their identity. Some form of harmony was reached by creating an interim governing body formed of members from each interested party, who agreed that the newly aligned institutions were now a school of the university. The continued demand from the university for full incorporation threatened this harmony, however, and it took a stroke of genius from Haldane to hold the peace. His solution was simple, but unexpected: he arranged it such that the report was signed unanimously, and part of that unanimity was an open confession of their disagreement. To show that they were not simply bypassing the issue, the committee recommended that a royal commission could be established at a later date to investigate the question and other matters concerning the constitution of the university. Thus, the actual founding of the new college could get under way despite the disagreement. The future of Imperial College London was secured. The college was formally incorporated on 8 July 1907.[68]

* * *

One thing becomes clear throughout these negotiations. Haldane was certainly high-minded and idealistic—he wanted the very best in scientific education at the heart of the empire—but he was also extremely pragmatic, allowing voices dissenting from his own high ideals to have their say. The key thing for him was that steps in the right direction were being taken. It is, indeed, a hallmark of the Haldanean approach that it is 'step by step'. How often do we see so-called reformers and radicals come undone because they seek an instantaneous utopia and fail to listen to, and respect, those whose utopias differ from their own? Haldane rarely made such a mistake.

Yet the radical nature of what has been called Haldane's educational 'blueprint' is not in question. What was the link at that time between schools, colleges and universities? It was hard to identify. What did Haldane envision? A unified system, permeated—one of Haldane's favourite words—by the spirit of the universities from the top down. These universities ought to be organised geographically into regions, serving their local areas. Teacher training ought to be an important university course, so that teachers could be equipped not only to teach well but also to teach in light of a truly emancipating educational experience, such as Haldane himself had undergone with Lotze. In such a way, the spirit of the university could be passed down to the schools. Haldane also sought a decentralised university system, which received the initiative for its own existence from the people who worked in and lived around it. They, too, should administer and control the university. The state's role was simply to foster and assist this initiative and control. In terms of curricula, Haldane was both progressive and conservative in setting forth the 'double function' of a university's teaching: it ought to promote pure culture, the love of learning for its own sake, while at the same time applying the findings of science to the life of the nation's industry.[69] This conception has been critiqued for Haldane's lack of adequate explanation for how these two functions can co-exist.[70] This may be a fair point, and Haldane's simple pointing to Germany as an example of their co-existence is likely to prove unsatisfying to many.[71] But it could be argued that the explanation is to be found in Haldane himself; he lived the solution. He was constantly engaged in activities which he enjoyed for their own sake (his wide reading in literature, for example, or his presidency of the Walter Scott, Emily Brontë and Goethe societies), but he was equally engaged in a multitude of enterprises very much orientated towards their use to society.[72] Perhaps the lack of adequate explanation is a result of Haldane's belief that such co-existence was obviously possible because he lived it every day. Whatever the case may be, Haldane wanted universities to be anything but inward looking. He wanted the curricular doors flung open, particularly to allow for all aspects of the applied sciences, so that what happened within their walls impacted the entirety of the nation.

Extra-mural work was the other manifestation of this. It was essential to Haldane that, through evening classes and free public lectures, something of the life of the university could enter into the lives of working men and women. Haldane's lecturing, in his early days in London, at the Working Men's College and at the St James's and Soho Radical Club; his later support for the Workers' Educational Association; his founding, in 1921, of the British Institute of Adult Education (explored later); and the way he directed funds towards the same cause as chairman of the Cassel Trust (also explored later)—all of this demonstrated his commitment to widening access to high-quality education. It was a commitment that sadly failed to take deep root in British thinking about the scope of university education. In the early years of the new universities of the 1960s—a time ripe for developing outreach opportunities—there was little material outcome of early enthusiasm for extra-mural teaching.[73]

But for all the radicalness of Haldane's blueprint, it was not dramatic. Here again, Haldanean pragmatism is evident. It was, in the view of Ashby and Anderson, 'politically practicable at every point and (equally essential) it would not need to be carried out all at once'.[74] Haldane was also aware that it was not enough just to state the ideal and expect the actions leading to that ideal to follow. If it were to succeed, he needed personally to be part of the process. In seeking a system whereby universities were decentralised and regionalised, capable of permeating the rest of the education system in their area by the quality and manner of their teaching, Haldane knew that new universities would have to be founded and, in some cases, existing examining universities reformed. London University was part of that reform, but there remained Victoria University in Manchester, the examining body serving three separate institutions: Owens College in the same city, University College Liverpool and Yorkshire College, Leeds. The success of Joseph Chamberlain's Birmingham University, founded in 1900, had given the public a taste of what it could be to have a real teaching university in the heart of a city apart from Oxford, Cambridge and Durham. Liverpool was especially keen to follow suit, but this would involve a complicated process of detaching the University College from the Victoria University and establishing an independent institution: Haldane's ideal challenge![75]

* * *

Opposition to the whole concept of multiplying teaching universities was rife. The essence of the opposition is captured in Mowatt's opinion that 'the multiplication of degree-giving bodies in a State is the certain forerunner of a depreciation in the value of a degree'.[76] This would lead inevitably to what the liberal thinker James Bryce apparently called 'Lilliputian Universities'.[77] Once again, the close cross-party working relationship with Balfour became important. Faced in Parliament with a mixture of apathy and strong opposition to university expansion, Balfour asked Haldane's advice. A powerful committee of the Privy Council was the answer; the Council was considered one of the most important crucibles for major educational decisions, and it was indeed a central enabling force utilised by Haldane in so many aspects of his working life. And with this particular committee, the history of university education in England was about to change.

Liverpool's readiness to petition for its own charter in April 1902 was the perfect occasion for the appointment of such a committee. To give it

weight, the big guns were called in: the Duke of Devonshire would preside, joined by Lord Rosebery, Lord Balfour of Burleigh, Lord James of
Hereford, and Sir Edward Fry. This, then, was a panel comprising, respectively, the Lord President of the Council, a former prime minister, the
Secretary for Scotland, a former Attorney General, and an ex-Lord Justice
of Appeal. A powerful panel indeed, and one that, on the face of it, could
boast of a certain impartiality. But even in its composition Haldane's hand
can be seen at play. All were well connected to Haldane, Rosebery and Fry
in particular; there was also a full knowledge of the Scottish universities in
Rosebery and Balfour of Burleigh; and, though three of the five were
Oxbridge men, they were not jealously attached to 'Oxford notions of
what a University ought to be'.[78]

Haldane's influence became more noticeable once the committee's
work got under way (the hearing lasted for three days, between 17 and
19 December 1902). Indeed, if it were not for the fact that Haldane was
made Privy Counsellor shortly before proceedings began, he would have
led the case for Liverpool himself. As an alternative, he made sure per-
suasive counsel was brought in, first of whom was Alfred Lyttelton, a man
who, though not greatly knowledgeable in educational affairs, was both
'tactful' and 'well known to the members of the Committee' (one senses
that 'well known' here means 'sympathetic', with the members predis-
posed to favour him).[79] Alongside him stood the indefatigable Sidney
Webb and the trusted John Kemp. Haldane, denied his place at the Bar,
became the principal witness for Liverpool. They were up against stiff
opposition in the guise of Lord Spencer, chancellor of the Victoria
University, and Lord Ripon, head of Yorkshire College, Leeds. But it was
advantage Haldane: 'We had worked out and knew our educational case
more thoroughly than our opponents had been able to do.'[80] Haldane
produced fact upon fact, figure upon figure, showing that adversaries in
Yorkshire were actually foolish to deny Liverpool the right to its own
university when the data showed that Yorkshire had quite enough educational institutions within its county lines to merit its own great university.
Haldane presented them with an attractive proposition: 'a great co-ordination of every kind of education' across the whole of Yorkshire, with
towns hosting schools of the university, and 'a great stimulus in the teaching of these institutions'.[81] In response to the question of whether degrees

would be cheapened by the existence of yet another degree-giving institution, Haldane found a remarkably simple answer. Degrees would be reviewed by external examiners to ensure their equality. This would be accompanied by a safeguard to ensure that no professor within an institution could overrule an external examiner.

But Haldane was thinking way beyond such mundane details; his evidence outlines 'a veritable manifesto'.[82] He spoke of an England in which a university education would be available to 'all those who are about to follow any profession or occupation which requires knowledge, reflection and judgement'. He made his case on the basis that the twentieth century's demands were absolutely unique: specialist knowledge was a prerequisite for success in the contemporary world. The 'trained intelligence' was paramount.[83] In such a context, how could England continue to deny the majority of its population access to the only institutions that could foster such intelligence? If it sought to remedy the present situation, only a great wave of university expansion, covering every major region of the land, would suffice.

Haldane's opponents were not a little peeved by the manner in which he escalated what was in reality the petition of one college to be separated from one university. The Privy Councillors thought differently. The tide of Haldane's argument appeared to sweep them away. There were other factors at play, of course. One important point was Rosebery's evident animosity towards Ripon and Acland (who was also giving evidence against Liverpool's case). These two had sat under Rosebery in his Cabinet of 1894–95, and the experience, for Rosebery at least, had not been a sweet one. According to the Duke of Devonshire, Rosebery's 'principal object has been to make them look ridiculous'.[84]

It was hard to see how the result could be anything but in Liverpool's favour: 16 February 1903 was a momentous day as the king in Council approved the committee's report recommending that the colleges at Liverpool and Manchester should receive separate charters granting them university status. In addition, it was stipulated that Leeds ought to be able to propose its own university for Yorkshire before the other charters were granted.

But the decision was far more wide-reaching than this. By setting such an official precedent for these 'civic' universities (so called on account of their bases in cities, though they are also known as 'red-brick' universities because of their building materials), it opened the doors for a transformation in the educational landscape of England.[85] No longer was it an accepted fact that the universities were the preserve of a wealthy elite; no longer were Oxford and Cambridge the sole models for teaching universities; no longer were educational institutions enslaved to the examining requirements of bodies without any real local knowledge. It was a transformation that would lead not just to Liverpool, Manchester and Leeds receiving royal charters, but also Bristol, Sheffield and Reading.

The committee's decision 'made educational history in England'.[86] Given Haldane's role in establishing the committee and in leading the charge for Liverpool's case, it would not be unreasonable to claim that Haldane, too, made history. Yet he has come under criticism for his claims around the part he played in the process. Sir Alfred Hopkinson, first vice-chancellor of the University of Manchester, felt that Haldane's *Autobiography* showed a lack of knowledge about the negotiations, and Ramsay Muir, influential on Liverpool's behalf, thought Haldane exaggerated his own importance. But the arguments in Haldane's defence are impressive. They are summed up, with admirable balance, in Ashby and Anderson's *Portrait of Haldane at Work on Education*:

> On some details Haldane's recollections were at fault and in his enthusiasm for the new pattern of civic universities, Haldane did tend to overlook the fact that other people, too, were enthusiastic. These are fair targets for criticism. But his critics overlooked (or were ignorant of) the formidable difficulty of turning airy aspirations into the unexciting legalese of charters and statutes. No one can say that without Haldane it would not have been done. But it is pretty clear that without Haldane it would not have been done so quickly, so smoothly, and so wisely. Rhetoric may conceive an idea: it takes negotiation to deliver it.[87]

* * *

If Haldane was the 'midwife' of university expansion, he also played a crucial role in nursing institutes of higher education into healthy financial positions.[88] Alongside his place on the board of trustees for the Carnegie Trust for the Universities of Scotland, Haldane was able to initiate, in 1904, a scheme that was to have far-reaching, long-lasting effects across Great Britain, through yet another chairmanship. In March of that year he

EDUCATION, EDUCATION, EDUCATION

122. Haldane: Thought as a preliminary to action. The most abstract of Haldane's thoughts were always based in the concrete world of human interaction. Haldane averred, 'I have lived for universities. They have been more to me than everything else'.

The Scottish Educational Tradition

123. Andrew Carnegie (1835–1919), who did so much to support widening educational access in Scotland and beyond, 1913. Haldane was a trustee of The Carnegie Trust for the Universities of Scotland, while his sister Elizabeth sat on The Carnegie United Kingdom Trust. The Scottish educational tradition of providing a wide breadth of access to high quality education significantly informed his approach to education.

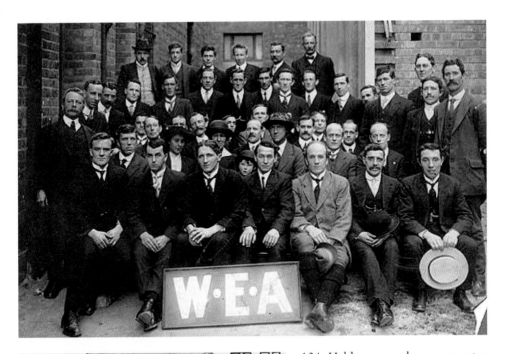

124. Haldane was a keen supporter of adult education, particularly the Workers' Educational Association, founded in 1903. It played an important role in providing university style education to those for whom formal university education was out of the question, 1915.

125. London School of Economics, Passmore Edwards Hall, Clare Market, Strand, 1902. Haldane provided Sidney Webb with the legal advice that led to its founding. He also secured key funding from Lord Rothschild for the building at Clare Market.

Lutyens's Proposal for Senate House for London University

126. With Haldane's encouragement, Sir Edwin Lutyens drew up plans between 1912 and 1914 for the new Senate House of London University in Bloomsbury, on a site optioned by Haldane from the Duke of Bedford. The plans were to be appropriate for 'The centre of the greatest university, in the capital city of the greatest empire of the world'. The Senate House was finally built, but to Charles Holden's design, on the same site in 1930.

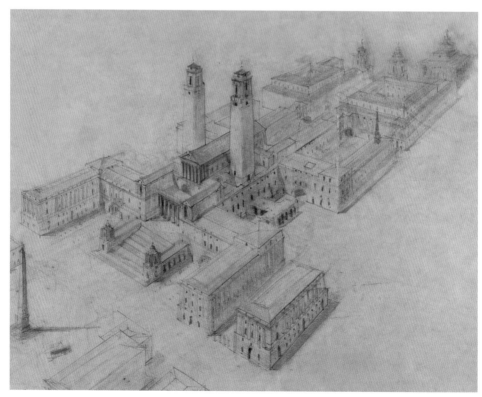

Alfred
Beit
Julius
Wernher

127. Imperial College founded 1907, with the Royal School of Mines as an integral part. Haldane was the principal founder of the College and persuaded Julius Wernher and Alfred Beit to provide core financing. Their statues above stand on each side of the main entrance.

128. Keys commemorating the many educational and military buildings opened by Haldane. His creation of the legal foundations for the 'civic' universities of Great Britain, led to the rapid expansion of universities across England, Ireland and Wales.

129, 130. Haldane opening the new buildings of University College Southampton in June 1914. The key, in verso, is displayed in the case above at the upper right.

131. Haldane, as Chancellor of the University of Bristol, was awarded an Honorary Doctorate of Law in 1912. He is seen above welcoming King George V, who opened the new Wills Building at Bristol in 1925 with Queen Mary.

Universitas McGill

AD MONTEM REGIUM, IN DOMINIO CANADENSI

Omnibus ad quos hae Litterae pervenerint, Salutem:

Cum Gradus Academici eo consilio instituti sint ut viri ingenio et doctrina praestantes aut qui bene meriti sunt de re publica ornamentis amplissimis ac praecipuis honoribus afficerentur, Nos Gubernatores Rector et Socii Universitatis et Collegii Magilliani virum egregium

Ricardum Burdon Haldane

ne honore merito ac debito careat, titulo graduque

Doctoris in utroque Iure

adornandum decrevimus.

Quod ut factum esse testemur Litteris hisce, quibus nomina rite subscripsimus, Sigillum Universitatis imprimendum curavimus.

Datae in Comitiis sollemnibus die _____ primo Mensis Septembris _____, Anno Domini, MCMXIII

_____ e Gubernatoribus

Johannes H. Nicholson
Tabularius

_____ Rector

132. Haldane was awarded honorary doctorates at ten universities, including McGill in Montreal, Quebec, in 1913 on the occasion when he delivered his lecture on 'Higher Nationality' to the joint meeting of the American and Canadian Bar Associations.

133. Haldane and Asquith received honorary degrees of Doctor of Laws from the University of Manchester on the same day in 1908.

was asked by Austen Chamberlain—son of Joseph, the founder of Birmingham University—to lead a Treasury committee to review the distribution of state grants to England's university colleges. He was joined by Mowatt, Henry Woods (former president of Trinity College, Oxford) and Charles Cripps (who later, as 1st Baron Parmoor, would sit beside Haldane as Labour's representative in the Lords). The recommendations of this committee are telling of Haldane's priorities. Alongside the expected principle that colleges would receive funds in proportion to their other incomes, and that some money should go towards books and equipment and superannuation, the final report also recommended that support ought to go directly to postgraduate research on 'special problems' and that teachers' salaries ought to be bolstered. It is no coincidence that an advance in research capacity and effective stimuli towards entering the teaching ranks were two matters close to Haldane's heart. It is equally indicative of the prevailing culture that these two specific recommendations were not taken up by the lacklustre Treasury (though later, 'in 1915 under the glare of war', Haldane's recommendations on postgraduate research in science were identified by the Advisory Council of Scientific and Industrial Research as 'the fundamental and most urgent need of the country').[89] Haldane's concerns were again evident in the report's proposal for financial aid to be provided to a wider range of academic disciplines; the polymathic Haldane desired a flourishing in medicine, engineering, law and architecture.

Most significantly, the report strongly suggested that an impartial committee ought to be established, bringing together members of the Treasury, academics, and the Board of Education. Such a committee could visit and inspect the colleges to ensure that the money was being appropriately and effectively spent. Unlike in previous arrangements, the Treasury would no longer send funds directly to the colleges; rather, they would come via this committee. The committee would report annually to the Treasury and their findings would be shared with Parliament. Here in embryo we have the University Grants Committee. This was the premier advisory body to the government on state funding to British universities until 1989, and its role lives on in the higher education funding councils of the present day. Once more, Haldane's immense educational legacy is in evidence.[90]

* * *

We shall return to tertiary education in a moment, but it is worthwhile remembering the brave role Haldane played in supporting Balfour's 1902 Education Act—an Act which aimed at the transformation of primary and secondary education in England and Wales.[91] It sought to do this by abolishing the school boards and establishing local education authorities (LEAs), which would seek to develop the existing elementary schools and establish new secondary schools—both operating under a unified system. Controversially, the LEAs would also support the existing 'voluntary schools'—schools predominantly run by the Church of England, though some were Roman Catholic—through aid from rates and taxes, while raising their standard by controlling their educational provision. The Church would maintain buildings and oversee religious instruction.

Unsurprisingly, the Nonconformists—many of whom were Liberals and Liberal Unionists—were furious. This was a Bill that not only would enhance the power of the deeply Tory, established Church, but also made it look as if those who dissented from such an establishment would actually have to support it financially! Haldane, however, rose above the religious dispute and supported the Bill, considering it 'a scheme showing earnestness in the endeavour to co-ordinate the whole of our education in a fashion of which hitherto we have had no example in this country'. But he was a lone voice crying from the desert of the Liberal benches. In his defence, Haldane could bang the hammer of 'national efficiency', the weapon brandished by many a politician at that time in the face of a growing threat from America and Germany's highly organised systems of state governance. The scheme, Haldane claimed in a Commons speech, 'recognises the necessity of co-ordinating education from top to bottom, and puts before the country a practical proposal towards that end'. Co-ordination and practicality were the twin pillars upon which Haldane built his support. On the one hand, the Act would create a link between primary and secondary education, as well as supporting a regionalised system, which so appealed to Haldane's desire for devolving educational power. On the other hand, it was the only genuine scheme open to the Conservatives at that time, and it contained conscience clauses which would allow dissent to be recognised. This is not to say that Haldane's support was wholesale. He was vocal in his desire to see far more done in bringing in the shaping influence of the universities, and he was clear in saying that the ideal would eventually be to secularise the education system. But Haldane, ever practical, saw that the world simply didn't work this way: 'I would rather see education more secular than it is in this country, but I am aware of the temperament of the people, and that being so we must deal with things as we find them.' And as for the universities: 'As it is, the scheme is enormous, and the right hon. Gentleman [Balfour] cannot cover the whole field of education, but I am not sure that the Bill will to any great extent carry out the end of making the University element in a large measure permeate our system of education.'[92] Despite these deficiencies it was an enormous step in the right direction, and therefore it received Haldane's support. In the end, the Bill was passed to the short-term detriment of the Tories, who would lose huge numbers of Liberal Unionist supporters on its account, but to the long-term benefit of secondary education in Britain, with over a thousand new secondary schools established by 1914, 349 of which were for girls.[93] The Act represented the first move towards the unification of the different stages of education in England and Wales that we know today.

* * *

Returning to higher education, it will be remembered that the question of the full incorporation of Imperial College into the University of London was left open in 1905. The royal commission that was mooted at that time came into effect in 1909 as the Royal Commission on University Education in London, under a man fresh from the reorganisation of one of the country's most complex institutions: the British army. That Haldane should take on this mammoth task while War Secretary (the commission was to sit for the following four years, issuing four reports, and Haldane was Lord Chancellor by the time its final report was issued) is testimony not only to his industry but also to his indomitably wide-ranging interests. He was joined by Lord Milner (former high commissioner for Southern Africa), Sir Robert Romer (former High Court judge), Sir Robert L. Morant (permanent secretary to the Board of Education), Laurence Currie (banker and director of Gresham Life Assurance, the Gresham Fire Insurance Societies, the Great Western Railway and the Union Discount Company), W. S. McCormick (first secretary of the Carnegie Trust for the Universities of Scotland; Haldane had secured his appointment to the Treasury Grants Committee in 1906, and he became the first chairman of the University Grants Committee in 1919), E. B. Sargant (former head of education for the Transvaal and Orange River Colony), and Louise Creighton (founder of the National Union of Women Workers).

The commission—much to the annoyance of the university senate—went far beyond the question of Imperial's incorporation. Instead, it identified its task as follows: 'To examine the existing provision for university education in London in the light of what we think ought to exist, and to make practical recommendations towards the realisation of the ideal.'[94] The characteristic stamp of Haldane—the establishment of an ideal and the practical scheme to meet it—was undeniable. So, too, was the equally tell-tale thoroughness of the commission's work: seventy-two additional meetings, on top of evidence hearings, to discuss proposals; the commissioning and digestion of a historical report on the university; the sifting of past reports and parliamentary papers; and the evidence of educational experts from a vast array of educational settings, a number of whom had travelled especially from Europe and North America to face the questioning commissioners. They were not to arrive at their conclusions lightly.

The commissioners reported four times in total, and the mass of evidence, examinations and recommendations make the reports somewhat overwhelming for the historian. But they are also a treasure trove in which the living voice, and even daily life, of Haldane can be found. For example, on the eighth day of hearing evidence, 17 February 1910, Sir Robert Morant opens proceedings by informing the witness, Dr William Garnett, educational adviser to the LCC, that 'Mr Haldane is extremely sorry that an unexpected summons of the Cabinet at 4 o'clock will compel his absence for the time being; he will be here as soon as possible, but is very sorry to be absent'.[95] Later, we can almost hear Haldane slip in and take his seat, the evidence recording that 'the chair was here vacated by Sir Robert Morant in favour of Mr Haldane',[96] who, a little later still, enters the questioning with his apologies: 'I am sorry I was detained, and could not get here before.' Haldane then dives straight into an examination of Garnett, which tells the reader far more about the former than it does about the latter:

> (Chairman) You speak of the nine Technical Universities with power to grant Degrees which have developed in Germany from polytechnics or trade

schools. ... I should like to ask you, in what sense is there any element of the trade school remaining in these technical schools in Germany to-day? Take, for instance, Charlottenburg, which is the principal one of them all. The working classes do not go there; it is a day college, and a day college for students who are mostly somewhere about the age of 20, and who have to pass an extremely stiff examination to get in, and indeed do not as a rule get there without the Abiturienten certificate. The portal of admission to this is as difficult, is it not, as admission to the University?—[Garnett responds] Yes; that is more comparable to the institutions at South Kensington, the old City and Guilds College, and the higher work of the Imperial College.[97]

Who is it that is giving evidence here, you might well ask.

It is clear from the final report that the commissioners' ideal university is very much in the image of Haldane's dream educational establishment. What is striking today is the humaneness of that vision, putting into question the utilitarianism of our modern universities, where 'impact' is everything, where the 'publish or perish' culture among academics often fosters competitiveness and insecurity and undermines the importance of teaching. The commission, on the other hand, was forthright in the purpose of a real university—'the spread of a pure love of learning'.[98] According to the commissioners, 'students and teachers should be brought together in living intercourse in the daily work of the University'; the professors ought to be people of inspiration, willing to come into close contact with undergraduates, in order to show what the true spirit of scholarship looks like. The effect would be to lift the aspirations of the students, who would then look to embody the pursuit of truth and knowledge themselves. Haldane's days in the lecture room of Lotze are clear between the lines. The report also diagnosed the difference between a degree and an education—something which we still today have not yet fully understood. In fact, it saw that the former could even hinder the latter. 'They [the students] cannot pursue knowledge both for its own sake and also for the sake of passing the test of an examination.'[99] The commissioners' idea of what incentivised a student showed a remarkable amount of respect for the student's intentions: students should not be obliged to attend their classes, since the high quality of the teaching would be enough to attract them (medicine and technology were the sensible exceptions to this generous rule). An atmosphere of freedom ought to be abroad within the university. In line with this, a strict centralised control of the curricula and the manner in which the courses were taught and examined ought to be relaxed. Professors should be of such a calibre that they could be trusted to keep the standards high. And, just as in the War Office command and administration were separated to allow for the 'thinking department' (namely, the General Staff) to get on with what it did best without the encumbrance of workaday details, so too did the commission seek for the university to maintain centralised control over finances, property and policies, to allow the professors to get on with their true vocation. This tension between centralisation and decentralisation, which marks so much of Haldane's work, is also highlighted in the commission's recommendations concerning higher education in the colonies. At that time, students affiliated to the university but based in the dominions were obliged to sit exactly the same examinations as those students based in Britain. In a sentence exhibiting the advanced thinking of the commissioners, the report asks the university to abandon 'once for all the pernicious theory underlying its present practice that the kind of education it thinks best for its own students must be the best for all peoples who own allegiance to the British flag'.[100] It took an entire generation until, in 1945, this enlightened recommendation was accepted.

The final report was published in April 1913, but its immediate recommendations were anathema to the individualistic spirit of many of the institutions that comprised the university. Here was a document calling for faculty, not institutional, control; for the eventual death of the external degree; for curricular and degree-giving diversity in an establishment famous for its monolithic nature. But at the governmental level, there was approval and a desire for action. Yet another committee was formed to develop plans for implementation. Unfortunately, for Haldane and the commissioners, it was the eve of war, and 'plans' were as far as it got.

In many ways, the outcome of the commission could be said to be one of the great disappointments of Haldane's life. The Hilton Young Committee, which met after the war to re-examine the commission's proposals, only really preserved the idea that the university would have centralised power over finances. Otherwise, few of the far-reaching and humane recommendations that we have outlined above were carried into effect. One or two lasting results were obtained, however. Just as it was Haldane who stood behind the move from Burlington House to the Imperial Institute in 1900, so too it is Haldane's report that stands behind London University's presence in the heart of Bloomsbury, the site now occupied principally by the university's School of Oriental and African Studies (SOAS), Birkbeck College and University College London (UCL). Haldane was enraptured by the idea of the university being largely located on a central site, a unified and geographically harmonious seat of learning. This sits strangely perhaps with his desire for devolving academic powers away from the administrative centre; one might expect that the very physical proximity of the faculties and institutions would encourage the centralists. But the idea of a 'university quarter' within the imperial capital had a magnetism that Haldane couldn't resist. The report articulated the argument based on the effect it would have on students and teachers alike, bringing them into closer contact and fostering an atmosphere of learning and exploration.[101] It also emphasised the effect such a site would have on the people of London more generally. A true 'university quarter ... would perhaps do more than anything else to impress the imagination of the great London public and to convince them that the University was a reality'.[102] The dominating symbolism of the British Museum and the proximity of University College made Bloomsbury an ideal choice. Characteristically, Haldane did not let his idea lie dormant. Before the final report of the commission was published, he gathered private trustees in order to purchase a plot of land belonging to the Duke of Bedford, situated directly behind the British Museum. In a fortnight the trustees raised £355,000 (today's £41 million),[103] and they had plans drawn up to reflect their hope of creating the grandest of educational settings. This was all classic Haldane, but on this occasion his enthusiasm got the better of him. Despite the support of the chancellor of the university (Lord Rosebery), Haldane was remiss in not sounding out the other important parties: the vice-chancellor, the senate, the convocation, the LCC. The money, as Crook puts it, 'was ignominiously returned'.[104]

Great schemes continued to be envisioned. Notably, the celebrated Edwin Lutyens—who appears throughout Haldane's life as a guiding architectural voice, even designing his library at Queen Anne's Gate—produced splendid plans for a London University embodying what he called the 'Classical High Game', all porticos and plinths, looking something like Bloomsbury's very own New Delhi. The plan never reached fruition and the location remained a controversial choice, particularly to representatives of King's College. The combination of a world war and institutional deadlock meant that many years passed before the scheme proposed by Haldane could come to fruition, this time under the guidance of William Beveridge, close friend of the Webbs, former director of the LSE, and vice-chancellor of the University between 1926 and 1928. Under his lead, Bloomsbury was confirmed as the final choice for the site in 1927, and it was Beveridge—when all looked dead and buried in the attempt to purchase the site—who secured a £400,000 donation from the Rockefeller Foundation to buy the land. The architect, when the moment came, was not Lutyens, but Charles Holden.

So Haldane did eventually get his dream of a university quarter in Bloomsbury. It was not the only aspect of his 1913 report that bore fruit. In the field of medicine, the commissioners' recommendations, according to L. P. le Quesne, 'had a seminal influence, and a direct line of thought can be traced from Haldane through the Goodenough Report (1944) on Medical Schools to the 1968 Royal Commission on Medical Education (the Todd Report).'[105] Hearing from the likes of Ernest Starling, Abraham Flexner and Sir William Osler—all men of eminence in the medical world—the report argued for the need for clinical professors (a position unknown at this time) to give a thoroughly scientific grounding to the medicine that was practised in hospitals and surgeries. Hitherto, a student would be rushed through the basic examinations of medical school under teachers of sciences ('in many cases not of marked ability')[106] in a manner akin to trade schools, the school having a purely professional, rather than educational, character. Clinicians themselves, to whom students then passed, found teaching 'a mere incident in a busy consultant's life', and had neither the time nor the training to apply themselves to clinical problems with the same sort of rigour that a chemist or a pharmacologist could.[107] The commissioners on university education in London therefore called for university medical schools in which 'the principal teachers of clinical medicine and surgery in all their branches ought to be university professors in the same sense as the principal teachers of chemistry or physiology'.[108] But the same recommendation needed to pass through another two large-scale reports (Goodenough and Todd) before the idea was fully accepted. Nevertheless, in the wake of the Haldane Commission, five clinical professors were appointed and the pre-clinical departments did become genuine university departments, leading research in a number of key areas. Fleming's discovery of penicillin, Charles Dodds's synthesis of stilboestrol, and Peter Medawar's revolutionary work on cellular immunity all took place in this new university context.

* * *

One dimension of education touched on in the report on university education in London, and of deep concern to Haldane, was what might be termed 'business education'.[109] This was education as it related to the directors, staff and workers of private corporations and public enterprises. Britain lagged behind Germany and the United States in the teaching of business and commerce in universities, and Haldane was energetic in his promotion of the need for management education at university level. Beginnings had been made. Rosebery, who was a director of the North Eastern Railway Company, arranged in 1902 to send some of their employees to the LSE for instruction in business management in a newly founded railway department. These were the early beginnings in Britain of the business school movement, initiated by the establishment of the commerce class in Birmingham University the same year. Haldane, as War Secretary, continued this new trend by starting in 1906 the army class at the LSE for selected mid-ranking officers, who were taught the art and the science of business administration.[110] After the war, as we shall see, Haldane also ensured that the largest proportion of the Cassel Trust's money for education—of which he was in charge as chairman—went to the development of the faculty of Commerce at the LSE.

But much more than action at the university level had to take place. It needed to start at earlier stages and embrace the many employees who would not go on to university. Trade schools were an important part in this. These institutions were designed for those elementary-school students not moving on to higher education but looking to be efficient and stimulated in their work. The educational opportunities for such a demographic in Britain before the war were almost non-existent. It is perhaps worthwhile to remind ourselves of the figures given earlier in this chapter, and used by Haldane to make his point about the shameful nature of the British track record in this regard. In 1916 90 per cent of young men and women received no formal education beyond the age of fourteen. In England and Wales 5.35 million of the 5.85 million young people between sixteen and twenty-five received no formal education whatsoever.[111] Whenever Haldane addressed the fortunate minority who did receive a formal education between these ages, he was always at pains to stress both the injustice of this and the stupidity of wasting such a 'vast reservoir of undeveloped talent'.[112] For British industry, here was an opportunity too good to be missed.

Speaking in March 1916 to the Union Society of University College (now UCL), Haldane posed this rhetorical question: 'Do the interests of the nation require that they too [wage earners belonging to the industrial classes] should be infused with the reflective habit which is born of knowledge?'[113] He answered with an emphatic 'Yes'.

Now, Haldane was realistic. He knew that complete equality in educational opportunities was not to be had, given the contingencies of nature and the complex societal structures that stood in its way. But those contingencies and structures could be fought against, if not overcome. One aspect of this fight had to involve what Haldane called 'the greatest educational discovery of the most recent years', that of the latent possibilities of 'vocational' training. This may not sound too significant to our ears. But this was 1916, not 2020. Moreover, Haldane's vision of such training had a breadth to it that would surprise those who simply thought of such training as the development of one specific skill set. Haldane's ideal would involve physical and spiritual training in addition to intellectual. He was aware that this would come at a financial cost to the country, but was keen to point out that this would be returned many times over—another example of Haldane taking the long view: 'Just as no worse economy can be made by a farmer than in starving the cultivation of the ground which is to produce his crops, so no worse economy can be made by the state than in starving the cultivation of the vast class on which it depends for efficient producers.'

Haldane was speaking in the midst of the war. He had been removed from office the previous year precisely because he was seen by a portion of the nation as a German sympathiser. It was in this context that he decided once again to return for illustration to the example of Germany. Despite all his qualifications about the 'murderous methods' of the German General Staff to achieve 'abstract purposes', and their violation of 'the moral law', it does seem remarkably brave—perhaps even fool-hardy—to go on to praise those 'other and quite legitimate preparations for ascendancy in the world which Germany has made and is still making'. The technical training of their young people as they began careers in their respective trades was just too appealing for him to keep silent about. 'The manufacturer depends more and more, as year succeeds year, on the machine and the skilled worker. The skilled workman is the intelligent workman.'[114]

Britain of course had its examples of skilled training. Haldane drew attention to preparatory training in the schools for metal working in Sheffield and, in his own constituency of Haddingtonshire, in agriculture. But what he saw in Germany was of a wholly different nature. Haldane believed that the roots of German success lay in the most modern form of continuation school as implemented by Dr Georg Kerschensteiner, the director of public schools in Munich (he had in fact written the introduction to the first English edition of Kerschensteiner's classic treatise in March 1914, just before the outbreak of war).[115]

The principle of these schools was to take those wanting to enter a special trade and use the studies necessary for that trade as a medium for imparting both trade skill and general knowledge.[116] Haldane explained that each school was dedicated to a different trade: metalworkers, wood-workers, engineers, plumbers, masons, butchers, bakers, waiters. Employers were compelled by law to send their young wage earners to the appropriate schools for a number of hours, which were taken out of the working time instead of the evening. Haldane saw the system as a modern substitute for apprenticeships. Before the war the system had been established in Munich, and Haldane believed that after the war it would be put into operation all over Germany.[117]

In Munich, a city with 600,000 inhabitants, almost all the boys on leaving elementary school at the age of fourteen went immediately to be taught trades which they had chosen. For four years they attended special and compulsory trade continuation schools which provided practical and theoretical work for eight to ten hours a week, taken out of their working hours. The system led to concentration rather than dissipation of energy. At the end of the four years many of them went on with voluntary instruction in higher technical schools, some inside and some outside working hours.

At the time war broke out, Haldane explained that the 'so-called apprentices' in the mechanical, optical and electrotechnical workshops in Munich attended four ascending sets of classes over four successive years for nine hours a week, at a time during the day when their minds were fresh and unwearied. The contrast was stark when compared with the British system, where so many children leaving school at the elementary level simply drifted into unqualified occupations.[118]

Haldane quoted Kerschensteiner in his pre-war foreword on the pleasure that the schools brought both to employers and employees. The employers were delighted by the successful work, but for the pupil the school was no longer, to quote Kerschensteiner, 'the horrid Continuation School that he must attend, but the school of his *own* special trade, the school of the trade in which his life's work would lie'. The pupil had a stake in the enterprise, and entered into a community with which he could identify—both aspects were key to its success. 'It was no longer the cold and intangible abstraction called "The State" which forced him to go to the school,' wrote Kerschensteiner, 'but he knew and felt a union of his fellows behind him taking an interest in his personal development, and in their ranks he could learn the duties of the individual to the society of which he formed a part.'[119]

Haldane saw the new system as bringing into union public and industrial interests. No wonder he was excited by this development, inspired by the change for good that it could bring about in Britain. Indeed, as we shall see later, he had already put a Bill before Parliament in 1914 outlining a comprehensive schooling system, which included continuation schools that would allow pupils to transition into trades. The onset of war, however, put this vision on hold—in Parliament, at least. The fact that his mid-war 1916 speech continued to stress this important lesson from the German education system shows just how vital vocational training was to Haldane. Less than twelve months earlier he had been forcibly excluded from public office on the grounds of his alleged sympathy for

Germany, and here he was praising that very nation's foresight in the vocational cause.

A cursory reading of Haldane's reflections on the relationship between education and industry might see him as instrumentalising the former for the sake of the latter. But it was precisely Kerschensteiner's emphasis on breaking the barriers of a purely utilitarian vocational training that so appealed to Haldane. Such barriers are broken, so Haldane says, 'by raising the training to a high level and making use of the passion for excellence which it awakens to inspire the learner with the desire for the knowledge which is wider, and of which his particular study is only the application in a concrete and specialised form'.[120] Personal experience had taught him that it was possible to study for a particular end and simultaneously create or indulge a love of learning for its own sake. Moreover, we should not lose sight of the support and initiative that Haldane offered towards the education of the worker in a non-vocational sense. His advocacy of the Workers' Educational Association and his founding of the British Institute of Adult Education in 1921 should serve as reminders that he was no narrow capitalist, interested in purely economic ends.

* * *

In 1916 Haldane had a chance to show this breadth of vision when he was offered the opportunity to impact the life of another major university, this time as chairman of the Royal Commission on University Education in Wales. The commission was established principally as a way of finding out how to relate a new national medical school at Cardiff to the University of Wales. This then widened to include the question of how colleges within the university—Bangor, Aberystwyth and Cardiff—and the medical school could receive Treasury grants in an effective manner. What the commission eventually reported on was the whole structure of the university: a report of typically Haldanean proportions. And let us not forget that in 1916, when Haldane took on the chairmanship, he also had his judicial business in hand, sat on a Privy Council committee on scientific and industrial research and a subcommittee on education reporting to Asquith's Reconstruction Committee, and chaired committees on air power and the conservation of coal.

For his Welsh work Haldane was joined by W. N. Bruce (chairman of the departmental committee enquiring into secondary education in Wales and assistant charity commissioner under the Endowed Schools Act), Sir William Osler (renowned Canadian physician and co-founder of Johns Hopkins Hospital), Sir Henry Jones (Welsh philosopher, professor of Moral Philosophy at Glasgow, and Haldane's fellow British Idealist),[121] Sir Owen Morgan Edwards (historian and former chief inspector of schools for Wales), Professor W. H. Bragg (1915 Nobel Prize winner in Physics), W. H. Hadow (vice-chancellor of the University of Durham), A. D. Hall (agricultural educationist), and Emily Penrose (principal of Somerville College, Oxford): a highly distinguished group, though, according to Haldane, 'it was no easy business to guide the fiery Welshmen'.[122] Once again, the workload was enormous: a full review of the history and structure of the university; thirty-one sessions for examination of witnesses; thirty-six sessions for deliberation. The final report was published in February 1918.

The Welsh people knew they were in safe hands. E. T. John, Liberal MP for East Denbighshire, commented in the *Times Educational Supplement*:

> The assistance of a statesman of genius so outstanding, of such conspicuous erudition so entirely sympathetic and appreciative as Lord Haldane is warmly welcomed. The catholicity of his temperament, with all its Continental implications arouses no prejudice in the Principality, while his intimate knowledge of Scottish conditions and his study of the problems of university administration peculiarly commend his appointment to the people of Wales.[123]

The warmth of Haldane's reception in Wales, as the commissioners travelled to the colleges in June 1916, was remarkable. Writing from Aberystwyth, Haldane could tell his mother: 'For the moment I am nearly as popular here in Wales as Lloyd George.'[124]

What became clear throughout proceedings was the need for a university that truly expressed the Welsh people and their unique spirit. What also became clear was the straitjacketing of the federal system that had been operative until that point, particularly in terms of the control exercised by the central authorities over examinations and curricula, coupled with their lack of control over teaching standards and the spending of public money.

Haldane addressed the first issue through proposing a total revamping of the University Court. At the point of reporting, the court was an ineffective mishmash of various groups concerned with education, numbering between 100 and 200 people, whose yearly gathering looked like an excuse for a giant tea party. The real business of the university was conducted by the council and the senate. But it was suggested to Haldane and the commissioners that it would be possible to lift the court beyond mere formality and give it real purpose in the life of the university and, indeed, of Wales. One of the witnesses, Mr W. George, the brother of Lloyd George, envisioned a 'real high festival of education'. This was the kind of thing to enthuse Haldane, who responded: 'And possibly it might sit in public so that the people might hear?'[125] An occasion resembling the Eisteddfod was proposed, gathering eminent speakers across a number of days to rouse the public to great educational ideals and establish standards of practice, setting the policy for the coming year and a tone of high quality. The report suggested that it could even function as 'a Parliament of higher education'.[126] The local authorities would have a greatly increased presence upon the court and the numbers would reach beyond 200; it would be the perfect setting for the discussion of 'great projects of reform and development'. Just as Haldane had sought to make the Army embedded within society through the Territorial system, so too did he think these great meetings of the court would enable the very highest in education to become 'part of the national life'.[127]

In terms of the recurring questions around finance and centralisation, the commission advised that the university should take charge of the Treasury grant and distribute to the colleges accordingly, and that it should control the appointment of professors and heads of department. Colleges, however, ought to have complete control in moulding their courses and in examinations. What Haldane sought was devolution not federalism. The commissioners' report also offered a wide range of further recommendations, covering topics as diverse as technology, agriculture, forestry, Celtic studies, music, commerce, extra-mural work and the founding of a university press. To the prime minister and Welshman Lloyd George, it was revolutionary, 'one of the most important documents, I think, in the history not merely of education in Wales, but of Wales itself'. His enthusiasm was coupled with practical proposals to make the vision a reality. The government 'should give £1 for £1. If you raise a penny rate, we will give the equivalent of it.'[128]

A devolved University of Wales could therefore take shape, though the grand ambitions for the University Court never quite materialised. Haldane, on the strength of his work for Wales and the liberality of his educational vision, became something of a hero in Welsh educational circles, if the testimony of the MP for the University is anything to go by. J. Herbert Lewis wrote to Haldane in November 1920:

> I feel I must send a line to thank you again for attending the meeting of the newly constituted University Court at Llandrindod. We all realised the trouble and inconvenience to which you put yourself in order to comply with the Prime Minister's request, and ours, and your speech—if you will allow me to say so, the very best I have ever heard on University education—was greatly appreciated by the members of the Court. W. N. Bruce [Haldane's fellow commissioner], with his balanced, unemotional mind, simply let himself go in talking about it. I have known him for 30 years & have never heard him speak so enthusiastically about anything.[129]

* * *

In Chapter 7 we looked at the significance of one of the final major chairmanships that Haldane undertook, that of the Machinery of Government Committee, whose report in 1918—the same year in which the Welsh Report was published—has come to be known as the Haldane Report. It is relevant here to mention this groundbreaking document in its relation to universities and research, for it was here that the seeds were sown for what came to be known, in the 1960s, as the 'Haldane Principle'.[130] That principle, in its modern guise, advocates that scientific experts should decide which scientific research projects the government ought to fund, while the government, which answers to the taxpayer, should set the broad strategic direction of that research. This avoids politicians channelling funding to serve their own short-term, politically expedient ends. Such has been the (not quite constant) guiding practice in the UK ever since the Haldane Report was published, and it finally became enshrined in law in 2017.[131]

It has been suggested that the 1918 report does not, as such, lay down this principle.[132] And yet the essence of the principle is widely acknowledged throughout the report's discussion on 'Research and Infor-mation'.[133] For instance, when considering the Medical Research Committee (which would become, as we shall see, the Medical Research Council), the report states: 'The Minister responsible for Health Insurance ... relies ... upon the Medical Research Committee to select the objects upon which they will spend their income, and to frame schemes for the efficient and economical performance of their work.' The report continues, 'The Minister has ... always received a full explanation of their schemes from the Committee before giving his approval, but he has never sought to control their work, or to suggest to them that they should follow one line of enquiry rather than another.'[134] As the report approvingly acknowledges, 'the judgement of the scientists who form the majority of the members of the Medical Research Committee as to the value of this understanding is clear.'[135]

The principle is also implied in the report's recommendations for a separate Department of Intelligence and Research, to which other depart-ments could refer problems; the fruits of the research undertaken would be at the disposal of every other department. The minister responsible for such a department would be 'free from any serious pressure of administra-tive duties, and is immune from any suspicion of being biased by adminis-trative considerations against the application of the results of research'.[136] The report goes on to suggest that the work of such a department could be expanded by new 'Advisory Councils', made up 'of persons with special knowledge and experience of the subject-matter standing referred to them'.[137] The Haldane Report is thus the originator of what we now know as research councils, the first of which was the Medical Research Council, established in 1920.[138] This was one of the key ways in which the report's primary recommendation became a reality. This recommendation stated that 'further provision is needed in the sphere of civil government for the continuous acquisition of knowledge and the prosecution of research, in order to furnish a proper basis for policy'.[139] Ehsan Masood, writing for *Nature* on 26 November 2018 to mark the centenary of Haldane's original report, outlined why Haldane's message remains essential. 'Today, from Istanbul to Islamabad, from Rome to Rio de Janeiro, a parade of authori-tarian leaders is advancing policies that fly in the face of evidence—on energy, emissions, the environment, economics, immigration and more.

HALDANE

Worse, these leaders are demanding that academics march to the beat of their drums.'[140]

The report's recommendation for a Department of Intelligence and Research was never realised. And yet, 'partly as a result of the Haldane Report', a Committee of Civil Research was established in 1925.[141] This attempted to root civil policy and administration in economic, scientific and statistical research, and gave the committee's president—the prime minister—the opportunity to summon expert advice in matters relating to these three branches of research. Due to a 'lack of enthusiasm on the part of the Prime Minister', the committee had become moribund by 1930, and was replaced with an Economic Advisory Council, which once again attempted to acknowledge the critical role of external expertise.[142] It has been argued that this, too, drifted into oblivion as a result of departmental suspicion of expert advice.[143] Haldane's passion for building policy according to dispassionate evidence was clearly not widely shared within Whitehall.

But the Haldane Report did bear lasting fruit in other ways. The establishment of the Medical Research Council under royal charter was the result of a clause in Christopher Addison's Ministry of Health Act 1919, which sought to put Haldane's suggestions on the autonomy of research into practice. In fact, 1919 proved somewhat of an *annus mirabilis* for Haldane, and can even be judged as the bedrock upon which university expansion, revolutionary changes in the training of doctors and the foundation of the NHS were based. So argues Sir Fred Dainton:

> For the world of learning and especially science and medicine in Britain, 1919 is a year to remember. It was then ... that the University Grants Committee was established under a Treasury minute. ... This made possible the steady increase in the flow of government resources to the universities and their rapid expansion in the 1960s without the infringement of any essential academic freedom. It was also the year in which, for the first time, the government, through the UGC, received and accepted bids from universities for resources to establish full-time chairs in medical subjects the occupants of which would have clinical responsibility for the care of patients. ... It was also the year in which Haldane's Committee enunciated the principles which should regulate the government's involvement in science and this, combined with Addison's far-sightedness, led to the establishment of the first Research Council to bear that title and, by implication,

246

secured the independence of the Department of Scientific and Industrial Research. When, in later years, other Research Councils were established their independence was never in question. Finally, on the 3 June 1919, the Ministry of Health Bill received the Royal Assent and just over three weeks later the Ministry of Health was established with Addison as its first Minister. It could be argued that this was a necessary precursor to the establishment of the National Health Service for, without the experience gained in the next two decades, it would have been difficult for the National Health Service to begin its work on 5 July 1948.[144]

* * *

Hidden legacies are rife when tracing the impact of Haldane's accomplishments. Alongside his role in establishing the independence of medical research stands his role in the origins of the comprehensive-school system in England and Wales, unified from top to bottom. Such a vision had long been Haldane's clarion call, and in 1912 he finally had the chance to lead a committee composed of ministers and educational experts and put together proposals for a scheme of full-scale reform, which he outlined in a major speech at the Manchester Reform Club on 10 January 1913. By 1914 a Bill was put before Parliament that had Haldane written all over it: it advocated a comprehensive system of schooling, continuation schools that would allow pupils to transition into trades, and the establishment of provincial associations to oversee regional educational reforms. Haldane played a central role in achieving both Cabinet approval and, the task that would prove really tricky, the approval of the Chancellor of the Exchequer, Lloyd George, so that the Bill could be catered for within the latter's Finance Bill. As ever, late-night, smoke-fuelled conversations, plenty of flattery, and dogged insistence finally achieved approval on both counts. And, as Ashby and Anderson point out, the priority of the outcome over the personal role that Haldane played was ever at the forefront of his utterances on the subject. When he spoke at the National Liberal Club after the Finance Bill was passed on 25 June 1914, he paid eloquent tribute to Lloyd George's capacities, achievements and contribution to the field of education. Following him, the Chancellor of the Exchequer thanked the Lord Chancellor:

> for his superb exposition. ... I have never regretted more than I do tonight that the Lord Chancellor has left the House of Commons. ... It was a great

speech and it displayed not merely the great intellectual qualities of the Lord Chancellor but … his thoroughly kind heart. What he did not reveal to you was that he had a great part not merely in the construction of this Budget, but in its initiation and in its inspiration.[145]

Despite the accumulating compliments, the Education Bill on this occasion came to nothing. Time ran out in Parliament and then, soon after, came the sweep of war, long-grassing the hard-won Bill.

But the fate of the Bill was not as unfortunate as that of the recommendations for the University of London. In 1916 Haldane was appointed to lead a subcommittee on education reporting to Asquith's Reconstruction Committee, and here he was able to expand upon the central tenets of the Bill. The priorities outlined by the subcommittee were 'the reorganisation of the final year at elementary school, raising the leaving age to fourteen, a system of continuation schools, and more secondary education'.[146] It included further enlightened suggestions, still relevant today, such as placing more emphasis on a pupil's school record when it came to entrance into university, rather than simply focusing on exams. Its weakness lay in its continued commitment to organise education according to large provinces, that would subsume local authorities. This sat badly with a number of civil servants, who saw such a proposal as 'quite out of touch with reality', and of course with local authority members.[147] As it turned out, external factors once again disrupted serious consideration of the subcommittee's memorandum. This time it was the fall of the government in December 1916.

Thankfully, the new president of the Board of Education was the brilliant H. A. L. Fisher, who was in deep sympathy with Haldane's objectives. In fact, on being offered the post, Fisher wrote to Gosse: 'I knew that they would not ask Haldane (much the best man for the purpose) to take up the work and I felt that I should probably be as helpful as any other outsider.'[148] The two (Haldane and Fisher) quickly fell into cahoots, as Fisher prepared a fresh Bill that would build upon the shipwrecked Bill of 1914, and expand into other areas such as nursery schooling and physical training. In October 1917 we find Fisher 'dining with Haldane … to discuss plans for waking up the country'.[149] Fisher tells his wife that he finds Haldane 'very anxious for the Bill before Xmas and is pulling all kinds of strings'.[150]

True to form, Haldane took Fisher's proposed Bill out on the road and to the people, speaking at Edinburgh, Dundee, Glasgow and Chelmsford across the autumn of 1917. Haldane's main theme in these speeches—the importance of establishing large provincial councils—was, however, gradually losing its place in the Bill, as it passed through its various readings in the Commons. Fisher had already chosen not to insist on large councils, but rather to establish provincial associations to which local education authorities might devolve administrative and educational functions. Eventually, the opposition from local authorities was so great that even this voluntary option to delegate power was removed and replaced with a mere provision for the federation of local education authorities in certain circumstances. But Fisher's compromise, disappointing as it was to Haldane, allowed the Bill a smooth passage through Parliament, and it became the Education Act 1918.[151] This was an enormous advance for the education system in England and Wales, and Haldane was not remiss in showing his praise for such a step. The Bill raised the compulsory age for school attendance from twelve to fourteen; it abolished fees in state education; it provided for continuation schools for young people between fourteen and eighteen to develop their vocational and practical training; it made arrangements for medical inspections, nursery schools and special needs education; and it linked secondary with higher education in a more definite way. Perhaps most importantly, while recognising the huge practical usefulness of an educated public, it emphasised the value of education in itself, showing the type of reverence for learning that was so vital to Haldane's thinking on human life and the structure of the state. A public triumph for Fisher; a personal triumph for Haldane.

* * *

Haldane remained engaged in what he called the 'missionary work' of education until his final days. Unsurprisingly, he continued to give much of his time to the promotion of adult education, forming from his home in Queen Anne's Gate the British Institute of Adult Education in 1921. The institute's first president, and honorary life president from 1926, Haldane spoke every year at its annual conference until 1927, the year before his death. Since then, the institute—known until recently as NIACE (National Institute of Adult Continuing Education) and now the Learning and Work Institute—has played a profoundly influential role in the cultural and social life of Britain. The British Film Institute and the Arts Council both have their origins in NIACE initiatives. The Haldane Memorial Trust continues to contribute to the institute's income.[152]

In his own time, Haldane was instrumental in marshalling funds for the purpose of adult education, most notably as the man charged with ensuring the responsible use of the German-born London banker Sir Ernest Cassel's £500,000 endowment for education.[153] Working closely with Fisher, Webb, Sir George Murray and, eventually, Philippa Fawcett of the LCC, Haldane as chairman played a pivotal role in ensuring the financial stability of a number of key educational projects. Fisher noted in his diary for 27 November 1918 that the following spending was decided:

150,000 for a Faculty of Commerce at L.[ondon] U.[niversity]
100,000 for Women's Education
50,000 for W.[orkers'] E.[ducational] A.[ssociation]
20,000 for Workman's Scholarship Continuation
100,000 for Foreign languages for *Clerks*
80,000 for Reserve[154]

The next month, Fisher told his wife: 'lunched with Haldane to discuss Cassel Trust. The old boy is full of beans and extraordinarily keen on every aspect of education, especially adult education.'[155] Incidentally, the planned Faculty of Commerce was to be housed at the LSE and Webb felt that a new director of the school was required to oversee its organisation. The candidate selected was none other than William Beveridge, who would go on to serve as director for another eighteen years, to be followed by the writing of the Beveridge Report in 1942, which would earn him the title 'father of the welfare state'. Under Beveridge's lead the LSE flourished, and his name is 'linked to an immensely fruitful period in its history in which the Sir Ernest Cassel Educational Trust [with Haldane at its head] played an ongoing part'.[156]

The extraordinary keenness for education noted by Fisher led Haldane to take one of the most courageous steps of his life. Nowhere in post-war Liberalism could he find an enthusiasm for education which corresponded with his own. By contrast, the Labour movement had placed education at the forefront of its desired reforms, and on the strength of this Haldane agreed, at Ramsay MacDonald's request, to enter the first Labour government in 1924. Interestingly, MacDonald offered Haldane the presidency of the Board of Education, but Haldane declined in favour of the Lord Chancellorship. It was a wise move, according to Ashby and Anderson:

> No more legislation was needed at that time, and he [Haldane] saw that he would be in a more influential position to determine the flow of public money as lord chancellor [Speaker of the House of Lords and the government's chief law officer] with a seat in the cabinet than in a lesser office.[157]

Nevertheless, Haldane's first speech in office set the tone for what was to follow over the next nine months of the government's life, as he called for more education in science: the natural topic for the new head of the judiciary!

The authenticity of Haldane's passion for education and his tireless endeavours in its cause (in 1920–21 he spoke on the issue at sixty meetings across the breadth of the UK) meant that honours showered in upon him. He laid the foundation stones of the University Colleges of Reading and of Nottingham. Over the course of his life he was awarded ten honorary doctorates, and served as Lord Rector of Edinburgh, 1905–8; chancellor of Bristol University (where the students, conscious of his work before the war, welcomed him in 1920 with the chant, 'Who saved England? … Haldane'), 1912–28; and president of Birkbeck, 1919–28. In June 1928, just before his death, he was appointed chancellor of St Andrews.[158]

When Haldane died two months later the hole at the centre of the British educational landscape was enormous. Bishop Charles Gore didn't hesitate to call it a 'disaster'.[159] Speaking in 1932 at one of the early Haldane Memorial Lectures at Birkbeck College, the vice-chancellor of the University of Liverpool, H. J. W. Hetherington, could claim: 'There is no University in these islands which is not in Lord Haldane's debt.'[160] Ashby and Anderson state the case even more strongly: 'But how much of his achievement is still visible? Our answer is that it lies in the foundations of our whole system of education.'[161]

9

WAR AND PEACE

Few men could have overcome the difficulties which confronted you <u>inside</u> the War Office when you began your scheme of reform.——Everything was done by those who ought to have known better to prevent any progress from being made! How you triumphed and gradually carried everyone with you was truly wonderful. ... I shall always feel proud that I was one of your humble supporters & was able quietly to look on and admire the genius which you displayed in handling the objectors!

Lieutenant General (later Field Marshal) Sir Douglas Haig to
R. B. Haldane, 1912[1]

Perhaps I saw more than almost anyone of the real value of the work that he did in those strenuous years before the war. And knowing all this at first hand, and reflecting on its consequences, I say without hesitation 'He saved the state.'

Major General J. E. B. Seely (Secretary of State for War, 1912–14) to
E. S. Haldane, 1928[2]

Haldane described the day he entered the War Office as Secretary of State as 'a day of the blackest fog that I can remember'.[3] It was 11 December 1905. Having received their seals of office from the king at Buckingham Palace late that afternoon, Haldane and his colleagues Grey (now Foreign Secretary) and Henry Fowler (Chancellor of the Duchy of Lancaster) set off through the soup-like haze to their respective departments in a brougham carriage. The carriage ground to a halt on the Mall, the driver totally unable to get his bearings. Haldane, feeling he might have a bit of luck determining their position if he got out for a moment, was singularly unsuccessful: he lost the carriage. Clutching his seals tightly, he plunged on through the horses' heads and the mud. He was exhausted when he eventually found the War Office on Pall Mall, and asked the soldier on duty for a glass of water. 'Certainly, sir: Irish or Scotch?'

It was an apt beginning. His road to the War Office had not been easy. With the Relugas Compact in tatters, Haldane described the week in which he had to decide whether or not to take office as 'the most miserable I have ever spent in my life'.[4] The department he was entering was itself lost in its own metaphorical fog. The two previous ministers to hold the seal, as we shall see, had failed to understand the place and its inner workings; it had become a graveyard for political careers. And yet, when Haldane left the War Office in 1912 it was, in the estimation of General Sir Ian Hamilton, 'a symmetrical and delectable garden'.[5]

Before looking at the deft ways in which Haldane managed to avoid the pitfalls experienced by his immediate predecessors, it is worthwhile reminding ourselves what constituted the essence of the so-called Haldane Reforms and why they were so significant. His principal achievement was the creation of the British Expeditionary Force (BEF), composed of six infantry divisions and a cavalry division, designed for rapid mobilisation and overseas combat. To make up for losses sustained by the BEF, Haldane formed a Special Reserve out of the existing Militia and elements of the Yeomanry. This was established on 1 April 1908 under the authorisation of the Territorial and Reserve Forces Act 1907. On the same date and under the same Act, Haldane created a Territorial Force (known until 2016 as the Territorial Army, now the Army Reserve), formed by the Volunteers and the other elements of the Yeomanry. This force was Haldane's attempt to ward off the cries for national conscription to raise an army of Continental proportions—a campaign headed by the powerful Lord Roberts, who had become a hero throughout the empire in light of his leadership during the Second Boer War (1899–1902). Haldane's Territorials provided, instead, a (much cheaper) voluntary force that remained only partially trained in peacetime, but which, upon the outbreak of war, could be swiftly trained to the necessary standards.[6] Though originally envisioned as a means of expanding the BEF, its purpose was altered towards home defence in response to external pressures.[7] Importantly, the Territorials were also provided with field artillery, companies of engineers, and crucial supply services, not least medical provision (Haldane's sister Elizabeth played a key role in the organisation of the Territorial Army Nursing Service).[8] In 1908 Haldane also organised an Officers' Training Corps (OTC) within the public schools and universities. This addressed the persistent shortage of officers, who would be needed not just to lead the BEF at the outset of any hostilities, but to provide for replacements following casualties, and to train and man the Territorial Force and the Reserves. Shortly afterwards, in 1909, Haldane created the Imperial General Staff, building on the already existing General Staff, which provided a 'thinking department' for the army, but in this case a thinking department that Haldane hoped would link, inform, and co-ordinate the armies of Britain's outlying dominions. Finally, though not commonly connected to his army reforms, between 1911 and 1912 Haldane was instrumental in laying the foundations for the Royal Flying Corps, which would become, in time, the Royal Air Force.

Military historians' perspectives on the role played by these bodies, particularly the BEF, during the opening months of the First World War have undergone some revision over the last decades, as have their views on Haldane's intentions in their creation. Until the 1970s Haldane's reputation as War Secretary was centred on a narrative that emphasised the critical assistance that the BEF—consisting of a mere 90,000 men when first deployed in August 1914, four-fifths of whom would be killed or wounded by Christmas—offered to the French army in its hour of direst need. The BEF's additional numbers, leading up to and during the Battle of the Marne, were seen as a vital component behind the forced retreat of General von Kluck's First Army on 7 September 1914, preventing the fall of Paris to the Germans and the occupation of the Channel ports that would inevitably have followed. The narrative especially praised the speed of the BEF's mobilisation and deployment, the professional nature of its soldiers and their devastating rifle fire, which led one German commanding officer at the Battle of Mons to lament the loss of 'my proud, beautiful battalion ... shot to pieces by the English, the English we laughed at'.[9] This 'contemptible little Army', as Kaiser Wilhelm II once reportedly called the BEF, would thereafter adopt the title of 'the Old Contemptibles' with pride. Haldane, as the creator of that force, was understandably proud too. His military and political allies, as we shall see, even went so far as to hail Haldane as the saviour of the British state. While he did not make such a claim himself, Haldane's 1920 book *Before the War* and his posthumously published *Autobiography* point out, not least for the benefit of all those who had attacked him as a German sympathiser, the work he and his colleagues had done before 1914 to prepare for conflict with Germany, stressing the way in which his reforms—notably the size and composition of the BEF—were specifically designed with such a conflict in mind.[10]

More recent historical scholarship has somewhat complicated that narrative. It tends to downplay the significance of the BEF and questions just how prepared Britain in fact was for Continental warfare when it broke out. A number of commentators have pointed out the ambiguity within pre-war British military thinking about the purpose of the BEF—was it for imperial defence or for Continental war or for both? There may have been a Continental strategy at play within the General Staff, but in many cases the actual organisation of the army pointed in other directions.[11] It was this ambiguity that meant that it was not a perfected instrument for European war when it came. Haldane's own post-war account is seen as bypassing this ambiguity, allowing the preparations for a war with Germany to dominate his version of events (a fair point, but this is understandable given the sheer volume of criticism he received for his apparently pro-German approach as War Secretary). Some historians also point out that certain actions for which Haldane had previously been praised are accolades more appropriately held by others. Yes, from the beginning of his time at the War Office Haldane did push for an army that could be rapidly deployed, but for that to become a reality it needed the skills of Sir Henry Wilson, who, as director of military operations from 1910, worked out the detailed plans for transporting the BEF to France. Too often, in earlier historical reflections on Haldane's achievements, Wilson had been left out of the picture.[12]

Yet Haldane's greatness as a Secretary of State for War is rarely in question. Where earlier historians had placed the emphasis on what he did to prepare the British army for the events of 1914, his exceptional abilities are now seen to be more specifically institutional and political. His truly formidable achievement was to create a deployable army to go overseas out of a genuinely chaotic situation within the army and an enormously difficult political climate. The army that emerged out of the Haldane Reforms was as efficient an instrument as was possible in the circumstances of the time. How he balanced the many differing demands upon him, allowing his reforms to win through in the end, was a masterpiece in statesmanship.[13] It is this masterpiece that we shall largely be exploring in the present chapter.

But before we come to that, we might still take a moment to reflect on the fate of Haldane's creations during the war. While the BEF ought not to steal the limelight from its much larger French counterpart in the fighting which culminated in the defence of Paris, that should not blind us to its critical importance in that endeavour and the enormous sacrifice made by its men in that cause. The Royal Flying Corps, again in conjunction with its French counterpart, also played a vital role in its careful observation of the movements of the German First Army. British and French aviation provided the crucial confirmation of the right moment to halt the Allied retreat and take the battle back to the Germans at the Marne.[14]

The young men who had entered the BEF, Special Reserve or the Territorials by means of Haldane's Officers' Training Corps should not be forgotten. Between 1907 and 1914, 4,000 boys who had served in their school OTCs had received commissions. In the first seven months of the war commissions were awarded to a further 21,000 who would serve as officers, with an additional 13,000 enlisting in the ranks.[15] As news of the deaths and injuries of so many of these young men filtered back to their schools and universities, the initial sense of the glory of the call to which their students had responded faded, to be replaced with a profound aware-ness of the sheer brutality of the conflict.[16] Nor did Haldane's Territorials escape that brutality, despite the new War Secretary Lord Kitchener's failure to capitalise upon the potential within the Territorial structure for rapid expansion, choosing instead to build up his own 'New Army'.[17] Before that army was ready, the Territorials were called in to supplement the BEF. By the end of 1914 twenty-three of their infantry battalions and six of their field companies of the Royal Engineers were in France. By April 1915 six complete Territorial Divisions had joined them.[18] According to Sir John French, 'without the assistance which the Territorials afforded between October, 1914, and June, 1915, it would have been impossible to have held the line in France and Belgium.'[19]

In sum, the Haldane Reforms clearly made a crucial difference to Britain's ability to engage effectively at the outset of the First World War, and granted the country an ability to absorb—for a limited but essential length of time—the monumental losses sustained by the BEF. Thus British forces played a significant attritional part in forcing the German retreat from the gates of Paris.

Haldane's role in the creation of these forces is little known today. Even less well known are the other revolutionary moves that he instigated while at the War Office, which fell outside the scope of his army reforms. These include the establishment of a Secret Service Bureau (today's MI5 and MI6) and the catalysing of the Boy Scout movement. But before exploring these neglected aspects of Haldane's tenure, what concerns us at the outset of this chapter are the conditions that stood in the War Secretary's way before any of these achievements were realised.

If we groan today about a major government department, such as the Department for Health and Social Care, its enormous cost, its inefficiencies and confusions, we would do well to compare it to the department that Haldane faced when he entered the War Office. For the financial year 2020, Healthcare accounts for 19 per cent of total UK public spending.[20] In 1905 army expenditure gulped down an equivalent of 20 per cent of overall outgoings, creating a wave of pressure on the new Campbell-Bannerman administration for drastic cuts.[21] Like the present NHS, the army had grown into its structure at the time in response to a set of historical conditions that no longer applied; it was either designed to meet needs that no longer existed or it wasn't designed at all, growing up reactively and organically in the face of unique crises. Making matters even worse for Haldane were the many loud and influential voices putting pressure on the new Secretary of State for War to reform the army in ways that were often mutually exclusive (conscription versus voluntary service, for example) and an atmosphere of animosity between these voices.

Haldane's response to the challenges that faced him was remarkable. As we explore that response and discover the principles and techniques he used to overcome these adversities, it will become clear just how relevant his approach remains.[22] We should ask ourselves: what could Haldane's form of statesmanship effect today? The crisis in our healthcare system would not be an inappropriate issue to have in mind.

* * *

To consider the desperate state of the army before, during and after the shambles of the Second Boer War is a suitable way of getting into the issues that Haldane had to pin down once he had battled through the December fog. He described the situation at the outbreak of the South African conflict as 'inconceivably confused'.[23] There was no General Staff to think through the larger principles of military action. As a result, the organisation of the army in time of peace did not correlate with what was required of it in time of war. When conflict arose in 1899, Britain was therefore unable to dispatch troops at speed without dismantling the regimental system or summoning the Reserves. In the Auxiliary Forces, meanwhile, certain units of the Militia simply refused to go. Haphazard arrangements meant huge inefficiency, so much so that a small band of Boer fighters almost toppled an army which, fully mobilised, could put over 400,000 men into the field.[24]

Shortly after Haldane's arrival at the War Office it was discovered, upon investigation, that it would take at least two months to put a mere 80,000 men on the Continent. The German army, by comparison, could boast over 600,000 men that year.[25] This disparity was significant because by January 1906 it had become clear, as Grey informed Haldane both by letter[26] and in person[27] that a major threat to Britain's interests, and the interests of her allies, lay in a growing militaristic spirit in Germany. It was likely, so Haldane was told, that this spirit would find expression in an invasion of France, and he was tasked to work out how the British army might aid the French in such a moment of peril. It was obvious to Haldane, and to his closest military advisers, that building an army on a Continental model would be highly impractical. Unlike Continental nations, Britain was an island, with the world's most powerful navy to defend its shores, and compulsory service would take a substantial time to implement fully, weakening the country for a time, not to mention the unacceptable financial burden on the taxpayer. But the army could and should be used overseas to defend Britain's imperial interests and the interests of her allies, and this required a force to be fashioned which could be rapidly mobilised, had sufficient numbers in reserve to replace casualties in war, and was supported with the necessary ancillary services to function in the field.[28]

The military powers on the Continent operated in the form of large divisions and corps, each corps consisting of two divisions.[29] An army without a single division was placed into Haldane's hands. The brigades he received remained without the necessary logistical and medical assistance for battle.[30] Of the ninety-nine batteries within the field artillery only forty-two could be mobilised, due to shortages in men and reserves. Meanwhile, huge sums of money were being sucked into home defence, despite the navy's evident ability to perform that function. To Haldane it seemed obvious that money could be freed up here and used to fashion a highly skilled, easily mobilised fighting force for overseas. But such financial decisions were fraught with danger.

To speak of freeing up money in one area of military expenditure for the purposes of building up another would have been, for radicals and militarists alike, an unthinkable manoeuvre. For the radicals—who had a considerable voice now that the reforming Campbell-Bannerman regime had been given a mandate by the nation—there was only one method of dealing with army expenditure: to cut it drastically and to use that money for the social reforms that had been promised to the people. For the militarists—who, within the Tory establishment, had a strong voice—there was likewise only one method: to increase expenditure to allow for conscription on a national level in order to compete with the powerful Continental armies. Haldane knew that if he wished to make any progress with military reform, he would have to satisfy, or at least defend himself against, both parties.

The problem mushrooms when we consider the scale of confusion and opposition Haldane faced when trying to reform the Auxiliary Forces. The Militia posed the largest problem. Its present state was one of negligible usefulness. No longer the 'Old Constitutional Force' of England, it had become a training ground—and not a very good one—for underage boys before they joined the Regular Army. In terms of its providing for home defence, there was little by way of organisation for actual combat, it lacked ancillary services, its training was deficient, and the quality of recruits was usually very poor. Furthermore, the Militia was now dependent on the Exchequer for roughly £2,000,000 a year. Haldane had two options: the Militia must either join the newly planned Territorial Force, functioning solely as a second-line body, or it must act as a reserve body to the Regulars. But those who supported the Militia had a powerful voice in Parliament and in the counties, and they were only going to sanction changes to so unique a body if they could claim equal status with Regular forces during time of war.[31] Their demands included a commitment that Militia officers should be interchangeable with officers of equal rank in the Line battalions; that militiamen should be exempt from civil obligations; and that all honours accorded to Line battalions should likewise be accorded to their attached Militia battalions. These requests were unacceptable to the War Office. This meant that legislation was almost unavoidable; changes would have to be made by force of law.[32]

The Volunteers posed a further problem. Hitherto, the commanding officers had been financially responsible for their units, receiving grants from the War Office for maintenance and training. Haldane wished to transfer the responsibility for finance and administration to County Associations (a term borrowed from Cromwell), headed by Lord Lieutenants, while the War Office would control military training. As things stood, a sense of system, so important to the Hegelian Haldane, was desperately needed. As Haldane told the Commons during the introduction of his second Army Estimates on 25 February 1907:

> Their [the Volunteers'] organisation, I think, is probably the most confused thing we have in the British constitution. They are paid twenty-two different ways. They get a capitation grant of 35s., which is practically a premium on the enlistments of inefficients. They have no supply organisation for war. If they were at war the colonel, whose business it is to provide socks, clothes, ammunition, and everything else, would have to carry these things with him in his saddle bags. The financial position of the commanding officers is deplorable. ... If he wants a drill hall for his corps and borrows money to enable him to build it, the Commissioners lend him money, but make him personally liable. If he does not get a capitation grant and his corps fails he has to make these things good.[33]

But the Volunteer commanders were up in arms (thankfully not literally). Their complaints were summed up by F. N. Maude: 'There is the principle of "growth" dependent on the zeal and interest of the one man who has most at stake in his venture [that is, the commanding officer]; and this incentive cannot be transferred to county association.'[34] There was also a general sense that recruitment would suffer considerably if the stricter regulations proposed by the War Office—in particular, fines for non-fulfilment of duties—were imposed.

The Yeomanry, out of which Haldane hoped to fashion a second line of cavalry, were in better shape than either the Militia or the Volunteers, but there remained difficulties. Worryingly, they lacked brigade organisation, staff and administrative services. They had their origins in the French Revolution and they had grown since then, without any plan and without relation to the requirements of strategy. Haldane was forced to point out: 'If we came to war nobody would quite know where to put them.'[35]

Here were three organisations, unrelated to each other, disorganised, leaking money, and ineffective in time of war. And yet they had 'histories and traditions and people who had been associated with them and were devotedly attached to them'.[36] To rebrand and reorganise these forces was Haldane's job, and he had to do it in the teeth of immense opposition.

* * *

All of these factors would have been sufficient cause for celebrating Haldane's achievement, even if he had inherited a harmonious and functioning department. But this was not the case. In the first instance, when he arrived at the War Office, the generals were at each other's throats. This was the very first knot Haldane sought to unravel. Within two weeks of taking office he could tell former Liberal prime minister and long-standing political ally, Lord Rosebery: 'My first task has been to get the Generals on to good terms with each other. As they are no longer on deadly terms with the S.[ecretary] of S.[tate] [Haldane himself, that is] this has not been difficult.'[37] After the confusion left in the wake of the two previous Conservative War Secretaries, William St John Brodrick and H. O. Arnold-Forster, it was imperative to establish order. That confusion had arisen out of their insistence on implementing preconceived plans without adequate consultation with the military experts. Haldane's tactic in restoring a sense of calm was to assure the generals that each of them would find in him a willing ear for their thoughts, concerns and ideas for reform.

Lieutenant General Sir Gerald Ellison—who, as Colonel Ellison, acted as Haldane's principal private secretary between 1905 and 1908—set out the three main voices that Haldane had to listen to upon taking office in a letter to Countess Haig in 1928. In the first instance, there was the older school of thought, which argued for a style of command and control that was improvisational and fluid. Then there was the younger school of thought, which knew that reform was necessary but hadn't grasped how extensive the reforms would need to be in order to produce a truly efficient army. Lastly, there were those who had a vested interest in the existing organisation of the Regular Army, Militia, Yeomanry and Volunteers, and who would fight against any significant institutional change.[38] Haldane claimed that he came with no preconceptions (though that is open to dispute)[39] and would refuse to side with a particular faction from the off. No doubt the generals were not only amused but relieved to hear Haldane say on arrival: 'I [am] a young and blushing virgin just united to a bronzed warrior ... it [is] not expected by the public that any result of the union should appear until nine months [have] passed.'[40] He would, he assured them, sound opinion from every side and make a considered judgment on what basis to proceed. This is not quite how events unfolded—upon entering office, he was determined to follow Admiral Jacky Fisher's example at the Admiralty, where Fisher attempted to cut ruthlessly unless funds were directly contributing to preparation for war;[41] he was also already a supporter of the 'Blue Water' principle, which considered the army's home defence functions unnecessary on account of the navy's dominance at sea; and the further principles that underpinned a two-line army were fashioned within his first month as Secretary of State. These principles concerning a two-line army were mainly developed in conversation with his private secretary Colonel Ellison over the Christmas recess at Cloan and January electioneering in Haddingtonshire.[42] But despite these early commitments, Haldane at least set a tone of consultation and openness. This certainly played its part in cooling the febrile atmosphere of a department rife with in-fighting. *The Times* military correspondent and avid Haldane supporter, Charles à Court Repington ('no other critic better advertised and justified his reform proposals'),[43] reflected on Haldane's remarkable capacity to change minds based on his strength of character, and expressed it thus: 'He comes, he smiles, he conquers.'[44] Or, as A. G. Gardiner humorously put it:

> You cannot resist a man who bursts with such enjoyment into the mess, smokes bigger and stronger cigars than anyone else, and obviously enjoys them more, knows as much about explosives as he does about the Westminster Confession, and with all these accomplishments does you the delicate honour of discussing his scheme with you as if your approval were the one thing in the world necessary to his complete happiness.[45]

Part of Haldane's success with the generals was surely the sheer joy he took in tackling the monumental task ahead of him. There was something in his constitution which made a difficult task the most favoured one. Less than two weeks into the job, he writes to his friend and librarian of the House of Lords, Edmund Gosse:

> I will make a confession of fickleness. I thought I loved the Law. But out of sight is out of mind. I am enjoying myself simply hugely. The dear Generals are angels—no other name is good enough for these simple, honourable, souls. I have already made changes which might alarm them (vide to-morrow's 'Times') and they gulp them down.
>
> Now I know what is to live! It is the best of fun—though my solemn predecessors, not being Scotsmen, never saw it. You never saw such a band of Reformers as I am trying to hold back. If I could only get three years here I could do something. It suits my habits of mind.[46]

Though the generals were largely acquiescent, there were other advisers who were not quite so willing to accept Haldane's approach. The then secretary of the Committee of Imperial Defence, Sir George Clarke, for instance, felt that Haldane, despite all his professions of open-mindedness, had fallen prey to Ellison's own flawed vision. The Territorial Force, claimed Clarke, was an idea implanted in Haldane's head by Ellison, whose thinking was 'doctrinaire' and 'academic', lacking in practical applicability. This could only lead to 'hopeless confusion' for Haldane.[47] By March 1906 Clarke felt that 'Haldane will make a considerably worse mess of it than A[rnold]-F[orster]'.[48] On reading Haldane's fourth memorandum on the Territorial Force, Clarke exclaimed: 'I wash my hands over the whole business if we are to be limited to the provisions of this Fourth Gospel according (mainly) to Ellison.'[49] But it was not that Haldane had failed to listen to Clarke's advice.[50] He did listen; he just rejected it in favour of the plans that he and Ellison had devised. Clarke had recommended a reanimated Militia, which would expand the Regulars in war and separate from them in peace. They would be raised under county authority, and formed in large and distinct units. But this would muddy the neat two-line distinction that was so integral to a cohesive force in war. Haldane was determined to stick firmly to his rigorously systematic approach. Meanwhile, Sir Henry Wilson, then commandant of the staff college at Camberley, was equally unsupportive, bitterly condemning Haldane's plans. He considered the lack of an officer reserve 'the worst part of the Scheme'. Everything Haldane suggested was, in Wilson's view, 'quite impractical'.[51]

Despite this resistance, Haldane adopted a safe approach that would maintain not only the majority of generals' support, but also broad cross-party support.[52] In the first instance, he took great care to implement the recommendations of the 1904 Esher Report (Ellison had been secretary to the committee)—particularly the proper formation of a General Staff—and could thereby show he was not simply acting according to his own lights—and, indeed, that he was following the advice of a body appointed by the Conservative Balfour. He kept in constant touch with Esher himself (Reginald Brett, 2nd Viscount Esher), who had chaired the 1904 committee and had sat on the Elgin Commission prior to that. This demonstrated Haldane's desire to remain true to the collective wisdom gathered since the end of the Boer War (and gathered specifically to remedy the defects highlighted by that war). Indeed, the relationship with Esher was critical in almost every aspect of the reforms. It was he who recommended Ellison as Haldane's private secretary, and encouraged Haldane to bring Haig back from India to act first as director of military training and then as director of staff duties. Esher also provided the incisive sounding board so necessary for any radical development.[53] Moreover, his political neutrality, his close relationships with many of the leading figures of the day, most importantly King Edward VII, and his willingness to reassure them of Haldane's sense and good judgment, guaranteed a certain amount of support in the places where it really mattered. As Esher's biographer, James Lees-Milne, put it: 'The better Regy [Esher] got to know Haldane the more fond he became, and more appreciative of his great gifts. He endeavoured, not without ultimate success, to convince the King that he was an exceptionally brilliant individual, as well as a lovable man.'[54]

Secondly, Haldane made sure the memoranda outlining proposed reforms were circulated to members of the Army Council for full consideration before any action was taken. Of course, there were those who disagreed with aspects of his plans, but because no genuinely viable alternatives could be offered, Haldane was able to argue from a position of strength. He could also enter into the debates of the House with the firm knowledge that every plan proposed had been thoroughly considered by 'the experts'. As he told his mother on 12 July 1906, before placing the Army Estimates for the coming year before the Commons: 'I go into action with no sense of certainty. The London Society opposition & that of the Conservative papers is very strong. But every link in the plan has been worked out & tested by experts.'[55] Two years later, Esher was reminding the king: 'Somebody may think of a better system, but so far no-one has *worked out in detail* a better plan than Mr Haldane and his military advisers.'[56]

* * *

The viability of Haldane's proposed reforms was principally related to affordability. By disbanding unnecessary infantry battalions, getting rid of excess artillery batteries and reducing forces at quiet garrisons overseas, then channelling a portion of the money saved into improving armaments, ammunition, equipment and ancillary services, Haldane could show that he could actually decrease military spending (as the radicals demanded), while at the same time increasing the army's capacity to enter the field of combat (as the militarists demanded).[57] It has even been suggested that the exact construction of the BEF 'was the fruit of cash constraints, not strategic reappraisal'.[58] In other words, it was the budget that dictated what the BEF looked like, not what might be needed on the Continent in the event of war with Germany (which, as we have seen, is what Haldane appears to suggest in his post-war writings).[59] But perhaps it is not necessary to be as black and white as this. Yes, budget concerns radically shaped what was possible, but throughout 1906 and again from 1910 onwards the British generals were in discussion with their French counterparts about the ways in which British troops might assist the French if they were on the receiving end of a German attack. These so-called military conversations proved highly controversial when they became public in 1911, partly because it turned out that only a very few members of the Cabinet knew of their existence and partly because some believed it placed a moral obligation on Britain to enter a war if France were attacked.[60] These discussions played a decisive role in understanding what kind of force would be needed if a moment of crisis came, and 'provided a focal point for reform' of the army—to the extent that such reform accorded with other imperial concerns and the financial constraints of the time, of course.[61] Haldane was naturally deeply sensitive to what those financial constraints were, and he won support from a number of radicals precisely because of this.

Another appealing aspect from a radical perspective was that the Territorial and Reserve Forces Bill of 1907 showed Haldane's commitment to the voluntary system. Conscription was unthinkable to the Liberal Party, and even to the majority of Conservatives. The Bill also ensured that Britain was unlikely to be led into any conflict with which the nation at large disagreed.[62] Although Haldane's scheme was seen as the last straw for the voluntary system, and would therefore catalyse conscription if it failed, it nevertheless maintained a crucial tenet of Liberalism (in time of peace, at least). And for the militarists who were convinced the scheme would collapse, conscription was only one step away, so to some extent they, too, were more willing to let Haldane have his moment.

Haldane was fortunate that the House and the nation were willing to give him time to show that his plans were possible—understandably, given the disastrous results of the previous War Secretaries' premature plans—but we shouldn't underestimate the skill with which Haldane made the case for taking his time. He ordered full reviews of each department within the War Office, which were able to show wastage at every turn; he then clearly demonstrated that certain steps could diminish that wastage, and how long it would take to instigate each of these steps. Of great importance was the fact that he set a reasonable financial cap on his spending (£28,000,000; roughly £3.4 billion today),[63] reassuring the radicals that army finances would remain within acceptable limits. He could also assure them that he was building his reforms on a Cardwellian structure, whereby every first battalion of a regiment was provided with a second, which would feed the first battalion abroad during peace time, and would form on mobilisation a fully ready second battalion with the aid of its reserves. Men would serve for seven years with the colours (that is, in the army) and five with the reserve. Edward Cardwell—famous for his efficiency and economy, and under whom Campbell-Bannerman (CB) had served when financial secretary of the War Office—was something of a hero among the Liberals. In this way, on 3 February 1907 CB could report to Captain Sinclair, his private secretary:

He [Haldane] dwelt on the fact of the Cardwell system being maintained, a committee of experts under General Miles having examined and approved the whole thing. Fleetwood and others having blessed the scheme financially. All is therefore for the best—the soldiers are delighted; the

Volunteers everywhere enthusiastic; Grey and Asquith very warm for it; [John] Burns and J.[ohn] M.[orley] most appreciative. Every bolthole was thus stopped! I could only congratulate him. ... He thus rides on the storm and directs the whirlwind.[64]

By the end of the parliamentary year, with the Territorial and Reserve Forces Act enshrined in law, CB—the man who thought he had condemned Haldane to a political graveyard by sending him to the War Office—was compelled to write to Haldane:

As this is the close of a Parliamentary Chapter, let me most sincerely & warmly congratulate you upon the great success you have wrought out of your complicated problem & your worrying labours over it. It is a great triumph to have carried such a large body of opinion with you, and I hope you will have as much satisfaction while you proceed to carry out & super-intend the working of the details of your magnum opus.[65]

* * *

Haldane was methodical and thoughtful in every respect, and such an approach is always difficult to refute. Having said that, his desire to keep all sides happy did not always mean that he won their complete support. As Esher observed: 'His weakness is that in wanting to please everybody, he satisfies no one.'[66] Though there is an element of truth here, this is surely an exaggeration—we know of a number of important individuals who were deeply satisfied with Haldane's approach,[67] and we also know of those he didn't even begin to try to placate.[68] But Esher's observation does bring to light a key technique that kept Haldane afloat as a minister, namely an ardent attempt to see his plans from his critics' perspective and to seek to work in such a way that he could meet their concerns, as far as possible. In all that Haldane did he thought through the consequences, considered the opposition, and sought a course of action that had the potential to be seen through to the end. Act with care; ensure longevity. That was Haldane's approach.

The essential factor in all this is that Haldane thought before he acted. That thought was dominated by an intense desire to work out the foun-dational principles upon which any action should rest, a desire that devel-oped out of his early philosophical studies.[69] No move was arbitrary, and every move was connected with every other. This began with 'a complete survey of the Army as a whole—with a view of getting in the end a definite objective'.[70] In this task he was supported by the best military brains he could find, initially Ellison and Charles Harris, principal clerk of the War Office;[71] then Haig (director of military training), Spencer Ewart (director of military operations) and Sir William Nicholson (quartermaster-general to the Forces in 1905, whom Haldane promoted to chief of the General Staff in 1908, then of the Imperial General Staff in 1909). That brains were a priority is shown when he writes to Rosebery in December 1905: 'I have eliminated from the Council one man who is better for the field than for the office and brought in Sir Wm. Nicholson—an acute big brain—but not a very easy man. Still I needed him badly.'[72] Haig's appointment was similarly grounded. As he told Esher: 'We want Haig badly, (1) he has brains, (2) he is a cavalry man.'[73] Given what we know of Haig's later reputation—'arguably the most reviled man in British history'—we may be surprised to hear of Haldane's admiration.[74] Now is not the time to debate his capacities as a commander-in-chief during the First World War (though it should be noted that his reputation is perhaps slowly on the mend), but we can at least draw attention to the fact that Esher—no fool—was a strong advocate on behalf of Haig's abilities in the early days of Haldane's time at the War Office.[75] Esher's advocacy was the reason that Haig came to Haldane's attention in the first place. It is also clear that the work Haig did in the years before the war under Haldane showed a man 'immensely able, co-operative, and loyal'.[76] As Edward Spiers has shown, it was Haig's efforts 'to study tactical problems in a highly practical manner' that brought to light 'a host of problems involved in the disembarking, moving, accommodating, and concentrating of troops'.[77] Haig was instrumental in showing the need for co-ordinating the activities of the various staffs and it was his work, in the form of the manual *Field Service Regulations Part II*, that addressed this issue to ensure the efficient organisation of the army in the field.[78]

It is true that Haldane did not utilise the Army Council to the extent that his forerunner did; he preferred, instead, to cut through the chaff and find minds—such as Haig's—he could rely on, irrespective of official positions and titles.[79] In that sense Haldane did not stand on ceremony, and he refused to be sucked into departmental machinations which would only

serve to delay and complicate his plans. The manner in which he and
Ellison worked together during the five weeks of the 1905–6 Christmas
recess and January electioneering in Scotland is a case in point. Here he
found clear thinking space, away from the demands of Whitehall, and the
chance to draw on the thinking power of a man who—though not of eminence in terms of rank—had been brought specially to Haldane's aid by
Esher, on account of his intimate knowledge of the Esher Committee's
findings and his advanced thinking on military organisation.

Much ink has been spent on attributing the origins of the Haldane
Reforms to other sources, particularly to Esher and Ellison, and even to
the Conservative leader Balfour,[80] and on arguing that Haldane sought
credit where credit wasn't due. It is no problem to admit that a number of
the defining features of the reforms had earlier precedents, and that some
of its central principles were already on the table before Haldane walked
into his new office.[81] But that is not to say that Haldane did not play a
decisive original part in the thinking side of the developments. Ellison
made Haldane's originality clear in his 'Reminiscences', and modern
scholars, such as Edward Spiers, have shown the features that bear his
distinctive marks. According to Ellison, Haldane's insistence that the
Regular forces should be primarily organised for overseas action justified
the claim that Haldane was the 'inventor' of the BEF; equally, Haldane's
idea that the Territorial Army should be constructed on the basis of County
Associations was entirely 'novel'. For Spiers, the whole notion of a 'nation
at arms' by which Haldane conceived the two-line structure of professional Regulars, backed by the Special Reserve and underwritten by citizens who made up the Territorials, bore a distinctly Germanic and militaristic overtone 'quite different' from anything Ellison had proffered in his
published writings, such as *Home Defence*.[82] In other words, it had Haldane's
fingerprints all over it.

The originality of Haldane's thinking should not, therefore, be overlooked; but perhaps more important is the unique way in which he implemented that thinking. Many eminent figures of the time considered this
manner of implementation to be his unmatched political achievement.
General Sir Ian Hamilton, a colourful character who held high military
positions throughout this period, put the case powerfully, if perhaps
slightly hyperbolically, in his book *The Soul and Body of an Army*. It makes

for entertaining reading and is worth quoting in full; it also brings out the connection between Cardwell and Haldane in a unique way:

> If Cardwell was the Castor of our military firmament, Haldane was its Pollux. How splendidly did he shine out during those dark nights when we might all of us 'sleep in our beds'—and a long last sleep it would have been had Haldane really believed in soporifics.

> Cardwell had left the Army in the following state:

> 1) Bare minimum garrisons for India and the overseas territories and fortresses;
> 2) Reserves for these foreign service troops which, by his clever organising skill, were represented to the taxpayer as being mere depots, whereas they were really duplicate training battalions capable of quickly taking the field as fighting battalions;
> 3) A disorganised mass of militia, yeomanry and volunteers, supposed to be adjuncts to the martello towers of the South coast, as defenders of our hearths and homes.

> Came Haldane the Organiser, and cut, pruned, shuffled, grafted, drafted until he had grouped (2) into an Expeditionary Force of six Divisions whilst making (3) partly into a special reserve for that Expeditionary Force and partly into fourteen fighting divisions, complete with engineers, artillery, cavalry, transport, supply and medical services. When I look back on this period and think of the jungle filled with hissing adders which Haldane broke up into a symmetrical and delectable garden, I do really feel uplifted to think I was privileged to watch his address, his artistry, his perseverance, and even to lend at times a hand. The war was won when Haldane stepped into the War Office: most miserably must we have lost it had he failed us. To say this is common justice—no more. We abound in Ministers who can spend more and produce less: Haldane spent less and less, yet quadrupled the value of the outfit![83]

It was Haldane's organisational skill that set him apart. It is likely, however, that many readers of Hamilton's remarks will still see it as an exaggeration to say that 'the war was won when Haldane stepped into the War Office'. It is striking, however, how many of Haldane's contemporaries shared this view, basing their case primarily on the BEF's contribution during the opening months of the First World War, as we discussed earlier. Haldane, in *Before the War*, outlined what the consequences would have been for Britain if the French and British armies had failed in halting the German progress towards Paris: 'if Germany succeeded in over-running France she might establish naval bases on the northern Channel ports of that country, quite close to our shores, and so, with the possible aid of the submarines, long-range guns and air-machines of the future, interfere materially with our naval position in the Channel and our fleet defenses against invasion.'[84] We saw at the top of this chapter what Seely, Haldane's successor at the War Office, thought of Haldane's role in this: 'He saved the state.' Major General Stanley von Donop, director of artillery at the War Office from 1911 before becoming master general of the ordnance in 1913, wrote in a similar vein to Elizabeth Haldane upon her brother's death:

> The immense debt the country owes to him for having reorganised the expeditionary force into a real fighting army, we who worked with him know only too well and we recognise that a disaster would have occurred in 1914 if we had not had the experience of his wise counsels and great powers of organisation, for the army which took the field and saved the situation was absolutely Lord Haldane's own creation. It will ever be to my mind a standing disgrace that his great work was so inadequately recognised by the country.[85]

Maurice Hankey, secretary to the Committee of Imperial Defence from 1912, saw matters similarly, reassuring Haldane on his ousting from government in 1915 that he, Hankey, at least recognised Haldane's achievement: 'It is in my opinion no exaggeration to say that it is to your foresight and patient organic reconstruction of our whole defence system, that we owe it that the allied cause, and with it the British Empire, did not collapse last August.'[86]

* * *

Haldane's 'patient organic reconstruction' in the face of so many challenges and doubters spoke volumes for his courage. That he took on such an apparently thankless task (as CB unkindly mused upon Haldane's appointment to the War Office: 'We shall now see how Schopenhauer gets on in the Kailyard')[87] with relish is the first thing that strikes one on reading his and others' letters from this time. Beatrice Webb even reports him as saying: 'The King signified that he would like me to take the War Office; it is exactly what I myself longed for. I have never been so happy in my life.'[88] And this about an office that was a known graveyard for political careers! There is in Haldane a very rare mixture of confidence, that could sometimes be perceived as arrogance, and a powerful humility, a willingness to be shaped by others' thoughts. These two sides of his character come together when he goes on to tell Webb, 'I shall spend three years observing and thinking. I shall succeed: I have always succeeded in everything I have undertaken.'[89] His confidence is rooted, it seems, in the very fact that he was so willing to observe, which, as we see by his approach at the War Office, was a readiness to listen to, and learn from, others.[90]

But not everyone was willing to offer constructive advice; not even within his own Cabinet. After Lloyd George went to the Exchequer and Churchill to the Board of Trade upon Asquith's accession to the premiership in 1908, Haldane knew he would have his task cut out for him. Both men were fiercely in favour of a drastically retrenched army. It was difficult for Lloyd George to attack Haldane outright, having been warned by Asquith that no change to military policy was to be considered.[91] But Churchill, who was apparently 'dazzled'[92] by the Welshman, was willing to be his mouthpiece and distribute amongst his Cabinet colleagues alternative, money-saving plans. Churchill issued three memoranda across the summer of 1908, arguing that the current organisation of the army bore no relation to the needs it had to meet—needs which, in Churchill's eyes, didn't amount to very much. Whatever dangers there might be from Russia on the Indian frontier, whatever tensions existed with Germany, these could be dealt with 'by skilful diplomacy and wise administration'.[93] Why build up a strong army, when all we really needed was a strong navy, though even that had ballooned out of all proportion to the tasks it faced? Haldane's response cleverly undercut his opponents' arguments. A. J. Anthony Morris put it this way: 'His [Haldane's] task now was to win over the waverers [in the Cabinet] and he chose to do this by attacking the strongest part of his opponents' case.'[94] With the help of Sir Charles Harris, he was able to show that the numbers, both financially and in personnel, were an absolute necessity, and he did so without any reference to the heated topic of possible conflict on the Continent.[95] The reductionists brought in a Treasury official to find a loophole in the costings. Nothing could be found. Haldane's justification for his activities was watertight. Churchill was forced to concede that any further savings could now only be minor economies. The support offered to Haldane during Cabinet debates by Prime Minister Asquith, Foreign Secretary Grey, and Secretary of State for India John Morley also played a crucial role in forcing Churchill to back down. They even made it clear that the government could break up if the campaign for reductions was pushed any further.[96]

It is interesting to note that Churchill would go on to become First Lord of the Admiralty in 1911 and a central figure in the building up of naval armaments (and its corresponding budget increases) before the outbreak of war. Haldane recognised Churchill's achievements in this sphere, but sought a different type of naval development. What he hoped for was a Naval War Staff on the same lines as the General Staff, and that these two bodies would work closely with each other. The navy, traditionally rather disdainful of the army, had been closed off from other branches of military organisation, and the First Sea Lord dominated naval planning for war. The dangers of such an approach became very clear when, in the summer of 1911 (a few months before Churchill took over at the Admiralty), a meeting of the Imperial Defence Committee was held, at which the First Lord of the Admiralty, Reginald McKenna, and the First Sea Lord, Sir Arthur Wilson, were present, as were Haldane as Secretary of State for War, and the chief of the Imperial General Staff, Sir William Nicholson. The meeting was chaired by Asquith, the prime minister. In the course of discussions it was revealed that the General Staff's carefully worked-out plans for the embarkation and transport of the British Expeditionary Force to the Continent in the event of war with Germany—plans in which the navy would play a central role—were utterly disregarded by the leaders at the Admiralty. According to Haldane, the Admiralty—or, rather, Sir Arthur Wilson's famous predecessor, Sir John (Jacky) Fisher—had worked out their own plans based on a hopelessly outdated scheme, one that failed to take any consideration of what was required of Britain in assisting the French, while simultaneously being totally oblivious to the German strategic railway system. The General Staff, on the other hand, had paid meticulous attention to every detail of the situation. Asquith therefore stipulated 'that the arrangements made must be carried out in accordance with the plan of the General Staff'.[97] It was a vindication of Haldane's insistence on carefully thought through staff work in preparation for conflict, and it showed up the lack of such staff work at the Admiralty. Their neglect in this regard infuriated Haldane, and to Asquith he threatened the resignation of his post at the War Office unless 'sweeping reform at the Admiralty' was made.[98]

That same evening Asquith and Haldane travelled up to Scotland, the former to Archerfield in East Lothian, the latter to Cloan. Asquith invited Haldane to come over to visit him the following day, intimating that the position of First Lord of the Admiralty might be offered to him. Although Haldane was devoted to the War Office, he could see that he was 'almost the only person available who was equipped to cope with the problem of the Naval War Staff'.[99] Haldane continues his account with this ominous image: 'I drove over to Archerfield as soon as I had got to Cloan. As I entered the approach I saw Winston Churchill standing at the door. I divined that he had heard of possible changes and had come down at once to see the Prime Minister.'[100]

Churchill was Home Secretary at the time, but visions of glory at the Admiralty were evidently haunting him. 'He felt to the quick the traditional glamour' of the office, claimed Violet Bonham Carter, 'the romance of sea-power, the part that it had played in our island history, the conviction that it was today the keystone of our safety and survival.'[101] Churchill made a tactical advance towards his goal by suggesting to Asquith that whoever did take on the role must be in the Commons, where he could defend and explain the changes over which he was presiding. Haldane had been elevated to the Lords that March, but he still felt that the work required at the Admiralty needed someone of his experience; and his was a unique experience. He returned to Archerfield the next day:

> Churchill was still there, and the Prime Minister shut me up in a room with him. I took the initiative. I told him that his imaginative power and vitality were greater than mine, and that physically he was better suited to be a War Minister. But at this critical moment it was not merely a question of such qualities. ... I said that, to be frank, I did not think Churchill's own type of mind was best for planning out the solution that was necessary for the problem which at the moment was confronting us.[102]

It was no good. Churchill was adamant, and Asquith yielded. 'This is a big thing,' said Churchill afterwards, 'the biggest thing that has ever come my way—the chance I should have chosen before all others. I shall pour into it everything I've got.'[103]

For Haldane it was a distressing blow. This is not to say that a new Naval War Staff totally failed to materialise. Haldane made a point of insisting that he and Churchill should work closely together to make Haldane's dream a reality. But the Staff that was created fell far below the standards of its counterpart at the War Office.[104] As R. C. K. Ensor has written: 'Its functions were purely advisory and its role subordinate. It did not develop into a General Staff. Nor had the Navy one when the European War broke out; and to this some of its serious shortcomings may be attributed.'[105] One can only wonder how history would have unfolded had Haldane been at the helm.

The debate about who ought to go to the Admiralty at least showed Churchill to be in accord with Haldane about certain fundamentals, principally the need for a Naval War Staff. Bearing in mind the ill-feeling that Churchill and Lloyd George were brewing up against Haldane in the economic debates of 1908, it is rather refreshing to find Haldane writing to his mother shortly after Churchill's appointment to the Admiralty:

> Winston and L.[loyd] G.[eorge] dined with me last night and we had a very useful talk. This is now a very harmonious Cabinet. It is odd to think that three years ago I had to fight those two for every penny for my army reforms. Winston is full of enthusiasm about the Admiralty and just as keen as I am on the War Staff. It is delightful to work with him. L.G. too has quite changed his attitude and is now very friendly to your 'bear', whom he used to call 'the Minister for Slaughter'.[106]

* * *

Part of the reason Haldane eventually won his Cabinet colleagues round was his clear ability to juggle the competing demands of a peacetime climate with possibilities of war. Shortly before Balfour left office he recognised his own failure to negotiate these demands: 'One of the greatest disappointments I have had to submit to in the last two or three years [has been] the failure to find, or to get adopted, some new organisation which would give greater power of military expansion in time of war, and, if possible, bring with it greater economies in time of peace.'[107] Haldane was able to walk the tightrope between these desired features by combining an ambitious 'nation at arms' concept with a financial cap. As Spiers has explained: 'The army, whose *raison d'être* was effective operation in war, had to remain for an indefinite period of peace as a burden on the Exchequer: only if this burden was tolerable could reform be accepted on a lasting basis.'[108]

Though financial restriction looked like a good thing from one angle, for many it remained a straitjacket that jeopardised the chances of the army properly discharging its duties. Public attacks upon Haldane, particularly in his early days at the War Office (before he confounded his critics by demonstrating the increased strength of the army on a reduced budget), were rife. His ability to take each attack with a quiet smile, and indeed humour, singles him out from most political personalities: He wrote to his mother:

> Your Bear is advancing on his way here—regardless of sticks & stones hurled at him. He does not mind the stings of bees if he can get his paw on the honey.
>
> Seriously I think I mind abuse less than most people. Here is Scotland [including his great friend Lord Rosebery] clamouring for the retention in Edin.[burgh] of the Scots Greys. But I cannot leave no officers & men at Piershill, & I have not £200,000 to build new barracks. If the public want economy they must put up with things.[109]

Haldane's capacity to shrug off abuse is anchored in the fact that he was acting upon solid principles. But he was also willing, where necessary, to make concessions, so long as those principles weren't fundamentally compromised. His steering of the Territorial and Reserve Forces Bill through Parliament in 1907 is a case in point. To the Yeomanry and Volunteer colonels he conceded more restrictions on the County Associations, granting far greater power to the Army Council over them. He postponed the new conditions of service for the Yeomanry in recognition that they would be affected by lower rates of pay. He even conceded, despite his views on the Blue Water Principle, to allow the Territorial Force to become solely for home defence, and not the overseas service for which it had originally been designed. But it was this that pacified many of his radical and Labour critics, who were uncomfortable with the 'expeditionary' side of Haldane's reforms.[110] Perhaps even more damaging to the original vision, Haldane also succumbed to the demand of the Conservatives that the Militia remain external to the Territorial Force. Instead, they were left to form a Special

Reserve to support the BEF. Although this would (and did) greatly hinder him in reaching the target of 300,000 Territorials, if he hadn't conceded on this point the Bill would have been wrecked, for it needed Conservative backing to pass through the Lords. Moreover, Haldane didn't make the decision single-handedly; he conferred with Esher, Repington, Ellison and Haig before capitulating. For Haldane, however, this significant and emasculating adjustment still did not change the principle of the scheme: that was the essential thing.

Even with these concessions, the fact that the Conservatives hadn't blocked a major Liberal Bill (it was in fact their first major Bill to pass through both Houses) was itself momentous.[111] This was thanks, in large part, to Haldane's good professional and personal relationship with the Conservative leader, A. J. Balfour—himself a philosopher-statesman, whom Haldane, alone of all his Liberal colleagues, had supported in seeing through the Education Act of 1902.[112] As Haldane explained in his *Autobiography*:

> The [Territorial and Reserve Forces] Bill was a large and formidable one, and I knew that difficulties would be made about finding time for it in the House of Commons. I met Balfour during a week-end at Windsor Castle and asked him whether he would help me. If he would assent to what in these days was wholly new, a time-table which would ensure full opportunity for disposal of the measure within a reasonable number of days, I would consult his convenience. He said that as the Unionist Government had not succeeded in disposing of the Army it was only right that we should have our chance. He knew our difficulties and he got Lord Lansdowne to agree to give us the like chance in the Lords. He added naturally that the Opposition could take no responsibility for our plan, on which Parliament itself must pronounce.[113]

Such magnanimous cross-party co-operation was critical to Haldane's successes, and not simply at the War Office. It shows that for Haldane—and indeed for Balfour—principle was above party and pride.[114]

In this sense, Haldane was also a pragmatist. He knew that without Conservative support his Bill had no chance of passing. It has been said that the Scottish political approach is marked by an attempt to formulate principles and then act upon them (what we today would be inclined to call a 'rationalist' approach, though Haldane would have described it as 'idealist'), while the Westminster approach is fundamentally one of pragmatism and, indeed, empiricism (asking, in other words: 'How much will this cost? Do we have evidence this will work?').[115] The Scot, to put it crudely, builds on reason, the Englishman on practical experience. With the blood of both nations coursing through his veins, it is perhaps no surprise that Haldane embodied both approaches. His reforms were based on a rational outworking of what the British army ought to be. Reason, in the Hegelian system, is the force that develops itself through all things and, for Haldane, the army was no exception. As he told his generals, he sought 'A Hegelian Army'.[116] Every aspect was to be an expression of its own inner reason: war overseas.[117] And yet Haldane knew that if such a scheme was ever to get off the ground, he needed to cater to those who had power to crush it, even if that meant adjusting its 'inner reason'; this is precisely what we see happening in 1907 as he guided the Bill through Parliament. So the Haldane Reforms are also deeply pragmatic in the sense that they were born out of a rejection of the impractical. No Bill could ever have got through such a Conservative-dominated House as the House of Lords was then if it had been unwilling to make concessions in an attempt to maintain the purity of its ideal. Haldane was willing to sacrifice the Bill's purity, on practical grounds, but not the ideal itself. His genius was in knowing when concessions make the achievement of one's goals impossible and when they do not. As Haldane's entry in the *Oxford Dictionary of National Biography* says:

> Haldane had a grasp of structures and relationships in politics which was very unusual in the English context. He declined to be bound by the usual empirical precedents of history and practice, and tried to see the essential purpose of institutions as they were and as they might be, and in this sense he brought his philosophical precepts directly to bear. He was then able to link this analysis with the practical skills of the political reformer. In that lay his distinctive contribution, one rarely matched in twentieth-century British public life.[118]

These 'practical skills' were tied to Haldane's ability to keep in mind other people's sensibilities. It was this quality, perhaps more than any other, that lay behind Haldane's military successes on an imperial level. At the Colonial Conference of 1907, where Haldane sought to, and did, achieve consent for 'a General Staff system for the Empire as a whole', he demonstrated his admirable qualities in this area. Though his plan aimed to make the War Office in London the nerve centre for the rest of the empire's military bodies, his speech made it clear to the delegates that London would refrain from any role in actually commanding the colonies. He had no intention, so he stated, to see their defence forces imposed upon by a centralised body with a 'rigid model'. By remaining purely advisory, the Imperial General Staff would avoid the label of a dictatorship and could therefore be seen as a helping hand in working out the intricacies of international defence. Haldane's long practice at the Bar representing the colonies in numerous cases, and his friendship with the Canadian prime minster, Sir Wilfrid Laurier, stood him in good stead for knowing precisely what their sensitivities concerning the role of 'the Motherland' were.[119] He would not allow his enthusiasm for a unified military system across the empire to overtake his caution around such a delicate topic. As Spiers remarks: 'Ever aware of Colonial sensitivities, he never deviated from his preference for a cautious, evolutionary approach towards limited objectives.'[120]

This speech reflected Haldane's wider imperial outlook. To speak about empire in positive terms today is almost to be automatically condemned, but Haldane's imperialism was actually far closer to the kind of thing that modern international unions strive towards. We have examined this in Chapter 6, but it is important to remember that what Haldane was seeking was what he called 'the development of intercommunication and mutual understanding'.[121] Centralised authority was not at all what Haldane longed for. He praised and advocated autonomy, but desired harmony between each expression of such freedom. Healthy co-operation between countries was his ambition, both in military matters and in wider political relationships.

* * *

So far we have looked at achievements brought about by force of mind and character; but we ought not to forget the important role that Haldane's physicality played in his successes. As Beatrice Webb wryly remarked: 'Plenitude, mental and physical, seemed to be his dominant feature.'[122] We know that, on entering office, Haldane would sit up until 2 a.m. reading works by notable military writers, predominantly German and French, such as Carl von Clausewitz, Paul Bronsart von Schellendorf and Ardant du Picq.[123] He is said to have survived on four hours' sleep (blessed with the handy knack of catching forty winks in the gaps between meetings and engagements), often in Edwardian rail carriages. In fact, rail travel was critical to national ventures, and few politicians could boast of putting it to better use. In an attempt to stir volunteer recruits to his new Territorials scheme, in January 1907 alone he spoke at gatherings in Glasgow, Liverpool, Manchester, Sheffield and London. (It should be remembered, too, that his political travels were interspersed with regular ten-hour overnight train rides from London to Auchterarder to see his ageing mother.) Every single week from August 1906 until March 1907, Haldane attended dinners and speaking engagements for the purpose of rousing support before the Bill was introduced to the House—'a punishing round of public appearances, encouraging, persuading, and berating the country as if his single-handed efforts would decide the fate of his scheme'.[124] He spoke to everyone he could find who could make an impression upon the project—from the lowliest country youth to the most powerful of county colonels.[125]

The fact that he spoke with as many people concerned in the reforms as possible represents another crucial technique behind his remarkable achievements. For Haldane, this didn't just mean gathering support before the Bill went to the House; it also meant making sure that, once the Bill was passed, support was maintained and put to good effect. Seeing Territorial numbers beginning to fall after an initial surge, Haldane in 1911 would travel as far and wide as Aberdeen and Barnstaple, Chelmsford and Ayr, to rally young men to the cause. In January the following year, within a space of fifteen days, he spoke in nine different towns, covering the Lowlands of Scotland, the Midlands, the north-east of England and London. He was at pains (sometimes literally) to show that his scheme was not the cold imposition of a system thought up in Whitehall, disconnected from the local communities upon whom the scheme depended. No, Haldane, at significant physical and temporal expense, brought the thinking of Whitehall into the local communities and made it personal to them, their lives and their hopes for their country. And when he could not be with them, he made a studied attempt to ensure that the correct information about his reforms was feeding back to the population. He did this primarily through interacting with influential voices in the newspapers 'patiently and dextrously, a courteous deftness he deployed in his treatment of all journalists'.[126] Haldane even created a department within the War Office specially designed to supply information, and encouraged propaganda. What he longed for was 'Good writing carefully read'.[127] This, he believed, along with his own personal encounters with critics and waverers, would be the key to his success.

Haldane had a wonderful capacity to bring people, and their differing perspectives, together. Again, Beatrice Webb remarked in her diary in July 1897, long before Haldane entered the War Office: 'This was a typical Haldane dinner on the night of the South African debate, typical of Haldane's weakness—his dilettante desire to be in every set; and of his strength—his diffusive friendship which enables him to bring about non-party measures.'[128] If this is a weakness, it is a very common and human one, and the positive effects in Haldane's case more than make up for it; it is not an exaggeration, as we discovered in our previous chapter, to say that the UK's extensive provisions for tertiary education are rooted in it. So too, in some respects, is the modern British army. Take, for example, the dinner held at Knowsley, the home of Lord Derby, on 15 February 1907, where Haldane brought Ellison, Haig and Lord Lucas (one of Haldane's private secretaries between 1907 and 1908) into dialogue with Derby and twelve Militia colonels—not a group inclined to accept reforms lightly. The evening lasted until 2 a.m. in discussion of the proposed Territorials scheme, ending in a unanimous promise of support from Derby and the colonels. This was typical of Haldane: widely divergent voices, with differing agendas, gathering in a comfortable setting over good food, good wine and, undoubtedly, good cigars—a setting where tensions could be mellowed and differences spoken about openly. We should not forget to add that such evenings tended to end with Haldane's plans in the ascendancy.

Haldane was also able to bring more wide-ranging perspectives together, through his open-mindedness concerning the practices of other nations. That openness was to be his undoing, too, of course, but in his early years at the War Office it allowed him to appropriate the best in Continental military organisation for the benefit of British forces. His interest was not simply confined to late-night reading of foreign military experts. Having accepted an invitation to attend the

Kaiser's autumn parade of his Guards in Berlin in 1906, he even organised a trip into the heart of the German General Staff's offices. Alongside significant discussions with Kaiser Wilhelm II, he was given free rein to examine their military arrangements (excepting 'confidential matters'). And Haldane certainly made an impression upon the Kaiser and German officials. His remarkable knowledge of their country, so unusual in a British minister, and his knowledge of their ways and customs created (alas only for a time) an unusual bond of sympathy between the two nations. On returning, he received this message from King Edward VII's secretary, Arthur Davidson:

> The King is exceedingly pleased at the success of your visit which he attributes entirely to you personally, & H.[is] M.[ajesty] says it is especially pleasing & gratifying to him to think that the knowledge you displayed of Germany & German military history, as well as of technical military works, was so accurate & extensive as to impress those you met, in the way it evidently did.[129]

But Haldane wasn't there to show off. He wanted to learn. What was discovered in Berlin appealed immensely to the efficiency-minded minister, for whom the 'thinking department' of an organisation ought to be as free as possible to think. As Haldane reflected in his *Autobiography*:

> In the course of the journey home Ellison and I talked much of what we had observed. We agreed that the great lesson lay in the way in which under the German system the Army in the field was free from the embarrassment of having to look after its transport and supplies. This last duty was a separately organised one, attended to by the administrative side to the exclusion of the General Staff. The latter dealt with command and with strategy and tactics, while all administrative work was handled only by the 'Intendantur,' which was the province of the War Office.[130]

Although Haldane was so open about his desire to learn from other nations, particularly Germany, he had, in essence, already recognised the importance of the need to distinguish between command and administration prior to his Berlin visit. Having read Spenser Wilkinson's *The Brain of an Army* in his first month in office, and digesting the Esher Report's recommendations of a General Staff system, he wrote to Wilkinson on 2 January 1906: 'I watch daily the people who ought to be thinking & teaching in the Army being loaded with Administrative details.'[131]

But we should not think that Haldane's fostering of the General Staff for thinking purposes meant that he neglected the effective development of the administrative side. Already in 1906, Haldane, the great apostle of education, made arrangements with the LSE for six-month courses to be available to officers, where subjects such as Business Administration, Economic and Commercial Theory, Accountancy, Statistics and Geography were on offer. He desired 'an administrative staff as real and as far reaching in the sphere of its operations' as the General Staff.[132] Between the first class starting in January 1907 and the outbreak of war in 1914, approximately thirty-one officers a year attended, mainly though not exclusively from the Army Service Corps.[133] Just because the administrative side of the army was principally orientated towards more mundane practical matters, that was no reason to fail to bring to bear the best thinking upon its execution. So long as Haldane had anything to do with them, all military activities were to be grounded in sound, educated thinking.

* * *

We know the positive effects upon the structure and achievements of the British army as a result of Haldane's passion for putting thinking first. But there is one area in which there has been a continued questioning of the consequences of his desire to set thought upon a pedestal: the (not so speedy) rise of British air power.[134] During the years of Haldane's incumbency of the War Office, the Wright brothers—famous for their pioneering developments in aviation—were on the lookout for commercial success, hoping to exploit the rising fears concerning national security that had opened up as a result of the rapid advancements in flight technology. They were looking, in other words, to secure a lucrative deal with a quivering government anxious to purchase a large supply of their aeroplanes. Haldane was an obvious target for negotiations. Working through an intermediary, Charles Flint, they arranged in 1907, for a negotiator, Lady Taylor (a Scottish aristocrat, and the widowed wife of a British general), to make contact with Haldane in the hope of securing a deal. After this led to a dead end in 1907, the brothers themselves travelled to England to meet the War Secretary in 1909. This, too, led nowhere. There is a fair amount of controversy over the discussions that took place, and a sense of disbelief, both by interested parties at the time and a number of subsequent commentators, that Haldane wrote off the Wright brothers as 'only clever empiricists'.[135]

With Germany, France, and the United States making immense strides each year in the race for mastery of the air, Britain at this time seemed to be stuck with its head in the sand. Indeed, General Sir William Nicholson, chief of the General Staff, was convinced that such developments would never have any bearing upon modern warfare. Haldane was not so closed-minded. He saw something of air travel's potential, certainly (he could not, of course, predict what we now know), but he wished to approach the whole issue with his characteristic thoroughness. Scientific study of the fundamentals of flight was the only way, so Haldane believed, of giving 'the most stable and rapid results'.[136] But when foreign nations are amassing aircraft that will very soon have the capacity to drop explosive chemicals on ports, factories and cities, the study of fundamentals might understandably be set aside for speedy acquisition of similar aircraft. Such was the repeated request of a number of influential personalities at the time, including press baron Lord Northcliffe, who would go on to punish Haldane with extraordinary severity for refusing to heed his pleas (see Chapter 7).

Haldane was unperturbed. All the information he had received suggested that the aircraft already developed needed considerable honing before they posed a major threat. At the time of Lady Taylor's interventions, Haldane was in close, but (to the wider public and to Lady Taylor) secret, consultation with Lieutenant John Dunne, who promised a home-grown, and greatly improved, alternative to the Wright brothers' designs (although the specifics of those designs remained unknown), and had begun work for the War Office at the Balloon Factory at Farnborough as early as June 1906. Contrary to the view that is sometimes expressed—that Haldane had no interest in the development of the aeroplane, favouring the airships that Count Ferdinand von Zeppelin had developed in Germany, the potential of which Haldane had learnt about during his trip to Berlin in the summer of 1906—it is clear that, behind the scenes, he was seeking to support the development of aeroplane technology. At first, this was by means of backing Dunne's work, having been assured that it would outstrip that of the Wrights. But when, in the summer of 1907, at a top-secret airfield at Blair Atholl in the Scottish Highlands, Haldane witnessed Dunne's efforts fail to get airborne, and when this was compounded the following year by another failure to get off the ground, Haldane changed tack. It had become clear to him that Dunne was just another 'clever empiricist'; his meagre progress was due to a lack of clear scientific grounding. This conviction led Haldane to establish, after taking advice from the Nobel Prize winner Lord Rayleigh and the director of the National Physical Laboratory, R. T. Glazebrook, the Advisory Committee for Aeronautics in 1909.

Representatives of the army and navy would sit upon the Advisory Committee, alongside a select group of scientists. Lord Rayleigh would chair the committee, and it would be based at the National Physical Laboratory at Teddington. Its purpose was to investigate the fundamentals of flight and build up 'the structure of the Air Service on a foundation of science',[137] as the Germans were doing, having set up their first ever lectureship in Aeronautics at Göttingen University that same year[138]—a move that was sure to arouse Haldane's envy and admiration. The committee would not only co-operate with the Aeronautical Society, the Aero Club and the Aerial League, it would critically work in collaboration with the Balloon Factory at Farnborough, which, after Dunne's abortive efforts, was reconstructed with the purpose of producing new types of dirigible, both heavier and lighter than air. The factory could put special questions to the committee for consideration, in a manner reminiscent of the way German industries related to the so-called Central-Stelle, as we saw in Chapter 8. Experiments with aeroplanes were not at an end, however. The government had an unusual arrangement with the Hon. C. S. Rolls, of car manufacturing fame, who had purchased a Wright aeroplane and would carry out experiments with it with the financial and logistical support of the War Office. Otherwise, the government would allow private enterprise to steer the development of aeroplane technology.

The two principal criticisms that Haldane faced, both at the time and posthumously, were as follows: firstly, that he had failed to heed the importance of developing aeroplane provision, culminating in his rejection of the offers emanating from the Wright brothers and their representative;[139] secondly, that he prioritised a slow scientific understanding of flight at the expense of practical advancements.[140] The brief outline of Haldane's actions sketched above, which reflects the best judgments of flight historian Alfred Gollin, suggests that he is guilty of neither of these charges. It could indeed be argued that he 'backed the wrong horse', as Gollin puts it,[141] by believing in Dunne's claim to be able to develop a superior aircraft to that of the Wrights. But his refusal to buy the Wright aeroplane must be seen in the context of having such assurances from Dunne and, after 1908, Rolls's own experiments with a Wright aeroplane on behalf of the War Office. Indeed, it should be noted that Haldane did not, in fact, categorically refuse Lady Taylor's overtures, but he did make demonstration of the Wright brothers' aeroplane a condition of any pur-chase that the War Office might make—a condition that was unacceptable to the Wrights, who were fearful of relinquishing secrets without a con-tract in place. It is simply not the case, then, that Haldane failed to heed the importance of developments in aeroplane technology. Having wit-nessed Dunne's failed attempts to get airborne and having received reports on attempts being made elsewhere, his 'empiricists' comment reflects his belief that experiments in flight were dominated by men lack-ing adequate scientific understanding, hence the establishment of the Advisory Committee for Aeronautics. And yet this did not put practical advancements on hold; these continued concomitantly with the scientific research carried out by the committee.

The work of the Advisory Committee proved to be of huge and lasting significance. It was, according to Gollin, 'a national institution. It was not controlled by either of the two services. It assisted the army and the navy. Eventually, British industry benefited from its endeavour. It later became concerned with aeronautical science in the universities.'[142] Indeed, the Committee was emulated in the United States in 1915 with the founding of the National Advisory Committee for Aeronautics (NACA), whose work was absorbed in 1958 into the newly founded National Aeronautics and Space Administration (NASA). Britain's 1909 Committee was undeni-ably Haldane's creation and, alongside his other efforts in the early days of developing Britain's Air Force ('many of which may never be known with certainty'),[143] it has led the aviation historian Percy Walker to acclaim Haldane as 'the ... saviour of British aviation'.[144] Indeed, in 1911 Haldane chaired a standing subcommittee of the CID which worked out the 'broad principles' of a national air service. The committee's strong membership included Churchill, Prince Louis of Battenberg (the Second Sea Lord),

Lord Esher, and Sir R. Chambers (permanent secretary to the Treasury). The resulting White Paper published on 11 April 1912 recommended a British aeronautical service to be called, with the king's approval, the Royal Flying Corps. It would consist of naval and military wings, and would boast of a central flying school. It would absorb the existing Air Battalion and work closely with the Advisory Committee for Aeronautics, while the Army Aircraft Factory at Farnborough would be renamed the Royal Aircraft Factory—where, according to Sir Henry Tizard, speaking in 1955, there ought to be 'a statue of Haldane, in his top hat, at the entrance gates'.[145] The Flying Corps received its royal warrant on 13 April, and the foundations of what would, on 1 April 1918, become the unified and independent Royal Air Force were essentially put in place.

Gollin sums up Haldane's legacy in light of these various controversies and achievements:

> In the same way that his contemporaries falsely condemned him as a pro-German, some of those he worked with and several aeronautical historians have denigrated his activities and achievements in the earliest days of British military aeronautics. However, these adverse opinions were largely incorrect. Haldane entirely deserved the title of 'saviour of British aviation'.[146]

* * *

An equally important founding role was the one that Haldane played in the creation of the Secret Service Bureau (SSB), which soon split into the Security Service and the Secret Intelligence Service—commonly known today as MI5 and MI6 respectively. The SSB was founded as a result of recommendations made by a 1909 sub-committee of the Committee of Imperial Defence, chaired by Haldane. The Liberal government tasked the subcommittee to consider 'the nature and extent of foreign espionage that is at present taking place within this country and the danger [to] which it may expose us'.[147] Two years previously, another subcommittee—this time chaired by Asquith, though Haldane served on it—had considered the potential threat of invasion from Germany at a time when the country was gripped by sensational talk about the menace of German spies in England. Initially sceptical, Haldane was eventually persuaded by Major James Edmonds, head of the counterespionage unit within the War Office

(MO3), that the threat was real. By the time of the opening meeting of the 1909 subcommittee, Haldane claimed that it 'was quite clear that a great deal of reconnaissance work is being conducted by Germans in this country', partly 'to enable important demolitions and destruction to be carried out in this country on or before the outbreak of war'.[148] By the second meeting Haldane viewed the gathering of intelligence as systematic, and believed that it was necessary for Britain to act in order 'to prevent them [Germany] in time of war or strained relations from availing themselves of the information they had collected, by injuring our defences, stores, or internal communications'. He went on to propose that five picked members of the subcommittee should meet to consider exactly 'how the secret service bureau could be established'.[149]

In July 1909, at the subcommittee's third meeting, the arrangements for the establishment and funding of the SSB were approved. In its declared objectives, the origins of what we now know of as MI5 and MI6 are clear. The bureau sought:

> to deal both with espionage in this country and with our own foreign agents abroad, and to serve as a screen between the Admiralty and the War Office on the one hand and those employed on secret service, or who have information they wish to sell to the British government, on the other.[150]

Such activities became crucial on the outbreak of war. According to MI5's official website, the organisation 'played a central role in the capture of most of Imperial Germany's intelligence agents in the UK at the start of World War I'.[151] But the SSB and its successors were kept top secret for many years, so much so that the biographies of Asquith and his Cabinet ministers (including Haldane) over half a century later contained no mention of them. It was not until the Security Service Act 1989 and the Intelligence Services Act 1994, which established MI5 and MI6 respectively as entities existing in law in their own right (rather than hidden under the cover of other parts of the defence department and budget), that these two organisations became 'official' in the eyes of the public. In 1992 the existing incumbents as heads of the two services—Sir Colin McColl of MI6 and Dame Stella Rimington of MI5—were for the first time identified whilst still in post.[152]

* * *

If Haldane's role in the establishment of these services is little known today, so too is the catalytic role he played, as War Secretary, in the creation of the Boy Scouts. This may sound like child's play after a discussion of MI5 and MI6, but, since its inception, the 'Scout and Guide Movements have attracted approximately 550,000,000 members worldwide'.[153] Tim Jeal—the biographer of the movement's founder, Robert Baden-Powell—has consequently argued that, 'With the exception of great religions and political ideologies, no international organisation can claim, more convincingly, to have had so major an impact on the social history of the developed world.'[154]

Baden-Powell was considered a national hero at the opening of the twentieth century for his leadership in the defence of Mafeking during the Second Boer War. As he withstood the Boer siege, which lasted from October 1899 to May 1900, he gave consent to the formation of the Mafeking Cadet Corps, which organised the boys of the town into a group capable of 'carrying messages from one part of the town to another, delivering mail, acting as orderlies, and sharing look-out duties.'[155] Baden-Powell had, as early as 1885, begun to collect material for a book on scouting within the army, and when it was published in November 1899—in the midst of the siege—his fame in South Africa 'turned a specialist military textbook into an instant best-seller'.[156] Baden-Powell believed the power of scouting to lie in its ability to develop self-reliance and initiative. Having seen the power of organising boys into quasi-military groups during his time in South Africa and then experiencing, upon his return to England, the effective contribution to society that clubs such as the Boys' Brigade could make, Baden-Powell started to develop the idea that training in scouting could be offered to boys as a way of developing their 'powers of observation' and ability to 'notice details'[157]—traits that would contribute, he believed, to effective citizenship and good character. In 1904 William Smith, the founder of the Boys' Brigade, encouraged Baden-Powell to rewrite his army scouting book in such a way that it would suit boys, but the latter was reluctant to devote his powers to such an endeavour until he was absolutely convinced it would actually be taken up by the nation's youth. It was Haldane's arrival at the War Office that convinced him.

Before his encounter with Haldane, Baden-Powell was toying with the difficult question of whether he ought to be devoting himself to developing

military or peacetime skills in those who would make up the future genera-
tions of the country. For Haldane, this was not an either/or. Tim Jeal writes:

> But as it happened, his [Baden-Powell's] single most important acquain-
> tanceship with a Liberal public figure was not destined to make him aban-
> don his efforts to persuade boys to learn to shoot in favour of promoting
> an exclusively pacific character-building programme. Instead it encouraged
> him to try to combine the two objectives within a single coherent frame-
> work. The Liberal in question was the new Secretary of State for War,
> Mr R. B. Haldane, a brilliant philosopher and lawyer with an awe-inspir-
> ingly innovative mind. It might seem strange that Baden-Powell should have
> got on so well with a man who was determined to reduce expenditure on
> the army, but from their first meeting on 1st May 1906 he was captivated
> by Haldane.[158]

The two met twice that month, and entered into correspondence. Haldane
'believed that the future of his Territorials would depend upon the quantity
and the patriotism of the boys now joining cadet corps and religious brigades'.[159] Baden-Powell's ideas around scouting's potential benefits to
society, and its military implications, must have been music to the War
Secretary's ears—though Haldane, in later years, was careful to state that
the Boy Scouts were 'an attempt to lay in the boy a foundation of character
upon which he may build a career in any direction'.[160]

May 1906 was a 'key month' in Baden-Powell's life. Five days after his
first encounter with Haldane, he finally shared a paper on the subject of
'Scouting for Boys' with the recently knighted Sir William Smith and a
further six notable public figures, including the great champion of conscription Lord Roberts. The timing of the dissemination, along with a
note in Baden-Powell's diary, four days before his second meeting with
Haldane, which simply reads 'Report for Army. Boy Scouts', leads Jeal
to believe 'that Haldane had given him the vital nudge which made him
complete his paper "Scouting for Boys" and send it to William Smith'.
Jeal continues: 'Stephe's [as Baden-Powell was known to intimates] split
nature as innovator and conformist had always required that he entertain
reasonable hopes of official blessing upon his proceedings before being
prepared to commit himself to them wholeheartedly. This was exactly
what Haldane provided at the perfect psychological moment.'[161] By July
1907 Baden-Powell seems to have envisioned a distinct Boy Scouts

movement.[162] But he evidently did not quite foresee the success that *Scouting for Boys* would achieve upon its publication the following year. Having ended his term as inspector general of cavalry in May 1907, Baden-Powell was concerned to ensure continuing financial security. While he was staying with Haldane at Cloan between 30 August and 1 September Haldane offered him a Territorial division, knowing that the power of his name would help draw recruits. Haldane was content to let Baden-Powell delay taking up the post until the following April so that he might complete a lecture tour on 'Scouting for Boys'. Baden-Powell, who was by now a lieutenant general, was initially reluctant—indeed, it was a 'relatively junior job' for one of his standing—but Haldane eventually 'flattered' him into accepting.[163]

Baden-Powell took command of the Northumbrian division of the Territorials in late March 1908, just over a month before *Scouting for Boys* appeared in book form. Part 1 had appeared as a periodical on British bookstalls that January, and by February independent Scout groups were popping up all over the country, alongside groups connected to the Boys' Brigade and the junior YMCA. The movement was enormously successful, so much so that Baden-Powell was knighted by Edward VII in October 1909 'for all his past services and especially the present one of raising Boy Scouts for the country'.[164]

In the spring of 1910 Baden-Powell decided that he had done all that he could in establishing the Northumbrian division on a firm footing. The Boy Scouts, however, 'were moving ahead with such vigour that far more of his time was required to keep the movement on the right track'.[165] Baden-Powell discussed his plan to bring his military career to an end with Haldane and Lord Roberts, and he was of course met with understanding. As Haldane wrote to him: 'I feel that this organization of yours has so important a bearing upon the future that probably the greatest service you can render to the country is to devote yourself to it.'[166] Given what we know of the reach that the Scouts and their related Guide movement were to have—their impact upon the lives of 550,000,000 young people worldwide—the wisdom of Baden-Powell's decision and Haldane's reflections upon it are incontrovertible.

* * *

WAR AND PEACE

Napoleon B. Haldane (and Citizen Buchanan) among the ruins of Bhrodrikh.

Original Drawing for Punch by E. T. Reed/

134. The weak leadership of previous War Ministers, notably William St John Brodrick, meant that when Haldane reached the War Office in 1905, it remained in a post-Boer War mess. This 1906 cartoon shows him as 'Napoleon B. Haldane among the ruins of Brodrikh'.

A Mounting Threat

135. The opening decade of the 20th century saw a mounting militaristic spirit within Germany. Kaiser Wilhelm II (pictured above reviewing his troops) considered the German army as a symbol of Germany's power and prestige.

136. The Entente Cordiale between France and Britain in 1904 laid the foundations for the highly controversial secret military discussions between the French and British General Staffs which Haldane developed, but without full Cabinet knowledge.

137. The 'Old War Office' in Pall Mall where Haldane, on a very foggy day in December 1905, first took office as Secretary of State for War. Later that year the War Office moved to new headquarters in Whitehall.

138. Despatch box used by Haldane as Secretary of State for War from 1905 to 1911 before being elevated in that role to the House of Lords.

139. Haldane, Lord Esher and Sir John French at Cloan 1906. Esher was deeply involved with Haldane in his War Office reforms. French became commander-in-chief of the British Expeditionary Force during the first year and a half of the war.

140. Douglas Haig returned in 1906 from India to serve in the War Office under Haldane, the start of a profound long-lasting relationship. Here, in 1912, Haig reviews, with Prince Alexander of Teck, the Royal Flying Corps, another Haldane inspired organization.

141. Colonel Ellison, walking with Haldane in Downing Street in 1906, whilst Haldane's Principal Private Secretary at the War Office. Their relationship was enormously productive, determining how Haldane structured the first and second lines of the Army.

Embedding Scientific Principles

142. The Wright Brothers' first successful flight on 17 December 1903. Haldane, who met the brothers in 1909, described them as 'only clever empiricists'. Haldane knew he had to develop Britain's capacities for air warfare, but – like every Haldane reform – wanted it to rest on sound scientific thinking.

143. To enhance scientific thinking, Haldane insisted on appointing the Nobel Laureate Lord Rayleigh (1842–1919) as the chairman of the Advisory Committee for Aeronautics in 1909. This was eventually to lead to the creation of the Royal Flying Corps in 1912. His critics felt this was all too slow.

144. Haldane talking to the Kaiser in Berlin in 1906, at the Kaiser's annual Guards' parade.

145. One of a set of four lithographs by R. Knötel (1904) of the Imperial Prussian Guard presented to Haldane by the Kaiser in Berlin 1906.

146. Statue of Achilles, by Johannes Gottfried Götz, also given to Haldane in Berlin by the Kaiser.

Haldane's First Major Government Success

147. The cartoon depicts Haldane reading the German philosopher Schopenhauer (whose work he'd previously translated) while awaiting news of the successful enactment of the Territorial and Reserve Forces Bill 1907. In order to achieve this Haldane had to overcome the supporters of the formidable Field Marshal Lord Roberts' campaign for national conscription. Despite their disagreements, Haldane and Lord Roberts remained on friendly terms.

148. Lord Roberts (1842–1914) on a visit to Cloan in 1906. Haldane and his mother can be seen in the background.

149. King Edward VII, at Haldane's request, presented colours at Windsor to the newly formed battalions of what would become the Territorial Army in 1909.

150. Haldane inspecting the Officers' Training Corps at his old school, the Edinburgh Academy in 1909.

151. 'A Late Beginner'. Cartoon of Haldane in 1912, a month before the creation of an Air Service, the Royal Flying Corps.

Imperial Cohesion

152. The 1907 Colonial Conference in London, which gathered together the prime ministers of the British Empire, gave Haldane the opportunity to promote the creation of an Imperial General Staff, which came into being in 1908.

153. The first Chief of the Imperial General Staff was Sir William Nicholson (1860–1933), whom Haldane had brought into the War Office in 1905 for his 'acute big brain', c. 1914.

154. Haldane reviewing the colonial troops before the coronation of George V in June 1911.

155. Haldane's most vital creation was the British Expeditionary Force, the 'Old Contemptibles'. Though small numerically, their skills were a crucial element in saving Paris from the German onslaught in the months after the onset of the war.

Army and Navy Co-operation

156. Churchill had originally resisted Haldane's plans for military expenditure, but ended up as one of the most vocal advocates for increased naval armaments as First Lord of the Admiralty. In 1911, Haldane had hoped the position would be offered to him, so that he might achieve his dream of a Naval War Staff to complement the Army's General Staff. Nevertheless, Churchill welcomed his support and, on the formation of the coalition goverment in May 1915, was distressed at Haldane's removal from the Cabinet (but perhaps not as distressed as his own demotion to Chancellor of the Duchy of Lancaster). Churchill and Haldane are photographed together on the doorstep of Haldane's London home, 28 Queen Anne's Gate, c. 1912.

Haldane's encouragement of Baden-Powell's scheme was inspired, in part, by the desire to lay a bedrock upon which his 'nation at arms' vision could become a reality. He was thinking for the long term. It was yet another example of his trademark thoughtfulness.

It is hard today to think of a government minister speaking so insistently about thinking as one of his or her department's primary disciplines. For the most part, immediate action is demanded. Few seem to ask the question: when and by whom was the action thought through? For Haldane, the imperative of statesmanship was that every action required a sound reason, and one that was intrinsically linked to, and advancing, the over-arching purpose of the department. Ultimately, it was this that set Haldane apart from all previous War Secretaries; it is what led Cyril Falls, one-time Chichele Professor of Military History at All Souls College, Oxford, to write in 1957:

> All qualifications made, the final judgement must be that he accomplished magnificent work in the reform of the Army. ... He combined imagination with industry and above all with the great gift for simplifying his problems before he started to solve them. Haldane's lucid mind blotted out the ines-sentials while realising the value of what would have appeared to others unimportant items. He wasted nothing. Haldane was not permitted to undergo the test of acting as Secretary of State for War in war itself. I sug-gest that he is the greatest peacetime holder of that Office in our annals.[167]

The undervaluing of thinking time lies, surely, at the root of much of our contemporary political despair. Can we recognise in our own generation, for instance, the picture of statesmanship that Edward Grey paints when describing Haldane's tenure in office?

> To develop and concentrate thought, to evolve policy, to translate policy into practice, to choose the best professional men and to set them to work—all this is the highest example of Statesmanship acting within the limits of a single, albeit a great Government Department. Haldane at the War Office was an example of Statesmanship in action.[168]

It is perhaps appropriate to draw this chapter to a close with this powerful description. While it insightfully captures the techniques and principles with which Haldane transformed the British army, it also challenges us to think of ways in which we, in our own time, might incarnate this spirit of statesmanship. It is clear that the present status quo is, in many respects, unsustainable—as it was in Haldane's time. But in learning about Haldane at the War Office it is also clear that an alternative mode of behaviour is capable of bringing about change that is lasting.

10

THE NEW STATE

We are citizens of the State and we owe duties to the State and to each other. The highest values we can reach are those we reach by self-sacrifice, by putting thoughts of ourselves aside, and by thinking of something nobler and greater.

Haldane, 'The Future of Democracy'[1]

Throughout the 1880s and 90s Haldane was at the vanguard of a political movement troubling both Conservative and mainstream Liberal alike. It was not, for the most part, a movement hailing an iconoclastic agenda, nor did it find in Irish Home Rule the political axis upon which all other policies should spin; as such, it went against Gladstone and the views emanating from the dominant platform for new ideas within his party, the National Liberal Federation, whose proposals were summed up in the Newcastle Programme of 1891.[2] The movement which Haldane was at that time spearheading—the so-called Liberal Imperialist movement or Lib Imps—opposed this agenda, and came worryingly, if deceptively, near to saying that the existing structure of things was, in fact, to be trusted.[3] According to historian Colin Matthew:

> [They sought] to interfere only at the margin of the economy, and, for the most part, by indirect means. Underlying this approach was a profoundly conservative conviction: the Liberal Imperialists believed that the existing economic and social structure of the nation was capable, with only minor adjustments, of maintaining both itself and the structure of the empire which was linked to it.[4]

This is not a description with which Haldane would have unconditionally agreed, but it is certainly true that he—ever practical—saw that there was a realism and boldness in saying, let's not be too bold! The Lib Imps wanted change, there was no doubt. But they knew what it meant to achieve it. They knew that Home Rule was a dead end; they knew that the House of Lords would stifle a radical agenda; they knew, most importantly in a world where utopian thinking is the surest way to practical undoing, that small adjustments to existing legislation could mean big changes in the daily lives of working people. Most of their proposals concerned domestic policy, despite the 'imperialist' tag. The largely restrained nature of these proposals should not hide the fact that they represented a concerted assault on the prevailing campaigns of both sides of the House; their power lay in their restraint.

The photographs of Haldane from that time show an unlikely warrior. Pale and portly, he was a picture of the well-fed but poorly slept King's Counsel. His colleagues on the war path, the future Foreign Secretary Sir Edward Grey and future prime minister H. H. Asquith, were still lithe with youth, visions of energy. But not visionaries. This was the role marked out for Haldane, and if one looks closely enough at those faded photographs, the eyes say it all.

It was a vision of empowerment, efficiency and equality; a vision not, at first sight, suggestive of restraint. Drawing on and informing what was known as the New Liberalism (a progressive approach to social issues that the Lib Imps shared with advocates of the Newcastle Programme),[5] Haldane's thinking encompassed nearly every aspect of the state—from taxation to housing, from education to women's suffrage—and it was built on one overarching principle, what he called 'the great principle of Liberalism in the widest sense, the principle of Liberty'.[6] The objective was a nation in which the working man or woman would be free from bonds of subjection, free from a domineering but distant government, free from prohibitive social and economic conditions that stifled the creative energy of individuals and their communities. But this was not merely a negative freedom; it was a freedom for as well as from. A society was imagined in which each member would be able to put their talents at the disposal of their neighbours, desirous to give and not just to receive. The policies that the Lib Imps advocated sought to unlock the mass of dormant talent within the nation—a move that was well tuned to the rising demand for 'National Efficiency', a movement which hoped to use the nation's resources, both human and material, in a far more effective manner than the slapdash approach that characterised traditional British politics. 'I want to see the latent talent in our democracy brought to light,' said Haldane, 'brought out of that vast reservoir of talent; I want to see it made actual, not only in the interest of the individual, but in that of the State.'[7] To create such a society proactive steps would have to be taken by the state, and a break would have to be made with older forms of laissez-faire Liberalism.[8]

In making an appeal to efficiency, the Lib Imps were playing a consciously non-partisan game. The efficiency movement was notable for the cross-party and cross-societal nature of its programme. It embraced great men—and women—from all wings of all parties. The historian G. R. Searle lists Rosebery, Haldane, Milner, L. S. Amery, Robert Morant, Professor Hewins (first director of the LSE), Sidney and Beatrice Webb and H. G. Wells to stress the catholicity of the group that campaigned for its success.[9] Haldane was certainly viewed as a central figure. A. G. Gardiner states that he is 'not sure whether Mr Haldane invented the word "efficiency", which has become the hardest worked vocable in politics. But whether he invented it or not, Mr Haldane is its recognised exponent. "Efficiency, and again efficiency, and always efficiency".'[10] As some commentators have pointed out, the term could ring hollow on the lips of many of its proponents as they struggled to articulate exactly what it meant to be 'efficient'. But, as we shall see, Haldane had no such difficulties.

Searle acknowledges that 'National Efficiency' in Haldane's time was not a homogeneous political ideology,[11] but he does attempt the following definition: 'one might describe the "National Efficiency" ideology as an attempt to discredit the habits, beliefs and institutions that put the British at a handicap in their competition with foreigners and to commend instead a social organization that more closely followed the German model.'[12] Such an approach appeared to place the characteristic efficiency of the German state above the traditional emphasis on liberty in Britain (hence the Lib Imps' refrain about putting the country on a 'business footing', as a way of counteracting the laxity of the older laissez-faire approach).[13] It was not, therefore, free from controversy. Indeed, Haldane's central position within a movement with such strong Germanic overtones would play a part in his public vilification in the early years of the war, and it certainly informed the decision to cast him from office in 1915.

Paul Kennedy, in his foreword to the 1990 second edition of Searle's seminal analysis of the efficiency movement,[14] notes that the greatest obstacles to any reform movements are usually psychological and cultural. Modern societies are complex and comprise many groups resistant to change, especially if the change embraces the adoption of foreign methods. Relative rather than absolute decline is a particularly difficult problem to face. What did it matter if the German economy was growing faster each year when the livelihood of the average worker in Britain was still improving? Without a national crisis or at least a sense of impending catastrophe, national efficiency movements have very little chance of winning the majority of votes, so Kennedy suggests, in a reasonably contented, liberal political culture. Haldane knew this, too. Already in 1896, writing on the 'New Liberalism', he saw that 'great changes in public opinion' were not achieved in the context of 'calm reasoning' but by 'an outburst over some particular event'.[15] And so it proved. It was a tragic vindication of Haldane's thesis that it took the horrors of the First World War to bring many of the issues over which he had campaigned to a head.

It is not surprising that the 'efficiency' concept had such appeal to Haldane. In its search for a set of governing principles upon which every aspect of national policy could be built,[16] the National Efficiency programme was at one with Haldane's philosophical methodology. It also tied into his sense of discomfort with political stagnation. We know of his impatience with the Liberal hang-up over Home Rule, which stultified any attempt to introduce effective domestic social policies. Similarly, then, his cry for efficiency was an expression of his exasperation at the complacency of the governing classes in the face of a rapidly changing world. The laissez-faire easy assurances of a people whose empire was so dominant, whose navy was so supreme, whose industrial technologies were so advanced, that they need not be anxious of their place in the world—the assurances, in other words, of the generation prior to Haldane's—were no longer tenable. Britain was witnessing its own decline as a so-called Great Power towards the end of the Victorian age, and a new approach was required to remedy this.

Intervention was now the order of the day, and it became evident that a more complex, richer notion of freedom was at large, one which found in regulatory, restrictive and compulsory measures a means whereby freedom (and efficiency and equality, too) could be more easily attained. As the organisational theorist and Haldane collaborator Mary Follett put it in 1920: 'We are freer under our present sanitary laws than without them; we are freer under compulsory education than without it. A highly organized state does not mean restriction of the individual but his greater liberty.'[17] A highly organised state, moreover, did not necessarily mean a centralised one (as we discovered in Chapter 4). Wherever power could be devolved to the local level, it should be. Involvement in decision-making from those most affected by the decisions was key to the material and spiritual prosperity of the nation.

Colin Matthew's magisterial coverage of this political movement, *The Liberal Imperialists*, makes it clear that Haldane was the architect of many of the policies embodying this new outlook. He, more than anyone else within the Liberals, was the intellectual powerhouse of the movement. This is the case both in terms of putting together actual legislation to challenge and adapt the laws of the day and in promoting policies on which a future Liberal government could stand. In terms of legislation, Matthew notes:

> They [the Lib Imps] took little interest in attacking the [Conservative] government, and devoted their energies to amending government bills constructively and to proposing their own. Typical of such activity was Haldane's amendment to the Irish Land Law Bill of 1887. ... Asquith's attempted amendment to the Local Government Act in 1888 ... and the Local Authorities (Land Purchase) Bill of 1891 and 1892.

> The last of these was their most radical, most substantial, and best organized attempt at legislation; the Bill gave councils powers for compulsory acquisition of land and powers to deal with unearned increment.[18]

The Land Purchase Bill, as we saw in Chapter 5, was Haldane's particular masterpiece. But Matthew also looks at education, temperance, housing reform, workers' accident compensation, unemployment, taxation, trade union disputes, and reform of the House of Lords, and finds in Haldane the driving creative force for thinking through these issues within this new mode of Liberalism.[19] We shall look later at the detail of some of this thinking and the way it reflects Haldane's understanding of what the state should be. For now, it is important to highlight two aspects of Matthew's analysis. Firstly, Haldane believed that one could operate within the broad existing structure of things and still fashion a greatly improved state; practicality and innovation needed to co-exist. Haldane was the embodiment of such co-existence. His political manoeuvrings towards the improvement of the state are entirely in keeping, therefore, with that combination of instincts that we have repeatedly emphasised in preceding chapters, the combination of pragmatism and idealism. Secondly, Haldane, continually inspired by that idealism, never stood still; deadlock was anathema to him; there was always another move to be played. This fact hints towards an intellectual and, indeed, spiritual conviction that motivated his work: that *Geist* (Spirit) was ever moving through the structures of the world, ever resolving the dilemmas of the time, ever developing the good that was already operative in those structures and dilemmas. The state was the stage on which that movement, resolution and development most evidently took place. And Haldane set himself to be one of the major actors within it. But what was the intellectual and professional background that made such action possible?

Yes, Haldane came from a family that placed a high value on liberty, that 'great principle of Liberalism'. But it rests on more than that. Its roots were deep within the Hegelian thinking in which he steeped himself throughout his life. That thinking showed not just the compatibility of individual self-expression and collective action, but also that such compatibility was the key to a healthy state—as we saw in Chapter 4. As Haldane's life drew on, he found himself engaging with other thinkers—particularly the British pluralists—equally sympathetic to a concept of a society that emphasised individual freedom in and through local groups.[20] From them, he drew insights into vital social and political dynamics that complemented his Hegel-orientated thoughts.[21] But his credo was not built on mere theory. Haldane made it his job—literally—to understand the concrete workings of states. Take his position, before ministerial office, as the leading barrister of his day representing Canadian provincial appeals before the Judicial Committee of the Privy Council (JCPC)—the court of last resort for (at that time) the whole of the empire, which Haldane would one day come to dominate as a judge. In this context, appearing seven times before the JCPC between 1894 and 1904, he heard first hand the demands of the provinces to be free to make their own decisions for their own communities. A close understanding of a particular region—its economic dynamics, its geographical possibilities and challenges, the mindset of its people, the social norms at play amongst them—was a prerequisite, it seemed, for the process of enacting laws that would actually function in a particular area and prove beneficial to the people. A distant federal government could rarely rival the provincial government in such understanding. Haldane's pleadings on behalf of the provinces inculcated a deep desire to see a state built from the bottom up, if conditions allowed. That it corresponded in such a coherent way with the philosophical worlds in which he moved and with new trends in Liberal thinking is a fact that may surprise the onlooker. Haldane saw it as the natural outworking of *Geist*, no doubt.

All the thinkers who went into the cocktail of Haldane's own thinking on the state were firm in one respect: that the state, despite the need to devolve political power, had a responsibility to provide for the essential, universal needs of human beings.[22] There was some divergence about what those needs were, but for Haldane, speaking towards the close of the war on 'The Future of Democracy', they came down to providing a living wage, good housing and, most importantly, high-quality education:

> The first principle … is that you must have a living wage, and the second principle is that you must have a decent home. Unless a man has a decent home for his wife and children and himself you will never get a good family, and without good families you will not get a good State. … You are hopelessly handicapped in the race of life unless you have knowledge, and it must be the concern of the State, in striving after the ideal of equality, to secure that every man and woman has a chance of knowing.[23]

Haldane's commitment to education was covered in Chapter 8, but his contribution to federalism—a dynamic that is crucial to enacting the twin pillars of the state that have just been mentioned, namely decentralisation and the maintenance of essential human needs—is equally worth exploring.[24]

* * *

In his capacity, from 1911 until his death in 1928, as a judge sitting upon the Judicial Committee of the Privy Council, Haldane took a leading role in the shaping of a major federal state, Canada. He sat on thirty-two Canadian appeals, delivering nineteen of the judgments: a formidable contribution.[25]

There are a number of competing views on Haldane's place in Canadian history. What can we say with any measure of certainty? His contribution revolves around his interpretation of the powers reserved to the federal government on the one hand and the provincial governments on the other, as set out respectively in sections 91 and 92 of the British North America Act 1867 (BNA Act). Depending on the way one interprets certain terms, it is possible to weigh power either towards the federal government or to the provincial governments. Much of the debate around Haldane's legacy turns on what constitutes a threat to the Peace, Order and Good Government of Canada (POGG), as mentioned in section 91 of the Act. For Haldane, the answer to this question determined in what situations the federal government could interfere with matters reserved to the provinces in normal circumstances. Another matter for debate concerned the extent to which certain powers reserved to the provinces, such as those relating to property and civil rights, could be made to include certain powers reserved for the federal government, such as trade and commerce. The scholarly consensus is that the answers Haldane provided to these questions in his JCPC rulings significantly reinforced the power of the provinces over the federal government. It is also claimed that he creatively reworked the interpretation of the BNA Act to allow for this reinforcement.[26]

The two classic judgments showcasing Haldane's new vision for Canada are *Board of Commerce* and *Snider*, where he limited the residual powers of the federal government so drastically that it required a national emergency on the scale of war or famine to justify its interference in the affairs of the provinces.[27] According to Haldane's judgments, only in such cases of emergency could the POGG of Canada be considered as truly under threat. Moreover, matters concerning trade and commerce and criminal law, which came within the scope of national interest, had previously been open to federal jurisdiction, though Haldane's judicial predecessor and hero, Lord Watson, had compromised this possibility to some extent. But with Haldane these federal powers were largely swept under the banner of property and civil rights (a move that some scholars would see as deeply against the original intention of the authors of the BNA Act). As property and civil rights were issues assigned in the BNA Act to the provinces, it became very difficult for the federal government to interfere in these previously accessible issues.[28] These issues could only become accessible when they rose to 'national dimensions' and, for Haldane, this meant something equivalent to a war or an emergency on a national scale. Such was the defining role that Haldane played in shaping the constitution that he was hailed, according to his own testimony, as the 'father of the Canadian constitution'.[29]

Yet, in Canada, criticisms of Haldane's constitutional legacy have dogged his reputation since his death. Two examples will suffice to show the complications involved. In the 1930s, at the height of the Great Depression, the Canadian prime minister R. B. Bennett decided to make a series of radio speeches outlining a 'New Deal' for the country, based on Roosevelt's model in the United States. These were radical proposals for a Conservative government—unemployment insurance (benefits, for instance), health and accident insurance, a minimum wage, a progressive taxation system, a maximum working week, fuller regulation of working conditions, a revision of old-age pensions and agricultural support programmes. The other political parties rallied behind the proposals, seeing in them a possible lifeline out of the country's desperate condition. Bennett, however, was knocked from the premiership by William Lyon Mackenzie King, the Liberal leader, in 1935, before the proposals could be taken any further. King, who adamantly believed the New Deal legislation to be unconstitutional, then referred the legislation to the JCPC to ascertain whether such reforms fell within federal jurisdiction. The committee, in a series of decisions in 1937, did indeed find the majority of the legislation to be unconstitutional.[30] The Weekly Rest in Industrial Undertakings Act, the Limitation of Hours of Work Act, the Minimum Wages Act, the Employment and Social Insurance Act and the National Products Marketing Act were judged totally invalid, as 'all these national issues turned out to be mere matters of property and civil rights in the provinces'.[31] The blame for this has subsequently fallen at Haldane's door.[32] According to modern commentator David Schneiderman, these losses 'represented the most significant series of defeats to federal power at the very time when the exercise of federal authority was considered critical to the survival of the nation'.[33] Referring to insights from Haldane critic Frank Scott, Schneiderman goes on to write that 'Haldane failed to see ... that the alternative to federal power was not necessarily the exercise of provincial power, but "anarchy" if the subject matter of the legislation did not lend itself to provincial control.'[34]

To respond to this criticism, we initially have to consider the justification for Haldane's particular reshaping of the constitution. I believe it is possible to mount a strong defence of this reshaping, given his time and his place, his thoughts regarding sovereignty and, indeed, the nature of Anglo-Saxon law itself. We have to remember on the one hand that Haldane considered it the duty of the statesman and of the judge to respond to the will of the people, for sovereignty inhered in that will—an idea explored in Chapter 4. Haldane of course recognised the difficulty of discovering what that will was, but his intimate knowledge of provincial grudges against a centralised federal control, and his friendships with a number of leading Canadians, may have suggested to him the direction in which public opinion was moving. On the other hand, we have to remember that Haldane believed, quite logically, that the more you could put decision-making into the hands of those most affected by those decisions, the better. One could respond with the argument that such beliefs don't change the fact that Haldane, to say the least, read against the grain of the BNA Act and perhaps even wilfully misinterpreted it. To say that trade and commerce and criminal law are largely inaccessible to federal control because they can usually be shielded by the provinces' jurisdiction over property and civil rights is already, some commentators claim, bad enough; then to argue that the 'Peace, Order, and Good Government' of the nation can only be considered under threat by national emergencies results in what one commentator has called the 'supreme joke of Canadian constitutional law'[35]—namely, the occasion on which Haldane tried to justify the JCPC's decision in 1882 to hold as valid the federal legislation over temperance in 1878, by claiming that the widespread drink problem of the time constituted a national emergency.[36] But we should not forget that his judgments came from a consensus of the judges sitting upon the committee's panels and that his predecessor Lord Watson had already begun pushing in similar interpretive directions.[37] Haldane was not, therefore, alone in his constitutional thinking. But there are further ways in which he might have defended himself.

Haldane would have pointed out that the times in which the Act was formulated were different from those in which he was passing judgments.

This being so, it was incumbent upon the judge to find ways of honouring the spirit of the Act, while at the same time responding to the conditions that confronted him at that precise time. Haldane, writing in 1921 and reflecting on the relativity involved in the interpretation of the British constitution, points to an analogous example in his own country (we remember, of course, that the British constitution, unlike the BNA Act, is unwritten; however, the BNA Act does clearly state that it wishes 'a Constitution similar in principle to that of the United Kingdom').[38] Haldane observes that it is no longer acceptable in Britain for the monarch to legislate without that legislation taking the form of a parliamentary Act, despite the fact that there were historical periods, such as the reign of James I of England and VI of Scotland, when the monarch exercised a far greater freedom of legislation. James, as the foremost exponent of the divine right of kings, believed he possessed 'the authority derived from God to rule without constitutional limit, indeed any earthly limit'.[39] Yet, according to Haldane, 'it was not long before the general sense of the British Community, as interpreted by the Judges generally', led to a rejection of this understanding of sovereignty. The point is still a highly relevant one, as the Brexit-related cases concerning prerogative power clearly demonstrate.[40] Indeed, in the case *Cherry and Miller* [2019] at paragraph 41, we find these words:

> Time and time again, in a series of cases since the 17th century, the Courts have protected Parliamentary sovereignty from threats posed to it by the use of prerogative powers, and in doing so have demonstrated that prerogative powers are limited by the principle of Parliamentary sovereignty.[41]

Haldane's point, ninety-eight years earlier, was that it is the general sense of the community, interpreted by the judiciary, that regulates the practice of the constitution.[42]

In terms of how this relates to Canada, Haldane would have seen that certain traditional interpretations of the BNA Act simply would not have allowed the judge to act appropriately in contemporary circumstances. The judge has to find novel ways of following the Act that permit him to respond in a manner that clearly corresponds to the general sense of the community. Long after Haldane's death this sense was in fact written into the Canadian Charter of Rights and Freedoms—in many ways a 'Bill of Rights'—which forms part of the Constitution Act 1982. The judiciary

305

was given a much-expanded role in arbitrating acts by both federal and provincial governments which in its opinion violated Charter rights. These rights in certain respects go beyond the principles of common law as originated in the United Kingdom, placing the judiciary in a position to judge, even in advance of specific legislation, what they believe to be the true underlying spirit of Canada's federation and of its individual provinces as they evolve and adjust over time.[43] As Haldane had already warned in 1921, 'The mind of the state never stands still, any more than does the mind of the individual. We have therefore not only to watch but to think, and to take heed lest our social organism gets encrusted with the products of an environment that is no longer suited to it.'[44]

To ensure that such watching and thinking found its way onto the judicial benches, it was Haldane's ideal that the judge should also be a statesman. For, as we have seen, the true statesman is one who can read the signs of the times, who can follow the complex twists and turns of public opinion, and the judge is the one who has the power to bring that opinion to bear within the law. Haldane was not alone in believing in the importance of such a combination. Haldane quotes President Wilson approvingly in this respect: 'It [the United States] never needed lawyers who are also statesmen more than it needs them now—needs them in its courts, in its legislatures, in its seats of executive authority—lawyers who can think in the terms of society itself.'[45]

Haldane's time at the Bar representing the provinces convinced him of the growing need for decentralisation and made him aware that new factors were always coming into play. In 1912—the year after he began sitting on the JCPC—we find him reflecting on the 'new problem' of the 'relation of the self-conscious and self-developing individual to the community' within advanced Western states. This raises what Haldane calls the 'great question' of the day: 'how the infinite value of the individual inner life, and the claims of the society of which the individual is a member and on which he is dependent are to be reconciled'.[46] Everything he heard at the Bar from the provinces backed up the view that power had to get closer to the wellsprings of sovereignty: the local groups, associations and corporations in which the best of that 'individual inner life' finds expression, reconciling the claims of that life with the wider claims of the community. This was indeed the pressing contemporary question.

Eight years later he wrote: 'the forms of all constitutions of the state are one-sided, if they are not able to contain the principle of free individuality'.[47] There is little doubt that Haldane saw the BNA Act in its traditional interpretation—that is, the interpretation that prevailed before his predecessor Lord Watson—as 'one-sided' and that he, in his capacity as a judge, needed to respond to the 'new problem' of the times, as that problem became apparent in public opinion. Not to do so would be to risk ignoring the source from which his own authority as a judge came, the authority of public opinion: 'it is the general opinion of the nation at the time when action has to be taken that is the ultimate source of authority'.[48] He was not afraid to say, in the British context, that 'Opinion has moulded ... the common law which the Judges administer',[49] and he believed this to be the case in Canada too. Speaking in Montreal in 1913, he quoted the famous words of the American authority Justice Oliver Wendell Holmes in endorsement of his point:

> The life of the law has not been logic; it has been experience. The felt necessities of the time, the prevalent moral and political theories, intentions of public policy, avowed or unconscious, even the prejudices which judges share with their fellow men, have had a good deal more to do than the syllogism in determining the rules [by] which men should be governed. The law embodies the story of a nation's development through many centuries, and it cannot be dealt with as if it contained only the axioms and corollaries of a book of mathematics.[50]

But for Haldane this was not a process that the judge ought simply to leave to history to prove; it was the judge's responsibility to ensure that the law continued to follow this human, experiential trajectory. If Hegel believed that the 'function of the supreme public authority is to adjust the old external structure to the new subjective attitudes',[51] Haldane did too.

These comments already, to some extent, vindicate Haldane's reshaping of the constitution. But what of its impact on the fate of Bennett's New Deal? It is always dangerous to indulge in counterfactual history, but Haldane does give indications that, had he been faced with the kind of crisis that Canada was experiencing in the 1930s, he would have once more shaped the constitution in a more centralised manner. He writes that 'In wartime, a highly centralized control may be essential. In peacetime it may be politically and ethically very undesirable.'[52] Though the crisis was a peacetime crisis, if Haldane had felt that it bore the hallmarks of a war-time emergency, then he may well have felt justified in allowing the federal government to implement its New Deal policies on the basis that the Peace, Order and Good Government of the land were under threat. The pliability of law was a constant theme of Haldane's and there is a strong case to be made that, if public opinion so demanded and the facts merited it, he would have gone against the grain of his previous provincial-orientated judgments in such exceptional circumstances—and he did himself do this on a number of occasions.[53] Having said that, we should note that the JCPC judges in 1937 did consider whether it could reasonably be said that Canada faced a situation of emergency, and they found that such a description did not meet the facts.[54]

A second criticism that has emerged concerns the apparent relativism that Haldane's jurisprudence seems to advocate. According to Frederick Vaughan's 2010 book *Viscount Haldane: 'The Wicked Step-father of the Canadian Constitution'*—which adopted Eugene Forsey's pejorative description of Haldane in its title[55]—Haldane's philosophical beliefs, particularly his reading of Hegel, led him to interpret the constitution in a way that was at variance with the intention of the Act's original authors.[56] Vaughan shows great sympathy with Haldane as a man, and seeks to do justice to the intellectual world that informed his legal perspective.[57] Indeed, before his death in 2018, Vaughan was a constant supporter of my own project to put Haldane back on the map as a major statesman of continuing relevance. He was ever ready to lend a hand towards this goal and helped me develop a fuller understanding of Haldane's place in Canada; I am deeply in his debt. But Vaughan maintained a critical stance, particularly in terms of what he saw as Haldane's contribution to a dangerous judicial relativism. For Vaughan, this stems back to Hegel's historicism, which he understood as follows:

> Hegel's most enduring contribution to modern public philosophy was his central thesis ... that ethical or moral standards change over time; what was wrong in one generation becomes right in a succeeding generation. Above all, it means there is no permanent notion of what constitutes justice. Justice becomes whatever the state says it is at any given historic epoch.[58]

Haldane was in thrall to such thinking, according to Vaughan, and his judgments were embodiments of this historicism, as he sought to enact whatever notions of justice prevailed at the time at which he passed judgment. Vaughan examines Haldane's commitment to understanding what he (Haldane) called the *Sittlichkeit* of a people—a word borrowed from Hegel and explored most fully by Haldane in his address to the special joint meeting of the American Bar Association and the Bar Association of Canada in Montreal in 1913, entitled 'Higher Nationality'. In German, *sittlich* means ethical, but *Sittlichkeit* does not have a direct translation in English. Haldane, however, unpacks it as follows: 'the system of habitual or customary conduct, ethical rather than legal, which embraces all those obligations of the citizen which it is "bad form" or "not the thing" to disregard'.[59] It is, if you like, something akin to social mores. *Sittlichkeit* is a system which is largely taken for granted within a society; it is for the most part unconsciously followed. For Vaughan, *Sittlichkeit* is closely related to the General Will and public opinion—notions explored in Chapter 4—as it encapsulates the prevailing attitudes within a society. Haldane, so the argument goes, believed that the law, over time, ought to reflect the changes that take place within a community's *Sittlichkeit*, will and opinion. In Haldane's day, the argument continues, this may not have been very damaging, but it was the start of a slippery slope and in more modern times Canadian law has followed Haldane's example and allowed for legislation that shows no basis in a universal moral truth—in other words, a truth that remains true for all times and all places.

Canada is well known for its progressive, and sometimes highly controversial, social policies. There is, for example, a universal right for a woman to have an abortion at any stage of her pregnancy—'a degree of permissiveness largely unseen elsewhere in the western world'.[60] Canada's 2014 prostitution laws outlawed the purchasing of sex, but not the selling of it, in an attempt to protect the safety rights of prostitutes. In 2018 marijuana was legalised for personal use. Vaughan, one of Canada's many Roman Catholics, felt deeply unsettled by the swing away from more 'traditional' values. The Civil Marriage Act of 2005, which legalised same-sex marriage, seemed to mark, for Vaughan, a decisive break with a universal moral code.

Vaughan did not blame Haldane for these particular laws, but he did consider him guilty of making relativity a fundamental feature of the Canadian constitution: 'It is no coincidence that he [Haldane] was the author of a book titled *The Reign of Relativity*, for as the times change so, too, must the public acceptance of the latest "progressive" social standard which the judges are called upon to weave into the fabric of the law.'[61]

For many, such an idea isn't problematic; it is even praiseworthy. Moreover, it seems hard to imagine how legislatures could do anything other than legislate in the context of their times. In my view, Vaughan's argument is not one that demands a rebuttal. What his argument does do, however, is raise the interesting question of how Haldane conceived of the relationship between *Sittlichkeit* (something akin to social mores, as I have said) and the law. What kind of relativity ought the law to show? And what role ought the judge to play?

Haldane's address on 'Higher Nationality' shines some light on this:

> The spirit of the community and its ideals may vary greatly. There may be a low level of 'Sittlichkeit'; and we have seen the spectacle of nations which have even degenerated in this respect. It may possibly conflict with law and morality, as in the case of the duel. But when a level is high in a nation we admire the system, for we see it not only guiding a people and binding them together for national effort, but affording the most real freedom of thought and action for those who in daily life habitually act in accordance with the General Will.[62]

This quotation suggests that Haldane did in fact believe in a universal standard of morality against which we can judge certain actions, in this case the duel. Indeed, the notion of higher and lower levels of *Sittlichkeit* suggests such a standard, as it appeals to a standard of measurement external to the individual systems of measurement belonging to particular communities. The key point is that, while the standard is universal, each person's knowledge of it is relative to the context in which they find themselves.

It is perhaps helpful to adopt the categories employed by Philip J. Kain, a noted Hegel scholar, who understands Hegel as a 'serious cultural relativist' as opposed to a 'vulgar cultural relativist'. Haldane fits the description of the former, who recognises that our thinking is formed and developed within particular cultural contexts and historical eras, and that these contexts and eras can greatly vary. But as Kain points out, this does not mean that certain cultures may not have access to what he calls 'real truth'. He elaborates:

> From the fact that there have been different scientific paradigms, must we conclude that there is no scientific truth or that one paradigm is just as good as another? Serious cultural relativism does not preclude truth, it just

implies that we cannot have access to it unless we come to understand it in and through a particular cultural and historical context.[63]

So the judge, while recognising that his own knowledge is relative, must to the best of his ability find what is truthful and beneficial in the latest social standard and, through his judgments, separate wheat from chaff, and thus raise the level of the community's *Sittlichkeit*; he performs a purifying function. But this influence must still act in response to the will of the people. The judge should not impose his own will. Even if he can envision ways of construing the law that would end various civic grievances, unless the people are ready for such a move, unless they will it, it is unlikely to be effective.[64] This explains why, for Haldane, the law must progress organically; it develops slowly as it follows and mirrors the best that is within the General Will. Novel, but artificial, interpretations of the law, lacking public support, will fail to achieve their purpose. The constitution of a state must always be a response to the people whose constitution it is, never an imposition upon them.

> It is Hegel who observes ... that every nation has the constitution which suits it and belongs to it. The state, he says, is the nation's spirit and depends on the character of its consciousness of itself. It is therefore idle to think of giving to a people a constitution *a priori* ... But, whatever the constitution, we come back in the end to its foundation. This must be the consent of the governed.[65]

All of Haldane's judgments on Canadian cases, and indeed on any case appearing before the JCPC, were attempts to reflect the spirit of the nation. The law, in his hands, was not a dead thing to be read off a piece of legislation; it was very much alive. Indeed, if Haldane were alive today, he would not be concerned that the interpretation of the Canadian constitution has moved on since his own time, and that some of his ways of reading it have been abandoned; on the contrary, he would have thought that only right.[66] Truth never stands still, as he was fond of saying. If Frederick Vaughan is correct about Haldane's role in introducing a strong streak of relativism into the constitution, then modern Canadians may even have Haldane to thank for the fact that their laws are recognisably reflective of their own time and their contemporary character as a people.

For those who support the current unity of the federation of Canada, it is also possible to consider Haldane and Lord Watson as having played a salvific role in maintaining that unity. That may sound extreme, but if we consider the circumstances of the 1995 Quebec referendum, then it could be proposed that the provincial autonomy that Watson and Haldane so radically championed provided just enough freedom for the province of Quebec to decide, ultimately, in favour of remaining part of the nation. The split of the vote was knife-edgingly close—50.6 per cent in favour of Quebec remaining in Canada with 49.4 per cent in favour of its secession—a margin of just over 1 per cent. Following that vote, the whole strength of the movement for an independent Quebec, promoted by the Parti Québécois, diminished significantly—although, as I write, its popularity is once again on the ascent. One could argue that if Watson and Haldane had not so effectively promoted greater provincial autonomy over so many years, it is possible that the degree of dissatisfaction in 1995 would have been that marginal degree greater than it actually was, with the consequence that Quebec would that year have seceded from Canada. The counter-argument of course is that Haldane's promotion of a greater level of devolution to the provinces was in itself the seed of the greater desire for provincial autonomy and, in the extreme, secession. If, like Haldane, you are convinced that strong states are built on a sense of autonomy amongst their constituent parts, the former is surely a more compelling argument. Haldane, on this view, posthumously played a vital role in saving the Canadian state through the judgments of the Judicial Committee which he so powerfully influenced. While there were obviously myriad other influences playing into the events of 1995, many of which might justifiably claim to have played a part in the 'saving' of Canada, they do not necessarily undermine the truth of the above statement. Of course, for those who do support Quebec's secession, then Haldane's role in Canadian history is perhaps less laudatory.

Whatever view one takes, what cannot be doubted is Haldane's commitment to seeing justice done in Canadian appeals. To confirm this, we only have to read one letter that seems to sum up the spirit of his approach.[67] Towards the close of 1913 Haldane received a missive from Sir Charles Fitzpatrick, the chief justice of Canada, reprimanding him for perfunctory and cavalier JCPC verdicts. For a moment, the usual Haldane spirit of equanimity trembles on the edge. His response, written on 29 December, shows a man for whom honour, integrity and hard work are everything. Clearly, Canada was the beneficiary of all three.

My dear Chief Justice,

I have your letter of the 12th. It contains several points which I must deal with (1) You seem to suggest that the case of Rex v. Cotton was decided perfunctorily, that we laid down that a Province cannot under S.92 of the Constitution Act direct the collection of taxes through a public office & that we treated the previous decisions of Woodruffe's case 'cavalierly'.

Now none of these things are so. I presided myself in Rex v. Cotton. We gave days to the hearing to which we devoted the energies of a judicial tribunal. We decided the point as to ultra vires because it was raised and pressed by the parties. We did not decide that the Province could not collect a tax through a public office. What we did decide was what was plainly in accordance with principle & with the previous decisions of Lord Selborne & others that the wording of a particular amendment which had been made to a previous & valid Act was an attempt to impose an indirect tax on property outside the Province. You say that there is a nasty feeling about the judgement of which I weighed every line personally.

Well. It is for you in Canada to say what you want. You need not keep the Appeal to the Privy Council. But so long as you do and I have anything to do with the Supreme Court of Imperial Justice I hope it will look at nothing but Law & Justice & Truth. We had better shut the Judicial Committee up than lend ourselves to any other standard. I know you do not mean otherwise, but there are ambiguous expressions in what you have written & I should be wanting in frankness if I did not say so.

Then (2) you say that leave to appeal has been too freely given. I was of that opinion myself, & told you so in September at Montreal, & you agreed except in the case of Quebec. As the result I consulted my colleagues & have sat on every application for leave to appeal from Canada which has been made since we resumed sittings in October.

If your Registrar will look into the records since then he will find that we have very effectively checked the stream of applications. Few of them have succeeded.

(3) You speak of myself as not giving personal attention to Canadian cases. I have sat in every case of importance since I became Chancellor & have instituted the Canada 'July'. I have bent the whole strength of our tribunal on cases from Canada even to the sacrifice of English work in the House of Lords of two judges—which was what the Imperial Conference asked for … And it certainly never gave more time or pains to Canadian cases. If we do not fall below the level reached in the Alberta, Fishery and Cotton cases, I shall be well content. But no lower standard will suffice. You must

take us or else do what you are quite within your rights in doing by abolishing the Appeal.

You must not mind me writing this freely but when I have been making some of the hardest efforts of my life I do not like to have them misinterpreted.

Believe me

Yours sincerely,

Haldane

* * *

We have spent quite some time analysing Haldane's role in the fashioning of the Canadian state. But what do his political actions at home tell us about his understanding of how the British state ought to operate?

Haldane articulates a central aspect of his views in an article on 'The Liberal Creed' in 1888, where he is clearly feeling his way towards a practical and fair solution to the land question:

> The first broad facts which require attention in seeking for a policy which is at once progressive and constructive are the relations which in reality obtain between the individual and the State. ... But for the State the capitalist classes could not have become what they are. Their relations to the State, in fact, enter into the very composition of the millionaires of Lombard Street, and the multitude of wealthy professional and trades people to whose prosperity the fortunes of these millionaires contribute. It is therefore perfectly just that the State, as the representative of the country, should charge as it were a rent for the fields which it provides for all these people to cultivate at such a profit—not such a rent as will take away the motives for their industry, but an equivalent which they will willingly pay as the price of the advantages for which it is paid.[68]

This is not a vision of a centralist, power-grabbing state, however. Haldane and his colleagues firmly believed that decisions around land ought to be devolved to local councils, though the government ought to set the broad limits within which they could act. Limits, in fact, is not quite the right word; powers would be better. For this was a vision of local empowerment, and for two reasons. One relates to what we have already said concerning the practical importance of devolution—proper understanding of local conditions, expression of freedom, allowing decision-making to get closer to the hands of those most affected by it—but the second relates to the practical challenges of the House of Commons; 'choked and overburdened ... under the existing system of local business', as Asquith described that House in 1895.

To give Asquith's words a little more context, they feature in the following important claim:

> Social legislation ... in the long run could not be adopted upon a large and really liberal scale until they amended their political machinery in three vital respects ... relieve the House of Commons, choked and overburdened as it was under the existing system of local business ... refer the transactions of local affairs to local bodies ... and thirdly the completion and climax of the whole ... readjustment of the function of the two Houses of Parliament.[69]

As this quotation hints, reform of the House of Lords was clearly essential if Liberal domestic legislation was to take off in a big way. The crisis of 1910—in which the Liberal government, backed by the king, threatened the Tory-dominated Lords with a mass creation of Liberal peers if the Lords refused to give free passage to money Bills sent to it from the Lower Chamber—made it clear just how real this hindrance was. But once again Haldane was the reasonable voice showing the way forward during the turbulent years before and, indeed, after the crisis. Crucially, he acted as mediator between Rosebery and Asquith during the 1892–95 government, where Rosebery was seen as representative of the 'menders' and Asquith of the 'enders' of the House of Lords. In typical Hegelian fashion, Haldane sought to show that in reality there was no real conflict between the two. They may have differed on the letter of the question, but in spirit they were one. Both positions were manifestations of the Liberal desire to see the constitution take its natural evolutionary course of 'development towards democracy'. Haldane's practical proposal was that the Lords ought to 'reserve a power of veto ... akin to that which the Home Rule Bill contemplated the Imperial Parliament should have over the Irish legislative body, a power to be exercised only when the spirit of the Constitution was being violated'.[70]

Haldane believed that this power of veto would be easier to swallow once the hereditary peerage came to an end—an inevitability for Haldane—and was replaced with 'an elite of talent'. All positions of authority should, in fact, be based on the same principle. Privilege, in other words, must never be automatic; it must be earned. But privilege there must be. Elitism should persist; elitism with a Haldanean twist:

> I think it is profoundly true that we are now on the way to see our old-fashioned aristocracy superseded. Quite painlessly and calmly you will put us poor Peers out of political existence, in a very delightful and easy way, I have no doubt; but we are going out of existence. And I am going to tell you what must take the place of the old-fashioned aristocracy. There is going to take its place an elite of talent. You will have your democracy, not on the footing of the Bolsheviks, but with every kind of differing authority, authority according to talent and capacity, only restrained so that the individual of great cleverness shall not be able to get more than the share which is justly his, having regard to the talent he possesses. With the elite of talent anyone, however meanly born, will have the opportunity of rising to the highest position. We have been getting on pretty fast towards that, but I want it done in a scientific way.[71]

Haldane was persuaded not just of the compatibility of elitism and justice, but of the necessity of their co-existence. Without the former, the state lacks effective leadership. Without the latter, it lacks a conscience. The state needs both if it is to function in a healthy manner. But if equality of opportunity was an essential component of the make-up of Haldane's desired state, this did not mean he wanted the Liberals to become the party simply of the underrepresented within society. His rhetoric was geared to take all demographics with him. He wanted to inspire the privileged classes with his vision so that they might begin to rethink their responsibilities. His was not a negative attack; it was a positive advance in which all could participate.

The desire to be a party that embraced the whole spectrum of society is one important reason why Haldane and Asquith, having entered Campbell-Bannerman's ministry in December 1905, resisted the idea of granting extra-legal privileges to the trade unions during discussions on the 1906 Trade Disputes Bill. The debate raised by this Bill concerned the trade unions' immunity from the possibility of being sued. This liberty had been widely assumed before the *Taff Vale* case of 1901, in which Haldane had acted as lead counsel for the union known as the Amalgamated Society of Railway Servants. The society's members had gone on strike in protest against the Taff Vale Railway Company's treatment of a member of staff who had been refused a pay increase, and who had been moved to a different station as a punishment for his continual requests. The company then brought in replacement workers, and this resulted in acts of sabotage by the strikers, seriously disrupting the company's ability to operate. Although the company then successfully sought resolution through collective bargaining, it still decided to sue for damages. In this too it was successful. But the Court of Appeal overturned the initial decision and the case then went up to the House of Lords, which restored the original verdict. Until this decision, the reason it had been assumed that trade unions were not liable for damages was based on the fact that they were unincorporated entities and were simply too large and unwieldy to be held accountable in the precise way the law seemed to require. But the decision in the Lords emphasised that the society was registered, and therefore enjoyed certain advantages concomitantly with certain responsibilities. As the then Lord Chancellor, Lord Halsbury, put it: 'If the legislature has created a thing which can own property, which can employ servants, or which can inflict injury, it must be taken, I think, to have impliedly given the power to make it suable in a court of law, for injuries purposely done by its authority and procurement.'[72] Their Lordships' decision that the union must be held responsible for damages caused by members acting in its name brought widespread outrage among the trade unions, and they exerted a huge amount of pressure on Parliament to have the law changed to protect their immunity. We have already seen what Haldane thought about responding to public opinion, and he was largely in favour of the unions' right to strike and maintain immunity. But he felt the concerns of their Lordships could be reconciled with the unions if it were possible to limit the law of agency, which would avoid a situation in which, as Asquith put it, 'the funds of a union might be made liable for the acts of persons who were really irresponsible agents, though their agency might be attributed to the union'.[73] Thus they sought to appease the unions, while at the same time guarding against eventualities in which someone or some group, acting in the name of their union 'in contemplation or furtherance of a trade dispute',[74] could break the law and not be held accountable for it. They lost their battle within the Cabinet, however. Campbell-Bannerman supported, instead, a private member's Bill that gave the widest sense of immunity to the unions. This the government decided to take up and champion. It was enshrined in law as the Trade Disputes Act 1906.

The Liberals became, in Matthew's words, 'the captives of an interest'.[75] It was a blow to the vision of Liberalism set out by Haldane. As Asquith said in 1895, 'the interests of the community as a whole ought to be paramount over the interests of any class, any interest, or any section'. This was 'the root and spring of Liberalism'.[76] Instead of granting privileges to one side, the state should play mediator between capital and labour. Rosebery's successful mediation during the coal strike of 1893 and the Scottish coal strike of 1894 demonstrated this key capacity of the state. Interestingly, it was Haldane who had prompted Asquith to reach out to Gladstone with the request for Rosebery to take up this role (just as Haldane believed that all aspects of reality could be traced back to the foundational role of the mind, so too, if we dig far enough, do we find him at the root of so many successful political manoeuvres). His belief in the mediatory role of the state was coupled with his insistence on the importance of bodies such as the trade unions. Not only could these allow for that expression of the collective willing of individuals that we have already seen to be so vital; they also acted as agencies providing labourers with their own necessities, relieving the governmental side of the state from certain responsibilities. Yes, state interference was no longer the *bête noire* of Liberalism; it was now a necessity on many fronts. But wherever it was possible to restrict interference and not jeopardise the interests of the community by doing so, then the state had a responsibility to hold back accordingly. Trade unions allowed the state, in its governmental form, to show such restraint.

Not only did Haldane desire the rights of labourers to be fairly upheld, he also felt that their working conditions could be made such that their daily tasks were no longer daily grinds. As things stood, 'Labour is discontented, because it does not have enough interest in its work; it is suffering from the monotony of being treated like a machine.'[77] If self-expression was critical to Haldane's understanding of citizens' involvement in the state, then it was crucial that their work should require—and indeed benefit from—the expression of their unique capacities. Could this be realistically achieved? Haldane thought a decisive step in that direction was, at least, possible. If we fast-forward from the debates of 1906 to 1918, we find him putting forward a proposal within the bounds of what he calls 'practical politics'. By that stage he had gained a wealth of knowledge concerning the condition of labourers through his 1917–18 chairmanship of the Ministry of Reconstruction's Coal Conservation Committee. Speaking on 'The Future of Democracy' to the Workers' Educational Association in Coventry, an address we have quoted elsewhere in this chapter, he reflected on the production of electrical power from coal. He noted that 'today we use eighty million tons of coal in the year to supply power for our industries in this country'. The majority of this coal, he lamented, was used to generate steam power, and 'the steam-engine is a very wasteful way of producing energy'. This waste was compounded by the widespread use of small engines. Optimistically, however, his committee saw the possibility for huge economies here:

> If you could take the coal at the pit-head and turn it on a great scale into steam at once ... the waste could be reduced to a minimum, and then, with great super-power stations generating electric power on a large scale, you would get the result that instead of eighty million tons of coal per year being used to produce the existing quantity of industrial power ... we should do it with only twenty-five million tons.

Haldane's proposal was that, because of the large deposits of coal at Britain's disposal and because other resources would surely supersede coal in the future, 'we can very well use the eighty million tons at one-third of the cost'. This leads to the conclusion that the 'workman with a combination of electrical tools might therefore put out three times as much and be paid three times the wage'.[78] Moreover, a six-hour day would then become possible. Haldane's excitement was palpable:

> It would be a concentrated day, requiring workmen who know a great deal and have knowledge enough to supervise the application of electrical energy. The workman would have to apply his mind very closely; like a Judge, he would have to attend to everything and never let his attention wander. Also, like a Judge, he would have to know a certain amount. But think, after six hours' work he would be able to spend time with his books, with his family, in the art gallery, in forming his mind, and generally in being more of a human being than he is now, when he is dog-tired at the end of the day.[79]

Haldane, who relished his judicial work, finding enormous satisfaction in its execution, evidently believed that this version of the workman's tasks would provide him with similar satisfaction. In fact, it was quite a thing in 1918 to compare a judge's work with that of the humble worker. It was the kind of move typical of Haldane. He could find nobility in any task if only it could embrace the working of the mind and fulfil the duties of the moment. And herein lay the key to abolishing class distinctions, one of the central tasks of Liberalism as Haldane construed it. Haldane was not a class leveller in the sense of reducing standards to the lowest common denominator. He believed the state had a duty to raise standards across all levels of society so that all working people, from judge to pit-worker, enjoyed equal dignity and reward in their work. Once again, education was the catalyst that would make such a state possible. The workman 'would have to be educated, and you must brush aside the idea that any illiterate person could do the work. ... Every workman will have something of the professor in him.'[80]

Inspiring stuff, but is it realistic and is it truly just? On the one hand, we might feel that this vision favours those with talent and intelligence, but leaves behind all else who struggle in these regards. Haldane would acknowledge that we cannot change the world from being one that favours talent and intelligence; it is in the order of nature that this is so. But he would add that the state should try its best to find ways of providing the less well accomplished with work suitable to their particular abilities, and in this way provide some form of job satisfaction. He by no means advocated that all work ought to require the same intellectual rigour. His point was simply that, where possible, work should be made interesting and engaging, and that our education system should be such that there are no barriers to applying oneself successfully to that work.

On the other hand, we might critique Haldane's vision of the engaged worker by pointing out the inevitability of monotony in any steady job. Unfortunately, he has already beaten us to it. The realist once more balances the idealist:

> Let us compare workmen with Judges. I am a fairly busy man. I am, among other things, a Judge of the Supreme Tribunal of the Empire, and I sit there daily from half-past ten to four listening to cases which are argued before us and on which we have to give judgements which are sometimes very difficult and laborious. Do you think there is no monotony in listening to speeches from half-past ten to four o'clock? I confess to you that I am haunted by the monotony of it. ... That is only one instance; but everyone, even in the most interesting occupation, has a feeling of monotony.[81]

Perhaps we might critique Haldane's vision from another angle. Surely his notion that the labourer would turn to books and art galleries at the end of his working day betrays the mind of a man living in a world quite removed from the realities of the labourer's predilections. Is this simply wishful thinking on Haldane's part? Again, he is one step ahead of us. He reminds us that for twenty-five years he represented a constituency whose members were mainly agricultural labourers, and what he says about his interactions with his constituents puts our own assumptions into question:

> I learned something of the ideals of democracy in the twenty-five years I represented them. When I went into those spotless and speckless cottages there I saw books, and there was an atmosphere of education there, and I used to feel that these men were not what was ordinarily understood by labourers, but were people with mind and knowledge just like what was possessed by their most highly educated neighbours. ... I have known a good many working men who read their Shakespeare, and some of them their Plato, too.[82]

When we remember the popularity of the new opportunities for adult education that were arising at this time—the evening classes offered by the Workers' Educational Association (WEA), for example—Haldane's assessment is clearly not as subjective as it might at first appear. Have we perhaps unjustly underestimated the character of the labourers of Haldane's day? Maybe we are the ones removed from the reality of those times.

* * *

Understanding what motivated people to become involved and interested in their work was vital if businesses and the economy were to thrive. Haldane knew better than most what 'job satisfaction' meant and how it could have a wider societal impact. His commitment to the work of the National Institute of Industrial Psychology, incorporated in February 1921, was a natural follow-on from his own personal experiences. Its foundation dates from two lectures delivered at the Royal Institution of Great Britain in 1918 by Dr Charles Myers, who was to become the institute's first full-time principal and the foremost representative of British psychology in its international relationships. He was at the time the director of the psychological laboratory in the University of Cambridge. He pointed out that there was no body in existence which was directly interested in utilising psychological and physiological knowledge in relation to industrial and commercial life. He suggested the formation of an appropriate institute of applied psychology in Great Britain. Henry Welch, a director of Harrisons & Crosfield, a pioneering company involved with the cultivation and marketing of tea and rubber, approached Myers with his long-held practical concerns as a businessman about the waste of human effort and ability caused by 'occupational misfits and by the existing haphazard methods of finding occupations for young people'.[83] A formidable partnership ensued.

All this was meat and drink to Haldane. He became a founding member of its council and advisory board[84] and was the principal speaker at its first annual meeting at the Mansion House in the City of London on 27 March 1922, to celebrate the achievements of its inaugural year.[85] As the institute built momentum and reputation, Balfour became its first president in 1924 and Haldane, in 1925, became, with Sir Charles Sherrington, one of its two vice-presidents, a position he held until his death in 1928. An appeal, in their three joint names, was launched in 1925 for £100,000 for the maintenance and the endowment of the institute.[86] The Carnegie United Kingdom Trust, of which Haldane's sister Elizabeth was a trustee and which had supported the work of the institute every year since its foundation, immediately increased its commitment. The Laura Spelman Rockefeller Foundation, which was shortly afterwards to provide the capital for the purchase of the Bloomsbury site as the new headquarters of the University of London, was also a significant contributor. The institute continued to promote the application of psychology and physiology within the fields of industry and commerce until the mid-1970s.

The question of how to get the most out of people was vital to Haldane. Given his own ability to squeeze every last bit of his energy and time in the service of the state, he knew what was possible—though, we might add, his bachelor status, his team of household servants, his wealth and his exceptional stamina usually went unrecognised as factors in his capacity to achieve so much in one lifetime. Nevertheless, he was convinced that vast portions of human potential were going untapped. Finding a way to access and develop this potential was therefore crucial. Equally important was discovering how, once tapped, to put the various talents of each individual to the benefit of the organisation, group, industry or business to which they belonged. It is in this regard that he was drawn to the thinking of Mary Follett, one of the pre-eminent thinkers in the United States in the fields of democracy and social organisation. Intellectually brilliant, her writing and her lectures maintain a continuing relevance even today.[87] As her biographer Joan C. Tonn writes, for many years her name rested in relative obscurity, but many of the notions promulgated in popular management books of the last thirty years (Tonn was writing in 2003) are close analogues to ideas Follett developed in the 1920s. Tonn argues that Follett's work in 'collaborative leadership, win-win forms of conflict resolution, worker empowerment, self-managed teams, valuing inclusivity and diversity, continuous improvement, cross functional coordination and corporate social responsibility' continues to resonate in the present.[88]

Haldane was first introduced to her work in 1920 by his friend the philosopher Bernard Bosanquet,[89] and it was typical of Haldane that, finding in her a kindred spirit, he should publicly embrace Follett's ideas and encourage her work. Indeed, quite out of the blue, Haldane wrote to Follett in January 1920 to request that she allow him to compose an introduction to her groundbreaking book *The New State*, in the hope that he might 'make the book known in my own country by pointing out its bearing on our own political problems'.[90] After some hesitancy[91]—would Haldane's endorsement imply that she belonged to a specific school of thought?—she accepted his offer, and a fruitful exchange ensued for the rest of Haldane's life.

In 1924, shortly before he became Lord Chancellor for a second time, she had invited Haldane (impressed by his understanding of her core intentions) to review the manuscript of her book *Creative Experience* and was amazed when he responded, having just taken office, with his acceptance. She wrote to him in gratitude for his suggestions:

> What fun that you are *doing* some of the things I can only write about. You will now probably have many opportunities to recognize and work with functional wholes, that is, at one and the same time to reject abstract wholes, and also the conceptions of those who think atomism is going to save their hugged-to-the-hearts individualism. It is so wonderful that England just at this moment should have a philosopher at the helm.[92]

Perhaps Ramsay MacDonald would have taken exception to this last statement.

Haldane had been out of office for a year by the time Follett arrived in Britain in mid-July 1926. Workplace militancy was high, and had been for two years, and there were numerous strikes. It was a good time to debate her theories with a philosopher and statesman. She went north and spent two nights at Cloan in mid-August. There she also met Elizabeth Haldane, and the discussions that ensued between the two about vocational guidance and placement and the significance of group activities sparked a friendship that was to be sustained after Haldane's death. Indeed, in one surviving letter there is even a hint of a romantic inclination from the side of Follett.[93] We don't know what Elizabeth's response was to this.

Haldane wrote about Follett on 17 August 1926 to Gosse: 'The great visit is over. The conversation was unbrokenly of the highest brow order. … Miss F[ollett] has a vast academic acquaintance. She is a really good thinker, but not very stirring socially. She lives for study and knows philosophy well. [She] was not much of a walker, although she proved a very good talker.' He then lamented that 'the Black Dog was barely more than civil. Someone seems to have instilled prejudice into his mind.'[94] And writing to Gosse a few days later he refers again to the Black Dog, saying that he had at last recovered his health and vigour. 'He seemed to be suffering from acute depression. The malicious suggestion was made that it was the outcome of jealousy of Miss Follett.'[95] This tells us something of the pleasure that Haldane had derived from the deep discussions during her visit.

Follett went on to lecture at Oxford after her stay at Cloan. She met there Lyndall Urwick, the co-founder in 1934 of Urwick, Orr & Partners, the great pioneer of the management consulting movement. More than forty years later he recalled that meeting. 'In two minutes flat,' Urwick remembered, 'I was at her feet, and I stayed there as long as she lived.' Her approach, as Urwick describes it, was almost pure Haldane. It was her ability to convey in that two-minute conversation Urwick's importance to her, in his experience, thoughts, everything about him—but that importance was rooted in the fact that he was an individual who was part of a whole. He was struck by her fascination with the human condition, not as something abstract, but as that which was embodied in unique persons, but could also not be reduced to single persons. She allowed Urwick to

THE NEW STATE

157. Haldane: A lifetime committed to the state. Haldane wrote that 'Responsible government is a complicated and difficult matter. It requires great tact and insight, as well as great courage, the essential qualities of character in the statesman'.

158. Cartoon in the *Westminster Gazette* July 1906 of 'The New War Office Agrippa: Mr Haldane developing the Negative'. The notion of efficiency guided Haldane in all of his political endeavours, making him a leading member of the cross-party initiative for National Efficiency. This programme involved a search for a set of governing principles upon which every aspect of national policy could be built, a concept at one with Haldane's philosophical methodology.

159. Haldane presiding at the Judicial Committee of the Privy Council at 9 Downing St., c. 1925, the 'Supreme Court' of the Empire. His remarkable series of judgements radically shifted power from the Canadian federal parliament to the provincial parliaments.

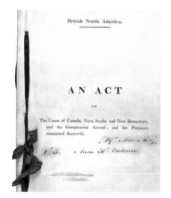

160. Above: The British North America Act 1867. Haldane's interpretation of this Act was informed by his philosophical commitment to building states from the bottom up.

161. Above right: The Federal Parliament of Canada, Ottawa, c. 1900 and, 162, lower right: The Provincial Parliament of Ontario, Toronto, c. 1915.

Group Organisation

Haldane was committed to developing healthy groups within society as a way of building a healthy state. His work in the law and his support of certain specialist organisations was a key part of this.

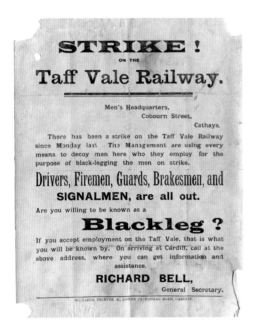

163. In 1900 Haldane acted as counsel on behalf of the union involved in the Taff Vale Railway strike in the defence of the legal action brought by the company. The case was lost by the union. Despite some reservations by Haldane as to the width of its scope, the Liberal government of 1906 enshrined in legislation the Trade Disputes Act giving immunity to unions from claims for damages during strikes.

164. The Mansion House in the City of London, c. 1900, where Haldane was the principal speaker for the annual meeting of the National Institute of Industrial Psychology in 1922. Haldane had been a founding member of the Institute the previous year.

165. Mary Parker Follett (1868–1933) wrote *The New State* in 1918. Haldane was deeply impressed by her book. He befriended her and wrote the introduction to the second edition. In 1926 Haldane invited her to stay at Cloan. Follett went on to lecture at Oxford and deeply inspired Lyndall Urmick, the pioneer of management consulting, c. 1918.

166. In 1922 Haldane helped create and became first president of the Institute of Public Administration devoted to promoting the science and practice of that profession. The prestigious Haldane medal was thereafter awarded annually by the institution.

Promoting International Co-operation

In August and September 1913, Haldane travelled to Montreal via New York at the invitation of a distinguished committee of Americans, including President Taft, and of Canadians, led by Prime Minister Robert Borden. He addressed the Bar Asssociations of America and Canada in joint session, delivering, on the subject of the 'Higher Nationality', the most important international address of his life.

167. Haldane crossed the Atlantic, accompanied by his sister Elizabeth, on the ill-fated R.M.S. *Lusitania*, which was sunk by a German U-boat off the coast of Ireland in May 1915, an act which influenced the United States' decision to declare war on Germany in 1917. Haldane's visit to North America necessitated the King giving exceptional permission for Haldane, as Lord Chancellor and Keeper of the Great Seal, to leave the shores of Britain.

168. En route to Montreal, Haldane travelled on the yacht of J.P. Morgan Jnr. up the Hudson River from New York to West Point, the US Military Academy, where he reviewed the largest parade of military cadets mounted until that time in the history of West Point.

Neglected Apostle of the League of Nations

In April 1915, whilst the war was in progress, Haldane, forward-looking as ever, wrote a prophetic memorandum to the Cabinet, the first paper laid before them to advocate the concept of a League of Nations. Haldane's thesis included most of the essential features adopted by the League of Nations at its post-war foundation in 1919. These comprised especially a collective guarantee against aggression, the formation of a representative Council and of a Permanent Court of International Justice.

169. Signing of League of Nations Geneva Protocol June 1925 by Sir Austen Chamberlain (centre) on behalf of the United Kingdom.

170. Haldane, in 1924 and, at 68 years old, visibly aged, returned for his second period of office as Lord Chancellor, this time in the first Labour government. He agreed with the prime minister, Ramsay MacDonald, that he should be relieved of certain judicial duties in order to devote more time to the Committee of Imperial Defence, of which he became chairman. At the fall of the Labour government later that year, Stanley Baldwin, the Conservative prime minister, invited Haldane to remain a member of the CID. Haldane used that office, with his restored judicial functions and his leadership of the Labour party in the House of Lords, to continue to shape the structure of the state both in Britain and Canada.

Centenary and Death of Mary Elizabeth Haldane

171. The Haldane family on Mary Haldane's 100th birthday in 1925. Front row: (l to r) J. S. Haldane, Lord Haldane, Elizabeth Haldane, Sir William Haldane; Middle row: J. B. S. Haldane, Lady Haldane, A. R. B. Haldane, Miss M. E. Haldane and T. G. N. Haldane (both of Foswell), and Miss A. Chinnery Haldane, B. Chinnery Haldane, and B. Chinnery Haldane (each of Gleneagles); back row: in centre Sir Aylmer Haldane. Others unknown.

172. Haldane's mother in her 98th year, 1923, with the protrait of her uncle Sir John Burdon Sanderson behind her bed. She died 16 days after her 100th birthday.

173. Philip de László's portrait of a noticeably thin Haldane, painted a few months before Haldane's death in August 1928.

HALDANE: THE STATESMAN
(1856–1928)

sense, in other words, the great web of interrelations between the human family, no constituent element of which was worthless or without interest. Urwick doubted 'if she had ever met anyone who was her intellectual superior' or 'ever met anyone without making them feel more important in themselves. Cleverness with no conceit, pity without patronage, sympathy with no superiority, interest without intrusion, it was a marvellous equipment.'[96] In this pen portrait it is clear why Follett's approach must have been so attractive to Haldane.

Follett's emphasis on the importance of the proper functioning of groups in their service to the state sheds light on why Haldane was so liberal in his support of public institutions. Wherever a body of committed and intelligent individuals came together to pool their ideas for the well-being of the state, it was almost an inevitability that Haldane's presence and support would surface somewhere within their affairs. The foundation, in 1922, of the Institute of Public Administration, devoted to the promotion of the science and practice of public administration, proved to be yet one more Haldane-backed initiative of significant importance. Haldane was, in fact, its first president. As Sir Frank Heath said of him, 'No one realised more clearly than Lord Haldane how much the success of any scheme for improving efficiency of public administration must depend upon the temper and equipment of the officials entrusted with its day-to-day business. He saw in the Institute ... useful means of influencing the temper and strengthening the equipment of civil servants both local and Imperial.'[97] The institute was for many years, until its dissolution in 1992, the leading independent British organisation concerned with policy-making and management in the public sector. It helped greatly to improve the effectiveness of public administration and to increase the wider public's understanding of the scope of activity and processes both within the United Kingdom and overseas. It was awarded a royal charter in 1954. Its work covered the entire public sector: the legislature, central and local government, publicly funded health services, public corporations, non-departmental and other statutory public bodies. It surveyed how these organisations interacted with each other and, importantly, with industry. At its inception, Sir William Beveridge hoped it would be a place in which 'Civil Servants may meet regularly to make a national pool of their ideas, to work out techniques of administration, by discussion and papers and so on; to educate themselves and incidentally the public as to what the Civil Service is and does'.[98]

But Haldane, in his inaugural presidential address to the institute, put its case more broadly. He referred to a comment made to him by a nameless 'distinguished public person' who had 'been engaged in making an investigation of the subject' to the effect that the country could, 'if the proper reforms were made, be governed at two-thirds of its present cost.'[99] Haldane admitted that this may have been too hopeful a view, but he was sure that waste lay at every turn, and that the reason for this could be found in the failure to think through what the true requirements of the nation were. This thinking through 'will not be accomplished without the co-operation and initiative of the Civil Service itself'.[100] He felt strongly that the institute should avoid the tendency of trade union organisations to become a body which merely protects individual interests. On the contrary, it should seek a much wider role in society. He believed that the Civil Service, if its members were themselves highly educated, could become one of the greatest educative influences within the nation. In this way, it could 'raise the standards in business and in life generally of those with whom it will have to be dealing constantly'.[101] One of the ways that Haldane envisioned such a raising of standards was for the Civil Service to keep in close touch with the universities, so that a fruitful interchange of ideas and skills on the highest level might occur. As is the case with many of Haldane's visions of harmonious co-operation between particular groups, this has taken a long time to materialise.[102]

* * *

We have spoken at length on Haldane's desire to see, and his work towards, improved working conditions for people of all sectors and classes. But we should not therefore think that he was all for championing a state in which the satisfaction of the individual was paramount. His address to the Workers' Educational Association in Coventry, quoted earlier, was given towards the close of a long and bloody war, a war that had seen the destruction of human life on a scale we can hardly imagine today. In the deaths of Patrick Haldane (the son of his youngest brother William), Raymond Asquith and Edward Horner, Haldane, too, had wit-

nessed the lives of those closest to him ravaged by the horror and brutality of the conflict. Could these countless acts of sacrifice have any meaning? For Haldane, they were expressive of what true citizenship meant.
His words at Coventry reach a crescendo as he tries to show their relationship to what true life within the state is. It is worth quoting him at
length again, for here perhaps more than anywhere else do we come to
the essence of his feelings for the state:

> We are citizens of the State and we owe duties to the State and to each
> other. The highest values we can reach are those we reach by self-sacrifice,
> by putting thoughts of ourselves aside, and by thinking of something nobler
> and greater. That is what our soldiers are doing in the fields of France to-
> day, and that is why our hearts go out to them, because theirs is the faith
> that there is something higher than life—the good of their country. We
> have to bear that in mind. There is a higher side in which we recognise
> society as there for more than mere self-help, as an organisation in which
> we can realise duties to the State, and realise more than merely personal
> aspirations. In an organised community like that we do not aim at or think
> of reward. We live for eternal justice. Your best man does not want reward
> for doing the right thing. It is the thing itself, the joy of quality, that makes
> all the difference to him. And so the ideal of the citizen of the State must
> be that it is quality and not quantity that counts, and that the real reward
> lies in self-sacrifice itself, even, it may be, in the giving of one's life.[103]

There remains one final feature to comment on regarding Haldane's
understanding of the state, and that concerns his emphasis on the importance of good relationships between states. We already know just how
much effort he applied to building a friendly rapport between Britain and
Germany: the countless speeches drawing attention to those aspects of the
German nation from which Britain could learn; his public praise of
Germany's scientific and educational advancements; his visits to the Kaiser
in 1906 and 1912, the latter specifically aimed at securing a consensus on
which a peace treaty could build. Despite these noble attempts, Haldane
failed to bring about the atmosphere of good feeling for which he so
longed. But his focus was not simply orientated towards the land of Kant
and Hegel.

I mentioned earlier Haldane's 1913 speech to the special joint meeting
of the American Bar Association and the Bar Association of Canada in
Montreal. As the first meeting of the American Bar Association outside the

United States, designed to mark 'the common basis of American and English Law', it was a remarkable occasion.[104] Even more remarkable perhaps was the fact of Haldane's physical presence there. In normal circumstances, the Lord Chancellor, as Keeper of the Great Seal (*Custos Sigilli*) was not allowed to leave British shores so long as he remained in that office. Haldane had to seek the king's permission to release him from this particular restriction for two weeks. It was deemed to be diplomatically advantageous for this transatlantic journey to go ahead, and the king gave leave for Haldane to put the Great Seal into the hands of a three-person commission, allowing him to travel with 'a comfortable constitutional conscience'.[105] (Fascinatingly, Haldane made his voyage on the ill-fated *Lusitania*, celebrated in its day for making the fastest crossing of the Atlantic and, briefly, as the world's largest passenger ship, destined to be sunk off the south coast of Ireland by a German U-boat in May 1915, an act which eventually led to the United States' decision to declare war on Germany in 1917.) The association's invitation, presented by its president and future UK ambassador, Frank B. Kellogg, had been endorsed by the highest authorities in both the United States and Canada—including President Taft himself, who wrote personally to Haldane seeking his acceptance—and it could achieve a double purpose of building a closer friendship with the United States while simultaneously affirming British ties with Canada.[106] It was, as Haldane pointed out to his audience, nearly a hundred years since the signing of the Treaty of Ghent, which ended the war of 1812 between the United States on the one side and Canada and Great Britain on the other. Haldane's speech was viewed as part of the 'process of coming to a deepening and yet more complete understanding of each other' since that time.[107] Moreover, it gave a platform from which a major British statesman could reach an audience of almost unprecedented magnitude, for the words of the speech would not just be confined to the ears of the lawyers in Montreal, but would be committed to print and published across both host nations. 'Through this organization you [Haldane] would reach every corner of America—United States and Canada', urged the US ambassador to France, Myron T. Herrick.[108] There is no doubt that Haldane took the preparation of the speech extremely seriously, sending Edmund Gosse six different drafts for consideration. Reflecting on their interaction at this time, Gosse wrote:

In the course of the many interviews we had on the subject, at 28 Queen Anne's Gate, and here at my own house, I was struck by the modesty and docility of the Lord Chancellor, who considered every one of my objections, and put nothing aside without attention. He was intensely desirous to produce an essay of real weight, capable by its form of pleasing the Americans and by its theme of awakening international reflection.[109]

What we discover in this speech are the foundations upon which can be established 'a true unison between Sovereign States'.[110] The critical concept that goes to the making of such foundations is embodied in that German word *Sittlichkeit*, defined, you will remember, as 'the system of habitual or customary conduct, ethical rather than legal, which embraces all those obligations of the citizen which it is "bad form" or "not the thing" to disregard'.[111] In Haldane's address this elides with the General Will, though it seems that there are some subtle differences. *Sittlichkeit* appears to be confined to the ethical sphere, whereas the General Will can go beyond this. Monarchy may, for example, represent the form of government determined by the General Will; this is not an ethical desire, but a political one.[112] Another difference lies in the fact that *Sittlichkeit* seems to be something citizens accept unconsciously and without reflection. The General Will can also be something that requires reflection before we are conscious of its existence, but, according to Haldane, it often has the character of showing itself in such a way that we cannot help but be aware of it. National acts of sacrifice and heroism, evident during times of conflict, are examples to which Haldane draws our attention. Of course, in many cases *Sittlichkeit* and the General Will do merge. In our culture, we find an instance of this when one person performs an act of service to another. It is taken for granted that the person to whom that act is directed ought to express gratitude in return. If they fail to do so, it is not only a breach of our 'habitual or customary conduct', a breach of our community's *Sittlichkeit*; it also goes against our will, and not simply our private and selfish will, that such an expression should be offered.

Leaving these technicalities aside, Haldane's proposition is a fairly simple one: 'Can nations form a group or community among themselves', he asks, 'within which a habit of looking to common ideals may grow up sufficiently strong to develop a General Will, and to make the binding power of these ideals a reliable sanction for their obligations to each other?'[113] This Will,

Haldane thinks, would form a common *Sittlichkeit* across the nations in question, and this would function as a basis for friendly and beneficent international relations between them. Haldane has reservations about this as a practical proposition applicable to *any* group of nations, given the state of things in the world at that time, but he feels that in the specific case of the United States, Canada and Great Britain there is much to be hopeful about. He sees in their 'common inheritance in traditions, in surroundings, and in ideals' the potential to build such mutual understanding.

This is important for a legal audience because he considers lawyers to be the chief agents, alongside governments, through which such mutuality can grow. His reasons are twofold. Firstly, systems of justice that have their roots in Anglo-Saxon law are peculiarly suited (as we have seen) to putting public opinion into a more definite form, and indeed they can even develop that form to a significant extent. Lawyers are capable, in other words, of shaping laws that reflect the General Will that Haldane hoped would emerge. Secondly, the tradition within all three countries is one in which lawyers play a large part in public affairs, 'and we influence our fellow-men in questions which go far beyond the province of the law'.[114] Their influence, he thinks, has a direct bearing on the *Sittlichkeit* of their nations. So lawyers must emphasise, in their public actions, the good feeling and shared values between the nations in the hope that they will sink into the intentions and wills of the people at large.

True to form, Haldane turns this into an affair of the spirit. He does not ask for treaties and written agreements. He is realistic enough to know that such things can never constitute real unison. For him, that unison 'must be sought for deeper down in an intimate social life'.[115] Here great opportunities and great responsibilities lie:

> It is easy to fail to realize how much an occasion like the assemblage in Montreal of the American Bar Association, on the eve of a great centenary, can be made to mean, and it is easy to let such an occasion pass with a too timid modesty. Should we let it pass now, I think a real opportunity for doing good will just thereby have been missed by you and me. We need say nothing; we need pass no cut-and-dried resolution. It is the spirit, not the letter, that is the one thing needful.[116]

Haldane's belief in the power of the spirit over the letter stands behind so much of what he sought to achieve in shaping both the British state and

330

other states beyond her shores. Of course, he was zealous in his determination to propose and enact legislation that would lead to improvements in the lives of his fellow citizens; the letter was still vital. But it meant nothing if it did not rest on an even more important foundation: the will of those for whom those goods were sought. Haldane's legendary stamina in travelling the length and breadth of the country to speak at public assemblies is a testimony to his conviction that what ultimately mattered was forming an educated, socially minded public opinion. This is the soil out of which beneficial legislation grows.

Although, in many ways, the vision that Haldane offered in 'Higher Nationality' never really materialised, he did achieve other, more concrete interventions of significance for international relations, which pushed in similar directions. One in particular stands out, and it was made in far more tense and dangerous circumstances than the atmosphere of Montreal in 1913. In April 1915, still within the first year of the greatest conflict the world had ever seen, Haldane, in the final months of his Lord Chancellorship, issued a prophetic Cabinet memorandum now held at the Public Record Office.[117] The document has led one commentator to hail Haldane as 'a conceptual godfather of the League of Nations and a strikingly accurate soothsayer of the impending Interwar period'.[118] The document does indeed show astonishing foresight. To do it justice one would have to read it in full. For this, sadly, there is little space. But Robert Joseph Gowen well summarises the memorandum's importance:

> Not only was Haldane the first to bring the League idea before the cabinet, but in doing so he unveiled most of its essential features: the collective guarantee against aggression found in articles 11 through 17, a select but representative Council to marshal information and mobilize public opinion, and a district court—the subsequent Permanent Court of International Justice—to deal with related 'justiciable' disputes.

Moreover, Haldane was able to paint the major factors that led to the League's establishment, as Gowen continues:

> With the easy touch of a clairvoyant, he adumbrates the quest for disarmament, the declining importance of British seapower, the growing weight of American influence, the ruptures with France and Russia, and, of course, the rise of a yet more powerful revanchist Germany.

331

Haldane was the first British statesman to lay the seeds of such an idea before the government. When the League movement began to build momentum the following year, it is perhaps no surprise that the government responded with such 'positive familiarity'. And yet, until Gowen wrote his article on Haldane as the 'Neglected Apostle of the League of Nations' in 1971, Haldane's name rarely appeared in discussions of the League's origins. The omission was indeed 'obviously unjust'.[119]

Although, on this occasion, Haldane's vision did materialise, other factors would come into play to render the League's work ineffectual, not least the crushing terms of the Treaty of Versailles. When these became known in 1919, Haldane wrote another prophetic, but far less hopeful message, this time to his mother:

> The peace terms make me anxious for the tranquillity of the world in the next generation. They are not high-minded terms. ... They [France] want to cripple Germany permanently. ... They can lay the seeds of war for the future. There is a liberal Germany which could be built up and a German culture which has its message for humanity, but this treaty submerges both in a state of misery and despair, which will in due course have their reactions.[120]

Within twenty years the Nazis were at the height of their power and the world was at war again.

* * *

But it would be wrong to end this final chapter with such a negative moment in history. Haldane's ability to see the latent possibilities for the rise of a 'liberal Germany' with a 'message for humanity' should remind us, more positively, of what he believed the state should be. We have seen throughout our discussion that a healthy functioning state, on Haldane's terms, is impossible without a meeting of interests between the state and the individuals who compose it. Only when citizens seek to embody a positive message for those around them—orienting themselves towards the well-being of their neighbours and communities—will the state come to have its own message for humanity.

In his tireless efforts for those closest to him and for the public good, Haldane certainly lived his own positive message. He found that in giving of himself, he discovered his true satisfaction and his true freedom; he sought in everything he did to embrace that which is of real quality and claimed to have thereby encountered a joy that the mere search after pleasure can never achieve. Haldane believed, as his speeches and writings repeatedly show, that the individual cultivation of this attitude lies at the foundation of the best form of states. As we develop in selflessness and in dedication to causes of value, we learn that, slowly, our own ends are becoming one and the same as the ends of the state. We no longer live in conflict with the state, but seek its goals because they are our own. But that does not cancel out individuality; far from it. As Haldane's own intense individuality showed, a person's uniqueness may even be enhanced in the service of the state.

AFTERWORD

Things done for gain are nought / But great things done, endure.
Shackleton's version of lines from Swinburne[1]

Over the years Haldane had often returned to Cloan drained by overwork or brought low by illness. At the end of July 1928, exhausted and ill, he came home to Scotland for the last time. Mortality was in the air. Three men intimately associated with Haldane had died that year: Haig on 29 January; Asquith on 15 February; and Edmund Gosse on 16 May. Haldane's sister Elizabeth, as at all critical times, was with him. She was worried, but the change was gradual, and it was only over the final few days that the downturn became grave. A number of years ago I happened to find her simple 'Letts' diary for 1928 in one of the bookcases at Cloan, in which she had jotted down a series of rather sad notes.

On 28 July she recorded that eighty members of the Boys' Brigade had come to tea. 'R. saw them and said goodbye,' she wrote. The same day an announcement was placed in *The Times* expressing Haldane's disappoint-ment that on account of ill health he had been unable to attend the lunch given that week by the British Academy to the Earl of Balfour. Two days later he reached his seventy-second birthday, but this passes unmentioned in her diary. On 4 August *The Times* reported that 'Lord Haldane, who is at Cloan, his Perthshire residence, had been ordered a complete rest'. That day, an address which Haldane had prepared as the president of the Brontë Society on 'The Genius of the Brontës' was read in his absence at the open-ing of the Old Howarth parsonage as a museum and library.

On 12 August, rather ominously, two doctors, Dr Matthew from Edinburgh and Dr Dunn from Auchterarder, came together to Cloan. This was immediately followed by the arrival the next day of Nurse Sarah

Turner from Glasgow. 14 and 15 August were simply marked 'anxious'. The next day, 'R. seemed brighter'. But Drs Matthew and Gunn returned on Saturday 18 August. He was 'very drowsy'.

And then we have her entry for Sunday, 19 August 1928. 'Sorrowful day. Passed away suddenly but peacefully at 3.5. All there from Foswell [his brother William's home]—boys, Dr Gunn & nurse.' She recorded on a folded sheet of Cloan writing paper the words of the last letter which he had sent, dictated to her only that morning. It was a message of reassurance to Frances Horner, on holiday in France, oblivious of the course of events. 'Getting on. All well. Love. A little tired but going on quite smoothly. Hope to write soon. Ever yours R.' And on the reverse of the sheet she wrote the third stanza of 'The Old Stoic' by Emily Brontë: 'Yes, as my swift days near their goal: / 'Tis all that I implore; / In life and death a changeless soul, / With courage to endure.' Haldane had used these words in his address to the Brontë Society.

The peace of Cloan was immediately disrupted. One hundred telegrams arrived within twenty-four hours, then letters and more letters. It was to be three weeks before Elizabeth could record in her diary that she had finished answering the nearly a thousand letters of sympathy. From every corner of the world they arrived, from family, friends, colleagues of many nationalities, often drawing on personal reminiscences of Haldane. Suddenly, it was as if the differences and the controversies that had beset his life were placed on one side. Many expressed their view, as did the obituaries in the very papers that had attacked him, that the passage of time could only work to restore him to the position of high honour that he so richly deserved.

Preparations for the burial were quickly put in place for the afternoon of Thursday 23 August. The internment would be at the graveside next to the family chapel at Gleneagles at 2.30 p.m., and would not be private. The events of that day were faithfully described by Kitty Inge, the wife of the dean of St Paul's, who had arrived at Cloan with her husband late the previous evening. In a long letter to Haldane's beloved Frances Horner, marooned with her family on holiday in France, some sense of the atmosphere can be gained.[2]

Haldane's body lay on a bed of Cloan heather in an oak coffin beneath the west window of the drawing room. Since his death four days earlier on

Sunday afternoon he had been at rest in his study 'among his beloved books, with the puritan simplicity of four little vases filled with flowers around him being the most moving thing of all'. Haldane had been brought down to the drawing room at noon, which Elizabeth Haldane 'had tried to make as beautiful as she could with just lovely greenery everywhere and on the coffin the three wreaths of the family'.

Kitty wrote of a great concourse of friends, 'Sir Ian Hamilton, black robed men, and others', standing together at the entrance to the room leaving Haldane and the young minister in a place apart 'in such simplicity which made one realise somehow the greatness of the Friend we had lost'. As the short funeral service commenced, the sun came out and through the west window lit the drawing room with a wonderful radiance. The minister started with the traditional words of comfort and consolation from the scriptures, before, as *The Times* reported the next day, expressing thanks 'for the services which Lord Haldane had rendered to his country, for the work that he had done in its hour of need, for the vision and foresight which lay behind that work and for the freedom Britain enjoyed today through his labours'. The choir from the Auchterarder Institute sang very simply 'O! God of Bethel' and the Scottish version of Psalm 121: 'I to the hills will lift mine eyes/ From whence doth come my aid.'

Just outside the north window a large farm lorry pulled by two black horses—the same lorry that had carried his mother's body on her own last journey from Cloan only three years previously at the age of 100—could be seen draped in purple cloth waiting to receive the coffin from the shoulders of the stalwart estate workers. 'It was so exactly as if the horses understood, just looking round with such intelligent eyes to the Master, and then as he was put onto his carriage they bowed their heads!'

It had been a grey and misty morning, but by the time the mourners emerged from Cloan's dark, low entrance hall into the open air at the front of the house the weather had cleared to reveal the spirit-enhancing vista stretching out before the house, from Ben Lomond in the west, along the Grampians, to the rising Cairngorms in the far north.

The Haldane family took up their assigned places in the cortège—the men on foot, the women in motor cars—behind the flower-covered cart and coffin and a second wagon bedecked with wreaths which had been sent from throughout Britain and the empire. Haldane's two brothers together with his three nephews, strode out behind, with the estate workers walking alongside. Down the drive and across the small glen they processed, 'such a wonderful sight as we wound in and out of those tortuous lanes', the journey to the 'Lang Toun' of Auchterarder watched over by 'men standing bare headed and the women true mourners with such true sorrowing faces'.

A body of sixty of Haldane's Territorials, led by four pipers, took up position at the head of the procession and the moving lament of the pipes could be heard as the cortège marched the 2 miles through Auchterarder and onwards to loop back into the foothills of the Ochils at Gleneagles. The procession had expanded to a mile in length by the time the coffin passed the hall and library which Andrew Carnegie had opened in Haldane and his sister's company thirty-two years before. Today all was silence except for the tolling of its bell. Kitty Inge noted that the shops and cottages had their blinds down and recalled 'silent knots of women and children, everyone really caring; there was a simplicity and dignity on the whole route, not one jarring note'.

Arriving at the small chapel and burial ground at the northern entrance to Gleneagles, whose 'great hills seemed to stand like sentinels', it was 'beautiful and impressive beyond words and yet so intimate as if the earth was waiting to receive a loved child to watch and guide'. Here a large number of mourners were gathered, 'the only note of colour being the Heads of the universities and their Mace-bearers, but never was there any formality, it was just a perfect loving tribute of those who loved and honoured their friend'. An ecumenical service was conducted at the graveside by Rev. Robert Gardner of Auchterarder Parish Church followed immediately by a private service within the small and ancient adjoining Gleneagles chapel at which Dean Inge and the Bishop of Glasgow officiated. Haldane was laid to rest.

But, as in life, where on so many occasions events involving Haldane had proved unpredictable, so it was to be in his death. For, in the morning, urgent news came from Gleneagles to Haldane's brother at Foswell and to Elizabeth at Cloan. During the night a deranged man, convinced that Lord Haldane was still alive, had dug open the newly filled grave. Even in death, Haldane was unable to rest wholly in peace.

* * *

But, as we have seen repeatedly in this book, Haldane continues to live on in modern Britain, and in Canada. What was it that secured the longevity of his work? I think it was the unusual combination of the principles that guided him and the techniques he used to build upon them. There is certainly more than just one 'Haldane Principle'; five, at the very least, stand out.[3]

1. The first principle is the importance of returning to first principles, in his insistence that thinking costs nothing and that thought must precede action. It is this that allowed Haldane to define the key questions, to see things whole, to fit each component element of his work into an organism that could live and breathe, develop and grow, over the long term. Hence the immense importance he placed on research, including independent research not designed to reflect a politically expedient agenda. Hence, too, his passion for being philosophically rigorous in all his undertakings. No politician of the modern age in Britain has ever attempted to put his or her philosophy into practice in the way Haldane did.

2. The second core principle is that investment in education is the best investment that any nation can make. Haldane's ability to act upon this conviction means that none can rival his contribution to the university landscape of Britain. Part of his success lay in some key Haldanean techniques: establishing principles; focus in approach; marshalling influential support; ensuring a sound financial footing for every endeavour; and, in his many speaking engagements and books, inspiring his audience with the loftiness of his cause.

3. The third principle is that decisions should ideally be taken as close as possible to the people that they affect. Haldane's stances on Home Rule for Ireland and on provincial autonomy in Canada show his commitment to this ideal. Haldane, inspired by his philosophical studies and friendships, believed that the more an individual feels a part of the decision-making process the more committed that individual will be to supporting that decision. This is where policies on sovereignty and devolution ought to begin. As Haldane explained in his 1913 speech on 'Higher Nationality' in Montreal, this applies both within and between individual nation-states. Here we see his vision of groups of nations working together to achieve higher objectives than they could individually.

4. The fourth Haldane principle is to balance realism with idealism, in the sense of recognising the importance of timing in relation to effecting change. Haldane saw, for instance, that there was no point in seeking to drive radical change at a pace which would simply be rejected by a House of Lords dominated by Conservatives. The compromises he made to get his army reforms through Parliament again illustrate the point. He was fully conscious that in politics a developed sense of timing, along with a subtle pragmatic approach, determines what can be achieved just as much as the ability to articulate the arguments. Connected to this was a desire to implement change at a pace that was concurrent with the General Will of the people. Statesmanship requires the cultivation of the capacity to identify the underlying sense of the direction of society, even if from time to time that direction may appear to be lost in the noisy maelstrom of competing mobs. Lasting and beneficial change comes when the statesman reacts to the General Will and not to the vacillations of short-term public outcries.

5. The fifth essential Haldane principle is a recourse to statesmanship rather than to politics. Haldane's approach to cross-party co-operation demonstrates the true difference in approach between the statesman and the politician. The statesman is someone who holds certain well-thought-through views and opinions that transcend day-to-day party-political life. In a representative democracy where a politician stands on the ticket of a particular party it is important that the electorate should be able to rely on their representative to support his or her colleagues. But there are occasions where, on certain matters, particularly of individual conscience, this proves impossible and an MP feels it necessary to abstain from voting or to vote against his own party. Haldane knew that cross-party co-operation often led to the most valuable policies. His legacy in education and defence amply bears out the wisdom of such a conviction.

But these principles would count for little if they were not underwritten by a fundamental idealistic belief in the transformational capacity of the human spirit and a corresponding goodness of character. It was Haldane's moral quality, and his depth, that lifted him to the highest level of statesmanship. John Buchan's pen portrait of Haldane seems to say it all:

His positive work belongs to history. So long as his friends live the man himself will be held in affectionate memory, for it would not be easy to overrate his essential goodness. He lived most fully the creed he preached. Whoever sought his advice was given the full benefit of his great powers of mind. There was nothing slipshod in his benevolence. He loved humanity and loved the State, not as an abstraction but as a community of lovable and fallible human beings. ... I think he was one of the least worldly men I have ever known. ... He enjoyed the various comforts vouchsafed to us in this melancholy vale—good food, good wine, good talk; but he always seemed to me to sit loose to the things of Time. When friends failed him he had no reproaches. He bore unjust attacks and popular distrust with a noble mag-nanimity. He lived his life as one who had a continuing vision of the unseen.[4]

Bearing this in mind, it is clear that our study of Haldane can be more than just a study of history; it can be read as a handbook of leadership and statesmanship.

I often think, and am sustained by the thought, that a 'Haldanean' approach to public affairs could be beneficial today. For example, in the United Kingdom, I ask myself whether the recently reordered Department of Health and Social Care could benefit in its supervision of the National Health Service, and the co-ordination of the work of that service with its social care functions, if it was to apply the holistic, principle-led Haldanean approach. Have the leaders of that department really been able to stand back from the ever-pressing immediate issues—an ageing population, bed shortages, the pressure to cut waiting times—to look at first principles? And, if they did so, are they prepared to ask themselves the core question as to that department's fundamental objective? If they determined that the objective was, for instance, the delivery of the greatest overall health of the nation with the maximum efficiency, would they then be prepared to judge each step rigorously against that clear standard? Could such a course deliver a different and much-improved structure, in a similar way to that which Haldane achieved when he addressed the issues facing the War Office? This might well require the restructuring and aggregation of some of the work of other government departments to co-ordinate more effec-tively within the Health Department an approach which incorporates the prevention of ill health, as well as its treatment.

In a post-Brexit age, this same holistic approach may well be appropriate in an area close to my personal and professional heart: the optimal enablement of Britain's international development policies. This could be especially important should Commonwealth countries determine to work more closely together in the future. Infrastructure investment internationally, to be effective, calls for a co-ordinated approach across development, foreign policy and trade and business departments. Haldane, as we have seen, was ever open to new and more effective departmental structures. Perhaps we need a new Haldane with a new Machinery of Government Report to help us navigate these uncharted waters? And, behind this, perhaps we need to insist—as Haldane did again and again—on a Civil Service and public administration system of the very highest general and specialist calibre to support the execution of good government. The creation of a new Royal Institute of Public Administration to replace the organisation which Haldane helped establish, and which met an untimely death in 1992, would surely promote a renewed search for excellence in this area.

Would Haldane's principle concerning the decision level at which political action is taken have helped to determine the most effective and publicly supportable split of activity between the European and the individual country level during the miserable period of confusion that led to the Brexit decision? Could it now help, within the United Kingdom, to resolve the issue of the break-up of the Union? Could a renewed commitment to devolving everything that can be efficiently devolved to national or regional assemblies result in greater support at the Union level for those essential matters that are best taken forward together?

At a time of appalling electoral disillusion with political leaders in many parts of the world, my sense is that Haldane's central principles and precepts have a continuing validity. Much of what he believed in should represent common ground between men and women of goodwill throughout society. If political parties themselves have to change because they no longer command the support of the people, so be it. Haldane lived through the age that saw the rise of the Labour Party and the end of the great Liberal Party he had known during much of his political life. The bravery of his change of allegiance from the latter to the former in his later years sets an example to all who are engaged in politics to examine their own allegiances and to ask themselves whether they truly meet the call of the principles in which they believe.

* * *

And, finally, what about the name and reputation of Haldane today? We are good at remembering in Britain, and the same can be said in Canada. We stand in seemingly ever increasing numbers on 11 November before the Cenotaph and other monuments across the country and the Commonwealth. Our great public spaces are replete with statues of statesmen, benefactors, educators and others who have enriched our local and national life. The history of our lands, our people and our heroes is rehearsed, in an endless stream of variations, on our television and cinema screens year after year.

For Haldane, there is a blue plaque on the face of his home at 28 Queen Anne's Gate, but his name and achievements are now largely forgotten. Nowhere is his statue to be found—and certainly not one in gold, as Asquith once proposed. There is time, of course. It would be a long-overdue accolade worthy of its subject. Who knows, maybe we will even yet see Haldane's large and benevolent figure (well, an actor's similar figure) illuminate our screens and meet us in our living rooms.

However things pan out in the future, great things done do endure. Haldane neither married nor had children. But if he were to return today to see the organisations to which he gave birth now grown to adulthood, I like to think that he would allow himself a moment of pleasure—before turning to new challenges.

ACKNOWLEDGEMENTS

In many different ways, as I said in the preface, I have been living ever more deeply with Haldane since the age of twelve. This accordingly includes the whole fifty years of life with Shellard, my wife. It is right that I should start by expressing my deepest thanks to her, to my children Milo, Coco and Rollo, to their spouses Katy, Barnes Oswald and Kate, to my grandchildren Ottilie, Bertie, Cosmo and Ivo Campbell and to my step-grandchildren Florence and Milo Oswald. Each of them can vouch for the constant presence of Haldane in their lives as well as my own. They now have the opportunity to read about him, rather than patiently hear about him. I dedicate this book to them all for their encouragement and patience.

The book would not have happened had not my parents, Wilson and Pearl Campbell, taken me to Cloan in 1959 to meet Graeme Haldane and his wife Billee. All four are now dead, but I hope they would be pleased that this book has come into being. As the preface also relates, I met that same day their son Dick Haldane, together with Robin, their daughter. This book would have been impossible without the support of Dick, his wife Jenny and their family who have welcomed my family to Cloan since they moved there in 1975. Whilst my debt to Dick and Jenny is total it, almost, goes without saying that I have complete editorial responsibility for the book, and all its blemishes.

Having never written a book of this type before, in the course of its planning it became clear that, to produce something meaningful, I would need professional assistance. As the principal Haldane family papers are deposited in the National Library of Scotland in Edinburgh, that was clearly the city in which to seek that help. Through my friend James Ferguson, I was introduced to Richard McLauchlan. He was at school at the Edinburgh Academy, Haldane's Alma Mater. He read theology at St

ACKNOWLEDGEMENTS

Andrews, where Haldane was chancellor at his death and where, in 1905, after delivering his Gifford Lectures, Haldane had been offered the chair of Moral Philosophy. Richard wrote his Ph.D. at Cambridge on spiritual dimensions within the poetry of R. S. Thomas, and then lived in Germany for a year, where he learnt the language. Here was the man who could help me interpret Haldane's philosophy and spirituality, and decode the correspondence in German between Haldane and Einstein. But much more than that, in deploying both his research and writing skills tirelessly in our joint cause, he has, for over five years, been my most intimate collaborator and fellow traveller in Haldane's footsteps. This book bears Richard's imprint just as much as my own. I thank him for all of his lucubration, friendship and enthusiasm. He and his wife Sabrina found time to marry and produce their son Magnus well within the period he has worked with me. I am most grateful to them all.

There are many others, over many years, to whom I am full of gratitude for their support and to whom I offer my particular thanks. In terms of archives held privately, my greatest debt is to Dick Haldane for freedom to roam at Cloan, to use much material unearthed there, and to reproduce many photographs within his family's possession. The Earl of Oxford and Asquith has allowed us to use, for the first time, the moving letters written to his great-grandmother Lady Horner by Lord Haldane. Patrick Campbell Fraser has permitted use of the diaries of Haldane's sister Elizabeth, his mother's aunt, which not least revealed the description of Asquith's insouciance in 'playing cards with the ladies' at Downing Street two nights before the outbreak of war.

So far as public archives are concerned, permission to quote from the extraordinarily extensive Haldane Papers, the Haig Papers, and the Papers of Dudley Sommer has been granted by the National Library of Scotland, and Richard and I are deeply grateful to Dr Heidi Eggington of the Manuscripts Division at the NLS for her kindness and helpfulness in responding to our request for permission. I extend that gratitude to Miss Jennifer Gosse for granting us permission to quote from the Gosse Papers at the Brotherton Library in Leeds; Virginia Brand and her fellow Trustees of the Asquith Bonham Carter Papers for the H.H. Asquith Papers at the Bodleian Library, Oxford; Christopher Osborn for the Margot Asquith Papers at the Bodleian; to the Warden and Scholars of New College

ACKNOWLEDGEMENTS

Oxford for the Milner Papers, again at the Bodleian; to the Edinburgh Academy for material within their archives; and to the Rothschild Archive London (where I received a wonderful welcome from Melanie Aspey) for the Rothschild Family Papers. To each of their librarians and archivists we extend our most grateful thanks. Quotes from the works and writings of Winston S. Churchill are here reproduced with permission of Curtis Brown, London on behalf of The Estate of Winston S. Churchill. My thanks to Niall Harman at Curtis Brown for his assistance. The London Library has been a formidable source of material and I thank all of their staff including Nathalie Belkin, their own archivist, for material on Haldane's vice presidency of the library, as well as Simon Blundell, the librarian of the Reform Club, London. I take pleasure in thanking those who helped us at the libraries of the London School of Economics and of Birkbeck College, the archive of drawings of Sir Edwin Lutyens at the Royal Institute of British Architects held at the Victoria and Albert Museum, the British Academy, the US Military Academy at West Point, National Liberal Club, London and the New Club, Edinburgh. It is also a pleasure to record Richard's and my thanks to Donald Mackintosh who assisted us with our research at the Bodleian and at the British Library.

For guidance or comments on particular chapters of the book Richard and I are most grateful to Andrew Chapman, Prof. Lindsay Paterson, Dr Jill Pellew, Prof. David Schneiderman, Sir Hew Strachan, the late Prof. Fred Vaughan and his wife Carol, and Prof. Andrew Vincent. As a new author, their patience and the thoughtfulness of their assistance has been most particularly appreciated. I also join Richard in thanking Will Ferguson, Sir Deian Hopkin, Jim Johnstone, Andrew McMillan, James Peoples QC and Dr Michael Wood for their contributions.

And then, as would be expected given the years in which this project has evolved to maturity, there are many individuals who have provided encouragement and support.

Within my own extended family I would particularly mention my brothers Malcolm, Andrew and Nicholas Campbell, Nicholas's wife Nicole, my nephew Barney Campbell, my sister Mary Du Croz and her husband David, Jo Shellard and Sue Wells.

In thanking the many friends who have been inspirational, made introductions or helped in numerous other ways—and who, above all, have exercised patience whilst waiting for the book finally to appear—I must start with Peter and Kay Sonneborn. Peter introduced me to Michael Dwyer at Hurst, who agreed to publish the book, and he in turn introduced me to Philip Cercone of McGill-Queen's University Press who are responsible for the North American edition published contemporaneously. Alexei Nabarro of Lexaeon has worked creatively and assiduously on the visualisation and presentation of the Haldane story. Rashid Amjad, Philip Borel, John Botts, Dermot and Vicky Butler, Prof. Stefan Buczacki, Simon Chester, David and Mary Ann Cooksey, Ray Dalio, Thierry Deau, Bita Esmaeli, Prof. David Gann, Brett Gutstein, Carolyn Hall, Thomas Hsu, Alice Hudson, Dominic Johnson, James Joll, John Kirkham, Elias Korosis, Peter Kulloi, Vera Lissauer, David Lough, Grant Manheim, Alexander McCall Smith, Gavin McGillivray, Tom McLean, Julia Prescot, David Reed, Jacob Rothschild, Lionel de Rothschild, Guy and Alison Stenhouse, Peter and Susie Stevenson and Prof. William Twining have each made contributions which I have valued. In this context, it is deeply sad that Peter Burt, Paul Cantor, Sue Davis, Frank Lissauer, Georgina Rhodes and Peter Waugh did not live to see the book completed.

For an inspirational tour in the footsteps of Haldane around Dalmeny and Barnbougle Castle, Richard and I are most grateful to the Countess of Rosebery. I also wish to record my appreciation of the courtesy of Alex and Alison Fortescue in allowing me to visit 28 Queen Anne's Gate on 19 July 2019, the centenary of the visit of Field Marshal Haig to Haldane after the Victory March.

Current and former colleagues at Campbell Lutyens have been particularly accommodating of the presence of Haldane in my life, especially over the last five years as work on the book became increasingly focused. Within their ranks I am particularly grateful for the enthusiastic interest shown by Ed Abel Smith, Richard Allsopp, Gordon Bajnai, Andrew Bentley, Alex Cass, Brian Chase, Bill Dacombe, Ali Floyd, David Gamble, Chiara Georgiadis, David Hall, Ed Hutton, Tom Fairhead, Takeshi Kadota, William Knight, Wayne Kozun, Thomas Liaudet, Colin McColl, Harry Noble, Ronak Patel, Peter Robertson, Andrew Sealey, James Shipperlee, James Sladden, Oliver Stocken, James Wardlaw, Peter Westmacott, Christopher Wright and Conrad Yan. Natasha Clark, Vanessa Evans and Maddie Watson have provided valuable support to me as has, most especially, Christine Campbell, for twenty years my ever-patient, ever-calm executive assistant.

ACKNOWLEDGEMENTS

My work at Campbell Lutyens has been much influenced by Haldane, not least in his inspirational long-term thinking and his willingness to take the path less travelled. It is, accordingly, a pleasure also to record my appreciation of all that I owe to our clients and counter-parties throughout the world and also to my colleagues at the Pacific Pension Institute and at the Long Term Infrastructure Investors Institute. There are far, far too many to mention individually and I ask for their indulgence in not seeking to do so. But I owe so much to so many who have inspired my thinking, have patiently listened to stories about Haldane and have shared their loves and stories of their own heroes with me. I thank each and every one of you deeply.

And, finally, both Richard and I wish to pay tribute to those who have been particularly supportive at Hurst Publishers in London and at McGill-Queen's University Press in Montreal. In addition to Michael Dwyer at Hurst, we have had constant editorial guidance from Lara Weisweiller-Wu; her wisdom and fine eye for detail have been invaluable. Daisy Leitch and Kathleen May must also be thanked for help with the book's production and marketing respectively. Mary Starkey and Erin Cunningham's proofreading assistance has been equally vital. In Montreal, at McGill-Queen's, we are most grateful to all of Philip Cercone's colleagues who have helped with the North American edition. Haldane, whilst Lord Chancellor, delivered his timeless lecture on 'Higher Nationality' at McGill in 1913, and was inducted as an honorary Doctor of Laws. It is entirely fitting that McGill-Queen's should be the North American publisher of this book.

John Campbell   London, February 2020

LIST OF SOURCES FOR ILLUSTRATIONS

The author and the publisher are grateful to the collections below, to the photographers Leonard Bentley (LB), John Campbell (JC), Milo Campbell (MC), Simon Jauncey (SJ), Justin Piperger (JP) and Caroline True (CT) for permission to reproduce their images in the plate sections of this book and to Lex Nabarro (LN) for his image editing.

1. Haldane's birthplace, Edinburgh (author's photograph; SJ).
2. J.A. Haldane, Haldane's grandfather (National Portrait Gallery, London NPG D 35111).
3. Robert Haldane, Haldane's great-uncle (National Gallery of Scotland).
4. First Earl of Eldon as Lord Chancellor, Haldane's great-great-uncle (University College, University of Oxford, Art UK).
5. Sir J.S. Burdon-Sanderson, Haldane's uncle (Wellcome Collection).
6. Haldane's mother's home, Jesmond (R.W. Haldane's collection; SJ).
7. Cloan, Haldane's Perthshire country home (R.W. Haldane's collection; JP).
8. Cloan today (author's photograph).
9. View north from Haldane's study at Cloan (R.W. Haldane's collection; JP).
10. View north to Grampians from Cloan (author's photograph).
11. Robert Haldane, Haldane's father (R.W. Haldane's collection; JC).
12. Mary Elizabeth Haldane, Haldane's mother (R.W. Haldane's collection; JP).
13. The young Haldane, 1874 (R.W. Haldane's collection; JP).
14. Geordie Haldane, Haldane's younger brother (R.W. Haldane's collection; JP).

15. John Scott Haldane, Haldane's second younger brother (R.W. Haldane's collection; JP).
16. Elizabeth Haldane, Haldane's sister, 1874 (R.W. Haldane's collection; JP).
17. William Haldane, Haldane's youngest brother (R.W. Haldane's collection; JP).
18. Geordie, Elizabeth and Richard Haldane, 1861 (R.W. Haldane's collection; JP).
19. Haldane in first year at Edinburgh Academy, 1866 (R.W. Haldane's collection; JP).
20. John, Richard and Geordie Haldane, 1870 (R.W. Haldane's collection; JP).
21. Göttingen University, early nineteenth century (Alamy).
22. Professor Hermann Lotze at Göttingen (R.W. Haldane's collection; JP).
23. Fräulein Helene Schlote (R.W. Haldane's collection; JC).
24. Inscription by Haldane to Helene Schlote (author's collection; JP).
25. Haldane's Diploma of Master of Arts, Edinburgh University (author's collection; JP).
26. Old College, Edinburgh University, early nineteenth century (Alamy).
27. Haldane with mother, sister and brother John Scott, 1879 (R.W. Haldane's collection; JP).
28. Haldane's mother aged 80, 1905 (R.W. Haldane's collection; JP).
29. Elizabeth Haldane, 1879 (R.W. Haldane's collection; JP).
30. Haldane and Elizabeth, c. 1905–10 (R.W. Haldane's collection; JP).
31. Elizabeth Haldane, 1920–25 (Wykeham Studios, P.A. Campbell Fraser).
32. Haldane with his dog Kaiser and Sir Ian Hamilton (R.W. Haldane's collection; JP).
33. Haldane with Kaiser, John Buchan and Archbishop of Canterbury (R.W. Haldane's collection; JP).
34. Haldane with his dog Bruce at Cloan (R.W. Haldane's collection; JP).
35. Haldane with Bruce and J.M. Barrie (R.W. Haldane's collection; JP).
36. Haldane's mother in old age, 1923 (R.W. Haldane's collection; JP).
37. Val Munro Ferguson, Haldane's fiancée (R.W. Haldane's collection; JP).
38. Elizabeth Haldane, c. 1905–10 (R.W. Haldane's collection; JP).

39. Helen Asquith, H.H. Asquith's first wife (R.W. Haldane's collection; JP).
40. H.H. Asquith as a young man (originally Violet Manners, Duchess of Rutland's drawing, in the Earl of Oxford and Asquith's collection; CT).
41. Frances Graham, *La Donna della Finestra*, 1879, by Dante Gabriel Rossetti (in Frances Horner, *Time Remembered: Reminiscences*, 1933; JP).
42. Frances Graham, 1875, by Sir Edward Burne-Jones (the Earl of Oxford and Asquith's collection; CT).
43. Frances Horner (neé Graham), c. 1910s (R.W. Haldane's collection; JP).
44. *The Golden Stairs*, 1880, by Sir Edward Burne-Jones (Tate Britain N04005).
45. Haldane in the Garden of Mells Manor, 1900 (National Portrait Gallery, London NPG Ax140130).
46. Commemorative blue plaque on 28 Queen Anne's Gate (author's photograph).
47. Haldane's London home, 28 Queen Anne's Gate (author's photograph).
48. Haldane in old age (author's collection and photograph).
49. Haldane with Winston Churchill and Edward and Dorothy Grey (R.W. Haldane's collection; JP).
50. Haldane's social world (author's collection; LN).
51. Lord and Lady Rothschild (Rothschild Archive London).
52. King Edward VII (Rothschild Archive London; Lionel de Rothschild's photograph).
53. Haldane at Balmoral, 1910 (R.W. Haldane's collection; JP).
54. Lady Rothschild's list of dinner guests, 1903 (Rothschild Archive London).
55. Haldane and Einstein outside 28 Queen Anne's Gate (R.W. Haldane's collection; JP).
56. Haldane and Einstein inside 28 Queen Anne's Gate (R.W. Haldane's collection; JP).
57. Portrait of Einstein, inscribed to Haldane (R.W. Haldane's collection; SJ).
58. Inscription to Haldane by Einstein (R.W. Haldane's collection; SJ).

59. *The Theory of Relativity* inscribed by Einstein for Graeme Haldane, Haldane's nephew (R.W. Haldane's collection; SJ).
60. Graeme Haldane's ticket to the Haldane-chaired Einstein lecture (R.W. Haldane's collection; JP).
61. Portrait of Edmund Gosse, 1885, by John Singer Sargent (Leeds University Brotherton Collection).
62. Academic Committee of the Royal Society of Literature (in Max Beerbohm, *Fifty Caricatures*, 1913; JP).
63. Unveiling of bronze bust of Sir Edmund Gosse (Max Beerbohm's drawing, in Evan Charteris, *Life and Letters of Sir Edmund Gosse*, 1931; JP).
64. Bronze bust of Sir Edmund Gosse (London Library; JP).
65. Oscar Wilde (public domain).
66. Wilde's *The Ballad of Reading Gaol* (author's collection; JP).
67. H.H. Asquith, c. 1915 (Library of Congress, Prints and Photographs Division).
68. Haldane's *carte postale* of Georg Wilhelm Friedrich Hegel (R.W. Haldane's collection; JC).
69. Haldane's *carte postale* of Johann Gottlieb Fichte (R.W. Haldane's collection; JC).
70. Haldane's *carte postale* of Bishop Berkeley (R.W. Haldane's collection; JC).
71. Graves of Fichte and Hegel, Berlin (public domain; Federico Leva).
72. Thomas Hill Green (public domain).
73. Haldane's hand resting on the *Works of T. H. Green* (R.W. Haldane's collection; JP).
74. Adam Smith (Library of Congress, Prints and Photographs Division #2004672780).
75. John Maynard Keynes (Alamy).
76. Harold Laski (Alamy).
77. Johann Wolfgang von Goethe, by Johann Heinrich Wilhelm Tischbein (Städelsches Kunstinstitut, Frankfurt).
78. Emily Brontë (National Portrait Gallery, London NPG 1725).
79. Robert Browning, by Herbert Rose Barraud, Wikimedia Commons.
80. John Morley, Secretary of State for India and Lord President of the Council, 1913, by John Collier (National Liberal Club's collection; JP).

81. Haldane's desk portrait of Gladstone (author's collection; JP).
82. Sidney and Beatrice Webb, c. 1895 (London School of Economics).
83. Beatrice Webb's book on the Factory Acts (R.W. Haldane's collection; JC).
84. Beatrice Webb's inscription to Haldane (R.W. Haldane's collection; JC).
85. Sidney and Beatrice Webb, 1928, by Sir William Nicholson (London School of Economics; JP).
86. Haldane, 1914, by Sir Arthur Stockdale Cope (UK Government Art Collection 0/637).
87. Keir Hardie in Trafalgar Square (Alamy).
88. 5th Earl of Rosebery, 1886, by Sir John Millais (the Earl and Countess of Rosebery's collection; SJ).
89. Balfour as Prime Minister, 1908, by John Singer Sargent (National Portrait Gallery, London NPG 6620).
90. Haldane's desk triptych of Balfour, Gladstone and Thomas Carlyle (author's collection; JP).
91. Sir Alfred Milner (Project Gutenberg).
92. Joseph Chamberlain (Alamy).
93. Emmeline Pankhurst (Alamy).
94. Haldane in Parliament Square, 1914 (R.W. Haldane's collection; JP).
95. Liberal Imperialists' signatures in visitors' book (the Earl and Countess of Rosebery's collection; JC).
96. Haldane with King Edward VII and house party (in Sir Frederick Maurice, *Haldane 1856–1915*, 1937; JP).
97. Haldane in relaxed mood, 1908 (R.W. Haldane's collection; JP).
98. Campbell-Bannerman Cabinet (R.W. Haldane's collection; JP).
99. Sir Henry Campbell-Bannerman (R.W. Haldane's collection; JP).
100. King Edward VII and Haldane at Marienbad (R.W. Haldane's collection; SJ).
101. H.H. Asquith as Chancellor of the Exchequer, 1908 (National Liberal Club; JP).
102. Sir Edward Grey, 1925, by Sir William Orpen (National Liberal Club; JP).
103. David Lloyd George as Chancellor of the Exchequer, 1911, by Christopher Williams (National Liberal Club; JP).

126. Lutyens's design for University of London (RIBA Drawings & Archives Collection RIBA127134; LN).
127. Imperial College (Kan-chane Gunawardena's photo).
128. Haldane's collection of ceremonial keys (R.W. Haldane's collection; SJ).
129. Ceremonial key to University College Southampton (R.W. Haldane's collection; JC).
130. Opening of University College Southampton (University of Southampton).
131. Haldane and King George V (University of Bristol, Library Special Collections DM251/17).
132. Haldane's doctoral diploma from McGill (author's collection; JP).
133. Haldane and Asquith at University of Manchester (in Sir Frederick Maurice, *Haldane 1865–1915*, 1937; JP).
134. Haldane depicted as 'Napoleon among the ruins of Bhrodrikh' (author's collection; JP).
135. Kaiser inspecting troops, 1914 (Library of Congress, Bain News Service Photograph Collection #2014689058).
136. Entente Cordiale, 1904 (Alamy).
137. Old War Office, Pall Mall (LB's photograph).
138. Haldane's despatch box as Secretary of State for War (R.W. Haldane's collection; SJ).
139. Haldane with Lord Esher and Sir John French (R.W. Haldane's collection; SJ).
140. Haig reviewing aircraft of Royal Flying Corps (Museum of Edinburgh, Haig Collection).
141. Colonel Ellison and Haldane in Downing Street (R.W. Haldane's collection; JP).
142. First flight, Wright Brothers (John T. Daniels, Library of Congress, Glass negatives from the Papers of Wilbur and Orville Wright #00652085; LN).
143. Lord Rayleigh (public domain).
144. Kaiser and Haldane talking at Berlin Parade (National Library of Scotland).
145. Lithograph of Imperial Prussian Guard presented to Haldane by the Kaiser (author's collection; JP).

146. Statue of Achilles presented to Haldane by the Kaiser (R.W. Haldane's collection; SJ).
147. Haldane awaits enactment of Territorial and Reserve Forces Bill (author's collection; JP).
148. Visit to Cloan of Field Marshal Lord Roberts (R.W. Haldane's collection; JP).
149. King Edward VII presents colours to Territorial Army Battalions (R.W. Haldane's collection; SJ).
150. Haldane inspects Officers' Training Corps of Edinburgh Academy (Edinburgh Academy).
151. Haldane, as 'a late beginner', promotes Air Service (author's collection; JP).
152. Colonial Prime Ministers' Conference (Auckland City Libraries, New Zealand).
153. General Sir William Nicholson (Library of Congress, George Grantham Bain Collection).
154. Haldane reviews colonial troops (Getty Images/Hulton Royals Collection).
155. British Expeditionary Force, 1914 (Imperial War Museum; coloured by Frank Augrandjean).
156. Churchill with Haldane outside 28 Queen Anne's Gate (R.W. Haldane's collection; JP).
157. Haldane (R.W. Haldane's collection; JP).
158. Haldane depicted as personification of National Efficiency (author's collection; JP).
159. Haldane presides at Judicial Committee of Privy Council (R.W. Haldane's collection; JP).
160. The British North America Act 1867 (Senate of Canada Archives).
161. Parliament of Canada, Ottawa, c. 1900 (National Archives of Canada).
162. Parliament of Ontario, Toronto, c. 1915 (public domain).
163. Taff Vale Railway strike poster (The National Archives, UK).
164. Mansion House, City of London (Alamy).
165. Mary Follett, author of *The New State* (Lyndall Fownes Urwick Archive; JP)
166. The Haldane Medal of the Institute of Public Administration (R.W. Haldane's collection; LN).

167. R.M.S. *Lusitania* (Library of Congress, George Grantham Bain Collection #2006677521; LN).
168. Haldane reviewing cadets, West Point (Library of Congress, Bain News Service Photograph Collection #2014694018; LN).
169. League of Nations, signature of Geneva Protocol (Alamy).
170. Haldane returns as Lord Chancellor, 1924 (R.W. Haldane's collection; JP).
171. Haldane and family on mother's 100th birthday, 1925 (R.W. Haldane's collection; JP).
172. Haldane's mother in her 98th year, 1923 (R.W. Haldane's collection; JP).
173. Haldane's final portrait, 1928, by Philip de László (National Portrait Gallery, London NPG 2364).
174 . Haldane, the statesman (Library of Congress, George Grantham Bain Collection #2014694016; LN).
175. Cover, back flap, John Campbell (MC).
176. Cover, back flap, Richard McLauchlan (The Edinburgh Academy).

NOTES

LIST OF ABBREVIATIONS IN NOTES

CB   HenryCampbell-Bannerman (Liberal prime minister Dec. 1905–Apr. 1908)
ESH   Elizabeth Sanderson Haldane (Haldane's sister)
FJH   Frances Jane Horner (Haldane's closest female friend)
MEH   Mary Elizabeth Haldane (Haldane's mother)
NLS   National Library of Scotland
RBH   Richard Burdon Haldane

PREFACE

1. R. B. Haldane, *Richard Burdon Haldane: An Autobiography* (London: Hodder & Stoughton, 1929), pp. 220–1.

INTRODUCTION

1. John Jolliffe, *Raymond Asquith: Life and Letters* (London: Collins, 1980), p. 70.
2. John Buchan, *Memory Hold-the-Door* (London: Hodder & Stoughton, 1940), p. 70.
3. Jolliffe, *Raymond Asquith*, pp. 70–1.
4. Obituary, Lord Haldane, *The Times*, 20 Aug. 1928.
5. Lionel Curtis (founder of the Royal Institute of International Affairs, 'Chatham House') to Dudley Sommer, 14 Nov. 1952, NLS, MS 20661, f. 159. Lionel Curtis also acknowledged his debt to Haldane in the support he offered in the development of Chatham House, writing to Haldane's sister Elizabeth upon her brother's death: 'To few if any of its members does the Royal Institute of International Affairs in its early years owe such as deep a debt as it does to him [Haldane]. His sympathy and advice was always unfailing and also his active help when needed. He seemed to live for the public service. The last time I saw him he was worn out trying to do the work of Lord Cave who was then on his deathbed. And yet he could give me the time that was needed. There never was a man whose octave was quite so wide. Was there ever before a profound metaphysician who could also give the nation the army which alone enabled it to survive the greatest struggle in history. The whole world mourns with you in your loss': 21 Aug. 1928, NLS, MS 6032, f. 219.
6. FJH to ESH, 25 Aug. 1928, NLS, MS 6033, f. 141.

7. E. S. Haldane, *From One Century to Another* (London: Alexander Maclehose & Co., 1937), p. 43.
8. Ibid.
9. See N. F. R. Crafts, 'The Industrial Revolution: Economic Growth in Britain, 1700–1860', *Refresh*, 4 (Spring 1987), p. 4.
10. For a history of the school and accounts of some of its notable alumni see Magnus Magnusson, *The Clacken and the Slate: The Story of the Edinburgh Academy 1824–1974* (London: Collins, 1974).
11. Haldane, *An Autobiography*, p. 5.
12. 'The Edinburgh Academy Chronicle', 1909, Edinburgh Academy Archives.
13. Haldane, *An Autobiography*, p. 7.
14. See RBH to MEH, 31 Oct. 1882, NLS, MS 5934, f. 148.
15. See RBH to MEH, 1 Nov. 1882, NLS, MS 5934, ff. 150–1; and Haldane, *An Autobiography*, p. 35.
16. Haldane, *An Autobiography*, p. 40, including above three quotations.
17. Quoted in Dudley Sommer, *Haldane of Cloan* (London: G. Allen & Unwin, 1960), p. 82.
18. 'UK Inflation Calculator', CPI Inflation Calculator. https://www.officialdata.org/uk/inflation/1905?amount=20000
19. Buchan, *Memory Hold-the-Door*, pp. 129–30.

1. A FAMILY TRADITION

1. John Burdon Sanderson to RBH, 5 Apr. 1874, NLS, MS 5901, ff. 14–15.
2. RBH to MEH, 6 Aug. 1890, NLS, MS 5944, ff. 243–4.
3. See Aylmer Haldane, *The Haldanes of Gleneagles* (Edinburgh and London: William Blackwood & Sons, 1929), p. 359.
4. For a full history up until 1929 of the extended Haldane family see Aylmer Haldane, *The Haldanes of Gleneagles*; for a very recent, but more restricted, history focusing on 'the owners of Gleneagles and the chiefs of the Haldane name' (p. xiii) see Neil Stacy's *The Haldanes of Gleneagles: A Scottish History from the Twelfth Century to the Present Day* (Edinburgh: Berlinn, 2017).
5. This title was considered 'a dignity next to that of Lord Chancellor': see Aylmer Haldane, *The Haldanes of Gleneagles*, pp. 15–19 and Alexander Haldane's *Memoirs of the Lives of Robert Haldane of Airthrey, and of his Brother James Alexander Haldane* (London: Hamilton, Adams, & Co., 1852), pp. 3–5.
6. For John Haldane's flourishing within the new political union see Stacy, *The Haldanes of Gleneagles*, pp. 104–7.
7. Such positions appear to be largely based on the manoeuvrings of his father, however, and the chair of Ecclesiastical History was 'a complete sinecure': see ibid., pp. 116 and 124.
8. See ibid., pp. 125–7; see also Aylmer Haldane, *The Haldanes of Gleneagles*, pp. 135–9.

9. See Stacy, *The Haldanes of Gleneagles*, pp. 141–2.

10. His father was Alexander Duncan of Lundie.

11. Michael A. Palmer, *Command at Sea: Naval Command and Control since the Sixteenth Century* (Cambridge, MA: Harvard University Press, 2009), p. 180.

12. 'Duncan, Adam, Viscount Duncan', *Oxford Dictionary of National Biography*.

13. 'Henri-Pierre Danloux: Adam Duncan, 1st Viscount Duncan of Camperdown, 1731–1804. Admiral', National Galleries of Scotland.

14. RBH to MEH, 4 Aug. 1883, NLS, MS 5936, f. 171.

15. Alexander Haldane, *Memoirs*, pp. 68–9.

16. Stacy, *The Haldanes of Gleneagles*, p. 213.

17. Ibid.

18. A. L. Drummond and J. Bulloch, *The Church in Victorian Scotland 1843–1874* (Edinburgh: St Andrews Press, 1975), p. 251.

19. See Haldane, *An Autobiography*, p. 27.

20. Alexander Haldane, *Memoirs*, p. 342. The equivalent sum today was calculated using 'UK Inflation Calculator', CPI Inflation Calculator. https://www.officialdata.org/uk/inflation/1810?amount=70000

21. RBH to MEH, 7 Nov. 1920, NLS, MS 6003, f. 205.

22. RBH to MEH, 15 Feb. 1892, NLS, MS 5947, ff. 62–3.

23. RBH to MEH, 8 Nov. 1894, NLS, MS 5952, f. 175.

24. RBH to MEH, 3 July 1903, NLS, MS 5970, ff. 7–8.

25. RBH to MEH, 5 Oct. 1903, NLS, MS 5970, ff. 101–2.

26. RBH to MEH, 18 Nov. 1903, NLS, MS 5970, f. 152.

27. RBH to MEH, 17 Feb. 1916, NLS, MS 5995, ff. 49–50.

28. RBH to MEH, 12 July 1916, NLS, MS 5996, ff. 15–16.

29. RBH to MEH, 31 July 1916, NLS, MS 5996, f. 43.

30. RBH to MEH, 6 Nov. 1920, NLS, MS 6003, f. 204 and RBH to MEH, 27 Mar. 1922, NLS, MS 6005, f. 55.

31. E. S. Haldane (ed.), *Mary Elizabeth Haldane: A Record of a Hundred Years (1825–1925)* (London: Hodder & Stoughton, 1925), p. 15.

32. His wife's father, Thomas Skinner, had also been Lord Mayor.

33. E. S. Haldane (ed.), *Mary Elizabeth Haldane*, p. 20.

34. Ibid.

35. Frederick Maurice, *Haldane 1856–1915: The Life of Viscount Haldane of Cloan K.T., O.M.* (London: Faber & Faber, 1937), p. 10.

36. E. S. Haldane (ed.), *Mary Elizabeth Haldane*, p. 36.

37. Haldane, *An Autobiography*, pp. 25–6.

38. E. S. Haldane (ed.), *Mary Elizabeth Haldane*, pp. 110–11.

39. RBH to MEH, 12 Dec. 1904, NLS, MS 5972, f. 165.

40. RBH to MEH, 12 June 1912, NLS, MS 5988, ff. 18–19.

41. 'Scott, John, first earl of Eldon', *ODNB*.

42. *Diary of Henry Greville*, 21 July 1864, quoted in 'Scott, John, first earl of Eldon', *ODNB*.

43. This is a phrase used by A. G. Gardiner in his essay on Haldane (mistakenly entitled 'Robert Burdon Haldane'!) in his *Prophets, Priests, & Kings* (London: J. M. Dent & Sons, 1914), p. 283.

44. 'Scott, John, first earl of Eldon', *ODNB*.

45. RBH to MEH, 25 Oct. 1880, NLS, MS 5930, ff. 182–3.

46. RBH to MEH, 27 June 1903, NLS, MS 5969, ff. 84–5.

47. H. Twiss, *The Public and Private Life of Lord Chancellor Eldon*, vol. 1 (London: John Murray, 1844), p. 196.

48. RBH to MEH, 5 Nov. 1904, NLS, MS 5972, f. 105.

49. RBH to MEH, 28 Aug. 1906, NLS, MS 5976, f. 92.

50. RBH to MEH, 17 Dec. 1906, NLS, MS 5976, ff. 177–8.

51. RBH to MEH, 20 July 1908, NLS, MS 5979, ff. 74–5.

52. RBH to MEH, 23 May 1909, NLS, MS 5981, f. 218.

53. RBH to MEH, 7 May 1910, NLS, MS 5983, f. 126.

54. RBH to MEH, 9 May 1910, NLS, MS 5983, ff. 127–8.

55. RBH to MEH, 12 May 1910, NLS, MS 5983, f. 132.

56. RBH to MEH, 6 Dec.1916, NLS, MS 5996, ff. 161–2.

57. H. B. Wheatley (ed.), *The Historical and the Posthumous Memoirs of Sir Nathaniel William Wraxall, 1772–1784*, vol. 5 (London: Bickers & Son, 1884), p. 75.

58. R. F. V. Heuston, *Lives of the Lord Chancellors, 1885–1940* (Oxford: Clarendon Press, 1964), p. 215.

59. 'Scott, William, Baron Stowell', *ODNB*.

60. RBH to MEH, 25 Jan. 1921, NLS, MS 6004, f. 11.

61. John Burdon Sanderson to RBH, 5 Apr. 1874, NLS, MS 5901, ff. 14–15.

62. R. B. Haldane, 'The Dedicated Life', in *Selected Addresses and Essays* (London: John Murray, 1928), p. 36.

2. THE HEAD AND THE HEART

1. RBH to FJH, 30 Oct. 1905. The letters are unpublished and quoted in this chapter by kind permission of the Earl of Oxford and Asquith.

2. T. G. N. Haldane, 'Viscount Haldane of Cloan: Graeme Haldane's Recollections', Nov. 1937, NLS, MS 20049, f. 204.

3. From the notes of Dudley Sommer, after a conversation with Lord Samuel on 2 Oct. 1952, NLS, MS 20666, f. 8.

4. Harold Nicolson to Dudley Sommer, 6 May 1960, NLS, MS 20664, f. 158.

5. E. S. Haldane (ed.), *Mary Elizabeth Haldane*, p. 45.

6. MEH to RBH, 18 Mar. 1911, NLS, MS 6009, ff. 46–7.

7. E. S. Haldane (ed.), *Mary Elizabeth Haldane*, pp. 46–7.

8. See E. S. Haldane, *From One Century to Another*, pp. 63–4.

9. This is somewhat equivalent to a solicitor in England; they are specially related to the Court of Session and have similar responsibilities as English conveyancing counsel. They also carry out financial business for their clients alongside their legal business.

10. Haldane, *An Autobiography*, p. 9.

11. E. S. Haldane, *From One Century to Another*, p. 43.

12. Ibid., p. 61.

13. MEH to RBH, 12 Apr. 1911, NLS, MS 6009, ff. 50–1.

14. E. S. Haldane (ed.), *Mary Elizabeth Haldane*, p. 114.

15. See particularly MEH to RBH, 29 July 1889, NLS, MS 6008, ff. 43–4; 13 May 1910, MS 6009, ff. 26–7.

16. RBH to MEH, 28 Jan. 1878, NLS, MS 5928, f. 49.

17. Elizabeth Joanna Haldane was thirty-five; Mary Abercromby Haldane was thirty-three; James Alexander Haldane was thirty-two; Margaret Isabella Haldane was thirty; Robert Camperdown Haldane was twenty-eight.

18. MEH to RBH, 12 Apr. 1911, NLS, MS 6009, ff. 50–1.

19. E. S. Haldane, *From One Century to Another*, pp. 143–4.

20. Haldane, *An Autobiography*, pp. 22–3.

21. See RBH to MEH, 17 May 1883, NLS, MS 5935, ff. 46–7; 1 May 1891, MS 5945, f. 106; and Haldane's note on his mother in E. S. Haldane (ed.), *Mary Elizabeth Haldane*, p. 126.

22. A classic Haldanean letter to his mother, at the moment she learns of the death of a relative in war, Guy Askew James Burdon Sanderson, brings both these features out: 'He has died for his country. You will feel this much, I know, but it is for the best. "In His Will is our peace." Dante said that, and it is true. And for Guy the best has come to him, and it is for us to accept the will of God': RBH to MEH, 22 Feb. 1917, NLS, MS 5997, ff. 60–1.

23. See RBH to MEH, 30 Mar. 1891, NLS, MS 5945, f. 65; 2 June 1896, MS 5995, f. 186; and 7 Apr. 1918, MS 5999, f. 121.

24. We should not forget a central figure within this home: the Haldanes' nanny, Betsy Ferguson, known as Baba. It is endearing to read Mary's account of Baba's words during her (Baba's) final illness: 'Eliz.[abe]th asked her whom she loved best in the world, and she thought for a while and then replied "Mr Richard"': MEH to RBH, 17 June 1898, NLS, MS 6008, ff. 87–8.

25. Violet Markham, *Friendship's Harvest* (London: Reinhardt, 1956), p. 49.

26. Andrew Seth and R. B. Haldane (eds.), *Essays in Philosophical Criticism* (London: Longmans, Green & Co., 1883), pp. 41–66.

27. K. C. Sehkar and S. S. C. Chakra Rao, 'John Scott Haldane: The Father of Oxygen Therapy', *Indian Journal of Anaesthesia*, 58, 3 (May–June 2014), p. 350; see also the highly entertaining biography of J. S. Haldane by Martin Goodman: *Suffer and Survive: Gas Attacks, Miners' Canaries, Spacesuits and the Bends: The Extreme Life of J. S. Haldane* (London: Simon & Schuster, 2007).

28. See RBH to MEH, 22 Apr. 1890, NLS, MS 5944, ff. 125–6.

29. Sir William Haldane, 'Some Early Recollections' (1 Mar. 1947), NLS, MS 20049, ff. 205–19.

30. RBH to MEH, 15 Feb. 1878, NLS, MS 5928, f. 94.

31. RBH to MEH, 10 Mar. 1896, NLS, MS 5955, f. 101.

32. For comments on 'higher standpoint' see R. B. Haldane, *The Pathway to Reality: Stage the First* (London: John Murray, 1903), pp. 113–14, 132, 295; for Matthew Arnold quotation see p. 102.

33. See particularly RBH to MEH, 6 Sept. 1914, NLS, MS 5992, ff. 65–6 and, again, 22 Sept. 1914, MS 5992, ff. 89–90.

34. MEH to RBH, 11 Mar. 1893, NLS, MS 6008, ff. 54–5.

35. MEH to RBH, 12 June 1890, NLS, MS 5944, ff. 168–9.

36. MEH to RBH, 24 Apr. 1897, NLS, MS 6008, ff. 83–4.

37. From the 'Note by Her Eldest Son' in E. S. Haldane (ed.), *Mary Elizabeth Haldane*, p. 126.

38. RBH to MEH, 23 Apr. 1897, NLS, MS 5957, f. 111.

39. RBH to MEH, 31 Oct. 1889, NLS, MS 5943, f. 90.

40. RBH to MEH, 13 Apr. 1896, NLS, MS 5955, f. 145.

41. See in particular RBH to MEH, 1 Nov. 1914, NLS, MS 5992, ff. 151–2; 10 July 1916, MS 5996, pp. 11–12; and 11 Mar. 1918, MS 5999, f. 101.

42. See MEH to RBH, 29 July 1906 and 13 Mar. 1911, NLS, MS 6008, ff. 166–7 and 41–3; 6 June 1915, MS 6009, ff. 121–2; and RBH to MEH, 22 June 1881, NLS, MS 5931, ff. 186–7; 24 July 1881, MS 5932, ff. 39–40.

43. RBH to MEH, 24 Apr. 1879, NLS, MS 5929, f. 81.

44. RBH to MEH, 14 Feb. 1898, NLS, MS 5959, f. 39.

45. RBH to MEH, 4 July 1906, NLS, MS 5976, f. 23.

46. RBH to MEH, 17 Nov. 1906, NLS, MS 5976, ff. 173–4.

47. RBH to MEH, 16 Nov. 1907, NLS, MS 5978, ff. 143–4.

48. The same could be applied to the German inscriptions from Hegel over the fireplace of Haldane's study at Cloan and on the bookcase of the library there.

49. See Frederick Vaughan, *Viscount Haldane: 'The Wicked Step-father of the Canadian Constitution'* (Toronto: University of Toronto Press, 2010), p. 151; but see Sommer to the contrary, *Haldane of Cloan*, pp. 123–4.

50. RBH to Gosse, 22 May 1918, Gosse Archive, Brotherton Library, Leeds, BC MS 19c Gosse.

51. RBH to Gosse, 3 Apr. 1921, Gosse Archive, Brotherton Library, Leeds, BC MS 19c Gosse.

52. RBH to Gosse, 29 Aug. 1921, Gosse Archive, Brotherton Library, Leeds, BC MS 19c Gosse.

53. RBH to Gosse, 6 Sept. 1921, Gosse Archive, Brotherton Library, Leeds, BC MS 19c Gosse.

54. RBH to Gosse, 10 May 1922, Gosse Archive, Brotherton Library, Leeds, BC MS 19c Gosse.

55. RBH to Gosse, 6 Sept. 1922, Gosse Archive, Brotherton Library, Leeds, BC MS 19c Gosse.

56. The letters themselves do not name Agnes, but there is a letter from T. G. N. Haldane

in the papers of Dudley Sommer, a previous biographer of Haldane, in which, after speaking with his aunt, Mrs Brown of Ichrachan, he discovered that Haldane was 'deeply attached to my great aunt, Agnes Kemp a sister of John Kemp. ... Aunt Agnes gave my uncle no encouragement and probably her affections lay elsewhere, but my uncle was her suitor for, I think, about 8 years, presumably round about 1880. Eventually he felt there was no chance of Aunt Agnes accepting him and subsequently, as you know, he became engaged to Miss Monroe [*sic*] Ferguson': 15 Sept. 1953, NLS, MS 20662, ff. 205–6.

57. RBH to MEH, 14 Mar. 1890, NLS, MS 5994, f. 94.

58. There are possible traces of this suggestion in some of Haldane's letters, but only very faint; for example, he refers to a friend of Val's who noticed that 'beautiful as her character was the real feminine side had never been developed either as regards me or her mother': RBH to MEH, 30 June 1890, NLS, MS 5944, f. 193. More obviously, Lord Asquith (Cyril Asquith, H. H. Asquith's fourth and youngest son) told Dudley Sommer that Val 'was not quite "natural"': conversation on 20 Jan. 1953, MS 20666, f. 20v. Val did live with singer and lecturer Mary Wakefield from 1895 until Val's death in 1897. Wakefield's biographer writes: 'It is needless to touch upon a sorrow to which, even ten years later, Mary Wakefield could hardly endure to allude': Rosa Newmarch, *Mary Wakefield: A Memoir* (Kendal: Atkinson & Pollitt, 1912), p. 111. See also Sophie Fuller and Lloyd Whitesell (eds), *Queer Episodes in Music and Modern Identity* (Urbana: University of Illinois Press, 2002), pp. 89–90.

59. RBH to MEH, 1 Mar. 1881, NLS, MS 5931, f. 76–7.

60. Munro's translation (adapted) of Lucretius' *De Rerum Natura*, ii. 7. Elizabeth Haldane provided this translation in a footnote on pp. 7–8 of Haldane, *An Autobiography*, but classical scholars may well find this a rather unsatisfactory rendering of the original Latin which Haldane provides in the main text!

61. These two remarks sum up Haldane's attitude at the time: 'The one thing is to occupy every moment with work': RBH to MEH, 23 Mar. 1881, NLS, MS 5931, f. 112. And: 'For myself there is practically only one way of living: ceaseless employment. I was up at 8 today at work & have arranged to continue this & to keep my hours absolutely full': RBH to MEH, 17 June 1881, NLS, MS 5931, f. 179.

62. RBH to MEH, 24 Feb. 1881, NLS, MS 5931, f. 68.

63. RBH to MEH, 26 Feb. 1881, NLS, MS 5931, f. 72.

64. RBH to MEH, 28 June 1881, NLS, MS 5931, f. 196.

65. RBH to MEH, 13 July 1881, NLS, MS 5932, f. 22.

66. RBH to MEH, 1 Mar. 1881, NLS, MS 5931, ff. 78–9 (the cataloguer has added a note reading: '2 March 1881?' to this letter).

67. See RBH to MEH, 29 Jan. 1889, NLS, MS 5942, ff. 20–1.

68. RBH to MEH, 11 Feb. 1889, NLS, MS 5942, f. 40.

69. See Edward M. Spiers's assessment of Haldane's reaction to the press's attack on him in his *Haldane: An Army Reformer* (Edinburgh: Edinburgh University Press, 1980), pp. 12–20.

70. RBH to MEH, 21 Apr. 1890, NLS, MS 5944, f. 194.

71. Julian of Norwich, *Revelations of Divine Love* (North Chelmsford, MA: Courier Corporation, 2012), p. 49.

72. RBH to MEH, 17 Apr. 1891, NLS, MS 5945, f. 89.

73. RBH to MEH, 13 Mar. 1890, NLS, MS 5944, f. 92.

74. RBH to MEH, 3 May 1892, NLS, MS 5947, ff. 137–8.

75. Haldane describes Sir John Horner thus: 'He was one of the most perfect gentlemen I ever knew, and also a considerable scholar. He had studied under Freeman the historian, with whom he was intimate, and he was himself an accomplished student of history': *An Autobiography*, p. 119. Sir John died in 1927. For details on the life of Raymond Asquith see Jolliffe, *Raymond Asquith*.

76. This description is taken from the back cover of Jane Abdy and Charlotte Gere's *The Souls: An Elite in English Society 1885–1930* (London: Sidgwick & Jackson, 1984).

77. See ibid., chapter 10, entitled 'Sir John and Lady Horner', pp. 126–33; for references to Haldane see pp. 16, 104, 127–8 and 170.

78. See Chapter 7.

79. Evidently a number of great men were intimately attached to her. Both Burne-Jones and Ruskin wrote what appear to be love letters to her, openly calling her 'darling', which is the same language Haldane uses. But the present Earl of Oxford and Asquith tells a story of Burne-Jones's attempting to steal a kiss from her behind a haystack in a field near Mells, which was thoroughly rejected. Was Haldane's expression of love similarly limited by her, one wonders?

80. RBH to FJH, 20 Sept. 1897 and 30 July 1909.

81. The letters suggest that this is a place of special significance for their relationship, and that it may be connected to Frances's fortieth birthday. As the Goethe book is inscribed on the day of Frances's fortieth, it is possible that the photo of the terrace was subsequently pasted into it as a memory of what happened that day.

82. In her memoirs, Frances intriguingly tells the following story: 'One Sunday morning [at Mells Park] he [Haldane] and I had a talk in the library, and when I rejoined Charty Ribblesdale and Daisy White they cross-questioned me eagerly. "Well, what is he like? What have you been talking about?" I said, "He's the most extraordinary person and we've had the most extraordinary conversation." "What about" said they; "Platonic marriage!" said I. This was a daring topic in those days, even for a matron, and they were duly interested': Frances Horner, *Time Remembered* (London: William Heinemann, 1933), p. 146. It is difficult not to ask whether this was a topic prompted by a discussion of Frances's marriage to Jack (Sir John) or of the relationship between Frances and Haldane. We shall never know.

83. 'Goethe, Johann Wolfgang von: To Charlotte Von Stein (An Charlotte von Stein in English)', Babelmatrix.

84. Frances records: 'I think after some years the wound closed, but it shook his confidence for a very long time': Horner, *Time Remembered*, p. 146.

85. RBH to FJH, 13 Sept. 1897.

86. RBH to FJH, 20 Sept. 1897.

87. RBH to FJH, 18 Oct. 1905.

88. RBH to FJH, 23 Nov. 1908.

89. RBH to FJH, 18 Sept. 1917.

90. RBH to FJH, 24 Aug. 1918.

91. RBH to FJH, 1 Jan. 1915.

92. RBH to FJH, 30 Oct. 1905.

93. RBH to FJH, 14 Feb. 1917.

94. RBH to FJH, 20 Dec. 1917.

95. RBH to FJH, 22 Sept. 1923.

96. RBH to FJH, 26 Dec. 1921.

97. 'UK Inflation Calculator', CPI Inflation Calculator. https://www.officialdata.org/ uk/inflation/1928?amount=5000

98. RBH to FJH, 11 Sept. 1897.

99. RBH to FJH, 14 Sept. 1897.

100. RBH to FJH, 30 Oct. 1905.

101. RBH to FJH, 8 Oct. 1908.

102. I found these leather-bound pocket appointment diaries given by Frances to Haldane in a dusty drawer at Cloan; they are now in the NLS, and can be found at Acc 13595, Items 3–18, spanning 1896–1915 (missing 1900/01/06/10).

103. RBH to FJH, 14 Dec. 1908.

104. RBH to FJH, 26 Mar. 1915.

105. RBH to FJH, 28 Mar. 1915.

106. RBH to FJH, 28 Mar. 1915.

107. In his memory, Frances—a passionate patron of the arts, like her father—commissioned the plinth designed by Sir Edwin Lutyens on which is placed the bronze horse and rider sculpture of Edward by Alfred Munnings, now standing in St Andrew's Church, Mells. This plinth, designed between 1920 and 1922, is echoed in the Cenotaph (1920), and stands close to another testimony of her patronage: the pale undecorated peacock memorial in gesso to Laura Lyttelton on the north wall of St Andrew's Church, which she commissioned from Burne-Jones. She also commissioned the stained-glass window by William Nicholson as a memorial to her husband Sir John Horner. In addition, she commissioned Lutyens's magnificent Mells War Memorial, surmounted by St George and the dragon, to those sons of the village who fell during the Great War. She was not the patron, it should be said, of Lutyens's brutalist memorial to the McKenna family in a corner of the Mells churchyard. That was Reginald McKenna.

108. RBH to FJH, 23 Nov. 1917.

109. RBH to FJH, 8 Oct. 1919.

110. RBH to FJH, 22 Sept. 1923.

111. 19 Aug. 1928. I have this manuscript note of ESH in my possession.

112. RBH to FJH, 16 June 1924.

113. Dudley Sommer's notebooks recall that both Lord Schuster and Lord Simon thought that Haldane 'rather liked to appear omniscient'. See NLS, MS 20666, ff. 7–10, conversation with Lord Simon on 2 Oct. 1952 and ff. 10–18, conversation with Lord Schuster on 7 Oct. 1952, quotation at MS 20666, f. 17.
114. Violet Bonham Carter to ESH, 22 Aug. 1928, NLS, MS 6033, ff. 14–15.
115. Lord Arnold to ESH, 21 Aug. 1928, NLS, MS 6032, f. 198.
116. Harold Begbie to ESH, 21 Aug. 1928, NLS, MS 6032, f. 199.
117. J. H. Morgan to ESH, 19 Dec. 1928, NLS, MS 6034, f. 233. In the Gosse Papers at the Brotherton Library in Leeds (BC MS 19c Gosse) there is also a delightful letter from Morley to Haldane that displays Morley's attitude to Haldane. It begins: 'My dear Haldane, You are known better to me than to most people as the kindest of men. So I expected no harsh usage, but your generosity of judgment and real magnanimity go beyond anything that I could look for.' The letter ends: 'It is a thing of which I may well be proud to have won, the rich friendship of one of your calibre. And this has been my good fortune for a long tale of years' (date unknown, but attached to Haldane's letter to Gosse on 26 Nov. 1917).

3. THE COMPANY OF FRIENDS

1. 25 Aug. 1928, NLS, MS 6033, ff. 126–7.
2. The Cloan visitors' book covering the fifty-year span of 1887–1937 still exists and is in the Haldane family's possession. It is a remarkable catalogue of names, but it is interesting to note that politicians feature far less frequently than men of science and letters or military and clerical figures. Sometimes there is the odd surprise, such as the moving messages of gratitude inscribed by wounded Belgian soldiers who first came to stay in a converted ward opposite the stable block in the late autumn of 1914.
3. Markham, *Friendship's Harvest*, p. 51.
4. Niall Ferguson, *The House of Rothschild: The World's Banker 1849–1999* (London: Penguin, 1998), p. 232.
5. Ibid., p. 240.
6. It is a pleasure to record my deep gratitude to Melanie Aspey, director of the Rothschild Archive London, and her staff, who patiently dug out visitors' books, ledgers containing lists of guests (and declinees) at lunches, dinners and other events at Tring, and numerous other letters and papers which have proved most helpful.
7. I am grateful to Jacob Rothschild for giving me this information about the visitors' book in his possession.
8. Haldane, *An Autobiography*, p. 162.
9. Ibid., p. 163.
10. UK Inflation Calculator, CPI Inflation Calculator. https://www.officialdata.org/uk/inflation/1915?amount=25000
11. Rothschild Archive, XI/130A/0/130 10 Jan. 1906.

12. Rothschild Archive, XI/130A/6A/30 9 Feb. 1912.

13. RBH to Lady Rothschild, 29 Aug. 1918, Rothschild Archive, 000/2278/24.

14. Constance Battersea, *Reminiscences* (London: Macmillan & Co., 1922), p. 198.

15. Ibid., pp. 207–8.

16. Quoted in Ferguson, *The House of Rothschild*, p. 22.

17. MEH to RBH, 2 Dec. 1918, NLS, MS 6009, f. 145. For Haldane's description of their friendship see *An Autobiography*, pp. 85–9. See also 'Brown, Peter Hume', *ODNB*.

18. RBH to Gosse, 29 May 1904, Gosse Papers, Brotherton Library, Leeds, BC MS 19c Gosse.

19. It is unclear to which book Haldane is referring.

20. RBH to MEH, 2 Apr. 1899, NLS, MS 5961, f. 64.

21. Haldane, *An Autobiography*, p. 86.

22. RBH to MEH, 1 May 1910, NLS, MS 5983, ff. 119–20. Haldane's confidence in his own abilities as a traveller are somewhat put into question by a story recorded by his nephew Graeme Haldane, who travelled with his uncle to Göttingen as a young man: 'We had been most royally received at the Dutch/German frontier by the Stationmaster. My uncle, wishing to show his appreciation gave the Stationmaster what he thought was a magnificent gift. I realised that the few-thousand mark note which he had presented into the Stationmaster's hand, with an air of great generosity, was worth rather less than a penny. So I hurriedly added a more substantial sum.' R. W. Haldane, *Thomas Graeme Nelson Haldane of Cloan, 1897–1981* (Edinburgh: Clark Constable, 1982), p. 48.

23. Quoted in Haldane, *An Autobiography*, p. 88.

24. RBH to MEH, 27 May 1912, NLS, MS 5987, ff. 208–9.

25. RBH to FJH, 29 Apr. 1919.

26. RBH to Edmund Gosse, 6 Apr. 1920, Gosse Archive, Brotherton Library, Leeds, BC MS 19c Gosse.

27. Haldane, *An Autobiography*, p. 113.

28. The following accounts are taken from ibid., pp. 166–7 (in which Haldane incorrectly records his visit taking place at Holloway Prison, where Wilde had previously been; Pentonville is, however, only a short distance away from where Holloway Prison was located) and Thomas Wright's *Oscar's Books* (London: Chatto & Windus, 2008), pp. 243–5, 249–51, 258, 299 and 319.

29. Haldane, *An Autobiography*, p. 166. Thomas Wright claims Haldane visited on 12 June, but Haldane's letter to his mother on 14 June confirms it was otherwise.

30. Wright, *Oscar's Books*, p. 243.

31. Haldane, *An Autobiography*, p. 167.

32. A full list of the titles can be found at p. 319 of Wright, *Oscar's Books*.

33. RBH to MEH, 20 Aug. 1895, NLS, MS 5954, f. 74.

34. Ibid., p. 249.

35. Ibid., p. 250.

36. Haldane, *An Autobiography*, p. 167.

37. Wright, *Oscar's Books*, p. 299.

38. Throughout the visit Haldane's nephew, Graeme Haldane (who, like his uncle, spoke German), acted as Einstein's guide. Einstein presented his book *Relativity: The Special and General Theory* (London: Methuen, 1920) to him with the inscription: 'Graeme Haldane, Albert Einstein, zum Andenken an unsere Begegnung in London im Juni 1921' ('In memory of our meeting in London in June 1921'). This book is now in the Haldane family's possession.

39. Quoted in Andrew Robinson, *Einstein on the Run: How Britain Saved the World's Greatest Scientist* (New Haven and London: Yale University Press, 2019), p. 76. Arthur Eddington, the distinguished Plumian Professor of Astronomy at Cambridge, who was also present—and whose measurements of the influence of gravitation on light on 29 May 1919 had famously confirmed Einstein's law of gravity—later noted of the remark to the archbishop that 'I can well understand him hastily shearing off the subject. … [I]n those days one had to become an expert in dodging persons who mixed up the fourth dimension with spiritualism. But surely the answer need not be preserved as though it were one of Einstein's more perspicacious utterances. The non-sequitur is obvious.' Quoted in Ronald Clark, *Einstein: The Life and Times* (New York: World Publishing Company, 1971), p. 276.

40. Clark, *Einstein: The Life and Times*, p. 337.

41. Walter Isaacson, *Einstein: His Life and Universe* (London: Pocket Books, 2008), p. 279.

42. Quoted in Sommer, *Haldane of Cloan*, p. 381.

43. *Nation & Athenaeum*, 18 June 1921, p. 431, quoted in Robinson, *Einstein on the Run*, pp. 78–81.

44. Horner, *Time Remembered*, p. 150.

45. Robinson, *Einstein on the Run*, pp. 78–81.

46. Quoted in Sommer, *Haldane of Cloan*, p. 382.

47. Quoted in ibid.

48. For details of Lindemann's life see Adrian Fort, *Prof: The Life of Frederick Lindemann* (London: Jonathan Cape, 2003).

49. Quoted in Robinson, *Einstein on the Run*, p. 82.

50. RBH to Einstein, 26 June 1921, in Diana K. Buchwald, Ze'ev Rosenkranz, Tilman Sauer, József Illy and Virginia Iris Holmes (eds), *The Collected Papers of Albert Einstein, Volume 12: The Berlin Years: Correspondence January–December 1921* (Princeton: Princeton University Press, 2009), p. 201.

51. See Diana K. Buchwald, József Illy, Ze'ev Rosenkranz and Tilman Sauer (eds), *The Collected Papers of Albert Einstein, Volume 13: The Berlin Years: Writings & Correspondence January 1922–March 1923* (Princeton: Princeton University Press, 2012), p. 481 n.1.

52. Einstein to RBH, 30 Aug. 1922, in Diana K. Buchwald, József Illy, Ze'ev Rosenkranz and Tilman Sauer (eds), *The Collected Papers of Albert Einstein, Volume 13: The Berlin Years: Writings & Correspondence January 1922–March 1923* (English translation supple-

ment), trans. Ann M. Hentschel and Osik Moses (Princeton: Princeton University Press, 2012), p. 266.

53. RBH to Einstein, undated letter from Cloan, NLS, MS 20260, f. 147, translated by my collaborator, Richard McLauchlan, as the letter is not included in *The Collected Papers of Albert Einstein*.

54. See RBH to Einstein, 23 Oct. 1922, in Buchwald et al. (eds), *The Collected Papers of Albert Einstein, Volume 13*, p. 591, and n. 2.

55. Gosse's biographer, Ann Thwaite, writing in the *Oxford Dictionary of National Biography*, states her belief that from the time of his appointment, Gosse's 'closest friend, now and until the end of his life, was Lord Haldane': 'Gosse, Sir Edmund William', *ODNB*.

56. Ann Thwaite, *Edmund Gosse: A Literary Landscape* (London: Secker & Warburg, 1984), p. 459.

57. 'Gosse, Sir Edmund William', *ODNB*.

58. Ibid.

59. RBH to Gosse, 17 June 1903, Gosse Archive, Brotherton Library, Leeds, BC MS 19c Gosse.

60. RBH to Gosse, 11 Nov. 1907, Gosse Archive, Brotherton Library, Leeds, BC MS 19c Gosse.

61. RBH to Gosse, 14 May 1919, Gosse Archive, Brotherton Library, Leeds, BC MS 19c Gosse.

62. Gosse Archive, Brotherton Library, Leeds, BC Gosse correspondence, Typescript, Slip-case lettered: MSS of AMERICAN ADDRESS. Gen, q, HAL.

63. A. C. Benson, quoted in Thwaite, *Edmund Gosse*, p. 453.

64. RBH to Gosse, 18 Aug. 1916, Gosse Archive, Brotherton Library, Leeds, BC MS 19c Gosse.

65. RBH to Gosse, 28 Nov. 1916, Gosse Archive, Brotherton Library, Leeds, BC MS 19c Gosse.

66. RBH to Gosse, 6 Dec. 1916, Gosse Archive, Brotherton Library, Leeds, BC MS 19c Gosse.

67. RBH to Gosse, 23 Aug. 1925, Gosse Archive, Brotherton Library, Leeds, BC MS 19c Gosse.

68. Thwaite, *Edmund Gosse*, p. 424.

69. RBH to Gosse, 3 Oct. 1908, Gosse Archive, Brotherton Library, Leeds, BC MS 19c Gosse.

70. RBH to Gosse, 19 June 1914, Gosse Archive, Brotherton Library, Leeds, BC MS 19c Gosse.

71. RBH to Gosse, 29 July 1914, Gosse Archive, Brotherton Library, Leeds, BC MS 19c Gosse.

72. Evan Charteris, *The Life and Letters of Sir Edmund Gosse* (London: William Heinemann, 1931), p. 367.

73. For details of the story see Thwaite, *Edmund Gosse*, p. 457.

74. Charteris, *Life and Letters*, p. 369.

75. Gosse to the editor of the *Morning Post*, 9 Jan. 1915, Gosse Archive, Brotherton Library, Leeds, BC MS 19c Gosse.

76. RBH to Gosse, 9 Jan. 1915, Gosse Archive, Brotherton Library, Leeds, BC MS 19c Gosse.

77. Thwaite, *Edmund Gosse*, p. 459.

78. Haldane, *An Autobiography*, p. 83.

79. Roy Jenkins, *Asquith* (London: Collins, 1964), p. 34.

80. RBH to MEH, 3 July 1899, NLS, MS 5962, f. 3.

81. Herbert Asquith, *Moments of Memory: Recollections and Impressions* (London: Hutchinson, 1937), pp. 13–14.

82. Haldane, *An Autobiography*, p. 103. Helen was the mother of Asquith's first five children, the eldest of whom was Raymond, whose pen portrait of Haldane opened the Introduction.

83. RBH to MEH, 10 Mar. 1917, NLS, MS 5997, ff. 88–9.

84. Haldane, *An Autobiography*, p. 101.

85. See Jenkins, *Asquith*, p. 29.

86. The Cloan visitors' book first records Asquith staying in October 1887. Asquith and Grey both stayed on the same occasion in September 1889, and their names and those of their families thereafter appear regularly. The last date on which Asquith is recorded as staying at Cloan is in October 1913, but his daughter Violet Bonham Carter came occasionally until 1923. Grey came regularly until 1922 and then returned in 1932, four years after Haldane's death, to visit Haldane's sister, Elizabeth.

87. 30 Oct. 1890, NLS, MS 6010, f. 77.

88. The book to which she is referring is W. H. Hudson's *Idle Days in Patagonia* (London: Chapman & Hall, 1893). *The London Times*, in its obituary of Hudson in 1922, considered him 'unsurpassed as an English writer on nature': 'The Naturalist who Inspired Ernest Hemingway and Many Others to Love the Wilderness', *Smithsonian*.

89. G. M. Trevelyan, *Grey of Fallodon* (London, New York, Toronto: Longmans, Green & Co., 1937), pp. 56–7.

90. Ibid., pp. 57–8.

91. Ibid., p. 58.

92. Ibid., pp. 146–7.

93. RBH to ESH, 4 Feb. 1906, NLS, MS 6011, ff. 24–5.

94. RBH to ESH, 16 Feb. 1906, NLS, MS 5975, ff. 69–70.

95. Letter to Katharine Lyttelton, quoted in Keith Robbins, *Sir Edward Grey* (London: Cassell, 1971), p. 154.

96. J. A. Spender and Cyril Asquith, *Life of Herbert Henry Asquith, Lord Oxford and Asquith*, vol. 2 (London: Hutchinson & Co., 1932), p. 167.

97. Oxford, Bodleian Library, MS. Eng. d. 3271, ff. 55–6.

98. FJH to ESH, 25 Aug. 1925, NLS, MS 6033, f. 141.

4. A PHILOSOPHY FOR LIFE

1. Edward Grey, Charles Harris, Frank Heath and Claud Schuster, *Viscount Haldane of Cloan: The Man and his Work* (London: Humphrey Milford/Oxford University Press, 1928), p. 3.
2. Stephen Hawking and Leonard Mlodinow, *The Grand Design: New Answers to the Ultimate Questions of Life* (London: Bantam, 2010), p. 13.
3. Matthew Arnold's words, quoted by Haldane in *The Pathway to Reality: Stage the First*, p. 102.
4. John Cornwell, 'The Grand Design: New Answers to the Ultimate Questions of Life by Stephen Hawking: Review', *Daily Telegraph*, 20 Sept. 2010.
5. Haldane, *An Autobiography*, p. 11.
6. Ibid.
7. Ibid., p. 13.
8. R. B. Haldane, 'The Soul of a People', in *Universities and National Life* (London: John Murray, 1910), p. 29.
9. See Johann Gottlieb Fichte, *The Vocation of Man*, trans. Peter Preuss (Indianapolis: Hackett, 1987), p. 75.
10. Ibid., p. 83.
11. Johann Gottlieb Fichte, *Fichte: Early Philosophical Writings*, trans. Daniel Breazeale (Ithaca: Cornell University Press, 1988), p. 172.
12. Ibid., p. 162.
13. Stewart Candlish has outlined a further four factors unconnected to actual philosophical argument: Russell's feelings about the beauty of mathematics and his loathing of metaphysics; idealism's 'vague, windy, and moralizing rhetoric' and the way its style soon became dated; the fading of the need for philosophy to act as a substitute for religion; and the decline of British imperialism, many of whose leading proponents were idealists. See the final chapter of Candlish's *The Russell–Bradley Dispute and its Significance for Twentieth-Century Philosophy* (Basingstoke and New York: Palgrave Macmillan, 2007), pp. 174–88. My thanks to Andrew Vincent, honorary professor in the School of Law and Politics at Cardiff University, for drawing my attention to Candlish's work.
14. Hence the antagonism that exists between the 'continental' and 'analytical' schools of philosophy.
15. Ryle is quoted by Ray Monk in 'The Man who Wasn't There', *Prospect Magazine*, Oct. 2019, p. 59, a piece on the philosopher R. G. Collingwood.
16. R. G. Collingwood, *An Autobiography* (Oxford: Clarendon Press, 1938), pp. 48–9. I am most grateful to Professor William Twining for enthusiastically recommending this autobiography to me. In his own autobiography, Twining refers to Collingwood's book as 'the most seminal book' in his intellectual development. See William Twining, *Jurist in Context: A Memoir* (Cambridge: Cambridge University Press, 2019), p. 23.
17. It is worth noting that Lotze does not appear to have directed Haldane towards Hegel. Given Haldane's own passion for Hegel (explored later in this chapter),

375

Andrew Vincent notes: 'With hindsight, it is … puzzling that Lotze—a leading figure in the neo-Kantian revival and the opposition to Hegel—remained a central influence on Haldane throughout his life': Andrew Vincent, 'German Philosophy and British Public Policy: Richard Burdon Haldane in Theory and Practice', *Journal of the History of Ideas*, 68, 1 (Jan. 2007), p. 161.

18. Haldane, *An Autobiography*, pp. 17–18.

19. Ibid., p. 18.

20. Ibid.

21. The volume in which this appears is now in my possession.

22. 'For myself, though I owe more than I can say to Green's gymnastics, both intellectual and moral, I never "worshipped at the Temple's inner shrine"': The Earl of Oxford and Asquith, KG, *Memories and Reflections*, vol. 1 (London: Cassell & Co., 1928), p. 19.

23. Seth and Haldane (eds), *Essays in Philosophical Criticism*. Green had died the year before, on 15 March 1882.

24. See Geoffrey Price, 'Science, Idealism and Higher Education in England: Arnold, Green and Haldane', *Studies in Higher Education*, 11, 1 (1986).

25. W. Caldwell, '*The Pathway to Reality* by Richard Burdon Haldane', *The Philosophical Review*, 13, 1 (Jan. 1904), p. 52. Commenting on the same volume, H. Rashdall wrote: 'Whatever view may be taken of his conclusions, there can be no question that he has given us a piece of solid and profound metaphysical thinking. Both from a metaphysical and a literary point of view, this is an extremely brilliant exposition of Hegelianism pure and simple—Hegelianism not of the right or of the left, but of the centre': '*The Pathway to Reality*. Being the Gifford Lectures Delivered in the University of St Andrews in the Session 1902–3. By Richard Burdon Haldane', *Mind*, NS, 12, 48 (Oct. 1903), p. 527. On the other side, F. Melian Stawell viewed the lectures in a different light: 'His [Haldane's] range of reading is extraordinarily wide, his sympathies many-sided, his command of expression remarkable, and his admiration for the great builders unfeigned. But too often the plain man, instead of realizing the principles of construction, will receive the impression of being whisked upstairs and downstairs with doors opened and shut in his face, until he would find it hard to say where a single passage led or what was the size of any room': '*The Pathway to Reality*. Being the Gifford Lectures Delivered in the University of St Andrews in the Session 1902–3. By Richard Burdon Haldane', *International Journal of Ethics*, 14, 2 (Jan. 1904), p. 254.

26. See J. H. Muirhead's assessment of Haldane in his *John Henry Muirhead: Reflections by a Journeyman in Philosophy* (London: George Allen & Unwin, 1942), p. 146.

27. Arthur Schopenhauer, *The World as Will and Idea*, trans. R. B. Haldane and John Kemp (London: Kegan Paul, Trench and Trübner & Co., 1883–6). This was a mammoth undertaking, accomplished across many late evenings. The following report to his mother is characteristic: 'J.K. & I had been at work upon our translation of Schopenhauer half the night and I did not get to bed until nearly 3. One has only the night time in which to do this work': 23 Feb. 1882, NLS, MS 5933, f. 76.

28. Haldane, *Pathway to Reality: Stage the First*, p. 312.

29. Haldane, *An Autobiography*, p. 16.

30. See Haldane, *The Pathway to Reality: Stage the First*, pp. 14–15 and 308; and R. B. Haldane, *Human Experience: A Study of its Structure* (New York: E. P. Dutton & Co., 1926), pp. 230–1.

31. Gardiner, *Prophets, Priests, & Kings*, p. 283.

32. 'I think that the greatest lesson that it [philosophy] can yield to-day is that the relativity of knowledge has among its consequences this, that all forms of knowledge are reconcilable if construed as aspects within one entirety': R. B. Haldane, *The Reign of Relativity* (London: John Murray, 1921), p. 413.

33. Hawking and Mlodinow, *The Grand Design*, pp. 61–2.

34. See Haldane, *The Pathway to Reality: Stage the First*, pp. 118–19.

35. See Haldane, *The Reign of Relativity*, esp. pp. 93 and 406; R. B. Haldane, *The Philosophy of Humanism and of Other Subjects* (London: John Murray, 1922), p. 47.

36. Haldane, *The Pathway to Reality: Stage the First*, pp. 8–9.

37. R. B. Haldane, 'The Doctrine of Degrees in Knowledge, Truth, and Reality' (London: Published for the British Academy by Humphrey Milford, Oxford University Press, 1919), p. 6. Haldane was elected a Fellow of the British Academy in 1914.

38. Esher Papers, ii. 267, quoted in A. J. Anthony Morris, 'Haldane's Army Reforms 1906–8: The Deception of the Radicals', *History*, 56, 186 (Feb. 1971), p. 24.

39. Markham, *Friendship's Harvest*, p. 56.

40. A. Seth Pringle-Pattison, 'Richard Burdon Haldane' (London: Published for the British Academy by Humphrey Milford, Oxford University Press, 1928), p. 33.

41. A helpful summary in more technical language can be found in Vincent, 'German Philosophy and British Public Policy', pp. 162–5.

42. An obvious question to ask is: what about the minds of animals? Haldane, that great dog lover, was particularly sensitive to this question and enjoyed pointing out the way in which dogs (it's not surprising they were always his go-to example) represent a different stage in the development of mind. He writes: 'The human self-consciousness is only an aspect, a stage, a plane, a degree in Reality. The dog and the angel disclose other degrees of the logical evolution of the categories of mind': R. B. Haldane, *The Pathway to Reality: Stage the First*, p. 129. See also Haldane's *Mind and Reality*, Affirmations series, part of God in the Modern World series (London: Ernest Benn Limited, 1928), p. 5. As an aside, the following observation from Haldane is particularly amusing: 'No one who has been in affectionate relations with a devoted dog can have failed to notice how his attitude to his master becomes one of regarding that master as a being of a superior order, to whom at time he accords something like reverence. There is here some analogy to nascent religion': Haldane, *Human Experience*, p. 138.

43. 'Das Geistige allein ist das Wirkliche', from section 24 of the *Phänomenologie des Geistes*. Haldane also had the words 'Dem Begriff nach, einmal ist allemal' carved into the fireplace of his study at Cloan. Literally translated it means 'According to

the Concept, once is always'. This is an adaption of two similar sentences in Hegel's lectures on the philosophy of religion. It captures the idea that the mind comprehends the universal in the particular through the use of reason.

44. See Haldane, 'The Doctrine of Degrees', pp. 31–2.

45. Ibid., p. 32.

46. Haldane, *The Philosophy of Humanism*, p. 22.

47. Edwards Spiers critically comments: 'Haldane, after five years in office, several severe eye infections, and the contraction of diabetes through over-work, was no longer the minister he had formerly been': Spiers, *Haldane*, p. 156.

48. R. B. Haldane, *The Conduct of Life* (London: John Murray, 1914), p. 20. Andrew Vincent acknowledges Haldane's debt to the thinking of the great F. H. Bradley, who makes a very similar point in his 'My Station and its Duties' in *Ethical Studies* (Oxford: Clarendon Press, 1876). See Vincent, 'German Philosophy and British Public Policy', p. 164.

49. Haldane, *An Autobiography*, p. 326.

50. Ibid., p. 184.

51. For a fuller analysis of how Haldane's philosophy shaped his army reforms see Vincent, 'German Philosophy and British Public Policy', pp. 167–70.

52. Jean-Jacques Rousseau, *The Social Contract*, trans. G. D. H. Cole (London: Everyman, 1913), p. 12.

53. See Bernard Bosanquet, *The Philosophical Theory of the State* (London: Macmillan, 1920), p. 221.

54. *Philosophy of Right* §260, quoted in Z. A. Pelczynski, 'Political Community and Individual Freedom in Hegel's Philosophy of the State', in Z. A. Pelczynski (ed.), *The State and Civil Society: Studies in Hegel's Political Philosophy* (Cambridge: Cambridge University Press, 1984), pp. 61–2; see also Andrew Vincent's comments in his *Theories of the State* (Oxford: Blackwell, 1987), p. 121: 'The individual [according to an early essay of Hegel] cannot be truly free in an indeterminate negative sense. Humans develop in the context of rules and customs and only the strong State has the flexibility and sensitivity to allow maximal play to human freedom.'

55. R. B. Haldane, 'The Future of Democracy' (London: Headley Bros., 1918), p. 21.

56. David Boucher and Andrew Vincent, *A Radical Hegelian: The Political and Social Philosophy of Henry Jones* (New York: St Martin's Press, 1994), pp. 96–7.

57. Haldane, 'Higher Nationality', in *Selected Addresses and Essays*, p. 79.

58. Ibid.

59. Ibid.

60. 'The ideal may be very high, or it may be of so ordinary a kind that we are not conscious of it without the effort of reflection': Haldane, 'Higher Nationality', p. 81.

61. Haldane, *The Reign of Relativity*, p. 368. The chapter on the state within *The Reign of Relativity* (pp. 367–81) represents Haldane's fully worked out thinking on the relationship between the individual and the state. For his thinking in less fleshed out form see R. B. Haldane, 'The Nature of the State', *Contemporary Review*, 117 (1920), p. 761.

62. R. B. Haldane, 'The New Liberalism', *Progressive Review*, 1, 2 (Nov. 1896), p. 133.

63. Haldane, *The Reign of Relativity*, p. 371; Sidney Webb was critical of Haldane on this point, writing to him in June 1921, on receiving *The Reign of Relativity*: 'I observe that Ministers to whom one could safely trust such an interpretation must be, not merely honest and candid, but also singularly free from innate or acquired prejudices, prepossessions and particularities; and (what is even more important) ought to be required to live in a social environment which did not bias them powerfully, even if unconsciously, in a direction different from that in which the general will was pressing. In short, no Ministry that I have ever known could be safely trusted to make correctly so delicate an interpretation': Sidney Webb to RBH, 13 June 1921, NLS, MS 5915, ff. 51–4.

64. See Haldane, *The Reign of Relativity*, p. 376.

65. *Philosophy of Right* § 265, quoted in Shlomo Avineri, *Hegel's Theory of the Modern State* (Cambridge: Cambridge University Press, 1972), p. 167.

66. See Vincent, *Theories of the State*, p. 121.

67. See *Philosophy of Right* § 290, quoted in Avineri, *Hegel's Theory of the Modern State*, p. 168.

68. See Harold Laski, *A Grammar of Politics* (London: George Allen & Unwin, 1925), pp. 54–5 and 68; Michael Newman, *Harold Laski: A Political Biography* (London: Merlin Press, 2009), p. 45; L. T. Hobhouse, *A Metaphysical Theory of the State* (London: George Allen & Unwin, 1951), pp. 82–3; P. Q. Hirst (ed.), *The Pluralist Theory of the State: Selected Writings of G. D. H. Cole, J. N. Figgis, and H. J. Laski* (London: Routledge, 1989), pp. 2 and 25.

69. See Newman, *Harold Laski*, p. 39.

70. See Chapter 10. For a good discussion of their relationship, and Follett's relationship with Elizabeth Haldane (which, on Follett's side at least, may have even had romantic overtones) see Joan C. Tonn's *Mary P. Follett: Creating Democracy, Transforming Management* (New Haven and London: Yale University Press, 2003), pp. 321–2, 377, 422–3, 436 and 455.

71. Mary Follett, *The New State: Group Organization the Solution of Popular Government* (New York: Longmans, Green & Co., third impression, 1920), pp. vii–viii.

72. Ibid., p. xii.

73. See ibid., p. 306.

74. See ibid., p. 69.

75. Critiquing the idealist notion of a General Will, L. T. Hobhouse observes: 'We come back again to the central point that the institutions of society are not the outcome of a unitary will but of the clash of wills, in which the selfishness and generally the bad in human nature is constantly operative, intermingled with but not always overcome by the better elements': Hobhouse, *A Metaphysical Theory of the State*, p. 83.

76. Seven years before the publication of *The New State*, we find Haldane foreshadowing Follett's rhetoric: 'They [citizens] cannot mark off or define their own individualities without reference to the individuality of others. And so they unconsciously find

themselves as in truth pulse-beats of the whole system, and themselves the whole system': Haldane, 'Higher Nationality', p. 76.

77. R. B. Haldane, 'The Liberal Creed', *Contemporary Review*, 54 (Oct. 1888), p. 465.

78. Haldane, *Human Experience*, p. 151.

79. Haldane, *The Pathway to Reality: Stage the First*, pp. 18–19.

80. Haldane, *The Pathway to Reality: Stage the First*, pp. 75–6.

81. Violet Bonham Carter, 'Haldane of Cloan: Scottish Lawyer who Shaped the British Army', *The Times*, 30 July 1956.

82. R. B. Haldane, *The Pathway to Reality: Stage the Second* (London: John Murray, 1904), p. 221.

83. Haldane writes in *The Sunday Times* in December 1922: 'We have emancipated women from the disabilities of their sex, but we have not emancipated the vast numbers in society generally who are, in point of status, unfree in a yet deeper sense, inasmuch as the conditions of mental freedom have not yet been put by the State within their reach': quoted in Frederick Maurice, *Haldane 1915–1928: The Life of Viscount Haldane of Cloan K.T., O.M.* (London: Faber & Faber, 1939), p. 138.

84. 'The function of education is not to create the higher attitudes of the soul, but only to render them more readily attainable. The good man may not be educated. The educated man may not be good. But education does render it easier for the mind to emancipate itself to higher levels': Haldane, *Human Experience*, p. 138.

85. Stephen E. Koss, *Lord Haldane: Scapegoat for Liberalism* (New York: Columbia University Press, 1969), p. 7.

86. Grey refines his views further: 'We speak of philosophy giving support; I am not satisfied this is the right way to express the truth about Haldane. It would perhaps be more true to say that it was his own innate strength that overcame the trials of life, and that his intellect found in philosophical conceptions and language a means of expressing the methods by which his nature conquered adversity': Grey et al., *Viscount Haldane of Cloan*, p. 3.

87. RBH to MEH, 9 July 1890, NLS, MS 5944, f. 209.

5. WEALTH AND THE NATION

1. Follett, *The New State*, p. xvi.

2. Haldane tended to view the death of his brother Geordie, aged sixteen, in this light, writing on 30 June 1912 to his mother: 'His was a beautiful life & one cannot regret that it closed early if to close early was to close so perfectly': NLS, MS 5988, ff. 45–6.

3. Published only a year earlier in 1873, although Mill was born in 1806. His treatise on *The Principles of Political Economy* was published 1848, *On Liberty* 1851 and *Utilitarianism* 1861.

4. RBH to John Burdon Sanderson, 24 Mar. 1874, NLS, MS 5901, ff. 10–12.

5. Haldane, 'The Liberal Creed', p. 467.

6. Ibid. See also his letter to a Göttingen friend upon his return to Scotland after his

time studying in Germany: 'I actually dislike my own country now. The people seem to think of nothing but how to make money and never how to attain to a high culture': quoted in Eric Ashby and Mary Anderson, *Portrait of Haldane at Work on Education* (London: Macmillan, 1974), p. 9.

7. J. B. Balfour, like Haldane, had been educated at the Edinburgh Academy and Edinburgh University. An advocate, he was elected Liberal MP for Clackmannan and Kinross; he became Lord Advocate in 1881, Privy Counsellor in 1882, and was appointed Lord Justice General of Scotland and Lord President of the Court of Session in 1899. In 1902 he entered the peerage as Baron Kinross of Glascune in the County of Haddingtonshire, Haldane's own constituency. Balfour died on 22 January 1905.

8. It is unclear whether he was unsuccessful or whether he turned down the lectureship.

9. On Sidgwick see RBH to Jane Burdon Sanderson, 22 Apr. 1883, NLS, MS 5902, f. 67. My thanks to Andrew Chapman for alerting me to the work of Henry George, and the correlations between George's thesis and Haldane's policy proposals. Although we have no *direct* evidence of Haldane engaging with the work of George, we do know that his brother, John, was influenced by George, thus increasing the likelihood of Haldane's knowledge of him even further. See Ian W. Archer (ed.), *Transactions of the Royal Historical Society: Volume 21: Sixth Series* (Cambridge: Cambridge University Press, 2012), p. 182.

10. RBH to Jane Burdon Sanderson, 13 Oct. 1884, NLS, MS 5902, f. 130.

11. G. R. Searle, *A New England? Peace and War, 1886–1918* (Oxford: Clarendon Press, 2005), p. 172.

12. Maurice, *Haldane 1856–1915*, p. 44.

13. Asquith, *Moments of Memory*, p. 50.

14. See Thomas Carlyle, *On Heroes, Hero-Worship and the Heroic in History* (London: Chapman & Hall, 1840). Carlyle's photograph stood in a triptych frame on Haldane's desk in Cloan, alongside photographs of Balfour and Gladstone, suggesting that Carlyle was also a hero of Haldane's.

15. Quoted in R. B. Haldane, *Life of Adam Smith* (London: Walter Scott, 1887), p. 34. Haldane also, we should note, loved Hume, and a portrait engraving of him, which I now possess, hung as an inspiration in his study.

16. Quoted in ibid., p. 74.

17. Ibid., p. 12.

18. Ibid.

19. Ibid.

20. Ibid., p. 77.

21. Ibid. p. 78.

22. Ibid., p. 95.

23. John Morley, *Notes on Politics and History* (London: Macmillan, 1914), p. 58.

24. 'Income Tax', *House of Commons Debates*, 21 April 1902, vol. 106, col. 828.

25. Haldane, *Life of Adam Smith*, p. 124.

26. See ibid., p. 133. It is hard to imagine Adam Smith making the following comment: 'I think there has been a remarkable development in what I may call the collectivist idea—it is not a very elegant, but it is the shortest, phrase I can find; I mean the desire that where it is possible the profits of industry, so far as they arise from the advantages of civilization and of the community, should be obtained for the community which has directly or indirectly created them, and should not be exploited by individuals: I mean the desire to vindicate the claims of labour to a larger share in the produce of industry as against capital': 'Social Problems: Speech by R. B. Haldane, Q.C., M.P. at Cambridge, on Saturday, May 30th, 1891', *Earl Grey Pamphlets Collection* (1891), p. 15.

27. Haldane, *Life of Adam Smith*, p. 133.

28. Ibid., pp. 133–4.

29. Ibid., p. 143.

30. The Bill was also sponsored by Grey, Acland, Ferguson and Buxton. Sidney Webb assisted in its drafting. See H. C. G. Matthew, *The Liberal Imperialists: The Ideas and Politics of a Post-Gladstonian Élite* (Oxford: Oxford University Press, 1973), p. 10.

31. Ibid.

32. R. B. Haldane, 'The Unearned Increment' (London: Eighty Club, 1892), p. 6.

33. Matthew, *The Liberal Imperialists*, pp. 10 and 242. It is interesting to note that the Royal Commission on Housing of 1884 had already complained that 'Landowners … profited by development to which they had contributed nothing at all': Maurice Bruce, *The Coming of the Welfare State* (London: B. T. Batsford Ltd, 1968), p. 211.

34. Haldane, 'The Unearned Increment', p. 4.

35. Ibid., p. 8.

36. In 1891 Haldane stated: 'But what we have to consider, and the only question to my mind, is, how are we best to promote the interests of the community, which of these ways is the best means for the realization of those collectivist ideas which have been in the air, and putting capital and labour on something more like a footing of equality, than is the case at the present time': 'Social Problems', p. 27.

37. Haldane, 'The Unearned Increment', p. 3.

38. Ibid., pp. 7–8.

39. Reinforcing this point, Haldane states: 'If what we value most in man were the qualities which enable the greatest wealth to be accumulated, the doctrine of contribution and State interference for the common good would be a mistake from beginning to end, and we should have simply to provide the best conditions for the operation of the Darwinian process of survival of the fittest to produce and accumulate. But so long as we recognize not only that there are moral ideals which are not being measured by material standards, but that man is something else than a wealth-producing animal, so long shall we who are Liberals continue to decline to bow ourselves down in the temple where Mr Herbert Spencer and Lord Bramwell worship': 'The Liberal Creed', p. 467.

40. A. S. Thompson, 'Tariff Reform: An Imperial Strategy, 1903–1913', *Historical Journal*, 40, 4 (1997), p. 1035.

41. R. B. Haldane, 'A Leap into the Unknown', speech delivered at East Linton, Haddingtonshire, 2 June 1903, published in *Army Reform and Other Addresses* (London: T. Fisher Unwin, 1907), p. 163.

42. Searle, *A New England?*, p. 336.

43. See ibid., p. 341.

44. Percy Ashley, *Modern Tariff History* (London: John Murray, 1904), pp. vii–viii.

45. Ibid., pp. viii–xiii.

46. RBH to MEH, 9 Dec. 1901, NLS, MS 5966, f. 177.

47. Ashley, *Modern Tariff History*, p. ix.

48. Author's Note to ibid.

49. Ibid., p. xiv.

50. Ibid., p. xvi.

51. Ibid., pp. xiv–xx.

52. Ibid., pp. xxi–xxii. There are other publications and speeches, printed or made before Ashley's book, in which Haldane gives further reasons why he regarded Chamberlain's scheme as a menace rather than a helpmate. See in particular the three speeches in the Fiscal Policy section of his *Army Reform and Other Addresses*, pp. 159–255.

53. R. H. Tawney, 'The Abolition of Economic Controls, 1918–1921', *Economic History Review*, 13, 1/2 (1943), p. 1.

54. Arthur Marwick, *The Deluge: British Society and the First World War* (London: Bodley Head, 1965), p. 228.

55. Ibid., pp. 228–9.

56. *Parliamentary Papers*, 1916, VIII, Cd. 8336, p. 8, quoted in Marwick, *The Deluge*, p. 229.

57. Marwick, *The Deluge*, p. 231.

58. See Chapter 8.

59. Roy Herbert, 'History of the DSIR: A Review of Sir Harry Melville's *The Department of Scientific and Industrial Research* (London: George Allen & Unwin, 1962)', *New Scientist*, 278 (15 Mar. 1962), p. 644. See also H. F. Heath and A. L. Hetherington, *Industrial Research and Development in the United Kingdom: A Survey* (London: Faber & Faber, 1946).

60. Marwick, *The Deluge*, p. 277.

61. Ibid.

62. Ibid.

63. Ibid., p. 278.

64. R. B. Haldane, 'The Problem of Nationalization' (London: George Allen & Unwin Ltd, 1921).

65. Ibid., pp. 3–4.

66. Isaac Kramnick and Barry Sheerman, *Harold Laski: A Life on the Left* (London: Hamish Hamilton, 1993), p. 145.

67. See David Schneiderman, 'Harold Laski, Viscount Haldane, and the Law of the Canadian Constitution in the Early Twentieth Century', *University of Toronto Law Journal*, 48, 4 (Autumn 1998); see also Chapters 4 and 10.

68. For a good overview of their relationship, and the figures Laski met through Haldane, see Kramnick and Sheerman, *Harold Laski*, pp. 162–4. For Laski's first-hand accounts of his encounters with Haldane see the many references to Haldane throughout the following: Oliver Wendell Holmes and Harold Joseph Laski, *Holmes–Laski Letters:The Correspondence of Mr Justice Holmes and Harold J. Laski, 1916–1935*, vol. 1 (Cambridge, MA: Harvard University Press, 1953).

69. Wendell Holmes and Laski, *Holmes–Laski Letters*, p. 257.

70. Haldane, 'The Problem of Nationalization', p. 4.

71. Ibid.

72. Ibid., p. 5.

73. Ibid., p. 15.

74. Ibid., p. 18. See also Chapter 9.

75. R. B. Haldane, 'The Problem of Nationalization', p. 20.

76. Ibid., p. 26.

77. Ibid., p. 23.

78. Ibid., p. 34.

79. Ibid., p. 35.

80. Ibid., p. 37.

81. Ibid.

82. Ibid., pp. 43–4.

83. Established as the British Economic Association in 1890, it became the Royal Economic Society upon receiving its royal charter in 1902.

84. For many years I considered myself unfortunate to have read Economics at Cambridge in the late 1960s at a time when Keynes's theories were still a cornerstone of the practice of political economy. The monetarism of Friedman was shortly to burst upon the scene and to play its diverting role for over thirty years until the recession of the first decade of the 2000s resurrected the relevance of Keynesianism. My undergraduate years were the years of influence of such professors as Lords Balogh and Kaldor, but Joan and Austin Robinson and others kept the Keynesian flag flying. It was many years later that I discovered that the austere Chinese-clothed Joan was the daughter of Major General Sir Frederick Maurice whose two-volume *Life of Viscount Haldane of Cloan* of 1937–9 was to become like a bible to me. My inadequacy in economics was a deterrent to engagement in discussion with Professor Robinson, but how I wish that I could have talked with her about her father and his love of Haldane.

85. On Keynes's resignation in June 1945 from the editorship after thirty-four years, the council of the RES dined him out at Brown's Hotel in Albemarle Street. He is reported to have given a scintillating speech which included sketches of the famous men who were members of the council when he took on the additional role of editor. He first mentioned Haldane, although his insights on our man were regrettably

not recorded in the report of the dinner in the *Journal*. But that report does capture Keynes describing Balfour as 'the most extraordinary *objet d'art* that ever embellished statesmanship' before proceeding to reminisce about other council members, naming Leonard Courtney, who had been secretary to John Stuart Mill, Alfred Marshall, the only professional economist among the vice-presidents, John Morley, Milner, Charles Booth and Sidney Webb. I have also always loved the idiosyncratic tribute he paid in that speech to Francis Ysidro Edgeworth, the founding editor of the *Journal*, who stayed on as Keynes's joint editor until his death in 1926, for whom he recalled Marshall's dictum, 'You will find Francis a most charming person, but be careful about Ysidro.' As the report in the *Journal* observed 'it was impossible to think of replacing such a company today' and Haldane was in different degrees intimate with each of them. See 'Current Topics', *Economic Journal*, 55, 218/219 (June–Sept. 1945).

86. 'Mr Haldane's Inaugural Address to the Congress', *Economic Journal*, 17, 65 (1 Mar. 1907).
87. Ibid., p. 2.
88. 'Annual Meeting of the Royal Economic Society: Discussion on the National Debt', *Economic Journal*, 35, 139 (Sept. 1925).
89. Ibid., p. 356.
90. Ibid., p. 364.
91. Ibid.
92. Ibid., pp. 364–5.
93. J. M. Keynes and H. D. Henderson, 'Can Lloyd George do it? The Pledge Examined' (London: The Nation and Athenaeum, 1929), p. 40.
94. Ibid., pp. 43–4.
95. Haldane, 'The Dedicated Life', p. 18.

6. A BRAVE NEW WORLD

1. Beatrice Webb, *Our Partnership*, ed. Barbara Drake and Margaret I. Cole (London: Longmans, Green & Co., 1948), p. 97.
2. Ibid., p. 96.
3. See George L. Bernstein, *Liberalism and Liberal Politics in Edwardian England* (Boston: Allen & Unwin, 1986), p. 6.
4. David Powell gives an excellently detailed analysis of the struggles connected to Liberalism's inclusive attitude to Labour in his 'The New Liberalism and the Rise of Labour, 1886–1906', *Historical Journal*, 29, 2 (June 1986).
5. For background to the role and activities of the club, see the closing pages of Haldane's 'The Unearned Increment'.
6. RBH to MEH, 20 Feb. 1882, NLS, MS 5933, f. 74.
7. R. B. Haldane, 'The New Liberalism', p. 139.
8. Maurice, *Haldane 1856–1915*, p. 59; see also Webb, *Our Partnership*, p. 32.

9. It was also recommended in the Minority Report for the Poor Law Commission, 1905–9, drafted largely by the Webbs. See Bruce, *The Coming of the Welfare State*, p. 210.

10. Ibid., p. 15.

11. On this uncomfortable skeleton in the closet of many left-leaning thinkers of the time see Jonathan Freedland, 'Eugenics: The Skeleton that Rattles Loudest in the Left's Closet', *The Guardian*, 17 Feb. 2012.

12. Sidney Webb, 'Socialism: True and False', Fabian Tract No. 51 (London: Fabian Society, 1899), p. 4.

13. Webb, *Our Partnership*, p. 97.

14. Ibid., p. 104.

15. Haldane, *An Autobiography*, p. 114. Interestingly, on 7 December 1923, only weeks before Ramsay MacDonald asked him to join the Labour government, Haldane wrote to his sister Elizabeth: 'The Liberals are in a hopeless position, apparently, tho' they will be of great use in the new House. I first saw things going wrong in 1909. I could then, I think, have averted the split with Labour. Now this is too late, but a new progressive party ought still, tho' not easily, be evolved. ... Yes—I think I could fashion a democratic programme. But only necessity will drive people to me': NLS, MS 6013, f. 165.

16. Webb, *Our Partnership*, p. 114.

17. Keir Hardie, 'The Labour Party: Its Aims and Policy', *National Review*, 46 (published by the proprietor at 23 Ryder Street, St James's, London, SW, Sept. 1905 to Feb. 1906), p. 1000. Maurice Bruce notes that, prior to 1914, 'except through the sympathetic influence of Liberals in social problems the working classes had singularly little influence on legislation': *The Coming of the Welfare State*, p. 24. See also Powell, 'The New Liberalism', p. 389.

18. Sidney Webb, 'Lord Rosebery's Escape from Houndsditch', *The Nineteenth Century*, 50 (1901), p. 386. See also Norman Mackenzie (ed.), *The Letters of Sidney and Beatrice Webb, Vol. II: Partnership 1892–1912* (Cambridge: Cambridge University Press, 1978), p. 169.

19. The first dinner covered the question 'How far and on what lines are closer political relations within the empire possible?' Other dinners looked at issues such as imperial preference, compulsory service, minimum standards of national well-being, how to increase the thinking element in administrative departments and Britain's relations with the great European powers—a discussion led by Grey.

20. By the 1907–8 session members included Lord Robert Cecil, Lord Milner, C. F. G. Masterman, H. Newbolt, F. S. Oliver and the soldier and *Times* journalist Charles à Court Repington.

21. E. S. Haldane, *From One Century to Another*, p. 222.

22. Webb, *Our Partnership*, 227–8.

23. Ibid., p. 97.

24. Haldane, 'The Future of Democracy', p. 18.

25. See Chapter 8.
26. Matthew, *The Liberal Imperialists*, p. 249.
27. The phrase is R. H. Tawney's, quoted in Sommer, *Haldane of Cloan*, p. 71.
28. RBH to MEH, 16 Apr. 1878, NLS, MS 5928, ff. 187–8.
29. See Koss, *Lord Haldane*, p. 10.
30. Jolliffe, *Raymond Asquith*, p. 26.
31. Haldane, *Thomas Graeme Nelson Haldane*, p. 40.
32. This is so in at least in some of the senses that Max Weber famously outlined in his *The Protestant Ethic and the Spirit of Capitalism* (London and New York: Routledge, 1992). For example, Weber claims that in the Calvinistic tradition, the way to assure oneself of one's salvation is 'intense worldly activity' (p. 112) and, within the ascetic tradition within Protestantism, 'waste of time is … the first and in principle the deadliest of sins' (p. 157).
33. It is interesting to note the following comment from Haldane in a letter to his sister Elizabeth in 1920, four years before taking up a post within a Labour government: 'I hear that a Committee has been appointed … to inquire as to why Liberals are going over to Labour. I wish they would call you & me as witnesses!': 28 Jan. 1920, NLS, MS 6013, f. 82.
34. Webb, *Our Partnership*, pp. 96–7.
35. Haldane, 'The New Liberalism', pp. 134–5.
36. See Haldane, *An Autobiography*, pp. 93–4.
37. Ibid., p. 106.
38. Ibid., p. 107.
39. G. Cecil, *Life of Robert, Marquis of Salisbury*, vol. 3 (London: Hodder & Stoughton, 1931), p. 275.
40. Haldane, 'The New Liberalism', p. 135.
41. Gladstone to Duke of Argyll, 30 Sept. 1885, in M. R. D. Foot and H. C. G. Matthew (eds), *The Gladstone Diaries with Cabinet Minutes and Prime-Ministerial Correspondence*, 14 vols. (Oxford: Clarendon Press, 1968–94), vol. 11, pp. 408–9.
42. See 'Cecil, Robert Arthur Talbot Gascoyne-, Third Marquess of Salisbury', *ODNB*.
43. *The Times*, 16 July 1891.
44. Andrew Roberts, *Salisbury: Victorian Titan* (London: Faber, 2011), pp. 282–4. We might note that Salisbury, for the 1902 Coronation Honours, put forward only two names from the opposition, recommending them for the Privy Council: Grey and Haldane. He had not consulted the Liberal leadership on this, so it is likely that their names were put forward on his own initiative. See Asquith to Balfour, 7 June 1911, Oxford, Bodleian Library, MS. Asquith 13, ff. 18–21.
45. RBH to MEH, 19 Nov. 1900, NLS, MS 5964, f. 150.
46. RBH to MEH, 28 June 1899, NLS, MS 5961, f. 188.
47. It should be noted that Chamberlain sent an ultimatum at the same time as Kruger's, which threatened war if complete equality was not granted; Kruger, however, had not yet received Chamberlain's message when he issued his. For Haldane's com-

ments on Kruger's role in the origins of the war see 'South African War—Mortality in Camps of Detention', *House of Commons Debates*, vol. 95, col. 607, https://api.parliament.uk/historic-hansard/commons/1901/jun/17/south-african-war-mortality-in-camps-of#S4V0095P0_19010617_HOC_292.

48. RBH to MEH, 19 Nov. 1900, NLS, MS 5964, f. 150.

49. Haldane, *An Autobiography*, p. 136.

50. 'Between June 1901 and May 1902, of the 115,000 people in the camps, almost 28,000 died, about 22,000 of them children. The death toll represented about 10 per cent of the Boer population. About 20,000 black people also died in other camps': '"Spin" on Boer Atrocities', *The Guardian*, 8 Dec. 2001.

51. Both quotations feature in Goodman, *Suffer and Survive*, pp. 162–3.

52. 'South African War—Mortality in Camps of Detention', vol. 95, col. 605.

53. *The Times*, 15 July 1901.

54. 'South African War—Mortality in Camps of Detention', vol. 95, col. 606.

55. Buchan, *Memory Hold-the-Door*, p. 128.

56. 'South African War—Mortality in Camps of Detention', vol. 95, col. 606; for Milner's initial support of the camps see 'Milner, Alfred, Viscount Milner', *ODNB*.

57. Milner to RBH, 8 Dec. 1901, Oxford, Bodleian Library, Milner dep. 185, ff. 287–92.

58. *The Times*, 25 July 1925.

59. 'Milner, Alfred, Viscount Milner', *ODNB*.

60. Quoted in Sommer, *Haldane of Cloan*, p. 108.

61. 'South African War—Peace Negotiations', *House of Commons Debates*, 28 Mar. 1901, vol. 92, col. 141, https://api.parliament.uk/historic-hansard/commons/1901/mar/28/south-african-war-peace-negotiations#S4V0092P0_19010328_HOC_355; the preceding quotation is also from col. 141.

62. Milner to RBH, 21 Jan. 1901, NLS, MS 5905, f. 55.

63. Maurice, *Haldane 1856–1915*, p. 145.

64. Buchan, *Memory Hold-the-Door*, pp. 131–2.

65. See Trevelyan, *Grey of Fallodon*, p. 87.

66. Channing to CB, 19 Nov. 1899, quoted in Stephen Koss, *The Pro-Boers: The Anatomy of an Antiwar Movement* (Chicago: University of Chicago Press, 1973), p. xxvi.

67. Angus Maddison, *The World Economy: A Millennial Perspective* (Paris: Organisation for Economic Co-operation and Development, 2001), p. 97.

68. Sarah Gertrude Millin, *Rhodes* (London: Chatto & Windus, 1933), p. 138.

69. Haldane, *An Autobiography*, pp. 93–4.

70. Ibid., p. 43.

71. See Haldane's 'East and West', *The Hibbert Journal*, 26, 4 (July 1928).

72. R. B. Haldane, *An Autobiography*, p. 351.

73. Quoted in Searle, *A New England?*, p. 320.

74. See Searle, *A New England?*, pp. 320–1.

75. See ibid., p. 321.

76. *New York Times*, 30 Aug. 1913.

77. Ministry of Reconstruction, *Report of the Machinery of Government Committee* (London: HMSO, 1918), Part I, para. 46, p. 14; for the broader discussion on 'Employment of women in the Civil Service' see paras 38–47, pp. 12–14.

78. RBH to ESH, 18 Nov. 1918, NLS, MS 6013, f. 47.

79. 'The Haldane Report 100 Years On', SoundCloud (see 6 mins 30).

80. E. S. Haldane (ed.), *Mary Elizabeth Haldane*, pp. 101–3. Haldane's sister, Elizabeth, even wrote a paper on women's rights at the age of nine, entitled 'Fair play or A few words for the lady doctors', which begins: 'I am going to say a few words for the lady doctors who, I think, are illtreated. What right have the men not to let ladies be whatever profession they choose?' This document is in my possession.

81. 'Final Balance Sheet', *House of Commons Debates*, 29 Apr. 1909, vol. 4, col. 548.

82. 'UK Inflation Calculator', CPI Inflation Calculator, https://www.officialdata.org/uk/inflation/1909?amount=5000

83. For comparison, Haldane's War Office budget that year was £28 million. For today's equivalent figure of the cost of old-age pensions in 1909 see 'UK Inflation Calculator', CPI Inflation Calculator, https://www.officialdata.org/uk/inflation/1909?amount=16000000

84. RBH to MEH, 4 May 1910, NLS, MS 5983, f. 123.

85. See Chapter 10.

7. A MAN FOR ALL SEASONS

1. Trevelyan, *Grey of Fallodon*, p. 278.

2. Haldane, *An Autobiography*, pp. 51–2.

3. Ibid., p. 71.

4. Quoted in Sommer, *Haldane of Cloan*, p. 136.

5. Haldane, *An Autobiography*, p. 74.

6. 'UK Inflation Calculator', CPI Inflation Calculator, https://www.officialdata.org/uk/inflation/1904?amount=1000.

7. Ibid., p. 75.

8. See George Dangerfield's classic, *The Strange Death of Liberal England* (London: Constable & Co., 1935).

9. Their earlier position is summed up in a letter from Haldane to Milner on 26 January 1902: 'You will be anxious to know what our group in the H. of Commons is doing. We are working with Rosebery. He is not an easy or altogether reliable chief—but he has the touch of genius, & he is very anti C.B. in reality, tho' he has tried to minimize our group's split with C.B. for the moment. What he wants to do is to make the split himself when the time comes. ... I rather quake over what he may say as to things outside the [Boer] war. He is too fond of surprising his friends! However, we are now working closely with him, & he knows our views': Oxford, Bodleian Library, MS. Milner dep. 215, ff. 121–3.

10. It should be noted, however, that Haldane and Asquith, having debated Asquith's suitability for the role at that time, expressed support for CB to be leader following Harcourt's resignation in December 1898 (CB took up the leadership of the party in February 1899). See CB to RBH, 29 Dec. 1898, Oxford, Bodleian Library, MS. Asquith 9, ff. 153–5 and Asquith's memorandum of events written the same months, ff. 109–28. But by 5 Oct. 1903 Haldane and Grey were urging Rosebery to lead the Liberals again and, as Haldane told Asquith in a letter that month (two years before Relugas), 'I said [to Rosebery] we would not serve under C.B. as long as he was leader in the H. of C.': Oxford, Bodleian Library, MS. Asquith 10, ff. 90–1.

11. Grey, rather unrealistically, felt that it was possible to approach CB with their idea in a non-threatening manner, telling Asquith on 2 Oct. 1905: 'I adhere to the opinion that it is too soon to put a pistol to C.B.'s head ... he should be told what we think & feel, but we want it to come to him in a friendly way & not as if we were trying to force him in a way, which he might think premature & unfriendly': Oxford, Bodleian Library, MS. Asquith 10, ff. 148–9. Haldane also claimed that they did not wish to put a 'pistol to his [CB's] head'; they just wanted to tell him their 'strong opinion of what is essential ... frankly though friendly': Haldane to Knollys, 19 Sept. 1905, Oxford, Bodleian Library, MS. Asquith 10, ff. 141–3.

12. Grey to Asquith, 24 Nov. 1905, Oxford, Bodleian Library, MS. Asquith 10, ff. 164–5. See Edmund Gosse's description of Alverstone's reaction to Haldane's advocacy in the 'Wee Frees' case before the House of Lords: 'Lord Alverstone, perfectly blank, with glassy eyes, is an evident Gallio, to whom all this ecclesiastical metaphysic is unintelligible and insane': Sommer, *Haldane of Cloan*, p. 136.

13. Grey to Asquith, 25 Nov. 1905, Oxford, Bodleian Library, MS. Asquith 10, ff. 168–70.

14. Asquith to RBH, 7 Oct. 1905, NLS, MS 5906, f. 244.

15. Haldane, *An Autobiography*, p. 179.

16. Ibid., pp. 177–8.

17. Ibid., pp. 171–2.

18. Horner, *Time Remembered*, p. 195.

19. I am aware, of course, that, when it comes to tracking the development of events that led to the outbreak of war, tensions between Britain and Germany ought not to overshadow the tensions at play in the Balkans and between the other empires and nations involved in the conflict. Christopher Clark's *The Sleepwalkers* (London: Penguin, 2012) is a masterful example of the ability to see the matter in its proper perspective.

20. See R. B. Haldane, *Before the War* (London: Cassell, 1920), pp. 182–3; Haldane, *An Autobiography*, p. 191; and the views of G. M. Trevelyan in his *Grey of Fallodon*, pp. 273–4. For the contrary perspective see David Owen, *The Hidden Perspective: The Military Conversations 1906–1914* (London: Haus Publishing, 1914).

21. G. Monger, *The End of Isolation: British Foreign Policy 1900–1907* (London: Thomas Nelson & Sons, 1963), p. 82.

22. For a full history of the naval armaments race see Robert K. Massie, *Dreadnought: Britain, Germany and the Coming of the Great War* (London: Vintage, 2007).

23. See Zara Steiner, 'Grey, Hardinge and the Foreign Office, 1906–10', *Historical Journal*, 10, 3 (1967), pp. 415 and 417.

24. Bertie to Mallet, 11 June 1904, quoted in Z. S. Steiner, *The Foreign Office and Foreign Policy, 1898–1914* (Cambridge: Cambridge University Press, 1969), p. 66.

25. FO 55/3, memorandum by Hardinge, 30 Oct. 1906, in Steiner, 'Grey, Hardinge and the Foreign Office', p. 418.

26. Haldane, *An Autobiography*, pp. 220–1.

27. Ibid., pp. 223–4.

28. *The Times*, 22 July 1911.

29. Haldane, *Before the War*, p. 71.

30. For a fuller account of his 'Mission' see ibid., pp. 72–81.

31. See RBH to MES, 15 Feb. 1912, NLS, MS 5987, ff. 59–60 and RBH to MES, 7 Mar. 1912, NLS, MS 5987, ff. 90–1.

32. Haldane, *Before the War*, p. 87.

33. See Chapter 9.

34. Major General J. E. B. Seely (Secretary of State for War, 1912–14) to ESH, 22 Aug. 1928, NLS, MS 6033, f. 36: see epigraph Chapter 9.

35. Haldane, *An Autobiography*, p. 288.

36. Mary wrote to Haldane before his birthday in his first year as War Secretary, well before there was a sign that he might be Lord Chancellor: 'Tomorrow is the anniversary of the day on which your appearance in the world gladdened the hearts of parents and grandparents. It was sunshine after clouds. Still I little guessed that I had a future minister of state for war. A Chancellor was more in my mind. He looked prematurely wise as he lay in his bassinette of pink silk & lace, his grandfather's gift. It is now 50 years ago or will be tomorrow at 3 pm. ... It has been a life of activity even from the first, and a life spent very much for others—which is the best': 29 July 1906, NLS, MS 6008, ff. 166–7.

37. RBH to MEH, 16 June 1912, NLS, MS 5988, ff. 23–4.

38. Quoted in 'The Lord Chancellor and the Privy Council—Address by the President of the Ontario Bar Association, Francis Dean Kerr K.C., of Peterborough, at the annual meeting of the Association held at Osgoode Hall, Toronto, on Thursday 23rd May 1924', NLS, MS 5925, f. 13.

39. The typescript of Elizabeth's diaries was generously made available to me by Patrick Campbell Fraser, the only son of Elsie Campbell Fraser, née Haldane, the second child and only daughter of Sir William Haldane, R. B. Haldane's youngest sibling.

40. Haldane, *An Autobiography*, pp. 103–4.

41. Typescript of ESH diaries, 8 August 1914.

42. See Koss, *Lord Haldane*, pp. 125–6.

43. The German businessman in question was the shipping magnate Albert Ballin of the Hamburg-America Line, a friend of Kaiser Wilhelm II. His letter to Haldane dated

1 Aug. 1914 recounted a dinner at Haldane's London home on 25 July, at which Grey and John Morley were also present. In the letter, Ballin refers to Grey and Haldane saying to him that 'England would only be induced to make a material intervention if Germany were to swallow up France'. In actual fact, instead of using the words 'swallow up', they had said 'attack'—a significant difference. Haldane refused to publish the letter when its existence became known, on the grounds that it was private correspondence and that he would need the consent of the other party, which was impossible to obtain once war was declared. To the public, it looked like a cover-up. As Dudley Sommer has written, Haldane's reason could be seen as 'quixotic to a degree, but it was in character with Haldane's principles'. See Sommer, *Haldane of Cloan*, pp. 309–10 and 318.

44. See Chapter 9; and Koss, *Lord Haldane*, pp. 144–5.

45. Quoted in Sommer, *Haldane of Cloan*, p. 341; see also Alfred Gollin, *The Impact of Air Power on the British People and their Government, 1909–1914* (London: Macmillan, 1989), pp. 94–5.

46. Koss, *Lord Haldane*, p. 134. Koss names the papers as follows: *National Review, John Bull, Blackwood's Magazine, The Times, Daily Mail, Daily Express* and *Morning Post*.

47. Koss lists the following figures: Leo Maxse, W. A. S. Hewins, F. S. Oliver, R. D. Blumenfeld, Geoffrey Robinson, Horatio Bottomley, and of course Lord Northcliffe himself. See Koss, *Lord Haldane*, p. 135.

48. Haldane, *An Autobiography*, p. 283.

49. White to Maxse, 4 Feb. 1915, Maxse Papers, quoted in Koss, *Lord Haldane*, p. 136.

50. Vincent, 'German Philosophy and British Public Policy', pp. 177–8.

51. Haldane, *An Autobiography*, p. 98.

52. Oxford, Bodleian Library, MS. Eng. d. 3212, ff. 42–3. Morley had in fact written a sympathetic letter to Haldane on 5 Aug. 1914, in which he said that he knew 'it must be more than personal pain to find yourself the enemy of Germany and the friend of Russia': NLS, MS 5910, f. 253.

53. Trevelyan, *Grey of Fallodon*, pp. 274–5.

54. There is a remarkable passage in Margot Asquith's diary recording a visit from Churchill's wife Clemmie to Downing Street on 9 June 1915. 'C.[lemmie said] The P.M!! That fool!! Why he has thrown his dearest friend & his most remarkable colleague Haldane & Winston to the wolves! She got up held me to the tea table & harangued me in fish-wife style on Henrys [*sic*] defects till I … said "Go Clemmie—leave the room—you are off yr. head"': Oxford, Bodleian Library, MS. Eng., d. 3212, ff. 111–13.

55. Sir Almeric Fitzroy records in his diary for 20 May 1915: 'Haldane is, I understand, very ill, and seeks a change in the interests of his health. A few days ago he had a heart seizure which caused the gravest anxiety.' *Memoirs*, vol. 1, second edition (London: Hutchinson & Co, 1925), p. 594. This is the only mention of such illness that I have found; Fitzroy's implication of Haldane's desire to leave (or at least change) office because of his bad health is a similar one-off. Bearing all the other factors in

mind, it is unlikely that Haldane would have seen this as an acceptable pretext for bowing out at that time. All other evidence suggests he did not actually desire to leave office.

56. Notably, in Margot Asquith's diary from this time (Oxford, Bodleian Library, MS. Eng., d. 3212, ff. 58–9), she records that her husband claimed that the real reason for Conservative dislike of Haldane went back to an occasion on which he (Haldane) had changed a sentence of his Commons speech in Hansard—the edited verbatim report of proceedings from both Houses of Parliament. The sentence related to what is known as the 'Curragh Incident' of March 1914 and concerned the government's policy regarding the use of troops in Ireland against the Ulster Volunteers. Haldane's additional word in Hansard, which he considered simply as a clarification, was viewed by some as the Lord Chancellor trying 'to deliberately mislead ... Parliament and the country' (as put by his detractor Leo Maxse in *The National Review*). For details of the story, including Maxse's quote, see Koss, *Lord Haldane*, pp. 107–14; for Haldane's account of his change in Hansard see *An Autobiography*, pp. 266–8.

57. Jenkins, *Asquith*, p. 362.

58. RBH to MEH, 25 May 1915, NLS, MS 5993, ff. 201–3.

59. See Violet Asquith Bonham Carter, *Winston Churchill as I Knew him* (London: Reprint Society, 1966), pp. 394–5; Trevelyan, *Grey of Fallodon*, p. 278; and Spender and Asquith, *Life of Herbert Henry Asquith*, p. 167.

60. Oxford, Bodleian Library, MS. Eng., d. 3212, f. 57. According to Austen Chamberlain, however, Asquith had himself already suggested Haldane's removal from office on 17 May, the first day of his discussions with Bonar Law. See Michael Brock and Eleanor Brock (eds), *Margot Asquith's Great War Diary 1914–1916: The View from Downing Street* (Oxford: Oxford University Press, 2014), p. cxiii.

61. See Spender and Asquith, *Life of Herbert Henry Asquith*, p. 167 and Jenkins, *Asquith*, p. 362. For the date around the final decision regarding Haldane's ejection see Margot Asquith's diary, in which she records a conversation on 23 May between Asquith and the Conservative leaders Bonar Law and Balfour, where Asquith pleads in Haldane's defence to no avail. The coalition was formed on 25 May. See Oxford, Bodleian Library, MS. Eng. d. 3212, ff. 58–9.

62. Spender and Asquith, *Life of Herbert Henry Asquith*, p. 167.

63. Jenkins, *Asquith*, p. 362.

64. Margot wrote almost immediately to Haldane, his sister Elizabeth, and his mother Mary. See Margot's diaries, Oxford, Bodleian Library, MS. Eng. d. 3271.

65. See Jenkins, *Asquith*, pp. 363f.

66. Quoted in Sommer, *Haldane of Cloan*, p. 329.

67. Quoted in ibid.

68. Oxford, Bodleian Library, MS. Eng. d. 3271, ff. 55–6.

69. Almeric Fitzroy, *Memoirs*, 2 vols (London: Hutchinson & Co., 1925), vol. 2, p. 595.

70. 'Beatrice Webb's typescript diary', 14 June 1915, LSE Digital Library.

71. Typescript of ESH diaries, 29 May 1915.

72. Haldane, *An Autobiography*, p. 286.

73. Trevelyan, *Grey of Fallodon*, p. 278.

74. Ibid.

75. Maurice, *Haldane 1915–1928*, p. 5.

76. Ibid., p. 6.

77. RBH to MEH, 22 Nov. 1915, NLS, MS 5994, ff. 171–2.

78. Maurice, *Haldane 1915–1928*, p. 2.

79. See Asquith to RBH, 8 Aug. 1916, NLS, MS 5913, ff. 50–1. For Grey's response see Koss, *Lord Haldane*, p. 90.

80. See draft letter from RBH to Asquith, 9 Aug. 1916, NLS, MS 5913, ff. 52–3.

81. Maurice, *Haldane 1915–1928*, p. 2.

82. Oxford, Bodleian Library, 12 Dec. 1916, MS. Asquith 17, f. 245.

83. RBH to Asquith, 18 Oct. 1926, Oxford, Bodleian Library, MS. Asquith 18, ff. 125–6.

84. See RBH to Gosse, 1 Aug. 1915, Gosse Archive, Brotherton Library, Leeds, BC MS 19c Gosse.

85. These words feature in manuscript notes by Gosse attached to Haldane's letter on 1 Aug. 1915 (see note above). Between 1906 and 1913 Sir John French made several visits to the Haldanes at Cloan, and Haldane always maintained a high regard for him.

86. Harold Begbie, *The Vindication of Great Britain: a study in diplomacy and strategy with reference to the illusions of her critics and the problems of the future* (London: Methuen, 1916).

87. RBH to Gosse, 9 Sept. 1917, Gosse Archive, Brotherton Library, Leeds, BC MS 19c Gosse.

88. RBH to Gosse, 12 Sept. 1917, Gosse Archive, Brotherton Library, Leeds, BC MS 19c Gosse.

89. RBH to Gosse, 18 Sept. 1918, Gosse Archive, Brotherton Library, Leeds, BC MS 19c Gosse.

90. See *An Autobiography*, pp. 287–8; but see Sommer, *Haldane of Cloan*, pp. 368–70. Sommer, I believe incorrectly, finds that the body of evidence suggests that Haig did not in fact call on Haldane immediately after the Victory March and that the visit took place at the same time as he presented Haldane with his Despatches—which cannot have been in July, as Haldane's *Autobiography* has it, but in December once Haig's Dispatches had been published. Sommer does, however, quote the words of Major General Sir John Davidson, a member of Haig's staff between 1916 and 1918, who was with Haig that July day and testified to his visit to Haldane. I have found further evidence to support the view that Haig did visit Haldane that day in a letter from Lady Haig to Haldane after the death of her husband. Lady Haig writes: 'I know the deep affection between you & Douglas & know you were the first Douglas went to see after that drive through London': 7 Mar. 1928, NLS, MS 5917, f. 86. Given the other evidence Sommer cites in favour of a December meeting between Haig and Haldane, it is extremely likely that both meetings took place.

91. Sommer, *Haldane of Cloan*, p. 370. The words are Major General Sir John Davidson's; see previous note.

92. See Haldane, *An Autobiography*, p. 288.

93. 'Minister to Enshrine Protection for Research Independence', BBC News. 24 Feb. 2017

94. J. R. Nethercote (adjunct professor with the Public Policy Institute at the Australian Catholic University), *Brisbane Times*, 6 Aug. 2013.

95. Ministry of Reconstruction, *Report of the Machinery of Government Committee*, Part II, X, pp. 72–5.

96. The Haldane Report also 'contributed to a new awareness of management' within government, details of which can be found in Jill Pellew, 'Practitioners versus Theorists: Early Attitudes of British Higher Civil Servants towards their Profession', *International Review of Administrative Sciences*, 49, 1 (Mar. 1983), p. 8.

97. It is easy to tell what Mary's attitude must have been in light of a 1908 letter about the churches in Scotland. See MEH to RBH, 29 May 1908, NLS, MS 6009, ff. 1–2.

98. Quoted in Sommer, *Haldane of Cloan*, p. 394.

99. RBH to Gosse, 4 Jan. 1924, Gosse Archive, Brotherton Library, Leeds, BC MS 19c Gosse.

100. For a considered assessment of Haldane's achievements during his two tenures as Lord Chancellor see Heuston, *Lives of the Lord Chancellors*.

101. White to Maxse, 4 Feb. 1915, Maxse Papers, quoted in Koss, *Lord Haldane*, p. 136.

102. In the final year of his life, he presided over a major nine-day Canadian constitutional case in February and March before delivering his intensely argued twenty-two-page judgment in June. His seventeen-page treatise on comparative religion and philosophy, published by the *Hibbert Journal* under the title 'East and West', appeared in July.

103. 22 Aug. 1928, NLS, MS 6033, f. 12.

104. Dean Inge to ESH, 20 Aug. 1928, NLS, MS 6032, f. 141.

8. EDUCATION, EDUCATION, EDUCATION

1. 16 June 1916, NLS, MS 5913, f. 24. It should be noted that F. S. Oliver was, in the words of Koss, 'by far the most eloquent of Haldane's critics and amongst the most insidious' (*Lord Haldane*, p. 148). Oliver was the great-grandfather of Katy Campbell, the wife of my elder son Milo. He was the partner of Frank Debenham in the successful business Debenham & Freebody. Highly erudite, he was an accomplished author, not least in 1915 of *Ordeal by Battle*, and in 1906 of a highly praised biography of Alexander Hamilton, which is also a classic text on federalism. A Conservative in politics, a devoted Milnerite and a strong supporter of Lord Roberts's campaign for compulsory military service, Oliver 'expressed in cogent if extreme philosophical terms the case against Haldane and Liberalism' (Koss, *Lord Haldane*, p. 148). I find it poignant and revealing of his qualities that he came to realise that some of Haldane's

achievements were in fact greatly meritorious. It is partly for this reason that I have chosen this epigraph, which reflects the considered judgment of one of Haldane's long-standing critics.

2. James Duff, 'The Scale and Scope of British Universities', Haldane Memorial Lecture, 1961 (London: Birkbeck College, 1961). Sir James Duff (1898–1970) was vice-chairman of the BBC 1960–5 and, 1937–60, alternating vice-chancellor and pro-vice-chancellor of the University of Durham.
3. See Carlyle, *On Heroes*. As we saw in Chapter 5 n. 15.
4. Haldane, 'The Soul of a People', p. 29.
5. R. B. Haldane, 'The Soul of a People', p. 19.
6. 'The Ideal of the University' (address to first meeting of the reconstructed court of the University of Wales, 25 Nov. 1920), quoted in Ashby and Anderson, *Portrait of Haldane*, p. xiii. This chapter is heavily indebted to the exceptional research and presentation of these two scholars. My limited archival work in this area is a result of their previous exhaustive achievements in uncovering the key material to prove Haldane's central role in education. I have attempted, however, to present the material in a more compressed format and to weave it together, along with other sources not available to Ashby and Anderson, in a manner that is fresh and original. In addition, Geoffrey Price makes the point that Ashby and Anderson, while fully recording Haldane's work as an educational reformer, paid less attention 'to the key role of his own intellectual advocacy of Hegelian principles, and to his own "conversion" in sustaining and energizing his extraordinary range of interests' : 'Science, Idealism and Higher Education', p. 10. This chapter lays particular stress on the early 'conversion' experience that was Haldane's own time at university as a key factor in driving his work in this arena.
7. Haldane, 'The Soul of a People', p. 18.
8. Haldane, 'The Dedicated Life', pp. 12–13.
9. R. B. Haldane, 'The Civic University', in *Selected Addresses and Essays*, p. 138.
10. Ibid., p. 140.
11. T. H. Green, *The Works of Thomas Hill Green*, ed. R. L. Nettleship, vol. 3 (London: Longmans Green, 1888), p. 409.
12. See Stephen K. Roberts (ed.), *A Ministry of Enthusiasm: Centenary Essays on the Workers' Educational Association* (London: Pluto Press, 2003), p. 97.
13. Roberts (ed.), *A Ministry of Enthusiasm*, p. 179.
14. 'University Finance', *House of Lords Debates*, 21 July 1920, vol. 41, col. 403.
15. Ashby and Anderson, *Portrait of Haldane*, p. 165.
16. 'Training of the Nation', *House of Lords Debates*, 12 July 1916, vol. 22, col. 660; Haldane, speaking in the same debate (col. 664), did recognise that, unlike Germany, there was still provision within Britain for 'the children of the workmen, who by bursaries and scholarships have a chance, if they have exceptional aptitude, of getting the benefit of secondary education'.
17. Ibid., col. 676.

18. R. B. Haldane, 'The Calling of the Preacher', in *Universities and National Life*, p. 43.

19. George Davie's *The Democratic Intellect* (Edinburgh: Edinburgh University Press, 1961) has become the standard go-to text for the representation of a distinct Scottish intellectual tradition. There are commentators, however, who would consider the lines that Davie draws as somewhat lacking in appropriate nuance. See, for example, Lindsay Paterson, 'George Davie and the Democratic Intellect', in G. Graham (ed.), *Oxford History of Scottish Philosophy* (Oxford: Oxford University Press, 2015), pp. 236–69.

20. 'Our History', Carnegie Trust. For more information on educational access in Scotland during Haldane's lifetime see R. D. Anderson, *Education and Opportunity in Victorian Scotland* (Edinburgh: Edinburgh University Press, 1983), which covers the period up until 1914. For the period between 1914 and 1939, see Chapter 5 of Lindsay Paterson, *Scottish Education in the Twentieth Century* (Edinburgh: Edinburgh University Press, 2003).

21. NLS, MS 5939, ff. 146–7.

22. Ashby and Anderson, *Portrait of Haldane*, p. 31.

23. Ibid., p. 126.

24. Haldane, *An Autobiography*, p. 124.

25. Webb's questions and Haldane's formal opinion can be read on pp. 25–9 of Sir Sidney Caine's *The History of the Foundation of the London School of Economics and Political Science* (London: University of London, 1963). Caine's review of the legal foundations of Haldane's opinion is somewhat critical, though he is thankful for the outcome: 'We may perhaps be grateful that the lawyers of the time were less perceptive of the true state of the law and therefore that the child was allowed to be born with however dubious an ancestry' (p. 33).

26. See Webb's description of the exact relationship of the LSE with the Hutchinson Trustees in Caine, *History*, pp. 8–10.

27. Ralf Dahrendorf, *LSE: A History of the London School of Economics and Political Science, 1896–1995* (Oxford: Oxford University Press, 1995), p. 3. This is quoted (p. 208) in a highly informative essay by Jill Pellew, covering the early histories of both the LSE and Imperial College, London, and the role of private benefactions, entitled 'A Metropolitan University Fit for Empire: The Role of Private Benefaction in the Early History of the London School of Economics and Political Science and Imperial College of Science and Technology, 1895–1930', in *History of Universities*, vol. 26/1 (Oxford: Oxford University Press, 2012).

28. Jill Pellew notes that both the Irish playwright George Bernard Shaw and Ramsay MacDonald (later to be first Labour prime minister, with Haldane in his Cabinet) criticised Webb for not using Hutchinson's money to promote socialism more directly. Pellew implies that Webb's belief that his actions had been justified was based on his consultation with Haldane. See 'A Metropolitan University Fit for Empire', p. 215.

29. Ibid., p. 237. It should be noted that Haldane was additionally a trustee and funder of the school's library and its building fund.

30. Ashby and Anderson, *Portrait of Haldane*, p. 34.

31. Buchan, *Memory Hold-the-Door*, pp. 129–30.

32. Ibid., p. 128.

33. 3 July 1897, Board of Education records, Public Records Office, 24/5, quoted in Ashby and Anderson, *Portrait of Haldane*, p. 35.

34. 15 Jan. 1897, Allchin Papers, quoted in Ashby and Anderson, *Portrait of Haldane*, pp. 33–4.

35. Haldane to Balfour, 16 Oct. 1897, quoted in Ashby and Anderson, *Portrait of Haldane*, p. 36.

36. 26 July 1897, from Webb, *Our Partnership*, pp. 99–100.

37. G. R. Searle, *The Quest for National Efficiency: A Study in British Politics and Political Thought, 1899–1914* (London: Ashfield Press, 1990), p. 125.

38. See Ashby and Anderson, *Portrait of Haldane*, pp. 36–7 for a full breakdown of Haldane's speech, though they overlook the fact that Dilke did not speak.

39. Gardiner, *Prophets, Priests, & Kings*, p. 283.

40. Haldane, *An Autobiography*, pp. 126–7.

41. Ibid., p. 127.

42. Ibid., pp. 127–8.

43. Ashby and Anderson, *Portrait of Haldane*, p. 37.

44. Haldane, *An Autobiography*, pp. 131–2.

45. J. Mordaunt Crook, 'The Architectural Image', in F. M. L. Thompson (ed.), *The University of London and the World of Learning* (London: Hambledon Press, 1990), p. 13.

46. Haldane, *An Autobiography*, p. 148.

47. Crook, 'The Architectural Image', p. 13.

48. Searle, *The Quest for National Efficiency*, p. 13.

49. R. B. Haldane, 'Great Britain and Germany—a Study in Education', in *Education and Empire* (London: John Murray, 1902), p. 6.

50. For this and preceding quotations from Haldane, see 'Great Britain and Germany—a Study in Education', pp. 9–19.

51. 'UK Inflation Calculator', CPI Inflation Calculator, https://www.officialdata.org/uk/inflation/1900?amount=100000

52. See Chapter 9.

53. Haldane, 'Great Britain and Germany—a Study in Education', p. 20.

54. Transcript of proceedings before the committee of council, 18 Dec. 1902, q. 238; Privy Council Records, Public Record Office, 8/605/89731, quoted in Ashby and Anderson, *Portrait of Haldane*, p. 45.

55. The hostility of British universities to industry should not be overstated, however. For an analysis that argues persuasively about their openness to industry see M. Sanderson, *The Universities and British Industry, 1850–1970* (London: Routledge & Kegan Paul, 1972).

56. Jill Pellew notes that this factor distinguished Imperial from the LSE: 'The intellectual rationale and professional milieu of the patrons of the LSE, who hoped to solve

social ills among the British population, might have been rather different from those of Imperial College, who wanted to educate young men fit to run and exploit the wealth of the Empire. Nevertheless, they all put their faith in the application of science': 'A Metropolitan University Fit for Empire', p. 204.

57. See Ashby and Anderson, *Portrait of Haldane*, pp. 52–3.

58. Ibid., p. 50.

59. Haldane, *An Autobiography*, p. 144. For further details of their careers see Pellew, 'A Metropolitan University Fit for Empire', p. 222. For a consideration of Wernher and Beit's contribution to the founding of Imperial College in the context of contemporary debates concerning how educational establishments deal with their connections to their colonial past (particularly their founders and funders) see Jill Pellew, 'Donors to an Imperial Project: Randlords as Benefactors to the Royal School of Mines, Imperial College of Science and Technology', in Jill Pellew and Lawrence Goldman (eds), *Dethroning Historical Reputations: Universities, Museums and the Commemoration of Benefactors* (London: School of Advanced Study, University of London, Institute of Historical Research, 2018).

60. R. Trevelyan, *Grand Dukes and Diamonds: The Wernhers of Luton Hoo* (London: Martin Secker & Warburg, 1991), p. 87. Beit also played an inglorious role in the Jameson Raid, a precursor to the Second Boer War (1899–1902). See Pellew, 'Donors to an Imperial Project', p. 39.

61. Passfield Papers, II, 4b, 36, quoted in Ashby and Anderson, *Portrait of Haldane*, p. 51.

62. Ashby and Anderson, *Portrait of Haldane*, p. 40.

63. Fitzroy's *Memoirs* are rich with Haldane-related material.

64. Lord Rosebery to Lord Monkswell, 27 June 1903, published in T. L. Humberstone, *University Reform in London* (1926), appendix 1, pp. 167–71, quoted in Ashby and Anderson, *Portrait of Haldane*, p. 5.

65. Morant to Lord Londonderry, 23 Jan. 1904, quoted in Ashby and Anderson, *Portrait of Haldane*, p. 54.

66. Haldane, 'The Civic University', p. 154.

67. Pellew, 'A Metropolitan University Fit for Empire', p. 218. Pellew's comment accords with the informed opinion of the authoritative Ashby and Anderson. It is for this reason that I disagree with the comments made by the official centenary historian of Imperial College Hannah Gay in her *The History of Imperial College London 1907–2007* (London: Imperial College Press, 2007), p. 64, fn. 7, in which she asserts that Haldane played a less central role than other commentators suggest. The evidence, in my view, strongly supports the claim that Haldane played an absolutely central role in the founding of Imperial. As Jill Pellew has written elsewhere, it is hard to accept Gay's judgment, as there 'is no denying the facts of his [Haldane's] membership of key bodies involved, of his ongoing involvement in the development of the University of London over several decades' and his 'relevant ideological thinking': Pellew, 'Donors to an Imperial Project', p. 41, fn. 23. Perhaps Gay's comments are a case of 'No prophet is accepted in his own country'.

68. It was not until 1929 that it became a fully integrated teaching college of London University. See Pellew, 'A Metropolitan University Fit for Empire', p. 226. For histories of Imperial College—bearing in mind the previous note—see Gay, *History* and A. R. Hall, *Science for Industry: A Short History of the Imperial College of Science and Technology and its Antecedents* (London: Imperial College Press, 1982).

69. Colin Matthew, usually so good on Haldane, fails to appreciate adequately the non-utilitarian dimension in his educational thinking. Matthew's focus on Haldane's vision of education as a means to secure the country's position as the leading manufacturing and industrial nation in the world fails to balance this with the repeated emphasis in Haldane's writings and speeches on the importance of education for its own sake. See particularly Matthew, *The Liberal Imperialists*, pp. 228–35. For a far more balanced view of Haldane's views on the purpose of education, where the paradox of the utility of education for its own sake is also importantly articulated, see Lindsay Paterson, *Social Radicalism and Liberal Education* (Exeter: Imprint Academic, 2015), p. 56.

70. See Andrew Vincent and Raymond Plant (eds), *Philosophy, Politics and Citizenship: The Life and Thought of the British Idealists* (Oxford: Basil Blackwell, 1984), p. 158.

71. 'Now in suggesting that reform of our education, particularly of our tertiary education, is essential, I am far from desiring to suggest that we ought to wish to see it entirely subordinated to utilitarian considerations. Culture is an end in itself, and if it is to be won it must be sought for its own sake. But the Germans have shown us how the University can fulfil a double function without slackening the effort after culture': Haldane, 'Great Britain and Germany—a Study in Education', p. 30.

72. My thanks to Dr Michael Wood for confirmation of Haldane's 1903–4 presidency of the Edinburgh Sir Walter Scott Society.

73. See Jill Pellew, 'The New British Campus Universities of the 1960s and their Localities', in Jill Pellew and Miles Taylor (eds), *Utopian Universities: A Global History of the New Campuses of the 1960s* (London: Bloomsbury Academic, forthcoming (2020)).

74. Ashby and Anderson, *Portrait of Haldane*, p. 46.

75. It is possible to raise the question—did Haldane have a preference for independent institutions based in single cities or for federal universities which united cities within a region? On different occasions he advocated one or the other. His desire, for instance, to champion Liverpool's cause does, at first, seem to stand in contrast to his vision for a regional federated west of England university, as articulated in a speech in Bristol in 1903. My sense is that he was guided by the size and capacity of the city in question; the larger the city, the more likely it was that an independent institution would thrive. My thanks to Jill Pellew for pointing out this apparent ambiguity in Haldane's thinking.

76. 'Birmingham University', 23 Mar. 1900; enclosure in memo to chancellor, 5 Dec. 1900; T 1/9653B/3328/1901, quoted in Ashby and Anderson, *Portrait of Haldane*, p. 62.

77. Ashby and Anderson, *Portrait of Haldane*, p. 62.

78. RBH to Joseph Chamberlain, 14 Aug. 1902, Joseph Chamberlain Papers, JC 11/15/2, quoted in Ashby and Anderson, *Portrait of Haldane*, p. 64.

79. Haldane, *An Autobiography*, p. 145. Interestingly, Sir Almeric Fitzroy recorded in his diary on 17 December that Lyttelton's opening before the committee was 'prolix and laboured, but that matters improved when Haldane was under examination and that it was a pity that Counsel [Lyttelton] had not shortened his own remarks and relied more on what he could extract from his principal witness [Haldane]': Fitzroy, *Memoirs*, vol. 1, p. 115.

80. Haldane, *An Autobiography*, p. 145.

81. Transcript of shorthand notes of evidence, 17 Dec. 1902, q. 196; Privy Council Records, Public Record Office, 8/605/89719, quoted in Ashby and Anderson, *Portrait of Haldane*, p. 65.

82. Ashby and Anderson, *Portrait of Haldane*, p. 66.

83. Transcript of shorthand notes of evidence, 18 Dec. 1902, q. 196; Privy Council Records, Public Record Office, 8/605/89731, quoted in Ashby and Anderson, *Portrait of Haldane*, p. 66–7.

84. Sir Almeric Fitzroy quoting the Duke of Devonshire in a diary entry of 6 Feb. 1903. See Fitzroy, *Memoirs*, vol. 1, p. 117.

85. Keith Vernon has argued that the 'issue at stake was a *fait accompli*', given the existence of Birmingham University. See Keith Vernon, *Universities and the State in England, 1850–1939* (London: RoutledgeFalmer, 2004), p. 156. But the key development that took place with the verdict of this committee of the Privy Council was the way in which it gave the precedent an official character, relevant across the country.

86. Ashby and Anderson, *Portrait of Haldane*, p. 68.

87. Ibid., p. 71.

88. On Haldane as 'midwife' see ibid.

89. Sir Frank Heath, 'Lord Haldane: His Influence on Higher Education and on Administration', in Grey et al., *Viscount Haldane of Cloan*, p. 23.

90. For a history of this important body see C. H. Shinn, *Paying the Piper: The Development of the University Grants Committee 1919–46* (London: Falmer Press, 1986).

91. It should be noted that the history of schooling in Scotland and its expansion was very different. See Anderson, *Education and Opportunity* and Paterson, *Scottish Education*.

92. 'Education (England and Wales)', *House of Commons Debates*, 24 Mar. 1902, vol. 105, cols. 900–5.

93. See Searle, *A New England?*, p. 333.

94. Royal Commission on University Education in London, *Final Report of the Commissioners* (London: HMSO, 1913), p. 2, para. 2, point III.

95. Royal Commission on University Education in London, *First Report of the Commissioners* (London: HMSO, 1910), p. 105, para. 1376.

96. Ibid., p. 112, para. 1430.

97. Ibid., p. 113, para. 1445.

98. Ibid., p. 188, para. 410.

99. Ibid., p. 36, para. 85.

100. Ibid., p. 185, para. 406.

101. Ibid., p. 44, para. 102. Haldane is also likely to have shared Sidney Webb's desire for 'London's university to be in close intellectual contact with, as well as in close physical proximity to, the bustling world of commerce, politics and practical activities': Searle, *The Quest for National Efficiency*, p. 76.

102. *Final Report of the Commissioners* (1913), p. 167, para. 371.

103. 'UK Inflation Calculator', CPI Inflation Calculator, https://www.officialdata.org/uk/inflation/1913?amount=355000

104. Crook, 'The Architectural Image', p. 16.

105. Thompson (ed.), *The University of London*, p. 138.

106. Ibid., p. 139.

107. F. Dainton, *Reflections on Universities and the National Health Services* (London: Nuffield Provincial Hospitals Trust, 1983), p. 61.

108. *Final Report of the Commissioners* (1913), p. 110, para. 253.

109. See ibid., p. 96, para. 219 for the mention of a professorship of Commerce.

110. See Chapter 9.

111. 'Training of the Nation', cols 660 and 676.

112. R. B. Haldane, 'National Education', in William Harbutt Dawson (ed.), *After-War Problems* (London: George Allen & Unwin, 1917), p. 86.

113. R. B. Haldane, 'The Student and the Nation', Foundation Oration 1916, University of London, University College, Union Society, p. 4.

114. This, and quotations from preceding paragraph, taken from Haldane, 'The Student and the Nation', pp. 5–14.

115. Georg Kerschensteiner, *The Schools and the Nation*, trans. C. K. Ogden (London: Macmillan, 1914).

116. Haldane, 'The Student and the Nation', p. 9.

117. Ibid., p. 11.

118. See Haldane, 'National Education'.

119. Kerschensteiner, *The Schools and the Nation*, p. xix.

120. Ibid., p. xxii.

121. See Boucher and Vincent, *A Radical Hegelian*.

122. RBH to MEH, 6 May 1916, NLS, MS 5995, ff. 137–8.

123. *Times Educational Supplement*, 6 June 1916, quoted in Ashby and Anderson, *Portrait of Haldane*, p. 125.

124. RBH to MEH, 29 June 1916, NLS, MS 5995, f. 205.

125. Qs14003ff., *appendix to final report*; 1918 [Cd8993] xiv, quoted in Ashby and Anderson, *Portrait of Haldane*, p. 128.

126. Royal Commission on University Education in Wales, *Final Report of the Commissioners* (London: HMSO, 1918), p. 60, para. 181.

127. 'The Ideal of the University' (1920), quoted in Ashby and Anderson, *Portrait of Haldane*, p. 129.

128. *Times Educational Supplement*, 22 Aug. 1918, quoted in Ashby and Anderson, *Portrait of Haldane*, pp. 130–1.

129. J. Herbert Lewis to RBH, 30 Nov. 1920, NLS, MS 5914, f. 260.

130. The term was coined by Quintin Hogg, later Viscount Hailsham, in 1964. See 'Clause 1.—(Administrative Provisions relating to New Ministries.)', *House of Commons Debates*, 9 Dec. 1964, vol. 703, cols. 1553–1686, esp. 1646. At col. 1651 Hogg refers to Haldane as 'a far more distinguished man than the Labour Party has ever harboured since or is ever likely to harbour again'.

131. 'Minister to Enshrine Protection for Research Independence'.

132. The UK Research and Innovation website states (not entirely accurately): 'Nowhere in his [Haldane's] report was any mention of the principle that we would recognise today as the one bearing his name.' This reading of the text did not stop the UKRI, in collaboration with the Institute for Government, hosting a special debate on 12 Dec. 2018, entitled Haldane 100, 'to mark the centenary and explore the continued relevance of Lord Haldane's report'. Speakers and panel members included Professor Sir Mark Walport, chief executive of UK Research and Innovation; Lord David Willetts, former minister for universities and science; and Minouche Shafik, director of the London School of Economics. See 'Haldane 100', UK Research and Innovation. The website for the Medical Research Council gives a very brief but just assessment of the place of Haldane's report with regards to their work in independence from government: 'History', Medical Research Council.

133. Ministry of Reconstruction, *Report of the Machinery of Government Committee*, Part 2, IV, pp. 22–35.

134. Ibid., para. 41, p. 29.

135. Ibid., para. 42, p. 29.

136. Ibid., para. 67(a), p. 34.

137. Ibid., para. 68, p. 34.

138. As mentioned, this did have its precursor in the Medical Research Committee, established in August 1913. The Haldane Report, however, redefines the operation of the committee along the lines of the (Haldane-inspired) Committee of Council for Scientific and Industrial Research—namely, to operate under the direction of a committee of the Privy Council. See Marwick, *The Deluge*, p. 230; also Ministry of Reconstruction, *Report of the Machinery of Government Committee*, Part II, IX, para. 15, p. 60.

139. Ibid. Part I, para. 56(a).

140. Ehsan Masood, 'A 100th Birthday Wish: Uphold Academic Freedom in Dark Times', *Nature* 563 (2018), https://www.nature.com/nature/volumes/563/issues/7733

141. Pellew, 'Practitioners versus Theorists', p. 8.

142. Ibid.

143. See Anthea Bennett, 'Advising the Cabinet—the Committee of Civil Research and

the Economic Advisory Council: A Brief Comparison', *Public Administration*, 56 (1978), pp. 53 and 65.

144. Dainton, *Reflections on Universities*, pp. 74–5. Sir Fred Dainton, later Lord Dainton, FRS FRSE (1914–97) was a professor of Chemistry, first at Leeds then Oxford, and became chair of the University Grants Committee in 1973. In 1970 he was made chairman of the Council for Scientific Policy. From 1978 until his death in 1997 Dainton was chancellor of the University of Sheffield.

145. *The Inwardness of the Budget; Speeches Delivered by the Rt. Hon.Viscount Haldane ... and the Rt. Hon, D. Lloyd George at the National Liberal Club on June 26, 1914* (1914), quoted in Ashby and Anderson, *Portrait of Haldane*, p. 118. The relationship between these two men would not remain so cordial. On 10 July 1915 Haldane, according to Margot Asquith's diary, described Lloyd George as 'a very treacherous little man', even 'a maniac', who has 'done nothing well in his life & rushes everything': Oxford, Bodleian Library, MS. Eng. d. 3213, f. 26.

146. Ashby and Anderson, *Portrait of Haldane*, p. 140.

147. H. W. Orange. 'Remarks on a Memo. Unsigned and undated, recd on Dec 12 1916', quoted in ibid., p. 142.

148. Fisher to Gosse, 8 Dec. 1916, in F. Russell Bryant (ed.), *Coalition Diaries and Letters of H. A. L. Fisher, 1916–1922*, vol. 1 (Lewiston, NY: Mellen Press, 2006), p. 84 (hereafter *Fisher Diaries*).

149. Fisher to Lettice Fisher, 15 Oct. 1917, in ibid., p. 149.

150. Fisher to Lettice Fisher, 18 Oct. 1917, in ibid., p. 152.

151. Not to be confused with the Education (Scotland) Act, 1918, which some claim to be an even more radical piece of legislation. See Lindsay Paterson, 'The Significance of the Education (Scotland) Act, 1918', *Scottish Affairs*, 27, 4 (2018).

152. See Howard Gilbert and Helen Prew (eds), *A Passion for Learning: Celebrating 80 Years of NIACE Support for Adult Learning* (Leicester: NIACE, 2001), though the section on Haldane has a number of factual inaccuracies.

153. For more on Cassel's background and career see Pellew, 'A Metropolitan University Fit for Empire', p. 223.

154. *Fisher Diaries*, p. 335. Jill Pellew notes: 'The core of this money [the money from the Cassel Trust] went to endow nine professorial posts—of which the first to be filled was the Ernest Cassel Professor of International Relations in 1924—and other lectureships': 'A Metropolitan University Fit for Empire', p. 232.

155. Fisher to Lettice Fisher, 17 Dec. 1918, *Fisher Diaries*, p. 341.

156. Pellew, 'A Metropolitan University Fit for Empire', p. 232.

157. Ashby and Anderson, *Portrait of Haldane*, pp. 156–7.

158. For reception at Bristol see ibid., pp. 155–6. The honorary doctorates were awarded by Bristol, Cambridge, Durham, Edinburgh, Göttingen, Liverpool, Manchester, McGill, Oxford and Sheffield.

159. Charles Gore to ESH, Aug. 1928 (precise date not given), NLS, MS 6033, f. 292.

160. H. J. W. Hetherington, *Theory and Practice* (Haldane Memorial Lecture, 1932), quoted in Ashby and Anderson, *Portrait of Haldane*, p. xiv.

161. Ashby and Anderson, *Portrait of Haldane*, p. 173.

9. WAR AND PEACE

1. 17 June 1912, NLS, MS 5909, ff. 259–60.

2. 22 Aug. 1928, NLS, MS 6033, f. 36.

3. Haldane, *An Autobiography*, p. 182.

4. Ibid., p. 181; see also Chapter 7.

5. Ian Hamilton, *The Soul and Body of an Army* (London: Edward Arnold & Co., 1921), p. 7.

6. The arguments in favour of the voluntary route were made in a book entitled *Compulsory Service: A Study of the Question in Light of Experience* (London: John Murray, 1910) by General Sir Ian Hamilton with an introduction by Haldane. Roberts swiftly attempted to rebut the book's claims in his *Fallacies and Facts: An Answer to 'Compulsory Service'* (London: John Murray, 1911). Haldane, unsurprisingly, believed that the advocates of the voluntary system got the better of the debate.

7. See Morris, 'Haldane's Army Reforms', p. 32; and Spiers, *Haldane*, p. 112.

8. For the origins of this service see E. S. Haldane, *The British Nurse in Peace and War* (London: John Murray, 1923), pp. 174–86. The defining figure in its establishment was General Sir Alfred Keogh, director-general of the Army Medical Service from 1905 to 1910 and, again, for the duration of the First World War. He served as rector of Haldane's beloved Imperial College London from 1910 to 1922. Ernest M. Teagarden comments: 'Certainly, when the First World War came and the Regular medical and nursing service proved to be inadequate the Territorial organization came to the rescue and performed steadfast service. The same could be said for the Voluntary Aid Detachments of the British Red Cross Society whose behind-the-line services helped Territorials and Regulars alike': *Haldane at the War Office* (New York: Gordon Press, 1976), p. 110. According to Elizabeth Haldane's entry in the *Oxford Dictionary of National Biography*, it was she who 'originated the Voluntary Aid Detachments': 'Haldane, Elizabeth Sanderson', *ODNB*.

9. See Robin Neillands, *The Old Contemptibles: The British Expeditionary Force 1914–1918* (London: John Murray, 2004), p. 136.

10. For historical perspectives which accepted and built upon Haldane's narrative, and did so in light of full access to a previously inaccessible range of historical papers from the pre-war period, see Nicholas d'Ombrain, *War Machinery and High Policy: Defence Administration in Peacetime Britain 1902–1914* (London: Oxford University Press, 1973) and J. McDermott, 'The Revolution in British Military Thinking from the Boer War to the Moroccan Crisis', *Canadian Journal of History*, 9, 2 (1974).

11. See Sir Hew Strachan, 'The British Army, its General Staff, and the Continental Commitment 1904–1914', in David French and Brian Holden Reid (eds), *The British*

General Staff: Reform and Innovation, 1890–1939 (London: Frank Cass, 2002), pp. 63–79.

12. Examples of the more recent historical perspective summarised in this paragraph can be found in John Gooch's *The Plans for War: The General Staff and British Military Strategy c. 1900–1916* (London: Routledge & Kegan Paul, 1974) and his *The Prospect of War: Studies in British Defence Policy 1847–1942* (London: Frank Cass, 1981). Edward Spiers's *Haldane* endorses Gooch's views. Sir Hew Strachan charts the history of the change of opinion amongst historians in 'The British Army'.

13. This, in essence, is one of the central claims of Edward Spiers, a representative historian of the modern perspective on Haldane as War Secretary. See the final chapter of his *Haldane*, pp. 187–200.

14. See Brigadier General E. L. Spears, *Liaison 1914: A Narrative of the Great Retreat* (London: William Heinemann, 1930), p. 416.

15. Anthony Seldon and David Walsh, *Public Schools and the Great War: The Generation Lost* (Barnsley: Pen and Sword Military, 2013), p. 30.

16. As Seldon and Walsh point out, 4,000 of the initial 7,000 officers deployed were casualties by Christmas 1914, of whom 1,220 were killed. See *Public Schools and the Great War*, p. 40. As an example of the public school contribution, Marlborough College, where my own three children went to school and where my brother-in-law David Du Croz was editor-in-chief of a magnificent centenary volume marking the sacrifice of the Marlborough College community during the Great War, provided in itself, through its OTC, 506 officers and 39 other ranks during that initial period. Over the whole period of the war, 749 Marlburians, teachers and staff were to give their lives in service to their country, 113 of whom were present in the whole school photograph taken in front of the cricket pavilion in July 1914. See David Du Croz (editor-in-chief), *Marlborough College and the Great War in 100 Stories* (Marlborough: Marlborough College, 2018). The impact on Haldane's own school, the Edinburgh Academy, has been poignantly described in Sarah Heintze and Alan Fyfe (eds), *Pro Patria Mori: The Edinburgh Academy at War, 1914–1918* (Edinburgh: Edinburgh Academy, 2015).

17. A number of military figures who had worked with Haldane at the War Office believed Kitchener would have built up the army more rapidly had he followed the structure and processes of the Territorial scheme. Haldane certainly believed that Kitchener fell short in this respect. The need for greatly expanded numbers was pressing as the scale of the conflict and the casualties became clear. Sir Hew Strachan's views on this are relevant to note, highlighting the discontinuities between General Staff strategy and army organisation: 'In 1914 the B.E.F. suffered a shattering defeat. The army survived, but it did so by effectively converting to the idea of a limited liability on the continent of Europe—at least until 1916. It had no option, for the general staff had embraced a continental strategy without creating a continental army. That was true organisationally and doctrinally, but it was above all true in terms of recruitment. Britain had no other option from the autumn of 1914 than to mark time, for

it now had to create the mass army which its strategy demanded of it': Strachan, 'The British Army', p. 78.

18. See Peter Dennis, *The Territorial Army, 1907–1940* (Woodbridge: published for the Royal Historical Society by the Boydell Press, 1987), pp. 33–4; and Ian F. W. Beckett, *Britain's Part-Time Soldiers: The Amateur Military Tradition 1558–1945* (Barnsley: Pen and Sword Military, 2011).

19. Field Marshal Viscount French of Ypres, *1914* (London: Constable & Co., 1919), p. 204.

20. 'What is the Total UK Public Spending', UK Public Spending.

21. For the year's overall expenditure see 'Public Spending Details for 1905', UK Public Spending. For army expenditure specifically see Haldane, *Army Reform and Other Addresses*, p. 3.

22. It is interesting to note Simon Giles Higgins's observation: 'Military history, if applied cautiously, provides a useful tool for decisions makers and ensures that they ask the right questions. Nearly every situation will have had something similar to it occur in the past and careful study of it can provide useful prompts to those responsible for asking the questions. But history does not provide prescriptive lessons only "approximate precedents"': 'How was Richard Haldane able to Reform the British Army? An Historical Assessment using a Contemporary Change Management Model' (Master of Philosophy Thesis, University of Birmingham, 2010), p. 10, published online at http://etheses.bham.ac.uk/1298/2/Higgens_MPhil_11.pdf

23. Haldane, *An Autobiography*, p. 185.

24. See Teagarden, *Haldane at the War Office*, p. 15.

25. 'Strength of the German Army (1890–1914)', German History in Documents and Images.

26. 8 Jan. 1906, NLS, MS 5907, f. 10.

27. See Haldane, *An Autobiography*, pp. 189–90.

28. As discussed earlier, there have been differing views amongst historians about the extent to which Haldane, in his post-war writings, reshaped the narrative to make it appear as if the German threat dominated strategic planning from as early as 1906, when in reality there were many threats, particularly imperial, that guided military strategy right up to the outbreak of war in 1914. In my view, Haldane's post-war focus on the preparations for Continental warfare (at the expense perhaps of a fully rounded historical picture) is accounted for by the sheer volume of vitriol he received for supposedly not heeding the German threat.

29. A division is a large military unit, and varies in size from about 10,000 (though it can on occasion be less than this) to 18,000 soldiers. A corps consists of two or more divisions, plus support troops, and can range from 50,000 (again, in some instances it can be less) to 100,000 soldiers.

30. A brigade is made up of three to five battalions. A battalion is a combat unit of 500 to 800 soldiers. A brigade tends to be 1,500 to 4,000 men strong.

31. See Rhodri Williams, *Defending the Empire: The Conservative Party and British Defence*

Policy 1899–1915 (New Haven and London: Yale University Press, 1991), pp. 100–19.

32. See Teagarden, *Haldane at the War Office*, pp. 90–1.

33. R. B. Haldane, 'On the Reform of the Army', in *Army Reform and Other Addresses*, p. 111.

34. F. N. Maude, 'The New Army Scheme', *Contemporary Review*, 91 (Apr. 1907), p. 520.

35. Haldane, 'On the Reform of the Army', p. 110.

36. Haldane, *An Autobiography*, p. 192.

37. RBH to Lord Rosebery, 19 Dec. 1905, NLS, MS 5906, f. 282.

38. Ellison to Lady Haig, 11 Sept. 1928, NLS, Haig Mss, Acc 3155.40q, quoted in Higgins, 'How was Richard Haldane able to Reform the British Army?', p. 56.

39. See Chapter 4 of Higgins, 'How was Richard Haldane able to Reform the British Army?'.

40. Haldane, *An Autobiography*, p. 183.

41. Haldane writes from Cloan to Asquith on 28 Dec 1905: 'I have Col. Ellison here and we have drawn up a memorandum on Economy in Army Administration. If the ideas work out I think I see my way to a substantial saving. I am dying to apply Fishers [*sic*] principle with regard to Navy Estimates, & have already found room for providing exclusive applications of it. No attempt at anything of the kind has yet been thought of—so far I can discover': Oxford, Bodleian Library, MS. Asquith 10, ff. 194–5. In the end, however, Fisher—unlike Haldane—did not in fact manage to save money.

42. Haldane issued two memoranda during this time, one on 1 January and the other on 1 February 1906, the second of which essentially set the principles of the reforms in stone. As Spiers comments, 'While amendments to detail and phraseology would be acceptable, there could be no departure from the original conception of an Expeditionary Force and a Territorial Army as outlined in the second memorandum': *Haldane*, p. 77.

43. A. J. Anthony Morris, *Reporting the First World War: Charles Repington*, The Times *and the Great War* (Cambridge: Cambridge University Press, 2015), p. 99.

44. Repington to Esher, 5 Oct. 1906, quoted in A. J. Anthony Morris, *The Scaremongers: The Advocacy of War and Rearmament 1896–1914* (London: Routledge & Kegan Paul, 2014), p. 116.

45. Gardiner, *Prophets, Priests, & Kings*, p. 286.

46. RBH to Gosse, 17 Dec. 1905, Brotherton Library, Leeds, BC MS 19c Gosse.

47. See Spiers, *Haldane*, p. 97.

48. Sir G. S. Clarke to Lord Esher, 21 Mar. 1906, Esher Mss. 10/38, quoted in Spiers, *Haldane*, p. 100.

49. Sir G. S. Clarke to Lord Esher, 30 Apr. 1906, Esher Mss. 10/38, quoted in Spiers, *Haldane*, p. 100.

50. On the day he took office, however, Haldane reported to his sister Elizabeth: 'Sir G. Clarke—a dry man but the greatest expert of the day—said to me quietly after two hours talk—"I prophesy that there has been nothing comparable to this appoint-

ment since Lord Cardwell's time'": 11 Dec. 1905, NLS, MS 6011, ff. 18–19. We might note that Viscount Esher's biographer regarded Clarke as 'an insensitive, clumsy, uncouth and infinitely boring man': James Lees-Milne, *The Enigmatic Edwardian: The Life of Reginald 2nd Viscount Esher* (London: Sidgwick & Jackson, 1986), p. 146. Clarke resigned as secretary of the CID in 1907. The highly influential Lord Esher wrote to the First Sea Lord Sir John Fisher in February 1907 that, 'In spite of Clarke and his numerous detractors, he [Haldane] has carried his *whole scheme*, one of the most controversial on record, right through the Cabinet': quoted in Lees-Milne, *The Enigmatic Edwardian*, p. 146. Clarke was made governor of Bombay in July 1907. Maurice Hankey was appointed naval assistant secretary to the CID in 1907, before succeeding as secretary of the CID in 1912. Unlike that with Clarke, Haldane's relationship with Hankey was a very close one, and each had immense respect for the other. See Stephen Roskill, *Hankey: Man of Secrets* (London: Collins, 1970).

51. See Spiers, *Haldane*, p. 136.

52. There were times, of course, when Haldane was ruffling more feathers than he was smoothing. According to Morley: 'The dangers to the Cabinet and its solidarity seem to be Ireland and Haldane': Morley to CB, 1 Jan. 1907, Campbell-Bannerman Papers, British Library, Add. MS. 41223, f. 208.

53. As Haldane tells Esher on 31 Dec. 1906: 'Yes. The New Year is a very important one. You have helped me enormously and if you give me the same splendid co-operation I am not without hope that we may land our fish': NLS, MS 5907, ff. 135–6. While Esher was undoubtedly critical to Haldane's success, it is going too far to give him the bulk of the recognition for the Haldane Reforms. Peter Fraser's *Lord Esher: A Political Biography* (London: Hart-Davis MacGibbon, 1973) argues that Esher and Ellison were the true originators of the reforms, while James Lees-Milne, in his *The Enigmatic Edwardian*, continues in this vein, though he also gives Balfour considerable credit. Correlli Barnett in his essay 'Radical Reform: 1902–14', in A. Perlmutter and V. P. Bennett (eds), *The Political Influence of the Military: A Comparative Reader* (New Haven: Yale University Press, 1980) sees Esher as the key figure in meeting the demands for military reform, downplaying Haldane's role to simple implementation of Esher's thinking. The principal authorities at the time, however, saw it very differently. Everyone knew that Esher was an influential figure, but Haig, Ellison, Sir Charles Harris, Colonel Seely, Charles à Court Repington, Sir Ian Hamilton, Sir William Nicholson and many others who were at the centre of military affairs at that time acknowledge that it is Haldane who bears the primary responsibility for the revolution in army organisation that took place at the beginning of the twentieth century. As Ellison told Elizabeth Haldane upon Haldane's death: 'This last week I have been compiling for Lady Haig's benefit some notes on those two wonderful years at the War Office 1906 to 7 in explanation of certain letters that General Haig wrote to me at that time and this labour of love has brought home to me more clearly than ever what a marvellous work Lord Haldane effected. No-one but he could have

done it': Ellison to ESH, 20 Aug. 1928, NLS, MS 6032, f. 101. The words of the head of the finance department at the War Office, Sir Charles Harris, are also perfectly clear on this matter: 'His fame as war minister rests secure on that incomparable little army "The Old Contemptibles" and on the Old Territorials who held the field in succession to them, of both of which he was the creator': Lord Harris to ESH, 20 Aug. 1928, NLS, MS 6032, f. 130.

54. Lees-Milne, *The Enigmatic Edwardian*, p. 164.

55. RBH to MEH, 12 July 1906, quoted in Spiers, *Haldane*, p. 61.

56. Esher to King Edward VII, 8 Apr. 1908, quoted in Reginald Brett, *Journals and Letters of Reginald, Viscount Esher*, vol. 2 (London: Ivor Nicholson & Watson, 1934), p. 302.

57. As Haldane wrote to CB: 'The whole question rests with our own people, and I think that if I can present this very temperately, not as a proposition for increasing the Army, but as one for putting a reduced Army on a business footing and producing, not only very substantial reductions in the Estimates—immediate and prospective—but an organization which can be—without destroying—diminished or expanded, according to policy, without, as under present conditions, damaging it, we may be able to carry our own people with us': RBH to HCB, 9 Jan. 1907, Campbell-Bannerman MSS., B.M. Add. MS. 41,230, f. 156, quoted in Spiers, *Haldane*, p. 107. Regarding the reduction in infantry battalions, nine were disbanded in total, including—controversially for Haldane the Scot—the Third Scots Guards.

58. Hew Strachan, *The Outbreak of the First World War* (Oxford: Oxford University Press, 2004), p. 33. See also Spiers, *Haldane*, p. 91.

59. Haldane put the matter bluntly in these terms: 'I believed we could obtain a finely organised Army for less money than at present, but that finer Army we must have, even though it cost more. I went to a meeting in the City within my first ten days of office, accompanied by Ellison and Lady Horner, and proclaimed this, adding that the Prime Minister had authorised me to say that if more money turned out to be essential we should have it. I was not prepared to go on with my work on any other footing': *An Autobiography*, p. 186.

60. See Chapter 7. Churchill's decision in the summer of 1912, while still First Lord of the Admiralty, to enter into a joint naval strategy with the French should not be left out of the picture. This allowed for the concentration of the British fleet in the North Sea and the French fleet in the Mediterranean. If this did not oblige Britain to enter into war on the side of France if France were attacked by Germany, then it is unclear what did. See Owen, *The Hidden Perspective*, p. 185. See also Churchill's letter to Haldane on 6 May 1912 outlining his arguments in favour of such a joint strategy (NLS, MS 5909, ff. 215–16), which includes some very Churchill-esque rhetoric: 'The war-plans for the last 5 years have provided for the evacuation of the Meditern [sic] as the first step consequent on a war with Germany, & all we are doing is to make peace dispositions wh approximate to war necessities. It wd be very foolish to lose England in safeguarding Egypt.' Or again, 'If she [France] is our friend, we shall not suffer. If she is not, we shall suffer. But if we win the big battle in the decisive

theatre, we can put everything else straight afterwards. If we lose it, there will not be any afterwards. London is the key of Egypt—don't lose that. Considering you propose to send the whole Br Army abroad, you ought to help me to keep the whole Br Navy at home. Whatever the French do, my counsel is the same, & is the first of all the laws of war—overpowering strength at the decisive point.'

61. Spiers's balanced assessment is as follows: 'A Continental commitment provided a focal point for reform and some key requirements, but it could not determine the content of reform. Peacetime requirements impinged upon and restricted the scope of the minister responsible; these were decisive at the time, even if too easily forgotten in retrospective writing': *Haldane*, p. 91. Historians John Gooch and Sir Hew Strachan argue that it was the advent of Sir Henry Wilson to the position of director of military operations in August 1910 (while Haldane was still in post) that really marked the point at which the military discussions with France gained firm substance, particularly in planning for the transportation of the BEF to France. It was at this point, so Gooch argues, that 'military planning, organization and mobilization concentrated exclusively on Europe': Gooch, *The Prospect of War*, p. 111 and *The Plans for War*, p. 166; Strachan, *The Outbreak of the First World War*, p. 33. See also S. R. Williamson, *The Politics of Grand Strategy: Britain and France Prepare for War, 1906–1914* (Cambridge, MA: Harvard University Press, 1969), p. 100 and Robbins, *Sir Edward Grey*, pp. 178–9.

62. See Morris, 'Haldane's Army Reforms', p. 32.

63. 'UK Inflation Calculator', CPI Inflation Calculator, https://www.officialdata.org/uk/inflation/1907?amount=28000000

64. HCB to Sinclair, 3 Feb. 1907, Campbell-Bannerman Papers, British Library, Add. MS. 41230, ff. 172–3. The last line is a reference to Joseph Addison's ode to the British victory at Blenheim, *The Campaign*, where the Duke of Marlborough, 'pleased th' Almighty's orders to perform, / Rides in the whirlwind, and directs the storm'.

65. CB to RBH, 3 Sept. 1907, NLS, MS 5907, ff. 180–1.

66. Esher Papers, ii. 267, quoted in Morris, 'Haldane's Army Reforms', p. 24.

67. For example, Ellison, Haig, Repington and Hamilton.

68. For example, Maxse. There are two sentences on p. 187 of Haldane's *Before the War* that would equally be applicable to the statements Haldane made before the outbreak of hostilities: 'It is not with any hope that these pages will satisfy the extremists of to-day that they have been written. They are intended for those who try to be dispassionate, and for them only, as a contribution to a vast heap of material that is being gathered together for consideration.'

69. See Haldane, *An Autobiography*, p. 30.

70. RBH to Lord Rosebery, 19 Dec. 1905, NLS, MS 5906, f. 282.

71. See Haldane, *An Autobiography*, p. 187.

72. RBH to Lord Rosebery, 19 Dec. 1905, NLS, MS 5906, f. 282.

73. RBH to Lord Esher, 19 Feb. 1906, MS 5907, f. 30. Interestingly, the historian Gary Sheffield draws on Haldane's admiration for Haig as evidence against those who

would accuse the commander-in-chief of the BEF of being 'several rounds short of a .303 Lee Enfield magazine'. Sheffield writes: 'There is plenty of evidence that Haig was not stupid. For one thing he worked closely with Richard Burdon Haldane in reforming the army before the First World War. Haldane, one of the greatest Secretaries of State for War Britain has ever had, possessed a formidable intellect— and yet admired Haig': *The Chief: Douglas Haig and the British Army* (London: Aurum Press, 2011), p. 6.

74. Nigel Jones, '*The Chief: Douglas Haig and the British Army* by Gary Sheffield: review', *The Telegraph* (11 Aug. 2011).

75. For overviews of the history of Haig's reputation and two more positive modern perspectives see the Introductions to Gary Mead's *The Good Soldier: The Biography of Douglas Haig* (London: Atlantic, 2007) and Sheffield's *The Chief*.

76. Spiers, *Haldane*, p. 150.

77. Ibid., pp. 152–3.

78. We might note that the Cloan visitors' book shows that Haig only stayed once, in 1907. On that occasion his fellow house guests were General Sir Ian Hamilton, Charles à Court Repington, the military correspondent of *The Times*, General Sir Edward Pemberton Leach VC, the GOC Scottish Command, and, curiously, although only for part of the time, three German military attachés.

79. See Spiers, *Haldane*, pp. 90, 150, 190.

80. James Lees-Milne's remark that 'the Haldane army reforms were to be as much Esher's and Balfour's as his own' is surely preposterous. See Lees-Milne, *The Enigmatic Edwardian*, p. 158.

81. See, for example, Ellison's comments in his 'Reminiscences', *Lancashire Lad Journal of the Loyal Regiment (North Lancashire)*, 55, 3 (Feb. 1936), p. 8 and Peter Fraser's comments in *Lord Esher* (p. 181) on Esher's advice around a 'striking force' before Haldane took office. See also Chapter 4 of Higgins's 'How was Richard Haldane able to Reform the British Army?'.

82. See Spiers, *Haldane*, pp. 96–7; also Haldane, *An Autobiography*, pp. 184–5.

83. Hamilton, *The Soul and Body of an Army*, pp. 6–7. It should be noted that Hamilton's point 3 was not in fact something Cardwell addressed; it had been addressed by Hugh Childers as Secretary of State for War between 1880 and 1882.

84. Haldane, *Before the War*, p. 43.

85. Stanley von Donop to ESH, 20 Aug. 1928, NLS, MS 6032, f. 191.

86. Hankey to RBH, 28 May 1915, quoted in Roskill, *Hankey*, pp. 176–7.

87. Haldane, *An Autobiography*, p. 182.

88. Webb, *Our Partnership*, pp. 325–6.

89. Ibid.

90. Haldane, towards the end of his life, was to reflect humbly on his youthful self-belief, writing in *An Autobiography* (p. 30): 'I [as a young man] was active and tenacious in a high degree, and was confident, probably to an undue extent, of my power to succeed in whatever I undertook.'

91. See Sommer, *Haldane of Cloan*, p. 213.

92. Morris, 'Haldane's Army Reforms', p. 26.

93. Memorandum to the Cabinet, 27 June 1908, quoted in ibid.

94. Morris, 'Haldane's Army Reforms', p. 26.

95. Repington wrote: 'We could not at this time so much as hint that we might ever be engaged upon the continent of Europe, because we were immediately treated to every kind of abuse for suggesting such a thing, and no one would look at any argument founded upon it. Our engagements to Belgium were regarded as ancient history, and nobody thought about them, or understood what they meant': Charles à Court Repington, *Vestigia* (London: Constable & Co., 1919), p. 278.

96. See Spiers, *Haldane*, p. 70.

97. Haldane, *An Autobiography*, p. 227. In October 1911, Esher noted a change of attitude in Asquith: 'We talked about the General Staff scheme of landing an army in France. The Prime Minister is opposed to this plan. He will not hear of the despatch of more than four Divisions. He has told Haldane so.': quoted in Sommer, *Haldane of Cloan*, p. 247.

98. Haldane, *An Autobiography*, p. 228.

99. Ibid., p. 230.

100. Ibid.

101. Bonham Carter, *Winston Churchill*, p. 239.

102. Haldane, *An Autobiography*, pp. 230–1.

103. Quoted in Bonham Carter, *Winston Churchill*, p. 237.

104. Haldane, *An Autobiography*, p. 232.

105. R. C. K. Ensor, *England, 1870–1914* (Oxford: Clarendon Press, 1960), p. 436.

106. Quoted in Sommer, *Haldane of Cloan*, pp. 248–9.

107. Balfour to Lord Roberts, 12 Aug. 1905, Roberts Papers, quoted in Koss, *Lord Haldane*, p. 42.

108. Spiers, *Haldane*, p. 73.

109. RBH to MEH, 17 Nov. 1906, NLS, MS 5976, ff. 173–4. On 16 November, the day before Haldane's letter was written, Rosebery had unveiled a memorial statue to the Scots Greys on Edinburgh's Princes Street, followed by a lunch at which he gave a speech. In his speech, Rosebery said: 'If the Scottish Liberal members of Parliament fail to move a Scottish Prime Minister and a Scottish Secretary for War to a sense of what is due to the claims of Scotland, I am afraid there is only one piece of advice I can offer, deleterious in its inference, poisonous in its source, and very likely to be disastrous in its result. It is, gentlemen, that you must cease to be a quiet, law-loving, God-fearing kingdom, and take up a different line—become an unruly, rebellious people, and you will have plenty of Scottish cavalry regiments (Laughter)': 'The Scots Greys Memorial', *The Scotsman*, 17 Nov. 1906.

110. See Spiers, *Haldane*, p. 112.

111. See ibid., p. 113.

112. See Chapter 8.

113. Haldane, *An Autobiography*, pp. 193–4; see also Koss, *Lord Haldane*, p. 53.

114. Even as early as 1900 Haldane was urging Liberals to unite with Conservatives to create an efficient army, as a way of defending the interests of the empire, not as a sign of heightened militarism. See Spiers, *Haldane*, p. 38.

115. A reflection made, in conversation with Richard McLauchlan, by Jim Johnston, clerk to the Finance and Constitution Committee at the Scottish Parliament, and member of the Executive Committee of the Study of Parliament Group.

116. Haldane, *An Autobiography*, p. 185.

117. Haldane, 'On the Reform of the Army', p. 46.

118. 'Haldane, Richard Burdon, Viscount Haldane', *ODNB*.

119. Spiers points out (see *Haldane*, p. 126) that the speech appears to have been drafted by Ellison, which is unsurprising given Haldane's heavy burden at the time of trying to get the Territorial Bill through Parliament. Nevertheless, it seems highly unlikely that the thrust of the speech did not come from Haldane, even if the actual words were put together by Ellison.

120. Ibid., p. 134.

121. See R. B. Haldane, 'The Cabinet and the Empire', 9 June 1903, *Proceedings of the Royal Colonial Institute* 34.

122. Webb, *Our Partnership*, p. 95.

123. Shane Leslie writes: 'Before taking office he had sent a friend to buy up all the books dealing with the subject of war. As his destination was still a secret, he did not wish to be seen making such an unusual purchase himself': 'Lord Haldane', in W. R. Inge (ed.), *The Post Victorians* (London: Ivor Nicholson & Watson, 1933), pp. 212–13.

124. Dennis, *The Territorial Army*, p. 16.

125. See Spiers, *Haldane*, p. 108.

126. Morris, *Reporting the First World War*, p. 99.

127. Ibid.

128. Webb, *Our Partnership*, pp. 141–2.

129. Arthur Davidson on behalf of the king to RBH, 9 Sept. 1906, NLS, MS 5907, ff. 94–7.

130. Haldane, *An Autobiography*, pp. 205–6.

131. RBH to Wilkinson, 2 Jan. 1906, Wilkinson Manuscripts, 13/32, quoted in Spiers, *Haldane*, p. 120.

132. R. B. Haldane at the London School of Economics, *The Times* (11 Feb. 1907), quoted in Spiers, *Haldane*, p. 151.

133. See Geoff Sloan, 'Haldane's Mackindergarten: A Radical Experiment in British Military Education?' *War in History*, 19, 3 (2012), p. 325.

134. The following paragraphs are highly indebted to the research and argumentation of Alfred Gollin in his *No Longer an Island: Britain and the Wright Brothers 1902–1909* (London: Heinemann, 1984) and *The Impact of Air Power*.

135. Haldane, *An Autobiography*, p. 232.

136. Ibid., p. 234.

137. Ibid., p. 233.
138. The position was held by Ludwig Prandtl. See Ernst Heinrich Hirschel, Horst Prem and Gero Madelung, *Aeronautical Research in Germany: From Lilienthal until Today* (Berlin: Springer Science & Business Media, 2012), p. 33.
139. See, for instance, E. Charles Vivian, *A History of Aeronautics* (London: W. Collins Sons & Co. 1921), p. 176 and Marvin W. McFarland, 'When the Airplane was a Military Secret', *The Air Power Historian*, 2, 4 (Oct. 1955), pp. 78–9.
140. For a good summary of criticisms of this kind see Chapter 14 of Gollin, *No Longer an Island*.
141. Ibid., p. 233.
142. Gollin, *The Impact of Air Power*, p. 46.
143. Percy Walker, *Early Aviation at Farnborough*, 2 vols (London: Macdonald & Co., 1974), vol. 1, p. 254.
144. Ibid., vol. 2, p. 273.
145. Henry Tizard, 'A Scientist in and out of the Civil Service', Haldane Memorial Lecture, 1955 (London: Birkbeck College, 1955), p. 4.
146. Gollin, *No Longer an Island*, p. 228.
147. 'Report and Proceedings of a Sub-Committee of the Committee of Imperial Defence Appointed by the Prime Minister to Consider the Question of Foreign Espionage in the United Kingdom', Oct. 1909, TNA CAB 16/8, quoted in Christopher Andrew, *The Defence of the Realm: The Authorised History of MI5* (London: Allen Lane, 2009), p. 3.
148. 'Report and Proceedings of a Sub-Committee of the Committee of Imperial Defence Appointed by the Prime Minister to Consider the Question of Foreign Espionage in the United Kingdom: First Meeting, Tuesday, 30th March, 1909', Oct. 1909, TNA CAB 16/8, quoted in Andrew, *The Defence of the Realm*, p. 19.
149. 'Report and Proceedings of a Sub-Committee of the Committee of Imperial Defence Appointed by the Prime Minister to Consider the Question of Foreign Espionage in the United Kingdom: Second Meeting, Tuesday, 20th April, 1909', Oct. 1909, TNA CAB 16/8, quoted in Andrew, *The Defence of the Realm*, p. 19. The members chosen were Sir Charles Hardinge, the permanent under-secretary (PUS) at the Foreign Office; Sir George Murray, the PUS at the Treasury; Sir Edward Henry, the commissioner of the Metropolitan Police; Major General Ewart, the director of military operations; and Rear Admiral A. E. Bethell, the director of naval intelligence.
150. Report and Proceedings of a Sub-committee of the Committee of Imperial Defence Appointed by the Prime Minister to Consider the Question of Foreign Espionage in the United Kingdom: Third Meeting, Monday, 12th July, 1909', Oct. 1909, TNA CAB 16/8, quoted in Andrew, *The Defence of the Realm*, p. 20.
151. 'The History of MI5', Security Service MI5.
152. I came to know Colin McColl, the chief of MI6, following his retirement from the service when for some fourteen years he became an advisory director of Campbell

Lutyens. He was the last incumbent as head of MI6 never to have his photograph disseminated in the public arena. To this day it is almost impossible to find his image on the internet.

153. Tim Jeal, *Baden-Powell: Founder of the Boy Scouts* (Yale: Yale University Press, 2001), p. ix.

154. Ibid.

155. Michael Rosenthal, *The Character Factory: Baden-Powell and the Origins of the Boy Scout Movement* (London: William Collins, 1986), p. 53.

156. Jeal, *Baden-Powell*, pp. 361–2.

157. Ibid., p. 362.

158. Ibid., p. 372.

159. Ibid., p. 373.

160. Ibid., quoting a speech made by Haldane in introducing an address by Baden-Powell to Royal United Service Institute (RUSI) members on 29 Mar. 1911, reported in the Journal of RUSI in May 1911.

161. Jeal, *Baden-Powell*, p. 373.

162. Ibid., pp. 386–7.

163. Ibid., p. 387.

164. Quoted in ibid., p. 422.

165. William Hillcourt, with Olave, Lady Baden-Powell, *Baden-Powell: The Two Lives of a Hero* (London: William Heinemann, 1964), p. 302.

166. Ibid.

167. Cyril Falls, 'Haldane and Defence', *Public Administration*, 35, 3 (Sept. 1957), p. 253.

168. Grey et al., *Viscount Haldane of Cloan*, p. 2.

10. THE NEW STATE

1. Haldane, 'The Future of Democracy', p. 19.

2. Alongside the main issue of Home Rule, the programme sought 'land reform; reform of the Lords; shorter parliaments; district and parish councils; registration reform and abolition of plural voting; local veto on drink sales; employers' liability for workers' accidents; Scottish and Welsh disestablishment': John Cannon (ed.), *A Dictionary of British History* (Oxford: Oxford University Press, 2009), p. 461.

3. Matthew, *The Liberal Imperialists*, p. 264. It should be noted that this agenda shifted somewhat upon Haldane's entry into office, when more fundamental changes became possible. The Liberal government's policies on income tax, death duties, excise duties and the payment of national insurance are more than 'minor adjustments'. But, as Haldane's friend Violet Markham remarked: 'the reforms [of the Liberal government] were made within the existing framework of a free capitalist society. Socialism as a philosophy of course existed but counted for so little as a political force that few people suspected that a giant was to grow from so puny a babe': *Friendship's Harvest*, p. 89.

4. Matthew, *The Liberal Imperialists*, p. 264.

5. See Bernstein, *Liberalism and Liberal Politics*, pp. 11 and 32.
6. Haldane, 'The New Liberalism', p. 141.
7. Haldane, 'The Future of Democracy', p. 17.
8. Maurice Bruce, however, notes that laissez-faire 'was rather more … an attitude of mind than a conscious political or economic creed. It can easily be shown that a perfect state of *laissez-faire* never in fact existed': *The Coming of the Welfare State*, p. 13.
9. See Searle's list in *The Quest for National Efficiency*, p. 2. Reading Wells's memoirs, it is strange to think of him in connection to Haldane. His assessment of Haldane is rather unkind, though not entirely so. While admitting a certain political affinity, Wells's dislike springs primarily from a lack of intellectual sympathy with Haldane, but he stoops lower than this in certain passages. He comments, for example: 'He [Haldane] was a self-indulgent man, with a large white face and an urbane voice that carried his words as it were on a salver, so that they seemed good even when they were not so. The "Souls," the Balfour set, in a moment of vulgarity had nicknamed him "Tubby."' But Wells does speak of his 'undeniably big brain' and hints that the nation would have been in safer hands during the war if Haldane had been War Secretary. See H. G. Wells, *Experiment in Autobiography: Discoveries and Conclusions of a Very Ordinary Brain (since 1866)* (London: Read Books, 2016), p. 712.
10. Gardiner, *Prophets, Priests, & Kings*, p. 287.
11. Searle, *The Quest for National Efficiency*, p. 54.
12. Ibid.
13. See ibid., pp. 86–92.
14. Ibid., pp. viii–x. See note 1 on page x for reference to Kennedy's own book.
15. Haldane, 'The New Liberalism', p. 133.
16. See Searle, *The Quest for National Efficiency*, p. 3.
17. Follett, *The New State*, p. 139.
18. Matthew, *The Liberal Imperialists*, pp. 9–10.
19. See ibid., pp. 224–64.
20. The British pluralists, in the sense I am using the name here, were those who sought the distribution of power across different groups within society rather than power solely emanating from a dominating, centralised source, such as government or monarch. For a good overview of their thinking see the Introduction to Hirst (ed.), *The Pluralist Theory of the State*. In terms of his engagement with pluralists, Haldane was attracted to certain aspects of L. T. Hobhouse's thinking, writing a preface for his *The Labour Movement* (London: T. Fisher Unwin, 1893), though Hobhouse later turned against Haldane and the Liberal Imperial wing of the Liberal Party for various reasons. See S. Collini, *Liberalism and Sociology: L. T. Hobhouse and Political Argument in England 1880–1914* (Cambridge: Cambridge University Press, 1979), p. 84. Haldane's longest-lasting interlocutor within the pluralist movement was Harold Laski. For more on this relationship see Chapters 4 and 5.
21. See Schneiderman, 'Harold Laski'.
22. Regarding T. H. Green's perspective see Sandra den Otter, 'Thinking in Communities:

Late Nineteenth-Century Liberals, Idealists and the Retrieval of Community', *Parliamentary History*, 16, 1 (Feb. 1997), p. 78; on Muirhead see Vincent and Plant (eds), *Philosophy, Politics and Citizenship*, p. 72; on Laski see Schneiderman, 'Harold Laski', p. 536.

23. Haldane, 'The Future of Democracy', p. 10.

24. For Mary Follett, 'true Hegelianism finds its actualised form in federalism': *The New State*, p. 267. For Harold Laski, 'functional federalism'—the theory that power over a particular issue ought to be devolved to the level of the federal system most suited to deal with that particular issue—was the principal form in which the state could 'take on a more interventionist role in securing the partial equalisation of economic and educational provision and in the reduction of the inequalities between different areas', helping to 'alleviate some of the obstacles to working-class participation': Newman, *Harold Laski*, pp. 50–1.

25. It should be noted that the committee issued only a single opinion in each case. Haldane could sign these on behalf of the committee, not on behalf of himself, as in other high courts.

26. See John T. Saywell's chapter on Haldane in his *The Lawmakers: Judicial Power and the Shaping of Canadian Federalism* (Toronto: University of Toronto Press, 2002), pp. 150–86 for a full overview of Haldane's place within Canadian legal history. Saywell's presentation does a good job of showing what was distinctively new in Haldane's rulings, though it is perhaps rather excessive in some of its judgments ('At times, his [Haldane's] observations and arguments were, if he meant or understood what he said, historically and legally absurd': p. 160) and curiously depicts Haldane 'exploding' (p. 161), 'angrily insisting' (p. 164) and 'storming' (p. 180) in response to those in disagreement with his views, alongside other rather unappealing descriptions of his interactions in court. This in no way correlates to any other portrayal of Haldane's handling of debates, and one wonders where Saywell got his sources for such descriptions. It is one of the defining caricatures of Haldane, according to every other account one reads, that he maintained an astonishing equanimity—sometimes to the annoyance of his opponents—in cases of disagreement. As for Haldane's creativity in his reading of the constitution, there is one voice of dissent, namely Stephen Wexler, who finds that he 'read the two lists of powers more or less as they were written'. See Stephen Wexler, 'The Urge to Idealize: Viscount Haldane and the Constitution of Canada', *McGill Law Journal*, 29 (1984), p. 642.

27. See pp. 175–84 in Saywell's *The Lawmakers* for an analysis of these two judgments and their importance.

28. Schneiderman is right to point out the exceptions, however: 'The Haldane-era jurisprudence did not consistently find for the provinces. In addition to finding Dominion capacity to prescribe the powers of federally incorporated companies, Lord Haldane affirmed federal jurisdiction over fisheries, marriage and divorce, and navigation and shipping. Provinces were also incapacitated from interfering with civil rights outside the province, from interfering with the office of the lieutenant governor, and

418

from imposing indirect taxes. So despite appearances, the Haldane record discloses a willingness to find constitutional authority, on occasion, for the federal government': 'Harold Laski', pp. 554–5.

29. RBH to MES, 20 July 1924, NLS, MS 5916, f. 122.

30. The Farmers' Creditors Arrangement Act, section 498A of the Criminal Code, the Dominion Trade and Industry Commission Act, except for section 14, were all maintained.

31. F. R. Scott, 'The Privy Council and Mr. Bennett's "New Deal" Legislation', *Canadian Journal of Economics and Political Science*, 3, 2 (May 1937), p. 234.

32. Scott actually considers the 1937 judgments to put an even narrower interpretation upon POGG than Haldane's, for 'it would appear that any element of permanence in the statute destroyed its claim to be an emergency legislation': ibid., p. 239.

33. Schneiderman, 'Harold Laski', p. 522.

34. Ibid.

35. F. R. Scott, 'The Development of Canadian Federalism', in *Essays on the Constitution* (Toronto: University of Toronto Press, 1977), pp. 46–7; see also Scott's withering analysis of this in his 'The Privy Council', p. 239, where the situation is described as adding 'an element of burlesque' to the law of the constitution. In addition, see Garth Stevenson, *Unfulfilled Union: Canadian Federalism and National Union*, 5th edn (Montreal: McGill-Queen's University Press, 2009), p. 53.

36. See Schneiderman, 'Harold Laski', p. 525.

37. See Chapter 6 in Vaughan's *Viscount Haldane*, entitled 'Haldane in the Shadow of Lord Watson', pp. 118–44.

38. See Haldane, *The Reign of Relativity*, pp. 372–4; for the BNA Act reference see 'British North America Act 1867'.

39. From a legal Note by James Peoples QC, written at the request of my collaborator Richard McLauchlan, to help clarify the legal position today regarding the monarch's prerogative power. Richard and I would like to thank James for taking the time and effort to produce the Note on our behalf. The following points linking Haldane's discussion to contemporary Brexit-related cases owe their place in this chapter to James's legal Note.

40. See *Miller v Secretary of State for Exiting the European Union* [2017] United Kingdom Supreme Court 5 (*Miller*). The second is *R (in the application of Miller) v The Prime Minister* and *Cherry and others v Advocate General for Scotland* [2019] United Kingdom Supreme Court 41 (*Cherry and Miller*). Paragraphs 40 to 47 of *Miller* are very relevant to our present discussion.

41. United Kingdom Supreme Court, 'Judgment: R (on the application of Miller) (Appellant) v The Prime Minister (Respondent) Cherry and others (Respondents) v Advocate General for Scotland (Appellant) (Scotland)', judgment given on 24 September 2019.

42. As he told his audience in Montreal in 1913: 'The law has grown by development through the influence of the opinion of society guided by its skilled advisers': 'Higher Nationality', in *Selected Addresses and Essays*, p. 65.

43. See The Constitution Act, 1982 (of Canada).

44. Haldane, *The Reign of Relativity*, pp. 428–9.

45. Quoted by Haldane in 'Higher Nationality', p. 64.

46. R. B. Haldane, 'Great Britain and Germany: A Study in National Characteristics' (New York: American Association for International Conciliation, 1912), p. 22.

47. Follett, *The New State*, p. vii.

48. Haldane, *The Reign of Relativity*, p. 371.

49. Ibid., p. 375.

50. Haldane, 'Higher Nationality', pp. 56–7; see also his comments on p. 62 regarding the 'influence of the judges in moulding the law'.

51. Z. A. Pelczynski, 'The Hegelian Concept of the State', in Z. A. Pelczynski (ed.), *Hegel's Political Philosophy: Problems and Perspectives* (Cambridge: Cambridge University Press, 1971), p. 19.

52. Schneiderman, 'Harold Laski', pp. 543–4.

53. See n. 28 above.

54. Scott, 'The Privy Council', p. 237.

55. Vaughan, *Viscount Haldane*, p. xii.

56. For a separate examination of the Hegelian influence on Haldane's Canadian record see also Jonathan Robinson, 'Lord Haldane and the British North America Act', *University of Toronto Law Journal*, 20, 1 (Winter 1970).

57. The question of Haldane's influence on the development of the Canadian constitution has aroused considerable political and academic controversy over much of the last century. In recent years this reached something of a peak following the publication of Vaughan's book in 2010 by the Osgoode Society for Canadian Legal History, established in 1979 to encourage research and writing in the history of Canadian law. Haldane's interpretation of the Canadian constitution involved a combination of philosophical and legal influences, neither of which are easy to pin down, and they are certainly difficult to balance. The book excited both critical acclaim and criticism. For those intrigued by both the intricacies of the debate and the polarisation of interpretation that exists, in addition to the papers and books already referenced in this chapter, I would recommend two reviews of Vaughan's book: David Schneiderman, 'Haldane Unrevealed', *McGill Law Journal*, 57, 3 (2012) and the much shorter review by Stephen Azzi of Carleton University: 'Book review: Viscount Haldane: "The Wicked Step-father of the Canadian Constitution". By Vaughan, Frederick', *The Historian*, 74, 3 (Fall 2012).

58. Vaughan, *Viscount Haldane*, p. 193.

59. Haldane, 'Higher Nationality', p. 68.

60. 'Social Issues in Canada', Canada Guide.

61. Vaughan, *Viscount Haldane*, p. 171.

62. Haldane, 'Higher Nationality', p. 72.

63. Philip J. Kain, *Hegel and the Other: A Study of the Phenomenology of Spirit* (Albany: SUNY Press, 2005), p. 234.

64. See particularly *The Reign of Relativity*, pp. 374–5. It is interesting to note that Haldane, in the last years of his life, was still seeking to rouse public opinion on possible legislation that he believed would cure a critical social problem. See his plea for a probation system in Scotland at the annual meeting of the Scottish Justices' and Magistrates' Association, as reported by the *Glasgow Herald* (14 Jan. 1928): 'Urging that an effort should be made to rouse public opinion to demand the necessary legislation he [Haldane] pointed out that England secured a statutory organisation of the system under the Criminal Justice Administration Act which was passed in 1925': NLS, MS 6105, f. 166.

65. Haldane, *The Reign of Relativity*, p. 376.

66. Haldane's particular understanding of what falls within 'trade and commerce' and 'criminal law' has largely been left behind, as has his interpretation of what constitutes 'national dimensions'. But his solidifying of provincial authority over a large number of private law subjects—a task he inherited from Lord Watson—continues to play an important part in modern Canada. It is certainly still the case that 'few judicial personalities figure so prominently in Canadian constitutional law as Lord Haldane': Schneiderman, 'Harold Laski', p. 521.

67. RBH to Sir Charles Fitzpatrick, 29 Dec. 1913, NLS, MS 5910, ff. 153–7.

68. Haldane, 'The Liberal Creed', pp. 465–6.

69. Asquith, in *The Times*, 10 July 1895, quoted in Matthew, *The Liberal Imperialists*, pp. 258–9. See also Ronald Munro Ferguson, in *The Scotsman*, 10 Oct. 1901, who called for rescuing the House of Commons by putting 'more trust in the great municipalities and county councils and through them advanc[ing] measures for social reform.' Quoted in Matthew, *The Liberal Imperialists*, p. 260.

70. R. B. Haldane, 'Lord Salisbury and the House of Lords', *National Review*, Jan. 1895, quoted in Matthew, *The Liberal Imperialists*, p. 262.

71. Haldane, 'The Future of Democracy', p. 18.

72. David Butler and Gareth Butler, *Twentieth-Century British Political Facts 1900–2000* (London: Palgrave Macmillan, 2000), p. 380.

73. 'Trades Unions and Trade Disputes Bill', *House of Commons Debates*, 10 Mar. 1905, vol. 142, col. 1097.

74. 'Trade Union and Labour Relations (Consolidation) Act 1992.

75. Matthew, *The Liberal Imperialists*, p. 249.

76. Asquith, in *The Times*, 31 Jan. 1895, quoted in Matthew, *The Liberal Imperialists*, p. 249. See also Powell, 'The New Liberalism', pp. 390–1.

77. Haldane, 'The Future of Democracy', p. 14.

78. Ibid., p. 15.

79. Ibid., pp. 15–16.

80. Ibid., pp. 16–17.

81. Ibid., pp. 12–13.

82. Ibid., p. 20.

83. Henry J. Welch and Charles S. Myers, *Ten Years of Industrial Psychology: An Account of*

the First Decade of the National Institute of Industrial Psychology (London: Sir Isaac Pitman & Sons, 1932), p. 3.

84. Ibid., p. 108.

85. Ibid., p. 23.

86. Ibid., p. 124.

87. Tonn, *Mary P. Follett*, p. 491.

88. Ibid., p. 492.

89. See RBH to Edmund Gosse, 8 Jan. 1920, Brotherton Library, Leeds, BC MS 19c Gosse.

90. Follett, *The New State*, p. v.

91. Tonn, *Mary P. Follett*, pp. 321–2.

92. Quoted in ibid., p. 423.

93. Ibid.

94. RBH to Edmund Gosse, 17 Aug. 1926, Brotherton Library, Leeds, BC MS 19c Gosse.

95. RBH to Edmund Gosse, 21 Aug. 1926, Brotherton Library, Leeds, BC MS 19c Gosse.

96. Tonn, *Mary P. Follett*, p. 427.

97. Sir Frank Heath, 'Lord Haldane: His Influence on Higher Education and on Administration', in Grey et al., *Viscount Haldane of Cloan*, p. 28.

98. Raymond Nottage and Freida Stack, 'The Royal Institute of Public Administration, 1922–1939', *Public Administration*, 50, 3 (1972), p. 282.

99. R. B. Haldane, 'An Organized Civil Service', *Journal of Public Administration*, 1, 1 (Jan. 1923), p. 15. See also his presidential address for 1923, 'The Constitutional Evolution of the Civil Service', *Public Administration*, 2, 1 (Mar. 1924).

100. Haldane, 'An Organized Civil Service', p. 15.

101. Ibid., p. 16. The institute's publication *Public Administration*, which continues independently despite the closure of the institute in 1992, has certainly contributed such raised standards. It was for many years the authoritative publication in its field. It still awards an annual Haldane Prize for the best paper in public administration.

102. See Pellew, 'Practitioners versus Theorists'. A recent example of creating 'opportunities for historians, policy makers and journalists to connect and learn from each other' is the 'History & Policy' project founded by a small group of academics in 2002.

103. Haldane, 'The Future of Democracy', p. 19.

104. Maurice, *Haldane 1856–1915*, p. 330.

105. Haldane, 'Higher Nationality', p. 54.

106. Kellogg was United States ambassador to the UK in 1924–5 and subsequently the forty-fifth United States Secretary of State, until 1929. Others who wrote personally to Haldane to seek his acceptance were the former American ambassador to the United Kingdom, Joseph H. Choate; the Attorney General of the United States, George W. Wickersham; the Canadian prime minister, Robert Borden; Borden's

predecessor and friend of Haldane, Wilfrid Laurier; the Chief Justice of Canada, Charles Fitzpatrick (who featured earlier in this chapter); and the United States ambassador to France, Myron T. Herrick.

107. Haldane, 'Higher Nationality', p. 87.
108. Myron T. Herrick to Haldane, 28 Jan. 1913, NLS, MS 5910, ff. 21–2.
109. From Gosse's handwritten preface to the 'Higher Nationality' correspondence, Brotherton Library, Leeds, BC Gosse correspondence, Typescript, Slip-case lettered: MSS of AMERICAN ADDRESS. Gen, q, HAL.
110. Haldane, 'Higher Nationality', p. 52.
111. Ibid., p. 68.
112. See Follett, *The New State*, p. vii and Haldane, *The Reign of Relativity*, p. 376.
113. Haldane, 'Higher Nationality', p. 82.
114. Ibid., p. 89.
115. Ibid., p. 52.
116. Ibid., p. 91.
117. Cab. 37/127/17.
118. Robert Joseph Gowen, 'Lord Haldane of Cloan (1856–1928), Neglected Apostle of the League of Nations', *Il Politico*, 36, 1 (Mar. 1971), p. 162.
119. This and the preceding quotations are from ibid., pp. 162–3. For a long but direct quotation from Haldane's original memorandum see pp. 164–8.
120. Quoted in Maurice, *Haldane 1915–1928*, p. 71.

AFTERWORD

1. Elizabeth Haldane records in her diary having met Shackleton—who, with Haldane, ranks as one of my great heroes—in March 1914. They discussed the nutritional requirements of polar explorers. Coincidentally, Shackleton bade farewell to King George V at Buckingham Palace on 4 August 1914, the day war broke out, before proceeding on his ill-fated expedition which sought to cross Antarctica.
2. The letter is now among the private papers of the Haldane family.
3. I am conscious that a whole book could be dedicated to a detailed analysis of Haldane's leadership principles and practice. His techniques have application across many different sectors of activity. Margot Morrell and Stephanie Capparell have done that work for Ernest Shackleton in *Shackleton's Way: Leadership Lessons from the Great Antarctic Explorer* (London: Nicholas Breasley Publishing, 2001). My friend Ray Dalio's recent publication, the widely read *Principles* (New York: Simon & Schuster, 2017), provides an equivalent analysis of management techniques with wide cross-sectoral application. Perhaps one day the same comprehensive work will be done for Haldane?
4. Buchan, *Memory Hold-the-Door*, pp. 132–3.

BIBLIOGRAPHY AND FURTHER READING

There have been three full-scale biographies which have attempted to capture Haldane in the round: Frederick Maurice's two-volume *Haldane*, published in 1937 and 1938; Dudley Sommer's *Haldane of Cloan*, published in 1960; and Jean Graham Hall and Douglas F. Martin's *Haldane: Statesman, Lawyer, Philosopher* (Chichester: Barry Rose Law Publishers Ltd, 1996). The last of these is fairly light, but the Maurice and Sommer volumes—full details of which can be found in the secondary literature section below—provide a solid bedrock for anyone who wants to understand the development of Haldane's statesmanship. Both biographies, however, are light on some of Haldane's most fundamental characteristics. Haldane's humanity and humour, for example, fail to come through, while his philosophy is under-represented. Their chronological approach, with its accompanying demands for keeping the narrative moving, also hampers deep dives into Haldane's central achievements. To grasp these in their fullness one needs to turn to studies focusing on individual aspects of his career. Eric Ashby and Mary Anderson's 1974 *Portrait of Haldane at Work on Education* is a superb guide to this dimension of his work. Edward M. Spiers's *Haldane: An Army Reformer*, which appeared in 1980, is similarly rigorous. For an understanding of the rise, fall and rise again of Haldane's political career, Stephen E. Koss's 1969 *Lord Haldane: Scapegoat for Liberalism* serves very well indeed. In terms of Haldane's influence on the Canadian constitution, Frederick Vaughan's 2010 *Viscount Haldane: 'The Wicked Step-father of the Canadian Constitution'* is the only book-length study of the topic, providing a provocative perspective on Haldane's philosophical foundations and his enormous contribution to the country. Full bibliographical details of each can be found below.

PRIMARY LITERATURE

Books

Haldane, R. B., *Life of Adam Smith* (London: Walter Scott, 1887).
———— *Education and Empire* (London: John Murray, 1902).
———— *The Pathway to Reality: Stage the First* (London: John Murray, 1903).
———— *The Pathway to Reality: Stage the Second* (London: John Murray, 1904).

———— *Army Reform and Other Addresses* (London: T. Fisher Unwin, 1907).

———— *Universities and National Life* (London: John Murray, 1910).

———— *The Conduct of Life* (London: John Murray, 1914).

———— *Before the War* (London: Cassell, 1920).

———— *The Reign of Relativity* (London: John Murray, 1921).

———— *The Philosophy of Humanism and of Other Subjects* (London: John Murray, 1922).

———— *Human Experience: A Study of its Structure* (New York: E. P. Dutton & Co., 1926).

———— *Selected Addresses and Essays* (London: John Murray, 1928).

———— *Richard Burdon Haldane: An Autobiography* (London: Hodder & Stoughton, 1929).

Selected Articles

Haldane, R. B., 'The Liberal Party and its Prospects', *Contemporary Review*, 53 (Jan. 1888), pp. 145–60.

———— 'The Liberal Creed', *Contemporary Review*, 54 (Oct. 1888), pp. 461–74.

———— 'Hegel and his Recent Critics', *Mind*, 13, 52 (Oct. 1888), pp. 585–9.

———— 'On Some Economic Aspects of Women's Suffrage', *Contemporary Review*, 57 (Dec. 1890), pp. 830–8.

———— 'Hegel', *Contemporary Review*, 20 (Feb. 1895), pp. 232–45.

———— 'The New Liberalism', *Progressive Review*, 1, 2 (Nov. 1896), pp. 133–43.

———— 'The Constitution of the Empire and the Development of its Councils', *Journal of the Society of Comparative Legislation*, 4, 1 (1902), pp. 11–18.

———— 'The Cabinet and the Empire', *Proceedings of the Royal Colonial Institute*, 34 (9 June 1903), pp. 325–8.

———— 'The Logical Foundations of Mathematics', *Mind*, NS, 18, 69 (Jan. 1909), pp. 1–39.

———— 'On Progress in Philosophical Research', *Proceedings of the Aristotelian Society*, NS, 16 (1915–16), pp. 32–62.

———— 'Training of the Workman', *The Herald* (2 Dec. 1916), p. 3.

———— 'New Ideals in Education', *Yale Review* (Jan. 1920), pp. 237–52.

———— 'The Nature of the State', *Contemporary Review*, 117 (1920), pp. 761–73.

———— 'The British Empire in its Wider Significance', *The Pilgrim*, 2, 1 (Oct. 1921), pp. 11–19.

———— 'An Organized Civil Service', *Journal of Public Administration*, 1, 1 (Jan. 1923), pp. 6–16.

———— 'The Constitutional Evolution of the Civil Service', *Public Administration*, 2, 1 (Mar. 1924), pp. 9–22.

———— 'Some New Machinery of Government', *Journal of Public Administration*, 3, 1 (Jan. 1925), pp. 6–9.

———— 'East and West', *Hibbert Journal*, 26, 4 (July 1928), pp. 590–607.

Pamphlets

Haldane, R. B., 'Social Problems: Speech by R. B. Haldane, Q.C., M.P. at Cambridge, on Saturday, May 30th, 1891', *Earl Grey Pamphlets Collection* (1891).

———— 'The Unearned Increment' (London: Eighty Club, 1892).

———— 'The Methods of Modern Logic and the Conception of Infinity: The Presidential Address to the Aristotelian Society', Aristotelian Society (4 Nov. 1907).

———— 'Great Britain and Germany: A Study in National Characteristics' (New York: American Association for International Conciliation, 1912).

———— 'National Education: A Speech delivered at the Reform Club, Manchester', Liberal Publication Department (10 Jan. 1913).

———— 'The Meaning of Truth in History', University of London Press (Mar. 1914).

———— 'Lord Haldane and National Duty: An Address on the War and How all can Help', Daily Chronicle (5 July 1915).

———— 'The Student and the Nation', Foundation Oration 1916, University of London, University College, Union Society.

———— 'An Address: Education after the War with Special Reference to Technical Instruction', Association of Technical Institutions (20 Oct. 1916).

———— 'The Future of the Boys' Brigade Organisation and the Cadet Movement', from *Proceedings of the Royal Philosophical Society of Glasgow* (Oct. 1917).

———— 'The Future of Democracy' (London: Headley Bros., 1918).

———— 'Symposium: Do Finite Individuals Possess a Substantive or an Adjectival Mode of Being?' Aristotelian Society (7 July 1918).

———— 'The Doctrine of Degrees in Knowledge, Truth, and Reality' (London: Published for the British Academy by Humphrey Milford, Oxford University Press, 1919).

———— 'The Problem of Nationalization' (London: George Allen & Unwin, 1921).

———— *Mind and Reality*, Affirmations series, part of the God in the Modern World series (London: Ernest Benn Limited, 1928).

SECONDARY LITERATURE AND MEDIA CITED

Books

Abdy, Jane, and Charlotte Gere, *The Souls: An Elite in English Society 1885–1930* (London: Sidgwick & Jackson, 1984).

Anderson, R. D., *Education and Opportunity in Victorian Scotland* (Edinburgh: Edinburgh University Press, 1983).

Andrew, Christopher, *The Defence of the Realm: The Authorised History of MI5* (London: Allen Lane, 2009).

Archer, Ian W. (ed.), *Transactions of the Royal Historical Society: Volume 21: Sixth Series* (Cambridge: Cambridge University Press, 2012).

Ashby, Eric, and Mary Anderson, *Portrait of Haldane at Work on Education* (London: Macmillan, 1974).

Ashley, Percy, *Modern Tariff History* (London: John Murray, 1904).

Asquith, Herbert, *Moments of Memory: Recollections and Impressions* (London: Hutchinson, 1937).

Avineri, Shlomo, *Hegel's Theory of the Modern State* (Cambridge: Cambridge University Press, 1972).

Battersea, Constance, *Reminiscences* (London: Macmillan & Co., 1922).

Beckett, Ian F. W., *Britain's Part-Time Soldiers: The Amateur Military Tradition 1558–1945* (Barnsley: Pen & Sword Military, 2011).

Beckett, Ian F. W., and Keith Simpson (eds), *A Nation in Arms: A Social Study of the British Army in the First World War* (Barnsley: Pen & Sword Military, 1985).

Begbie, Harold, *The Vindication of Great Britain: a study in diplomacy and strategy with reference to the illusions of her critics and the problems of the future* (London: Methuen, 1916).

Bernstein, George L., *Liberalism and Liberal Politics in Edwardian England* (Boston: Allen & Unwin, 1986).

Bonham Carter, Violet Asquith, *Winston Churchill as I Knew him* (London: Reprint Society, 1966).

Bosanquet, Bernard, *The Philosophical Theory of the State* (London: Macmillan, 1920).

Boucher, David, and Andrew Vincent, *A Radical Hegelian: The Political and Social Philosophy of Henry Jones* (New York: St Martin's Press, 1994).

Bradley, F. H., *Ethical Studies* (Oxford: Clarendon Press, 1876).

Brett, Reginald, *Journals and Letters of Reginald, Viscount Esher*, vol. 2 (London: Ivor Nicholson & Watson, 1934).

Brock, Michael, and Eleanor Brock (eds), *Margot Asquith's Great War Diary 1914–1916: The View from Downing Street* (Oxford: Oxford University Press, 2014).

Bruce, Maurice, *The Coming of the Welfare State* (London: B. T. Batsford, 1968).

Bryant, F. Russell (ed.), *Coalition Diaries and Letters of H. A. L. Fisher, 1916–1922*, vol. 1 (Lewiston, NY: Mellen Press, 2006).

Buchan, John, *Memory Hold-the-Door* (London: Hodder & Stoughton, 1940).

Buchwald, Diana K., Ze'ev Rosenkranz, Tilman Sauer, József Illy and Virginia Iris Holmes (eds), *The Collected Papers of Albert Einstein, Volume 12: The Berlin Years: Correspondence January–December 1921* (Princeton: Princeton University Press, 2009).

Buchwald, Diana K., József Illy, Ze'ev Rosenkranz and Tilman Sauer (eds), *The*

Collected Papers of Albert Einstein, Volume 13: The Berlin Years: Writings & Correspondence January 1922–March 1923 (Princeton: Princeton University Press, 2012).

Buchwald, Diana K., József Illy, Ze'ev Rosenkranz, Tilman Sauer (eds), *The Collected Papers of Albert Einstein, Volume 13: The Berlin Years: Writings & Correspondence January 1922–March 1923 (English translation supplement)*, trans. Ann M. Hentschel and Osik Moses (Princeton: Princeton University Press, 2012).

Butler, David, and Gareth Butler, *Twentieth-Century British Political Facts 1900–2000* (London: Palgrave Macmillan, 2000).

Caine, Sidney, *The History of the Foundation of the London School of Economics and Political Science* (London: University of London, 1963).

Candlish, Stewart, *The Russell–Bradley Dispute and its Significance for Twentieth-Century Philosophy* (Basingstoke and New York: Palgrave Macmillan, 2007).

Cannon, John (ed.), *A Dictionary of British History* (Oxford: Oxford University Press, 2009).

Carlyle, Thomas, *On Heroes, Hero-Worship and the Heroic in History* (London: Chapman & Hall, 1840).

Cecil, G., *Life of Robert, Marquis of Salisbury*, vol. 3 (London: Hodder & Stoughton, 1931).

Charteris, Evan, *The Life and Letters of Sir Edmund Gosse* (London: William Heinemann, 1931).

Clark, Christopher, *The Sleepwalkers: How Europe Went to War in 1914* (London: Penguin, 2012).

Clark, Ronald, *Einstein: The Life and Times* (New York: World Publishing Company, 1971).

Collingwood, R. G., *An Autobiography* (Oxford: Clarendon Press, 1938).

Collini, S., *Liberalism and Sociology: L. T. Hobhouse and Political Argument in England 1880–1914* (Cambridge: Cambridge University Press, 1979).

Dahrendorf, Ralf, *LSE: A History of the London School of Economics and Political Science, 1896–1995* (Oxford: Oxford University Press, 1995).

Dainton, F., *Reflections on Universities and the National Health Services* (London: Nuffield Provincial Hospitals Trust, 1983).

Dalio, Ray, *Principles* (New York: Simon & Schuster, 2017).

Dangerfield, George, *The Strange Death of Liberal England* (London: Constable, 1935).

Davie, George, *The Democratic Intellect* (Edinburgh: Edinburgh University Press, 1961).

Dawson, William Harbutt (ed.), *After-War Problems* (London: George Allen & Unwin, 1917).

Dennis, Peter, *The Territorial Army, 1907–1940* (Woodbridge: published for the Royal Historical Society by the Boydell Press, 1987).

d'Ombrain, Nicholas, *War Machinery and High Policy: Defence Administration in Peacetime Britain 1902–1914* (London: Oxford University Press, 1973).

Drummond, A. L., and J. Bulloch, *The Church in Victorian Scotland 1843–1874* (Edinburgh: St Andrews Press, 1975).

Du Croz, David (editor-in-chief), *Marlborough College and the Great War in 100 Stories* (Marlborough: Marlborough College, 2018).

Earl of Oxford and Asquith, KG, *Memories and Reflections*, vol. 1 (London: Cassell & Co., 1928).

Einstein, A., *Relativity: The Special and General Theory* (London: Methuen, 1920).

Ensor, R. C. K., *England, 1870–1914* (Oxford: Clarendon Press, 1960).

Ferguson, Niall, *The House of Rothschild: The World's Banker 1849–1999* (London: Penguin, 1998).

Fichte, Johann Gottlieb, *The Vocation of Man*, trans. Peter Preuss (Indianapolis: Hackett, 1987).

——— *Fichte: Early Philosophical Writings*, trans. Daniel Breazeale (Ithaca: Cornell University Press, 1988).

Fitzroy, Almeric, *Memoirs*, 2 vols (London: Hutchinson & Co., 1925).

Follett, Mary, *The New State: Group Organization the Solution of Popular Government* (New York: Longmans, Green & Co., third impression, 1920).

Foot, M. R. D., and H. C. G. Matthew (eds), *The Gladstone Diaries with Cabinet Minutes and Prime-Ministerial Correspondence*, 14 vols (Oxford: Clarendon Press, 1968–94).

Fort, Adrian, *Prof: The Life of Frederick Lindemann* (London: Jonathan Cape, 2003).

Fraser, Peter, *Lord Esher: A Political Biography* (London: Hart-Davis MacGibbon, 1973).

French, David, and Brian Holden Reid (eds.), *The British General Staff: Reform and Innovation, 1890–1939* (London: Frank Cass, 2002).

French, Field Marshal Viscount of Ypres, *1914* (London: Constable & Co., 1919).

Fuller, Sophie, and Lloyd Whitesell (eds), *Queer Episodes in Music and Modern Identity* (Urbana: University of Illinois Press, 2002).

Gardiner, A. G., *Prophets, Priests, & Kings* (London: J. M. Dent & Sons, 1914).

Gay, Hannah, *The History of Imperial College London 1907–2007* (London: Imperial College Press, 2007).

Gilbert, Howard and Helen Prew (eds), *A Passion for Learning: Celebrating 80 Years of NIACE Support for Adult Learning* (Leicester: NIACE, 2001).

Gollin, Alfred, *No Longer an Island: Britain and the Wright Brothers 1902–1909* (London: Heinemann, 1984).

——— *The Impact of Air Power on the British People and their Government, 1909–1914* (London: Macmillan, 1989).

Gooch, John, *The Plans for War: The General Staff and British Military Strategy c. 1900–1916* (London: Routledge & Kegan Paul, 1974).

BIBLIOGRAPHY AND FURTHER READING

———— *The Prospect of War: Studies in British Defence Policy 1847–1942* (London: Frank Cass, 1981).

Goodman, Martin, *Suffer and Survive: Gas Attacks, Miners' Canaries, Spacesuits and the Bends: The Extreme Life of J. S. Haldane* (London: Simon & Schuster, 2007).

Graham, G. (ed.), *Oxford History of Scottish Philosophy* (Oxford: Oxford University Press, 2015).

Green, T. H., *The Works of Thomas Hill Green*, ed. R. L. Nettleship, vol. 3 (London: Longmans Green, 1888).

Grey, Edward, Charles Harris, Frank Heath and Claud Schuster, *Viscount Haldane of Cloan: The Man and his Work* (London: Humphrey Milford for Oxford University Press, 1928).

Haldane, Alexander, *Memoirs of the Lives of Robert Haldane of Airthrey, and of his Brother James Alexander Haldane* (London: Hamilton, Adams, & Co., 1852).

Haldane, Aylmer, *The Haldanes of Gleneagles* (Edinburgh and London: William Blackwood & Sons, 1929).

Haldane, E. S., *The British Nurse in Peace and War* (London: John Murray, 1923).

———— (ed.), *Mary Elizabeth Haldane: A Record of a Hundred Years (1825–1925)* (London: Hodder & Stoughton, 1925).

———— *From One Century to Another* (London: Alexander Maclehose & Co., 1937).

Haldane, R. W., *Thomas Graeme Nelson Haldane of Cloan, 1897–1981* (Edinburgh: Clark Constable, 1982).

Hall, A. R., *Science for Industry: A Short History of the Imperial College of Science and Technology and its Antecedents* (London: Imperial College Press, 1982).

Hamilton, Ian, *Compulsory Service: A Study of the Question in Light of Experience* (London: John Murray, 1910).

———— *The Soul and Body of an Army* (London: Edward Arnold & Co., 1921).

Hawking, Stephen, and Leonard Mlodinow, *The Grand Design: New Answers to the Ultimate Questions of Life* (London: Bantam Books, 2010).

Heath, H. F., and A. L. Hetherington, *Industrial Research and Development in the United Kingdom: A Survey* (London: Faber & Faber, 1946).

Heintze, Sarah, and Alan Fyfe (eds), *Pro Patria Mori: The Edinburgh Academy at War, 1914–1918* (Edinburgh: Edinburgh Academy, 2015).

Heuston, R. F. V., *Lives of the Lord Chancellors, 1885–1940* (Oxford: Clarendon Press, 1964).

Hillcourt, William, with Olave, Lady Baden-Powell, *Baden-Powell: The Two Lives of a Hero* (London: William Heinemann, 1964).

Hirschel, Ernst Heinrich, Horst Prem and Gero Madelung, *Aeronautical Research in Germany: From Lilienthal until Today* (Berlin: Springer Science & Business Media, 2012).

Hirst, P. Q. (ed.), *The Pluralist Theory of the State: Selected Writings of G. D. H. Cole, J. N. Figgis, and H. J. Laski* (London: Routledge, 1989).

431

Hobhouse, L. T., *The Labour Movement* (London: T. Fisher Unwin, 1893).

———— *A Metaphysical Theory of the State* (London: George Allen & Unwin, 1951).

Horner, Frances, *Time Remembered* (London: William Heinemann, 1933).

Hudson, W. H., *Idle Days in Patagonia* (London: Chapman & Hall, 1893).

Inge, W. R. (ed.), *The Post Victorians* (London: Ivor Nicholson & Watson, 1933).

Isaacson, Walter, *Einstein: His Life and Universe* (London: Pocket Books, 2008).

Jeal, Tim, *Baden-Powell: Founder of the Boy Scouts* (Yale: Yale University Press, 2001).

Jenkins, Roy, *Asquith* (London: Collins, 1964).

Jolliffe, John, *Raymond Asquith: Life and Letters* (London: Collins, 1980).

Julian of Norwich, *Revelations of Divine Love* (North Chelmsford, MA: Courier Corporation, 2012).

Kain, Philip J., *Hegel and the Other: A Study of the Phenomenology of Spirit* (Albany: SUNY Press, 2005).

Kerschensteiner, Georg, *The Schools and the Nation*, trans. C. K. Ogden (London: Macmillan, 1914).

Koss, Stephen E., *Lord Haldane: Scapegoat for Liberalism* (New York: Columbia University Press, 1969).

———— *The Pro-Boers: The Anatomy of an Antiwar Movement* (Chicago: University of Chicago Press, 1973).

Kramnick, Isaac, and Barry Sheerman, *Harold Laski: A Life on the Left* (London: Hamish Hamilton, 1993).

Laski, Harold, *A Grammar of Politics* (London: George Allen & Unwin, 1925).

Lees-Milne, James, *The Enigmatic Edwardian: The Life of Reginald 2nd Viscount Esher* (London: Sidgwick & Jackson, 1986).

Mackenzie, Norman (ed.), *The Letters of Sidney and Beatrice Webb, Vol. II: Partnership 1892–1912* (Cambridge: Cambridge University Press, 1978).

Maddison, Angus, *The World Economy: A Millennial Perspective* (Paris: Organisation for Economic Co-operation and Development, 2001).

Magnusson, Magnus, *The Clacken and the Slate: The Story of the Edinburgh Academy 1824–1974* (London: Collins, 1974).

Markham, Violet, *Friendship's Harvest* (London: Reinhardt, 1956).

Marwick, Arthur, *The Deluge: British Society and the First World War* (London: The Bodley Head, 1965).

Massie, Robert K., *Dreadnought: Britain, Germany and the Coming of the Great War* (London: Vintage, 2007).

Matthew, H. C. G., *The Liberal Imperialists: The Ideas and Politics of a Post-Gladstonian Élite* (Oxford: Oxford University Press, 1973).

Maurice, Frederick, *Haldane 1856–1915: The Life of Viscount Haldane of Cloan K.T., O.M.* (London: Faber & Faber, 1937).

———— *Haldane 1915–1928: The Life of Viscount Haldane of Cloan K.T., O.M.* (London: Faber & Faber, 1939).

Mead, Gary, *The Good Soldier: The Biography of Douglas Haig* (London: Atlantic, 2007).

Millin, Sarah Gertrude, *Rhodes* (London: Chatto & Windus, 1933).

Monger, G., *The End of Isolation: British Foreign Policy 1900–1907* (London: Thomas Nelson & Sons, 1963).

Morley, John, *Notes on Politics and History* (London: Macmillan, 1914).

Morrell, Margot, and Stephanie Capparell, *Shackleton's Way: Leadership Lessons from the Great Antarctic Explorer* (London: Nicholas Breasley Publishing, 2001).

Morris, A. J. Anthony, *The Scaremongers: The Advocacy of War and Rearmament 1896–1914* (London: Routledge & Kegan Paul, 2014).

———— *Reporting the First World War: Charles Repington*, The Times *and the Great War* (Cambridge: Cambridge University Press, 2015).

Muirhead, J. H., *John Henry Muirhead: Reflections by a Journeyman in Philosophy* (London: George Allen & Unwin, 1942).

Neillands, Robin, *The Old Contemptibles: The British Expeditionary Force 1914–1918* (London: John Murray, 2004).

Newman, Michael, *Harold Laski: A Political Biography* (London: Merlin Press, 2009).

Newmarch, Rosa, *Mary Wakefield: A Memoir* (Kendal: Atkinson & Pollitt, 1912).

Owen, David, *The Hidden Perspective: The Military Conversations 1906–1914* (London: Haus Publishing, 1914).

Palmer, Michael A., *Command at Sea: Naval Command and Control since the Sixteenth Century* (Cambridge, MA: Harvard University Press, 2009).

Paterson, Lindsay, *Scottish Education in the Twentieth Century* (Edinburgh: Edinburgh University Press, 2003).

———— *Social Radicalism and Liberal Education* (Exeter: Imprint Academic, 2015).

Pelczynski, Z. A. (ed.), *Hegel's Political Philosophy: Problems and Perspectives* (Cambridge: Cambridge University Press, 1971).

———— *The State and Civil Society: Studies in Hegel's Political Philosophy* (Cambridge: Cambridge University Press, 1984).

Pellew, Jill, and Lawrence Goldman (eds), *Dethroning Historical Reputations: Universities, Museums and the Commemoration of Benefactors* (London: School of Advanced Study, University of London, Institute of Historical Research, 2018).

Pellew, Jill, and Miles Taylor (eds), *Utopian Universities: A Global History of the New Campuses of the 1960s* (London: Bloomsbury Academic, forthcoming (2020)).

Perlmutter, A., and V. P. Bennett (eds), *The Political Influence of the Military: A Comparative Reader* (New Haven: Yale University Press, 1980).

Repington, Charles à Court, *Vestigia* (London: Constable & Co., 1919).

Robbins, Keith, *Sir Edward Grey* (London: Cassell & Co., 1971).

Roberts, Andrew, *Salisbury: Victorian Titan* (London: Faber, 2011).

Roberts, Frederick, *Fallacies and Facts: An Answer to 'Compulsory Service'* (London: John Murray, 1911).

Roberts, Stephen K. (ed.), *A Ministry of Enthusiasm: Centenary Essays on the Workers' Educational Association* (London: Pluto Press, 2003).

Robinson, Andrew, *Einstein on the Run: How Britain Saved the World's Greatest Scientist* (New Haven and London: Yale University Press, 2019).

Rosenthal, Michael, *The Character Factory: Baden-Powell and the Origins of the Boy Scout Movement*, (London: William Collins, 1986).

Roskill, Stephen, *Hankey: Man of Secrets* (London: Collins, 1970).

Rousseau, Jean-Jacques, *The Social Contract*, trans. G. D. H. Cole (London: Everyman, 1913).

Sanderson, M., *The Universities and British Industry, 1850–1970* (London: Routledge & Kegan Paul, 1972).

Saywell, John T., *The Lawmakers: Judicial Power and the Shaping of Canadian Federalism* (Toronto: University of Toronto Press, 2002).

Schopenhauer, Arthur, *The World as Will and Idea*, trans. R. B. Haldane and John Kemp (London: Kegan Paul, Trench and Trübner & Co., 1883–6).

Scott, F. R., *Essays on the Constitution* (Toronto: University of Toronto Press, 1977).

Searle, G. R., *The Quest for National Efficiency: A Study in British Politics and Political Thought, 1899–1914* (London: Ashfield Press, 1990).

———— *A New England? Peace and War, 1886–1918* (Oxford: Clarendon Press, 2005).

Seldon, Anthony, and David Walsh, *Public Schools and the Great War: The Generation Lost* (Barnsley: Pen & Sword Military, 2013).

Seth, Andrew, and R. B. Haldane (eds), *Essays in Philosophical Criticism* (London: Longmans, Green & Co., 1883).

Sheffield, Gary, *The Chief: Douglas Haig and the British Army* (London: Aurum Press, 2011).

Shinn, C. H., *Paying the Piper: The Development of the University Grants Committee 1919–46* (London: Falmer Press, 1986).

Sommer, Dudley, *Haldane of Cloan* (London: G. Allen & Unwin, 1960).

Spears, E. L., *Liaison 1914: A Narrative of the Great Retreat* (London: William Heinemann, 1930).

Spender, J. A., and Cyril Asquith, *Life of Herbert Henry Asquith, Lord Oxford and Asquith*, vol. 2 (London: Hutchinson & Co., 1932).

Spiers, Edward M., *Haldane: An Army Reformer* (Edinburgh: Edinburgh University Press, 1980).

Stacy, Neil, *The Haldanes of Gleneagles: A Scottish History from the Twelfth Century to the Present Day* (Edinburgh: Berlinn, 2017).

Steiner, Z. S., *The Foreign Office and Foreign Policy, 1898–1914* (Cambridge: Cambridge University Press, 1969).

Stevenson, Garth, *Unfulfilled Union: Canadian Federalism and National Union*, 5th edn (Montreal: McGill-Queen's University Press, 2009).

Strachan, Hew, *The Outbreak of the First World War* (Oxford: Oxford University Press, 2004).

Teagarden, Ernest M., *Haldane at the War Office* (New York: Gordon Press, 1976).

Thompson, F. M. L. (ed.), *The University of London and the World of Learning* (London: Hambledon Press, 1990).

Thwaite, Ann, *Edmund Gosse: A Literary Landscape* (London: Secker & Warburg, 1984).

Tonn, Joan C., *Mary P. Follett: Creating Democracy, Transforming Management* (New Haven and London: Yale University Press, 2003).

Trevelyan, G. M., *Grey of Fallodon* (London, New York, Toronto: Longmans, Green & Co., 1937).

Trevelyan, R., *Grand Dukes and Diamonds: The Wernhers of Luton Hoo* (London: Martin Secker & Warburg, 1991).

Tuchman, Barbara, *The Guns of August* (New York: Presidio Press, 2004).

Twining, William, *Jurist in Context: A Memoir* (Cambridge: Cambridge University Press, 2019).

Twiss, H., *The Public and Private Life of Lord Chancellor Eldon*, vol. 1 (London: John Murray, 1844).

Vaughan, Frederick, *Viscount Haldane: 'The Wicked Step-father of the Canadian Constitution'* (Toronto: University of Toronto Press, 2010).

Vernon, Keith, *Universities and the State in England, 1850–1939* (London: RoutledgeFalmer, 2004).

Vincent, Andrew, *Theories of the State* (Oxford: Blackwell, 1987).

Vincent, Andrew, and Raymond Plant (eds), *Philosophy, Politics and Citizenship: The Life and Thought of the British Idealists* (Oxford: Basil Blackwell, 1984).

Vivian, E. Charles, *A History of Aeronautics* (London: W. Collins Sons & Co., 1921).

Walker, Percy, *Early Aviation at Farnborough*, 2 vols (London: Macdonald & Co., 1974).

Webb, Beatrice, *Our Partnership*, ed. Barbara Drake and Margaret I. Cole (London: Longmans, Green & Co., 1948).

Weber, Max, *The Protestant Ethic and the Spirit of Capitalism* (London and New York: Routledge, 1992).

Welch, Henry J., and Charles S. Myers, *Ten Years of Industrial Psychology: An Account of the First Decade of the National Institute of Industrial Psychology* (London: Sir Isaac Pitman & Sons, 1932).

Wells, H. G., *Experiment in Autobiography: Discoveries and Conclusions of a Very Ordinary Brain (since 1866)* (London: Read Books, 2016).

Wendell Holmes, Oliver, and Harold Joseph Laski, *Holmes–Laski Letters: The Correspondence of Mr Justice Holmes and Harold J. Laski, 1916–1935*, vol. 1 (Cambridge, MA: Harvard University Press, 1953).

Wheatley, H. B. (ed.), *The Historical and the Posthumous Memoirs of Sir Nathaniel William Wraxall, 1772–1784*, vol. 5 (London: Bickers & Son, 1884).

Williams, Rhodri, *Defending the Empire: The Conservative Party and British Defence Policy 1899–1915* (New Haven and London: Yale University Press, 1991).

Williamson, S. R., *The Politics of Grand Strategy: Britain and France Prepare for War, 1906–1914* (Cambridge, MA: Harvard University Press, 1969).

Wright, Thomas, *Oscar's Books* (London: Chatto & Windus, 2008).

Articles

'Annual Meeting of the Royal Economic Society: Discussion on the National Debt', *Economic Journal*, 35, 139 (Sept. 1925), pp. 351–65.

Azzi, Stephen, 'Book Review: Viscount Haldane: "The Wicked Step-father of the Canadian Constitution". By Vaughan, Frederick', *The Historian*, 74, 3 (Fall 2012), pp. 640–1.

Bennett, Anthea, 'Advising the Cabinet—the Committee of Civil Research and the Economic Advisory Council: A Brief Comparison', *Public Administration*, 56 (1978), pp. 51–71.

Caldwell, W., '*The Pathway to Reality* by Richard Burdon Haldane', *Philosophical Review*, 13, 1 (Jan. 1904), pp. 51–7.

Crafts, N. F. R., 'The Industrial Revolution: Economic Growth in Britain, 1700–1860', *Refresh*, 4 (Spring, 1987), pp. 1–4.

'Current Topics', *Economic Journal*, 55, 218/219 (June–Sept. 1945), pp. 298–300.

den Otter, Sandra, 'Thinking in Communities: Late Nineteenth-Century Liberals, Idealists and the Retrieval of Community', *Parliamentary History*, 16, 1 (Feb. 1997), pp. 67–84.

Ellison, Gerald, 'Reminiscences', *Lancashire Lad, Journal of the Loyal Regiment (North Lancashire)*, 55, 3 (Feb. 1936), pp. 5–9.

Falls, Cyril, 'Haldane and Defence', *Public Administration*, 35, 3 (Sept. 1957), pp. 245–53.

Gowen, Robert Joseph, 'Lord Haldane of Cloan (1856–1928), Neglected Apostle of the League of Nations', *Il Politico*, 36, 1 (Mar. 1971), pp. 161–8.

Hardie, Keir, 'The Labour Party: Its Aims and Policy', *National Review*, 46 (published by the proprietor at 23 Ryder Street, St James's, London, SW, Sept. 1905 to Feb. 1906).

Herbert, Roy, 'History of the DSIR: A Review of Sir Harry Melville's *The Department of Scientific and Industrial Research* (London: George Allen & Unwin, 1962)', *New Scientist*, 278 (15 Mar. 1961), p. 644.

Masood, Ehsan, 'A 100th Birthday Wish: Uphold Academic Freedom in Dark

Times', *Nature* 563 (2018), https://www.nature.com/nature/volumes/563/issues/7733

Maude, F. N., 'The New Army Scheme', *Contemporary Review*, 91 (Apr. 1907), pp. 516–24.

McDermott, J., 'The Revolution in British Military Thinking from the Boer War to the Moroccan Crisis', *Canadian Journal of History*, 9, 2 (1974), pp. 159–78.

McFarland, Marvin W., 'When the Airplane was a Military Secret', *The Air Power Historian*, 2, 4 (Oct. 1955), pp. 70–82.

Morris, A. J. Anthony, 'Haldane's Army Reforms 1906–8: The Deception of the Radicals', *History*, 56, 186 (Feb. 1971), pp. 17–34.

'Mr Haldane's Inaugural Address to the Congress', *Economic Journal*, 17, 65 (1 Mar. 1907), pp. 2–6.

Nottage, Raymond, and Freida Stack, 'The Royal Institute of Public Administration, 1922–1939', *Public Administration*, 50, 3 (1972), pp. 281–304.

Paterson, Lindsay, 'The Significance of the Education (Scotland) Act, 1918', *Scottish Affairs*, 27, 4 (2018), pp. 401–24.

Pellew, Jill, 'Practitioners versus Theorists: Early Attitudes of British Higher Civil Servants towards their Profession', *International Review of Administrative Sciences*, 49, 1 (Mar. 1983), pp. 4–12.

———— 'A Metropolitan University Fit for Empire: The Role of Private Benefaction in the Early History of the London School of Economics and Political Science and Imperial College of Science and Technology, 1895–1930', in *History of Universities*, vol. 26/1 (Oxford: Oxford University Press, 2012), pp. 201–45.

Powell, David, 'The New Liberalism and the Rise of Labour, 1886–1906', *Historical Journal*, 29, 2 (June 1986), pp. 369–93.

Price, Geoffrey, 'Science, Idealism and Higher Education in England: Arnold, Green and Haldane', *Studies in Higher Education*, 11, 1 (1986), pp. 5–16.

Rashdall, H., '*The Pathway to Reality*. Being the Gifford Lectures Delivered in the University of St Andrews in the Session 1902–3. By Richard Burdon Haldane', *Mind*, NS, 12, 48 (Oct. 1903), pp. 527–35.

Robinson, Jonathon, 'Lord Haldane and the British North America Act', *University of Toronto Law Journal*, 20, 1 (Winter 1970), pp. 55–69.

Schneiderman, David, 'Harold Laski, Viscount Haldane, and the Law of the Canadian Constitution in the Early Twentieth Century', *University of Toronto Law Journal*, 48, 4 (Autumn 1998), pp. 521–60.

———— 'Haldane Unrevealed', *McGill Law Journal*, 57, 3 (2012), pp. 597–626.

Scott, F. R., 'The Privy Council and Mr. Bennett's "New Deal" Legislation', *Canadian Journal of Economics and Political Science*, 3, 2 (May 1937), pp. 234–41.

Sehkar, K. C., and S. S. C. Chakra Rao, 'John Scott Haldane: The Father of Oxygen Therapy', *Indian Journal of Anaesthesia*, 58, 3 (May–June 2014), pp. 350–2.

Sloan, Geoff, 'Haldane's Mackindergarten: A Radical Experiment in British Military Education?' *War in History*, 19, 3 (2012), pp. 322–52.

Stawell, F. Melian, '*The Pathway to Reality*. Being the Gifford Lectures Delivered in the University of St Andrews in the Session 1902–3. By Richard Burdon Haldane', *International Journal of Ethics*, 14, 2 (Jan. 1904), pp. 253–7.

Steiner, Zara, 'Grey, Hardinge and the Foreign Office, 1906–10', *Historical Journal*, 10, 3 (1967), pp. 415–39.

Tawney, R. H., 'The Abolition of Economic Controls, 1918–1921', *Economic History Review*, 13, 1/2 (1943), pp. 1–30.

Thompson, A. S., 'Tariff Reform: An Imperial Strategy, 1903–1913', *Historical Journal*, 40, 4 (1997), pp. 1033–54.

Vincent, Andrew, 'German Philosophy and British Public Policy: Richard Burdon Haldane in Theory and Practice', *Journal of the History of Ideas*, 68, 1 (Jan. 2007), pp. 157–79.

Webb, Sidney, 'Lord Rosebery's Escape from Houndsditch', *The Nineteenth Century*, 50 (1901), pp. 366–86.

Wexler, Stephen, 'The Urge to Idealize: Viscount Haldane and the Constitution of Canada', *McGill Law Journal*, 29 (1984), pp. 608–47.

Newspaper articles

Bonham Carter, Violet, 'Haldane of Cloan: Scottish Lawyer who Shaped the British Army', *The Times*, 30 July 1956.

Cornwell, John, 'The Grand Design: New Answers to the Ultimate Questions of Life by Stephen Hawking: Review', *Daily Telegraph*, 20 Sept. 2010.

Jones, Nigel, '*The Chief: Douglas Haig and the British Army* by Gary Sheffield: Review', *The Telegraph*, 11 Aug. 2011.

Monk, Ray, 'The Man who Wasn't There', *Prospect Magazine*, Oct. 2019.

Obituary, Lord Haldane, *The Times*, 20 Aug 1928.

'The Scots Greys Memorial', *The Scotsman*, 17 Nov. 1906.

Pamphlets

Keynes, J. M., and H. D. Henderson, 'Can Lloyd George do it? The Pledge Examined' (London: The Nation and Athanaeum, 1929).

Pringle-Pattison, A. Seth, 'Richard Burdon Haldane' (London: Published for the British Academy by Humphrey Milford, Oxford University Press, 1928).

Webb, Sidney, 'Socialism: True and False', Fabian Tract No. 51 (London: Fabian Society, 1899).

Websites

'Beatrice Webb's typescript diary', 14 June 1915, LSE Digital Library (last accessed 30 Nov. 2019).

'British North America Act 1867' (last accessed 2 Dec. 2019).

BIBLIOGRAPHY AND FURTHER READING

'Brown, Peter Hume', *Oxford Dictionary of National Biography* (last accessed 2 Dec. 2019).

'Cecil, Robert Arthur Talbot Gascoyne-, Third Marquess of Salisbury', *Oxford Dictionary of National Biography* (last accessed 18 Nov. 2019).

'Clause 1.—(Administrative Provisions relating to New Ministries.)', *House of Commons Debates*, 9 Dec. 1964, vol. 703, cols 1553–1686 (last accessed 30 Nov. 2019).

The Constitution Act, 1982 (of Canada) (last accessed 3 Dec. 2019).

'Duncan, Adam, Viscount Duncan', *Oxford Dictionary of National Biography* (last accessed 2 Dec. 2019).

'Education (England and Wales)', *House of Commons Debates*, 24 Mar. 1902, vol. 105, cols. 900–5 (last accessed 28 Nov. 2019).

'Final Balance Sheet', *House of Commons Debates*, 29 Apr. 1909, vol. 4, col. 548 (last accessed 18 Nov. 2018).

Freedland, Jonathan, 'Eugenics: The Skeleton that Rattles Loudest in the Left's Closet', *The Guardian*, 17 Feb. 2012 (last accessed 2 Dec. 2019).

'Goethe, Johann Wolfgang von: To Charlotte Von Stein (An Charlotte von Stein in English)', Babelmatrix (last accessed 4 Aug. 2017).

'Gosse, Sir Edmund William', *Oxford Dictionary of National Biography* (last accessed 2 Dec. 2019).

'Haldane, Elizabeth Sanderson', *Oxford Dictionary of National Biography* (last accessed 12 Nov. 2019).

'Haldane, Richard Burdon, Viscount Haldane', *Oxford Dictionary of National Biography* (last accessed 12 Nov. 2019).

'Haldane 100', UK Research and Innovation (last accessed 15 Nov. 2019).

'The Haldane Report 100 Years On', SoundCloud (last accessed 21 June 2019).

'Henri-Pierre Danloux: Adam Duncan, 1st Viscount Duncan of Camperdown, 1731–1804. Admiral', National Galleries of Scotland (last accessed 2 Dec. 2019).

'History', Medical Research Council (last accessed 15 Nov. 2019).

'The History of MI5', Security Service MI5 (last accessed 2 Dec. 2019).

'Income Tax', *House of Commons Debates*, 21 Apr. 1902, vol. 106, col. 828 (last accessed 2 Dec. 2019).

'Milner, Alfred, Viscount Milner', *Oxford Dictionary of National Biography* (last accessed 18 Nov. 2019).

'Minister to Enshrine Protection for Research Independence', BBC News, 24 Feb. 2017 (last accessed 2 Dec. 2019).

'The Naturalist Who Inspired Ernest Hemingway and Many Others to Love the Wilderness', *Smithsonian* (last accessed 30 Oct. 2019).

'Our History', Carnegie Trust (last accessed 2 Dec. 2019).

'Public Spending Details for 1905', UK Public Spending (last accessed 30 Sept. 2019).

'Scott, John, first earl of Eldon', *Oxford Dictionary of National Biography* (last accessed 2 Dec. 2019).

'Scott, William, Baron Stowell', *Oxford Dictionary of National Biography* (last accessed 2 Dec. 2019).

'Social Issues in Canada', Canada Guide (last accessed 2 Dec. 2019).

'South African War—Mortality in Camps of Detention', *House of Commons Debates*, 17 June 1901, vol. 95, cols 605–7 (last accessed 2 Dec. 2019).

'South African War—Peace Negotiations', *House of Commons Debates*, 28 Mar. 1901, vol. 92, col. 141 (last accessed 2 Dec. 2019).

'"Spin" on Boer Atrocities', *The Guardian*, 8 Dec. 2001 (last accessed 2 Dec. 2019).

'Strength of the German Army (1890–1914)', German History in Documents and Images (last accessed 2 Dec. 2019).

'Trade Union and Labour Relations (Consolidation) Act 1992 (last accessed 2 Dec. 2019).

'Trades Unions and Trade Disputes Bill', *House of Commons Debates*, 10 Mar. 1905, vol. 142, col. 1097 (last accessed 2 Dec. 2019).

'Training of the Nation', *House of Lords Debates*, 12 July 1916, vol. 22, cols 660–76 (last accessed 28 Nov. 2019).

'UK Inflation Calculator', CPI Inflation Calculator (last accessed 2 Dec. 2019).

——— https://www.officialdata.org/uk/inflation/1905?amount=20000 (last accessed 2 Dec. 2019).

——— https://www.officialdata.org/uk/inflation/1810?amount=70000 (last accessed 2 Dec. 2019).

——— https://www.officialdata.org/uk/inflation/1928?amount=5000 (last accessed 2 Dec. 2019).

——— https://www.officialdata.org/uk/inflation/1915?amount=25000 (last accessed 2 Dec. 2019).

——— https://www.officialdata.org/uk/inflation/1909?amount=5000 (last accessed 12 Feb. 2020).

——— https://www.officialdata.org/uk/inflation/1909?amount=16000000 (last accessed 12 Feb. 2020).

——— https://www.officialdata.org/uk/inflation/1904?amount=1000 (last accessed 12 Feb. 2020).

——— https://www.officialdata.org/uk/inflation/1900?amount=100000 (last accessed 13 Feb. 2020).

——— https://www.officialdata.org/uk/inflation/1913?amount=355000 (last accessed 13 Feb. 2020).

——— https://www.officialdata.org/uk/inflation/1907?amount=28000000 (last accessed 13 Feb. 2020).

'University Finance', *House of Lords Debates*, 21 July 1920, vol. 41, col. 403 (last accessed 28 Nov. 2019).

'What is the Total UK Public Spending', UK Public Spending (last accessed 2 Dec. 2019).

Government Reports and Royal Commissions

Ministry of Reconstruction, *Report of the Machinery of Government Committee* (London: HMSO, 1918).
Royal Commission on University Education in London, *First Report of the Commissioners* (London: HMSO, 1910).
———— *Final Report of the Commissioners* (London: HMSO, 1913).
Royal Commission on University Education in Wales, *Final Report of the Commissioners* (London: HMSO, 1918).

Typescripts

Elizabeth Sanderson Haldane's diaries, in the possession of Patrick Campbell Fraser.

Lectures

Henry Tizard, 'A Scientist in and out of the Civil Service', Haldane Memorial Lecture, 1955 (London: Birkbeck College, 1955).

Unpublished thesis

Higgins, Simon Giles, 'How was Richard Haldane able to Reform the British Army? An Historical Assessment using a Contemporary Change Management Model' (Master of Philosophy thesis, University of Birmingham, 2010).

FURTHER READING

Chapter 1—A Family Tradition

Calder, Jenni, *The Nine Lives of Naomi Mitchison* (London: Virago Press, 1997).
Christie, Ella and Alice King Stewart, *A Long Look at Life by Two Victorians* (London: Seeley, Service, n.d.).
Haldane, E. S., 'Scottish Family Life in the Seventies', *Quarterly Review*, 514 (Oct. 1932), pp. 259–72.
Haldane, John (ed.), *Philosophy and Public Affairs: Royal Institute of Philosophy Supplement 45* (Cambridge: Cambridge University Press, 2000).
Haldane, J. S., *The Philosophy of a Biologist* (Oxford: Oxford University Press, 1935).
Joseph, H. W. B., 'John Scott Haldane, an Address', *Oxford Magazine* (7 May 1936), pp. 547–9.
Mitchison, Naomi, *You May Well Ask: A Memoir 1920–1940* (London: Victor Gollancz, 1979).

Stewart, Averil, *'Alicella': A Memoir of Alice King Stewart and Ella Christie* (London: John Murray, 1955).

Chapter 2—The Head and the Heart

MacCarthy, Fiona, *The Last Pre-Raphaelite: Edward Burne-Jones and the Victorian Imagination* (London: Faber & Faber, 2011).

Chapter 3—The Company of Friends

Asquith, H. H., *Occasional Addresses* (London: Macmillan & Co., 1918).

Bellows, William, *Edmund Gosse: Some Memories* (London: R. Cobden-Sanderson, 1929).

Bonham Carter, Mark (ed.), *The Autobiography of Margot Asquith* (London: Eyre & Spottiswoode, 1962).

Bonham Carter, Mark, and Mark Pottle (eds), *Lantern Slides: The Diaries and Letters of Violet Bonham Carter 1904–1914* (London: Weidenfeld & Nicolson, 1996).

Bruce, Sir Robert, *Greystones: Musings without Dates (by a City Man)* (London: Alexander Maclehose, 1932).

Churchill, Winston S., *Great Contemporaries* (London: Odhams Press, 1937).

Clark, Ronald W., *Einstein: The Life and Times* (New York: World Publishing Company, 1971).

Davenport-Hines, Richard, *Ettie: The Intimate Life and Dauntless Spirit of Lady Desborough* (London: Weidenfeld & Nicolson, 2008).

De Courcy, Anne, *Margot at War: Love and Betrayal in Downing Street 1912–16* (London: Weidenfeld & Nicolson, 2014).

Desmet, Ronnie, 'Whitehead and the British Reception of Einstein's Relativity: An Addendum to Victor Lowe's Whitehead Biography', *Process Studies Supplement*, Issue 11 (2007).

———— 'Did Whitehead and Einstein Actually Meet?' in Franz Riffert and Hans-Joachim Sander (eds), *Researching with Whitehead: System and Adventure* (Freiburg: Verlag Karl Alber, 2008).

Egremont, Max, *Balfour: A Life of Arthur James Balfour* (London: William Collins, 1980).

Ellenberger, Nancy W., 'The Souls and London "Society" at the End of the Nineteenth Century', *Victorian Studies*, 25, 2 (Winter 1982), pp. 133–60.

Hamer, D. A., *John Morley: Liberal Intellectual in Politics* (London: Clarendon Press, 1968).

Hume Brown, P., *Life of Goethe, with a Prefatory Note by Viscount Haldane*, 2 vols (London: John Murray, 1920).

Hussey, Christopher, *The Life of Sir Edwin Lutyens* (London: Country Life, 1950).

James, Robert Rhodes, *Rosebery: A Biography of Archibald Philip, Fifth Earl of Rosebery* (London: Weidenfeld & Nicolson, 1963).

BIBLIOGRAPHY AND FURTHER READING

Jenkins, Roy, *Mr. Balfour's Poodle: Peers v. People* (London: Collins, 1954).

Koss, Stephen, *Asquith* (London: Allen Lane, 1976).

Lambert, Angela, *Unquiet Souls: The Indian Summer of the British Aristocracy 1880–1918* (London: Macmillan, 1984).

Levine, Naomi B., *Politics, Religion and Love: The Story of H. H. Asquith, Venetia Stanley and Edwin Montagu, Based on the Life and Letters of Edwin Samuel Montagu* (New York: New York University Press, 1991).

Lownie, Andrew, *John Buchan: The Presbyterian Cavalier* (London: Constable, 1995).

McKinstry, Leo, *Rosebery: Statesman in Turmoil* (London: John Murray, 2005).

Morley, John, Viscount, *Recollections*, 2 vols (London: Macmillan, 1918).

Nordmann, Charles, *Einstein and the Universe: A Popular Exposition of the Famous Theory*, translated by Joseph McCabe, preface by Rt. Hon. the Viscount Haldane, O.M. (London: T. Fisher Unwin, 1922).

Oxford, Margot, *More Memories* (London: Cassell, 1933).

Politicus, *Viscount Grey of Fallodon* (London: Methuen, 1934).

Pringle-Pattison, A. Seth, *Man's Place in the Cosmos and Other Essays* (Edinburgh: William Blackwood, 1902).

Renton, Claudia, *Those Wild Wyndhams: Three Sisters at the Heart of Power* (London: William Collins, 2014).

Rothschild, Miriam, *Dear Lord Rothschild: Birds, Butterflies and History* (London: Hutchison, 1983).

Stewart, Graham, *Friendship and Betrayal: Ambition and the Limits of Loyalty* (London: Weidenfeld & Nicolson, 2007.

Waterhouse, Michael, *Edwardian Requiem: A Life of Sir Edward Grey* (London: Biteback Publishing, 2013).

Chapter 4—A Philosophy for Life

Balfour, Arthur James, *Papers Read Before the Synthetic Society 1896–1908* (London: Spottiswoode & Co., 1909).

Begbie, Harold, *Painted Windows: A Study in Religious Personality (by a Gentleman with a Duster)* (London: Mills & Boon, 1922).

Beiser, Frederick C. (ed.), *The Cambridge Companion to Hegel* (Cambridge: Cambridge University Press, 1993).

Beiser, Frederick C., *Hegel* (London: Routledge, 2005).

Bosanquet, Bernard (ed.), *Aspects of the Social Problem by Various Writers* (London: Macmillan, 1895).

Boucher, David (ed.), *The Scottish Idealists: Selected Philosophical Writings* (Exeter: Imprint Academic, 2004).

Boucher, David, and Andrew Vincent, *British Idealism: A Guide for the Perplexed* (London: Continuum, 2012).

Carter, Matt, *T. H. Green and the Development of Ethical Socialism* (Exeter: Imprint Academic, 2003).

BIBLIOGRAPHY AND FURTHER READING

Cropsey, Joseph, *Political Philosophy and the Issues of Politics* (Chicago: University of Chicago Press, 1977).

Cunningham, G. Watts, *Problems of Philosophy: An Introductory Survey*, with a foreword by Viscount Haldane K.T. O.M. (London: George G. Harrap, 1925).

Freeden, Michael, *The New Liberalism: An Ideology of Social Reform* (Oxford: Oxford University Press, 1978).

Green, Thomas Hill, *Lectures in the Principles of Political Obligation*, with an introduction by Lord Lindsay of Birker (London: Longmans Green, 1941).

Mander, W. J., *British Idealism: A History* (Oxford: Oxford University Press, 2011).

Muirhead, J. H. (ed.), *Contemporary British Philosophy: Personal Statements, First Series: Viscount Haldane and Others* (London: George Allen, 1924).

———— *Bernard Bosanquet and his Friends: Letters Illustrating the Sources and the Development of his Philosophical Opinions* (London: George Allen & Unwin, 1935).

Nicholson, Peter P., *The Political Philosophy of the British Idealists: Selected Studies* (Cambridge: Cambridge University Press, 1990).

Pringle-Pattison, A. Seth, *The Balfour Lectures on Realism: Delivered in the University of Edinburgh* (Edinburgh: William Blackwood, 1933).

Rockow, Lewis, *Contemporary Political Thought in England* (London: Leonard Parsons, 1925).

Rogers, R. A. P., 'Mr. Haldane on Hegel's Continuity and Cantorian Philosophy', *Mind*, NS, 18, 70 (Apr. 1909), pp. 252–4.

Russell, Bertrand, 'Mr. Haldane on Infinity', *Mind*, NS, 66 (Apr. 1908), pp. 238–42.

———— *The Autobiography*, vol. 1 (London: George Allen & Unwin, 1967).

Seth, James, *A Study of Ethical Principles*, 10th edn (Edinburgh: William Blackwood, 1908).

Smith, Steven B., *Hegel's Critique of Liberalism: Rights in Context* (Chicago: University of Chicago Press, 1989).

Strauss, Leo, *What is Political Philosophy? And Other Studies* (Chicago: University of Chicago Press, 1959).

Sweet, William (ed.), *Bernard Bosanquet and the Legacy of British Idealism* (Toronto: University of Toronto Press, 2007).

Taylor, Charles, *Hegel* (Cambridge: Cambridge University Press, 1975).

Turner, J. E., 'Dr. Wildon Carr and Lord Haldane on Scientific Relativity', *Mind*, NS, 31, 121 (Jan. 1922), pp. 40–52.

Twining, William, *Jurist in Context: A Memoir* (Cambridge: Cambridge University Press, 2019).

Vincent, Andrew, 'The Hegelian State and International Politics', *Review of International Studies*, 9, 3 (July 1983), pp. 191–205.

———— 'Becoming Green', *Victorian Studies*, 48, 3 (Spring 2006), pp. 487–504.

Whitehead, Alfred North, *Adventures of Ideas* (Cambridge: Cambridge University Press, 1933).

Chapter 5—Wealth and the Nation

Allfrey, Anthony, *Edward VII and his Jewish Court* (London: Weidenfeld & Nicolson, 1991).

Coats, A. W., 'Political Economy and the Tariff Reform Campaign of 1903', *Journal of Law & Economics*, 11, 1 (Apr. 1968), pp. 181–229.

Cole, G. D. H., 'Beatrice Webb as an Economist', *Economic Journal*, 53, 212 (Dec. 1943), pp. 422–37.

Cropsey, Joseph, *Polity and Economy: With Further Thoughts on the Principles of Adam Smith* (South Bend, IN: St. Augustine's Press, 2001).

Cunningham, William, *The Wisdom of the Wise: Three Lectures on Free Trade Imperialism, including 'The Right Hon. R. B. Haldane and Economic Science'* (Cambridge: Cambridge University Press, 1906).

Emy, H. V., 'The Impact of Financial Policy on English Party Politics before 1914', *Historical Journal*, 15, 1 (Mar. 1972), pp. 103–31.

Harrod, R. F., *The Life of John Maynard Keynes* (London: Macmillan, 1951).

Leverhulme, Lord, *The Six-hour Day & Other Industrial Questions*, with an introduction by Viscount Haldane of Cloan (New York: Henry Holt, 1919).

Pellew, Jill, *The Home Office 1848–1914: From Clerks to Bureaucrats* (London: Heinemann, 1982).

Rowntree, B. Seebohm, *The Human Factor in Business* (London: Longmans Green, 1921).

Shield Nicholson, J., 'The Economics of Imperialism', *Economic Journal*, 20, 78 (June 1910), pp. 155–71.

Skidelsky, Robert, *John Maynard Keynes*, vol. 1: *Hopes Betrayed 1883–1920* (London: Macmillan, 1983).

Tawney, R. H., *The Sickness of an Acquisitive Society* (London: Fabian Society, 1920).

Wallas, Graham, *The Great Society: A Psychological Analysis* (London: Macmillan, 1914).

Chapter 6—A Brave New World

Adams, R. J. Q., *Balfour: The Last Grandee* (London: John Murray, 2007).

Balfour, Lady Frances, *Ne Obliviscaris: Dinna Forget*, 2 vols (London: Hodder & Stoughton, 1930).

Beloff, Max, *Britain's Liberal Empire 1897–1921* (London: Macmillan, 1969).

Bevir, Mark, 'Fabianism, Permeation and Independent Labour', *Historical Journal*, 39, 1 (Mar. 1996), pp. 179–96.

———— *The Making of British Socialism* (Princeton: Princeton University Press, 2011).

Brown, Jane, *Lutyens and the Edwardians: An English Architect and his Clients* (London: Viking, 1996).

Cannadine, David, *The Decline and Fall of the British Aristocracy* (New Haven: Yale University Press, 1990).

Carter, Hugh, *The Social Theories of L. T. Hobhouse* (Chapel Hill: University of North Carolina Press, 1927).

Churchill, Randolph S., *Winston S. Churchill*, vol. 2: *Young Statesman 1901–14* (London: Heinemann, 1967).

Clarke, Peter, *The Locomotive of War: Money, Empire, Power and Guilt* (London: Bloomsbury, 2017).

Curtis, Lionel, *With Milner in South Africa* (Oxford: Basil Blackwell, 1951).

Dutton, David, *Austen Chamberlain: Gentleman in Politics* (Bolton: Ross Anderson Publications, 1985).

Eyck, Frank, *G. P. Gooch: A Study in History and Politics* (London: Macmillan, 1982).

Gilmour, David, *Curzon* (London: John Murray, 1994).

Gollin, A. M., *Proconsul in Politics: A Study of Lord Milner in Opposition and in Power* (London: Anthony Blond, 1964).

Green, E. H. H., and D. M. Tanner (eds), *The Strange Survival of Liberal England: Political Leaders, Moral Values and the Reception of Economic Debate* (Cambridge: Cambridge University Press, 2007).

Guttsman, W. L., 'Aristocracy and the Middle Class in the British Political Elite 1886–1916', *British Journal of Sociology*, 5, 1 (Mar. 1954), pp. 12–32.

Halpérin, Vladimir, *Lord Milner and the Empire: The Evolution of British Imperialism* (London: Odhams Press, 1952).

Jackson, Alvin, *Home Rule: An Irish History 1800–2000* (London: Weidenfeld & Nicolson, 2003).

Jacobson, Peter D., 'Rosebery and Liberal Imperialism', *Journal of British Studies*, 13, 1 (Nov. 1973), pp. 83–107.

Jalland, Pat, *Women, Marriage and Politics 1860–1914* (Oxford: Oxford University Press, 1986).

James, Robert Rhodes, *The British Revolution: British Politics, 1880–1939* (London: Hamish Hamilton, 1976).

Jenkins, Roy, *Gladstone* (London: Macmillan, 1995).

Judd, Denis, and Keith Surridge, *The Boer War* (London: John Murray, 2002).

Koss, Stephen, *Nonconformity in Modern British Politics* (London: B. T. Batsford, 1975).

Massingham, H. J. and Hugh Massingham, (eds), *The Great Victorians* (including 'Lord Haldane' by Shane Leslie) (London: Ivor Nicholson & Watson, 1933).

Morgan, David, *Suffragists and Liberals: The Politics of Woman Suffrage in Britain* (Oxford: Basil Blackwell, 1975).

Newton, Lord, *Lord Lansdowne: A Biography* (London: Macmillan & Co., 1929).

Nicholson, A. P., *The Real Men in Public Life: Forces and Factors in the State* (London: W. Collins Sons, 1928).

Pakenham, Thomas, *The Boer War* (London: Weidenfeld & Nicholson, 1979).

Pankhurst, Sylvia, *The Suffragette Movement: An Intimate Account of Persons and Ideals* (London: Virago, 1977).

Pugh, Martin D., *The March of Women: A Revisionist Analysis of the Campaign for Women's Suffrage, 1866–1914* (Oxford: Oxford University Press, 2000).

———— *Speak for Britain! A New History of the Labour Party* (London: The Bodley Head, 2010).

Ridley, Jane, *Bertie: A Life of Edward VII* (London: Chatto & Windus, 2012).

Schneider, Fred D., 'Fabians and the Utilitarian Idea of Empire', *Review of Politics*, 35, 4 (Oct. 1973), pp. 501–22.

Searle, G. R., *The Liberal Party: Triumph and Disintegration, 1886–1929* (London: Macmillan, 1992).

Semmel, Bernard, *Imperialism and Social Reform: English Social-Imperial Thought 1895–1914* (London: George Allen & Unwin, 1960).

Weinroth, Howard S., 'The British Radicals and the Balance of Power', *Historical Journal*, 13, 4 (Dec. 1970), pp. 653–82.

Wolin, Sheldon S., *Politics and Vision: Continuity and Innovation in Western Political Thought* (Boston: Little, Brown & Co., 1960).

Chapter 7—A Man for All Seasons

Addison, Christopher, *Four and a Half Years: A Personal Diary from June 1914 to January 1919*, 2 vols (London: Hutchinson, 1934).

Begbie, Harold, *The Glass of Fashion: Some Social Reflections (by a Gentleman with a Duster)* (New York: G. P. Putnam's Sons, 1921).

———— *The Mirrors of Downing Street: Some Political Reflections (by a Gentleman with a Duster)* (New York: G. P. Putnam's Sons, 1921).

Blake, Robert, *The Unknown Prime Minister: The Life and Times of Andrew Bonar Law 1858–1923* (London: Eyre & Spottiswoode, 1955).

Brock, Michael, and Eleanor Brock, *H. H. Asquith: Letters to Venetia Stanley* (Oxford: Oxford University Press, 1982).

Buczacki, Stefan, *My Darling Mr Asquith: The Extraordinary Life and Times of Venetia Stanley* (Stratford-upon-Avon: Cato & Clarke, 2016).

Chamberlain, Sir Austen, *Politics from Inside: An Epistolary Chronicle 1906–1914* (London: Cassell, 1936).

Charmley, John, *Splendid Isolation? Britain, the Balance of Power and the Origins of the First World War* (London: Hodder & Stoughton, 1999).

Crewe, Marquess of, *Lord Rosebery*, 2 vols (London: John Murray, 1931).

Cudlipp, Hugh, *The Prerogative of the Harlot: Press Barons & Power* (London: The Bodley Head, 1980).

Cross, Colin, *The Liberals in Power (1905–1914)* (London: Barrie & Rockliff, 1963).

David, Edward (ed.), *Inside Asquith's Cabinet: From the Diaries of Charles Hobhouse* (London: John Murray, 1977).

Ferguson, Niall, *The Pity of War 1914–1918* (London: Allen Lane, 1998).

Gilbert, Martin, *Winston S. Churchill, 1874–1965*, vol. 3: *1914–1916* (London: Heinemann, 1971).

———— *Winston S. Churchill, Volume III, Companion, Part 1, Documents, July 1914– April 1915* (London: Heinemann, 1972).

———— *Winston S. Churchill, Volume III, Companion, Part 2, Documents, May 1915– December 1916* (London: Heinemann, 1972).

Grigg, John, *Lloyd George: War Leader 1916–1918*, 4 vols (London: Allen Lane, 2001).

Harris, José F., and Cameron Hazlehurst, 'Campbell-Bannerman as Prime Minister', *History*, 55, 185 (1970), pp. 360–83.

Hattersley, Roy, *David Lloyd George: The Great Outsider* (London: Little Brown, 2010).

Hazelhurst, Cameron, *Politicians at War: July 1914 to May 1915: A Prologue to the Triumph of Lloyd George* (London: Jonathan Cape, 1971.

Koss, Stephen, *The Rise and Fall of the Political Press in Britain* (London: Fontana, 1990).

Lee Thompson, J., *Northcliffe: Press Baron in Politics, 1865–1922* (London: John Murray, 2000).

Lloyd, T. O., *Empire to Welfare State: English History 1906–1985*, 3rd edn (Oxford: Oxford University Press, 1986).

Lowther, Fred L., *In Northcliffe's Service* (Sydney: Cornstalk Publishing, 1927).

MacMillan, Margaret, *The War that Ended Peace: How Europe Abandoned Peace for the First World War* (London: Profile Books, 1913).

———— *Peacemakers: The Paris Conference of 1919 and its Attempt to End War* (London: John Murray, 2001).

Marquand, David, *Ramsay Macdonald* (London: Jonathan Cape, 1977).

Nicolson, Harold, *King George the Fifth: His Life and Reign* (London: Constable & Co, 1952).

Nock, Albert Jay, *Introduction to How Diplomats Make War, By a British Statesman* (New York: B. W. Huebsch, 1915).

Pugh, Martin D., 'Asquith, Bonar Law and the First Coalition', *Historical Journal*, 17, 4 (Dec. 1974), pp. 813–36.

Raymond, E. T., *Uncensored Celebrities* (New York: Henry Holt, 1919).

Roberts, Andrew, *Churchill: Walking with Destiny* (London: Allen Lane, 2018).

Rowland, Peter, *The Last Liberal Governments: The Promised Land 1905–1910* and *Unfinished Business 1911–1914*, 2 vols (London: Barrie & Rockliff, 1968/ Barrie & Jenkins, 1971).

Salter, Arthur, *Personality in Politics: Studies of Contemporary Statesmen* (London: Faber & Faber, 1947).

Spender, J. A., *The Life of The Right Hon. Sir Henry Campbell-Bannerman, G.C.B.*, 2 vols (London: Hodder & Stoughton, 1923).

———— *Life, Journalism and Politics*, 2 vols (London: Cassell & Co., 1927).

Taylor, A. J. P., *English History, 1914–1945* (Oxford: Oxford University Press, 1965).

Toye, Richard, *Lloyd George & Churchill: Rivals for Greatness* (London: Macmillan, 2007).

Wilson, John, *A Life of Sir Henry Campbell-Bannerman* (London: Constable, 1973).

Wilson, Trevor, *The Downfall of the Liberal Party 1914–1935* (London: Collins, 1966).

———— (ed.), *The Political Diaries of C. P. Scott 1911–1928* (London: Collins, 1970).

Chapter 8—Education, Education, Education

Anderson, Robert, 'Secondary Schools and Scottish Society in the Nineteenth Century', *Past & Present*, 109 (Nov. 1985), pp. 176–203.

Argles, Michael, *South Kensington to Robbins: An Account of English Technical and Scientific Education since 1851* (London: Longmans, 1964).

Beveridge, Janet, *An Epic of Clare Market: Birth and Early Days of the London School of Economics* (London: G. Bell, 1960).

Beveridge, William H., *Full Employment in a Free Society* (London: George Allen & Unwin, 1944).

———— *The London School of Economics and its Problems 1919–1937* (London: George Allen & Unwin, 1960).

Brennan, Edward J. T., 'Sidney Webb and the London Technical Education Board. III The Education Act of 1902', *The Vocational Aspect of Education*, 13, 27 (1961), pp. 146–71.

Clarke, Sabine, 'Pure Science with a Practical Aim: The Meanings of Fundamental Research in Britain, circa 1916–50', *Isis, The History of Science Society*, 101, 2 (June 2010), pp. 285–311.

Delisle Burns, C., *A Short History of Birkbeck College (University of London)* (London: University of London Press, 1924).

Edgerton, David, 'The Haldane Principle and Other Invented Traditions in Science Policy', History & Policy, Policy Papers (last accessed 9 Dec. 2018).

Fara, Patricia, *A Lab of One's Own: Science and Suffrage in the First World War* (Oxford: Oxford University Press, 2018).

Fort, G. Seymour, *Alfred Beit: A Study of the Man and his Work* (London: Ivor Nicholson & Watson, 1932).

Foster, C. D., 'Civil Service Fusion: The Period of "Companionable Embrace" in Contemporary Perspective', *Parliamentary Affairs*, 54 (2001), pp. 425–41.

Foster, Sir Gregory, *The University of London: History, Present Resources & Future Possibilities* (London: University of London Press, 1922).

Gordon, Peter, and John White, *Philosophers as Educational Reformers: The Influence of Idealism on British Educational Thought and Practice* (London: Routledge & Kegan Paul, 1979).

Hand, J. E. (ed.), *Science in Public Affairs*, with a preface by the Right Hon. R. B. Haldane (London: George Allen, 1906).

Hankey, Lord, 'The Control of External Affairs', *Royal Institute of International Affairs*, 22, 2 (Mar. 1946), pp. 161–73.

Harris, José, *William Beveridge: A Biography* (Oxford: Clarendon Press, 1977).

Hayek, F. A., 'The London School of Economics 1895–1945', *Economica*, NS, 13, 49 (Feb. 1946), pp. 1–31.

Hennessy, Peter, '"Harvesting the Cupboards": Why Britain has Produced no Administrative Theory or Ideology in the 20th Century', *Transactions of the Royal Historical Society*, Sixth Series, 4 (1994), pp. 203–19.

Hewins, W. A. S., 'The London School of Economics and Political Science', *Special Report on Educational Subjects, No. 2*, ed. M. E. Sadler (London: HMSO, Education Department, 1898, C 8943), pp. 76–98.

Hughes, Alan, 'Open Innovation, the Haldane Principle, and the New Production of Knowledge: Science Policy and University–Industry Links in the UK after the Financial Crisis', Working Papers wp425, Centre for Business Research, University of Cambridge (2011).

Hull, Andrew, 'The Public Science of the British Scientific Community and the Origins of the Department of Scientific and Industrial Research, 1914–16', *British Journal for the History of Science*, 32, 4 (Dec. 1999), pp. 461–81.

Landsborough Thomson, A., 'Half a Century of Medical Research: Volume One: Origins and Policy of the Medical Research Council (UK)' (Medical Research Council, 1987) [pamphlet].

Lockyer, Sir Norman, *Education and National Progress: Essays and Addresses 1870–1905*, with an introduction by the Right Honourable R. B. Haldane, KC, MP (London: Macmillan, 1906).

MacKenzie, Norman, and Jeanne MacKenzie, *The First Fabians* (London: Quartet Books, 1979).

——— (eds), *The Diary of Beatrice Webb*, 4 vols (London: Virago, 1982–5).

Mansbridge, Albert, *An Adventure in Working Class Education: Being the Story of the Workers' Educational Association 1903–1915* (London: Longmans Green, 1920).

Marsh, Neville, *The History of Queen Elizabeth College: One Hundred Years of University Education in Kensington* (London: King's College, 1986).

Nasaw, David, *Andrew Carnegie* (London: Penguin, 2006).

Oliver, Frederick Scott, *Alexander Hamilton: An Essay on American Union* (Edinburgh: Thomas Nelson & Sons, 1906).

Privy Council, 'Report of Committee of Privy Council for Scientific and Industrial Research, 1916–17, Uncorrected proof' (London: HMSO, 1917).

Seymour-Jones, Carole, *Beatrice Webb: Woman of Conflict* (London: Alison & Busby, 1992).

Sherington, Geoffrey, 'The 1918 Education Act: Origins, Aims and Development', *British Journal of Educational Studies*, 24, 1 (Feb. 1976), pp 66–85.

———— *English Education Social Change and War 1911–20* (Manchester: Manchester University Press, 1981).

Stanley, Oliver (ed.), *The Way Out: Essays on the Meaning and Purpose of Adult Education by Members of the British Institute of Adult Education* (Oxford: Oxford University Press, 1923).

Stocks, Mary, *The Workers' Educational Association: The First Fifty Years* (London: George Allen & Unwin, 1953).

Wade, O. L., 'The Legacy of Richard Burdon Haldane: The University Clinical Units and their Future', Inaugural lecture at opening of Whitla Medical Building, Queen's University, Belfast (28 May 1976).

Wheatcroft, Geoffrey, *The Randlords: The Men who Made South Africa* (London: Weidenfeld, 1991).

Chapter 9—War and Peace

Adams, R. J. Q., and Philip P. Poirier, *The Conscription Controversy in Great Britain, 1900–1918* (Columbus: Ohio State University Press, 1987).

Aron, Raymond, *Clausewitz: Philosopher of War*, trans. Christine Booker and Norman Stone (Englewood Cliffs, NJ: Prentice-Hall, 1985).

Arthur, Sir George, *Life of Lord Kitchener*, 3 vols (London: Macmillan & Co., 1920).

Asquith, H. H., *The Genesis of the War* (London: Cassell, 1923).

Baker, Harold, *The Territorial Force: A Manual of its Law, Organisation and Administration*, with an introduction by the Right Honourable R. B. Haldane (London: John Murray, 1909).

Beckett, Ian F. W., and Keith Simpson (eds), *A Nation in Arms: A Social Study of the British Army in the First World War* (Barnsley: Pen & Sword Military, 1985).

Bloor, David, *The Enigma of the Aerofoil: Rival Theories in Aerodynamics, 1909–1930* (Chicago: University of Chicago Press, 2011).

Buchan, John, *A History of the Great War*, vol. 1 (London: Thomas Nelson, 1921).

Calleo, David, *The German Problem Reconsidered: Germany and the World Order, 1870 to the Present* (Cambridge: Cambridge University Press, 1978).

Callwell, C. E., *Field-Marshal Sir Henry Wilson: His Life and Diaries*, 3 vols (London: Cassell, 1927).

Cassar, George H., *Asquith as War Leader* (London: Hambledon Press, 1994).

Cecil, Lamar, *Alfred Ballin: Business and Politics in Imperial Germany 1888–1918* (Princeton: Princeton University Press, 1967).

Coogan, John W., and Peter F. Coogan, 'The British Cabinet and the Anglo-French Staff Talks, 1905–1914: Who Knew What and When Did he Know it?' *Journal of British Studies*, 24, 1 (Jan. 1985), pp. 110–31.

Edgerton, David, *England and the Aeroplane: Militarism, Modernity and Machines* (London: Penguin, 1991).

Esher, Oliver, *Journals and Letters of Reginald Viscount Esher*, 4 vols (London: Ivor Nicholson & Watson, 1934–8).

Fischer, Fritz, *Germany's Aims in the First World War* (London: Chatto & Windus, 1967).

Fromkin, David, *Europe's Last Summer: Who Started the Great War in 1914?* (New York: Alfred A. Knopf, 2004).

Gooch, John, *Studies in British Defence Policy 1847–1942* (London: Frank Cass, 1981).

Hamilton, Keith, *Bertie of Thame: Edwardian Ambassador* (Woodbridge: Boydell Press, 1990).

Harris, J. P., *Douglas Haig and the First World War* (Cambridge: Cambridge University Press, 2008).

Hastings, Max, *Catastrophe: Europe Goes to War 1914* (London: William Collins, 2013).

Heffer, Simon, *Staring at God: Britain in the Great War* (London: Random House, 2019).

Herrmann, David G., *The Arming of Europe and the Making of the First World War* (Princeton: Princeton University Press, 1996).

Hiley, Nicholas, 'The Failure of British Counter-Espionage against Germany, 1907–1914', *Historical Journal*, 28, 4 (Dec. 1985), pp. 835–62.

Hinsley, F. H. (ed.), *British Foreign Policy under Sir Edward Grey* (Cambridge: Cambridge University Press, 1977).

Hirsch, Felix E., 'Hermann Oncken and the End of an Era', *Journal of Modern History*, 18, 2 (June 1946), pp. 148–59.

HMSO, 'Report of the (Haldane) Committee on the Education and Training of Officers', *Parliamentary Papers*, Cmd. 2031, vol. VII (1924).

Holmes, Richard, *The Little Field-Marshal: Sir John French* (London: Jonathan Cape, 1981).

Howard, Michael (ed.), *Soldiers and Governments: Nine Studies in Civil–Military Relations* (Bloomington: Indiana University Press, 1959).

Langhorne, Richard, 'The Naval Question in Anglo-German Relations, 1912–1914', *Historical Journal*, 14, 2 (June 1971), pp. 359–70.

Lee, John, *A Soldier's Life: General Sir Ian Hamilton 1853–1947* (London: Macmillan, 2000).

Lennox, Lady Algernon Gordon (ed.), *The Diary of Lord Bertie of Thame 1914–1918*, 2 vols (London: Hodder & Stoughton, 1924).

BIBLIOGRAPHY AND FURTHER READING

Liddle, Peter (ed.), *Britain Goes to War: How the First World War Began to Reshape the Nation* (Barnsley: Pen & Sword Military, 2015).

Liddell Hart, B. H., *History of the First World War* (London: Cassell, 1970).

Lloyd George, David, *War Memories*, 3 vols (London: Ivor Nicholson & Watson, 1933).

Lomas, David, *Mons 1914: The BEF's Tactical Triumph* (London: Osprey, 1997).

Lutz, Hermann, *Lord Grey and the World War* (London: George Allen & Unwin, 1928).

Luvaas, Jay, *The Education of an Army: British Military Thought, 1815–1940* (Chicago: University of Chicago Press, 1964).

Lynn-Jones, M., 'Détente and Deterrence: Anglo-German Relations, 1911–1914', *International Security*, 11, 2 (Fall 1986), pp. 121–50.

Mackay, Ruddock F., *Fisher of Kilverstone* (Oxford: Oxford University Press, 1973).

MacGregor Dawson, R., 'The Cabinet Minister and Administration: The British War Office, 1903–1916', *Canadian Journal of Economics and Political Science*, 5, 4 (Nov. 1939), pp. 451–78.

MacKintosh, John P., 'The Role of the Committee of Imperial Defence', *English Historical Review*, 77, 304 (July 1962), pp. 490–503.

Mallinson, Allan, *1914: Fight the Good Fight: Britain, the Army and the Coming of the First World War* (London: Bantam Press, 2013).

————— *Too Important for the Generals: Losing and Winning the First World War* (London: Bantam Press, 2016).

Marder, Arthur J., *From the Dreadnought to Scapa Flow: The Royal Navy in the Fisher Era, 1904–1919*, vol. 1. (Oxford: Oxford University Press, 1961).

Marshall-Cornwall, General Sir James, *Haig: As Military Commander* (London: B. T. Batsford, 1973).

Massie, Robert K., *Castles of Steel: Britain, Germany, and the Winning of the Great War at Sea* (New York: Random House, 2003).

McDonough, Frank, *The Conservative Party and Anglo-German Relations, 1905–1914* (Basingstoke: Palgrave Macmillan, 2007).

McMeekin, Sean, *July 1914: Countdown to War* (London: Icon Books, 1913).

Mommsen, Wolfgang J., *Imperial Germany, 1867–1918: Politics, Culture, and Society in an Authoritarian State* (London: Arnold, 1995).

Morris, A. J. A. *The Scaremongers: The Advocacy of War and Rearmament 1896–1914* (London: Routledge & Kegan Paul, 1984).

Morris, Jan, *Fisher's Face* (London: Viking, 1995).

Mowat, R. B., 'Great Britain and Germany in the Early Twentieth Century', *English Historical Review*, 46, 183 (July 1931), pp. 423–41.

Oliver, Frederick Scott, *Ordeal by Battle* (London: Macmillan, 1915).

Otte, T. G., *The World's Descent into War, Summer 1914* (Cambridge: Cambridge University Press, 2014).

Pattison, Michael, 'Scientists, Inventors and the Military in Britain, 1915–19: The Munitions Inventions Department', *Social Studies of Science*, 13, 4 (9 Nov. 1983), pp. 521–68.

Philpott, William J., 'The Making of the Military Entente, 1904–1914: France, the British Army, and the Prospect of War', *English Historical Review*, 128, 534 (Sept. 2013), pp. 1155–85.

Poe, Bryce II, 'British Army Reforms, 1902–1914', *Military Affairs*, 31, 3 (Autumn 1967), pp. 131–8.

Powell, Geoffrey, *Plumer, the Soldiers' General: A Biography* (Barnsley: Pen & Sword Military Classics, 1990).

Repington, Charles à Court, *The Foundations of Reform: By the Military Correspondent of* The Times (London: Simpkin, Marshall and Co., 1908).

———— *The First World War 1914–1918: Personal Experiences of Lieut-Col C. à Court Repington*, 2 vols (London: Constable & Co., 1920).

Röhl, John C. G., *The Kaiser and his Court: Wilhelm II and the Government of Germany* (Cambridge: Cambridge University Press, 1994).

———— *Wilhelm II: Into the Abyss of War and Exile, 1900–1941* (Cambridge: Cambridge University Press, 2014).

Scott, Douglas (ed.), *Douglas Haig: The Preparatory Prologue 1860–1914 Diaries and Letters* (Barnsley: Pen & Sword Military, 2006).

Sheffield, Gary, and John Bourne (eds), *Douglas Haig: War Diaries and Letters 1914–1918* (London: Weidenfeld & Nicolson, 2005).

Simpson, Keith, *The Old Contemptibles: A Photographic History of the British Expeditionary Force August to December 1914* (London: George Allen & Unwin, 1981).

Spiers, Edward M., 'Learning from Haldane', Commentary, Royal United Services Institute (19 Aug. 2010).

———— 'University Officers' Training Corps and the First World War', Council of Military Education Committees of the United Kingdom, COMEC Occasional Paper, no. 4 (*c.* 2015).

Steiner, Zara S., *Britain and the Origins of the First World War* (Basingstoke: Macmillan Education, 1977).

Strachan, Hew, *The First World War*, vol. 1: *To Arms* (Oxford: Oxford University Press, 2001).

Terraine, John, *Mons: The Retreat to Victory* (London: B.T. Batsford, 1960).

———— *Douglas Haig: The Educated Soldier* (London: Hutchinson, 1963).

Watson, Peter, *The German Genius: Europe's Third Renaissance, the Second Scientific Revolution, and the Twentieth Century* (London: Simon & Schuster, 2010).

Worthington, Ian, 'Militarization and Officer Recruiting: The Development of the Officers Training Corps', *Military Affairs*, 43, 2 (Apr. 1979), pp. 90–6.

BIBLIOGRAPHY AND FURTHER READING

Chapter 10—The New State

Anderson, Ellen, *Judging Bertha Wilson: Law as Large as Life* (Toronto: University of Toronto Press, 2001).

Beaudry, Jonas-Sébastien, 'The Empire's Sentinels: The Privy Council's Quest to Balance Idealism and Pragmatism', *Birkbeck Law Review*, 1, 1 (Apr. 2013), pp. 15–62.

Dicey, A. V., *Lectures on the Relation between Law and Public Opinion in England during the Nineteenth Century* (London: Macmillan & Co., 1905).

———— *Introduction to the Study of the Law of the Constitution* (London: Macmillan & Co., 1915).

Eaton, William, 'Canadian Judicial Review and the Federal Distribution of Power', *American Journal of Comparative Law*, 7, 1 (Winter 1958), pp. 47–70.

Elliott, W. Y., *The Pragmatic Revolt in Politics: Syndicalism, Fascism and the Constitutional State* (New York: Macmillan, 1928).

Forsey, Eugene, 'Constitutional Aspects of the Canadian Economy', *Proceedings of the Academy of Political Science*, 32, 2 (1976), pp. 53–62.

Gibson, Dale, 'Founding Fathers-in-Law: Judicial Amendment of the Canadian Constitution', *Law and Contemporary Problems*, 55, 1 (Winter 1992), pp. 261–84.

Girard, Philip, *Bora Laskin: Bringing Law to Life* (Toronto: University of Toronto Press, 2005).

Goldring, John, 'The Privy Council as a Constitutional Court: Canadian Antecedents of Australian Constitutional Interpretation', *Australian–Canadian Studies*, 10, 2 (1992), pp. 1–36.

Gwyn, Richard, *Nation Maker: Sir John A. Macdonald: His Life and Times*, vol. 2: *1867–1891* (Toronto: Vintage Canada, 2012).

Hobhouse, L. T., *The Metaphysical Theory of the State: A Criticism* (London: George Allen & Unwin, 1918).

Hogg, Peter W., *Constitutional Law of Canada* (Toronto: The Carswell Company, 1977).

Jennings, Ivor, 'Constitutional Interpretation: The Experience of Canada', *Harvard Law Review*, 51, 1 (Nov. 1937), pp. 1–39.

Kennedy, W. P. M., *The Constitution of Canada: An Introduction to its Development and Law* (Oxford: Oxford University Press, 1922).

Lamb, Peter, 'Harold Laski (1893–1950): Political Theorist of a World in Crisis', *Review of International Studies*, 25, 2 (Apr. 1999), pp. 329–42.

Laski, Harold J., *Authority in the Modern State* (New Haven: Yale University Press, 1919).

Lazar, Harvey, and Tom McIntosh (eds), *Canada: The State of the Federation 1998/99* (Montreal and Kingston: McGill-Queen's University Press, 1999).

Lederman, William R. (ed.), *The Courts and the Canadian Constitution* (Toronto: McClelland & Stewart, 1964).

BIBLIOGRAPHY AND FURTHER READING

Levy, David W., *Herbert Croly of the New Republic: The Life and Thought of an American Progressive* (Princeton: Princeton University Press, 1985).

Lewis, Geoffrey, *Lord Atkin* (London: Butterworths, 1983).

Mallory, J. R., *Social Credit and the Federal Power in Canada* (Toronto: University of Toronto Press, 1954).

MacCormick, Neil, *Questioning Sovereignty: Law, State and Nation in the European Commonwealth* (Oxford: Oxford University Press, 1999).

Oliver, Frederick Scott [Pacificus], *Federalism and Home Rule* (London: John Murray, 1910).

———— *The Alternatives to Civil War* (London: John Murray, 1913).

Olmsted, Richard A., *Decisions of the Judicial Committee of the Privy Council relating to the British North America Act, 1867 and the Canadian Constitution 1867–1954*, 2 vols (Ottawa: Queen's Printer, 1954).

Paret, Peter, *Clausewitz and the State* (Oxford: Oxford University Press, 1976).

Pollard, A. F., *The Evolution of Parliament: Second Edition* (London: Longmans Green, 1920).

Risk, R. C. B., 'Constitutional Scholarship in the Late Nineteenth Century: Making Federalism Work', *University of Toronto Law Journal*, 46, 3 (Summer 1996), pp. 427–57.

Romney, Paul, *The Attorney General for Ontario in Court, Cabinet, and Legislature 1791–1899* (Toronto: Osgoode Society, 1986).

———— *How Canadians Forgot their Past and Imperilled Confederation* (Toronto: University of Toronto Press, 1999).

Rosenberg, Kate, *How Britain is Governed*, preface by Viscount Haldane of Cloan (London: The Labour Publishing Company, 1925).

Society of Civil Servants, *The Development of the Civil Service: Lectures Delivered before the Society of Civil Servants 1920–21* (London: P. S. King, 1922).

Thomas, Rosamund M., *The British Philosophy of Administration: A Comparison of British and American Ideas 1900–1939* (London: Longman, 1978).

Vaughan, Frederick, *The Canadian Federalist Experiment: From Defiant Monarchy to Reluctant Republic* (Montreal and Kingston: McGill-Queen's University Press, 2003).

Vaughan, Frederick, with Patrick Kyba and O. P. Dwivedi, *Contemporary Issues in Canadian Politics* (Scarborough, Ont.: Prentice-Hall, 1970).

Watson, John, *The State in Peace and War* (Glasgow: James Maclehose, 1919).

Winkler, Henry R., 'The Development of the League of Nations Idea in Great Britain', *Journal of Modern History*, 20, 2 (June 1948), pp. 95–112.

Wright, John de P., 'The Judicial Committee of the Privy Council', *GreenBag*, 10, 3 (Spring 2007).

INDEX

Note: Page numbers followed by "*n*" refer to notes.

INDEX

INDEX

INDEX

Grey, Dorothy (wife of Edward
Grey), 78–81, 162

Grey, Sir Edward (later Viscount
Grey of Fallodon), 382n30,
386n19

Haldane and, xx, xxi, xxiii, 52,
59, 73, 75–6, 78–81, 83, 110,
147–53, 175–9, 182, 184,
186–7, 190–91, 193–4, 253,
259, 268, 274, 293, 296,
374n86, 380n86, 387n44,
390n10, 391–2n43, 394n79

Gunn, Dr, 335–6

Haddingtonshire (East Lothian), xxii,
171, 239, 263, 381n7

Hadow, Sir William H., 242

Haig, Countess, 262, 394n90

Haig, Sir Douglas (later 1st Earl Haig
of Bemersyde), xix, xx, 182,
194–5, 253, 265, 269, 278, 282,
335, 394n90, 409n53, 411–2n73,
412n75 and 78

Haldane Army Reforms, see Army

Haldane Report 1918, see Machinery
of Government Committee and
Report

Haldane, Elizabeth Sanderson
(Haldane's sister), 4, 5, 19, 30,
32–4, 40, 52, 55, 61, 63, 66, 78,
81, 151, 166, 183, 189, 194, 199,
206, 254, 272, 322, 324, 335–8,
346, 361n5, 365nn17 and 24,
367n60, 374n86, 379n70, 386n15,
387n33, 389n80, 391n39, 393n64,
404n8, 408n50, 409n53, 423n1

Haldane, Geordie (brother of
Haldane), 5, 34–6, 110, 380n2

Haldane, Brigadier-General George,
14

Haldane, Graeme (Haldane's

nephew), 27, 56, 153, 371n22,
372n38

Haldane, Helen, 14

Haldane, James Alexander (paternal
grandfather), 15, 16

Haldane, Sir John, 13

Haldane, John of Gleneagles, 14

Haldane, John Scott 'J.S.' (brother of
Haldane), 5, 30, 32–4, 158, 180,
337, 365n27, 381n9

Haldane, Mary Elizabeth (Haldane's
mother), 5, 18, 19, 28–30, 32,
35–6, 38, 68, 167, 206, 365n24,
367n58, 391n36, 395n97

'Haldane Principle', 195–6, 218,
244–6, 339–40, 403n132

Haldane, Patrick (son of Haldane,
John of Gleneagles), 14, 326

Haldane, Richard Burdon (later 1st
Viscount Haldane of Cloan)
birth, education and early life
baptism, 31–2
birth, 4
early days in London, 8,
112–15, 206–7
Edinburgh Academy, 6–7
Edinburgh University, 7, 61,
85, 90–3, 205, 206
family life, 4, 5–6, 28–34
Göttingen University, 7, 31, 35,
75, 85–7, 89–90, 92, 202
Bar, career at the, 8–9, 21, 76,
163, 209, 280
destined for English Bar, 19
early successes, 8
earnings, 8
goes 'Special', 172
influence on later Canadian
judgements, 8–9, 300–1,
306
Real Property Law and Convey-

465

INDEX

INDEX

Jesus Christ, 28, 85, 96

John, E. T., 242

Jones, Sir Henry, 91, 102, 242

Jowett, Benjamin, 7

Judicial Committee of the Privy
Council (JCPC), xxii, 8–9, 183,
195, 300–14

Julian of Norwich, 44

Junior YMCA, 292

Kain, Philip J., 310

Kaiser (Haldane's dog), 39, 40, 63

Kant, Immanuel, 89, 101, 327, 376

Kay, Sir Edward Ebenezer, 13

Kellogg, Frank B., 328, 422–3n106

Kemp, Agnes, 41–44, 77, 367n56

Kemp, John, 7, 41, 77, 92, 226,
367n56

Kennedy, Paul, 298, 417n14

Kensington, Lord, 147

Keogh, Sir Alfred, 405n8

Kerschensteiner, Georg, 239–241

Keynes, John Maynard (1st Baron
Keynes), 136–141, 384n84,
384–5n85

King's College, University of
London, 67

Kirkcaldy, 116

Kitchener, 74, 158–9, 192, 257,
406–7n17

von Kluck, Alexander, 255

Knowsley, 282

Knox, John, 61

Koss, Stephen, 110, 185, 392n46,
393n56, 395n1

Kruger, Paul (President of Transvaal),
157, 387–8n47

Labour government (1924), 147

Labour ministry, 197–8

labour movement, 148, 250

Labour Party, 113

Labour Representation Committee
(1900), 148

laissez-faire, 149, 297–8, 417n8

Lansdowne, Lord, 164, 278

Laski, Harold, 105, 131–3, 154,
379n68, 384n68

Lassalle, Ferdinand, 206

Laura Spelman Rockefeller
Foundation, 322

Laurier, Wilfrid, 280, 422–3n106

Learning and Work Institute, 249,
see National Institute of Adult
Continuing Education

Lees-Milne, James, 265, 409–10n53,
412n80

Lewis, J. Herbert, 244

Liberalism, 113, 125, 146–151,
155–7, 168, 230–1, 267, 295–
300, 314–18, 382n33, 385n4,
386n17, 395n1, 404n145, 416n3,
421n69

Liberal Administrations, xx, 117,
121, 165, 168, 175–6, 182,
186, 278

Liberal Imperialism, 75, 149–51,
159–62, 174–5, 296, 417n20

Liberal Party, 5, 60, 78–80, 114,
124, 139, 155–6, 159, 169,
187, 190, 194, 242, 342,
381n7, 386n15, 387n33,
390n10

Liberal Policy and Haldane, 1, 9,
27, 76, 78, 122–3, 146–8,
155–7, 159–61, 166, 174–5,
197, 206, 210, 212, 250, 262,
267, 291, 295–300, 314–18,
320, 386n15, 387n44, 400n69,
413n109, 414n114

Liberals and women's suffrage,
165, 166, 169

INDEX

INDEX

Tennyson, Alfred (1st Baron Tennyson), 70
Territorial and Reserve Forces Act (1907), see Army
Territorial Army Nursing Service, see Army
Territorial Force (later Territorial Army, now Army Reserve), see Army
Thomson, Sir Joseph John, 67
Thwaite, Ann, 373n55
Times Educational Supplement, 242
Times, The, 2, 20, 53, 167, 185, 193, 263–4, 335, 337, 374n88, 386n20, 392n46, 412n78, 421n69
von Tirpitz, Alfred, 181
Tizard, Sir Henry, 288
Tonn, Joan C., 323, 379n70
Tory, 185, 230, 260, 315
Toynbee Hall, 115, 153–4
Trade Disputes Act (1906), 316–7
Trade schools, 233, 236–7, 239–40, 247
Trade unions, 113–4, 150, 232, 299, 316–18, 326
Trafalgar Square, xxi, 114–5
Treasury, The, 220, 229
Treasury Grants Committee (1906), 231, 233–4, 243, 246
Tring Park, 58, 81
Triple Entente, 178
Twining, William, 375n16

UK Research and Innovation, 403n132
Unearned Increment, 120, 121, 136, 299
unemployment, 114, 131, 139–40, 299, 303
Union Society of University College (London), 238

United Free Church of Scotland, 172–4, 196–7
United Presbyterian Church, 172
United States, 66, 124, 126–8, 166, 215, 237, 285, 287, 303, 306, 323, 328, 330, 422–3n106
Universities, xxiii, 7, 202, 204, 217, 223–9, 231–3, 237, 244, 246, 396n6, 398n55, 440n71
  Berlin, 218
  Birmingham, 33, 225, 229, 237, 401n85, 407n22
  Bristol, xxiii, 198–9, 228, 251, 400n75, 404n158
  Edinburgh, 7, 33, 61, 85, 90, 92, 205, 206, 251, 381n7
  Göttingen, 7, 31, 35, 75, 85, 89, 90, 92, 111, 181, 202, 286, 371n22, 380–1n6, 404n158
  Leeds, xxiii, 228
  'Lilliputian Universities', 225
  Liverpool, xxiii, 225–8, 251
  London, xix, xxi, xxiii, 23, 174, 183, 207–8, 211, 219, 225, 231–7, 248, 322, 402n101
  Manchester, xxiii, 225–8
  National University of Ireland, Dublin, xxiii, 213–4
  Nottingham, xxiii, 251
  Owens College, Manchester, 225
  Queen's University, Belfast, xxiii, 213–4
  Reading, xxiii, 228, 251
  School of Oriental and African Studies (SOAS), 235
  Scottish, 205–6
  Sheffield, xxiii, 228, 404n144
  Southampton, xxiii
  St Andrews, 172, 199
  University College London (UCL), 206, 235